INSTITUTES

OF THE

CHRISTIAN RELIGION.

BY

JOHN CALVIN.

TRANSLATED FROM THE ORIGINAL LATIN, AND COLLATED WITH
THE AUTHOR'S LAST EDITION IN FRENCH,

BY JOHN ALLEN.

Non tamen omnino potuit mors invida totum
Tollere Calvinum terris ; æterna manebunt
Ingenii monumenta tui ; et livoris iniqui
Languida paulatim cum flamma resederit, omnes
Religio quâ pura nitet se fundet in oras
Fama tui. . . . . BUCHANAN

SIXTH AMERICAN EDITION, REVISED AND CORRECTED.

IN TWO VOLUMES.

VOL. I.

WIPF & STOCK · Eugene, Oregon

Wipf and Stock Publishers
199 W 8th Ave, Suite 3
Eugene, OR 97401

Institutes of the Christian Religion Vol. 1
Translated from the Original Latin,
and Collated With the Author's Last Edition in French
By Calvin, John and Allen, John
ISBN 13: 978-1-60899-378-9
Publication date 12/24/2009
Previously published by Presbyterian Board of Publication
and Sabbath - School Work, 1902

ADVERTISEMENT.

The Presbyterian Board of Publication, in introducing to the public a new edition of the inimitable "Institutes of the Christian Religion," do not wish to be regarded as adopting all the sentiments and forms of expression of the venerated writer; although they agree with him in his general views, and admire the skill and learning with which he has pointed out the relative positions and bearings of the great doctrines of revelation. Calvin was better qualified than any of his contemporaries, to present revealed truth in a connected and systematic form. His great natural abilities, his profound erudition, his well balanced and discriminating judgment, and his habits of diligent investigation, eminently fitted him to prepare such a work as the "Institutes," in which the doctrines of the gospel are so clearly developed and harmonized, that the system has been closely associated with his name, from the period of its publication until the present time.

The honour of Calvin consisted, not in suggesting ingenious theories and speculations, but in his general accuracy in interpreting the Holy Scriptures, and in detecting and pointing out the connection of Scripture doctrines, which, instead of being insulated, were shown to occupy their respective places in forming a complete and perfect system of Divine truth. The doctrines embraced in the formularies of the Presbyterian Church are termed Calvinistic, from their general accordance with Calvin's interpretation of scriptural truth; but the admission of this term, as explanatory of their general character, is not understood as by any means implying an entire coincidence in the views of Calvin, or a submission to his authority as an umpire in theological controversies. Although a learned and pious, he was a fallible man; and his opinions, although deserving of profound respect, are not to be blindly followed.

While admitting that the "Institutes," considering the times and circumstances in which they were written, form an invaluable body of divinity, still it must be acknowledged, that some of the doctrines therein maintained have been more luminously set forth in modern times. We would especially mention as an instance the doctrine of justification through the imputed righteousness of Christ. Some of the expressions of Calvin on the subject of reprobation may be regarded as too unqualified, and we can no further endorse them than as they are incorporated in the Presbyterian Confession of Faith. The most decidedly objectionable feature in the "Christian Institutes," is to be found in the explanation of the Fourth Commandment, where the author asserts the abrogation of the Sabbath. In Calvin's view, this ordinance was a mere type of better blessings, and, with the types and ceremonies of the old dispensation, was done away by the introduction of a new and better dispensation. In this opinion there can be no doubt that he greatly erred; and so universal is the conviction of the Church on the perpetual obligation of the Sabbath as a moral institution, that no danger is to be apprehended from a contrary view, even under the sanction of so great a name as that of Calvin. In justice to his opinion on this subject, however, it should be stated, that he distinctly recognized not only the propriety but the necessity of a consecration of stated days for public religious services, without which regulation, he declares that "it is so far from being possible to preserve order and decorum, that if it were abolished, the Church would be in imminent danger of immediate convulsion and ruin." It is much to be lamented that so great a mind should have been led astray on so important a point by attempting to avoid an opposite extreme.

The Board of Publication have been induced to undertake this edition, by the very generous offer of the First and Second Presbyterian Churches in Baltimore, of which the Rev. John Backus and the Rev. Dr. R. J. Breckinridge are respectively Pastors, to defray the expense of stereotyping the work. Under the direction of the Executive Committee of the Board, the translation has been diligently compared throughout with the original Latin and French, and various corrections have been made to convey the meaning of the author more distinctly and accurately. This laborious duty has been performed by a member of the Publishing Committee. The intrinsic excellence of the work, taken in connection with the attractive style, and comparative cheapness, of the present edition, induces the Committee to hope, that it may be widely circulated and carefully studied, both by the clergy and laymen of the Presbyterian Church.

In behalf of the Executive Committee,

WILLIAM M. ENGLES, Editor.

THE

TRANSLATOR'S PREFACE.

THE English Reader is here presented with a translation of one of the principal theological productions of the sixteenth century. Few persons, into whose hands this translation is likely to fall, will require to be informed that the Author of the original work was one of an illustrious triumvirate, who acted a most conspicuous part in what has been generally and justly denominated THE REFORMATION. Of that important revolution in ecclesiastical affairs, so necessary to the interests of true religion, and productive of such immense advantages even to civil society, LUTHER, ZUINGLE, and CALVIN, were honoured, by the providence of God, to be the most highly distinguished instruments. It is no degradation to the memory of the many other ornaments of that age, to consider them as brilliant satellites in the firmament of the Church, revolving round these primary luminaries, to whom they were indebted for much of that lustre which they diffused over the earth; while they were all together revolving around one and the same common centre, though, it must be confessed, with considerable varieties of approximation, velocity, and obliquity in their courses; yet all deriving more or less copious communications of light from the great Sun of the moral system, THE TRUE LIGHT OF THE WORLD.

Differing in the powers of their minds, as well as in the temperament of their bodily constitutions, placed in different circumstances, and called to act in different scenes, these leading Reformers, though engaged in the same common cause, displayed their characteristic and peculiar excellences; which, it is no disparagement of that cause to admit, were likewise accompanied by peculiar failings. It is not the design of this preface to portray and discriminate their respective characters. They alike devoted their lives and labours to rescue Christianity from the absurdities, superstitions, and vices by which it had been so deplorably deformed, mutilated, and obscured, and to recall the attention of mankind from the doubtful traditions of men to the unerring word of God. But while they were all distinguished Reformers, Calvin has been generally acknowledged to have been the most eminent theologian of the three.

Such was the superiority of the talents and attainments of Calvin to those of most other great men, that the strictest truth is in danger of being taken for exaggeration. It is impossible for any candid and intelligent person to have even a slight acquaintance with his writings, without admiring his various knowledge, extensive learning, profound penetration, solid judgment, acute reasoning, pure morality, and fervent piety.

His COMMENTARIES on the Scriptures have been celebrated for a juster method of exposition than had been exhibited by any preceding writer. Above a hundred years after his death, Poole, the author of the Synopsis, in the preface to that valuable work, says, " Calvin's Commentaries abound in solid discussions of theological subjects, and practical improvements of them. Subsequent writers have borrowed most of their materials from Calvin, and his interpretations adorn the books even of those who repay the obligation by reproaching their master." And nothing can more satisfactorily evince the high estimation to which they are still entitled from the biblical student, than the following testimony, given, after the lapse of another century, by the late learned Bishop Horsley : " I hold the memory of Calvin in high veneration: his works have a place in my library; and in the study of the Holy Scriptures, he is one of the commentators whom I frequently consult."

But perhaps, of all the writings of Calvin, none has excited so much attention as his INSTITUTES OF THE CHRISTIAN RELIGION.

His original design in commencing this work is stated by himself, in the beginning of his dedication, to have been to supply his countrymen, the French, with an elementary compendium for their instruction in the principles of true religion. But we learn from Beza that, by the time of its completion, existing circumstances furnished the Author with an additional motive for sending it into the world, during his residence at Basil, whither he had retired to avoid the persecution which was then raging in France against all the dissentients from the Church of Rome. Francis the First, king of France, courted the friendship of the Protestant princes of Germany; and knowing their detestation of the cruelties which he employed against his subjects of the reformed religion, he endeavoured to excuse his conduct by alleging that he caused none to be put to death except some few fanatics; who, so far from taking the word of God as the rule of their faith, gave themselves up to the impulses of their disordered imaginations, and even openly avowed a contempt of magistrates and sovereign princes. Unable to bear such foul aspersions of his brethren, Calvin determined on the immediate publication of this treatise, which he thought would serve as an answer to the calumnies circulated by the enemies of the truth, and as an apology for his pious and persecuted countrymen.

The Dedication to Francis is one of the most masterly compositions of modern times. The purity, elegance, and energy of style; the bold, yet respectful, freedom of address; the firm attachment to the Divine word; the Christian fortitude in the midst of persecution; the triumphant refutation of the calumnies of detractors; with other qualities which distinguish this celebrated remonstrance, will surely permit no reader of taste or piety to withhold his concurrence from the general admiration which it has received.

The Author composed this treatise in Latin and French, and though, at its first appearance, it was little more than an outline of what it afterwards became, it was received with uncommon approbation, and a second edition of it was soon required. How many editions it passed through during his life, it is difficult, if not impossible, now to ascertain; but it obtained a very extensive circulation, and was reprinted several times, and every time was further improved and enlarged by him, till, in the year 1559, twenty-three years after the first impression, he put the finishing hand to his work, and published it in Latin and French, with his last corrections and additions.

The circulation which it enjoyed was not confined to persons capable of reading it in the languages in which it was written. It was translated into High Dutch, Low Dutch, Italian, and Spanish.

Soon after the publication of the Author's last edition, it was translated from the Latin into English. In this language it appears to have reached six editions in the life of the Translator. A reflection on the small number of persons who may be supposed to have had inclination and ability to read such a book at that period, compared with the number of readers in the present age, may excite some wonder that there should have been a demand for so many editions. But no surprise at this circumstance will be felt by any person acquainted with the high estimation in which the works of the Author were held by the venerable Reformers of the Church of England, and their immediate successors, as well as by the great majority of religious people in this country. This is not a question of opinion, but an undeniable fact. Dr. Heylin, the admirer and biographer of Archbishop Laud, speaking of the early part of the seventeenth century, says, that Calvin's " Book of Institutes was, for the most part, the foundation on which the young divines of those times did build their studies." The great Dr. Saunderson, who was chaplain to King Charles I., and, after the restoration of Charles II., was created Bishop of Lincoln, says, " When I began to set myself to the study of divinity as my proper business, Calvin's Institutions were recommended to me, as they were generally to all young scholars in those times, as the best and perfectest system of divinity, and the fittest to be laid as a ground-work in the study of this profession. And, indeed, my expectation was not at all deceived in the reading of those Institutions." *

The great changes which have taken place in our language render it difficult to form a correct opinion of the merits of Mr. Norton's translation, which was first published about two hundred and fifty years ago. It must give rather a favourable idea of its execution, that it was carefully revised by the Rev. David Whitehead, a man of learning and piety, who, in the reign of Henry VIII., was nominated by Archbishop Cranmer to a bishopric in Ireland, and, soon after the accession of Queen Elizabeth, was solicited by that Princess to fill the metropolitan see of Canterbury, but declined the preferment. But, whatever were the merits or defects of that translation at its first appearance, it has long been too antiquated, uncouth, and obscure, to convey any just idea of the original work, and abounds with passages which, to the modern English reader, cannot but be altogether unintelligible.

The intrinsic excellence of the book, its importance in the history of theological controversy, the celebrity of the

---

* It is not uncommon, among persons of a certain class, to represent the leading principles of Calvin as unfavourable to practical religion, and to that kind of preaching which is adapted to affect the hearts and consciences of the hearers. A reference to the most able and intelligent theologians and preachers who have held those principles, and upon whom they may reasonably be concluded to have exerted their genuine and fullest influence, will amply evince the inaccuracy of this representation. Of the excellent divine quoted above, King Charles I. was wont to say, that " he carried his ears to hear other preachers, but his conscience to hear Mr. Saunderson."

Author, the application of his name to designate the leading principles of the system he maintained, and the frequent collision of sentiment respecting various parts of that system, combine with other considerations to render it a matter of wonder, that it has not long ago been given to the English public in a new dress. The importance of it has also been much increased by the recent controversy respecting Calvinism, commenced by Dr. Tomline, the present Bishop of Lincoln, in which such direct and copious reference has been made to the writings of this Reformer, and especially to his CHRISTIAN INSTITUTES. These circumstances and considerations have led to the present translation and publication, which, from the very respectable encouragement it has received, the Translator trusts will be regarded as an acceptable service to the religious public.

Among the different methods of translation which have been recommended, he has adopted that which appeared to him best fitted to the present undertaking. A servile adherence to the letter of the original, the style of which is so very remote from the English idiom, he thought would convey a very inadequate representation of the work; such extreme fidelity, to use an expression of Cowper's, being seldom successful, even in a faithful transmission of the precise sentiments of the author to the mind of the reader. A mere attention to the ideas and sentiments of the original, to the neglect of its style and manner, would expose the Translator of a treatise of this nature to no small danger of misrepresenting the meaning of the Author, by too frequent and unnecessary deviations from his language. He has, therefore, aimed at a medium between servility and looseness, and endeavoured to follow the style of the original as far as the respective idioms of the Latin and English would admit.

After the greater part of the work had been translated, he had the happiness to meet with an edition in French of which he has availed himself in translating the remainder, and in the revision of what he had translated before. Every person, who understands any two languages, will be aware that the ambiguity of one will sometimes be explained by the precision of another; and, notwithstanding the acknowledged superiority of the Latin to the French in most of the qualities which constitute the excellence of a language, the case of the article is not the only one in which Calvin's French elucidates his Latin.

The scriptural quotations which occur in the work, the Translator has given, generally, in the words of our common English version; sometimes according to the readings in the margin of that version; and, in a few instances, he has literally translated the version adopted by the Author, where the context required his peculiar reading to be preserved. Almost all the writers of that age, writing chiefly in a dead language, were accustomed to speak of their adversaries in language which the polished manners of the modern times have discarded, and which would now be deemed illiberal and scurrilous. Where these cases occur, the Translator has not thought himself bound to a literal rendering of every word, or at liberty to refine them entirely away, but has adopted such expressions as he apprehends will give a faithful representation of the spirit of the Author to modern readers.

Intending this work as a complete system of theology, the Author has made it the repository of his sentiments on all points of faith and practice. The whole being distributed into four parts, in conformity to the Apostles' Creed, and this plan being very different from that of most other bodies of divinity, the Translator has borrowed from the Latin edition of Amsterdam a very perspicuous general syllabus, which will give the reader a clear view of the original design and plan of the treatise.

He would not be understood to represent these Institutes as a perfect summary of Christian doctrines and morals, or to profess an unqualified approbation of all the sentiments they contain. This is a homage to which no uninspired writings can ever be entitled. But the simplicity of the method; the freedom from the barbarous terms, captious questions, minute distinctions, and intricate subtilties of many other Divines; the clearness and closeness of argument; the complete refutation of the advocates of the Romish Church, sometimes by obvious conclusions from their professed principles, sometimes by clear proofs of the absurdities they involve; the intimate knowledge of ecclesiastical history; the intimate acquaintance with former theological controversies; the perspicuity of scriptural interpretation; and the uniform spirit of genuine piety, which pervade the book, cannot escape the observation of any judicious reader.

It has been advised by some persons that the translation should be accompanied by a few notes, to elucidate and enforce some passages, and to correct others; but, on all the consideration which the Translator has been able to give to this subject, he has thought it would be best to content himself with the humble office of placing the sentiments of Calvin before the reader, with all the fidelity in his power, without any addition or limitation. He hopes that the present publication will serve the cause of true religion, and that the reputation of the work itself will sustain no diminution from the form in which it now appears.

London, *May* 12, 1813.

CONTENTS.

The Author's Preface to the edition published in 1559............p. 17
Dedication. 20
General Syllabus. 41

BOOK I.

Chap. I. The connection between the knowledge of God and the knowledge of ourselves.
Chap. II. The nature and tendency of the knowledge of God.
Chap. III. The mind of man naturally endued with the knowledge of God.
Chap. IV. This knowledge extinguished or corrupted, partly by ignorance, partly by wickedness.
Chap. V. The knowledge of God conspicuous in the formation and continual government of the world.
Chap. VI. The guidance and teaching of the Scripture necessary to lead to the knowledge of God the Creator.
Chap. VII. The testimony of the Spirit necessary to confirm the Scripture, in order to the complete establishment of its authority. The suspension of its authority, on the judgment of the Church, an impious fiction.
Chap. VIII. Rational proofs to establish the belief of the Scripture.
Chap. IX. The fanaticism which discards the Scripture, under the pretence of resorting to immediate revelations, subversive of every principle of piety.
Chap. X. All idolatrous worship discountenanced in the Scripture, by its exclusive opposition of the true God to all the fictitious deities of the heathen.
Chap. XI. Unlawfulness of ascribing to God a visible form. All idolatry a defection from the true God.
Chap. XII. God contradistinguished from idols, that he may be solely and supremely worshipped.
Chap. XIII. One Divine essence, containing three persons, taught in the Scripture since the beginning.

Chap. XIV. The true God distinguished in the Scripture from all fictitious ones, by the creation of the world.
Chap. XV. The state of man at his creation; the faculties of the soul, the Divine image, free-will, and the original purity of his nature.
Chap. XVI. God's preservation and support of the world by his power and his government of every part of it by his providence.
Chap. XVII. The proper application of this doctrine to render it useful to us.
Chap. XVIII. God uses the agency of the impious, and inclines their minds to execute his judgments, yet without the least stain of his perfect purity.

BOOK II.

Chap. I. The fall and defection of Adam the cause of the curse inflicted on all mankind, and of the degeneracy from their primitive condition. The doctrine of original sin.
Chap. II. Man in his present state despoiled of freedom of will, and subjected to a miserable slavery.
Chap. III. Every thing that proceeds from the corrupt nature of man worthy of condemnation.
Chap. IV. The operation of God in the hearts of men.
Chap. V. A refutation of the objections commonly urged in the support of free-will.
Chap. VI. Redemption for lost man to be sought in Christ.
Chap. VII. The law given not to confine the ancient people to itself, but to encourage their hope of salvation in Christ, till the time of his coming.
Chap. VIII. An exposition of the moral law.
Chap. IX. Christ, though known to the Jews under the law, yet clearly revealed only in the gospel.
Chap. X. The similarity of the Old and New Testaments.
Chap. XI. The difference of the two Testaments.
Chap. XII. The necessity of Christ becoming man, in order to fulfil the office of Mediator.
Chap. XIII. Christ's assumption of real humanity.
Chap. XIV. The union of the two natures constituting the person of the Mediator.
Chap. XV. The consideration of Christ's three offices, prophetical, regal, and sacerdotal, necessary to our knowing the end of his mission from the Father, and the benefits which he confers on us.
Chap. XVI. Christ's execution of the office of a Redeemer to procure our salvation; his death, resurrection, and ascension to heaven.
Chap. XVII. Christ truly and properly said to have merited the grace of God and salvation for us.

BOOK III.

Chap. I. What is declared concerning Christ rendered profitable to us by the secret operation of the Spirit.
Chap. II. Faith defined, and its properties described.
Chap. III. On repentance.
Chap. IV. The sophistry and jargon of the schools concerning repentance very remote from the purity of the gospel. On confession and satisfaction.
Chap. V. The supplements to their doctrine of satisfactions, indulgences, and purgatory.
Chap. VI. The life of a Christian. Scriptural arguments and exhortations to it.
Chap. VII. Summary of the Christian life. Self-denial.
Chap. VIII. Bearing the cross, which is a branch of self-denial.
Chap. IX. Meditation on the future life.
Chap. X. The right use of the present life and its supports.
Chap. XI. Justification by faith. The name and thing defined.
Chap. XII. A consideration of the Divine tribunal necessary to a serious conviction of gratuitous justification.
Chap. XIII. Two things necessary to be observed in gratuitous justification.
Chap. XIV. The commencement and continual progress of justification.
Chap. XV. Boasting of the merit of works equally subversive of God's glory in the gift of righteousness, and of the certainty of salvation.
Chap. XVI. A refutation of the injurious calumnies of the Papists against this doctrine.
Chap. XVII. The harmony between the promises of the law and those of the gospel.
Chap. XVIII. Justification from works not to be inferred from the promise of a reward.
Chap. XIX. On Christian liberty.
Chap. XX. On prayer, the principal exercise of faith, and the medium of our daily reception of Divine blessings.
Chap. XXI. Eternal election, or God's predestination of some to salvation, and of others to destruction.
Chap. XXII. Testimonies of Scripture in confirmation of this doctrine.
Chap. XXIII. A refutation of the calumnies generally, but unjustly, urged against this doctrine.
Chap. XXIV. Election confirmed by the Divine call. The destined destruction of the reprobate procured by themselves.
Chap. XXV. The final resurrection.

BOOK IV.

Chap. I. The true Church, and the necessity of our union with her, being the mother of all the pious.
Chap. II. The true and false Church compared.
Chap. III. The teachers and ministers of the Church, their election and office.
Chap. IV. The state of the ancient Church, and the mode of government practised before the Papacy.
Chap. V. The ancient form of government entirely subverted by the Papal tyranny.
Chap. VI. The primacy of the Roman see.
Chap. VII. The rise and progress of the Papal power to its present eminence attended with the loss of liberty to the Church, and the ruin of all moderation.
Chap. VIII. The power of the Church respecting articles of faith, and its licentious perversion under the Papacy, to the corruption of all purity of doctrine.
Chap. IX. Councils; their authority.
Chap. X. The power of legislation, in which the pope and his adherents have most cruelly tyrannized over the minds, and tortured the bodies of men.
Chap. XI. The jurisdiction of the Church, and its abuse under the Papacy.
Chap. XII. The discipline of the Church; its principal use in censures and excommunication.
Chap. XIII. Vows; the misery of rashly making them.
Chap. XIV. The sacraments.
Chap. XV. Baptism.
Chap. XVI. Pædobaptism perfectly consistent with the institution of Christ, and the nature of the sign.
Chap. XVII. The Lord's supper and its advantages.
Chap. XVIII. The Papal mass not only a sacrilegious profanation of the Lord's supper, but a total annihilation of it.
Chap. XIX. The five other ceremonies, falsely called sacraments, proved not to be sacraments; their true nature explained.
Chap. XX. On civil government.

THE

AUTHOR'S PREFACE

TO

AN EDITION PUBLISHED IN THE YEAR 1559,

WITH HIS

LAST CORRECTIONS AND ADDITIONS.

In the first edition of this work, not expecting that success which the Lord, in his infinite goodness, hath given, I handled the subject for the most part in a superficial manner, as is usual in small treatises. But when I understood that it had obtained from almost all pious persons such a favourable acceptance as I never could have presumed to wish, much less to hope; while I was conscious of receiving far more attention than I had deserved, I thought it would evince great ingratitude, if I did not endeavour at least, according to my humble ability, to make some suitable return for the attentions paid to me — attentions of themselves calculated to stimulate my industry. Nor did I attempt this only in the second edition; but in every succeeding one the work has been improved by some further enlargements. But though I repented not the labour then devoted to it, yet I never satisfied myself, till it was arranged in the order in which it is now published; and I trust I have here presented to my readers what their judgments will unite in approving. Of my diligent application to the accomplishment of this service for the Church of God, I can produce abundant proof. For, last winter, when I thought that a quartan ague would speedily terminate in my death, the more my disorder increased, the less I spared myself, till I had finished this book, to leave it behind me, as some grateful return to such kind solicitations of the religious public. Indeed, I would rather it had been done sooner; but it is soon enough, if well enough. I shall think it has appeared at the proper time, when I shall find it to have been more beneficial than before to the Church of God. This is my only wish.

I should indeed be ill requited for my labour, if I did not content myself with the approbation of God alone, despising equally the foolish and perverse judgments of ignorant men, and the calumnies and detractions of the wicked. For though God hath wholly devoted my mind to study the enlargement of his kingdom, and the promotion of general usefulness; and I have the testimony of my own conscience, of angels, and of God himself, that, since I undertook the office of a teacher in the Church, I have had no other object in view than to profit the Church by maintaining the pure doctrine of godliness; yet I suppose there is no man more slandered or calumniated than myself. When this Preface was actually in the press, I had certain information, that at Augsburg, where the States of the Empire were assembled, a report had been circulated of my defection to popery, and received with unbecoming eagerness in the courts of the princes. This is the gratitude of those who cannot be unacquainted with the numerous proofs of my constancy, which not only refute such a foul calumny, but, with all equitable and humane judges, ought to preserve me from it. But the devil, with all his host, is deceived, if he think to overwhelm me with vile falsehoods, or to render me more timid, indolent, or dilatory, by such indignities. For I trust that God, in his infinite goodness, will enable me to persevere with patient constancy in the career of his holy calling; of which I afford my pious readers a fresh proof in this edition.

Now, my design in this work has been to prepare and qualify students of theology for the reading of the divine word, that they may have an easy introduction to it, and be enabled to proceed in it without any obstruction. For I think I have given such a comprehensive summary, and orderly arrangement of all the branches of religion, that, with proper attention, no person will find any difficulty in determining what ought to be the principal objects of his research in the Scripture, and to what end he ought to refer any thing it contains. This way, therefore, being prepared, if I should hereafter publish any expositions of the Scripture, I shall have no need to introduce long discussions respecting doctrines, or digressions on common topics, and therefore shall always compress them within a narrow compass. This will relieve the pious reader from great trouble and tediousness, provided he come previously furnished with the necessary information, by a knowledge of the present work. But as the reason of this design is very evident in my numerous Commentaries, I would rather have it known from the fact itself, than from my declaration.

Farewell, friendly reader; and if you receive any benefit from my labours, let me have the assistance of your prayers with God our Father.

GENEVA, 1st *August*, 1559.

DEDICATION.

To His Most Christian Majesty, Francis, *King of the French, and his Sovereign, John Calvin wisheth peace and salvation in Christ.*

When I began this work, Sire, nothing was further from my thoughts than writing a book which would afterwards be presented to your Majesty. My intention was only to lay down some elementary principles, by which inquirers on the subject of religion might be instructed in the nature of true piety. And this labour I undertook chiefly for my countrymen, the French, of whom I apprehended multitudes to be hungering and thirsting after Christ, but saw very few possessing any real knowledge of him. That this was my design, the book itself proves by its simple method and unadorned composition. But when I perceived that the fury of certain wicked men in your kingdom had grown to such a height, as to leave no room in the land for sound doctrine, I thought I should be usefully employed, if in the same work I delivered my instructions to them, and exhibited my confession to you, that you may know the nature of that doctrine, which is the object of such unbounded rage to those madmen who are now disturbing the country with fire and sword. For I shall not be afraid to acknowledge, that this treatise contains a summary of that very doctrine, which, according to their clamours, deserves to be punished with imprisonment, banishment, proscription, and flames, and to be exterminated from the face of the earth. I well know with what atrocious insinuations your ears have been filled by them, in order to render our cause most odious in your esteem; but your clemency should lead you to consider that, if accusation be accounted a sufficient evidence of guilt, there will be an end of all innocence in words and actions. If any one, indeed, with a view to bring an odium upon the doctrine which I am endeavouring to defend, should allege that it has long ago been condemned by the general consent, and suppressed by many judicial decisions, this will be only equivalent to saying, that it has been sometimes violently rejected through the influence and power of its adversaries, and sometimes insidiously and fraudulently oppressed by falsehoods, artifices, and calumnies. Violence is displayed, when sanguinary sentences are passed against it without the cause being heard; and fraud, when it is unjustly accused of sedition and mischief. Lest any one should suppose that these our complaints are unfounded, you yourself, Sire, can bear witness of the false calumnies with which you hear it daily traduced; that its only tendency is to wrest the sceptres of kings out of their hands, to overturn all the tribunals and judicial proceedings, to subvert all order and governments, to disturb the peace and tranquillity of the people, to abrogate all laws, to scatter all properties and possessions, and, in a word, to involve every thing in total confusion. And yet you hear the smallest portion of what is alleged against it; for such horrible things are circulated amongst the vulgar, that, if they were true, the whole world would justly pronounce it and its abettors worthy of a thousand fires and gibbets. Who, then, will wonder at its becoming the object of public odium, where credit is given to such most iniquitous accusations? This is the cause of the general consent and conspiracy to condemn us and our doctrine. Hurried away with this impulse, those who sit in judgment pronounce for sentences the prejudices they brought from home with them; and think their duty fully discharged if they condemn none to be punished but such as are convicted by their own confession, or by sufficient proofs. Convicted of what crime? Of this condemned doctrine, they say. But with what justice is it condemned? Now, the ground of defence was not to abjure the doctrine itself, but to maintain its truth. On this subject, however, not a word is allowed to be uttered.

Wherefore I beseech you, Sire, — and surely it is not an unreasonable request, — to take upon yourself the entire cognizance of this cause, which has hitherto been confusedly and carelessly agitated, without any order of law, and with outrageous passion rather than judicial gravity. Think not that I am now meditating my own individual defence, in order to effect a safe return to my native country; for, though I feel the affection which every man ought to feel for it, yet, under the existing circumstances, I regret not my removal from it. But I plead the cause of all the godly, and consequently of Christ himself, which, having been in these times persecuted and trampled on in all ways in your kingdom, now lies in a most deplorable state; and this indeed rather through the tyranny of certain Pharisees, than with your knowledge. How this comes to pass is foreign to my present purpose to say; but it certainly lies in a most afflicted state. For the ungodly have gone to such lengths, that the truth of Christ, if not vanquished, dissipated, and entirely destroyed, is buried, as it were, in ignoble obscurity, while the poor, despised church is either destroyed by cruel massacres, or driven away into banishment, or menaced and terrified into total silence. And still they continue their wonted madness and ferocity, pushing violently against the wall already bent, and finishing the ruin they have begun. In the mean time, no one comes forward to plead the cause against such furies. If there be any persons desirous of appearing most favourable to the truth, they only venture an opinion, that forgiveness should be extended to the error and imprudence of ignorant people. For this is the language of these moderate men, calling *that* error and imprudence which they know to be the certain truth of God, and *those* ignorant people, whose understanding they perceive not to have been so despicable to Christ, but that he has favoured them with the mysteries of his heavenly wisdom. Thus all are ashamed of the Gospel. But it shall be yours, Sire, not to turn away your ears or thoughts from so just a defence, especially in a cause of such importance as the maintenance of God's glory unimpaired in the world, the preservation of the honour of divine truth, and the continuance of the kingdom of Christ uninjured among us. This is a cause worthy of your attention, worthy of your cognizance, worthy of your throne. This consideration constitutes true royalty, to acknowledge yourself in the government of your kingdom to be the minister of God. For where the glory of God is not made the end of the government, it is not a legitimate sovereignty, but a usurpation. And he is deceived who expects lasting prosperity in that kingdom which is not ruled by the sceptre of God, that is, his holy word; for that heavenly oracle cannot fail, which declares that "where there is no vision, the people perish." (*a*) Nor should you be seduced from this pursuit by a contempt of our meanness. We are fully conscious to ourselves how very mean and abject we are, being miserable sinners before God, and accounted most despicable by men; being (if you please) the refuse of the world, deserving of the vilest appellations that can be found; so that nothing remains for us to glory in before God, but his mercy alone, by which, without any merit of ours, we have been admitted to the hope of eternal salvation, and before men nothing but our weakness, the slightest confession of which is esteemed by them as the greatest disgrace. But our doctrine must stand, exalted above all the glory, and invincible by all the power of the world; because it is not ours, but the doctrine of the living God, and of his Christ, whom the Father hath constituted King, that he may have dominion from sea to sea, and from the river even to the ends of the earth, and that he may rule in such a manner, that the whole earth, with its strength of iron and with its splendour of gold and silver, smitten by the rod of his mouth, may be broken to pieces like a potter's vessel; (*b*) for thus do the prophets foretell the magnificence of his kingdom.

Our adversaries reply, that our pleading the word of God is a false pretence, and that we are nefarious corrupters of it. But that this is not only a malicious calumny, but egregious impudence, by reading our confession, you will, in your wisdom, be able to judge. Yet something further is necessary to be said, to excite your attention, or at least to prepare your mind for this perusal. Paul's direction, that every prophecy be framed "according to the analogy of faith," (*c*) has fixed an invariable standard by which all interpretation of Scripture ought to be tried. If our principles be examined by this rule of faith, the victory is ours. For what is more consistent with faith than to acknowledge ourselves naked of all virtue, that we may be clothed by God; empty of all good, that we may

(*a*) Prov. xxix. 18. (*b*) Dan. ii. 34. Isaiah xi. 4. Psalm ii. 9.
(*c*) Rom. xii. 6.

be filled by him; slaves to sin, that we may be liberated by him; blind, that we may be enlightened by him; lame, that we may be guided; weak, that we may be supported by him; to divest ourselves of all ground of glorying, that he alone may be eminently glorious, and that we may glory in him? When we advance these and similar sentiments, they interrupt us with complaints that this is the way to overturn, I know not what blind light of nature, pretended preparations, free will, and works meritorious of eternal salvation, together with all their supererogations; because they cannot bear that the praise and glory of all goodness, strength, righteousness, and wisdom, should remain entirely with God. But we read of none being reproved for having drawn too freely from the fountain of living waters; on the contrary, they are severely upbraided who have "hewed them out cisterns, broken cisterns, that can hold no water." (d) Again, what is more consistent with faith, than to assure ourselves of God being a propitious Father, where Christ is acknowledged as a brother and Mediator? than securely to expect all prosperity and happiness from Him, whose unspeakable love towards us went so far, that "he spared not his own Son, but delivered him up for us?" (e) than to rest in the certain expectation of salvation and eternal life, when we reflect upon the Father's gift of Christ, in whom such treasures are hidden? Here they oppose us, and complain that this certainty of confidence is chargeable with arrogance and presumption. But as we ought to presume nothing of ourselves, so we should presume every thing of God; nor are we divested of vain glory for any other reason than that we may learn to glory in the Lord. What shall I say more? Review, Sire, all the parts of our cause, and consider us worse than the most abandoned of mankind, unless you clearly discover that we thus "both labour and suffer reproach, because we trust in the living God," (f) because we believe that "this is life eternal, to know the only true God, and Jesus Christ whom he hath sent." (g) For this hope some of us are bound in chains, others are lashed with scourges, others are carried about as laughing-stocks, others are outlawed, others are cruelly

(d) Jer ii 13 (e) Rom. viii. 32. (f) 1 Tim. iv. 10.
(g) John xvii. 3.

tortured, others escape by flight; but we are all reduced to extreme perplexities, execrated with dreadful curses, cruelly slandered, and treated with the greatest indignities. Now, look at our adversaries, (I speak of the order of priests, at whose will and directions others carry on these hostilities against us,) and consider a little with me by what principles they are actuated. The true religion, which is taught in the Scriptures, and ought to be universally maintained, they readily permit both themselves and others to be ignorant of, and to treat with neglect and contempt. They think it unimportant what any one holds or denies concerning God and Christ, provided he submits his mind with an implicit faith (as they call it) to the judgment of the Church. Nor are they much affected, if the glory of God happens to be violated with open blasphemies, provided no one lift a finger against the primacy of the Apostolic See, and the authority of their holy Mother Church. Why, therefore, do they contend with such extreme bitterness and cruelty for the mass, purgatory, pilgrimages, and similar trifles, and deny that any piety can be maintained without a most explicit faith, so to speak, in these things; whereas they prove none of them from the Word of God? Why, but because their belly is their god, their kitchen is their religion; deprived of which they consider themselves no longer as Christians, or even as men. For though some feast themselves in splendour, and others subsist on slender fare, yet all live on the same pot, which, without this fuel, would not only cool, but completely freeze. Every one of them, therefore, who is most solicitous for his belly, is found to be a most strenuous champion for their faith. Indeed, they universally exert themselves for the preservation of their kingdom, and the repletion of their bellies; but not one of them discovers the least indication of sincere zeal.

Nor do their attacks on our doctrine cease here; they urge every topic of accusation and abuse to render it an object of hatred or suspicion. They call it novel, and of recent origin, — they cavil at it as doubtful and uncertain, — they inquire by what miracles it is confirmed, — they ask whether it is right for it to be received contrary to the consent of so many holy fathers, and the custom of the highest antiquity, — they urge us to confess that it is schismatical in stirring up opposition against the Church, or that the Church was wholly extinct for many ages, during which no such thing was known. — Lastly, they say all arguments are unnecessary; for that its nature may be determined by its fruits, since it has produced such a multitude of sects, so many factious tumults, and such great licentiousness of vices. It is indeed very easy for them to insult a deserted cause with the credulous and ignorant multitude; but, if we had also the liberty of speaking in our turn, this acrimony, which they now discover in violently foaming against us with equal licentiousness and impunity, would presently cool.

In the first place, their calling it novel is highly injurious to God, whose holy word deserves not to be accused of novelty. I have no doubt of its being new to them, to whom Jesus Christ and the Gospel are equally new. But those who know the antiquity of this preaching of Paul, "that Jesus Christ died for our sins, and rose again for our justification," (*h*) will find no novelty among us. That it has long been concealed, buried, and unknown, is the crime of human impiety. Now that the goodness of God has restored it to us, it ought at least to be allowed its just claim of antiquity.

From the same source of ignorance springs the notion of its being doubtful and uncertain. This is the very thing which the Lord complains of by his prophet; that "the ox knoweth his owner, and the ass his master's crib," (*i*) but that his people know not him. But however they may laugh at its uncertainty, if they were called to seal their own doctrine with their blood and lives, it would appear how much they value it. Very different is our confidence, which dreads neither the terrors of death, nor even the tribunal of God.

Their requiring miracles of us is altogether unreasonable; for we forge no new Gospel, but retain the very same whose truth was confirmed by all the miracles ever wrought by Christ and the apostles. But they have this peculiar advantage above us, that they can confirm their faith by continual miracles even to this day. But the truth is, they allege miracles which are calculated to unsettle a mind otherwise well established, they

(*h*) Rom. iv. 25. 1 Cor. xv. 3, 17.   (*i*) Isaiah i. 3.

are so frivolous and ridiculous, or vain and false. Nor, if they were ever so preternatural, ought they to have any weight in opposition to the truth of God, since the name of God ought to be sanctified in all places and at all times, whether by miraculous events, or by the common order of nature. This fallacy might perhaps be more specious, if the Scripture did not apprize us of the legitimate end and use of miracles. For Mark informs us, that the miracles which followed the preaching of the apostles were wrought in confirmation (*k*) of it, and Luke tells us, that (*l*) "the Lord gave testimony to the word of his grace," when "signs and wonders" were "done by the hands" of the apostles. Very similar to which is the assertion of the apostle, that "salvation was confirmed" by the preaching of the Gospel, "God also bearing witness with signs, and wonders, and divers miracles." (*m*) But those things which we are told were seals of the Gospel, shall we pervert to undermine the faith of the Gospel? Those things which were designed to be testimonials of the truth, shall we accommodate to the confirmation of falsehood? It is right, therefore, that the doctrine, which, according to the evangelist, claims the first attention, be examined and tried in the first place; and if it be approved, then it ought to derive confirmation from miracles. But it is the characteristic of sound doctrine, given by Christ, that it tends to promote, not the glory of men, but the glory of God. (*n*) Christ having laid down this proof of a doctrine, it is wrong to esteem those as miracles which are directed to any other end than the glorification of the name of God alone. And we should remember that Satan has his wonders, which, though they are juggling tricks rather than real miracles, are such as to delude the ignorant and inexperienced. Magicians and enchanters have always been famous for miracles; idolatry has been supported by astonishing miracles; and yet we admit them not as proofs of the superstition of magicians or idolaters. With this engine also the simplicity of the vulgar was anciently assailed by the Donatists, who abounded in miracles. We therefore give the same answer now to our adversaries as Augustine (*o*) gave to the Donatists, that our Lord hath cautioned us against these miracle-mongers by his prediction, that there

(*k*) Mark xvi. 20.   (*l*) Acts xiv. 3.   (*m*) Heb. ii. 3, 4.
(*n*) John vii. 18. viii. 50.   (*o*) In Joan. tract. 13.

should arise false prophets, who, by various signs and lying wonders, "should deceive (if possible) the very elect." (*p*) And Paul has told us, that the kingdom of Antichrist would be "with all power, and signs, and lying wonders." (*q*) But these miracles (they say) are wrought, not by idols, or sorcerers, or false prophets, but by saints; as if we were ignorant, that it is a stratagem of Satan to "transform" himself "into an angel of light." (*r*) At the tomb of Jeremiah, (*s*) who was buried in Egypt, the Egyptians formerly offered sacrifices and other divine honours. Was not this abusing God's holy prophet to the purposes of idolatry? Yet they supposed this veneration of his sepulchre to be rewarded with a cure for the bite of serpents. What shall we say, but that it has been, and ever will be, the most righteous vengeance of God to "send those who receive not the love of the truth strong delusions, that they should believe a lie"? (*t*) We are by no means without miracles, and such as are certain, and not liable to cavils. But those under which they shelter themselves are mere illusions of Satan, seducing the people from the true worship of God to vanity.

Another calumny is their charging us with opposition to the fathers, — I mean the writers of the earlier and purer ages, — as if those writers were abettors of their impiety; whereas, if the contest were to be terminated by this authority, the victory in most parts of the controversy — to speak in the most modest terms — would be on our side. But though the writings of those fathers contain many wise and excellent things, yet in some respects they have suffered the common fate of mankind: these very dutiful children reverence only their errors and mistakes, but their excellences they either overlook, or conceal, or corrupt; so that it may be truly said to be their only study to collect dross from the midst of gold. Then they overwhelm us with senseless clamours, as despisers and enemies of the fathers. But we do not hold them in such contempt, but that, if it were consistent with my present design, I could easily support by their suffrages most of the sentiments that we now maintain. But while we make use of their writings, we always remember that "all things are ours," to serve us, not to have

---

(*p*) Matt. xxiv. 24.   (*q*) 2 Thess. ii. 9.   (*r*) 2 Cor. xi. 14.
(*s*) Hierom. in præf. Jerem.   (*t*) 2 Thess. ii. 10, 11.

dominion over us, and that "we are Christ's" (*v*) alone, and owe him universal obedience. He who neglects this distinction will have nothing decided in religion; since those holy men were ignorant of many things, frequently at variance with each other, and sometimes even inconsistent with themselves. There is great reason, they say, for the admonition of Solomon, "not to transgress or remove the ancient landmarks, which our fathers have set." (*w*) But the same rule is not applicable to the bounding of fields, and to the obedience of faith, which ought to be ready to "forget her own people and her father's house." (*x*) But if they are so fond of allegorizing, why do they not explain the apostles, rather than any others, to be those fathers, whose appointed landmarks it is so unlawful to remove? For this is the interpretation of Jerome, whose works they have received into their canons. But if they insist on preserving the landmarks of those whom they understand to be intended, why do they at pleasure so freely transgress them themselves? There were two fathers, (*y*) of whom one said, that our God neither eats nor drinks, and therefore needs neither cups nor dishes; the other, that sacred things require no gold, and that gold is no recommendation of that which is not purchased with gold. This landmark therefore is transgressed by those who in sacred things are so much delighted with gold, silver, ivory, marble, jewels, and silks, and suppose that God is not rightly worshipped, unless all things abound in exquisite splendour, or rather extravagant profusion. There was a father (*z*) who said he freely partook of flesh on a day when others abstained from it, because he was a Christian. They transgress the landmarks therefore when they curse the soul that tastes flesh in Lent. There were two fathers, (*a*) of whom one said, that a monk who labours not with his hands is on a level with a cheat or a robber; and the other, that it is unlawful for monks to live on what is not their own, notwithstanding their assiduity in contemplations, studies, and prayers; and they have transgressed this landmark by placing the idle and distended carcasses of monks in cells and brothels, to be pam-

(*v*) 1 Cor. iii. 21, 23.   (*w*) Prov. xxii. 28.   (*x*) Psalm xlv. 10.
(*y*) Acat. in lib. 11. cap. 16. Trip. Hist. Amb. lib. 2. de Off. c. 28.
(*z*) Spiridion. Trip. Hist. lib. 1. c. 10.
(*a*) Trip. Hist. lib 8. c. 1. August. de Opere Mon. c. 17.

pered on the substance of others. There was a father (*b*) who said, that to see a painted image of Christ, or of any saint, in the temples of Christians, is a dreadful abomination. Nor was this merely the sentence of an individual; it was also decreed by an ecclesiastical council, that the object of worship should not be painted on the walls. They are far from confining themselves within these landmarks, for every corner is filled with images. Another father (*c*) has advised that, after having discharged the office of humanity towards the dead by the rites of sepulture, we should leave them to their repose. They break through these landmarks by inculcating a constant solicitude for the dead. There was one of the fathers (*d*) who asserted that the substance of bread and wine in the eucharist ceases not, but remains, just as the substance of the human nature remains in the Lord Christ united with the divine. They transgress this landmark therefore by pretending that, on the words of the Lord being recited, the substance of bread and wine ceases, and is transubstantiated into his body and blood. There were fathers (*e*) who, while they exhibited to the universal Church only one eucharist, and forbade all scandalous and immoral persons to approach it, at the same time severely censured all who, when present, did not partake of it. How far have they removed these landmarks, when they fill not only the churches, but even private houses, with their masses, admit all who choose to be spectators of them, and every one the more readily in proportion to the magnitude of his contribution, however chargeable with impurity and wickedness! They invite none to faith in Christ and a faithful participation of the sacraments; but rather for purposes of gain bring forward their own work instead of the grace and merit of Christ. There were two fathers, (*f*) of whom one contended that the use of Christ's sacred supper should be wholly forbidden to those who, content with partaking of one kind, abstained from the other; the other strenuously maintained that Christian people ought not to be refused the blood of their Lord, for the confession of whom they are required to shed their own. These landmarks also

(*b*) Epiph. Epist. ab. Hier. vers. Con. Eliber. c. 36. (*c*) Amb. de Abra. lib. 1. c. 7.
(*d*) Gelas. Pap. in Conc. Rom.
(*e*) Chrys. in 1 Cap. Ephes. Calix. Papa de Cons. dist. 2.
(*f*) Gelas. can. Comperimus de Cons. dist. 2. Cypr. Epist. 2. lib. 1, de Laps.

they have removed, in appointing, by an inviolable law, that very thing which the former punished with excommunication, and the latter gave a powerful reason for disapproving. There was a father (*g*) who asserted the temerity of deciding on either side of an obscure subject, without clear and evident testimonies of Scripture. This landmark they forgot when they made so many constitutions, canons, and judicial determinations, without any authority from the word of God. There was a father (*h*) who upbraided Montanus with having, among other heresies, been the first imposer of laws for the observance of fasts. They have gone far beyond this landmark also, in establishing fasts by the strictest laws. There was a father (*i*) who denied that marriage ought to be forbidden to the ministers of the Church, and pronounced cohabitation with a wife to be real chastity; and there were fathers who assented to his judgment. They have transgressed these landmarks by enjoining on their priests the strictest celibacy. There was a father who thought that attention should be paid to Christ only, of whom it is said, "Hear ye him," and that no regard should be had to what others before us have either said or done, only to what has been commanded by Christ, who is preëminent over all. This landmark they neither prescribe to themselves, nor permit to be observed by others, when they set up over themselves and others any masters rather than Christ. There was a father (*k*) who contended that the Church ought not to take the precedence of Christ, because his judgment is always according to truth; but ecclesiastical judges, like other men, may generally be deceived. Breaking down this landmark also, they scruple not to assert, that all the authority of the Scripture depends on the decision of the Church. All the fathers, with one heart and voice, have declared it execrable and detestable for the holy word of God to be contaminated with the subtleties of sophists, and perplexed by the wrangles of logicians. Do they confine themselves within these landmarks, when the whole business of their lives is to involve the simplicity of the Scripture in endless controversies, and worse

(*g*) August. lib. 2. de Pec. Mer. cap. ult.
(*h*) Apollon. de quo Eccl. Hist. lib. 5. cap. 11, 12.
(*i*) Paphnut. Trip. Hist. lib. 2. c. 14.   Cypr. Epist. 2. lib. 2.
(*k*) Aug. cap. 2. contr. Cresc. Grammatic.

than sophistical wrangles? so that if the fathers were now restored to life, and heard this art of wrangling, which they call speculative divinity, they would not suspect the dispute to have the least reference to God. But if I would enumerate all the instances in which the authority of the fathers is insolently rejected by those who would be thought their dutiful children, my address would exceed all reasonable bounds. Months and years would be insufficient for me. And yet such is their consummate and incorrigible impudence, they dare to censure us for presuming to transgress the ancient landmarks.

Nor can they gain any advantage against us by their argument from custom; for, if we were compelled to submit to custom, we should have to complain of the greatest injustice. Indeed, if the judgments of men were correct, custom should be sought among the good. But the fact is often very different. What appears to be practised by many soon obtains the force of a custom. And human affairs have scarcely ever been in so good a state as for the majority to be pleased with things of real excellence. From the private vices of multitudes, therefore, has arisen public error, or rather a common agreement of vices, which these good men would now have to be received as law. It is evident to all who can see, that the world is inundated with more than an ocean of evils, that it is overrun with numerous destructive pests, that every thing is fast verging to ruin, so that we must altogether despair of human affairs, or vigorously and even violently oppose such immense evils. And the remedy is rejected for no other reason, but because we have been accustomed to the evils so long. But let public error be tolerated in human society; in the kingdom of God nothing but his eternal truth should be heard and regarded, which no succession of years, no custom, no confederacy, can circumscribe. Thus Isaiah once taught the chosen people of God: "Say ye not, A confederacy, to all to whom this people shall say, A confederacy;" that is, that they should not unite in the wicked consent of the people; "nor fear their fear, nor be afraid," but rather "sanctify the Lord of hosts," that he might "be their fear and their dread." (*l*) Now, therefore, let them, if they please, object against us past ages and present examples; if we "sanctify the Lord of hosts,"

(*l*) Isaiah viii. 12, 13.

we shall not be much afraid. For, whether many ages agree in similar impiety, he is mighty to take vengeance on the third and fourth generation; or whether the whole world combine in the same iniquity, he has given an example of the fatal end of those who sin with a multitude, by destroying all men with a deluge, and preserving Noah and his small family, in order that his individual faith might condemn the whole world. Lastly, a corrupt custom is nothing but an epidemical pestilence, which is equally fatal to its objects, though they fall with a multitude. Besides, they ought to consider a remark, somewhere made by Cyprian, (*m*) that persons who sin through ignorance, though they cannot be wholly exculpated, may yet be considered in some degree excusable; but those who obstinately reject the truth offered by the Divine goodness, are without any excuse at all.

Nor are we so embarrassed by their dilemma as to be obliged to confess, either that the Church was for some time extinct, or that we have now a controversy with the Church. The Church of Christ has lived, and will continue to live, as long as Christ shall reign at the right hand of the Father, by whose hand she is sustained, by whose protection she is defended, by whose power she is preserved in safety. For he will undoubtedly perform what he once promised, to be with his people "even to the end of the world." (*n*) We have no quarrel against the Church, for with one consent we unite with all the company of the faithful in worshipping and adoring the one God and Christ the Lord, as he has been adored by all the pious in all ages. But our opponents deviate widely from the truth when they acknowledge no Church but what is visible to the corporeal eye, and endeavour to circumscribe it by those limits within which it is far from being included. Our controversy turns on the two following points:—first, they contend that the form of the Church is always apparent and visible; secondly, they place that form in the see of the Roman Church and her order of prelates. We assert, on the contrary, first, that the Church may exist without any visible form; secondly, that its form is not contained in that external splendour which they fool-

---

(*m*) Epist. 3. lib. 2. et in Epist. ad Julian. de Hæret. baptiz.
(*n*) Matt xxviii. 20.

ishly admire, but is distinguished by a very different criterion, *viz.* the pure preaching of God's word, and the legitimate administration of the sacraments. They are not satisfied unless the Church can always be pointed out with the finger. But how often among the Jewish people was it so disorganized, as to have no visible form left? What splendid form do we suppose could be seen, when Elias deplored his being left alone? (*o*) How long, after the coming of Christ, did it remain without any external form? How often, since that time, have wars, seditions, and heresies, oppressed and totally obscured it? If they had lived at that period, would they have believed that any Church existed? Yet Elias was informed that there were "left seven thousand" who had "not bowed the knee to Baal." Nor should we entertain any doubt of Christ's having always reigned on earth ever since his ascension to heaven. But if the pious at such periods had sought for any form evident to their senses, must not their hearts have been quite discouraged? Indeed it was already considered by Hilary in his day as a grievous error, that people were absorbed in foolish admiration of the episcopal dignity, and did not perceive the dreadful mischiefs concealed under that disguise. For this is his language : (*p*) "One thing I advise you — beware of Antichrist, for you have an improper attachment to walls; your veneration for the Church of God is misplaced on houses and buildings; you wrongly introduce under them the name of peace. Is there any doubt that they will be seats of Antichrist? I think mountains, woods, and lakes, prisons and whirlpools, less dangerous; for these were the scenes of retirement or banishment in which the prophets prophesied." But what excites the veneration of the multitude in the present day for their horned bishops, but the supposition that those are the holy prelates of religion whom they see presiding over great cities? Away, then, with such stupid admiration. Let us rather leave it to the Lord, since he alone "knoweth them that are his," (*q*) sometimes to remove from human observation all external knowledge of his Church. I admit this to be a dreadful judgment of God on the earth; but if it be deserved by the impiety of men, why do we attempt to resist the righteous vengeance of God? Thus the Lord punished the ingrati-

(*o*) 1 Kings xix. 14, 18.   (*p*) Contr. Auxent.   (*q*) 2 Tim. ii. 19.

tude of men in former ages; for, in consequence of their resistance to his truth, and extinction of the light he had given them, he permitted them to be blinded by sense, deluded by absurd falsehoods, and immerged in profound darkness, so that there was no appearance of the true Church left; yet, at the same time, in the midst of darkness and errors, he preserved his scattered and concealed people from total destruction. Nor is this to be wondered at; for he knew how to save in all the confusion of Babylon, and the flame of the fiery furnace. But how dangerous it is to estimate the form of the Church by I know not what vain pomp, which they contend for; I shall rather briefly suggest than state at large, lest I should protract this discourse to an excessive length. The Pope, they say, who holds the Apostolic see, and the bishops anointed and consecrated by him, provided they are equipped with mitres and crosiers, represent the Church, and ought to be considered as the Church. Therefore they cannot err. How is this?—Because they are pastors of the Church, and consecrated to the Lord. And did not the pastoral character belong to Aaron, and the other rulers of Israel? Yet Aaron and his sons, after their designation to the priesthood, fell into error when they made the golden calf. (*r*) According to this mode of reasoning, why should not the four hundred prophets, who lied to Ahab, have represented the Church? (*s*) But the Church remained on the side of Micaiah, solitary and despised as he was, and out of his mouth proceeded the truth. Did not those prophets exhibit both the name and appearance of the Church, who with united violence rose up against Jeremiah, and threatened and boasted, "the law shall not perish from the priest, nor counsel from the wise, nor the word from the prophet"? (*t*) Jeremiah is sent singly against the whole multitude of prophets, with a denunciation from the Lord, that the "law shall perish from the priest, counsel from the wise, and the word from the prophet." (*v*) And was there not the like external respectability in the council convened by the chief priests, scribes, and Pharisees, to consult about putting Christ to death? (*w*) Now, let them go and adhere to the external appearance, and thereby make Christ and all the prophets schismatics, and, on the other

(*r*) Exod. xxxii. 4.   (*s*) 1 Kings xxii. 6, 11—23.   (*t*) Jer. xviii. 18.
    (*v*) Jer. iv. 9.   (*w*) Matt. xxvi. 3, 4.

hand, make the ministers of Satan instruments of the Holy Spirit. But if they speak their real sentiments, let them answer me sincerely, what nation or place they consider as the seat of the Church, from the time when, by a decree of the council of Basil, Eugenius was deposed and degraded from the pontificate, and Amadeus substituted in his place. They cannot deny that the council, as far as relates to external forms, was a lawful one, and summoned not only by one pope, but by two. There Eugenius was pronounced guilty of schism, rebellion, and obstinacy, together with all the host of cardinals and bishops who had joined him in attempting a dissolution of the council. Yet afterwards, assisted by the favour of princes, he regained the quiet possession of his former dignity. That election of Amadeus, though formally made by the authority of a general and holy synod, vanished into smoke; and he was appeased with a cardinal's hat, like a barking dog with a morsel. From the bosom of those heretics and rebels have proceeded all the popes, cardinals, bishops, abbots, and priests, ever since. Here they must stop. For to which party will they give the title of the Church? Will they deny that this was a general council, which wanted nothing to complete its external majesty, being solemnly convened by two papal bulls, consecrated by a presiding legate of the Roman see, and well regulated in every point of order, and invariably preserving the same dignity to the last? Will they acknowledge Eugenius to be a schismatic, with all his adherents, by whom they have all been consecrated? Either, therefore, let them give a different definition of the form of the Church, or, whatever be their number, we shall account them all schismatics, as having been knowingly and voluntarily ordained by heretics. But if it had never been ascertained before, that the Church is not confined to external pomps, they would themselves afford us abundant proof of it, who have so long superciliously exhibited themselves to the world under the title of the Church, though they were at the same time the deadly plagues of it. I speak not of their morals, and those tragical exploits with which all their lives abound, since they profess themselves to be Pharisees, who are to be heard and not imitated. I refer to the very doctrine itself, on which they found their claim to be considered as the Church. If you devote a portion of your leisure, Sire, to the perusal of our writings, you will clearly discover that doctrine to be a fatal pestilence of souls, the firebrand, ruin, and destruction of the Church.

Finally, they betray great want of candour, by invidiously repeating what great commotions, tumults, and contentions, have attended the preaching of our doctrine, and what effects it produces in many persons. For it is unfair to charge it with those evils which ought to be attributed to the malice of Satan. It is the native property of the Divine word, never to make its appearance without disturbing Satan, and rousing his opposition. This is the most certain and unequivocal criterion by which it is distinguished from false doctrines, which are easily broached when they are heard with general attention, and received with applauses by the world. Thus, in some ages, when all things were immerged in profound darkness, the prince of this world amused and diverted himself with the generality of mankind, and, like another Sardanapalus, gave himself up to his ease and pleasures in perfect peace; for what would he do but amuse and divert himself, in the quiet and undisturbed possession of his kingdom? But when the light shining from above dissipated a portion of his darkness — when that Mighty One alarmed and assaulted his kingdom — then he began to shake off his wonted torpor, and to hurry on his armour. First, indeed, he stirred up the power of men to suppress the truth by violence at its first appearance; and when this proved ineffectual, he had recourse to subtlety. He made the Catabaptists, and other infamous characters, the instruments of exciting dissensions and doctrinal controversies, with a view to obscure and finally to extinguish it. And now he continues to attack it in both ways; for he endeavours to root up this genuine seed by means of human force, and at the same time tries every effort to choke it with his tares, that it may not grow and produce fruit. But all his attempts will be vain, if we attend to the admonitions of the Lord, who hath long ago made us acquainted with his devices, that we might not be caught by him unawares, and has armed us with sufficient means of defence against all his assaults. But to charge the word of God with the odium of seditions, excited against it by wicked and rebellious men, or of sects raised by impostors, — is not this extreme malignity? Yet it is not without example in former times. Elias was asked whether it was not he "that troubled Israel." (*x*) Christ was represented by the Jews as guilty of sedition. (*y*) The apostles were accused of stirring up popular commotions. (*z*) Wherein does this differ from the conduct of those who, at the present day, impute to us all the disturbances, tumults, and contentions, that break out against us? But the proper answer to such accusations has been taught us by Elias, that the dissemination of errors and the raising of tumults is not chargeable on us, but on those who are resisting the power of God. But as this one reply is sufficient to repress their temerity, so, on the other hand, we must meet the weakness of some persons, who are frequently disturbed with such offences, and become unsettled and wavering in their minds. Now, that they may not stumble and fall amidst this agitation and perplexity, let them know that the apostles in their day experienced the same things that now befall us. There were "unlearned and unstable" men, Peter says, who "wrested" the inspired writings of Paul "to their own destruction." (*a*) There were despisers of God, who, when they heard that "where sin abounded grace did much more abound," immediately concluded, Let us "continue in sin, that grace may abound." When they heard that the faithful were "not under the law," they immediately croaked, "We will sin, because we are not under the law, but under grace." (*b*) There were some who accused him as an encourager of sin. Many false apostles crept in, to destroy the churches he had raised. "Some preached" the gospel "of envy and strife, not in sincerity," maliciously "supposing to add affliction to his bonds." (*c*) In some places the Gospel was attended with little benefit. "All were seeking their own, not the things of Jesus Christ." (*d*) Others returned "like dogs to their vomit, and like swine to their wallowing in the mire." (*e*) Many perverted the liberty of the spirit into the licentiousness of the flesh. Many insinuated themselves as brethren, who afterwards brought the pious into dangers. Various contentions were excited among the brethren themselves. What was to be done by the apostles in such circumstances? Should they not have dissembled for a time, or

(*x*) 1 Kings xviii. 17.　　(*y*) Luke xxiii. 2, 5.　　(*z*) Acts xvii. 6. xxiv. 5.
(*a*) 2 Pet. iii. 16.　　(*b*) Rom. v. 20. vi. 1, 14, 15.　　(*c*) Phil. i. 15, 16.
(*d*) Phil. ii. 21.　　(*e*) 2 Pet. ii. 22.

rather have rejected and deserted that Gospel which appeared to be the nursery of so many disputes, the cause of so many dangers, the occasion of so many offences? But in such difficulties as these, their minds were relieved by this reflection, that Christ is the "stone of stumbling and rock of offence," (*f*) "set for the fall and rising again of many, and for a sign which shall be spoken against;" (*g*) and armed with this confidence, they proceeded boldly through all the dangers of tumults and offences. The same consideration should support us, since Paul declares it to be the perpetual character of the Gospel, that it is "a savour of death unto death in them that perish," (*h*) although it was rather given us to be the "savour of life unto life," and "the power of God to" the "salvation" of the faithful; (*i*) which we also should certainly experience it to be, if we did not corrupt this eminent gift of God by our ingratitude, and pervert to our destruction what ought to be a principal instrument of our salvation.

But I return to you, Sire. Let not your Majesty be at all moved by those groundless accusations with which our adversaries endeavour to terrify you; as that the sole tendency and design of this new Gospel — for so they call it — is to furnish a pretext for seditions, and to gain impunity for all crimes. "For God is not the author of confusion, but of peace;" (*k*) nor is "the Son of God," who came to "destroy the works of the devil, the minister of sin." (*l*) And it is unjust to charge us with such motives and designs, of which we have never given cause for the least suspicion. Is it probable that we are meditating the subversion of kingdoms? — we, who were never heard to utter a factious word, whose lives were ever known to be peaceable and honest while we lived under your government, and who, even now in our exile, cease not to pray for all prosperity to attend yourself and your kingdom! Is it probable that we are seeking an unlimited license to commit crimes with impunity? in whose conduct, though many things may be blamed, yet there is nothing worthy of such severe reproach! Nor have we, by Divine Grace, profited so little in the Gospel, but that our life may be an example to our detractors of chastity, liberality, mercy, temperance, patience,

(*f*) 1 Pet. ii. 8.   (*h*) 2 Cor. ii. 15, 16.   (*k*) 1 Cor. xiv. 33.
(*g*) Luke ii. 34.   (*i*) Rom. i. 16.   (*l*) 1 John iii. 8. Gal. ii. 17.

modesty, and every other virtue. It is an undeniable fact, that we sincerely fear and worship God, whose name we desire to be sanctified both by our life and by our death; and envy itself is constrained to bear testimony to the innocence and civil integrity of some of us, who have suffered the punishment of death for that very thing which ought to be accounted their highest praise. But if the Gospel be made a pretext for tumults, which has not yet happened in your kingdom; if any persons make the liberty of divine grace an excuse for the licentiousness of their vices, of whom I have known many, — there are laws and legal penalties, by which they may be punished according to their deserts; only let not the Gospel of God be reproached for the crimes of wicked men. You have now, Sire, the virulent iniquity of our calumniators laid before you in a sufficient number of instances, that you may not receive their accusations with too credulous an ear. — I fear I have gone too much into the detail, as this preface already approaches the size of a full apology; whereas I intended it not to contain our defence, but only to prepare your mind to attend to the pleading of our cause; for, though you are now averse and alienated from us, and even inflamed against us, we despair not of regaining your favour, if you will only once read with calmness and composure this our confession, which we intend as our defence before your Majesty. But, on the contrary, if your ears are so preoccupied with the whispers of the malevolent, as to leave no opportunity for the accused to speak for themselves, and if those outrageous furies, with your connivance, continue to persecute with imprisonments, scourges, tortures, confiscations, and flames, we shall indeed, like sheep destined to the slaughter, be reduced to the greatest extremities. Yet shall we in patience possess our souls, and wait for the mighty hand of the Lord, which undoubtedly will in time appear, and show itself armed for the deliverance of the poor from their affliction, and for the punishment of their despisers, who now exult in such perfect security. May the Lord, the King of kings, establish your throne with righteousness, and your kingdom with equity.

BASIL, 1st August, 1536.

GENERAL SYLLABUS.

The design of the Author in these Christian Institutes is twofold, relating, First, to the knowledge of God, as the way to attain a blessed immortality; and, in connection with and subservience to this, Secondly, to the knowledge of ourselves.

In the prosecution of this design, he strictly follows the method of the Apostles' Creed, as being most familiar to all Christians. For as the Creed consists of four parts, the first relating to God the Father, the second to the Son, the third to the Holy Spirit, the fourth to the Church; so the Author distributes the whole of this work into Four Books, corresponding respectively to the four parts of the Creed; as will clearly appear from the following detail: —

I. The first article of the Creed relates to God the Father, and to the creation, conservation, and government of all things, which are included in his omnipotence.

So the first book is on the knowledge of God, considered as the Creator, Preserver, and Governor of the universe at large, and of every thing contained in it. It shows both the nature and tendency of the true knowledge of the Creator — that this is not learned in the schools, but that every man from his birth is self-taught it — Yet that the depravity of men is so great as to corrupt and extinguish this knowledge, partly by ignorance, partly by wickedness; so that it neither leads him to glorify God as he ought, nor conducts him to the attainment of happiness — And though this internal knowledge is assisted by all the creatures around, which serve as a mirror to display the Divine perfections, yet that man does not profit by it — Therefore, that to those, whom it is God's will to bring to an intimate and saving knowledge of himself, he gives his written word; which introduces observations on the sacred Scripture — That he has therein revealed himself; that not the Father only, but the Father, Son, and Holy Spirit, united, is the Creator of heaven and earth; whom neither the knowledge innate by nature, nor the very beautiful mirror displayed to us in the world, can, in consequence of our depravity, teach us to know so as to glorify him. This gives occasion for treating of the revelation of God in the Scripture, of the unity of the Divine Essence, and the trinity of Persons. — To prevent man from attributing to God the blame of his own voluntary blindness, the Author shows the state of man at his creation, and treats of the image of God, free-will, and the primitive integrity of nature. — Having finished the subject of creation, he proceeds to the conservation and government of all things, concluding the first book with a full discussion of the doctrine of divine providence.

II. But since man is fallen by sin from the state in which he was created, it is necessary to come to Christ. Therefore it follows in the Creed, "And in Jesus Christ, his only Son our Lord," &c.

So in the second book of the Institutes our Author treats of the knowledge of God as the Redeemer in Christ; and having shown the fall of man, leads him to Christ the Mediator. Here he states the doctrine of original sin — that man possesses no inherent strength to enable him to deliver himself from sin and the impending curse, but that, on the contrary, nothing can proceed from him, antecedently to reconciliation and renovation, but what is deserving of condemnation — Therefore, that, man being utterly lost in himself, and incapable of conceiving even a good thought by which he may restore himself, or perform actions acceptable to God, he must seek redemption out of himself, in Christ — That the Law was given for this purpose, not to confine its observers to itself, but to conduct them to Christ; which gives occasion to introduce an exposition of the Moral Law — That he was known, as the Author of salvation, to the Jews under the Law, but more fully under the Gospel, in which he is manifested to the world. — Hence follows the doctrine of the similarity and difference of the Old and New Testament, of the Law and Gospel. — It is next stated, that, in order to the complete accomplishment of salvation, it was necessary for the eternal Son of God to become man, and that he actually assumed a real human nature: — it is also shown how these two natures constitute one person — That the office of Christ, appointed for the acquisition and application of complete salvation by his merit and efficacy, is sacerdotal, regal, and prophetical. — Next follows the manner in which Christ executed his office, or actually performed the part of a Mediator, being an exposition of the Articles respecting his death, resurrection, and ascension to heaven. — Lastly, the Author shows the truth and propriety of affirming that Christ merited the grace of God and salvation for us.

III. As long as Christ is separate from us, he profits us nothing. Hence the necessity of our being ingrafted into him, as branches into a vine. Therefore the doctrine concerning Christ is followed, in the third part of the Creed, by this clause, "I believe in the Holy Spirit," as being the bond of union between us and Christ.

So in the third book our Author treats of the Holy Spirit, who unites us to Christ — and consequently of faith, by which we embrace Christ, with his twofold benefit, free righteousness, which he imputes to us, and regeneration, which he commences within us, by bestowing repentance upon us. — And to show that we have not the least room to glory in such faith as is unconnected with the pursuit of repentance, before proceeding to the full discussion of justification, he treats at large of repentance and the continual exercise of it, which Christ, apprehended by faith, produces in us by his Spirit. — He next fully discusses the first and chief benefit of Christ when united to us by the Holy Spirit, that is, justification — and then treats of prayer, which resembles the hand that actually receives those blessings to be enjoyed, which faith knows, from the word of promise, to be laid up with God for our use. — But as all men are not united to Christ, the sole Author of salvation, by the Holy Spirit, who creates and preserves faith in us, he treats of God's eternal election; which is the cause that we, in whom he foresaw no good but what he intended freely to bestow, have been favoured with the gift of Christ, and united to God by the effectual call of the Gospel. — Lastly, he treats of complete regeneration, and the fruition of happiness; that is, the final resurrection, towards which our eyes must be directed, since in this world the felicity of the pious, in respect of enjoyment, is only begun.

IV. But as the Holy Spirit does not unite all men to Christ, or make them partakers of faith, and on those to whom he imparts it he does not ordinarily bestow it without means, but employs for this purpose the preaching of the Gospel and the use of the sacraments, with the administration of all discipline, therefore it follows in the Creed, "I believe in the Holy Catholic Church," whom, though involved in eternal death, yet, in pursuance of the gratuitous election, God has freely reconciled to himself in Christ, and made partakers of the Holy Spirit, that, being ingrafted into Christ, they may have communion with him as their head, whence flows a perpetual remission of sins, and a full restoration to eternal life.

So in the fourth book our Author treats of the Church — then of the means used by the Holy Spirit in effectually calling from spiritual death, and preserving the church — the word and sacraments — baptism and the Lord's supper — which are as it were Christ's regal sceptre, by which he commences his spiritual reign in the Church by the energy of his Spirit, and carries it forwards from day to day during the present life, after the close of which he perfects it without those means.

And as political institutions are the asylums of the Church in this life, though civil government is distinct from the spiritual kingdom of Christ, our Author instructs us respecting it as a signal blessing of God, which the Church ought to acknowledge with gratitude of heart, till we are called out of this transitory state to the heavenly inheritance, where God will be all in all.

This is the plan of the Institutes, which may be comprised in the following brief summary: —

Man, created originally upright, being afterwards ruined, not partially, but totally, finds salvation out of himself, wholly in Christ; to whom being united by the Holy Spirit, freely bestowed, without any regard of future works, he enjoys in him a twofold benefit, the perfect imputation of righteousness, which attends him to the grave, and the commencement of sanctification, which he daily increases, till at length he completes it at the day of regeneration or resurrection of the body, so that in eternal life and the heavenly inheritance his praises are celebrated for such stupendous mercy.

INSTITUTES

OF THE

CHRISTIAN RELIGION.

BOOK I.

ON THE KNOWLEDGE OF GOD THE CREATOR.

ARGUMENT.

The first book treats of the knowledge of God the Creator; but, this being chiefly manifested in the creation of man, man also is made the subject of discussion. Thus the principal topics of the whole treatise are two — the knowledge of God, and the knowledge of man. In the first chapter, they are considered together; in the following chapters, separately; yet some things are introduced, which may be referred to either or both. What respects the Scripture and images may belong to the knowledge of God; what respects the formation of the world, the holy angels, and the devils, to the knowledge of man; and what respects the manner in which God governs the world, to both.

On the first of these topics, the knowledge of God, this book shows,

First, What kind of knowledge God himself requires—Chap. II.

Secondly, Where it must be sought—Chap. III.—IX., as follows:

1. Not in man; because, though the human mind is naturally endued with it, yet it is extinguished, partly by ignorance, partly by wickedness—Chap. III. IV.
2. Nor in the structure of the world; because, though it shines there with the brightest evidence, testimonies of that kind, however plain, are, through our stupidity, wholly useless to us—Chap. V.
3. But in the Scripture—Chap. VI.—IX.

Thirdly, What kind of a being God is—Chap. X.
Fourthly, The impiety of ascribing to God a visible form, with observations on the adoration and origin of images—Chap. XI.
Fifthly, The reasonableness that God alone should be supremely worshipped—Chap. XII.
Lastly, The unity of the Divine Essence, and the distinction of three Persons—Chap. XIII.
On the other of these topics, the knowledge of man, it contains,
First, A dissertation on the creation of the world, and on the good and evil angels, all which relate to man—Chap. XIV.
Secondly, Proceeding to man himself, an examination of his nature and powers—Chap. XV.
But, in order to a clearer illustration of the knowledge of God and man, the three remaining chapters treat of the government of all human actions and of the whole world, in opposition to fortune and fate, stating the pure doctrine, and showing its use; and conclude with proving that, though God uses the agency of the wicked, he is pure from all pollution, and chargeable with no blame.

CHAPTER I.

THE CONNECTION BETWEEN THE KNOWLEDGE OF GOD AND THE KNOWLEDGE OF OURSELVES.

True and substantial wisdom principally consists of two parts, the knowledge of God, and the knowledge of ourselves. But, while these two branches of knowledge are so intimately connected, which of them precedes and produces the other, is not easy to discover. For, in the first place, no man can take a survey of himself but he must immediately turn to the contemplation of God, in whom he "lives and moves;" (a) since it is evident that the talents which we possess are not from ourselves, and that our very existence is nothing but a subsistence in God alone. These bounties, distilling to us by drops from heaven, form, as it were, so many streams conducting us to the fountain-head. Our poverty conduces to a clearer display of the infinite fulness of God. Especially, the miserable ruin, into which we have been plunged by the defection of the first man, compels us to raise our eyes towards heaven, not only as hungry and famished, to seek thence a supply for our wants,

(a) Acts xvii. 2.

but, aroused with fear, to learn humility. For, since man is subject to a world of miseries, and has been spoiled of his divine array, this melancholy exposure discovers an immense mass of deformity: every one, therefore, must be so impressed with a consciousness of his own infelicity, as to arrive at some knowledge of God. Thus a sense of our ignorance, vanity, poverty, infirmity, depravity, and corruption, leads us to perceive and acknowledge that in the Lord alone are to be found true wisdom, solid strength, perfect goodness, and unspotted righteousness; and so, by our imperfections, we are excited to a consideration of the perfections of God. Nor can we really aspire toward him, till we have begun to be displeased with ourselves. For who would not gladly rest satisfied with himself? where is the man not actually absorbed in self-complacency, while he remains unacquainted with his true situation, or content with his own endowments, and ignorant or forgetful of his own misery? The knowledge of ourselves, therefore, is not only an incitement to seek after God, but likewise a considerable assistance towards finding him.

II. On the other hand, it is plain that no man can arrive at the true knowledge of himself, without having first contemplated the divine character, and then descended to the consideration of his own. For, such is the native pride of us all, we invariably esteem ourselves righteous, innocent, wise, and holy, till we are convinced, by clear proofs, of our unrighteousness, turpitude, folly, and impurity. But we are never thus convinced, while we confine our attention to ourselves, and regard not the Lord, who is the only standard by which this judgment ought to be formed. Because, from our natural proneness to hypocrisy, any vain appearance of righteousness abundantly contents us instead of the reality; and, every thing within and around us being exceedingly defiled, we are delighted with what is least so, as extremely pure, while we confine our reflections within the limits of human corruption. So the eye, accustomed to see nothing but black, judges that to be very white, which is but whitish, or perhaps brown. Indeed, the senses of our bodies may assist us in discovering how grossly we err in estimating the powers of the soul. For if at noon-day we look either on the ground, or at any surrounding objects, we conclude our vision to be very strong and piercing; but when we raise our eyes and steadily look at the sun, they are at once dazzled and confounded with such a blaze of brightness, and we are constrained to confess, that our sight, so piercing in viewing terrestrial things, when directed to the sun, is dimness itself. Thus also it happens in the consideration of our spiritual endowments. For as long as our views are bounded by the earth, perfectly content with our own righteousness, wisdom, and strength, we fondly flatter ourselves, and fancy we are little less than demigods. But, if we once elevate our thoughts to God, and consider his nature, and the consummate perfection of his righteousness, wisdom, and strength, to which we ought to be conformed, — what before charmed us in ourselves under the false pretext of righteousness, will soon be loathed as the greatest iniquity; what strangely deceived us under the title of wisdom, will be despised as extreme folly; and what wore the appearance of strength, will be proved to be most wretched impotence. So very remote from the divine purity is what seems in us the highest perfection.

III. Hence that horror and amazement with which the Scripture always represents the saints to have been impressed and disturbed, on every discovery of the presence of God. For when we see those, who before his appearance stood secure and firm, so astonished and affrighted at the manifestation of his glory, as to faint and almost expire through fear, — we must infer that man is never sufficiently affected with a knowledge of his own meanness, till he has compared himself with the Divine Majesty. Of this consternation we have frequent examples in the Judges and Prophets; so that it was a common expression among the Lord's people — "We shall die, because we have seen God." (*b*) Therefore the history of Job, to humble men with a consciousness of their pollution, impotence, and folly, derives its principal argument from a description of the Divine purity, power, and wisdom. And not without reason. For we see how Abraham, the nearer he approached to behold the glory of the Lord, the more fully acknowledged himself to be but "dust and ashes;" (*c*) and how Elias (*d*) could not bear his approach without covering his face, his appearance is so formidable. And what can man do, all vile and corrupt, when fear constrains even the cherubim themselves to veil their faces? This is what the prophet Isaiah speaks of — "the moon shall be confounded, and the sun ashamed, when the Lord of hosts shall reign:" (*e*) that is, when he shall make a fuller and nearer exhibition of his splendour, it shall eclipse the splendour of the brightest object besides. But, though the knowledge of God and the knowledge of ourselves be intimately connected, the proper order of instruction requires us first to treat of the former, and then to proceed to the discussion of the latter.

(*b*) Judg. xiii. 22.
(*c*) Gen. xviii. 27.
(*d*) 1 Kings xix. 13.
(*e*) Isaiah vi. 2; xxiv. 23.

CHAPTER II.

THE NATURE AND TENDENCY OF THE KNOWLEDGE OF GOD.

By the knowledge of God, I intend not merely a notion that there is such a Being, but also an acquaintance with whatever we ought to know concerning Him, conducing to his glory and our benefit. For we cannot with propriety say, there is any knowledge of God where there is no religion or piety. I have no reference here to that species of knowledge by which men, lost and condemned in themselves, apprehend God the Redeemer in Christ the Mediator; but only to that first and simple knowledge, to which the genuine order of nature would lead us, if Adam had retained his innocence. For though, in the present ruined state of human nature, no man will ever perceive God to be a Father, or the Author of salvation, or in any respect propitious, but as pacified by the mediation of Christ; yet it is one thing to understand, that God our Maker supports us by his power, governs us by his providence, nourishes us by his goodness, and follows us with blessings of every kind, and another to embrace the grace of reconciliation proposed to us in Christ. Therefore, since God is first manifested, both in the structure of the world and in the general tenor of Scripture, simply as the Creator, and afterwards reveals himself in the person of Christ as a Redeemer, hence arises a twofold knowledge of him; of which the former is first to be considered, and the other will follow in its proper place. For though our mind cannot conceive of God, without ascribing some worship to him, it will not be sufficient merely to apprehend that he is the only proper object of universal worship and adoration, unless we are also persuaded that he is the fountain of all good, and seek for none but in him. This I maintain, not only because he sustains the universe, as he once made it, by his infinite power, governs it by his wisdom, preserves it by his goodness, and especially reigns over the human race in righteousness and judgment, exercising a merciful forbearance, and defending them by his protection; but because there cannot be found the least particle of wisdom, light, righteousness, power, rectitude, or sincere truth which does not proceed from him, and claim him for its author: we should therefore learn to expect and supplicate all these things from him, and thankfully to acknowledge what he gives us. For this sense of the divine perfections is calculated to teach us piety, which produces religion. By piety, I mean a reverence and love of God, arising from a knowledge of his benefits. For, till men are sensible that they owe every thing to God, that they are supported by his paternal care, that he is the Author of all the blessings they enjoy, and that nothing should be sought independently of him, they will never voluntarily submit to his authority; they will never truly and cordially devote themselves to his service, unless they rely upon him alone for true felicity.

II. Cold and frivolous, then, are the speculations of those who employ themselves in disquisitions on the essence of God, when it would be more interesting to us to become acquainted with his character, and to know what is agreeable to his nature. For what end is answered by professing, with Epicurus, that there is a God, who, discarding all concern about the world, indulges himself in perpetual inactivity? What benefit arises from the knowledge of a God with whom we have no concern? Our knowledge of God should rather tend, first, to teach us fear and reverence; and, secondly, to instruct us to implore all good at his hand, and to render him the praise of all that we receive. For how can you entertain a thought of God without immediately reflecting, that, being a creature of his formation, you must, by right of creation, be subject to his authority? that you are indebted to him for your life, and that all your actions should be done with reference to him? If this be true, it certainly follows that your life is miserably corrupt, unless it be regulated by a desire of obeying him, since his will ought to be the rule of our conduct. Nor can you have a clear view of him without discovering him to be the fountain and origin of all good. This would produce a desire of union to him, and confidence in him, if the human mind were not seduced by its own depravity from the right path of investigation. For, even at the first, the pious mind dreams not of any imaginary deity, but contemplates only the one true God; and, concerning him, indulges not the fictions of fancy, but, content with believing him to be such as he reveals himself, uses the most diligent and unremitting caution, lest it should fall into error by a rash and presumptuous transgression of his will. He who thus knows him, sensible that all things are subject to his control, confides in him as his Guardian and Protector, and unreservedly commits himself to his care. Assured that he is the author of all blessings, in distress or want he immediately flies to his protection, and expects his aid. Persuaded of his goodness and mercy, he relies on him with unlimited confidence, nor doubts of finding in his clemency a remedy provided for all his evils. Knowing him to be his Lord and Father, he concludes that he ought to mark his government in all things, revere his majesty, endeavour to promote his glory, and obey his commands. Perceiving him to be a just Judge, armed with severity for the punishment of crimes, he keeps his tribunal always in view, and is restrained by fear from provoking his wrath. Yet he is not so terrified at the apprehension of his justice, as to wish to evade it, even if escape were possible; but loves him as much in punishing the wicked as in blessing the pious, because he believes it as necessary to his glory to punish the impious and abandoned, as to reward the righteous with eternal life. Besides, he restrains himself from sin, not merely from a dread of vengeance, but because he loves and reveres God as his Father, honours and worships him as his Lord, and, even though there were no hell, would shudder at the thought of offending him. See, then, the nature of pure and genuine religion. It consists in faith, united with a serious fear of God, comprehending a voluntary reverence, and producing legitimate worship agreeable to the injunctions of the law. And this requires to be the more carefully remarked, because men in general render to God a formal worship, but very few truly reverence him; while great ostentation in ceremonies is universally displayed, but sincerity of heart is rarely to be found.

CHAPTER III.

THE HUMAN MIND NATURALLY ENDUED WITH THE KNOWLEDGE OF GOD.

We lay it down as a position not to be controverted, that the human mind, even by natural instinct, possesses some sense of a Deity. For that no man might shelter himself under the pretext of ignorance, God hath given to all some apprehension of his existence, (*f*) the memory of which he frequently and insensibly renews; so that, as men universally know that there is a God, and that he is their Maker, they must be condemned by their own testimony, for not having worshipped him and consecrated their lives to his service. If we seek for ignorance of a Deity, it is nowhere more likely to be found, than among tribes the most stupid and furthest from civilization. But, as the celebrated Cicero observes, there is no nation so barbarous, no race so savage, as not to be firmly persuaded of the being of a God. (*g*) Even those who in other respects appear to differ but little from brutes, always

(*f*) Rom. i. 20.   (*g*) Cicer. de Natur. Deor. lib. i.   Lactant. Inst. lib. iii. cap. 10

retain some sense of religion; so fully are the minds of men possessed with this common principle, which is closely interwoven with their original composition. Now, since there has never been a country or family, from the beginning of the world, totally destitute of religion, it is a tacit confession, that some sense of the Divinity is inscribed on every heart. Of this opinion, idolatry itself furnishes ample proof. For we know how reluctantly man would degrade himself to exalt other creatures above him. His preference of worshipping a piece of wood or stone, to being thought to have no god, evinces the impression of a Deity on the human mind to be very strong, the obliteration of which is more difficult than a total change of the natural disposition; and this is certainly changed, whenever man leaves his natural pride, and voluntarily descends to such meannesses under the notion of worshipping God.

II. It is most absurd, then, to pretend, as is asserted by some, that religion was the contrivance of a few subtle and designing men, a political machine to confine the simple multitude to their duty, while those who inculcated the worship of God on others, were themselves far from believing that any god existed. I confess, indeed, that artful men have introduced many inventions into religion, to fill the vulgar with reverence, and strike them with terror, in order to obtain the greater command over their minds. But this they never could have accomplished, if the minds of men had not previously been possessed of a firm persuasion of the existence of God, from which the propensity to religion proceeds. And that they who cunningly imposed on the illiterate, under the pretext of religion, were themselves wholly destitute of any knowledge of God, is quite incredible. For though there were some in ancient times, and many arise in the present age, who deny the existence of God, yet, in spite of their reluctance, they are continually receiving proofs of what they desire to disbelieve. We read of no one guilty of more audacious or unbridled contempt of the Deity than Caligula; yet no man ever trembled with greater distress at any instance of Divine wrath, so that he was constrained to dread the Divinity whom he professed to despise. This you may always see exemplified in persons of similar character. For the most audacious contemners of God are most alarmed, even at the noise of a falling leaf. Whence arises this, but from the vengeance of the Divine Majesty, smiting their consciences the more powerfully in proportion to their efforts to fly from it? They try every refuge to hide themselves from the Lord's presence, and to efface it from their minds; but their attempts to elude it are all in vain. Though it may seem to disappear for a moment, it presently returns with increased violence; so that, if they have any remission of the anguish of conscience, it resembles the sleep of persons intoxicated, or subject to frenzy, who enjoy no placid rest while sleeping, being continually harassed with horrible and tremendous dreams. The impious themselves, therefore, exemplify the observation, that the idea of a God is never lost in the human mind.

III. It will always be evident to persons of correct judgment, that the idea of a Deity impressed on the mind of man is indelible. That all have by nature an innate persuasion of the Divine existence, a persuasion inseparable from their very constitution, we have abundant evidence in the contumacy of the wicked, whose furious struggles to extricate themselves from the fear of God are unavailing. Though Diagoras, and others like him, turn to ridicule what all ages have believed of religion; (*h*) though Dionysius scoff at the judgment of Heaven, — it is but a forced laughter, for the worm of a guilty conscience torments them within, worse than if they were seared with hot irons. I agree not with Cicero, that errors in process of time become obsolete, and that religion is increased and ameliorated daily. For the world, as will shortly be observed, uses its utmost endeavours to banish all knowledge of God, and tries every method of corrupting his worship. I only maintain, that while the stupid insensibility which the wicked wish to acquire, to promote their contempt of God, preys upon their minds, yet the sense of a Deity, which they ardently desire to extinguish, is still strong, and frequently discovers itself. Whence we infer, that this is a doctrine, not first to be learned in the schools, but which every man from his birth is self-taught, and which, though many strain every nerve to banish it from them, yet nature itself permits none to forget. Now, if the end for which all men are born and live, be to know God, — and unless the knowledge of God have reached this point, it is uncertain and vain, — it is evident, that all who direct not every thought and action of life to this end, are degenerated from the law of their creation. Of this the heathen philosophers themselves were not ignorant. This was Plato's meaning, when he taught that the chief good of the soul consists in similitude to God, when the soul, having a clear knowledge of him, is wholly transformed into his likeness. (*i*) The reasoning also of Gryllus, in Plutarch, is very accurate, when he affirms, that men entirely destitute of religion, not only do not excel the brutes, but are in many respects far more wretched, being obnoxious to evil under so many forms, and always dragging on a tumultuous

---

(*h*) Cicer. de Nat. Deor. lib. 1 & 3. Valer. Maxim. lib. 1, cap. 1.
(*i*) In Phæd. & Theæt.

and restless life. The worship of God is therefore the only thing which renders men superior to brutes, and makes them aspire to immortality.

CHAPTER IV.

THIS KNOWLEDGE EXTINGUISHED OR CORRUPTED, PARTLY BY IGNORANCE, PARTLY BY WICKEDNESS.

While experience testifies that the seeds of religion are sown by God in every heart, we scarcely find one man in a hundred who cherishes what he has received, and not one in whom they grow to maturity, much less bear fruit in due season. Some perhaps grow vain in their own superstitions, while others revolt from God with intentional wickedness; but all degenerate from the true knowledge of him. The fact is, that no genuine piety remains in the world. But, in saying that some fall into superstition through error, I would not insinuate that their ignorance excuses them from guilt; because their blindness is always connected with pride, vanity, and contumacy. Pride and vanity are discovered, when miserable men, in seeking after God, rise not, as they ought, above their own level, but judge of him according to their carnal stupidity, and leave the proper path of investigation in pursuit of speculations as vain as they are curious. Their conceptions of him are formed, not according to the representations he gives of himself, but by the inventions of their own presumptuous imaginations. This gulf being opened, whatever course they take, they must be rushing forwards to destruction. None of their subsequent attempts for the worship or service of God can be considered as rendered to him; because they worship not him, but a figment of their own brains in his stead. This depravity Paul expressly remarks: " Professing themselves to be wise, they became fools." (k) He had before said, "they became vain in their imaginations." But lest any should exculpate them, he adds that they were deservedly blinded, because, not content within the bounds of sobriety, but arrogating to themselves more than was right, they wilfully darkened, and even infatuated themselves with pride, vanity, and perverseness. Whence it follows, that their folly is inexcusable, which originates not only in a vain curiosity, but in false confidence, and an immoderate desire to exceed the limits of human knowledge.

(k) Rom. i. 22.

II. David's assertion, that "the fool hath said in his heart, There is no God," (*l*) is primarily, as we shall soon see in another place, to be restricted to those who extinguish the light of nature, and wilfully stupefy themselves. For we see many, become hardened by bold and habitual transgressions, striving to banish all remembrance of God, which the instinct of nature is still suggesting to their minds. To render their madness more detestable, he introduces them as expressly denying the existence of God; not that they deprive him of his being, but because they rob him of his justice and providence, shutting him up as an idler in heaven. Now, as nothing would be more inconsistent with Deity, than to abandon the government of the world, leave it to fortune, and connive at the crimes of men, that they might wanton with impunity, — whoever extinguishes all fear of the heavenly judgment, and indulges himself in security, denies that there is any God. After the impious have wilfully shut their own eyes, it is the righteous vengeance of God upon them, to darken their understandings, so that, seeing, they may not perceive. (*m*) David is the best interpreter of his own meaning, in another place, where he says, "The wicked have no fear of God before their eyes;" (*n*) and again, that they encourage themselves in their iniquities with the flattering persuasion that God doth not see them. (*o*) Though they are constrained to acknowledge the existence of God, yet they rob him of his glory, by detracting from his power. For as God, according to the testimony of Paul, "cannot deny himself," (*p*) because he perpetually remains like himself, — those who feign him to be a vain and lifeless image, are truly said to deny God. It must also be remarked, that, though they strive against their own natural understanding, and desire not only to banish him thence, but even to annihilate him in heaven, their insensibility can never prevail, so as to prevent God from sometimes recalling them to his tribunal. But as no dread restrains them from violent opposition to the divine will, it is evident, as long as they are carried away with such a blind impetuosity, that they are governed by a brutish forgetfulness of God.

III. Thus is overthrown the vain excuse pleaded by many for their superstition; for they satisfy themselves with any attention to religion, however preposterous, not considering that the Divine Will is the perpetual rule to which true religion ought to be conformed; that God ever continues like himself; that he is no spectre or phantasm, to be metamorphosed according to the fancy of every individual. It is easy to see how superstition mocks God with hypocritical services, while it attempts

(*l*) Psalm xiv. 1.   (*m*) Isaiah vi. 9.   (*n*) Psalm xxxvi. 1.
(*o*) Psalm x. 11.   (*p*) 2 Tim. ii. 13.

to please him. For, embracing only those things which he declares he disregards, it either contemptuously practises, or even openly rejects, what he prescribes and declares to be pleasing in his sight. Persons who introduce newly-invented methods of worshipping God, really worship and adore the creature of their distempered imaginations; for they would never have dared to trifle in such a manner with God, if they had not first feigned a god conformable to their own false and foolish notions. Wherefore the apostle pronounces a vague and unsettled notion concerning the Deity to be ignorance of God. "When ye knew not God, (says he,) ye did service unto them which by nature were no gods." (*q*) And in another place he speaks of the Ephesians as having been "without God," (*r*) while they were strangers to a right knowledge of the only true God. Nor, in this respect, is it of much importance, whether you imagine to yourself one god or more; for in either case you depart and revolt from the true God, and, forsaking him, you have nothing left you but an execrable idol. We must therefore decide, with Lactantius, that there is no legitimate religion unconnected with truth.

IV. Another sin is, that they never think of God but against their inclinations, nor approach him till their reluctance is overcome by constraint; and then they are influenced, not by a voluntary fear, proceeding from reverence of the Divine Majesty, but by a servile and constrained fear, extorted by the divine judgment, which they dread because it is inevitable, at the same time that they hate it. Now, to impiety, and to this species of it alone, is applicable that assertion of Statius, that fear first made gods in the world. (*s*) They, whose minds are alienated from the righteousness of God, earnestly desire the subversion of that tribunal, which they know to be established for the punishment of transgressions against it. With this disposition, they wage war against the Lord, who cannot be deprived of his judgment; but when they apprehend his irresistible arm to be impending over their heads, unable to avert or evade it, they tremble with fear. That they may not seem altogether to despise him, whose majesty troubles them, they practise some form of religion; at the same time not ceasing to pollute themselves with vices of every kind, and to add one flagitious act to another, till they have violated every part of God's holy law, and dissipated all its righteousness. It is certain, at least, that they are not prevented by that pretended fear of God from enjoying pleasure and satisfaction in their sins, practising self-adulation, and preferring the indulgence of their own carnal intemperance to the salutary restraints of the

(*q*) Gal. iv. 8.   (*r*) Eph. ii. 12.   (*s*) Statii Thebaid. lib. 3.

Holy Spirit. But that being a false and vain shadow of religion, and scarcely worthy even to be called its shadow, — it is easy to infer the wide difference between such a confused notion of God, and the piety which is instilled only into the minds of the faithful, and is the source of religion. Yet hypocrites, who are flying from God, resort to the artifices of superstition, for the sake of appearing devoted to him. For whereas the whole tenor of their life ought to be a perpetual course of obedience to him, they make no scruple of rebelling against him in almost all their actions, only endeavouring to appease him with a few paltry sacrifices. Whereas he ought to be served with sanctity of life and integrity of heart, they invent frivolous trifles and worthless observances, to conciliate his favour. They abandon themselves to their impurities with the greater licentiousness, because they confide in being able to discharge all their duty to him by ridiculous expiations. In a word, whereas their confidence ought to be placed on him, they neglect him, and depend upon themselves or on other creatures. At length they involve themselves in such a vast accumulation of errors, that those sparks which enable them to discover the glory of God are smothered, and at last extinguished by the criminal darkness of iniquity. That seed, which it is impossible to eradicate, a sense of the existence of a Deity, yet remains; but so corrupted as to produce only the worst of fruits. Yet this is a further proof of what I now contend for, that an idea of God is naturally engraved on the hearts of men, since necessity extorts a confession of it, even from reprobates themselves. In the moment of tranquillity, they facetiously mock the Divine Being, and with loquacious impertinence derogate from his power. But if any despair oppress them, it stimulates them to seek him, and dictates concise prayers, which prove that they are not altogether ignorant of God, but that what ought to have appeared before had been suppressed by obstinacy.

CHAPTER V.

THE KNOWLEDGE OF GOD CONSPICUOUS IN THE FORMATION AND CONTINUAL GOVERNMENT OF THE WORLD.

As the perfection of a happy life consists in the knowledge of God, that no man might be precluded from attaining felicity, God hath not only sown in the minds of men the seed of religion, already mentioned, but hath manifested himself in the formation of every part of the world, and daily presents himself to public view, in such a manner, that they cannot open their eyes without being constrained to behold him. His essence indeed is incomprehensible, so that his Majesty is not to be perceived by the human senses; but on all his works he hath inscribed his glory in characters so clear, unequivocal, and striking, that the most illiterate and stupid cannot exculpate themselves by the plea of ignorance. The Psalmist therefore, with great propriety, exclaims, " He covereth himself with light as with a garment ; " (*t*) as if he had said, that his first appearance in visible apparel was at the creation of the world, when he displayed those glories which are still conspicuous on every side. In the same place, the Psalmist compares the expanded heavens to a royal pavilion ; — he says that "he layeth the beams of his chambers in the waters ; maketh the clouds his chariot ; walketh upon the wings of the wind ; " and maketh the winds and the lightnings his swift messengers. And because the glory of his power and wisdom is more refulgently displayed above, heaven is generally called his palace. And, in the first place, whithersoever you turn your eyes, there is not an atom of the world in which you cannot behold some brilliant sparks at least of his glory. But you cannot at one view take a survey of this most ample and beautiful machine in all its vast extent, without being completely overwhelmed with its infinite splendour. Wherefore the author of the Epistle to the Hebrews elegantly represents the worlds as the manifestations of invisible things ; (*v*) for the exact symmetry of the universe is a mirror, in which we may contemplate the otherwise invisible God. For which reason the Psalmist (*w*) attributes to the celestial bodies a language universally known ; for they afford a testimony of the Deity too evident to escape the observation even of the most ignorant people in the world. But the Apostle more distinctly asserts this manifestation to men of what was useful to be known concerning God ; " for the invisible things of him from the creation of the world are clearly seen, being understood by the things that are made, even his eternal power and godhead." (*x*)

II. Of his wonderful wisdom, both heaven and earth contain innumerable proofs ; not only those more abstruse things, which are the subjects of astronomy, medicine, and the whole science of physics, but those things which force themselves on the view of the most illiterate of mankind, so that they cannot open their eyes without being constrained to witness them. Adepts, indeed, in those liberal arts, or persons just

---

(*t*) Psalm civ. 2.   (*v*) Heb. xi. 3.   (*w*) Psalm xix. 1, 3.   (*x*) Rom. i. 20.

initiated into them, are thereby enabled to proceed much further in investigating the secrets of Divine Wisdom. Yet ignorance of those sciences prevents no man from such a survey of the workmanship of God, as is more than sufficient to excite his admiration of the Divine Architect. In disquisitions concerning the motions of the stars, in fixing their situations, measuring their distances, and distinguishing their peculiar properties, there is need of skill, exactness, and industry; and the providence of God being more clearly revealed by these discoveries, the mind ought to rise to a sublimer elevation for the contemplation of his glory. But since the meanest and most illiterate of mankind, who are furnished with no other assistance than their own eyes, cannot be ignorant of the excellence of the Divine skill, exhibiting itself in that endless, yet regular variety of the innumerable celestial host, — it is evident, that the Lord abundantly manifests his wisdom to every individual on earth. Thus it belongs to a man of preëminent ingenuity to examine, with the critical exactness of Galen, the connection, the symmetry, the beauty, and the use of the various parts of the human body. But the composition of the human body is universally acknowledged to be so ingenious, as to render its Maker the object of deserved admiration.

III. And therefore some of the philosophers (*y*) of antiquity have justly called man a microcosm, or world in miniature; because he is an eminent specimen of the power, goodness, and wisdom of God, and contains in him wonders enough to occupy the attention of our minds, if we are not indisposed to such a study. For this reason, Paul, having remarked that the blind " might feel after God and find him," immediately adds, that " he is not far from every one of us;" (*z*) because every man has undoubtedly an inward perception of the celestial goodness, by which he is quickened. But if, to attain some ideas of God, it be not necessary for us to go beyond ourselves, what an unpardonable indolence is it in those who will not descend into themselves that they may find him! For the same reason, David, having briefly celebrated the wonderful name and honour of God, which are universally conspicuous, immediately exclaims, " What is man, that thou art mindful of him?" (*a*) Again, " Out of the mouths of babes and sucklings thou hast ordained strength." Thus declaring not only that the human race is a clear mirror of the works of God, but that even infants at the breast have tongues so eloquent for the publication of his glory, that there is no necessity for other orators; whence he hesitates not to produce them as fully

(*y*) Macrob. lib. 2. de Somn. Scip. c. 12. Boet. de Defin. Arist. lib. 1. de Hist. Animal.   (*z*) Acts xvii. 27.   (*a*) Psalm viii. 2, 4.

capable of confuting the madness of those whose diabolical pride would wish to extinguish the name of God. Hence also what Paul quotes from Aratus, that "we are the offspring of God;" (b) since his adorning us with such great excellence has proved him to be our Father. So, from the dictates of common sense and experience, the heathen poets called him the Father of men. Nor will any man freely devote himself to the service of God, unless he have been allured to love and reverence him, by first experiencing his paternal love.

IV. But herein appears the vile ingratitude of men — that, while they ought to be proclaiming the praises of God for the wonderful skill displayed in their formation, and the inestimable bounties he bestows on them, they are only inflated with the greater pride. They perceive how wonderfully God works within them, and experience teaches them what a variety of blessings they receive from his liberality. They are constrained to know, whether willingly or not, that these are proofs of his divinity: yet they suppress this knowledge in their hearts. Indeed, they need not go out of themselves, provided they do not, by arrogating to themselves what is given from heaven, smother the light which illuminates their minds to a clearer discovery of God. Even in the present day, there are many men of monstrous dispositions, who hesitate not to pervert all the seeds of divinity sown in the nature of man, in order to bury in oblivion the name of God. How detestable is this frenzy, that man, discovering in his body and soul a hundred vestiges of God, should make this very excellence a pretext for the denial of his being! They will not say that they are distinguished from the brutes by chance; but they ascribe it to nature, which they consider as the author of all things, and remove God out of sight. They perceive most exquisite workmanship in all their members, from the head to the feet. Here also they substitute nature in the place of God. But above all, the rapid motions of the soul, its noble faculties, and excellent talents, discover a Divinity not easily concealed; unless the Epicureans, like the Cyclops, from this eminence should audaciously wage war against God. Do all the treasures of heavenly wisdom concur in the government of a worm five feet in length? and shall the universe be destitute of this privilege? To state that there is in the soul a certain machinery corresponding to every part of the body, is so far from obscuring the divine glory, that it is rather an illustration of it. Let Epicurus answer; what concourse of atoms in the concoction of food and drink distributes part into excrements and part into blood, and causes the several members to perform

(b) Acts xvii. 28.

their different offices with as much diligence as if so many souls by common consent governed one body?

V. But my present concern is not with that sty of swines: I rather address those who, influenced by preposterous subtilties, would indirectly employ that frigid dogma of Aristotle to destroy the immortality of the soul, and deprive God of his rights. For, because the organs of the body are directed by the faculties of the soul, they pretend the soul to be so united to the body as to be incapable of subsisting without it; and by their eulogies of nature do all they can to suppress the name of God. But the powers of the soul are far from being limited to functions subservient to the body. For what concern has the body in measuring the heavens, counting the number of the stars, computing their several magnitudes, and acquiring a knowledge of their respective distances, of the celerity or tardiness of their courses, and of the degrees of their various declinations? I grant, indeed, the usefulness of astronomy, but only remark that, in these profound researches relating to the celestial orbs, there is no corporeal coöperation, but that the soul has its functions distinct from the body. I have proposed one example, whence inferences may readily be drawn by the readers. The manifold agility of the soul, which enables it to take a survey of heaven and earth; to join the past and the present; to retain the memory of things heard long ago; to conceive of whatever it chooses by the help of imagination; its ingenuity also in the invention of such admirable arts, — are certain proofs of the divinity in man. Besides, in sleep, it not only turns and moves itself round, but conceives many useful ideas, reasons on various subjects, and even divines future events. What shall we say, but that the vestiges of immortality impressed upon man are absolutely indelible? Now, what reason can be given, why man, who is of divine original, should not acknowledge his Creator? Shall we indeed, by the judgment with which we are endued, discern right from wrong, and shall there be no judge in heaven? Shall we, even in our sleep, have some remains of intelligence, and shall there be no God to govern the world? Shall we be esteemed the inventers of so many useful arts, that God may be defrauded of his praise? Whereas experience abundantly teaches, that all we have is variously distributed to us by some superior Being. The clamour of some, about a secret inspiration animating the whole world, is not only weak, but altogether profane. They are pleased with the celebrated passage of Virgil —

> "Know, first, a spirit, with an active flame,
> Fills, feeds, and animates this mighty frame;
> Runs through the watery worlds, the fields of air,
> The ponderous earth, the depths of heaven; and there
> Glows in the sun and moon, and burns in every star.

> Thus, mingling with the mass, the general soul
> Lives in the parts, and agitates the whole.
> From that celestial energy began
> The low-browed brute, th' imperial race of man,
> The painted birds who wing th' aërial plain,
> And all the mighty monsters of the main;
> Their souls at first from high Olympus came," &c. (c)

Just as if the world, which is a theatre erected for displaying the glory of God, were its own creator! For thus writes the same poet in another place, following the common opinion of the Greeks and Latins —

> " Led by such wonders, sages have opined,
> That bees have portions of a heavenly mind;
> That God pervades, and, like one common soul,
> Fills, feeds, and animates the world's great whole;
> That flocks, herds, beasts, and men, from him receive
> Their vital breath; in him all move and live;
> That souls discerpt from him shall never die,
> But back resolved to God and heaven shall fly,
> And live for ever in the starry sky." (d)

See the efficacy of that jejune speculation concerning a universal mind animating and actuating the world, in the production and encouragement of piety in the human heart. This more fully appears also from the profane expressions of the filthy Lucretius, which are deductions from the same principle. (e) Its true tendency is to set up a shadowy deity, and to banish all ideas of the true God, the proper object of fear and worship. I confess, indeed, that the expression, that nature is God, may be used in a pious sense by a pious mind; but, as it is harsh and inconsistent with strict propriety of speech, nature being rather an order prescribed by God, it is dangerous in matters so momentous, and demanding peculiar caution, to confound the Deity with the inferior course of his works.

VI. Let us remember, then, in every consideration of our own nature, that there is one God, who governs all natures, and who expects us to regard him, to direct our faith to him, to worship and invoke him. For nothing is more preposterous than to enjoy such splendid advantages, which proclaim within us their divine origin, and to neglect the Author who bountifully bestows them. Now, what illustrious specimens of his power have we to arrest our attention! unless it be possible for us not to know what strength is required to sustain with his word this immense fabric of heaven and earth; now by his mere nod to shake the heaven with roaring peals of thunder, to consume whatever he choose with lightnings, and set the atmosphere on fire with the flame; now to disturb it with

(c) Æneid vi. Pitt's Translation. (d) Georg. iv. Warton's Translation.
(e) De Rerum Natur. lib. 1.

tempests in various forms, and immediately, if he please, to compose all to instantaneous serenity; to restrain, suspended as it were in air, the sea, which, by its elevation, seems to threaten the earth with continual devastation; now raising it in a tremendous manner, by the tumultuous violence of the winds, and now appeasing the waves to render it calm. To this purpose are the numerous praises of the power of God, drawn from the testimonies of nature, particularly in the book of Job, and in the prophecies of Isaiah; which I now purposely omit, as they will be more suitably introduced, when I discuss the scriptural account of the creation of the world. Only I wished at present to hint, that this way of seeking God, by tracing the lineaments which, both above and below us, exhibit such a lively adumbration of him, is common to aliens, and to those who belong to his family. His power leads us to the consideration of his eternity; because he, from whom all things derive their origin, must necessarily be eternal and self-existent. But if we inquire the reason that induced him first to create all things, and now to preserve them, we shall find the sole cause to be his own goodness. But though this be the only cause, it should be more than sufficient to attract us to love him; since, according to the Psalmist, (*f*) there is no creature that does not participate in the effusions of his mercy.

VII. In the second species of his works, such as happen out of the ordinary course of nature, the proofs of his perfections are equally clear. For he so regulates his providence in the government of human society, that, while he exhibits, in innumerable ways, his benignity and beneficence to all, he likewise declares, by evident and daily indications, his clemency to the pious, and his severity to the wicked and ungodly. For no doubt can be entertained respecting his punishment of flagitious crimes; inasmuch as he clearly demonstrates himself to be the guardian and avenger of innocence, in prospering with his blessing the life of good men, in assisting their necessities, assuaging and comforting their sorrows, alleviating their calamities, and providing in all things for their safety. Nor should it perplex or eclipse his perpetual rule of righteousness, that he frequently permits the wicked and guilty for a time to exult in impunity; but suffers good men to be undeservedly harassed with much adversity, and even to be oppressed by the iniquitous malice of the ungodly. We ought rather to make a very different reflection; that, when he clearly manifests his wrath in the punishment of one sin, he hates all sins; and that, since he now passes by many sins unpunished, there will be a judgment hereafter, till which the punishment is de-

(*f*) Psalm cxlv. 9.

ferred. So, also, what ample occasion he supplies us for the consideration of his mercy, while, with unwearied benignity, he pursues the miserable, calling them back to himself with more than paternal indulgence, till his beneficence overcomes their depravity!

VIII. To this end the Psalmist, (*g*) mentioning that God, in desperate cases, suddenly and wonderfully succors, beyond all expectation, those who are miserable and ready to perish, either protecting from beasts of prey such as are wandering in deserts, and, at length, reconducting them into the right way, or supplying with food the needy and hungry, or delivering captives from dreary dungeons and iron chains, or bringing the shipwrecked safe into port, or healing the diseases of some who are almost dead, or scorching the earth with excessive heat and drought, or fertilizing it with the secret showers of his mercy, or elevating the meanest of the vulgar, or degrading nobles from their dignified stations,—the Psalmist, I say, having proposed such examples as these, infers from them that what are accounted fortuitous accidents, are so many proofs of his heavenly providence, especially of his paternal clemency; and that hence the pious have cause to rejoice, while the mouths of the impious and reprobate are stopped. But, since the majority of men, immersed in their errors, are blind amidst the greatest opportunities of seeing, he accounts it a rare instance of singular wisdom discreetly to consider these works of God; (*h*) from the sight of which, some, who, in other instances, discover the greatest acuteness, receive no benefit. And, notwithstanding all the displays of the glory of God, scarcely one man in a hundred is really a spectator of it. His power and wisdom are equally conspicuous. His power is illustriously manifested, when the ferocity of the impious, universally deemed insuperable, is quelled in an instant, their arrogance subdued, their strongest fortresses demolished, their weapons and armour broken in pieces, their strength diminished, their machinations confounded, and they fall by their own exertions; when the audacity, which exalted itself above the heavens, is thrown down to the centre of the earth; when, on the contrary, "the poor are raised out of the dust, and the needy out of the dunghill;" (*i*) the oppressed and afflicted extricated from distressing extremities, and the desperate restored to a good hope; when the unarmed are victorious over those who are armed, the few over the many, the weak over the strong. But his wisdom is eminently displayed in ordering every dispensation at the best possible time, confounding the greatest worldly sagacity, "taking the wise in their own craftiness," (*k*) and

(*g*) Psalm cvii.
(*h*) Psalm cvii. 43.
(*i*) Psalm cxiii. 7.
(*k*) 1 Cor. iii. 19.

finally disposing all things according to the dictates of the highest reason.

IX. We see that there is no need of any long or laborious argumentation, to obtain and produce testimonies for illustrating and asserting the Divine Majesty; since, from the few which we have selected and cursorily mentioned, it appears that they are every where so evident and obvious, as easily to be distinguished by the eyes, and pointed out with the fingers. And here it must again be observed, that we are invited to a knowledge of God; not such as, content with empty speculation, merely floats in the brain, but such as will be solid and fruitful, if rightly received and rooted in our hearts. For the Lord is manifested by his perfections: perceiving the influence and enjoying the benefits of which, we must necessarily be more acutely impressed with such a knowledge, than if we imagined a Deity of whose influence we had no perception. Whence we conclude this to be the right way, and the best method of seeking God; not with presumptuous curiosity to attempt an examination of his essence, which is rather to be adored than too curiously investigated; but to contemplate him in his works, in which he approaches and familiarizes, and, in some measure, communicates himself to us. To this the Apostle referred, when he said, that he is not to be sought far off, since, by his attribute of omnipresence, he dwells in every one of us. (*l*) Therefore David, having before confessed his greatness ineffable, after he descends to the mention of his works, adds, that he will "declare this greatness." (*m*) Wherefore it becomes us also to apply ourselves to such an investigation of God, as may fill our understanding with admiration, and powerfully interest our feelings. And, as Augustine somewhere teaches, being incapable of comprehending him, and fainting, as it were, under his immensity, we must take a view of his works, that we may be refreshed with his goodness. (*n*)

X. Now, such a knowledge ought not only to excite us to the worship of God, but likewise to awaken and arouse us to the hope of a future life. For when we consider, that the specimens given by the Lord, both of his clemency and of his severity, are only begun, and not completed, we certainly should esteem these as preludes to greater things, of which the manifestation and full exhibition are deferred to another life. When we see that pious men are loaded with afflictions by the impious, harassed with injuries, oppressed with calumnies, and vexed with contumelious and opprobrious treatment; that the wicked, on the contrary, flourish, prosper, obtain ease and dignity, and all with impunity, — we should immediately con-

(*l*) Acts xvii. 27.   (*m*) Psalm cxlv. 6.   (*n*) Aug. in Psal. cxliv.

clude, that there is another life, to which is reserved the vengeance due to iniquity, and the reward of righteousness. Moreover, when we observe the faithful frequently chastised by the Lord's rod, we may conclude, with great certainty, that the impious shall not always escape his vengeance. For that is a wise observation of Augustine — " If open punishment were now inflicted for every sin, it would be supposed that nothing would be reserved till the last judgment. Again, if God now did not openly punish any sin, it would be presumed that there was no divine providence." (*o*) It must therefore be confessed, that in each of the works of God, but more especially in the whole considered together, there is a bright exhibition of the divine perfections; by which the whole human race is invited and allured to the knowledge of God, and thence to true and complete felicity. But, though those perfections are most luminously portrayed around us, we only discover their principal tendency, their use, and the end of our contemplation of them, when we descend into our own selves, and consider by what means God displays in us his life, wisdom, and power, and exercises towards us his righteousness, goodness, and mercy. For, though David justly complains that unbelievers are fools, because they consider not the profound designs of God in the government of mankind, (*p*) yet there is much truth in what he says in another place — that the wonders of Divine Wisdom in this respect exceed in number the hairs of our head. (*q*) But as this argument must be treated more at large in due course, I at present omit it.

XI. But, notwithstanding the clear representations given by God in the mirror of his works, both of himself and of his everlasting dominion, such is our stupidity, that, always inattentive to these obvious testimonies, we derive no advantage from them. For, with regard to the structure and very beautiful organization of the world, how few of us are there, who, when lifting up their eyes to heaven, or looking round on the various regions of the earth, direct their minds to the remembrance of the Creator, and do not rather content themselves with a view of his works, to the total neglect of their Author! And with respect to those things that daily happen out of the ordinary course of nature, is it not the general opinion, that men are rolled and whirled about by the blind temerity of fortune, rather than governed by the providence of God? Or if, by the guidance and direction of these things, we are ever driven (as all men must sometimes be) to the consideration of a God, yet, when we have rashly conceived an idea of some deity, we soon slide into our own carnal dreams, or depraved

(*o*) De Civit. Dei. lib. 1, cap. 8.   (*p*) Psalm xcii. 6.   (*q*) Psalm xl. 12.

inventions, corrupting by our vanity the purity of divine truth. We differ from one another, in that each individual imbibes some peculiarity of error; but we perfectly agree in a universal departure from the one true God, to preposterous trifles. This disease affects, not only the vulgar and ignorant, but the most eminent, and those who, in other things, discover peculiar sagacity. How abundantly have all the philosophers, in this respect, betrayed their stupidity and folly! For, to spare others, chargeable with greater absurdities, Plato himself, the most religious and judicious of them all, loses himself in his round globe. (r) And what would not befall others, when their principal men, whose place it was to enlighten the rest, stumble upon such gross errors! So also, while the government of human actions proves a providence too plainly to admit of a denial, men derive no more advantage from it, than if they believed all things to be agitated forwards and backwards by the uncertain caprice of fortune; so great is our propensity to vanity and error! I speak exclusively of the excellent of mankind, not of the vulgar, whose madness in the profanation of divine truth has known no bounds.

XII. Hence that immense flood of errors, which has deluged the whole world. For every man's understanding is like a labyrinth to him; so that it is not to be wondered at, that the different nations were drawn aside into various inventions, and even that almost every individual had his own particular deity. For, amidst the union of temerity and wantonness with ignorance and darkness, scarcely a man could be found who did not frame to himself some idol or phantasm instead of God. Indeed, the immense multitude of gods proceeding from the mind of man, resembles the ebullition of waters from a vast and ample spring, while every one, with an extreme licentiousness of error, invents one thing or another concerning God himself. It is not necessary here to compose a catalogue of the superstitions which have perplexed the world; for it would be an endless task; and, without a word more being said, the horrible blindness of the human mind sufficiently appears from such a multiplicity of corruptions. I pass over the rude and unlearned vulgar. But among the philosophers, (s) who attempted with reason and learning to penetrate heaven, how shameful is the diversity! In proportion to the vigour of his natural genius, and the polish acquired by art and science, each of them seemed to give the more specious colouring to his own opinion; but, on a close inspection, you will find them all fading colours. The Stoics said, in their own opinion very

---

(r) Plut. de Philosoph. placitis, lib. 1. Plato in Timæo. Cic lib. 1, de Natur. Deor.   (s) Lactant. Institut. div.

shrewdly, that from all the parts of nature may be collected various names of God, but yet that the one God is not therefore divided; (*t*) as if we were not already too much inclined to vanity, without being further and more violently seduced into error, by the notion of such a various abundance of gods. The mystical theology of the Egyptians also shows that they all sedulously endeavoured to preserve the appearance of reason in the midst of their folly. (*v*) And any thing apparently probable might at first sight, perhaps, deceive the simple and incautious; but there never was any human invention by which religion was not basely corrupted. And this confused diversity imboldened the Epicureans, and other gross despisers of piety, to reject all idea of God. For, seeing the wisest of men contending with each other for contrary opinions, they hesitated not, from their dissensions, and from the frivolous and absurd doctrines maintained by the different parties, to infer, that it was vain and foolish for men to torment themselves with investigations concerning God, who does not exist. And this they thought they might do with impunity, supposing that a compendious denial of any God at all would be better than feigning uncertain gods, and thereby occasioning endless controversies. They reason very ignorantly, or rather endeavour to conceal their own impiety behind the ignorance of men, which not at all justifies any encroachment on God. But from the general confession, that there is no subject productive of so many dissensions among the learned as well as the unlearned, it is inferred, that the minds of men, which err so much in investigations concerning God, are extremely blind and stupid in celestial mysteries. Others commend the answer of Simonides, (*w*) who, being asked by Hiero the Tyrant what God was, requested a day to consider it. When the tyrant, the next day, repeated the inquiry, he begged to be allowed two days longer; and, having often doubled the number of days, at length answered, "The longer I consider the subject, the more obscure it appears to me." He prudently suspended his opinion on a subject so obscure to him; yet this shows that men, who are taught only by nature, have no certain, sound, or distinct knowledge, but are confined to confused principles; so that they worship an unknown God.

XIII. Now, it must also be maintained, that whoever adulterates the pure religion, (which must necessarily be the case of all who are influenced by their own imagination,) he is guilty of a departure from the one God. They will profess, indeed, a different intention; but what they intend, or what

---

(*t*) Seneca, lib. 4, de benef., &c.
(*v*) Plutarch. lib. 1, de Isid. & Osirid. Cic. lib. 1, de Nat. Deor.
(*w*) Cic. lib. de Nat. Deor.

they persuade themselves, is of little importance; since the Holy Spirit pronounces all to be apostates, who, in the darkness of their minds, substitute demons in the place of God. For this reason Paul declares the Ephesians to have been "without God" (*x*) — till they had learned from the gospel the worship of the true God. Nor should this be restricted to one nation only, since, in another place, he asserts of men in general, that they "became vain in their imaginations," (*y*) after the majesty of the Creator had been discovered to them in the structure of the world. And therefore the Scripture, to make room for the only true God, condemns, as false and lying, whatever was formerly worshipped as divine among the Gentiles, (*z*) and leaves no Deity but in Mount Sion, where flourished the peculiar knowledge of God. Indeed, among the Gentiles, the Samaritans, in the days of Christ, seemed to approach very nearly to true piety; yet we hear, from the mouth of Christ, that they "worshipped they knew not what;" (*a*) whence it follows, that they were under a vain and erroneous delusion. In fine, though they were not all the subjects of gross vices, or open idolaters, there was no pure and approved religion, their notions being founded only in common sense. For, though there were a few uninfected with the madness of the vulgar, this assertion of Paul remains unshaken, that "none of the princes of this world knew the wisdom of God." (*b*) But if the most exalted have been involved in the darkness of error, what must be said of the dregs of the people! Wherefore it is not surprising if the Holy Spirit reject, as spurious, every form of worship which is of human contrivance; because, in the mysteries of heaven, an opinion acquired by human means, though it may not always produce an immense mass of errors, yet always produces some. And though no worse consequence follow, it is no trivial fault to worship, at an uncertainty, an unknown god; of which, however, Christ pronounces all to be guilty who have not been taught by the law what god they ought to worship. And indeed the best legislators have proceeded no further than to declare religion to be founded upon common consent. And even Socrates, in Xenophon, (*c*) praises the answer of Apollo, which directed that every man should worship the gods according to the rites of his country, and the custom of his own city. But whence had mortals this right of determining, by their own authority, what far exceeds all the world? or who could so acquiesce in the decrees of the rulers or the ordinances of the people, as without hesitation to receive a god delivered

(*x*) Ephes. ii. 12. (*y*) Rom. i. 21. (*z*) Hab. ii. 18, 20.
(*a*) John iv. 22. (*b*) 1 Cor. ii. 8.
(*c*) Xenoph. de Dict. et Fact. Socrat. lib. 1. Cic. de Legib. lib. 2.

to him by the authority of man? Every man will rather abide by his own judgment, than be subject to the will of another. Since, then, the following of the custom of a city, or the consent of antiquity, in divine worship, is too weak and frail a bond of piety, it remains for God himself to give a revelation concerning himself from heaven.

XIV. Vain, therefore, is the light afforded us in the formation of the world to illustrate the glory of its Author; which, though its rays be diffused all around us, is insufficient to conduct us into the right way. Some sparks, indeed, are kindled, but smothered before they have emitted any great degree of light. Wherefore the Apostle, in the place before cited, says, " By faith we understand that the worlds were framed by the word of God;" (d) thus intimating, that the invisible Deity was represented by such visible objects, yet that we have no eyes to discern him, unless they be illuminated through faith by an internal revelation of God. Nor does Paul, where he observes, that "that which may be known of God is manifest" (e) in the creation of the world, design such a manifestation as human sagacity may comprehend; but rather shows, that its utmost extent is to render men inexcusable. The same writer also, though in one place (f) he denies that God is to be traced far off, seeing he dwells within us, yet teaches, in another place, (g) the consequences of such a proximity. God, says he, " in times past suffered all nations to walk in their own ways. Nevertheless he left not himself without witness, in that he did good, and gave us rain from heaven, and fruitful seasons, filling our hearts with food and gladness." (h) Though the Lord, then, is not destitute of a testimony concerning himself, while with various and most abundant benignity he sweetly allures mankind to a knowledge of him, yet they persist in following their own ways, their pernicious and fatal errors.

XV. But whatever deficiency of natural ability prevents us from attaining the pure and clear knowledge of God, yet, since that deficiency arises from our own fault, we are left without any excuse. Nor indeed can we set up any pretence of ignorance, that will prevent our own consciences from perpetually accusing us of indolence and ingratitude. Truly it would be a defence worthy to be admitted, if a man should plead that he wanted ears to hear the truth, for the publication of which even the mute creatures are supplied with most melodious voices; if he should allege that his eyes are not capable of seeing what is demonstrated by the creatures without the help

(d) Heb. xi. 3. (e) Rom. i. 19. (f) Rom. i. 20.
(g) Acts xvii. 27. (h) Acts xiv. 16, 17.

of the eyes; if he should plead mental imbecility, while all the irrational creatures instruct us. Wherefore we are justly excluded from all excuse for our uncertain and extravagant deviations, since all things conspire to show us the right way. But, however men are chargeable with sinfully corrupting the seeds of divine knowledge, which, by the wonderful operation of nature, are sown in their hearts, so that they produce no good and fair crop, yet it is beyond a doubt, that the simple testimony magnificently borne by the creatures to the glory of God, is very insufficient for our instruction. For as soon as a survey of the world has just shown us a deity, neglecting the true God, we set up in his stead the dreams and phantasms of our own brains; and confer on them the praise of righteousness, wisdom, goodness, and power, due to him. We either obscure his daily acts, or pervert them by an erroneous estimate; thereby depriving the acts themselves of their glory, and their Author of his deserved praise.

CHAPTER VI.

THE GUIDANCE AND TEACHING OF THE SCRIPTURE NECESSARY TO LEAD TO THE KNOWLEDGE OF GOD THE CREATOR.

Though the light which presents itself to all eyes, both in heaven and in earth, is more than sufficient to deprive the ingratitude of men of every excuse, since God, in order to involve all mankind in the same guilt, sets before them all, without exception, an exhibition of his majesty, delineated in the creatures, — yet we need another and better assistance, properly to direct us to the Creator of the world. Therefore he hath not unnecessarily added the light of his word, to make himself known unto salvation, and hath honoured with this privilege those whom he intended to unite in a more close and familiar connection with himself. For, seeing the minds of all men to be agitated with unstable dispositions, when he had chosen the Jews as his peculiar flock, he enclosed them as in a fold, that they might not wander after the vanities of other nations. And it is not without cause that he preserves us in the pure knowledge of himself by the same means; for, otherwise, they who seem comparatively to stand firm, would soon fall. For, as persons who are old, or whose eyes are by any means become dim, if you show them the most beautiful book, though they perceive something written, but can scarcely read two words together, yet, by the assistance of spectacles, will begin to read distinctly, — so the Scripture, collecting in our minds the otherwise confused notions of Deity, dispels the darkness, and gives us a clear view of the true God. This, then, is a singular favour, that, in the instruction of the Church, God not only uses mute teachers, but even opens his own sacred mouth; not only proclaims that some god ought to be worshipped, but at the same time pronounces himself to be the Being to whom this worship is due; and not only teaches the elect to raise their view to a Deity, but also exhibits himself as the object of their contemplation. This method he hath observed toward his Church from the beginning; beside those common lessons of instruction, to afford them also his word; which furnishes a more correct and certain criterion to distinguish him from all fictitious deities. And it was undoubtedly by this assistance that Adam, Noah, Abraham, and the rest of the patriarchs, attained to that familiar knowledge which distinguished them from unbelievers. I speak not yet of the peculiar doctrine of faith which illuminated them into the hope of eternal life. For, to pass from death to life, they must have known God, not only as the Creator, but also as the Redeemer; as they certainly obtained both from his word. For that species of knowledge, which related to him as the Creator and Governor of the world, in order, preceded the other. To this was afterwards added the other internal knowledge, which alone vivifies dead souls, and apprehends God, not only as the Creator of the world, and as the sole Author and Arbiter of all events, but also as the Redeemer in the person of the Mediator. But, being not yet come to the fall of man and the corruption of nature, I also forbear to treat of the remedy. Let the reader remember, therefore, that I am not yet treating of that covenant by which God adopted the children of Abraham, and of that point of doctrine by which believers have always been particularly separated from the profane nations, since that is founded on Christ; but am only showing how we ought to learn from the Scripture, that God, who created the world, may be certainly distinguished from the whole multitude of fictitious deities. The series of subjects will, in due time, lead us to redemption. But, though we shall adduce many testimonies from the New Testament, and some also from the Law and the Prophets, in which Christ is expressly mentioned, yet they will all tend to prove, that the Scripture discovers God to us as the Creator of the world, and declares what sentiments we should form of him, that we may not be seeking after a deity in a labyrinth of uncertainty.

II. But, whether God revealed himself to the patriarchs by oracles and visions, or suggested, by means of the ministry of men, what should be handed down by tradition to their posterity, it is beyond a doubt that their minds were impressed with a firm assurance of the doctrine, so that they were persuaded and convinced that the information they had received came from God. For God always secured to his word an undoubted credit, superior to all human opinion. At length, that the truth might remain in the world in a continual course of instruction to all ages, he determined that the same oracles which he had deposited with the patriarchs should be committed to public records. With this design the Law was promulgated, to which the Prophets were afterwards annexed, as its interpreters. — For, though the uses of the law were many, as will be better seen in the proper place; and particularly the intention of Moses, and of all the prophets, was to teach the mode of reconciliation between God and man, (whence also Paul calls Christ "the end of the law,") (*i*) — yet I repeat again, that, beside the peculiar doctrine of faith and repentance, which proposes Christ as the Mediator, the Scripture distinguishes the only true God by certain characters and titles, as the Creator and Governor of the world, that he may not be confounded with the multitude of false gods. Therefore, though every man should seriously apply himself to a consideration of the works of God, being placed in this very splendid theatre to be a spectator of them, yet he ought principally to attend to the word, that he may attain superior advantages. And, therefore, it is not surprising, that they who are born in darkness grow more and more hardened in their stupidity; since very few attend to the word of God with teachable dispositions, to restrain themselves within the limits which it prescribes, but rather exult in their own vanity. This, then, must be considered as a fixed principle, that, in order to enjoy the light of true religion, we ought to begin with the doctrine of heaven; and that no man can have the least knowledge of true and sound doctrine, without having been a disciple of the Scripture. Hence originates all true wisdom, when we embrace with reverence the testimony which God hath been pleased therein to deliver concerning himself. For obedience is the source, not only of an absolutely perfect and complete faith, but of all right knowledge of God. And truly in this instance God hath, in his providence, particularly consulted the true interests of mankind in all ages.

III. For, if we consider the mutability of the human mind, — how easy its lapse into forgetfulness of God; how great its propensity to errors of every kind; how violent its rage for the perpetual fabrication of new and false religions, — it will be easy

(*i*) Rom. x. 4.

to perceive the necessity of the heavenly doctrine being thus committed to writing, that it might not be lost in oblivion, or evaporate in error, or be corrupted by the presumption of men. Since it is evident, therefore, that God, foreseeing the inefficacy of his manifestation of himself in the exquisite structure of the world, hath afforded the assistance of his word to all those to whom he determined to make his instructions effectual, — if we seriously aspire to a sincere contemplation of God, it is necessary for us to pursue this right way. We must come, I say, to the word, which contains a just and lively description of God as he appears in his works, when those works are estimated, not according to our depraved judgment, but by the rule of eternal truth. If we deviate from it, as I have just observed, though we run with the utmost celerity, yet, being out of the course, we shall never reach the goal. For it must be concluded, that the light of the Divine countenance, which even the Apostle says "no man can approach unto," (*j*) is like an inexplicable labyrinth to us, unless we are directed by the line of the word; so that it were better to halt in this way, than to run with the greatest rapidity out of it. Therefore David, inculcating the necessity of the removal of superstitions out of the world, that pure religion may flourish, frequently introduces God as "reigning;" (*k*) by the word "reigning," intending, not the power which he possesses, and which he exercises in the universal government of nature, but the doctrine in which he asserts his legitimate sovereignty; because errors can never be eradicated from the human heart, till the true knowledge of God is implanted in it.

IV. Therefore the same Psalmist, having said, that "the heavens declare the glory of God, and the firmament showeth his handy-work; day unto day uttereth speech, and night unto night showeth knowledge," (*l*) afterwards proceeds to the mention of the word: "The law of the Lord is perfect, converting the soul: the testimony of the Lord is sure, making wise the simple: the statutes of the Lord are right, rejoicing the heart: the commandment of the Lord is pure, enlightening the eyes." For, though he also comprehends other uses of the law, yet he suggests, in general, that, since God's invitation of all nations to him by the view of heaven and earth is ineffectual, this is the peculiar school of the children of God. The same is adverted to in the twenty-ninth Psalm, where the Psalmist, having preached the terrors of the Divine voice, which in thunders, in winds, in showers, in whirlwinds, and in tempests, shakes the earth, makes the mountains tremble, and breaks the cedars, adds, at length, towards the close, " in

(*j*) 1 Tim. vi. 16.   (*k*) Ps. xciii. xcvi., &c.   (*l*) Ps. xix. 1, &c.

his temple doth every one speak of his glory;" because unbelievers are deaf to all the voices of God, which resound in the air. So, in another Psalm, after describing the terrible waves of the sea, he concludes thus: "Thy testimonies are very sure: holiness becometh thine house, O Lord, for ever." (*m*) Hence also proceeds the observation of Christ to the Samaritan woman, that her nation and all others worshipped they knew not what; and that the Jews were the only worshippers of the true God. (*n*) For, since the human mind is unable, through its imbecility, to attain any knowledge of God without the assistance of his sacred word, all mankind, except the Jews, as they sought God without the word, must necessarily have been wandering in vanity and error.

CHAPTER VII.

THE TESTIMONY OF THE SPIRIT NECESSARY TO CONFIRM THE SCRIPTURE, IN ORDER TO THE COMPLETE ESTABLISHMENT OF ITS AUTHORITY. THE SUSPENSION OF ITS AUTHORITY ON THE JUDGMENT OF THE CHURCH, AN IMPIOUS FICTION.

BEFORE I proceed any further, it is proper to introduce some remarks on the authority of the Scripture, not only to prepare the mind to regard it with due reverence, but also to remove every doubt. For, when it is admitted to be a declaration of the word of God, no man can be so deplorably presumptuous, unless he be also destitute of common sense and of the common feelings of men, as to dare to derogate from the credit due to the speaker. But since we are not favoured with daily oracles from heaven, and since it is only in the Scriptures that the Lord hath been pleased to preserve his truth in perpetual remembrance, it obtains the same complete credit and authority with believers, when they are satisfied of its divine origin, as if they heard the very words pronounced by God himself. The subject, indeed, merits a diffuse discussion, and a most accurate examination. But the reader will pardon me, if I attend rather to what the design of this work admits, than to what the extensive nature of the present subject requires. But there has very generally prevailed a most pernicious error, that the Scriptures have only so much weight as is conceded to them by the suffrages of the Church; as though the eternal

(*m*) Ps. xciii. 5.   (*n*) John iv. 22.

and inviolable truth of God depended on the arbitrary will of men. For thus, with great contempt of the Holy Spirit, they inquire, Who can assure us that God is the author of them? Who can with certainty affirm, that they have been preserved safe and uncorrupted to the present age? Who can persuade us that this book ought to be received with reverence, and that expunged from the sacred number, unless all these things were regulated by the decisions of the Church? It depends, therefore, (say they,) on the determination of the Church, to decide both what reverence is due to the Scripture, and what books are to be comprised in its canon. Thus sacrilegious men, while they wish to introduce an unlimited tyranny, under the name of the Church, are totally unconcerned with what absurdities they embarrass themselves and others, provided they can extort from the ignorant this one admission, that the Church can do every thing. But, if this be true, what will be the condition of those wretched consciences, which are seeking a solid assurance of eternal life, if all the promises extant concerning it rest only on the judgment of men? Will the reception of such an answer cause their fluctuations to subside, and their terrors to vanish? Again, how will the impious ridicule our faith, and all men call it in question, if it be understood to possess only a precarious authority depending on the favour of men!

II. But such cavillers are completely refuted even by one word of the Apostle. He testifies that the church is " built upon the foundation of the apostles and prophets." (o) If the doctrine of the prophets and apostles be the foundation of the Church, it must have been certain, antecedently to the existence of the Church. Nor is there any foundation for this cavil, that though the Church derive its origin from the Scriptures, yet it remains doubtful what writings are to be ascribed to the prophets and apostles, unless it be determined by the Church. For if the Christian Church has been from the beginning founded on the writings of the prophets and the preaching of the apostles, wherever that doctrine is found, the approbation of it has certainly preceded the formation of the Church; since without it the Church itself had never existed. It is a very false notion, therefore, that the power of judging of the Scripture belongs to the Church, so as to make the certainty of it dependent on the Church's will. Wherefore, when the Church receives it, and seals it with her suffrage, she does not authenticate a thing otherwise dubious or controvertible; but, knowing it to be the truth of her God, performs a duty of piety, by treating it with immediate veneration. But, with regard to the question, How shall we be persuaded of its divine

(o) Eph. ii. 20.

original, unless we have recourse to the decree of the Church? this is just as if any one should inquire, How shall we learn to distinguish light from darkness, white from black, sweet from bitter? For the Scripture exhibits as clear evidence of its truth, as white and black things do of their colour, or sweet and bitter things of their taste.

III. I know, indeed, that they commonly cite the opinion of Augustine, where he says, "that he would not believe the Gospel unless he were influenced by the authority of the Church." (*p*) But how falsely and unfairly this is cited in support of such a notion, it is easy to discover from the context. He was in that contending with the Manichees, who wished to be credited, without any controversy, when they affirmed the truth to be on their side, but never proved it. Now, as they made the authority of the Gospel a pretext in order to establish the credit of their Manichæus, he inquires what they would do if they met with a man who did not believe the Gospel; with what kind of persuasion they would convert him to their opinion. He afterwards adds, " Indeed, I would not give credit to the Gospel," &c., intending, that he himself, when an alien from the faith, could not be prevailed on to embrace the Gospel as the certain truth of God, till he was convinced by the authority of the Church. And is it surprising that any one, yet destitute of the knowledge of Christ, should pay a respect to men? Augustine, therefore, does not there maintain that the faith of the pious is founded on the authority of the Church, nor does he mean that the certainty of the Gospel depends on it; but simply, that unbelievers would have no assurance of the truth of the Gospel, that would win them to Christ, unless they were influenced by the consent of the Church. And a little before, he clearly confirms it in these words : " When I shall have commended my own creed, and derided yours, what judgment, think you, ought we to form, what conduct ought we to pursue, but to forsake those who invite us to acknowledge things that are certain, and afterwards command us to believe things that are uncertain ; and to follow those who invite us first to believe what we cannot yet clearly see, that, being strengthened by faith, we may acquire an understanding of what we believe ; our mind being now internally strengthened and illuminated, not by men, but by God himself?" These are the express words of Augustine ; whence the inference is obvious to every one, that this holy man did not design to suspend our faith in the Scriptures on the arbitrary decision of the Church, but only to show (what we all confess to be true) that they who

---

(*p*) Contr. Epist. Fundam. cap. 5.

are yet unilluminated by the Spirit of God, are, by a reverence for the Church, brought to such a docility as to submit to learn the faith of Christ from the Gospel; and that thus the authority of the Church is an introduction to prepare us for the faith of the Gospel. For we see that he will have the certainty of the pious to rest on a very different foundation. Otherwise I do not deny his frequently urging on the Manichees the universal consent of the Church, with a view to prove the truth of the Scripture, which they rejected. Whence his rebuke of Faustus, "for not submitting to the truth of the Gospel, so founded, so established, so gloriously celebrated, and delivered through certain successions from the apostolic age." But he nowhere insinuates that the authority which we attribute to the Scripture depends on the definitions or decrees of men: he only produces the universal judgment of the Church, which was very useful to his argument, and gave him an advantage over his adversaries. If any one desire a fuller proof of this, let him read his treatise "Of the Advantage of Believing;" where he will find, that he recommends no other facility of believing, than such as may afford us an introduction, and be a proper beginning of inquiry, as he expresses himself; yet that we should not be satisfied with mere opinion, but rest upon certain and solid truth.

IV. It must be maintained, as I have before asserted, that we are not established in the belief of the doctrine till we are indubitably persuaded that God is its Author. The principal proof, therefore, of the Scriptures is every where derived from the character of the Divine Speaker. The prophets and apostles boast not of their own genius, or any of those talents which conciliate the faith of the hearers; nor do they insist on arguments from reason; but bring forward the sacred name of God, to compel the submission of the whole world. We must now see how it appears, not from probable supposition, but from clear demonstration, that this use of the divine name is neither rash nor fallacious. Now, if we wish to consult the true interest of our consciences; that they may not be unstable and wavering, the subjects of perpetual doubt; that they may not hesitate at the smallest scruples, — this persuasion must be sought from a higher source than human reasons, or judgments, or conjectures — even from the secret testimony of the Spirit. It is true that, if we were inclined to argue the point, many things might be adduced which certainly evince, if there be any God in heaven, that he is the Author of the Law, and the Prophecies, and the Gospel. Even though men of learning and deep judgment rise up in opposition, and exert and display all the powers of their minds in this dispute, yet, unless they are wholly lost to all sense of shame, this confession will be extorted from them, that the Scripture exhibits the plainest evidences that it is God who speaks in it, which manifests its doctrine to be divine. And we shall soon see, that all the books of the sacred Scripture very far excel all other writings. If we read it with pure eyes and sound minds, we shall immediately perceive the majesty of God, which will subdue our audacious contradictions, and compel us to obey him. Yet it is acting a preposterous part, to endeavour to produce sound faith in the Scripture by disputations. Though, indeed, I am far from excelling in peculiar dexterity or eloquence, yet, if I were to contend with the most subtle despisers of God, who are ambitious to display their wit and their skill in weakening the authority of Scripture, I trust I should be able, without difficulty, to silence their obstreperous clamour. And, if it were of any use to attempt a refutation of their cavils, I would easily demolish the boasts which they mutter in secret corners. But though any one vindicates the sacred word of God from the aspersions of men, yet this will not fix in their hearts that assurance which is essential to true piety. Religion appearing, to profane men, to consist wholly in opinion, in order that they may not believe any thing on foolish or slight grounds, they wish and expect it to be proved by rational arguments, that Moses and the prophets spake by divine inspiration. But I reply, that the testimony of the Spirit is superior to all reason. For, as God alone is a sufficient witness of himself in his own word, so also the word will never gain credit in the hearts of men, till it be confirmed by the internal testimony of the Spirit. It is necessary, therefore, that the same Spirit, who spake by the mouths of the prophets, should penetrate into our hearts, to convince us that they faithfully delivered the oracles which were divinely intrusted to them. And this connection is very suitably expressed in these words: "My Spirit that is upon thee, and my word which I have put in thy mouth, shall not depart out of thy mouth, nor out of the mouth of thy seed, nor out of the mouth of thy seed's seed, for ever." (*q*) Some good men are troubled that they are not always prepared with clear proof to oppose the impious, when they murmur with impunity against the divine word; as though the Spirit were not therefore denominated a "seal," and "an earnest," for the confirmation of the faith of the pious; because, till he illuminate their minds, they are perpetually fluctuating amidst a multitude of doubts.

V. Let it be considered, then, as an undeniable truth, that they who have been inwardly taught by the Spirit, feel an

(*q*) Isaiah lix. 21.

entire acquiescence in the Scripture, and that it is self-authenticated, carrying with it its own evidence, and ought not to be made the subject of demonstration and arguments from reason; but it obtains the credit which it deserves with us by the testimony of the Spirit. For though it conciliate our reverence by its internal majesty, it never seriously affects us till it is confirmed by the Spirit in our hearts. Therefore, being illuminated by him, we now believe the divine original of the Scripture, not from our own judgment or that of others, but we esteem the certainty, that we have received it from God's own mouth by the ministry of men, to be superior to that of any human judgment, and equal to that of an intuitive perception of God himself in it. We seek not arguments or probabilities to support our judgment, but submit our judgments and understandings as to a thing concerning which it is impossible for us to judge; and that not like some persons, who are in the habit of hastily embracing what they do not understand, which displeases them as soon as they examine it, but because we feel the firmest conviction that we hold an invincible truth; nor like those unhappy men who surrender their minds captives to superstitions, but because we perceive in it the undoubted energies of the Divine power, by which we are attracted and inflamed to an understanding and voluntary obedience, but with a vigour and efficacy superior to the power of any human will or knowledge. With the greatest justice, therefore, God exclaims by Isaiah, (*r*) that the prophets and all the people were his witnesses; because, being taught by prophecies, they were certain that God had spoken without the least fallacy or ambiguity. It is such a persuasion, therefore, as requires no reasons; such a knowledge as is supported by the highest reason, in which, indeed, the mind rests with greater security and constancy than in any reasons; it is, finally, such a sentiment as cannot be produced but by a revelation from heaven. I speak of nothing but what every believer experiences in his heart, except that my language falls far short of a just explication of the subject. I pass over many things at present, because this subject will present itself for discussion again in another place. Only let it be known here, that that alone is true faith which the Spirit of God seals in our hearts. And with this one reason every reader of modesty and docility will be satisfied: Isaiah predicts that " all the children " of the renovated Church " shall be taught of God." (*s*) Herein God deigns to confer a singular privilege on his elect, whom he distinguishes from the rest of mankind. For what is the beginning of true learning but a prompt alac-

---

(*r*) Isaiah xliii. 10. (*s*) Isaiah liv. 13.

rity to hear the voice of God? By the mouth of Moses he demands our attention in these terms: "Say not in thine heart, Who shall ascend into heaven? or, Who shall descend into the deep? The word is even in thy mouth." (*t*) If God hath determined that this treasury of wisdom shall be reserved for his children, it is neither surprising nor absurd, that we see so much ignorance and stupidity among the vulgar herd of mankind. By this appellation I designate even those of the greatest talents and highest rank, till they are incorporated into the Church. Moreover, Isaiah, observing that the prophetical doctrine would be incredible, not only to aliens, but also to the Jews, who wished to be esteemed members of the family, adds, at the same time, the reason — Because the arm of the Lord will not be revealed to all. (*v*) Whenever, therefore, we are disturbed at the paucity of believers, let us, on the other hand, remember that none, but those to whom it was given, have any apprehension of the mysteries of God.

CHAPTER VIII.

RATIONAL PROOFS TO ESTABLISH THE BELIEF OF THE SCRIPTURE.

WITHOUT this certainty, better and stronger than any human judgment, in vain will the authority of the Scripture be either defended by arguments, or established by the consent of the Church, or confirmed by any other supports; since, unless the foundation be laid, it remains in perpetual suspense. Whilst, on the contrary, when, regarding it in a different point of view from common things, we have once religiously received it in a manner worthy of its excellence, we shall then derive great assistance from things which before were not sufficient to establish the certainty of it in our minds. For it is admirable to observe how much it conduces to our confirmation, attentively to study the order and disposition of the Divine Wisdom dispensed in it, the heavenly nature of its doctrine, which never savours of any thing terrestrial, the beautiful agreement of all the parts with each other, and other similar characters adapted to conciliate respect to any writings. But our hearts are more strongly confirmed, when we reflect that we are constrained to admire it more by the dignity of the subjects than by the beauties of the language. For even this did not happen without the particular providence of God, that the sublime mys-

(*t*) Deut. xxx. Rom. x.   (*v*) Isaiah liii. 1.

teries of the kingdom of heaven should be communicated, for the most part, in a humble and contemptible style ; lest, if they had been illustrated with more of the splendour of eloquence, the impious might cavil that their triumph is only the triumph of eloquence. Now, since that uncultivated and almost rude simplicity procures itself more reverence than all the graces of rhetoric, what opinion can we form, but that the force of truth in the sacred Scripture is too powerful to need the assistance of verbal art? Justly, therefore, does the apostle argue that the faith of the Corinthians was founded, "not in the wisdom of men, but in the power of God," because his preaching among them was, "not with enticing words of man's wisdom, but in demonstration of the Spirit and of power." (*x*) For the truth is vindicated from every doubt, when, unassisted by foreign aid, it is sufficient for its own support. But that this is the peculiar property of the Scripture, appears from the insufficiency of any human compositions, however artificially polished, to make an equal impression on our minds. Read Demosthenes or Cicero ; read Plato, Aristotle, or any others of that class ; I grant that you will be attracted, delighted, moved, and enraptured by them in a surprising manner ; but if, after reading them, you turn to the perusal of the sacred volume, whether you are willing or unwilling, it will affect you so powerfully, it will so penetrate your heart, and impress itself so strongly on your mind, that, compared with its energetic influence, the beauties of rhetoricians and philosophers will almost entirely disappear ; so that it is easy to perceive something divine in the sacred Scriptures, which far surpasses the highest attainments and ornaments of human industry.

II. I grant, indeed, that the diction of some of the prophets is neat and elegant, and even splendid ; so that they are not inferior in eloquence to the heathen writers. And by such examples the Holy Spirit hath been pleased to show, that he was not deficient in eloquence, though elsewhere he hath used a rude and homely style. But whether we read David, Isaiah, and others that resemble them, who have a sweet and pleasant flow of words, or Amos the herdsman, Jeremiah, and Zechariah, whose rougher language savours of rusticity, — that majesty of the Spirit, which I have mentioned, is every where conspicuous. I am not ignorant that Satan in many things imitates God, in order that, by the fallacious resemblance, he may more easily insinuate himself into the minds of the simple ; and has therefore craftily disseminated, in unpolished and even barbarous language, the most impious errors, by which

(*x*) 1 Cor. ii. 4.

multitudes have been miserably deceived, and has often used obsolete forms of speech as a mask to conceal his impostures. But the vanity and fraud of such affectation are visible to all men of moderate understanding. With respect to the sacred Scripture, though presumptuous men try to cavil at various passages, yet it is evidently replete with sentences which are beyond the powers of human conception. Let all the prophets be examined; not one will be found, who has not far surpassed the ability of men; so that those to whom their doctrine is insipid must be accounted utterly destitute of all true taste.

III. This argument has been copiously treated by other writers; wherefore it may suffice at present merely to hint at a few things which chiefly relate to the subject in a general view. Beside what I have already treated on, the antiquity of the Scripture is of no small weight. For, notwithstanding the fabulous accounts of the Greek writers concerning the Egyptian theology, yet there remains no monument of any religion, but what is much lower than the age of Moses. Nor does Moses invent a new deity; he only makes a declaration of what the Israelites had, through a long series of years, received by tradition from their forefathers concerning the eternal God. For what does he aim at, but to recall them to the covenant made with Abraham? If he had advanced a thing till then unheard of, it would not have been received; but their liberation from the servitude in which they were detained must have been a thing well known to them all; so that the mention of it immediately excited universal attention. It is probable also that they had been informed of the number of four hundred years. Now, we must consider, if Moses (who himself preceded all other writers by such a long distance of time) derives the tradition of his doctrine from so remote a beginning, how much the sacred Scripture exceeds in antiquity all other books.

IV. Unless any would choose to credit the Egyptians, who extend their antiquity to six thousand years before the creation of the world. But since their garrulity has been ridiculed even by all the profane writers, I need not trouble myself with refuting it. Josephus, in his book against Appion, cites from the most ancient writers testimonies worthy of being remembered; whence we may gather, that the doctrine contained in the law has, according to the consent of all nations, been renowned from the remotest ages, although it was neither read nor truly understood. Now, that the malicious might have no room for suspicion, nor even the wicked any pretence for cavilling, God hath provided the most excellent remedies for both these dangers. When Moses relates what Jacob had, almost three hundred years before, by the spirit of inspiration pronounced concerning his posterity, how does he disgrace his own tribe! He even brands it, in the person of Levi, with perpetual infamy. "Simeon," says he, "and Levi, instruments of cruelty are in their habitations. O my soul, come not thou into their secret: unto their assembly, mine honour, be not thou united." (y) He certainly might have been silent on that disgraceful circumstance, not only to spare his father, but also to avoid aspersing himself, as well as all his family, with part of the same ignominy. How can any suspicion be entertained of him, who, voluntarily publishing, from the inspiration of the Holy Spirit, that the first of the family from which he was descended was guilty of detestable conduct, neither consults his own personal honours, nor refuses to incur the resentment of his relations, to whom this must undoubtedly have given offence? When he mentions also the impious murmurings of Aaron, his brother, and Miriam, his sister, (z) shall we say that he spake according to the dictates of the flesh, or obeyed the command of the Holy Spirit? Besides, as he enjoyed the supreme authority, why did he not leave to his own sons, at least, the office of the high-priesthood, but place them in the lowest station? I only hint at a few things out of many. But in the law itself many arguments will every where occur, which challenge a full belief, that, without controversy, the legation of Moses was truly divine.

V. Moreover, the miracles which he relates, and which are so numerous and remarkable, are so many confirmations of the law which he delivered, and of the doctrine which he published. For that he was carried up into the mountain in a cloud; that he continued there forty days, deprived of all human intercourse; that, in the act of proclaiming the law, his face shone as with the rays of the sun; that lightnings flashed all around; that thunders and various noises were heard through the whole atmosphere; that a trumpet sounded, but a trumpet not blown by human breath; that the entrance of the tabernacle was concealed from the view of the people by an intervening cloud; that his authority was so miraculously vindicated by the horrible destruction of Korah, Dathan, and Abiram, and all their impious faction; that a rock smitten with a rod immediately emitted a river; that manna rained from heaven at his request; (a) — are not all these so many testimonies from heaven of his being a true prophet? If any one object that I assume, as granted, things which are the subjects of controversy, this cavil is easily answered. For, as Moses published all these things in an assembly of the people, what room was there for fiction among those who had been eye-

(y) Gen. xlix. 5. (z) Num. xii. 1.
(a) Exod. xxiv. 18; xxxiv. 29; xix. 16; xl. 34. Num. xvi. 24, &c.; xx. 11; xi. 9.

witnesses of the events? Is it probable that he would make his appearance in public, and, accusing the people of infidelity, contumacy, ingratitude, and other crimes, boast that his doctrine had been confirmed in their sight by miracles which they had never seen?

VI. For this also is worthy of being remarked, that all his accounts of miracles are connected with such unpleasant circumstances, as were calculated to stimulate all the people, if there had been but the smallest occasion, to a public and positive contradiction; whence it appears, that they were induced to coincide with him only by the ample conviction of their own experience. But since the matter was too evident for profane writers to take the liberty of denying the performance of miracles by Moses, the father of lies has suggested the calumny of ascribing them to magical arts. But by what kind of conjecture can they pretend to charge him with having been a magician, who had so great an abhorrence of that superstition, as to command, that he who merely consulted magicians and soothsayers should be stoned? (*b*) Certainly no impostor practises such juggling tricks, who does not make it his study, for the sake of acquiring fame, to astonish the minds of the vulgar. But what is the practice of Moses? Openly avowing that himself and his brother Aaron are nothing, (*c*) but that they only execute the commands of God, he sufficiently clears his character from every unfavourable aspersion. Now, if the events themselves be considered, what incantation could cause manna to rain daily from heaven sufficient to support the people, and, if any one laid up more than the proper quantity, cause it to putrefy, as a punishment from God for his unbelief? Add also the many serious examinations which God permitted his servant to undergo, so that the clamour of the wicked can now be of no avail. For as often as this holy servant of God was in danger of being destroyed, at one time by proud and petulant insurrections of all the people, at another by the secret conspiracies of a few, — how was it possible for him to elude their inveterate rage by any arts of deception? And the event evidently proves, that by these circumstances his doctrine was confirmed to all succeeding ages.

VII. Moreover, who can deny that his assigning, in the person of the patriarch Jacob, the supreme power to the tribe of Judah, proceeded from a spirit of prophecy, (*d*) especially if we consider the eventual accomplishment of this prediction? Suppose Moses to have been the first author of it; yet after he committed it to writing, there elapsed four hundred years

---

(*b*) Lev. xx. 6. (*c*) Exod. xvi. 7. (*d*) Gen. xlix. 10.

in which we have no mention of the sceptre in the tribe of Judah. After the inauguration of Saul, the regal power seemed to be fixed in the tribe of Benjamin. When Samuel anointed David, what reason appeared for transferring it? Who would have expected a king to arise out of the plebeian family of a herdsman? And of seven brothers, who would have conjectured that such an honour was destined for the youngest? And by what means did he attain a hope of the kingdom? Who can assert that this unction was directed by human art, or industry, or prudence, and was not rather a completion of the prediction of heaven? And in like manner do not his predictions, although obscure, concerning the admission of the Gentiles into the covenant of God, which were accomplished almost two thousand years after, clearly prove him to have spoken under a divine inspiration? I omit other predictions, which so strongly savour of a divine inspiration, that all who have the use of their reason must perceive that it is God who speaks. In short, one song of his is a clear mirror in which God evidently appears. (*e*)

VIII. But in the other prophets this is yet far more conspicuous. I shall only select a few examples; for to collect all would be too laborious. When, in the time of Isaiah, the kingdom of Judah was in peace, and even when they thought themselves safe in the alliance of the Chaldeans, Isaiah publicly spake of the destruction of the city and the banishment of the people. (*f*) Now, even if to predict long before things which then seemed false, but have since appeared to be true, were not a sufficiently clear proof of a divine inspiration, to whom but God shall we ascribe the prophecies which he uttered concerning their deliverance? He mentions the name of Cyrus, by whom the Chaldeans were to be subdued, and the people restored to liberty. (*g*) More than a century elapsed after this prophecy before the birth of Cyrus; for he was not born till about the hundredth year after the prophet's death. No man could then divine, that there would be one Cyrus, who would engage in a war with the Babylonians, who would subjugate such a powerful monarchy, and release the people of Israel from exile. Does not this bare narration, without any ornaments of diction, plainly demonstrate that Isaiah delivered the undoubted oracles of God, and not the conjectures of men? Again, when Jeremiah, just before the people were carried away, limited the duration of their captivity to seventy years, and predicted their liberation and return, must not his tongue have been under the direction of the Spirit of God? (*h*) What impudence must it be to deny

(*e*) Deut. xxxii.
(*f*) Isaiah xxxix. 6.
(*g*) Isaiah xlv. 1.
(*h*) Jer. xxv. 11, 12.

that the authority of the prophets has been confirmed by such proofs, or that what they themselves assert, in order to vindicate the credit due to their declarations, has been actually fulfilled! "Behold, the former things are come to pass, and new things do I declare: before they spring forth, I tell you of them." (*i*) I shall not speak of Jeremiah and Ezekiel, who, living in distant countries, but prophesying at the same time, so exactly accord in their declarations, as though they had mutually dictated the words to each other. What shall we say of Daniel? Has not he prophesied of the events of nearly six hundred years in such a connected series, as if he were composing a history of transactions already past and universally known? If pious men properly consider these things, they will be sufficiently prepared to curb the petulance of the wicked; for the demonstration is too clear to be liable to any cavils.

IX. I know what is objected by some clamorous men, who would ostentatiously display the force of their understanding in opposing divine truth. For they inquire, Who has assured us that Moses and the prophets actually wrote those books which bear their names? They even dare to question whether such a man as Moses ever existed. But if any man should call in question the existence of Plato, or Aristotle, or Cicero, who would deny that such madness ought to receive corporal punishment? The law of Moses has been wonderfully preserved, rather by the providence of heaven than by the endeavours of men. And though, through the negligence of the priests, it lay for a short time concealed, since it was found by the pious king Josiah, it has continued in the hands of men through every succeeding age. (*k*) Nor, indeed, did Josiah produce it as a thing unknown or new, but as what had always been public, and the memory of which was then famous. The protograph had been appointed to be kept in the temple, and a transcript of it to be deposited in the royal archives; (*l*) only the priests had discontinued their ancient custom of publishing the law, and the people themselves had neglected their wonted reading of it: yet there scarcely passed an age in which its sanction was not confirmed and renewed. Were they, who had the writings of David, ignorant of Moses? But, to speak of all at once, it is certain, that their writings descended to posterity only from hand to hand, (so to speak,) through a long series of years transmitted from the fathers, who partly had heard them speak, and partly learned from others who heard them, while it was fresh in their memory, that they had thus spoken.

X. With regard to what they object from the history of the

(*i*) Isaiah xlii. 9.   (*k*) 2 Kings xxii. 8.   (*l*) Deut. xvii. 18.

Maccabees, to diminish the credit of the Scripture, nothing could be conceived more adapted to establish it. But first let us divest it of their artificial colouring, and then retort upon them the weapon which they direct against us. When Antiochus, say they, commanded all the books to be burned, whence proceeded the copies which we now have? I, on the contrary, inquire, where they could so speedily be fabricated. For it is evident, that, as soon as the persecution subsided, they immediately appeared, and were, without controversy, acknowledged as the same by all pious men; who, having been educated in their doctrine, had been familiarly acquainted with them. Nay, even when all the impious, as if by a general conspiracy, so wantonly insulted the Jews, no man ever dared to charge them with forging their books. For, whatever be their opinion of the Jewish religion, yet they confess that Moses was the author of it. What, then, do these clamorous objectors, but betray their own consummate impudence, when they slander, as supposititious, books whose sacred antiquity is confirmed by the consent of all histories? But, to waste no more useless labour in refuting such stale calumnies, let us rather consider how carefully the Lord preserved his own word, when, beyond all hope, he rescued it from the fury of the most cruel of tyrants, as from a devouring fire;— that he endued the pious priests and others with so much constancy, that they hesitated not to redeem this treasure, if necessary, with their lives, to transmit it to posterity; and that he frustrated the most diligent inquisition of so many governors and soldiers. Who is there but must acknowledge it to have been an eminent and wonderful work of God, that those sacred monuments, which the impious had flattered themselves were utterly destroyed, were soon public again, as it were, fully restored to mankind, and, indeed, with far greater honour? For soon after followed the Greek Translation, which published them throughout the world. Nor was God's preserving the tables of his covenant from the sanguinary edicts of Antiochus, the only instance of his wonderful operation, but that, amidst such various miseries, with which the Jewish nation was diminished and laid waste, and at last nearly exterminated, these records still remained entire. The Hebrew language lay not only despised, but almost unknown; and surely, had not God consulted the interest of religion, it had been totally lost. For how much the Jews, after their return from captivity, departed from the genuine use of their native language, appears from the prophets of that age; which it is therefore useful to observe, because this comparison more clearly evinces the antiquity of the law and the prophets. And by whom hath God preserved to us the doctrine of salvation contained in the law and the prophets, that Christ might be manifested in due time? By his most inveterate enemies, the Jews; whom Augustine therefore justly denominates the librarians of the Christian Church, because they have furnished us with a book of which themselves make no use.

XI. If we proceed to the New Testament, by what solid foundations is its truth supported? Three Evangelists recite their history in a low and mean style. Many proud men are disgusted with that simplicity, because they attend not to the principal points of doctrine; whence it were easy to infer, that they treat of heavenly mysteries which are above human capacity. They who have a spark of ingenuous modesty will certainly be ashamed, if they peruse the first chapter of Luke. Now, the discourses of Christ, a concise summary of which is comprised in these three Evangelists, easily exempt their writings from contempt. But John, thundering from his sublimity, more powerfully than any thunderbolt, levels to the dust the obstinacy of those whom he does not compel to the obedience of faith. Let all those censorious critics whose supreme pleasure consists in banishing all reverence for the Scripture out of their own hearts and the hearts of others, come forth to public view. Let them read the Gospel of John: whether they wish it or not, they will there find numerous passages, which, at least, arouse their indolence; and which will even imprint a horrible brand on their consciences to restrain their ridicule. Similar is the method of Paul and of Peter, in whose writings, though the greater part be blind, yet their heavenly majesty attracts universal attention. But this one circumstance raises their doctrine sufficiently above the world, that Matthew, who had before been confined to the profit of his table, and Peter and John, who had been employed in fishing-boats,— all plain, unlettered men,— had learned nothing in any human school which they could communicate to others. And Paul, from not only a professed, but a cruel and sanguinary enemy, being converted to a new man, proves, by his sudden and unhoped for change, that he was constrained, by a command from heaven, to vindicate that doctrine which he had before opposed. Let these men deny that the Holy Spirit descended on the Apostles; or, at least, let them dispute the credibility of the history; yet the fact itself loudly proclaims, that they were taught by the Spirit, who, though before despised as some of the meanest of the people, suddenly began to discourse in such a magnificent manner on the mysteries of heaven.

XII. Besides, there are also other very substantial reasons why the consent of the Church should have its weight. For it is not an unimportant consideration, that, since the publication of the Scripture, so many generations of men should have agreed in voluntarily obeying it; and that however Satan, together with the whole world, has endeavoured by strange methods to suppress or destroy it, or utterly to erase and obliterate it from the memory of man, yet it has always, like a palm-tree, risen superior to all opposition, and remained invincible. Indeed, there has scarcely ever been a sophist or orator of more than common abilities, who has not tried his strength in opposing it; yet they have all availed nothing. All the powers of the earth have armed themselves for its destruction; but their attempts have all evaporated into smoke. How could it have so firmly resisted attacks on every quarter, if it had been supported only by human power? Indeed, an additional proof of its Divine origin arises from this very circumstance, that, notwithstanding all the strenuous resistance of men, it has, by its own power, risen superior to every danger. Moreover, not one city, or one nation, only, has conspired to receive and embrace it; but, as far as the world extends, it has obtained its authority by the holy consent of various nations, who agreed in nothing besides. And as such an agreement of minds, so widely distant in place, and so completely dissimilar in manners and opinions, ought to have great influence with us, since it is plain that it was effected only by the power of heaven, so it acquires no small weight from a consideration of the piety of those who unite in this agreement; not indeed of all, but of those, who, it hath pleased the Lord, should shine as luminaries in his Church.

XIII. Now, with what unlimited confidence should we submit to that doctrine, which we see confirmed and witnessed by the blood of so many saints! Having once received it, they hesitated not, with intrepid boldness, and even with great alacrity, to die in its defence: transmitted to us with such a pledge, how should we not receive it with a firm and unshaken conviction? Is it therefore no small confirmation of the Scripture, that it has been sealed with the blood of so many martyrs? especially when we consider that they died to bear testimony to their faith, not through intemperate fanaticism, as is sometimes the case with men of erroneous minds, but through a firm and constant, yet sober zeal for God. There are other reasons, and those neither few nor weak, by which the native dignity and authority of the Scripture are not only maintained in the minds of the pious, but also completely vindicated against the subtleties of calumniators; but such as alone are not sufficient to produce firm faith in it, till the heavenly Father, discovering his own power therein, places its authority beyond all controversy. Wherefore the Scripture will then only be effectual to produce the saving knowledge of God, when the certainty of it shall be founded on the internal persuasion of the Holy Spirit. Thus those human testimonies, which contribute to its confirmation, will not be useless, if they follow that first and principal proof, as secondary aids to our imbecility. But those persons betray great folly, who wish it to be demonstrated to infidels that the Scripture is the word of God, which cannot be known without faith. Augustine therefore justly observes, (*m*) that piety and peace of mind ought to precede, in order that a man may understand somewhat of such great subjects.

CHAPTER IX.

THE FANATICISM WHICH DISCARDS THE SCRIPTURE, UNDER THE PRETENCE OF RESORTING TO IMMEDIATE REVELATIONS, SUBVERSIVE OF EVERY PRINCIPLE OF PIETY.

Persons who, abandoning the Scripture, imagine to themselves some other way of approaching to God, must be considered as not so much misled by error as actuated by frenzy. For there have lately arisen some unsteady men, who, haughtily pretending to be taught by the Spirit, reject all reading themselves, and deride the simplicity of those who still attend to (what they style) the dead and killing letter. But I would ask them, what spirit that is, by whose inspiration they are elevated to such a sublimity, as to dare to despise the doctrine of the Scripture, as puerile and mean. For, if they answer that it is the Spirit of Christ, how ridiculous is such an assurance! for that the apostles of Christ, and other believers in the primitive Church, were illuminated by no other Spirit, I think they will concede. But not one of them learned, from his teaching, to contemn the Divine word; they were rather filled with higher reverence for it, as their writings abundantly testify. This had been predicted by the mouth of Isaiah. For where he says, "My Spirit that is upon thee, and my words which I have put in thy mouth, shall not depart out of thy mouth, nor out of the mouth of thy seed, for ever," (*n*) he does not confine people under the old dispensation to the external letter, as though they were children learning to read, but declares, that it will be the true and complete felicity of the new Church, under the reign of Christ, to be governed by the word of God, as well as by his Spirit.

(*m*) Lib. de Util. Credend.   (*n*) Isaiah lix. 21.

Whence we infer, that these persons are guilty of detestable sacrilege, in disjoining these two things, which the prophet has connected in an inviolable union. Again; Paul, after he had been caught up into the third heaven, did not cease to study the doctrine of the law and the prophets; as he also exhorted Timothy, a teacher of more than common excellence, to "give attendance to reading." (*o*) And worthy of remembrance is his eulogium on the Scripture, that it " is profitable for doctrine, for reproof, for correction, for instruction in righteousness; that the man of God may be perfect." (*p*) How diabolical, then, is that madness which pretends that the use of the Scripture is only transient and temporary, which guides the sons of God to the highest point of perfection! I would also ask them another question — whether they have imbibed a different spirit from that which the Lord promised to his disciples? Great as their infatuation is, I do not think them fanatical enough to hazard such an avowal. But what kind of Spirit did he promise? One, truly, who should "not speak of himself," (*q*) but suggest and instil into their minds those things which he had orally delivered. The office of the Spirit, then, which is promised to us, is not to feign new and unheard of revelations, or to coin a new system of doctrine, which would seduce us from the received doctrine of the Gospel, but to seal to our minds the same doctrine which the Gospel delivers.

II. Hence we readily understand that it is incumbent on us diligently to read and attend to the Scripture, if we would receive any advantage or satisfaction from the Spirit of God; (thus also Peter (*r*) commends those who studiously attended to the doctrine of the prophets, which yet might be supposed to have retired after the light of the Gospel was risen;) but, on the contrary, that if any spirit, neglecting the wisdom of the word of God, obtrude on us another doctrine, he ought justly to be suspected of vanity and falsehood. For, as Satan transforms himself into an angel of light, what authority will the Spirit have with us, unless we can distinguish him by the most certain criterion? We find him clearly designated, indeed, in the word of the Lord; but these unhappy men are fondly bent on delusion, even to their own destruction, seeking a spirit rather from themselves than from him. But they plead, that it is unworthy of the Spirit of God, to whom all things ought to be subject, to be made subject to the Scripture; as though it were ignominious to the Holy Spirit to be every where equal and uniform, in all things invariably consistent with himself. If he were to be conformed to the rules of

(*o*) 1 Tim. iv. 13. (*q*) John xvi. 13.
(*p*) 2 Tim. iii. 16, 17. (*r*) 2 Pet. i. 19.

men, or of angels, or of any other beings, I grant he might then be considered as degraded, or even reduced to a state of servitude; but while he is compared with himself, and considered in himself, who will assert that he is thereby injured? This is bringing him to the test of examination. I confess it is. But it is the way which he has chosen for the confirmation of his majesty among us. We ought to be satisfied, as soon as he communicates himself to us. But, lest the spirit of Satan should insinuate himself under his name, he chooses to be recognized by us from his image, which he hath impressed in the Scriptures. He is the author of the Scriptures: he cannot be mutable and inconsistent with himself. He must therefore perpetually remain such as he has there discovered himself to be. This is not disgraceful to him; unless we esteem it honourable for him to alter and degenerate from himself.

III. But their cavilling objection, that we depend on "the letter that killeth," shows, that they have not escaped the punishment due to the despisers of the Scripture. For it is sufficiently evident, that Paul is there contending against the false apostles, (*s*) who, recommending the law to the exclusion of Christ, were seducing the people from the blessings of the New Covenant, in which the Lord engages to engrave his law in the minds of believers, and to inscribe it on their hearts. The letter therefore is dead, and the law of the Lord slays the readers of it, where it is separated from the grace of Christ, and only sounds in the ears, without affecting the heart. But if it be efficaciously impressed on our hearts by the Spirit, — if it exhibit Christ, — it is the word of life, "converting the soul, making wise the simple," &c. (*t*) But in the same place the Apostle also calls his preaching "the ministration of the Spirit;" (*v*) doubtless intending, that the Holy Spirit so adheres to his own truth, which he hath expressed in the Scriptures, that he only displays and exerts his power where the word is received with due reverence and honour. Nor is this repugnant to what I before asserted, that the word itself has not much certainty with us, unless when confirmed by the testimony of the Spirit. For the Lord hath established a kind of mutual connection between the certainty of his word and of his Spirit; so that our minds are filled with a solid reverence for the word, when by the light of the Spirit we are enabled therein to behold the Divine countenance; and, on the other hand, without the least fear of mistake, we gladly receive the Spirit, when we recognize him in his image, that is, in the word. This is the true state of the case. God did

(*s*) 2 Cor. iii. 6.   (*t*) Psalm xix. 7.   (*v*) 2 Cor. iii. 8.

not publish his word to mankind for the sake of momentary ostentation, with a design to destroy or annul it immediately on the advent of the Spirit; but he afterwards sent the same Spirit, by whose agency he had dispensed his word, to complete his work by an efficacious confirmation of that word. In this manner Christ opened the understanding of his two disciples; (*w*) not that, rejecting the Scriptures, they might be wise enough of themselves, but that they might understand the Scriptures. So when Paul exhorts the Thessalonians to "quench not the Spirit," (*x*) he does not lead them to empty speculations independent of the word; for he immediately adds, "despise not prophesyings;" clearly intimating, that the light of the Spirit is extinguished when prophecies fall into contempt. What answer can be given to these things, by those proud fanatics, who think themselves possessed of the only valuable illumination, when, securely neglecting and forsaking the Divine word, they, with equal confidence and temerity, greedily embrace every reverie which their distempered imaginations may have conceived? A very different sobriety becomes the children of God; who, while they are sensible that, exclusively of the Spirit of God, they are utterly destitute of the light of truth, yet are not ignorant that the word is the instrument, by which the Lord dispenses to believers the illumination of his Spirit. For they know no other Spirit than that who dwelt in and spake by the apostles; by whose oracles they are continually called to the hearing of the word.

CHAPTER X.

ALL IDOLATROUS WORSHIP DISCOUNTENANCED IN THE SCRIPTURE, BY ITS EXCLUSIVE OPPOSITION OF THE TRUE GOD TO ALL THE FICTITIOUS DEITIES OF THE HEATHEN.

But, since we have shown that the knowledge of God, which is otherwise exhibited without obscurity in the structure of the world, and in all the creatures, is yet more familiarly and clearly unfolded in the word, it will be useful to examine, whether the representation, which the Lord gives us of himself in the Scripture, agrees with the portraiture which he had before been pleased to delineate in his works. This is indeed an extensive subject, if we intended to dwell on a particular

(*w*) Luke xxiv. 27, &c. (*x*) 1 Thess. v. 19.

discussion of it. But I shall content myself with suggesting some hints, by which the minds of the pious may learn what ought to be their principal objects of investigation in Scripture concerning God, and may be directed to a certain end in that inquiry. I do not yet allude to the peculiar covenant which distinguished the descendants of Abraham from the rest of the nations. For in receiving, by gratuitous adoption, those who were his enemies into the number of his children, God even then manifested himself as a Redeemer; but we are still treating of that knowledge which relates to the creation of the world, without ascending to Christ the Mediator. But though it will be useful soon to cite some passages from the New Testament, (since that also demonstrates the power of God in the creation, and his providence in the conservation of the world,) yet I wish the reader to be apprized of the point now intended to be discussed, that he may not pass the limits which the subject prescribes. At present, then, let it suffice to understand how God, the former of heaven and earth, governs the world which he hath made. Both his paternal goodness, and the beneficent inclinations of his will, are every where celebrated; and examples are given of his severity, which discover him to be the righteous punisher of iniquities, especially where his forbearance produces no salutary effects upon the obstinate.

II. In some places, indeed, we are favoured with more explicit descriptions, which exhibit to our view an exact representation of his genuine countenance. For Moses, in the description which he gives of it, certainly appears to have intended a brief comprehension of all that it was possible for men to know concerning him—" The Lord, the Lord God, merciful and gracious, long suffering, and abundant in goodness and truth, keeping mercy for thousands, forgiving iniquity, and transgression, and sin, and that will by no means clear the guilty; visiting the iniquity of the fathers upon the children, and upon the children's children." (*y*) Where we may observe, first, the assertion of his eternity and self-existence, in that magnificent name, which is twice repeated; and secondly, the celebration of his attributes, giving us a description, not of what he is in himself, but of what he is to us, that our knowledge of him may consist rather in a lively perception, than in vain and airy speculation. Here we find an enumeration of the same perfections which, as we have remarked, are illustriously displayed both in heaven and on earth—clemency, goodness, mercy, justice, judgment, and truth. For power is comprised in the word Elohim, God. The prophets distin-

---

(*y*) Exod. xxxiv. 6.

guish him by the same epithets, when they intend a complete exhibition of his holy name. But, to avoid the necessity of quoting many passages, let us content ourselves at present with referring to one Psalm; (z) which contains such an accurate summary of all his perfections, that nothing seems to be omitted. And yet it contains nothing but what may be known from a contemplation of the creatures. Thus, by the teaching of experience, we perceive God to be just what he declares himself in his word. In Jeremiah, where he announces in what characters he will be known by us, he gives a description, not so full, but to the same effect — "Let him that glorieth glory in this, that he understandeth and knoweth me, that I am the Lord, which exercise loving-kindness, judgment, and righteousness in the earth." (a) These three things it is certainly of the highest importance for us to know — mercy, in which alone consists all our salvation; judgment, which is executed on the wicked every day, and awaits them in a still heavier degree to eternal destruction; righteousness, by which the faithful are preserved, and most graciously supported. When you understand these things, the prophecy declares that you have abundant reason for glorying in God. Nor is this representation chargeable with an omission of his truth, or his power, or his holiness, or his goodness. For how could we have that knowledge, which is here required, of his righteousness, mercy, and judgment, unless it were supported by his inflexible veracity? And how could we believe that he governed the world in judgment and justice, if we were ignorant of his power? And whence proceeds his mercy, but from his goodness? If all his ways, then, are mercy, judgment, and righteousness, holiness also must be conspicuously displayed in them. Moreover, the knowledge of God, which is afforded us in the Scriptures, is designed for the same end as that which we derive from the creatures: it invites us first to the fear of God, and then to confidence in him; that we may learn to honour him with perfect innocence of life, and sincere obedience to his will, and to place all our dependence on his goodness.

III. But here I intend to comprise a summary of the general doctrine. And, first, let the reader observe, that the Scripture, in order to direct us to the true God, expressly excludes and rejects all the gods of the heathen; because, in almost all ages, religion has been generally corrupted. It is true, indeed, that the name of one supreme God has been universally known and celebrated. For those who used to worship a multitude of deities, whenever they spake according

(z) Psalm cxlv.   (a) Jer. ix. 24.

to the genuine sense of nature, used simply the name of God, in the singular number, as though they were contented with one God. And this was wisely remarked by Justin Martyr, who for this purpose wrote a book *On the Monarchy of God*, in which he demonstrates, from numerous testimonies, that the unity of God was a principle universally impressed on the hearts of men. Tertullian also proves the same point from the common phraseology. (*b*) But since all men, without exception, have by their own vanity been drawn into erroneous notions, and so their understandings have become vain, all their natural perception of the Divine unity has only served to render them inexcusable. For even the wisest of them evidently betray the vagrant uncertainty of their minds, when they wish for some god to assist them, and in their vows call upon unknown and fabulous deities. Besides, in imagining the existence of many natures in God, though they did not entertain such absurd notions as the ignorant vulgar concerning Jupiter, Mercury, Venus, Minerva, and the rest, they were themselves by no means exempt from the delusions of Satan; and, as we have already remarked, whatever subterfuges their ingenuity has invented, none of the philosophers can exculpate themselves from the crime of revolting from God by the corruption of his truth. For this reason Habakkuk, after condemning all idols, bids us to seek "the Lord in his holy temple," (*c*) that the faithful might acknowledge no other God than Jehovah, who had revealed himself in his word.

CHAPTER XI.

UNLAWFULNESS OF ASCRIBING TO GOD A VISIBLE FORM. ALL IDOLATRY A DEFECTION FROM THE TRUE GOD.

Now, as the Scripture, in consideration of the ignorance and dulness of the human understanding, generally speaks in the plainest manner, — where it intends to discriminate between the true God and all false gods, it principally contrasts him with idols; not that it may sanction the more ingenious and plausible systems of the philosophers, but that it may better detect the folly and even madness of the world in researches concerning God, as long as every one adheres to his own speculations. That exclusive definition, therefore, which

---

(*b*) Lib. de Idolol. Vid. Aug. Epist. 43 et 44.   (*c*) Hab. ii. 20.

every where occurs, reduces to nothing whatever notions of the Deity men may form in their own imaginations; since God alone is a sufficient witness concerning himself. In the mean time, since the whole world has been seized with such brutal stupidity, as to be desirous of visible representations of the Deity, and thus to fabricate gods of wood, stone, gold, silver, and other inanimate and corruptible materials, we ought to hold this as a certain principle, that, whenever any image is made as a representation of God, the Divine glory is corrupted by an impious falsehood. Therefore God, in the law, after having asserted the glory of Deity to belong exclusively to himself, when he intends to show what worship he approves or rejects, immediately adds, "Thou shalt not make unto thee any graven image, or any likeness." In these words he forbids us to attempt a representation of him in any visible figure; and briefly enumerates all the forms by which superstition had already begun to change his truth into a lie. For the Persians, we know, worshipped the sun; and the foolish heathen made for themselves as many gods as they saw stars in the heavens. There was scarcely an animal, indeed, which the Egyptians did not consider as an image of God. The Greeks appeared wiser than the rest, because they worshipped the Deity under the human form. (d) But God compares not idols with each other, as though one were better or worse than another; but rejects, without a single exception, all statues, pictures, and other figures, in which idolaters imagined that he would be near them.

II. This it is easy to infer from the reasons which he annexes to the prohibition. First, in the writings of Moses: "Take ye therefore good heed unto yourselves; for ye saw no manner of similitude, on the day that the Lord spake unto you in Horeb, out of the midst of the fire: ye heard the voice of the words, but saw no similitude; lest ye corrupt yourselves, and make you a graven image, the similitude of any figure," &c. (e) We see how expressly God opposes his "voice" to every "manner of similitude," to show, that whoever desires visible representations of him, is guilty of departing from him. It will be sufficient to refer to one of the Prophets, Isaiah, (f) who insists more than all the others on this argument, that the Divine Majesty is dishonoured by mean and absurd fiction, when he that is incorporeal is likened to a corporeal form; he that is invisible, to a visible image; he that is a spirit, to inanimate matter; and he that fills immensity, to a log of wood, a small stone, or a lump of gold. Paul also reasons in the same manner: "Forasmuch, then, as we are the offspring of God, we

---

(d) Maximus Tyrius, Plat. Serm. 38.   (e) Deut. iv. 15.
(f) Isaiah xl. 18; xli. 7, 29; xlvi. 5, &c.

ought not to think that the Godhead is like unto gold, or silver, or stone, graven by art and man's device." (*g*) Whence it follows, that whatever statues are erected, or images painted, to represent God, they are only displeasing to him, as being so many insults to the Divine Majesty. And why should we wonder at the Holy Spirit thundering forth such oracles from heaven, since he compels the blind and wretched idolaters to make a similar confession on earth? Well known is the complaint of Seneca, which is cited by Augustine: "They dedicate (says he) the vilest and meanest materials to represent the sacred, immortal, and inviolable gods; and give them some a human form, and some a brutal one, and some a double sex, and different bodies; and they confer the name of gods upon images which, if animated, would be accounted monsters." Hence it further appears that the pretence set up by the advocates for idols, that they were forbidden to the Jews because they were prone to superstition, is only a frivolous cavil, to evade the force of the argument. As if truly that were peculiarly applicable to one nation, which God deduces from his eternal existence, and the invariable order of nature! Besides, Paul was not addressing the Jews, but the Athenians, when he refuted the error of making any similitude of God.

III. Sometimes indeed God hath discovered his presence by certain signs, so that he was said to be seen "face to face;" (*h*) but all the signs which he ever adopted, were well calculated for the instruction of men, and afforded clear intimations of his incomprehensible essence. For "the cloud, and the smoke, and the flame," (*i*) though they were symbols of celestial glory, nevertheless operated as a restraint on the minds of all, to prevent their attempting to penetrate any further. Wherefore even Moses (to whom he manifested himself more familiarly than to any other) obtained not by his prayers a sight of the face of God, but received this answer: "Thou canst not see my face; for there shall no man see my face and live." (*k*) The Holy Spirit once appeared in the form of a dove; (*l*) but, as he presently disappeared again, who does not perceive that by this momentary symbol the faithful are taught that they should believe the Spirit to be invisible? that, being content with his power and grace, they might make no external representation of him. The appearances of God in the human form were preludes to his future manifestation in Christ. Therefore the Jews were not permitted to make this a pretext for erecting a symbol of Deity in the figure of a man. "The mercy seat" (*m*) also, from which, under the law, God displayed the presence of his power, was so constructed, as to suggest that the best contemplation of the

(*g*) Acts xvii. 29. (*i*) Deut. iv. 11. (*l*) Matt. iii. 16.
(*h*) Exod. xxxiii. 11. (*k*) Exod. xxxiii. 20. (*m*) Exod. xxv. 17, 18, &c.

Divine Being is when the mind is transported beyond itself with admiration. For "the cherubim" covered it with their extended wings; the veil was spread before it; and the place itself was sufficiently concealed by its secluded situation. It is manifestly unreasonable therefore to endeavour to defend images of God and of the saints, by the example of those cherubim. For, pray, what was signified by those little images but that images are not calculated to represent the Divine mysteries? since they were formed in such a manner as, by veiling the mercy seat with their wings, to prevent not only the eyes, but all the human senses, from prying into God, and so to restrain all temerity. Moreover, the Prophet describes the seraphim whom he saw in a vision, as having "their faces covered;" (n) to signify, that the splendour of the Divine glory is so great, that even the angels themselves cannot steadfastly behold it; and the faint sparks of it, which shine in the angels, are concealed from our view. The cherubim, however, of which we are now speaking, are acknowledged by all persons of sound judgment to have been peculiar to the old state of tutelage under the legal dispensation. To adduce them, therefore, as examples for the imitation of the present age, is quite absurd. For that puerile period, as I may call it, for which such rudiments were appointed, is now past. And, indeed, it is a shameful consideration, that heathen writers are more expert interpreters of the Divine law than the papists. Juvenal reproaches and ridicules the Jews for worshipping the white clouds and Deity of heaven. This language, indeed, is perverse and impious; but in denying that there was any image of God among them, he speaks with more truth than the papists, who idly pretend that there was some visible figure of him. But as that nation frequently broke out into idolatry, with great and sudden impetuosity, resembling the violent ebullition of water from a large spring, hence let us learn the strong propensity of the human mind to idolatry, lest, imputing to the Jews a crime common to all, we should be fascinated by the allurements of sin, and sleep the sleep of death.

IV. To the same purpose is that passage, "The idols of the heathen are silver and gold, the work of men's hands;" (o) for the Prophet concludes, from the very materials, that they are no gods, whose images are made of gold or of silver; and takes it for granted, that every conception we form of the Deity, merely from our own understandings, is a foolish imagination. He mentions gold and silver rather than clay or stone, that the splendour or the value of the materials may procure no reverence for the idols. But he concludes in general, that nothing is more improbable, than that gods should be manufactured

(n) Isaiah vi. 2.   (o) Psalm cxxxv. 15.

from any inanimate matter. At the same time he insists equally on another point — that it is presumption and madness in mortal men, who are every moment in danger of losing the fleeting breath which they draw, to dare to confer upon idols the honour due to God. Man is constrained to confess that he is a creature of a day, and yet he will have a piece of metal to be worshipped as a god, of the deity of which he is the author; for whence did idols originate, but in the will of men? There is much propriety in that sarcasm of a heathen poet, who represents one of their idols as saying, "Formerly, I was the trunk of a wild fig-tree, a useless log; when the artificer, after hesitating whether he would make me a stool or a deity, at length determined that I should be a god." (p)

A poor mortal, forsooth, who is, as it were, expiring almost every moment, will, by his workmanship, transfer to a dead stock the name and honour of God. But as that Epicurean, in his satirical effusions, has paid no respect to any religion, — leaving this sarcasm, and others of the same kind, we should be stung and penetrated by the rebuke which the Prophet (q) has given to the extreme stupidity of those, who, with the same wood, make a fire to warm themselves, heat an oven for baking bread, roast or boil their meat, and fabricate a god, before which they prostrate themselves, to address their humble supplications. In another place, therefore, he not only pronounces them transgressors of the law, but reproaches them for not having learned from the foundations of the earth; (r) since, in reality, there is nothing more unreasonable than the thought of contracting the infinite and incomprehensible God within the compass of five feet. And yet this monstrous abomination, which is manifestly repugnant to the order of nature, experience demonstrates to be natural to man. It must be further observed, that idols are frequently stigmatized as being the works of men's hands, unsanctioned by Divine authority; in order to establish this principle, that all modes of worship which are merely of human invention, are detestable. The Psalmist aggravates this madness, forasmuch as men implore the aid of dead and insensible things, who are imbued with understanding to know that all things are directed solely by the power of God. But since the corruption of nature carries all nations in general, and each individual in particular, to such an excess of frenzy, the Spirit at length thunders out this direful imprecation: "Let those that make them be like unto them and every one that trusteth in them." (s) Let it be observed, that all similitudes are equally as much forbidden as graven images; which refutes the foolish subterfuge of the Greeks; for they think themselves quite safe, if they

(p) Hor. Sat. lib. I, 8.
(q) Isaiah xliv. 9—20.
(r) Isaiah xl. 21.
(s) Psalm cxv. 8.

make no sculpture of Deity, while in pictures they indulge greater liberty than any other nations. But the Lord prohibits every representation of him, whether made by the statuary, or by any other artificer, because all similitudes are criminal and insulting to the Divine Majesty.

V. I know that it is a very common observation, that images are the books of the illiterate. Gregory said so; but very different is the decision of the Spirit of God, in whose school had Gregory been taught, he would never have made such an assertion. For, since Jeremiah pronounces that "the stock is a doctrine of vanities," (*t*) since Habakkuk represents "a molten image" as "a teacher of lies," (*v*) — certainly the general doctrine to be gathered from these passages is, that whatever men learn respecting God from images is equally frivolous and false. If any one object, that the Prophets only reprehended those who abuse images to the impious purposes of superstition, — that indeed I grant; but affirm also, what is evident to every one, that they utterly condemn what is assumed by the papists as an indubitable axiom, that images are substitutes for books. For they contrast images with the true God, as contraries, which can never agree. This comparison, I say, is laid down in those passages which I have just cited; that, since there is only one true God, whom the Jews worshipped, there can be no visible figures made, to serve as representations of the Divine Being, without falsehood and criminality; and all who seek the knowledge of God from such figures are under a miserable delusion. Were it not true, that all knowledge of God, sought from images, is corrupt and fallacious, it would not be so uniformly condemned by the Prophets. This at least must be granted to us, that, when we maintain the vanity and fallaciousness of the attempts of men to make visible representations of God, we do no other than recite the express declarations of the Prophets.

VI. Read likewise what has been written on this subject by Lactantius and Eusebius, who hesitate not to assume as a certainty, that all those whose images are to be seen, were mortal men. Augustine also confidently asserts the unlawfulness, not only of worshipping images, but even of erecting any with reference to God. Nor does he advance any thing different from what had, many years before, been decreed by the Elibertine council, the thirty-sixth chapter of which is as follows: "It hath been decreed, that no pictures be had in the churches, and that what is worshipped or adored be not painted on the walls." But most remarkable is what Augustine elsewhere cites from Varro, and to the truth of which he

---

(*t*) Jer. x. 8.   (*r*) Hab. ii. 18.

subscribes — "That they who first introduced images of the gods, removed fear and added error." If this had been a mere assertion of Varro alone, it might have perhaps but little authority; yet it should justly fill us with shame, that a heathen, groping as it were in the dark, attained so much light as to perceive that corporeal representations were unworthy of the Divine Majesty, being calculated to diminish the fear of God, and to increase error among mankind. The fact itself demonstrates this to have been spoken with equal truth and wisdom; but Augustine, having borrowed it from Varro, advances it as his own opinion. And first he observes that the most ancient errors concerning God, in which men were involved, did not originate from images, but were increased by them, as by the superaddition of new materials. He next explains that the fear of God is thereby diminished, and even destroyed; since the foolish, ridiculous, and absurd fabrication of idols would easily bring his Divinity into contempt. Of the truth of this second remark, I sincerely wish that we had not such proofs in our own experience. Whoever, therefore, desires to be rightly instructed, he must learn from some other quarter than from images, what is to be known concerning God.

VII. If the papists have any shame, let them no longer use this subterfuge, that images are the books of the illiterate; which is so clearly refuted by numerous testimonies from Scripture. Yet, though I should concede this point to them, it would avail them but little in defence of their idols. What monsters they obtrude in the place of Deity is well known. But what they call the pictures or statues of their saints — what are they but examples of the most abandoned luxury and obscenity? which if any one were desirous of imitating, he would deserve corporal punishment. Even prostitutes in brothels are to be seen in more chaste and modest attire, than those images in their temples, which they wish to be accounted images of virgins. Nor do they clothe the martyrs in habits at all more becoming. Let them adorn their idols, then, with some small degree of modesty, that the pretence of their being books of some holiness, if not less false, may be less impudent. But even then, we will reply, that this is not the method to be adopted in sacred places for the instruction of the faithful, whom God will have taught a very different doctrine from any that can be learned from such insignificant trifles. He hath commanded one common doctrine to be there proposed to all, in the preaching of his word, and in his sacred mysteries; to which they betray great inattention of mind, who are carried about by their eyes to the contemplation of idols. Whom, then, do the papists call illiterate, whose ignorance will suffer them to be taught only by images? Those, truly, whom the Lord acknowledges as his disciples; whom he honours with the revelation of his heavenly philosophy; whom he will have instructed in the healthful mysteries of his kingdom. I confess, indeed, as things are now circumstanced, that there are at present not a few who cannot bear to be deprived of such books. But whence arises this stupidity, but from being defrauded of that teaching which alone is adapted to their instruction? In fact, those who presided over the churches, resigned to idols the office of teaching, for no other reason but because they were themselves dumb. Paul testifies, that in the true preaching of this gospel, Christ is "evidently set forth," and, as it were, "crucified before our eyes." (*w*) To what purpose, then, was the erection of so many crosses of wood and stone, silver and gold, every where in the temples, if it had been fully and faithfully inculcated, that Christ died that he might bear our curse on the cross, expiate our sins by the sacrifice of his body, cleanse us by his blood, and, in a word, reconcile us to God the Father? From this simple declaration they might learn more than from a thousand crosses of wood or stone; for perhaps the avaricious fix their minds and their eyes more tenaciously on the gold and silver crosses, than on any part of the Divine word.

VIII. Respecting the origin of idols, the generally received opinion agrees with what is asserted in the book of Wisdom; (*x*) namely, that the first authors of them were persons who paid this honour to the dead, from a superstitious reverence for their memory. I grant that this perverse custom was very ancient, and deny not that it greatly contributed to increase the rage of mankind after idolatry; nevertheless, I cannot concede that it was the first cause of that evil. For it appears from Moses, that idols were in use long before the introduction of that ostentatious consecration of the images of the dead, which is frequently mentioned by profane writers. When he relates that Rachel stole her father's idols, (*y*) he speaks as of a common corruption. Whence we may infer, that the mind of man is, if I may be allowed the expression, a perpetual manufactory of idols. After the deluge, there was, as it were, a regeneration of the world; but not many years elapsed before men fabricated gods according to their own fancy. And it is probable, that while the holy patriarch was yet alive, his posterity were addicted to idolatry, so that, with the bitterest grief, he might, with his own eyes, behold the earth which God had lately purged from its corruptions by such a dreadful judgment,

---

(*w*) Gal. iii. 1. (*x*) Wisdom xiv. 15. (*y*) Gen. xxxi. 19.

again polluted with idols. For Terah and Nachor, before the birth of Abraham, were worshippers of false gods, as is asserted by Joshua (*z*) Since the posterity of Shem so speedily degenerated, what opinion must we entertain of the descendants of Ham, who had already been cursed in their father? The true state of the case is, that the mind of man, being full of pride and temerity, dares to conceive of God according to its own standard; and, being sunk in stupidity, and immersed in profound ignorance, imagines a vain and ridiculous phantom instead of God. These evils are followed by another; men attempt to express in the work of their hands such a deity as they have imagined in their minds. The mind then begets the idol, and the hand brings it forth. The example of the Israelites proves this to have been the origin of idolatry, namely, that men believe not God to be among them, unless he exhibit some external signs of his presence. "As for this Moses," they said, "we wot not what is become of him; make us gods which shall go before us." (*a*) They knew, indeed, that there was a God, whose power they had experienced in so many miracles; but they had no confidence in his being present with them, unless they could see some corporeal symbol of his countenance, as a testimony of their Divine Guide. They wished, therefore, to understand, from the image going before them, that God was the leader of their march. Daily experience teaches, that the flesh is never satisfied, till it has obtained some image, resembling itself, in which it may be foolishly gratified, as an image of God. In almost all ages, from the creation of the world, in obedience to this stupid propensity, men have erected visible representations, in which they believed God to be presented to their carnal eyes.

IX. Such an invention is immediately attended with adoration; for when men supposed that they saw God in images, they also worshipped him in them. At length, both their eyes and their minds being wholly confined to them, they began to grow more stupid, and to admire them, as though they possessed some inherent divinity. Now, it is plain that men did not rush into the worship of images, till they had imbibed some very gross opinion respecting them; not, indeed, that they believed them to be gods, but they imagined that something of Divinity resided in them. When you prostrate yourself, therefore, in adoration of an image, whether you suppose it to represent God or a creature, you are already fascinated with superstition. For this reason the Lord hath prohibited, not only the erection of statues made as representations of him, but also the consecration of any inscriptions or monuments to

(*z*) Joshua xxiv. 2.   (*a*) Exod. xxxii. 1.

stand as objects of worship. For the same reason, also, another point is annexed to the precept in the law concerning adoration. For as soon as men have made a visible figure of God, they attach Divine power to it. Such is the stupidity of men, that they confine God to any image which they make to represent him, and therefore cannot but worship it. Nor is it of any importance, whether they worship simply the idol, or God in the idol; it is always idolatry, when Divine honours are paid to an idol, under any pretence whatsoever. And as God will not be worshipped in a superstitious or idolatrous manner, whatever is conferred on idols is taken from him. Let this be considered by those who seek such miserable pretexts for the defence of that execrable idolatry, with which, for many ages, true religion has been overwhelmed and subverted. The images, they say, are not considered as gods. Neither were the Jews so thoughtless as not to remember, that it was God by whose hand they had been conducted out of Egypt, before they made the calf. But when Aaron said that those were the gods by whom they had been liberated from Egypt, they boldly assented; (*b*) signifying, doubtless, that they would keep in remembrance, that God himself was their deliverer, while they could see him going before them in the calf. Nor can we believe the heathen to have been so stupid, as to conceive that God was no other than wood and stone. For they changed the images at pleasure, but always retained in their minds the same gods; and there were many images for one god; nor did they imagine to themselves gods in proportion to the multitude of images: besides, they daily consecrated new images, but without supposing that they made new gods. Read the excuses, which, Augustine says, (*c*) were alleged by the idolaters of the age in which he lived. When they were charged with idolatry, the vulgar replied, that they worshipped, not the visible figure, but the Divinity that invisibly dwelt in it. But they, whose religion was, as he expresses himself, more refined, said, that they worshipped neither the image, nor the spirit represented by it; but that in the corporeal figure they beheld a sign of that which they ought to worship. What is to be inferred from this, but that all idolaters, whether Jewish or Gentile, have been guided by the notion which I have mentioned? Not content with a spiritual knowledge of God, they thought that they should receive more clear and familiar impressions of him by means of images. After they had once pleased themselves with such a preposterous representation of God, they ceased not from being deluded with new fallacies, till they imagined that God

(*b*) Exod. xxxii. 4—6.   (*c*) In Psalm cxiii.

displayed his power in images. Nevertheless, the Jews were persuaded that, under such images, they worshipped the eternal God, the one true Lord of heaven and earth; and the heathen, that they worshipped their false gods, whom they pretended to be inhabitants of heaven.

X. Those who deny that this has been done in time past, and even within our own remembrance, assert an impudent falsehood. For why do they prostrate themselves before images? And when about to pray, why do they turn themselves towards them, as towards the ears of God? For it is true, as Augustine says, (d) "That no man prays or worships thus, looking on an image, who is not impressed with an opinion that he shall be heard by it, and a hope that it will do for him as he desires." Why is there so great a difference between images of the same god, that one is passed by with little or no respect, and another is honoured in the most solemn manner? Why do they fatigue themselves with votive pilgrimages, in going to see images resembling those which they have at home? Why do they at this day fight, even to slaughter and destruction, in defence of them, as of their country and religion, so that they could part with the only true God more easily than with their idols? Yet I am not here enumerating the gross errors of the vulgar, which are almost infinite, and occupy nearly the hearts of all; I only relate what they themselves allege, when they are most anxious to exculpate themselves from idolatry. "We never," say they, "call them our gods." Nor did the Jews or heathen in ancient times call them their gods; and yet the Prophets, in all their writings, were constantly accusing them of fornication with wood and stone, only on account of such things as are daily practised by those who wish to be thought Christians; that is, for worshipping God, by corporeal adoration before figures of wood or stone.

XI. I am neither ignorant, nor desirous of concealing, that they evade the charge by a more subtle distinction, which will soon be noticed more at large. They pretend that the reverence which they pay to images is εἰδωλοδουλεια, (service of images,) but deny that it is εἰδωλολατρεια (worship of images.) For in this manner they express themselves, when they maintain, that the reverence which they call *dulia*, may be given to statues or pictures, without injury to God. They consider themselves, therefore, liable to no blame, while they are only the servants of their idols, and not worshippers of them; as though worship were not rather inferior to service. And yet, while they seek to shelter themselves under a Greek term, they contradict themselves in the most childish manner. For

---

(d) In Psalm cxiii.

since the Greek word λατρεύειν signifies nothing else but to worship, what they say is equivalent to a confession that they adore their images, but without adoration. Nor can they justly object, that I am trying to insnare them with words: they betray their own ignorance in their endeavours to raise a mist before the eyes of the simple. But, however eloquent they may be, they will never be able, by their rhetoric, to prove one and the same thing to be two different things. Let them point out, I say, a difference in fact, that they may be accounted different from ancient idolaters. For as an adulterer, or homicide, will not escape the imputation of guilt, by giving his crime a new and arbitrary name, so it is absurd that these persons should be exculpated by the subtle invention of a name, if they really differ in no respect from those idolaters whom they themselves are constrained to condemn. But their case is so far from being different from that of former idolaters, that the source of all the evil is a preposterous emulation, with which they have rivalled them by exercising their minds in contriving, and their hands in forming, visible symbols of the Deity.

XII. Nevertheless, I am not so scrupulous as to think that no images ought ever to be permitted. But since sculpture and painting are gifts of God, I wish for a pure and legitimate use of both; lest those things, which the Lord hath conferred on us for his glory and our benefit, be not only corrupted by preposterous abuse, but even perverted to our ruin. We think it unlawful to make any visible figure as a representation of God, because he hath himself forbidden it, and it cannot be done without detracting, in some measure, from his glory. Let it not be supposed that we are singular in this opinion; for that all sound writers have uniformly reprobated the practice, must be evident to persons conversant with their works. If, then, it be not lawful to make any corporeal representation of God, much less will it be lawful to worship it for God, or to worship God in it. We conclude, therefore, that nothing should be painted and engraved but objects visible to our eyes: the Divine Majesty, which is far above the reach of human sight, ought not to be corrupted by unseemly figures. The subjects of those arts consist partly of histories and transactions, partly of images and corporeal forms, without reference to any transactions. The former are of some use in information or recollection; the latter, as far as I see, can furnish nothing but amusement. And yet it is evident, that almost all the images, which have hitherto been set up in the churches, have been of this latter description. Hence it may be seen, that they were placed there, not with judgment and discrimination, but from a foolish and inconsiderate passion for them. I say nothing here of the impropriety and indecency conspicuous in most of them, and the wanton licentiousness displayed in them by the painters and statuaries, at which I have before hinted: I only assert, that even if they were intrinsically faultless, still they would be altogether unavailing for the purposes of instruction.

XIII. But, passing over that difference also, let us consider, as we proceed, whether it be expedient to have any images at all in Christian temples, either descriptive of historical events, or representative of human forms. In the first place, if the authority of the ancient Church have any influence with us, let us remember, that for about five hundred years, while religion continued in a more prosperous state, and purer doctrine prevailed, the Christian churches were generally without images. They were then first introduced, therefore, to ornament the churches, when the purity of the ministry had begun to degenerate. I will not dispute what was the reason which influenced the first authors of them; but if you compare one age with another, you will see that they were much declined from the integrity of those who had no images. Who can suppose, that those holy fathers would have permitted the Church to remain so long destitute of what they judged useful and salutary for it? The fact was, that, instead of omitting them through ignorance or negligence, they perceived them to be of little or no use, but, on the contrary, pregnant with much danger; and, therefore, intentionally and wisely rejected them. This is asserted in express terms by Augustine: "When they are fixed," says he, "in those places in an honourable elevation, to attract the attention of those who are praying and sacrificing, though they are destitute of sense and life, yet, by the very similitude of living members and senses, they affect weak minds, so that they appear to them to live and breathe," &c. (e) And in another place: "For that representation of members leads, and, as it were, constrains, the mind, which animates a body, to suppose that body to be endued with perception, which it sees to be very similar to its own," &c. And a little after: "Idols have more influence to bow down an unhappy soul, because they have a mouth, eyes, ears, and feet, than to correct it, because they neither speak, nor see, nor hear, nor walk." This indeed appears to be the reason of John's exhortation to "keep ourselves," not only from the worship of idols, but "from idols" themselves. And we have found it too true, that, through the horrible frenzy, which, almost to the total destruction of piety, hath heretofore possessed the world, as soon as images are set up in churches, there is, as it were, a standard of idol-

(e) Epist. 49. De Civ. Dei. lib. iv. cap. 31.

atry erected; for the folly of mankind cannot refrain from immediately falling into idolatrous worship. But, even if the danger were less, yet, when I consider the use for which temples were designed, it appears to me extremely unworthy of their sanctity, to receive any other images, than those natural and expressive ones, which the Lord hath consecrated in his word; I mean Baptism, and the Supper of the Lord, and the other ceremonies, with which our eyes ought to be more attentively engaged, and more sensibly affected, than to require any others formed by human ingenuity. Behold the incomparable advantages of images! the loss of which, if you believe the papists, nothing can compensate.

XIV. The remarks already made on this subject, I think, would be sufficient, if it were not necessary to take some notice of the Council of Nice; not that very celebrated one, which was convened by Constantine the Great, but that which was held about eight hundred years ago, by the command, and under the auspices, of the Empress Irene. For that Council decreed, not only that images should be had in churches, but also that they should be worshipped. And, notwithstanding what I have advanced, the authority of the Council would raise a strong prejudice on the contrary side. Though, to confess the truth, I am not much concerned at this, as I am to show the reader their extreme madness, whose fondness for images exceeded any thing that was becoming in Christians. But let us despatch this point first: the present advocates for the use of images, allege the authority of that Nicene Council in their defence. There is a book extant, written in refutation of this practice, under the name of Charlemagne; which, from the diction, we may conclude was composed at the same time. In this work are recited the opinions of the bishops who attended the Council, and the arguments they used in the controversy. John, the delegate of the Eastern churches, said, "God created man in his own image;" and hence he inferred that we ought to have images. The same prelate thought that images were recommended to us by this sentence: "Show me thy face, for it is glorious." Another, to prove that they ought to be placed on the altars, cited this testimony: "No man lighteth a candle, and putteth it under a bushel." Another, to show the contemplation of these to be useful to us, adduced a verse from a Psalm: "The light of thy countenance, O Lord, is sealed upon us." Another pressed this comparison into his service: "As the patriarchs used the sacrifices of the heathen, so Christians ought to have the images of saints, instead of the idols of the heathen." In the same manner they tortured that expression, "Lord, I have loved the beauty of thy house." But the most ingenious of all was their interpretation of this passage: "As we have heard, so have we seen;" that therefore God is known, not only by the hearing of his word, but by the contemplation of images. Similar is the subtlety of Bishop Theodore: "God is glorious in his saints." And in another place it is said, "In the saints that are in the earth:" therefore this ought to be referred to images. But their impertinencies and absurdities are so disgusting, that I am quite ashamed to repeat them.

XV. When they dispute concerning adoration, they bring forward Jacob's worshipping of Pharaoh, and of the staff of Joseph, and of the inscription erected by himself; although, in this last instance, they not only corrupt the sense of the Scripture, but allege what is nowhere to be found. These passages also, "Worship his footstool;" "Worship in his holy hill;" and, "All the rich of the people shall supplicate thy face;" they consider as apposite and conclusive proofs. If any one wished to represent the advocates for images in a ridiculous point of view, could he possibly ascribe to them greater and grosser instances of folly? But, that no doubt of this might remain, Theodosius, bishop of Mira, defends the propriety of worshipping images from the dreams of his archdeacon, as seriously as if he had an immediate revelation from heaven. Now, let the advocates of images go and urge upon us the decree of that Council; as though those venerable fathers had not entirely destroyed all their credit by such puerile treatment of the sacred Scriptures, or such impious and shameful mutilation of them.

XVI. I come now to those prodigies of impiety, which it is wonderful that they ever ventured to broach; and more wonderful still, that they have not been opposed with universal detestation. It is right to expose this flagitious madness, that the worship of images may at least be deprived of the pretence of antiquity, which the papists falsely urge in its favour. Theodosius, bishop of Amorum, denounces an anathema against all who are averse to the worship of images. Another imputes all the calamities of Greece and the East to the crime of not having worshipped them. What punishments, then, did the Prophets, Apostles, and Martyrs deserve, in whose time images were unknown? They add further, If the image of the emperor be met by processions with perfumes and incense, much more is this honour due to the images of the saints. Constantius, bishop of Constance, in Cyprus, professes his reverence for images, and avows that he will pay them the same worship and honour as is due to the Trinity, the source of all life; and whoever refuses to do the same, he anathematizes and dismisses with the Manichees and Marcionites. And, lest you should suppose this to be the private opinion of an individual, they all declare their assent to it. John, the delegate of the Eastern churches, carried by the fervour of his zeal to still greater lengths, asserts it to be better to admit all the brothels of the world into one city, than to reject the worship of images. At length it was unanimously decreed, that the Samaritans were worse than all heretics, and that the adversaries of images were worse than the Samaritans. But, that the farce might not want its usual plaudit, they add this clause : " Let them rejoice and exult, who have the image of Christ, and offer sacrifice to it." Where is now the distinction of *latria* and *dulia*, with which they attempt to deceive both God and men? For the Council gives the same honour, without any exception, to images and to the living God.

CHAPTER XII.

GOD CONTRADISTINGUISHED FROM IDOLS, THAT HE MAY BE SOLELY AND SUPREMELY WORSHIPPED.

WE said, at the beginning, that the knowledge of God consists not in frigid speculation, but is accompanied by the worship of him. We also cursorily touched on the right method of worshipping him, which will be more fully explained in other places. I now only repeat, in few words, that whenever the Scripture asserts that there is but one God, it contends not for the bare name, but also teaches, that whatever belongs to the Deity, should not be transferred to another. This shows how pure religion differs from idolatry. The Greek word ευσέβια certainly signifies right worship, since even blind mortals, groping in the dark, have always perceived the necessity of some certain rule, that the worship of God may not be involved in disorder and confusion. Although Cicero ingeniously and correctly derives the word *religion* from a verb signifying "to read over again," or "to gather again;" yet the reason he assigns for it, that good worshippers often recollect, and diligently reconsider what is true, is forced and far-fetched. I rather think the word is opposed to a liberty of wandering without restraint ; because the greater part of the world rashly embrace whatever they meet with, and also ramble from one thing to another; but piety, in order to walk with a steady step, collects itself within its proper limits. The word *superstition* also appears to me to import a discontent with the method and order prescribed, and an accumulation of a superfluous mass of vain things. But to leave the consideration of words, it has been generally admitted, in all ages, that religion is corrupted and perverted by errors and falsehoods; whence we infer, that when we allow ourselves any thing from inconsiderate zeal, the pretext alleged by the superstitious is altogether frivolous. Although this confession is in the mouths of all, they betray, at the same time, a shameful ignorance, neither adhering to the one true God, nor observing any discrimination in his worship, as we have before shown. But God, to assert his own right, proclaims that he is "jealous," and will be a severe avenger, if men confound him with any fictitious deity; and then, to retain mankind in obedience, he defines his legitimate worship. He comprises both in his law, where he first binds the faithful to himself, as their sole legislator; and then prescribes a rule for the right worship of him according to his will. Now, of the law, since the uses and ends of it are various, I shall treat in its proper place: at present, I only remark, that it sets up a barrier to prevent men turning aside to corrupt modes of worship. Let us remember, what I have already stated, that, unless every thing belonging to Divinity remain in God alone, he is spoiled of his honour, and his worship is violated. And here it is necessary to animadvert more particularly on the subtle fallacies of superstition. For it revolts not to strange gods, in such a manner as to appear to desert the supreme God, or to degrade him to a level with others; but, allowing him the highest place, it surrounds him with a multitude of inferior deities, among whom it distributes his honours; and thus, in a cunning and hypocritical manner, the glory of Divinity is divided among many, instead of remaining wholly in one. Thus the ancient idolaters, Jews as well as Gentiles, imagined one God, the Father and Governor of all, and subordinate to him a vast multitude of other deities; to whom, in common with the supreme God, they attributed the government of heaven and earth. Thus the saints, who departed out of this life some ages ago, are exalted to the society of God, to be worshipped, and invoked, and celebrated like him. We suppose, indeed, the glory of God not to be sullied with this abomination; whereas it is, in a great measure, suppressed and extinguished, except that we retain some faint notion of his supreme power; but, at the same time, deceived with such impostures, we are seduced to the worship of various deities.

II. On this account was invented the distinction of *latria* and *dulia*, as they express themselves, by which they conceived they might safely ascribe divine honours to angels and deceased men. For it is evident, that the worship which papists pay to the saints, differs not in reality from the worship of God; for they adore God and them promiscuously; but when they are accused of it, they evade the charge with this subterfuge, that they preserve inviolate to God what belongs to him, because they leave him λατρεια. But since the question relates to a thing, not to a word, who can bear their careless trifling on the most important of all subjects? But, to pass this also, they will gain nothing at last by their distinction, but that they render worship to God alone, and service to the saints. For λατρεια, in Greek, signifies the same as *cultus* in Latin, [and *worship* in English;] but δουλεια properly signifies *servitus*, [*service;*] and yet, in the Scriptures, this distinction is sometimes disregarded. But, suppose it to be a constant distinction, it remains to be inquired, what is the meaning of each term. Λατρεια is *worship;* δουλεια is *service*. Now, no one doubts, that to serve is more than to worship or honour. For it would be irksome to serve many persons, whom you would not refuse to honour. So unjust is the distribution, to assign the greater to the saints, and leave to God that which is less. But many of the ancients, it is urged, have used this distinction. What is that to the purpose, if every one perceives it to be not only improper, but altogether frivolous?

III. Leaving these subtleties, let us consider the subject itself. Paul, when he reminds the Galatians what they had been before they were illuminated in the knowledge of God, says, that they " did service to them which by nature were no gods."(*f*) Though he mentions not λατρεια, (worship,) is their idolatry therefore excusable? He certainly condemns that perverse superstition, which he denominates δουλεια, (service,) equally as much as if he had used the word λατρεια, (worship.) And when Christ repels the assault of Satan with this shield, "It is written, Thou shalt worship the Lord thy God," (*g*) the word λατρεια came not into the question; for Satan required nothing but προσκυνησις, (prostration, or adoration.) So, when John is reprehended by an angel, for having fallen on his knees before him, (*h*) we must not understand that John was so stupid as to intend to transfer to an angel the honour due exclusively to God. But since all worship, that is connected with religion, cannot but savour of Divine, he could not (προσκυνειν) prostrate himself before the angel, without detracting from the glory of God. We read, indeed, frequently, of men having been worshipped; but that was civil honour, so to speak; religion has a different design; and no sooner is religion connected with worship, or homage, than it produces a profanation of the Divine honour. We may see the same in Cornelius, who had not made such a small progress in piety, as not to ascribe supreme worship to God alone. When

(*f*) Gal. iv. 8. (*g*) Matt. iv. 10. (*h*) Rev. xix. 10; xxii. 8, 9.

he " fell down " before Peter, therefore, it certainly was not with an intention of worshipping him instead of God: (*i*) yet Peter positively forbade him to do it. And why was this, but because men never so particularly distinguish between the worship or homage of God, and that of the creatures, as to avoid transferring to a creature what belongs exclusively to God? Wherefore, if we desire to have but one God, let us remember, that his glory ought not, in the least, to be diminished; but that he must retain all that belongs to him. Therefore Zechariah, when speaking of the restoration of the Church, expressly declares, not only that "there shall be one Lord," but also " that his name shall be one ; " (*k*) signifying, without doubt, that he will have nothing in common with idols. Now, what kind of worship God requires, will be seen, in due course, in another place. For he hath been pleased, in his law, to prescribe to mankind what is lawful and right; and so to confine them to a certain rule, that every individual might not take the liberty of inventing a mode of worship according to his own fancy. But, since it is not proper to burden the reader, by confounding many subjects together, I shall not enter on that point yet; let it suffice to know, that no religious services can be transferred to any other than God alone, without committing sacrilege. At first, indeed, superstition ascribed Divine honours either to the sun, or to the other stars, or to idols. Afterwards followed ambition, which, adorning men with the spoils of God, dared to profane every thing that was sacred. And although there remained a persuasion, that they ought to worship a supreme God, yet it became customary to offer sacrifices promiscuously to genii, and inferior deities, and deceased heroes. So steep is the descent to this vice, to communicate to a vast multitude that which God particularly challenges to himself alone!

CHAPTER XIII.

ONE DIVINE ESSENCE, CONTAINING THREE PERSONS, TAUGHT IN THE SCRIPTURES FROM THE BEGINNING.

What is taught in the Scriptures concerning the immensity and spirituality of the essence of God, should serve not only to overthrow the foolish notions of the vulgar, but also to refute the subtleties of profane philosophy. One of the ancients, (*l*)

(*i*) Acts x. 25.   (*k*) Zech. xiv. 9.   (*l*) Seneca, Præf. lib. I. Quæst. Nat.

in his own conception very shrewdly, said, that whatever we see, and whatever we do not see, is God. But he imagined that the Deity was diffused through every part of the world. But, although God, to keep us within the bounds of sobriety, speaks but rarely of his essence, yet, by those two attributes, which I have mentioned, he supersedes all gross imaginations, and represses the presumption of the human mind. For, surely, his immensity ought to inspire us with awe, that we may not attempt to measure him with our senses; and the spirituality of his nature prohibits us from entertaining any earthly or carnal speculations concerning him. For the same reason, he represents his residence to be "in heaven;" for though, as he is incomprehensible, he fills the earth also; yet, seeing that our minds, from their dulness, are continually dwelling on the earth, in order to shake off our sloth and inactivity, he properly raises us above the world. And here is demolished the error of the Manichees, who, by maintaining the existence of two original principles, made the devil, as it were, equal to God. This certainly was both dividing the unity of God, and limiting his immensity. For their daring to abuse certain testimonies of Scripture betrayed a shameful ignorance; as the error itself evidenced an execrable madness. The Anthropomorphites also, who imagined God to be corporeal, because the Scripture frequently ascribes to him a mouth, ears, eyes, hands, and feet, are easily refuted. For who, even of the meanest capacity, understands not, that God lisps, as it were, with us, just as nurses are accustomed to speak to infants? Wherefore, such forms of expression do not clearly explain the nature of God, but accommodate the knowledge of him to our narrow capacity; to accomplish which, the Scripture must necessarily descend far below the height of his majesty.

II. But he also designates himself by another peculiar character, by which he may be yet more clearly distinguished: for, while he declares himself to be but One, he proposes himself to be distinctly considered in Three Persons, without apprehending which, we have only a bare and empty name of God floating in our brains, without any idea of the true God. Now, that no one may vainly dream of three gods, or suppose that the simple essence of God is divided among the three Persons, we must seek for a short and easy definition, which will preserve us from all error. But since some violently object to the word Person, as of human invention, we must first examine the reasonableness of this objection. When the Apostle denominates the Son the express image of the hypostasis of the Father, he undoubtedly ascribes to the Father some subsistence, in which he differs from the Son. For to understand this word as synonymous with Essence, (as some interpreters have done, as though Christ, like wax impressed with a seal, represented in himself the substance of the Father,) were not only harsh, but also absurd. For the essence of God being simple and indivisible, he who contains all in himself, not in part, or by derivation, but in complete perfection, could not, without impropriety, and even absurdity, be called the express image of it. But since the Father, although distinguished by his own peculiar property, hath expressed himself entirely in his Son, it is with the greatest reason asserted that he hath made his hypostasis conspicuous in him; with which the other appellation, given him in the same passage, of "the brightness of his glory," exactly corresponds. From the words of the Apostle, we certainly conclude, that there is in the Father a proper hypostasis, which is conspicuous in the Son. And thence also we easily infer the hypostasis of the Son, which distinguishes him from the Father. The same reasoning is applicable to the Holy Spirit; for we shall soon prove him also to be God; and yet he must, of necessity, be considered as distinct from the Father. But this is not a distinction of the essence, which it is unlawful to represent as any other than simple and undivided. It follows, therefore, if the testimony of the Apostle be credited, that there are in God three *hypostases*. And, as the Latins have expressed the same thing by the word *person*, it is too fastidious and obstinate to contend about so clear a matter. If we wish to translate word for word, we may call it *subsistence*. Many, in the same sense, have called it *substance*. Nor has the word *person* been used by the Latins only; but the Greeks also, for the sake of testifying their consent to this doctrine, taught the existence of three πρόσωπα (persons) in God. But both Greeks and Latins, notwithstanding any verbal difference, are in perfect harmony respecting the doctrine itself.

III. Now, though heretics rail at the word *person*, or some morose and obstinate men clamorously refuse to admit a name of human invention; since they cannot make us assert that there are three, each of whom is entirely God, nor yet that there are more gods than one, how very unreasonable is it to reprobate words which express nothing but what is testified and recorded in the Scriptures! It were better, say they, to restrain not only our thoughts, but our expressions also, within the limits of the Scripture, than to introduce exotic words, which may generate future dissensions and disputes; for thus we weary ourselves with verbal controversies; thus the truth is lost in altercation; thus charity expires in odious contention. If they call every word exotic, which cannot be found in the Scriptures in so many syllables, they impose on us a law which is very unreasonable, and which condemns all interpretation, but what is composed of detached texts of Scripture connected together. But if by exotic they mean that which is curiously contrived, and superstitiously defended, which tends to contention more than to edification, the use of which is either unseasonable or unprofitable, which offends pious ears with its harshness, and seduces persons from the simplicity of the Divine word, I most cordially embrace their modest opinion. For I think that we ought to speak of God with the same religious caution, which should govern our thoughts of him; since all the thoughts that we entertain concerning him merely from ourselves, are foolish, and all our expressions absurd. But there is a proper medium to be observed: we should seek in the Scriptures a certain rule, both for thinking and for speaking; by which we may regulate all the thoughts of our minds, and all the words of our mouths. But what forbids our expressing, in plainer words, those things which, in the Scriptures, are, to our understanding, intricate and obscure, provided our expressions religiously and faithfully convey the true sense of the Scripture, and are used with modest caution, and not without sufficient occasion? Of this, examples sufficiently numerous are not wanting. But, when it shall have been proved, that the Church was absolutely necessitated to use the terms Trinity and Persons, if any one then censures the novelty of the words, may he not be justly considered as offended at the light of the truth? as having no other cause of censure, but that the truth is explained and elucidated?

IV. But such verbal novelty (if it must have this appellation) is principally used, when the truth is to be asserted in opposition to malicious cavillers, who elude it by crafty evasions; of which we have too much experience in the present day, who find great difficulty in refuting the enemies of pure and sound doctrine: possessed of serpentine lubricity, they escape by the most artful expedients, unless they are vigorously pursued, and held fast when once caught. Thus the ancients, pestered with various controversies against erroneous dogmas, were constrained to express their sentiments with the utmost perspicuity, that they might leave no subterfuges to the impious, who availed themselves of obscure expressions, for the concealment of their errors. Unable to resist the clear testimonies of the Scriptures, Arius confessed Christ to be God, and the Son of God; and, as though this were all that was necessary, he pretended to agree with the Church at large. But, at the same time, he continued to maintain that Christ was created, and had a beginning like other creatures. To draw the versatile subtlety of this man from its concealment, the ancient Fathers proceeded further, and declared Christ to be the eternal Son of the Father, and consubstantial with the Father. Here impiety openly discovered itself, when the Arians began inveterately to hate and execrate the name ὁμοούσιος, (consubstantial.) But if, in the first instance, they had sincerely and cordially confessed Christ to be God, they would not have denied him to be consubstantial with the Father. Who can dare to censure those good men, as quarrelsome and contentious, for having kindled such a flame of controversy, and disturbed the peace of the Church on account of one little word? That little word distinguished Christians, who held the pure faith, from sacrilegious Arians. Afterwards arose Sabellius, who considered the names of Father, Son, and Holy Spirit, as little more than empty sounds; arguing, that they were not used on account of any real distinction, but were different attributes of God, whose attributes of this kind are numerous. If the point came to be controverted, he confessed, that he believed the Father to be God, the Son God, and the Holy Spirit God; but he would readily evade all the force of this confession, by adding, that he had said no other than if he had called God potent, and just, and wise. And thus he came to another conclusion, that the Father is the Son, and that the Holy Spirit is the Father, without any order or distinction. The good doctors of that age, who had the interest of religion at heart, in order to counteract the wickedness of this man, maintained, on the contrary, that they ought really to acknowledge three peculiar properties in one God. And, to defend themselves against his intricate subtleties, by the plain and simple truth, they affirmed, that they truly subsisted in the one God; or, what is the same, that in the unity of God there subsisted a trinity of Persons.

V. If, then, the words have not been rashly invented, we should beware lest we be convicted of fastidious temerity in rejecting them. I could wish them, indeed, to be buried in oblivion, provided this faith were universally received, that the Father, Son, and Holy Spirit, are the one God; and that nevertheless the Son is not the Father, nor the Spirit the Son, but that they are distinguished from each other by some peculiar property. I am not so rigidly precise as to be fond of contending for mere words. For I observe that the ancients, who otherwise speak on these subjects with great piety, are not consistent with each other, nor, in all cases, with themselves. For what forms of expression, adopted by councils, does Hilary excuse! To what extremes does Augustine sometimes proceed! How different are the Greeks from the Latins! But of this variation, let one example suffice: when the Latins would translate the word ὁμοούσιος, they called it *consubstantial*, signifying the *substance* of the Father and the Son to be one, and thus using *substance* for *essence*. Whence also Jerome, writing to Damasus, pronounces it to be sacrilege to say that there are three *substances* in God. Yet, that there are three *substances* in God, you will find asserted in Hilary more than a hundred times. But how perplexed is Jerome on the word *hypostasis!* For he suspects some latent poison in the assertion, that there are three *hypostases* in God. And if any one uses this word in a pious sense, he refrains not from calling it an improper expression; if, indeed, he was sincere in this declaration, and did not rather knowingly and wilfully endeavour to asperse, with a groundless calumny, the bishops of the East, whom he hated. He certainly discovers not much ingenuousness in affirming that, in all the profane schools, οὐσία (essence) is the same as ὑπόστασις, (hypostasis,) which the trite and common use of the words universally contradicts. More modesty and liberality are discovered by Augustine, who, though he asserts that the word *hypostasis*, in this sense, is new to Latin ears, yet leaves the Greeks their usual phraseology, and even peaceably tolerates the Latins, who had imitated their language; and the account of Socrates, in the sixth book of his Tripartite History, seems to imply, that it was by ignorant men that it had first been improperly applied to this subject. The same Hilary accuses the heretics of a great crime, in constraining him, by their wickedness, to expose to the danger of human language those things which ought to be confined within the religion of the mind; plainly avowing that this is to do things unlawful, to express things inexpressible, to assume things not conceded. A little after, he largely excuses himself for his boldness in bringing forward new terms; for, when he has used the names of nature, Father, Son, and Spirit, he immediately adds, that whatever is sought further, is beyond the signification of language, beyond the reach of our senses, beyond the conception of our understanding. And, in another place, he pronounces that happy were the bishops of Gaul, who had neither composed, nor received, nor even known, any other confession but that ancient and very simple one, which had been received in all the churches from the days of the Apostles. Very similar is the excuse of Augustine, that this word was extorted by necessity, on account of the poverty of human language on so great a subject, not for the sake of expressing what God is, but to avoid passing it over in total silence, that the Father, Son, and Spirit are three. This moderation of those holy men should teach us, not to pass such severe censures on those who are unwilling to subscribe to expressions adopted by us, provided they are not actuated by pride, perverseness, or disingenuous subtlety. But let them also, on the other hand, consider the great necessity which constrains us to use such language, that, by degrees, they may at length be accustomed to a useful phraseology.

Let them also learn to beware, since we have to oppose the Arians on one side, and the Sabellians on the other, lest, while they take offence at both these parties being deprived of all opportunity of evasion, they cause some suspicion that they are themselves the disciples either of Arius or of Sabellius. Arius confesses, "that Christ is God;" but maintains also, "that he was created, and had a beginning." He acknowledges that Christ is "one with the Father;" but secretly whispers in the ears of his disciples, that he is "united to him," like the rest of the faithful, though by a singular privilege. Say that he is *consubstantial*, you tear off the mask from the hypocrite, and yet you add nothing to the Scriptures. Sabellius asserts, "that the names Father, Son, and Spirit, are expressive of no distinction in the Godhead." Say that they are three, and he will exclaim, that you are talking of "three gods." Say, "that in the one essence of God there is a trinity of Persons," and you will at once express what the Scriptures declare, and will restrain such frivolous loquacity. Now, if any persons are prevented, by such excessive scrupulousness, from admitting these terms, yet not one of them can deny, that, when the Scripture speaks of one God, it should be understood of a unity of substance; and that, when it speaks of three in one essence, it denotes the Persons in this trinity. When this is honestly confessed, we have no further concern about words. But I have found, by long and frequent experience, that those who pertinaciously contend about words, cherish some latent poison; so that it were better designedly to provoke their resentment, than to use obscure language for the sake of obtaining their favour.

VI. But, leaving the dispute about terms, I shall now enter on the discussion of the subject itself. What I denominate a Person, is a subsistence in the Divine essence, which is related to the others, and yet distinguished from them by an incommunicable property. By the word *subsistence* we mean something different from the word *essence*. For, if the *Word* were simply God, and had no peculiar property, John had been guilty of impropriety in saying that he was always *with God*. (*l*) When he immediately adds, that *the Word* also *was God*, he reminds us of the unity of the essence. But because he could not be *with God*, without subsisting in the Father, hence arises that subsistence, which, although inseparably connected with the essence, has a peculiar mark, by which it is distinguished from it. Now, I say that each of the three subsistences has a relation to the others, but is distinguished from them by a peculiar property. We particularly use the word

(*l*) John i. 1.

relation, (or *comparison,*) here, because, when mention is made simply and indefinitely of God, this name pertains no less to the Son and Spirit, than to the Father. But whenever the Father is compared with the Son, the property peculiar to each distinguishes him from the other. Thirdly, whatever is proper to each of them, I assert to be incommunicable, because whatever is ascribed to the Father as a character of distinction, cannot be applied or transferred to the Son. Nor, indeed, do I disapprove of the definition of Tertullian, if rightly understood: "That there is in God a certain distribution or economy, which makes no change in the unity of the essence."

VII. But before I proceed any further, I must prove the Deity of the Son and of the Holy Spirit; after which we shall see how they differ from each other. When the Scripture speaks of *the Word of God*, it certainly were very absurd to imagine it to be only a transient and momentary sound, emitted into the air, and coming forth from God himself; of which nature were the oracles, given to the fathers, and all the prophecies. It is rather to be understood of the eternal wisdom residing in God, whence the oracles, and all the prophecies, proceeded. For, according to the testimony of Peter, (*m*) the ancient Prophets spake by the Spirit of Christ no less than the Apostles and all the succeeding ministers of the heavenly doctrine. But, as Christ had not yet been manifested, we must necessarily understand that the Word was begotten of the Father before the world began. And if the Spirit that inspired the Prophets was the Spirit of the Word, we conclude, beyond all doubt, that the Word was truly God. And this is taught by Moses, with sufficient perspicuity, in the creation of the world, in which he represents the Word as acting such a conspicuous part. For why does he relate that God, in the creation of each of his works, said, Let this or that be done, but that the unsearchable glory of God may resplendently appear in his image? Captious and loquacious men would readily evade this argument, by saying, that the *Word* imports an order or command; but the Apostles are better interpreters, who declare, that the worlds were created by the Son, and that he "upholds all things by the word of his power." (*n*) For here we see that the *Word* intends the nod or mandate of the Son, who is himself the eternal and essential Son of the Father. Nor, to the wise and sober, is there any obscurity in that passage of Solomon, where he introduces Wisdom as begotten of the Father before time began, and presiding at the creation of the world, and over all the works of God. For, to pretend that this denotes some temporary ex-

---

(*m*) 1 Pet. i. 11. (*n*) Heb. i. 2, 3.

pression of the will of God, were foolish and frivolous; whereas God then intended to discover his fixed and eternal counsel, and even something more secret. To the same purpose also is that assertion of Christ, "My Father worketh hitherto, and I work." (o) For, by affirming that, from the beginning of the world, he had continually coöperated with the Father, he makes a more explicit declaration of what had been briefly glanced at by Moses. We conclude, therefore, that God spake thus at the creation, that the Word might have his part in the work, and so that operation be common to both. But John speaks more clearly than all others, when he represents *the Word*, who from the beginning *was God with God*, as in union with the Father, the original cause of all things. For to the Word he both attributes a real and permanent essence, and assigns some peculiar property; and plainly shows how God, by speaking, created the world. Therefore, as all Divine revelations are justly entitled *the word of God*, so we ought chiefly to esteem that substantial Word the source of all revelations, who is liable to no variation, who remains with God perpetually one and the same, and who is God himself.

VIII. Here we are interrupted by some clamorous objectors, who, since they cannot openly rob him of his divinity, secretly steal from him his eternity. For they say, that the Word only began to exist, when God opened his sacred mouth in the creation of the world. But they are too inconsiderate in imagining something new in the substance of God. For, as those names of God, which relate to his external works, began to be ascribed to him after the existence of those works, as when he is called the Creator of heaven and earth, so piety neither acknowledges nor admits any name, signifying that God has found any thing new to happen to himself. For, could any thing, from any quarter, effect a change in him, it would contradict the assertion of James, that "every good gift and every perfect gift is from above, and cometh down from the Father of lights, with whom is no variableness or shadow of turning." (p) Nothing, then, is more intolerable, than to suppose a beginning of that Word, which was always God, and afterwards the Creator of the world. But they argue, in their own apprehension most acutely, that Moses, by representing God as having then spoken for the first time, implies also, that there was no Word in him before; than which nothing is more absurd. For it is not to be concluded, because any thing begins to be manifested at a certain time, that it had no prior existence. I form a very different conclusion; that, since, in the very instant when God said, "Let there be light," (q) the power of the Word

(o) John v. 17.   (p) James i. 17.   (q) Gen. i. 3.

was clearly manifested, the Word must have existed long before. But if any one inquires, how long, he will find no beginning. For he limits no certain period of time, when he himself says, "O Father, glorify thou me with thine own self, with the glory which I had with thee before the world was." (*r*) Nor is this omitted by John; for, before he descends to the creation of the world, he declares that the Word "was in the beginning with God." (*s*) We therefore conclude again, that the Word, conceived of God before time began, perpetually remained with him, which proves his eternity, his true essence, and his divinity.

IX. Though I advert not yet to the person of the Mediator, but defer it to that part of the work which will relate to redemption, yet, since it ought, without controversy, to be believed by all, that Christ is the very same Word clothed in flesh, any testimonies which assert the Deity of Christ, will be very properly introduced here. When it is said, in the forty-fifth Psalm, "Thy throne, O God, is for ever and ever," the Jews endeavour to evade its force, by pleading that the name Elohim is applicable also to angels, and to men of dignity and power. But there cannot be found in the Scripture a similar passage, which erects an eternal throne for a creature; for he is not merely called God, but is also declared to possess an eternal dominion. Besides, this title is never given to a creature, without some addition, as when it is said that Moses should be "a god to Pharaoh." (*t*) Some read it in the genitive case, "Thy throne is of God," which is extremely insipid. I confess, indeed, that what is eminently and singularly excellent, is frequently called Divine; but it sufficiently appears from the context, that such a meaning would be uncouth and forced, and totally inapplicable here. But, if their perverseness refuse to yield this point, there certainly is no obscurity in Isaiah, where he introduces Christ as God, and as crowned with supreme power, which is the prerogative of God alone. "His name," says he, "shall be called the Mighty God, the Father of eternity," &c. (*v*) Here also the Jews object, and invert the reading of the passage in this manner: "This is the name by which the mighty God, the Father of eternity, shall call him," &c.; so that they would leave the Son only the title of Prince of peace. But to what purpose would so many epithets be accumulated in this passage on God the Father, when the design of the prophet is to distinguish Christ by such eminent characters as may establish our faith in him? Wherefore, there can be no doubt that he is there denominated the Mighty God, just as, a little before, he is called Immanuel. But nothing can be required plainer than a passage in Jeremiah, that this should be the name

(*r*) John xvii. 5. (*s*) John i. 2. (*t*) Exod. vii. 1. (*v*) Isaiah ix. 6.

whereby the Branch of David shall be called "Jehovah our righteousness." (*w*) For since the Jews themselves teach, that all other names of God are mere epithets, but that this alone, which they call ineffable, is a proper name expressive of his Essence, we conclude, that the Son is the one eternal God, who declares, in another place, that he "will not give his glory to another." (*x*) This also they endeavour to evade, because Moses imposed this name on an altar which he built, and Ezekiel on the city of the new Jerusalem. But who does not perceive, that the altar was erected as a monument of Moses having been exalted by God, and that Jerusalem is honoured with the name of God, only as a testimony of the Divine presence? For thus speaks the prophet: "The name of the city shall be, Jehovah is there." (*y*) But Moses expresses himself thus: He "built an altar, and called the name of it Jehovah-nissi," (my exaltation.) (*z*) But there is more contention about another passage of Jeremiah, where the same title is given to Jerusalem in these words: "This is the name wherewith she shall be called, Jehovah our righteousness." (*a*) But this testimony is so far from opposing the truth which we are defending, that it rather confirms it. For, having before testified that Christ is the true Jehovah, from whom righteousness proceeds, he now pronounces that the church will have such a clear apprehension of it, as to be able to glory in the same name. In the former place, then, is shown the original cause of righteousness, in the latter the effect.

X. Now, if these things do not satisfy the Jews, I see not by what cavils they can evade the accounts of Jehovah having so frequently appeared in the character of an angel. An angel is said to have appeared to the holy fathers. He claims for himself the name of the eternal God. If it be objected, that this is spoken with regard to the character which he sustains, this by no means removes the difficulty. For a servant would never rob God of his honour, by permitting sacrifice to be offered to himself. But the angel, refusing to eat bread, commands a sacrifice to be offered to Jehovah. He afterwards demonstrates that he is really Jehovah himself. Therefore Manoah and his wife conclude, from this evidence, that they have seen, not a mere angel, but God himself. Hence he says, "We shall surely die, because we have seen God." When his wife replies, "If the Lord were pleased to kill us, he would not have received" a sacrifice "at our hands," (*b*) she clearly acknowledges him to be God, who before is called an angel. Moreover, the reply of the angel himself removes every doubt: "Why askest thou after my name, seeing it is wonderful?" So much the more detes-

(*w*) Jer. xxiii. 6. (*y*) Ezek. xlviii. 35. (*a*) Jer. xxxiii. 16.
(*x*) Isaiah xlii. 8. (*z*) Exod. xvii. 15. (*b*) Judges xiii. 22, 23.

table is the impiety of Servetus, in asserting that God never appeared to Abraham and the other patriarchs, but that they worshipped an angel in his stead. But the orthodox doctors of the church have truly and wisely understood and taught, that the same chief angel was the Word of God, who even then began to perform some services introductory to his execution of the office of Mediator. For though he was not yet incarnate, he descended, as it were, in a mediatorial capacity, that he might approach the faithful with greater familiarity. His familiar intercourse with men gave him the name of an angel; yet he still retained what properly belonged to him, and continued the ineffably glorious God. The same truth is attested by Hosea, who, after relating the wrestling of Jacob with an angel, says, "The Lord (Jehovah) God of hosts; Jehovah is his memorial." (c) Servetus again cavils, that God employed the person of an angel; as though the prophet did not confirm what had been delivered by Moses, — "Wherefore is it that thou dost ask after my name?" And the confession of the holy patriarch, when he says, "I have seen God face to face," (d) sufficiently declares, that he was not a created angel, but one in whom resided the fulness of Deity. Hence, also, the representation of Paul, that Christ was the conductor of the people in the wilderness; because, though the time of his humiliation was not yet arrived, the eternal Word then exhibited a type of the office to which he was appointed. Now, if the second chapter of Zechariah be strictly and coolly examined, the angel who sends another angel is immediately pronounced the God of hosts, and supreme power is ascribed to him. I omit testimonies innumerable on which our faith safely rests, although they have little influence on the Jews. For when it is said in Isaiah, "Lo, this is our God; we have waited for him, and he will save us; this is Jehovah;" (e) all who have eyes may perceive that this is God, who arises for the salvation of his people. And the emphatical repetition of these pointed expressions forbids an application of this passage to any other than to Christ. But still more plain and decisive is a passage of Malachi, where he prophesies, that "the Lord, who was then sought, should come into his temple." (f) The temple was exclusively consecrated to the one Most High God; yet the prophet claims it as belonging to Christ. Whence it follows, that he is the same God that was always worshipped among the Jews.

XI. The New Testament abounds with innumerable testimonies. We must, therefore, endeavour briefly to select a few, rather than to collect them all. Though the Apostles spake of him after he had appeared in flesh as the Mediator,

(c) Hosea xii. 5.
(d) Gen. xxxii. 29, 30.
(e) Isaiah xxv. 9.
(f) Mal. iii. 1.

yet all that I shall adduce will be adapted to prove his eternal Deity. In the first place, it is worthy of particular observation, that the apostle represents those things which were predicted concerning the eternal God, as either already exhibited in Christ, or to be accomplished in him at some future period. The prediction of Isaiah, that the Lord of Hosts would be "for a stone of stumbling, and for a rock of offence to both the houses of Israel," (*g*) Paul asserts to have been fulfilled in Christ. (*h*) Therefore he declares, that Christ is the Lord of Hosts. There is a similar instance in another place : " We shall all stand," says he, " before the judgment-seat of Christ. For it is written, As I live, saith the Lord, every knee shall bow to me, and every tongue shall confess to God." (*i*) Since God, in Isaiah, (*k*) declares this concerning himself, and Christ actually exhibits it in his own person, it follows, that he is that very God, whose glory cannot be transferred to another. The apostle's quotation from the Psalms also, in his Epistle to the Ephesians, is evidently applicable to none but God : " When he ascended up on high, he led captivity captive : " (*l*) understanding that ascension to have been prefigured by the exertions of the Divine power in the signal victories of David over the heathen nations, he signifies, that the text was more fully accomplished in Christ. Thus John attests that it was the glory of the Son which was revealed in a vision to Isaiah ; whereas the prophet himself records that he saw the majesty of God. (*m*) And those praises which the Apostle, in the Epistle to the Hebrews, ascribes to the Son, beyond all doubt most evidently belong to God : " Thou, Lord, in the beginning, hast laid the foundation of the earth ; and the heavens are the works of thine hands," &c. Again, " Let all the angels of God worship him." (*n*) Nor is it any misapplication of them, when he refers them to Christ ; since all that is predicted in those Psalms has been accomplished only by him. For it was He who arose and had mercy upon Zion ; it was He who claimed as his own the dominion over all nations and islands. And why should John, after having affirmed, at the commencement of his Gospel, (*o*) that the Word was always God, have hesitated to attribute to Christ the majesty of God ? And why should Paul have been afraid to place Christ on the tribunal of God, (*p*) after having so publicly preached his Divinity, when he called him " God blessed for ever ? " (*q*) And, to show how consistent he is with himself on this subject, he says, also, that " God was manifest in the flesh." (*r*)

(*g*) Isaiah viii. 14.
(*h*) Rom. ix. 33.
(*i*) Rom. xiv. 10, 11.
(*k*) Isaiah xlv. 23.
(*l*) Eph. iv. 8. Psalm lxviii. 18.
(*m*) John xii. 41. Isaiah vi. 1.
(*n*) Heb. i. 6, 10.
(*o*) John i. 1, 14.
(*p*) 2 Cor. v. 10.
(*q*) Rom. ix. 5.
(*r*) 1 Tim. iii. 16.

If he is "God blessed for ever," he is the same to whom this apostle, in another place, affirms all glory and honour to be due. And he conceals not, but openly proclaims, that, "being in the form of God," he "thought it not robbery to be equal with God, but made himself of no reputation." (*s*) And, lest the impious might object, that he is a sort of artificial God, John goes further, and affirms, that "This is the true God, and eternal life;" (*t*) although we ought to be fully satisfied by his being called God, especially by a witness who expressly avers that there are no more gods than one; I mean Paul, who says, "though there be that are called gods, whether in heaven or in earth; to us there is but one God, of whom are all things." (*v*) When we hear, from the same mouth, that "God was manifested in the flesh," that "God hath purchased the Church with his own blood,"— why do we imagine a second God, whom he by no means acknowledges? And there is no doubt that all the pious were of the same opinion. Thomas, likewise, by publicly confessing him to be "his Lord and God," declares him to be the same true God whom he had always worshipped. (*w*)

XII. If we judge of his Divinity from the works which the Scriptures attribute to him, it will thence appear with increasing evidence. For when he said, that he had, from the beginning, continually coöperated with the Father, the Jews, stupid as they were about his other declarations, yet perceived, that he assumed to himself Divine power; and, therefore, as John informs us, they "sought the more to kill him; because he not only had broken the sabbath, but said also that God was his Father, making himself equal with God." (*x*) How great, then, must be our stupidity, if we perceive not this passage to be a plain assertion of his Divinity! To preside over the world by his almighty providence, and to govern all things by the nod of his own power, (which the Apostle attributes to him,) (*y*) belongs exclusively to the Creator. And he participates with the Father, not only in the government of the world, but also in all other offices, which cannot be communicated to creatures. The Lord proclaims, by the prophet, "I, even I, am he that blotteth out thy transgressions, for mine own sake." (*z*) According to this declaration, when the Jews thought that Christ committed an injury against God, by undertaking to forgive sins, (*a*) he not only asserted in express terms, that this power belonged to him, but proved it by a miracle. We see, therefore, that he hath not the ministry, but the power of remission of sins, which the Lord de-

(*s*) Philip. ii. 6.
(*t*) 1 John v. 20.
(*r*) 1 Cor. viii. 5, 6.
(*w*) John xx. 28.
(*x*) John v. 18.
(*y*) Heb. i. 3.
(*z*) Isaiah xliii. 25.
(*a*) Matt. ix. 6.

clares shall never be transferred from himself to another. Is it not the prerogative of God alone to examine and penetrate the secret thoughts of the heart? Yet Christ possessed that power; which is a proof of his Divinity.

XIII. But with what perspicuity of evidence does it appear in his miracles! Though I grant that the Prophets and Apostles performed miracles similar and equal to his, yet there is a considerable difference in this respect, that they, in their ministry, dispensed the favours of God, whereas his miracles were performed by his exertions of his own power. He sometimes, indeed, used prayer, that he might glorify the Father; but, in most instances, we perceive the manifest displays of his own power. And how should not he be the true author of miracles, who, by his own authority, committed the dispensation of them to others? For the Evangelists relate, that he gave his Apostles power to raise the dead, to heal the leprous, to cast out devils, &c. (*b*) And they performed that ministry in such a manner, as plainly to discover, that the power proceeded solely from Christ. "In the name of Jesus Christ," says Peter, "arise and walk." (*c*) It is no wonder, therefore, that Christ should bring forward his miracles, (*d*) to convince the incredulity of the Jews, since, being performed by his own power, they afforded most ample evidence of his Divinity. Besides, if out of God there be no salvation, no righteousness, no life, but Christ contains all these things in himself, it certainly demonstrates him to be God. Let it not be objected, that life and salvation are infused into him by God; for he is not said to have received salvation, but to be himself salvation. And if no one be good but God alone, (*e*) how can *he* be a mere man who is, I will not say good and righteous, but goodness and righteousness itself? Even from the beginning of the creation, according to the testimony of an Evangelist, "in him was life; and the life" then existed as "the light of men." Supported by such proofs, therefore, we venture to repose our faith and hope on him; whereas we know that it is impious and sacrilegious for any man to place his confidence in creatures. He says, "Ye believe in God, believe also in me." (*f*) And in this sense Paul interprets two passages of Isaiah — "Whosoever believeth on him shall not be ashamed." Again, "There shall be a root of Jesse, that shall rise to reign over the Gentiles; in him shall the Gentiles trust." (*g*) And why should we search for more testimonies from Scripture, when this declaration occurs so frequently, "He that believeth on me hath everlasting life"? (*h*)

(*b*) Matt. x. 8. Mark iii. 15.   (*c*) Acts iii. 6.   (*d*) John v. 36; x. 37.
    (*e*) Matt. xix. 17.   (*f*) John xiv. 1.
(*g*) Isaiah xxviii. 16; xi. 10. Rom. x. 11; xv. 12.   (*h*) John vi. 47.

The invocation, arising from faith, is also directed to him; which, nevertheless, peculiarly belongs, if any thing peculiarly belongs, to the Divine majesty. For a prophet says, " Whosoever shall call on the name of the Lord (Jehovah) shall be delivered." (*i*) And Solomon, " The name of the Lord is a strong tower: the righteous runneth into it, and is safe." (*k*) But the name of Christ is invoked for salvation: it follows, therefore, that he is Jehovah. Moreover, we have an example of such invocation in Stephen, when he says, " Lord Jesus, receive my spirit." (*l*) And afterwards in the whole Church, as Ananias testifies in the same book: " Lord, I have heard by many of this man, how much evil he hath done to thy saints — that call on thy name." (*m*) And to make it more clearly understood, that "all the fulness of the Godhead dwelleth bodily in Christ," the Apostle confesses that he had introduced among the Corinthians no other doctrine than the knowledge of him, and that this had been the only subject of his preaching. (*n*) What a remarkable and important consideration is it, that the name of the Son only is preached to us, whereas God commands us to glory in the knowledge of himself alone! (*o*) Who can dare to assert that *he* is a mere creature, the knowledge of whom is our only glory? It must also be remarked, that the salutations prefixed to the epistles of Paul implore the same blessings from the Son as from the Father; whence we learn, not only that those things, which our heavenly Father bestows, are obtained for us by his intercession, but that the Son, by a communion of power, is himself the author of them. This practical knowledge is unquestionably more certain and solid than any idle speculation. For then the pious mind has the nearest view of the Divine presence, and almost touches it, when it experiences itself to be quickened, illuminated, saved, justified, and sanctified.

XIV. Wherefore the proof of the Deity of the Spirit must be derived principally from the same sources. There is no obscurity in the testimony of Moses, in the history of the creation, that the Spirit of God was expanded on the abyss or chaos; (*p*) for it signifies, not only that the beautiful state of the world which we now behold owes its preservation to the power of the Spirit, but that, previously to its being thus adorned, the Spirit was engaged in brooding over the confused mass. The declaration of Isaiah bids defiance to all cavils: "And now the Lord God, and his Spirit, hath sent me." (*q*) For the Holy Spirit is united in the exercise of supreme

(*i*) Joel ii. 32.
(*k*) Prov. xviii. 10.
(*l*) Acts vii. 59.
(*m*) Acts ix. 13, 14.
(*n*) 1 Cor. ii. 2.
(*o*) Jer. ix. 24.
(*p*) Gen. i. 2.
(*q*) Isaiah xlviii. 16.

power in the mission of Prophets, which is a proof of his Divine majesty. But the best confirmation, as I have remarked, we shall derive from familiar experience. For what the Scriptures ascribe to him, and what we ourselves learn by the certain experience of piety, is not at all applicable to any creature. For it is he who, being universally diffused, sustains and animates all things in heaven and in earth. And this very thing excludes him from the number of creatures, that he is circumscribed by no limits, but transfuses through all his own vigorous influence, to inspire them with being, life, and motion: this is clearly a work of Deity. Again, if regeneration to an incorruptible life be more important and excellent than any present life, what must we think of him from whose power it proceeds? But the Scripture teaches, in various places, that he is the author of regeneration by a power not derived, but properly his own; and not of regeneration only, but likewise of the future immortality. Finally, to him, as well as to the Son, are applied all those offices which are peculiar to Deity. For he "searcheth even the deep things of God," (r) who admits no creature to a share in his councils. He bestows wisdom and the faculty of speech; (s) whereas the Lord declares to Moses, that this can only be done by himself. (t) So through him we attain to a participation of God, to feel his vivifying energy upon us. Our justification is his work. From him proceed power, sanctification, truth, grace, and every other blessing we can conceive; since there is but one Spirit, from whom every kind of gifts descends. For this passage of Paul is worthy of particular attention: "There are diversities of gifts, and there are differences of administrations, but the same Spirit;" (u) because it represents him, not only as the principle and source of them, but also as the author; which is yet more clearly expressed a little after in these words: "All these worketh that only and the self-same Spirit, dividing to every man severally as he will." For if he were not a subsistence in the Deity, judgment and voluntary determination would never be ascribed to him. Paul, therefore, very clearly attributes to the Spirit Divine power, and thereby demonstrates him to be an hypostasis or subsistence in God.

XV. Nor does the Scripture, when it speaks of him, refrain from giving him the appellation of God. For Paul concludes that we are the temple of God, because his Spirit dwelleth in us. (v) This must not be passed over without particular notice; for the frequent promises of God, that he will choose us for a temple for himself, receive no other accomplishment, than by

(r) 1 Cor. ii. 10, 16.   (s) 1 Cor. xii. 8.   (t) Exod. iv. 11.
(u) 1 Cor. xii. 4, &c.   (v) 1 Cor. iii. 16; vi. 19. 2 Cor. vi. 16.

the inhabitation of his Spirit in us. Certainly, as Augustine excellently observes, "If we were commanded to erect to the Spirit a temple of wood and stone, forasmuch as God is the sole object of worship, it would be a clear proof of his Divinity; how much clearer, then, is the proof, now that we are commanded, not to erect one, but to be ourselves his temples!" And the Apostle calls us sometimes the temple of God, and sometimes the temple of the Holy Spirit, both in the same signification. Peter, reprehending Ananias for having "lied to the Holy Ghost," told him that he had "not lied unto men, but unto God." (*w*) And where Isaiah (*x*) introduces the Lord of hosts as the speaker, Paul (*y*) informs us that it is the Holy Spirit who speaks. Indeed, while the Prophets invariably declare, that the words which they utter are those of the Lord of hosts, Christ and the Apostles refer them to the Holy Spirit; whence it follows, that he is the true Jehovah, who is the primary author of the prophecies. Again, God complains that his anger was provoked by the perverseness of the people; Isaiah, in reference to the same conduct, says, that "they vexed his Holy Spirit." (*z*) Lastly, if blasphemy against the Spirit be not forgiven, either in this world or in that which is to come, (*a*) whilst a man may obtain pardon who has been guilty of blasphemy against the Son, this is an open declaration of his Divine majesty, to defame or degrade which is an inexpiable crime. I intentionally pass over many testimonies which were used by the fathers. To them there appeared much plausibility in citing this passage from David, "By the word of the Lord were the heavens made, and all the host of them by the breath of his mouth;" (*b*) to prove that the creation of the world was the work of the Holy Spirit, as well as of the Son. But since a repetition of the same thing twice is common in the Psalms, and in Isaiah "the spirit of his mouth" means the same as "his word," this is but a weak argument. Therefore I have determined to confine myself to a sober statement of those evidences on which pious minds may satisfactorily rest.

XVI. As God afforded a clearer manifestation of himself at the advent of Christ, the three Persons also then became better known. Among many testimonies, let us be satisfied with this one: Paul connects together these three, Lord, Faith, and Baptism, (*c*) in such a manner as to reason from one to another. Since there is but one faith, hence he proves that there is but one Lord; since there is but one baptism, he shows that there is also but one faith. Therefore, if we are initiated by baptism into the faith and religion of one God, we must necessarily suppose

---

(*w*) Acts v. 3, 4.　　(*x*) Isaiah vi. 9.　　(*y*) Acts xxviii. 25.
(*z*) Isaiah lxiii. 10.　　(*a*) Matt. xii. 31.　Mark iii. 29.　Luke xii. 10.
　　(*b*) Psalm xxxiii. 6.　　(*c*) Ephes. iv. 5.

him to be the true God, into whose name we are baptized. Nor can it be doubted but that in this solemn commission, "Baptize them in the name of the Father, and of the Son, and of the Holy Ghost," Christ intended to testify, that the perfect light of faith was now exhibited. For this is equivalent to being baptized into the name of the one God, who hath clearly manifested himself in the Father, Son, and Spirit; whence it evidently appears, that in the Divine Essence there exist three Persons, in whom is known the one God. And truly, since faith ought not to be looking about hither and thither, or to be wandering through the varieties of inconstancy, but to direct its views towards the one God, to be fixed on him, and to adhere to him,—it may easily be proved from these premises, that, if there be various kinds of faith, there must also be a plurality of gods. Baptism, being a sacrament of faith, confirms to us the unity of God, because it is but one. Hence, also, we conclude, that it is not lawful to be baptized, except into the name of the one God; because we embrace the faith of him, into whose name we are baptized. What, then, was intended by Christ, when he commanded baptism to be administered in the name of the Father, and of the Son, and of the Holy Spirit, but that one faith ought to be exercised in the Father, Son, and Spirit? and what is that but a clear testimony, that the Father, the Son, and the Holy Spirit, are the one God? Therefore, since it is an undeniable truth, that there is one God, and only one, we conclude the Word and Spirit to be no other than the very Essence of the Deity. The greatest degree of folly was betrayed by the Arians, who confessed the Divinity of the Son, but denied him to possess the substance of God. Nor were the Macedonians free from a similar delusion, who would explain the term "Spirit" to mean only the gifts of grace conferred upon man. For as wisdom, understanding, prudence, fortitude, and the fear of the Lord, proceed from him, so he alone is the Spirit of wisdom, prudence, fortitude, and piety. Nor is he himself divided according to the distribution of his graces; but, as the Apostle declares, how variously soever they are divided, he always remains one and the same. (*d*)

XVII. On the other hand, also, we find in the Scriptures a distinction between the Father and the Word, between the Word and the Spirit; in the discussion of which the magnitude of the mystery reminds us that we ought to proceed with the utmost reverence and sobriety. I am exceedingly pleased with this observation of Gregory Nazianzen: "I cannot think of the *one*, but I am immediately surrounded with the splendour of the *three;* nor can I clearly discover the *three*, but I

(*d*) 1 Cor. xii. 11.

am suddenly carried back to the *one.*" Wherefore let us not imagine such a trinity of Persons, as includes an idea of separation, or does not immediately recall us to the unity. The names of Father, Son, and Spirit, certainly imply a real distinction; let no one suppose them to be mere epithets, by which God is variously designated from his works; but it is a distinction, not a division. The passages already cited show, that the Son has a property, by which he is distinguished from the Father; because the Word had not been with God, or had his glory with the Father, unless he had been distinct from him. He likewise distinguishes the Father from himself, when he says, "that there is another that beareth witness of him." (*e*) And to the same effect is what is declared in another place, that the Father created all things by the Word; which he could not have done, unless he had been in some sense distinct from him. Besides, the Father descended not to the earth, but he who came forth from the Father. The Father neither died nor rose again, but he who was sent by the Father. Nor did this distinction commence at the incarnation, but it is evident, that, before that period, he was the only begotten in the bosom of the Father. (*f*) For who can undertake to assert, that the Son first entered into the bosom of the Father, when he descended from heaven to assume a human nature? He, therefore, was in the bosom of the Father before, and possessed his glory with the Father. The distinction between the Holy Spirit and the Father is announced by Christ, when he says, that he "proceedeth from the Father." (*g*) But how often does he represent him as another, distinct from himself! as when he promises that "another Comforter" (*h*) should be sent, and in many other places.

XVIII. I doubt the propriety of borrowing similitudes from human things, to express the force of this distinction. The fathers sometimes practise this method; but they likewise confess the great disproportion of all the similitudes which they introduce. Wherefore I greatly dread, in this instance, every degree of presumption; lest the introduction of any thing unseasonable should afford an occasion of calumny to the malicious, or of error to the ignorant. Yet it is not right to be silent on the distinction which we find expressed in the Scriptures; which is this — that to the Father is attributed the principle of action, the fountain and source of all things; to the Son, wisdom, counsel, and the arrangement of all operations; and the power and efficacy of the action is assigned to the Spirit. Moreover, though eternity belongs to the Father,

(*e*) John v. 32; viii. 16, 18. (*g*) John xv. 26.
(*f*) John i. 18. (*h*) John xiv. 16.

and to the Son and Spirit also, since God can never have been destitute of his wisdom or his power, and in eternity we must not inquire after any thing prior or posterior, — yet the observation of order is not vain or superfluous, while the Father is mentioned as first; in the next place the Son, as from him; and then the Spirit, as from both. For the mind of every man naturally inclines to the consideration, first, of God; secondly, of the wisdom emanating from him; and lastly, of the power by which he executes the decrees of his wisdom. For this reason the Son is said to be from the Father, and the Spirit from both the Father and the Son; and that in various places, but nowhere more clearly than in the eighth chapter of the Epistle to the Romans, where the same Spirit is indifferently denominated " the Spirit of Christ," and " the Spirit of him that raised up Christ from the dead," and that without any impropriety. For Peter also testifies that it was the Spirit of Christ by whom the prophets prophesied; (*i*) whereas the Scripture so frequently declares that it was the Spirit of God the Father.

XIX. This distinction is so far from opposing the most absolute simplicity and unity of the Divine Being, that it affords a proof that the Son is one God with the Father, because he has the same Spirit with him; and that the Spirit is not a different substance from the Father and the Son, because he is the Spirit of the Father and of the Son. For the whole nature is in each hypostasis, and each has something peculiar to himself. The Father is entirely in the Son, and the Son entirely in the Father, according to his own declaration, " I am in the Father, and the Father in me; " (*k*) nor do ecclesiastical writers allow that one is divided from the other by any difference of essence. " These distinctive appellations," says Augustine, " denote their reciprocal relations to each other, and not the substance itself, which is but one." This explanation may serve to reconcile the opinions of the fathers, which would otherwise appear totally repugnant to each other. For sometimes they state that the Son originates from the Father, and at other times assert that he has essential Divinity from himself, and so is, together with the Father, the one first cause of all. Augustine, in another place, admirably and perspicuously explains the cause of this diversity, in the following manner: " Christ, considered in himself, is called God; but with relation to the Father, he is called the Son." And again, " The Father, considered in himself, is called God; but with relation to the Son, he is called the Father. He who, with relation to the Son, is called the Father, is not the Son;

(*i*) 1 Pet. i. 11. (*k*) John xiv. 10, 11.

he who, with relation to the Father, is called the Son, is not the Father; they who are severally called the Father and the Son, are the same God." Therefore, when we speak simply of the Son, without reference to the Father, we truly and properly assert him to be self-existent, and therefore call him the sole first cause; but, when we distinctly treat of the relation between him and the Father, we justly represent him as originating from the Father. The first book of Augustine on the Trinity is entirely occupied with the explication of this subject; and it is far more safe to rest satisfied with that relation which he states, than by curiously penetrating into the sublime mystery, to wander through a multitude of vain speculations.

XX. Therefore, let such as love sobriety, and will be contented with the measure of faith, briefly attend to what is useful to be known; which is, that, when we profess to believe in one God, the word *God* denotes a single and simple essence, in which we comprehend three Persons, or hypostases; and that, therefore, whenever the word *God* is used indefinitely, the Son and Spirit are intended as much as the Father; but when the Son is associated with the Father, that introduces the reciprocal relation of one to the other; and thus we distinguish between the Persons. But, since the peculiar properties of the Persons produce a certain order, so that the original cause is in the Father, whenever the Father and the Son or Spirit are mentioned together, the name of God is peculiarly ascribed to the Father: by this method the unity of the essence is preserved, and the order is retained; which, however, derogates nothing from the Deity of the Son and Spirit. And indeed, as we have already seen that the Apostles assert him to be the Son of God, whom Moses and the Prophets have represented as Jehovah, it is always necessary to recur to the unity of the essence. Wherefore it would be a detestable sacrilege for us to call the Son another God different from the Father; because the simple name of God admits of no relation; nor can God, with respect to himself, be denominated either the one or the other. Now, that the name "Jehovah," in an indefinite sense, is applicable to Christ, appears even from the words of Paul: "for this thing I besought the Lord thrice;" (*l*) because, after relating the answer of Christ, "My grace is sufficient for thee," he immediately subjoins, "That the power of Christ may rest upon me." For it is certain that the word "Lord" is there used for "Jehovah;" and to restrict it to the person of the Mediator, would be frivolous and puerile, since it is an absolute declaration, containing

(*l*) 2 Cor. xii. 8, 9.

no comparison between the Son and the Father. And we know that the Apostles, following the custom of the Greek translators, invariably use the word Κυριος, (Lord,) instead of Jehovah. And, not to seek far for an example of this, Paul prayed to the Lord in no other sense than is intended in a passage of Joel, cited by Peter: "Whosoever shall call on the name of the Lord shall be saved." (*m*) But for the peculiar ascription of this name to the Son, another reason will be given in its proper place; suffice it at present to observe that, when Paul had prayed to God absolutely, he immediately subjoins the name of Christ. Thus also the whole Deity is by Christ himself denominated "a Spirit." For nothing opposes the spirituality of the whole Divine essence, in which are comprehended the Father, the Son, and the Spirit; which is plain from the Scripture. For as we there find God denominated a Spirit, so we find also the Holy Spirit, forasmuch as he is an hypostasis of the whole essence, represented both as the Spirit of God, and as proceeding from God.

XXI. But since Satan, in order to subvert the very foundations of our faith, has always been exciting great contentions concerning the Divine essence of the Son and Spirit, and the distinction of the Persons; and in almost all ages has instigated impious spirits to vex the orthodox teachers on this account; and is also endeavouring, in the present day, with the old embers, to kindle a new flame; it becomes necessary here to refute the perverse and fanciful notions which some persons have imbibed. Hitherto it has been our principal design to instruct the docile, and not to combat the obstinate and contentious; but now, having calmly explained and proved the truth, we must vindicate it from all the cavils of the wicked; although I shall make it my principal study, that those who readily and implicitly attend to the Divine word, may have stable ground on which they may confidently rest. On this, indeed, if on any of the secret mysteries of the Scripture, we ought to philosophize with great sobriety and moderation; and also with extreme caution, lest either our ideas or our language should proceed beyond the limits of the Divine word. For how can the infinite essence of God be defined by the narrow capacity of the human mind, which could never yet certainly determine the nature of the body of the sun, though the object of our daily contemplation? How can the human mind, by its own efforts, penetrate into an examination of the essence of God, when it is totally ignorant of its own? Wherefore let us freely leave to God the knowledge of himself. For "he alone," as Hilary says, "is a competent witness for him-

(*m*) Joel ii. 28—32. Acts ii. 16—21.

self, being only known by himself." And we shall certainly leave it to him, if our conceptions of him correspond to the manifestations which he has given us of himself, and our inquiries concerning him are confined to his word. There are extant on this argument five homilies of Chrysostom against the Anomœi; which, however, were not sufficient to restrain the presumptuous garrulity of those sophists. For they discovered no greater modesty in this instance than in every other. The very unhappy consequences of this temerity should warn us to study this question with more docility than subtlety, and not allow ourselves to investigate God any where but in his sacred word, or to form any ideas of him but such as are agreeable to his word, or to speak any thing concerning him but what is derived from the same word. But if the distinction of Father, Son, and Spirit, in the one Deity, as it is not easy to be comprehended, occasions some understandings more labour and trouble than is desirable, let them remember that the mind of man, when it indulges its curiosity, enters into a labyrinth; and let them submit to be guided by the heavenly oracles, however they may not comprehend the height of this mystery.

XXII. To compose a catalogue of the errors, by which the purity of the faith has been attacked on this point of doctrine, would be too prolix and tedious, without being profitable; and most of the heretics so strenuously exerted themselves to effect the total extinction of the Divine glory by their gross reveries, that they thought it sufficient to unsettle and disturb the inexperienced. From a few men there soon arose numerous sects, of whom some would divide the Divine essence, and others would confound the distinction which subsists between the Persons. But if we maintain, what has already been sufficiently demonstrated from the Scripture, that the essence of the one God, which pertains to the Father, to the Son, and to the Spirit, is simple and undivided, and, on the other hand, that the Father is, by some property, distinguished from the Son, and likewise the Son from the Spirit, the gate will be shut, not only against Arius and Sabellius, but also against all the other ancient heresiarchs. But since our own times have witnessed some madmen, as Servetus and his followers, who have involved every thing in new subtleties, a brief exposure of their fallacies will not be unuseful. The word *Trinity* was so odious and even detestable to Servetus, that he asserted all Trinitarians, as he called them, to be Atheists. I omit his impertinent and scurrilous language, but this was the substance of his speculations: That it is representing God as consisting of three parts, when three Persons are said to subsist in his essence, and that this triad is merely imaginary, being repugnant to the Divine unity.

At the same time, he maintained the Persons to be certain external ideas, which have no real subsistence in the Divine essence, but give us a figurative representation of God, under this or the other form; and that in the beginning there was no distinction in God, because the Word was once the same as the Spirit; but that, after Christ appeared God of God, there emanated from him another God, even the Spirit. Though he sometimes glosses over his impertinencies with allegories, as when he says, that the eternal Word of God was the Spirit of Christ with God, and the reflection of his image, and that the Spirit was a shadow of the Deity, yet he afterwards destroys the Deity of both, asserting that, according to the mode of dispensation, there is a part of God in both the Son and the Spirit; just as the same Spirit, substantially diffused in us, and even in wood and stones, is a portion of the Deity. What he broached concerning the Person of the Mediator, we shall examine in the proper place. But this monstrous fiction, that a Divine Person is nothing but a visible appearance of the glory of God, will not need a prolix refutation. For when John pronounces that the Word (Λογος) was God before the creation of the world, he sufficiently discriminates him from an ideal form. But if then also, and from the remotest eternity, that Word (Λογος) who was God, was with the Father, and possessed his own glory with the Father, he certainly could not be an external or figurative splendour; but it necessarily follows, that he was a real hypostasis, subsisting in God himself. But although no mention is made of the Spirit, but in the history of the creation of the world, yet he is there introduced, not as a shadow, but as the essential power of God, since Moses relates that the chaotic mass was supported by him. (*n*) It then appeared, therefore, that the eternal Spirit had always existed in the Deity, since he cherished and sustained the confused matter of the heaven and earth, till it attained a state of beauty and order. He certainly could not then be an image or representation of God, according to the dreams of Servetus. But in other places he is constrained to make a fuller disclosure of his impiety, saying that God, in his eternal reason, decreeing for himself a visible Son, has visibly exhibited himself in this manner; for if this be true, there is no other Divinity left to Christ, than as he has been appointed a Son by an eternal decree of God. Besides, he so transforms those phantasms, which he substitutes instead of the hypostases, that he hesitates not to imagine new accidents or properties in God. But the most execrable blasphemy of all is, his promiscuous confusion of the Son of God and the Spirit with all the creatures. For he asserts that in the Divine essence there are parts and divisions, every por-

---

(*n*) Gen. i. 2.

tion of which is God; and especially that the souls of the faithful are coëternal and consubstantial with God; though in another place he assigns substantial Deity, not only to the human soul, but to all created things.

XXIII. From the same corrupt source has proceeded another heresy, equally monstrous. For some worthless men, to escape the odium and disgrace which attended the impious tenets of Servetus, have confessed, indeed, that there are three Persons, but with this explanation, that the Father, who alone is truly and properly God, hath created the Son and Spirit, and transfused his Deity into them. Nor do they refrain from this dreadful manner of expressing themselves, that the Father is distinguished from the Son and Spirit, as being the sole possessor of the Divine essence. Their first plea in support of this notion is, that Christ is commonly called the Son of God; whence they conclude that no other is properly God but the Father. But they observe not, that although the name of God is common also to the Son, yet that it is sometimes ascribed to the Father ($\kappa\alpha\tau'$ $\dot{\varepsilon}\xi o\chi\eta\nu$) by way of eminence, because he is the fountain and original of the Deity; and this in order to denote the simple unity of the essence. They object, that if he is truly the Son of God, it is absurd to account him the Son of a Person. I reply, that both are true; that he is the Son of God, because he is the Word begotten of the Father before time began, for we are not yet speaking of the Person of the Mediator; and to be explicit, we must notice the Person, that the name of God may not be understood absolutely, but for the Father; for if we acknowledge no other to be God than the Father, it will be a manifest degradation of the dignity of the Son. Whenever mention is made of the Deity, therefore, there must no opposition be admitted between the Father and the Son, as though the name of the true God belonged exclusively to the Father. For surely the God who appeared to Isaiah, was the only true God; (*o*) whom, nevertheless, John affirms to have been Christ. (*p*) He likewise, who by the mouth of Isaiah declared that he was to be a rock of offence to the Jews, was the only true God; (*q*) whom Paul pronounces to have been Christ. (*r*) He who proclaims by Isaiah, "As I live, every knee shall bow to me," (*s*) is the only true God; but Paul applies the same to Christ. (*t*) To the same purpose are the testimonies recited by the Apostle — "Thou, Lord, hast laid the foundation of the earth and the heavens;" and "Let all the angels of God worship him." (*v*) These ascriptions belong only to the one true God; whereas

(*o*) Isaiah vi. 1. (*q*) Isaiah viii. 14. (*s*) Isaiah xlv. 23.
(*p*) John xii. 41. (*r*) Rom. ix. 33. (*t*) Rom. xiv. 11.
(*v*) Heb. i. 6, 10. Psalm cii. 25; xcvii. 7.

he contends that they are properly applied to Christ. Nor is there any force in that cavil, that what is proper to God is transferred to Christ, because he is the brightness of his glory. For, since the name Jehovah is used in each of these passages, it follows that in respect of his Deity he is self-existent. For, if he is Jehovah, he cannot be denied to be the same God, who in another place proclaims by Isaiah, "I am the first and I am the last; and beside me there is no God." (*w*) That passage in Jeremiah also deserves our attention — "The gods that have not made the heavens and the earth, even they shall perish from the earth, and from under these heavens;" (*x*) while, on the contrary, it must be acknowledged, that the Deity of the Son of God is frequently proved by Isaiah from the creation of the world. But how shall the Creator, who gives existence to all, not be self-existent, but derive his essence from another? For whoever asserts that the Son owes his essence to the Father, denies him to be self-existent. But this is contradicted by the Holy Spirit, who gives him the name of Jehovah. Now, if we admit the whole essence to be solely in the Father, either it will be divisible, or it will be taken away from the Son; and so, being despoiled of his essence, he will be only a titular god. The Divine essence, according to these triflers, belongs solely to the Father, inasmuch as he alone possesses it, and is the author of the essence of the Son. Thus the Divinity of the Son will be a kind of emanation from the essence of God, or a derivation of a part from the whole. Now, they must of necessity concede, from their own premises, that the Spirit is the Spirit of the Father only; because if he be a derivation from the original essence, which belongs exclusively to the Father, he cannot be accounted the Spirit of the Son; which is refuted by the testimony of Paul, where he makes him common to Christ and the Father. Besides, if the Person of the Father be expunged from the Trinity, wherein will he differ from the Son and Spirit, but in being himself the sole Deity? They confess that Christ is God, and yet differs from the Father. Some distinctive character is necessary, also, to discriminate the Father from the Son. They who place this in the essence, manifestly destroy the true Deity of Christ, which cannot exist independently of the essence, that is, of the entire essence. The Father certainly cannot differ from the Son, unless he have something peculiar to himself, which is not common to the Son. What will they find, by which to distinguish him? If the difference be in the essence, let them tell us whether he has communicated the same to the Son. But this could not

(*w*) Isaiah xliv. 6. (*x*) Jer. x. 11.

be done partially; for it would be an abomination to fabricate a demigod. Besides, this would miserably dismember the Divine essence. The necessary conclusion then is, that it is entirely and perfectly common to the Father and the Son. And if this be true, there cannot, in respect of the essence, be any difference between them. If it be objected that the Father, notwithstanding this communication of his essence, remains the only God with whom the essence continues, then Christ must be a figurative god, a god in appearance and name only, not in reality; because nothing is more proper to God than TO BE, according to that declaration, "I AM hath sent me unto you." (y)

XXIV. We might readily prove from many passages the falsehood of their assumption, that, whenever the name of God is mentioned absolutely in the Scripture, it means only the Father. And in those places which they cite in their own defence, they shamefully betray their ignorance, since the Son is there added; from which it appears, that the name of God is used in a relative sense, and therefore is particularly restricted to the Person of the Father. Their objection, that, unless the Father alone were the true God, he would himself be his own Father, is answered in a word. For there is no absurdity in the name of God, for the sake of dignity and order, being peculiarly given to him, who not only hath begotten of himself his own wisdom, but is also the God of the Mediator, of which I shall treat more at large in its proper place. For since Christ was manifested in the flesh, he is called the Son of God, not only as he was the eternal Word begotten of the Father before time began, but because he assumed the person and office of a Mediator, to unite us to God. And since they so presumptuously exclude the Son from Divine honours, I would wish to be informed, when he declares that there is none good but the one God, (z) whether he deprives himself of all goodness. I speak not of his human nature, lest they should object, that, whatever goodness it had, it was gratuitously conferred on it. I demand whether the eternal Word of God be good or not. If they answer in the negative, they are sufficiently convicted of impiety; and if in the affirmative, they cut the throat of their own system. But though, at the first glance, Christ seems to deny himself the appellation of good, he furnishes, notwithstanding, a further confirmation of our opinion. For, as that is a title which peculiarly belongs to the one God, forasmuch as he had been saluted as good, merely according to a common custom, by his rejection of false honour, he suggested that the goodness

(y) Exod. iii. 14. (z) Matt. xix. 17.

which he possessed was Divine. I demand, also, when Paul affirms that God alone is immortal, wise, and true, (*a*) whether he thereby degrades Christ to the rank of those who are mortal, unwise, and false. Shall not he then be immortal who from the beginning was life itself, and the giver of immortality to angels? Shall not he be wise who is the eternal Wisdom of God? Shall not he be true who is truth itself? I demand further, whether they think that Christ ought to be worshipped. For, if he justly claims this as his right, that every knee should bow before him, (*b*) it follows that he is that God, who, in the law, prohibited the worship of any one but himself. If they will have this passage in Isaiah, "I am, and there is no God besides me," to be understood solely of the Father, I retort this testimony on themselves; since we see that whatever belongs to God is attributed to Christ. Nor is there any room for their cavil, that Christ was exalted in the humanity in which he had been abased; and that, with regard to his humanity, all power was given to him in heaven and in earth; because, although the regal and judicial majesty extends to the whole Person of the Mediator, yet, had he not been God manifested in the flesh, he could not have been exalted to such an eminence, without God being in opposition to himself. And Paul excellently determines this controversy, by informing us that he was equal with God, before he abased himself under the form of a servant. (*c*) Now, how could this equality subsist, unless he had been that God whose name is JAH and JEHOVAH, who rides on the cherubim, whose kingdom is universal and everlasting? No clamour of theirs can deprive Christ of another declaration of Isaiah: "Lo, this is our God, we have waited for him;" (*d*) since in these words he describes the advent of God the Redeemer, not only for the deliverance of the people from exile in Babylon, but also for the complete restoration of the church. Nor do they gain any thing by another cavil, that Christ was God in his Father. For although we confess, in point of order and degree, that the Father is the fountain of the Deity, yet we pronounce it a detestable figment, that the essence belongs exclusively to the Father, as though he were the author of the Deity of the Son; because, on this supposition, either the essence would be divided, or Christ would be only a titular and imaginary god. If they admit that the Son is God, but inferior to the Father, then in him the essence must be begotten and created, which in the Father is unbegotten and uncreated. I know that some scorners ridicule our concluding a distinction of Persons from the words of Moses, where he introduces God thus speak-

---

(*a*) 1 Tim. i. 17.   (*b*) Phil. ii. 10.   (*c*) Phil. ii. 6, 7.   (*d*) Isaiah xxv. 9

ing: "Let us make man in our image." (e) Yet pious readers perceive how frigidly and foolishly Moses would have introduced this conference, if in one God there had not subsisted a plurality of Persons. Now, it is certain that they whom the Father addressed, were uncreated; but there is nothing uncreated, except the one God himself. Now, therefore, unless they grant that the power to create, and the authority to command, were common to the Father, the Son, and the Spirit, it will follow, that God did not speak thus within himself, but directed his conversation to some exterior agents. Lastly, one place will easily remove their two objections at once. For when Christ himself declares, that God is a Spirit, it would be unreasonable to restrict this solely to the Father, as though the Word were not also of a spiritual nature. But if the name of Spirit is equally as applicable to the Son as to the Father, I conclude that the Son is comprehended under the indefinite name of God. Yet he immediately subjoins, that none are approved worshippers of the Father, but those who worship him in spirit and in truth. (f) Whence follows another consequence, that, because Christ performs the office of a Teacher, in a station of inferiority, he ascribes the name of God to the Father, not to destroy his own Deity, but by degrees to raise us to the knowledge of it.

XXV. But they deceive themselves in dreaming of three separate individuals, each of them possessing a part of the Divine essence. We teach, according to the Scriptures, that there is essentially but one God; and, therefore, that the essence of both the Son and the Spirit is unbegotten. But since the Father is first in order, and hath of himself begotten his wisdom, therefore, as has before been observed, he is justly esteemed the original and fountain of the whole Divinity. Thus God, indefinitely, is unbegotten; and the Father also is unbegotten with regard to his Person. They even foolishly suppose, that our opinion implies a quaternity; whereas they are guilty of falsehood and calumny, in ascribing to us a figment of their own; as though we pretended that the three Persons are as so many streams proceeding from one essence, when it is evident, from our writings, that we separate not the Persons from the essence, but, though they subsist in it, make a distinction between them. If the persons were separated from the essence, there would perhaps be some probability in their argument; but then there would be a trinity of Gods, not a trinity of persons contained in one God. This solves their frivolous question, whether the essence concurs to the formation of the Trinity; as though we imagined three Gods to descend from it. Their objection,

(e) Gen. i. 26.   (f) John iv. 24.

that then the Trinity would be without God, is equally impertinent. Because, though it concurs not to the distinction as a part or member, yet the Persons are not independent of it, nor separate from it; for the Father, unless he were God, could not be the Father; and the Son is the Son only as he is God. Therefore we say, that the Deity is absolutely self-existent; whence we confess, also, that the Son, as God, independently of the consideration of Person, is self-existent; but as the Son, we say, that he is of the Father. Thus his essence is unoriginated; but the origin of his Person is God himself. And, indeed, the orthodox writers, who have written on the Trinity, have referred this name only to the Persons; since to comprehend the essence in that distinction, were not only an absurd error, but a most gross impiety. For it is evident that those who maintain that the Trinity consists in a union of the Essence, the Son, and the Spirit, annihilate the essence of the Son and of the Spirit; otherwise the parts would be destroyed by being confounded together; which is a fault in every distinction. Finally, if the words *Father* and *God* were synonymous — if the Father were the author of the Deity — nothing would be left in the Son but a mere shadow; nor would the Trinity be any other than a conjunction of the one God with two created things.

XXVI. Their objection, that Christ, if he be properly God, is not rightly called the Son of God, has already been answered; for when a comparison is made between one Person and another, the word *God* is not used indefinitely, but is restricted to the Father, as being the fountain of the Deity, not with regard to the essence, as fanatics falsely pretend, but in respect of order. This is the sense in which we ought to understand that declaration of Christ to his Father: "This is life eternal, that they might know thee, the only true God, and Jesus Christ, whom thou hast sent." (*g*) For, speaking in the capacity of Mediator, he holds an intermediate station between God and men; yet without any diminution of his majesty. For, although he abased himself, yet he lost not his glory with the Father, which was hidden from the world. Thus the Apostle to the Hebrews, (*h*) though he acknowledges that Christ was made for a short time inferior to the angels, yet, nevertheless, hesitates not to assert, that he is the eternal God, who laid the foundation of the earth. We must remember, therefore, that whenever Christ, in the capacity of Mediator, addresses the Father, he comprehends, under the name of God, the Divinity which belongs also to himself. Thus, when he said to his

(*g*) John xvii. 3.   (*h*) Heb. i. 10; ii. 9.

Apostles, "I go unto the Father, for my Father is greater than I," (*i*) he attributes not to himself a secondary Divinity, as if he were inferior to the Father with respect to the eternal essence, but because, having obtained the glory of heaven, he gathers together the faithful to a participation of it with him; he represents the Father to be in a station superior to himself, just as the illustrious perfection of the splendour which appears in heaven excels that degree of glory which was visible in him during his incarnate state. For the same reason, Paul says, in another place, that Christ "shall deliver up the kingdom to God, even the Father, that God may be all in all." (*k*) Nothing would be more absurd than to deny perpetual duration to the Deity of Christ. Now, if he will never cease to be the Son of God, but will remain for ever the same as he has been from the beginning, it follows, that by the name *Father* is intended the one sole Divine essence, which is common to them both. And it is certain that Christ descended to us, in order that, exalting us to the Father, he might at the same time exalt us to himself also, as being one with the Father. It is therefore neither lawful nor right to restrict the name of God exclusively to the Father, and to deny it to the Son. For even on this very account John asserts him to be the true God, (*l*) that no one might suppose, that he possessed only a secondary degree of Deity, inferior to the Father. And I wonder what can be the meaning of these fabricators of new gods, when, after confessing that Christ is the true God, they immediately exclude him from the Deity of the Father; as though there could be any true God but one alone, or as though a transfused Divinity were any thing but a novel fiction.

XXVII. Their accumulation of numerous passages from Irenæus, where he asserts the Father of Christ to be the only and eternal God of Israel, is a proof either of shameful ignorance, or of consummate wickedness. For they ought to have considered, that that holy man was then engaged in a controversy with some madmen, who denied that the Father of Christ was the same God that has spoken by Moses and the Prophets, but maintained that he was I know not what sort of phantasm, produced from the corruption of the world. His only object, therefore, is to show that no other God is revealed in the Scripture than the Father of Christ, and that it is impious to imagine any other; and therefore we need not wonder at his frequently concluding, that there never was any other God of Israel than he who was preached by Christ and his Apostles. So, now, on the other hand, when a different error is to be opposed, we

(*i*) John xiv. 28.   (*k*) 1 Cor. xv. 24.   (*l*) 1 John v. 20.

shall truly assert, that the God who appeared formerly to the patriarchs, was no other than Christ. If it be objected that it was the Father, we are prepared to reply, that, while we contend for the Divinity of the Son, we by no means reject that of the Father. If the reader attends to this design of Irenæus, all contention will cease. Moreover, the whole controversy is easily decided by the sixth chapter of the third book, where the good man insists on this one point: That he who is absolutely and indefinitely called God in the Scripture, is the only true God; but that the name of God is given absolutely to Christ. Let us remember that the point at issue, as appears from the whole treatise, and particularly from the forty-sixth chapter of the second book, was this: That the appellation of Father is not given in an enigmatical and parabolical sense to one who is not truly God. Besides, in another place he contends, that the Son is called God, as well as the Father, by the Prophets and Apostles. He afterwards states how Christ, who is Lord, and King, and God, and Judge of all, received power from him who is God of all; and that is with relation to the subjection in which he was humbled even to the death of the cross. And a little after he affirms, that the Son is the Creator of heaven and earth, who gave the law by the hand of Moses, and appeared to the patriarchs. Now, if any one pretends that Irenæus acknowledges the Father alone as the God of Israel. I shall reply, as is clearly maintained by the same writer, that Christ is one and the same; as also he applies to him the prophecy of Habakkuk: "God shall come from the south." To the same purpose is what we find in the ninth chapter of the fourth book: "Therefore Christ himself is, with the Father, the God of the living." And in the twelfth chapter of the same book he states, that Abraham believed in God, inasmuch as Christ is the Creator of heaven and earth, and the only God.

XXVIII. Their pretensions to the sanction of Tertullian are equally unfounded, for, notwithstanding the occasional harshness and obscurity of his mode of expression, yet he unequivocally teaches the substance of the doctrine which we are defending; that is, that whereas there is one God, yet by dispensation or economy there is his Word; that there is but one God in the unity of the substance, but that the unity, by a mysterious dispensation, is disposed into a trinity; that there are three, not in condition, but in degree; not in substance, but in form; not in power, but in order. He says, indeed, that he maintains the Son to be second to the Father; but he applies this only to the distinction of the Persons. He says somewhere, that the Son is visible; but after having stated arguments on both sides, he concludes that, as the Word, he is invisible. Lastly, his assertion that the Father is designated by his Person, proves him to be at the greatest distance from the notion which we are refuting. And though he acknowledges no other God than the Father, yet the explanations which he gives in the immediate context show that he speaks not to the exclusion of the Son, when he denies the existence of any other God than the Father; and that therefore the unity of Divine government is not violated by the distinction of persons. And from the nature and design of his argument it is easy to gather the meaning of his words. For he contends, in opposition to Praxeas, that although God is distinguished into three Persons, yet neither is there a plurality of gods, nor is the unity divided. And because, according to the erroneous notion of Praxeas, Christ could not be God, without being the Father, therefore Tertullian bestows so much labour upon the distinction. His calling the Word and Spirit a portion of the whole, though a harsh expression, yet is excusable; since it has no reference to the substance, but only denotes the disposition and economy, which belongs solely to the Persons, according to the testimony of Tertullian himself. Hence also that question, "How many Persons suppose you that there are, O most perverse Praxeas, but as many as there are names?" So, a little after, "that they may believe the Father and the Son, both in their names and Persons." These arguments, I conceive, will suffice to refute the impudence of those who make use of the authority of Tertullian in order to deceive the minds of the simple.

XXIX. And certainly, whoever will diligently compare the writings of the fathers, will find in Irenæus nothing different from what was advanced by others who succeeded him. Justin Martyr is one of the most ancient; and he agrees with us in every point. They may object that the Father of Christ is denominated the one God by him as well as by the rest. The same is asserted also by Hilary, and even in harsher terms: he says, that eternity is in the Father; but does this imply a denial of the Divine essence to the Son? On the contrary, he had no other design than to maintain the same faith which we hold. Nevertheless, they are not ashamed to cull out mutilated passages, in order to induce a belief that he patronized their error. If they wish any authority to be attached to their quotation of Ignatius, let them prove that the Apostles delivered any law concerning Lent, and similar corruptions; for nothing can be more absurd than the impertinencies which have been published under the name of Ignatius. Wherefore their impudence is more intolerable, who disguise themselves under such false colours for the purpose of deception. Moreover, the consent of antiquity manifestly appears from this circumstance, that in the Nicene Council, Arius never dared to defend himself by the authority of any approved writer; and not one of the Greek or Latin fathers, who were there united against him, excused himself as at all dissenting from his predecessors. With regard to Augustine, who experienced great hostility from these disturbers, his diligent examination of all the writings of the earlier fathers, and his respectful attention to them, need not be mentioned. If he differs from them in the smallest particulars, he assigns the reasons which oblige him to dissent from them. On this argument also, if he finds any thing ambiguous or obscure in others, he never conceals it. Yet he takes it for granted, that the doctrine which those men oppose has been received without controversy from the remotest antiquity; and yet that he was not uninformed of what others had taught before him, appears even from one word in the first book of his Treatise on the Christian Doctrine, where he says, that unity is in the Father. Will they pretend that he had then forgotten himself? But he elsewhere vindicates himself from this calumny, where he calls the Father the fountain of the whole Deity, because he is from no other; wisely considering that the name of God is especially ascribed to the Father, because, unless the original be from him, it is impossible to conceive of the simple unity of the Deity. These observations, I hope, will be approved by the pious reader, as sufficient to refute all the calumnies, with which Satan has hitherto laboured to pervert or obscure the purity of this doctrine. Finally, I trust that the whole substance of this doctrine has been faithfully stated and explained, provided my readers set bounds to their curiosity, and are not unreasonably fond of tedious and intricate controversies. For I have not the least expectation of giving satisfaction to those who are pleased with an intemperance of speculation. I am sure I have used no artifice in the omission of any thing, from a supposition that it would make against me. But, studying the edification of the Church, I have thought it better not to touch upon many things, which would be unnecessarily burdensome to the reader, without yielding him any profit. For to what purpose is it to dispute, whether the Father be always begetting? For it is foolish to imagine a continual act of generation, since it is evident that three Persons have subsisted in God from all eternity.

CHAPTER XIV.

THE TRUE GOD CLEARLY DISTINGUISHED IN THE SCRIPTURE FROM ALL FICTITIOUS ONES BY THE CREATION OF THE WORLD.

ALTHOUGH Isaiah (*m*) brings a just accusation of stupidity against the worshippers of fictitious deities, for not having learned, from the foundations of the earth, and the circuit of the heavens, who was the true God, yet such is the slowness and dulness of our minds, as to induce a necessity for a more express exhibition of the true God, lest the faithful should decline to the fictions of the heathen. For, since the most tolerable description given by the philosophers, that God is the soul of the world, is utterly vain and worthless, we require a more familiar knowledge of him, to prevent us from wavering in perpetual uncertainty. Therefore he hath been pleased to give us a history of the creation, on which the faith of the Church might rest, without seeking after any other God than him whom Moses has represented as the former and builder of the world. The first thing specified in this history is the time, that by a continued series of years the faithful might arrive at the first original of the human race, and of all things. This knowledge is eminently useful, not only to contradict the monstrous fables formerly received in Egypt and other countries, but also to give us clearer views of the eternity of God, and to fill us with greater admiration of it. Nor ought we to be moved with that profane sneer, that it is marvellous that God did not form the design of creating heaven and earth at an earlier period, but suffered an immeasurable duration to pass away unemployed, since he could have made them many thousands of ages before ; whereas the continuance of the world, now advancing to its last end, has not yet reached six thousand years. For the reason why God deferred it so long, it would be neither lawful nor expedient to inquire ; because, if the human mind strive to penetrate it, it will fail a hundred times in the attempt ; nor, indeed, could there be any utility in the knowledge of that which God himself, in order to prove the modesty of our faith, has purposely concealed. Great shrewdness was discovered by a certain pious old man, who, when some scoffer ludicrously inquired what God had been doing before the creation of the world, replied that he had been making hell for over curious men. This admonition, no less

(*m*) Isaiah xl. 21.

grave than severe, should repress the wantonness which stimulates many, and impels them to perverse and injurious speculations. Lastly, let us remember that God, who is invisible, and whose wisdom, power, and justice, are incomprehensible, has placed before us the history of Moses, as a mirror which exhibits his lively image. For as eyes, either dim through age, or dull through any disease, see nothing distinctly without the assistance of spectacles, so, in our inquiries after God, such is our imbecility, without the guidance of the Scripture we immediately lose our way. But those who indulge their presumption, since they are now admonished in vain, will perceive too late, by their horrible destruction, how much better it would have been to look up to the secret counsels of God with reverential awe, than to disgorge their blasphemies to darken the heaven. Augustine justly complains, that it is an offence against God, to inquire for any cause of things, higher than his will. He elsewhere prudently cautions us, that it is as absurd to dispute concerning an infinite duration of time, as concerning an infinite extent of place. However extensive the circuit of the heavens, yet certainly it has some dimensions. Now, if any one should expostulate with God, that the vacuity of space is a hundred times larger, would not such arrogance be detested by all pious persons? The same madness is chargeable on those who censure the inaction of God, for not having, according to their wishes, created the world innumerable ages before. To gratify their inordinate curiosity, they desire to pass beyond the limits of the world; as though, in the very ample circumference of heaven and earth, we were not surrounded by numerous objects capable of absorbing all our senses in their inestimable splendour; as though, in the course of six thousand years, God had not given us lessons sufficient to exercise our minds in assiduous meditation on them. Then let us cheerfully remain within these barriers with which God has been pleased to circumscribe us, and as it were to confine our minds, that they might not be wandering in the boundless regions of uncertain conjecture.

II. To the same purpose is the narration of Moses, that the work of God was completed, not in one moment, but in six days. For by this circumstance also we are called away from all false deities to the only true God, who distributed his work into six days, that it might not be tedious to us to occupy the whole of life in the consideration of it. For though, whithersoever we turn our eyes, they are constrained to behold the works of God, yet we see how transient our attention is, and, if we are touched with any pious reflections, how soon they leave us again. Here, also, human reason murmurs, as though such progressive works were inconsistent with the power of

Deity; till, subdued to the obedience of faith, it learns to observe that rest, to which the sanctification of the seventh day invites us. Now, in the order of those things, we must diligently consider the paternal love of God towards the human race, in not creating Adam before he had enriched the earth with an abundant supply of every thing conducive to his happiness. For had he placed him in the earth while it remained barren and vacant, had he given him life before there was any light, he would have appeared not very attentive to his benefit. Now, when he has regulated the motions of the sun and the stars for the service of man, replenished the earth, the air, and the waters, with living creatures, and caused the earth to produce an abundance of all kinds of fruits sufficient for sustenance, he acts the part of a provident and sedulous father of a family, and displays his wonderful goodness towards us. If the reader will more attentively consider with himself these things, which I only hint at as I proceed, he will be convinced that Moses was an authentic witness and herald of the one God, the Creator of the world. I pass over what I have already stated, that he not only speaks of the mere essence of God, but also exhibits to us his eternal Wisdom and his Spirit, in order that we may not dream of any other God except him who will be known in that express image.

III. But before I begin to enlarge on the nature of man, something must be said concerning angels. Because, though Moses, in the history of the creation, accommodating himself to the ignorance of the common people, mentions no other works of God than such as are visible to our eyes, yet, when he afterwards introduces angels as ministers of God, we may easily conclude, that he is their Creator, whom they obey, and in whose service they are employed. Though Moses, therefore, speaking in a popular manner, does not, in the beginning of his writings, immediately enumerate the angels among the creatures of God, yet nothing forbids our here making a plain and explicit statement of those things which the Scripture teaches in other places; because, if we desire to know God from his works, such an excellent and noble specimen should by no means be omitted. Besides, this point of doctrine is very necessary for the confutation of many errors. The excellence of the angelic nature has so dazzled the minds of many, that they have supposed them to be injured, if they were treated as mere creatures, subject to the government of one God. Hence they were falsely pretended to possess a kind of divinity. Manichæus has also arisen, with the sect which he founded, who imagined to himself two original principles, God and the devil; and attributed to God the origin of all good things, but referred evil natures to the production of the devil. If our minds were bewildered in this wild and incoherent system, we should not leave God in full possession of his glory in the creation of the world. For, since nothing is more peculiar to God than eternity and self-existence, does not the ascription of this to the devil dignify him with a title of Divinity? Now, where is the omnipotence of God, if such an empire be conceded to the devil, as that he can execute whatever he pleases, notwithstanding the aversion of the Divine will, or opposition of the Divine power? But the only foundation of the system of Manichæus, that it is unlawful to ascribe to a good God the creation of any evil thing, in no respect affects the orthodox faith, which admits not that any thing in the universe is evil in its nature; since neither the depravity and wickedness of men and devils, nor the sins which proceed from that source, are from mere nature, but from a corruption of nature; nor from the beginning has any thing existed, in which God has not given a specimen both of his wisdom and of his justice. To oppose these perverse notions, it is necessary to raise our minds higher than our eyes can reach. And it is very probable that it was with this design, when, in the Nicene creed, God is called the Creator of all things, that particular mention is made of things invisible. Yet it shall be my study to observe the limit which the rule of piety prescribes, lest, by indulging an unprofitable degree of speculation, I should lead the reader astray from the simplicity of the faith. And certainly, since the Spirit invariably teaches us in a profitable manner, but, with regard to things of little importance to edification, either is wholly silent, or but lightly and cursorily touches on them,—it is also our duty cheerfully to remain in ignorance of what it is not for our advantage to know.

IV. Since angels are ministers of God appointed to execute his commands, (n) that they are also his creatures, ought to be admitted without controversy. And does it not betray obstinacy rather than diligence, to raise any contention concerning the time or the order in which they were created? Moses narrates, that "the heavens and the earth were finished, and all the host of them:" (o) to what purpose is it anxiously to inquire, on what day, besides the stars and the planets, the other more concealed hosts of heaven began to exist? Not to be too prolix, let us remember on this point (as on the whole doctrine of religion) to observe one rule of modesty and sobriety; which is, not to speak, or think, or even desire to know, concerning obscure subjects, any thing beyond the information given us in the Divine word. Another rule to be

(n) Psalm ciii. 20.   (o) Gen. ii. 1.

followed is, in reading the Scripture, continually to direct our attention to investigate and meditate upon things conducive to edification; not to indulge curiosity or the study of things unprofitable. And, since the Lord has been pleased to instruct us, not in frivolous questions, but in solid piety, the fear of his name, true confidence, and the duties of holiness, let us content ourselves with that knowledge. Wherefore, if we wish to be truly wise, we must forsake the vain imaginations propagated by triflers concerning the nature, orders, and multitude of angels. I know that these things are embraced by many persons with greater avidity, and dwelt upon with more pleasure, than such things as are in daily use. But, if it be not irksome to be the disciples of Christ, it should not be irksome to follow that method which he has prescribed. Then the consequence will be, that, content with his discipline, we shall not only leave, but also abhor, those unprofitable speculations from which he calls us away. No man can deny that great subtlety and acuteness is discovered by Dionysius, whoever he was, in many parts of his treatise on the Celestial Hierarchy; but, if any one enters into a critical examination of it, he will find the greatest part of it to be mere babbling. But the duty of a theologian is, not to please the ear with empty sounds, but to confirm the conscience by teaching things which are true, certain, and profitable. A reader of that book would suppose that the author was a man descended from heaven, giving an account of things that he had not learned from the information of others, but had seen with his own eyes. But Paul, who was "caught up to the third heaven," (p) not only has told us no such things, but has even declared, that it is not lawful for men to utter the secret things which he had seen. Taking our leave, therefore, of this nugatory wisdom, let us consider, from the simple doctrine of the Scripture, what the Lord has been pleased for us to know concerning his angels.

V. We are frequently informed in the Scripture, that angels are celestial spirits, whose ministry and service God uses for the execution of whatever he has decreed; and hence this name is given to them, because God employs them as messengers to manifest himself to men. Other appellations also, by which they are distinguished, are derived from a similar cause. They are called Hosts, because, as life-guards, they surround their prince, aggrandizing his majesty, and rendering it conspicuous; and, like soldiers, are ever attentive to the signal of their leader; and are so prepared for the performance of his commands, that he has no sooner signified his will than

(p) 2 Cor. xii. 1, &c.

they are ready for the work, or rather are actually engaged in it. Such a representation of the throne of God is exhibited in the magnificent descriptions of the Prophets, but particularly of Daniel; where he says, when God had ascended the judgment-seat, that "thousand thousands ministered unto him, and ten thousand times ten thousand stood before him." (*q*) Since by their means the Lord wonderfully exerts and declares the power and strength of his hand, thence they are denominated Powers. (*r*) Because by them he exercises and administers his government in the world, therefore they are called sometimes Principalities, sometimes Powers, sometimes Dominions. Lastly, because the glory of God in some measure resides in them, they have also, for this reason, the appellation of Thrones; (*s*) although on this last name I would affirm nothing, because a different interpretation is equally or even more suitable. But, omitting this name, the Holy Spirit often uses the former ones, to magnify the dignity of the angelic ministry. Nor, indeed, is it right that no honour should be paid to those instruments, by whom God particularly exhibits the presence of his power. Moreover, they are more than once called gods; because in their ministry, as in a mirror, they give us an imperfect representation of Divinity. Though I am pleased with the interpretation of the old writers, on those passages where the Scripture records the appearance of an angel of God to Abraham, Jacob, Moses, and others, (*t*) that Christ was that angel, yet frequently, where mention is made of angels in general, this name is given to them. Nor should this surprise us; for, if that honour be given to princes and governors, because, in the performance of their functions, they are vicegerents of God, the supreme King and Judge, (*v*) there is far greater reason for its being paid to angels, in whom the splendour of the Divine glory is far more abundantly displayed.

VI. But the Scripture principally insists on what might conduce most to our consolation, and the confirmation of our faith — that the angels are the dispensers and administrators of the Divine beneficence towards us; and therefore it informs us, that they guard our safety, undertake our defence, direct our ways, and exercise a constant solicitude that no evil befall us. The declarations are universal, belonging primarily to Christ the head of the Church, and then to all the faithful: "He shall give his angels charge over thee, to keep thee in all thy ways. They shall bear thee up in their hands, lest thou dash thy foot against a stone." (*w*) Again, "The angel of the Lord encampeth round about them that fear him, and de-

(*q*) Daniel vii. 10. (*r*) Ephes. i. 21. (*s*) Col. i. 16.
(*t*) Gen. xviii. 2; xxxii. 1, 28. Josh. v. 13. Judges vi. 11; xiii. 3, 22.
(*v*) Psalm lxxxii. 6. (*w*) Psalm xci. 11, 12.

livereth them." (*x*) In these passages God shows that he delegates to his angels the protection of those whom he has undertaken to preserve. Accordingly, the angel of the Lord consoles the fugitive Hagar, and commands her to be reconciled to her mistress. (*y*) Abraham promises his servant that an angel should be the guide of his journey. (*z*) Jacob, in his benediction of Ephraim and Manasseh, prays that the angel of the Lord, by whom he had been redeemed from all evil, would cause them to prosper. (*a*) Thus an angel was appointed to protect the camp of the Israelites; (*b*) and whenever it pleased God to deliver them from the hands of their enemies, he raised up avengers by the ministry of angels. (*c*) And finally, to supersede the necessity of adducing more examples, angels ministered to Christ and attended him in all his difficulties; they announced his resurrection to the women, and his glorious advent to the disciples. (*d*) And thus, in the discharge of their office as our protectors, they contend against the devil and all our enemies, and execute the vengeance of God on those who molest us; as we read that an angel of God, to deliver Jerusalem from a siege, slew a hundred and eighty-five thousand men in the camp of the king of Assyria in one night. (*e*)

VII. But whether each of the faithful has a particular angel assigned him for his defence, I cannot venture certainly to affirm. When Daniel introduces the angel of the Persians and the angel of the Greeks, (*f*) he clearly signifies that certain angels are appointed to preside over kingdoms and provinces. Christ also, when he says that the angels of children always behold the face of the Father, (*g*) suggests, that there are certain angels who are charged with their safety. But I know not whether this justifies the conclusion, that every one of them has his particular guardian angel. Of this, indeed, we may be certain, that not one angel only has the care of every one of us, but that they all with one consent watch for our salvation. For it is said of all the angels together, that they rejoice more over one sinner turned to repentance, than over ninety and nine just persons who have persevered in their righteousness. (*h*) Of more than one angel it is said, that they carried the soul of Lazarus into the bosom of Abraham. (*i*) Nor is it in vain that Elisha shows his servant so many fiery chariots, which were peculiarly assigned to him for his protection. (*k*) There is one place which seems clearer than the rest in confirmation of this

(*x*) Psalm xxxiv. 7.   (*y*) Gen. xvi. 9.   (*z*) Gen. xxiv. 7.
(*a*) Gen. xlviii. 16.   (*b*) Exod. xiv. 19; xxiii. 20.   (*c*) Judges ii. 1; vi. 11; xiii. 3, &c.
(*d*) Matt. iv. 11.   Luke xxii. 43.   Matt. xxviii. 5.   Luke xxiv. 4, 5.   Acts i. 10.
(*e*) 2 Kings xix. 35.   Isaiah xxxvii. 36.   (*f*) Daniel x. 13, 20; xii. 1.
(*g*) Matt. xviii. 10.   (*h*) Luke xv. 7.   (*i*) Luke xvi. 22.   (*k*) 2 Kings vi. 17

point. For when Peter, on his liberation from prison, knocked at the door of the house in which the brethren were assembled, as they could not suppose it to be Peter himself, they said it was his angel. (*l*) This conclusion seems to have arisen in their minds from the common opinion that each of the faithful has his guardian angel assigned him. But here it may also be replied, that nothing prevents this being understood of any one of the angels, to whom the Lord might have committed the care of Peter on that occasion, and who yet might not be his perpetual guardian; as it is vulgarly imagined that every person has two angels, a good one and a bad one, according to the heathen notion of different genii. But it is not worth while anxiously to investigate what it little concerns us to know. For if any one be not satisfied with this, that all the orders of the celestial army watch for his safety, I see not what advantage he can derive from knowing that he has one particular angel given him for his guardian. But those who restrict to one angel the care which God exercises over every one of us, do a great injury to themselves, and to all the members of the Church; as though those auxiliaries had been promised in vain, who, by surrounding and defending us on all sides, contribute to increase our courage in the conflict.

VIII. Let those, who venture to determine concerning the multitude and orders of the angels, examine on what foundation their opinions rest. Michael, I confess, is called in Daniel "the great prince," and in Jude "the archangel." (*m*) And Paul informs us that it will be an archangel, who, with the sound of a trumpet, shall summon men to judgment. (*n*) But who, from these passages, can determine the degrees of honour among the angels, distinguish the individuals by their respective titles, and assign to every one his place and station? For the two names which are found in the Scripture, Michael and Gabriel, and the third, if you wish to add it from the history of Tobias, (*o*) may appear, from their significations, to be given to angels on account of our infirmity; though I would rather leave this undetermined. With respect to their numbers, we hear, from the mouth of Christ, of many legions; (*p*) from Daniel, of many myriads: (*q*) the servant of Elisha saw many chariots; and their being said to encamp round about them that fear God, (*r*) is expressive of a great multitude. It is certain that spirits have no form; and yet the Scripture, on account of the slender capacity of our minds, under the names of cherubim and seraphim, represents angels to us as having wings, to prevent our doubting that they will always attend, with

(*l*) Acts xii. 15. (*m*) Daniel xii. 1. Jude, ver. 9. (*n*) 1 Thess. iv. 16.
(*o*) Daniel x. 13, 21; viii. 16; ix. 21. Luke i. 19, 26. Tob. iii. 17; v. 5.
(*p*) Matt. xxvi. 53. (*q*) Daniel vii. 10. (*r*) Psalm xxxiv. 7.

incredible celerity, to afford us assistance as soon as our cases require it; as though the lightning darted from heaven were to fly to us with its accustomed velocity. All further inquiries on both these points, we should consider as belonging to that class of mysteries, the full revelation of which is deferred to the last day. Wherefore let us remember that we ought to avoid too much curiosity of research, and presumption of language.

IX. But this, which is called in question by some restless men, must be received as a certain truth, that angels are ministering spirits, whose service God uses for the protection of his people, and by whom he dispenses his benefits among mankind, and executes his other works. It was the opinion of the ancient Sadducees, indeed, that the term *angels* signified nothing but the motions which God inspires into men, or those specimens which he gives of his power. But this foolish notion is repugnant to so many testimonies of Scripture, that it is surprising how such gross ignorance could have been tolerated among that people. For, to omit the places before cited, where mention is made of thousands and legions of angels; where joy is attributed to them; where they are said to sustain the faithful in their hands, to carry their souls into rest, to behold the face of the Father, (s) and the like, — there are others which most clearly evince, that they are spirits possessing an actual existence and their own peculiar nature. For the declarations of Stephen and Paul, — that the law was given by the hand of angels, (t) and of Christ, that the elect, after the resurrection, shall be like angels; that the day of judgment is not known even to the angels; that he then will come with his holy angels, (v) — however tortured, must necessarily be thus understood. Likewise, when Paul charges Timothy, before Christ and the elect angels, to keep his precepts, (w) he intends, not unsubstantial qualities or inspirations, but real spirits. Nor otherwise is there any meaning in what we read in the Epistle to the Hebrews, that Christ is made more excellent than the angels, that the world is not subject to them, that Christ assumed not their nature, but the nature of man, (x) unless we understand that there are happy spirits, to whom these comparisons may apply. And the author of the same epistle explains himself, where he places angels and the souls of the faithful together in the kingdom of God. (y) Besides, we have already quoted, that the angels of children always behold the face of God; that we are always defended by their protection; that they rejoice for our safety; that they

---

(s) Luke xv. 10; iv. 10; xvi. 22. Psalm xci. 12. Matt. iv. 6; xviii. 10.
(t) Acts vii. 53. Gal. iii. 19.
(v) Matt. xxii. 30; xxiv. 36; xxv. 31. Luke ix. 26. (w) 1 Tim. v. 21.
(x) Heb. i. 4; ii. 16. (y) Heb. xii. 22, 23.

admire the manifold grace of God in the church ; (*z*) and are subject to Christ as their head. (*a*) The same truth is proved by their having so often appeared to the patriarchs in the form of men, conversed with them, and been entertained by them. And Christ himself, on account of the preëminence which he obtains in the capacity of Mediator, is called an angel. (*b*) I have thought proper cursorily to touch on this point, in order to fortify the simple against those foolish and absurd notions, which were disseminated by Satan many ages ago, and are frequently springing up afresh.

X. It remains for us to encounter the superstition, which generally insinuates itself into men's minds when angels are said to be the ministers and dispensers of all our blessings. For human reason soon falls into an opinion, that there is no honour that ought not to be paid to them. Thus it happens that what belongs solely to God and Christ, is transferred to them. Thus we see, that for some ages past the glory of Christ has in many ways been obscured; while angels have been loaded with extravagant honours without the authority of the word of God. And among the errors which we combat in the present day, there is scarcely one more ancient than this. For even Paul appears to have had a great controversy with some, who exalted angels in such a manner as almost to degrade Christ to an inferior station. Hence the solicitude with which he maintains, in the Epistle to the Colossians, not only that Christ is to be esteemed above angels, but also that he is the author of all blessings to them, (*c*) in order that we may not forsake him and turn to them, who are not even sufficient for themselves, but draw from the same fountain as we do. Since the splendour of the Divine majesty, therefore, is eminently displayed in them, there is nothing more natural than for us to fall down with astonishment in adoration of them, and to attribute every thing to them which exclusively belongs to God. Even John, in the Revelation, confesses this to have happened to himself; but adds at the same time, that he was thus answered: "See thou do it not: I am thy fellow-servant: worship God." (*d*)

XI. But this danger we shall happily avoid, if we consider why God is accustomed to provide for the safety of the faithful, and to communicate the gifts of his beneficence by means of angels, rather than by himself to manifest his own power without their intervention. He certainly does this not from necessity, as though he were unable to do without them; for whenever he pleases he passes them by, and performs his work with a mere nod of his power; so far is he from being indebt-

(*z*) 1 Peter i. 12. (*a*) Heb. i. 6. (*b*) Mal. iii. 1.
(*c*) Col. i. 16, 20. (*d*) Rev. xix. 10; xxii. 8, 9.

ed to their assistance for relieving him in any difficulty. This, therefore, conduces to the consolation of our imbecility, that we may want nothing that can either raise our minds to a good hope, or confirm them in security. This one thing, indeed, ought to be more than sufficient for us, that the Lord declares himself to be our Protector. But while we see ourselves encompassed with so many dangers, so many annoyances, such various kinds of enemies,—such is our weakness and frailty, that we may sometimes be filled with terror, or fall into despair, unless the Lord enables us, according to our capacity, to discover the presence of his grace. For this reason he promises, not only that he will take care of us himself, but also that we shall have innumerable life-guards, to whom he has committed the charge of our safety; and that, as long as we are surrounded by their superintendence and protection, whatever danger may threaten, we are placed beyond the utmost reach of evil. I confess, indeed, that it is wrong for us, after that simple promise of the protection of God alone, still to be looking around to see from what quarter our aid may come. But since the Lord, from his infinite clemency and goodness, is pleased to assist this our weakness, there is no reason why we should neglect this great favour which he shows us. We have an example of this in the servant of Elisha, who, when he saw that the mountain was besieged by an army of Syrians, (c) and that no way of escape was left, was filled with consternation, as though himself and his master had been ruined. Then Elisha prayed that God would open his eyes, and he immediately saw the mountain full of horses and chariots of fire; that is, of a multitude of angels who were to guard him and the Prophet. Encouraged by this vision, he came to himself again, and was able to look down with intrepidity on the enemies, the sight of whom before had almost deprived him of life.

XII. Therefore, whatever is said concerning the ministry of angels, let us direct it to this end, that, overcoming all diffidence, our hope in God may be more firmly established. For the Lord has provided these guards for us, that we may not be terrified by a multitude of enemies, as though they could prevail in opposition to his assistance, but may have recourse to the sentiment expressed by Elisha, "There are more for us than against us." How preposterous is it, then, that we should be alienated from God by angels, who are appointed for this very purpose, to testify that his aid is more especially present with us! But they do alienate us from him, unless they lead us directly to him, to regard him, call on him, and celebrate him as our only helper; unless they are considered by us as

(c) 2 Kings vi. 15, 16, 17.

his hands, which apply themselves to do nothing without his direction; unless they attach us to Christ, the only Mediator, to depend entirely on him, to lean upon him, to aspire to him, and to rest satisfied in him. For what is described in the vision of Jacob (*f*) ought to be firmly fixed in our minds, that the angels descend to the earth to men, and ascend from earth to heaven, by a ladder above which stands the Lord of hosts. This implies, that it is only through the intercession of Christ, that we are favoured with the ministry of angels, as he himself affirms: "Hereafter ye shall see heaven open, and the angels descending upon the Son of man." (*g*) Therefore the servant of Abraham, having been commended to the care of an angel, (*h*) does not therefore invoke him for his aid, but, trusting to that committal, pours out his prayers before the Lord, and entreats him to display his mercy towards Abraham. For as God does not make them the ministers of his power and goodness, in order to divide his glory with them, so neither does he promise his assistance in their ministry, that we may divide our confidence between them and him. Let us take our leave, therefore, of that Platonic philosophy, which seeks access to God by means of angels, and worships them in order to render him more propitious to us; which superstitious and curious men have endeavoured from the beginning, and even to this day persevere in attempting, to introduce into our religion.

XIII. The design of almost every thing that the Scripture teaches concerning devils, is that we may be careful to guard against their insidious machinations, and may provide ourselves with such weapons as are sufficiently firm and strong to repel the most powerful enemies. For when Satan is called the god and prince of this world, (*i*) the strong man armed, (*k*) the prince of the power of the air, (*l*) a roaring lion, (*m*) these descriptions only tend to make us more cautious and vigilant, and better prepared to encounter him. This is sometimes signified in express words. For Peter, after having said that "the devil, as a roaring lion, walketh about seeking whom he may devour," immediately subjoins an exhortation to "resist him, steadfast in the faith." And Paul, having suggested that "we wrestle not against flesh and blood, but against principalities, against powers, against the rulers of the darkness of this world, against spiritual wickedness," (*n*) immediately commands us to put on suitable armour for so great and so perilous a conflict. Wherefore, having been previously warned that we are perpetually threatened by an enemy, and an enemy desperately bold

(*f*) Gen. xxviii. 12.
(*g*) John i. 51.
(*h*) Gen. xxiv. 7, 12, 27, 52.
(*i*) 2 Cor. iv. 4. John xii. 31.
(*k*) Matt. xii. 29. Luke xi. 21.
(*l*) Ephes. ii. 2.
(*m*) 1 Peter v. 8, 9.
(*n*) Ephes. vi. 12, &c.

and extremely strong, skilled in every artifice, indefatigable in diligence and celerity, abundantly provided with all kinds of weapons, and most expert in the science of war, let us make it the grand object of our attention, that we suffer not ourselves to be oppressed with slothfulness and inactivity, but, on the contrary, arousing and collecting all our courage, be ready for a vigorous resistance; and as this warfare is terminated only by death, let us encourage ourselves to perseverance. But, above all, conscious of weakness and ignorance, let us implore the assistance of God, nor attempt any thing but in reliance on him; since he alone can supply us with wisdom, and strength, and courage, and armour.

XIV. But, the more to excite and urge us to such conduct, the Scripture announces that there are not one, or two, or a few enemies, but great armies who wage war against us. For even Mary Magdalene is said to have been delivered from seven demons, by whom she was possessed; (*o*) and Christ declares it to be a common case, that, if you leave the place open for the re-entrance of a demon who has once been ejected, he associates with himself seven spirits more wicked still, and returns to his vacant possession. (*p*) Indeed, one man is said to have been possessed by a whole legion. (*q*) By these passages, therefore, we are taught, that we have to contend with an infinite multitude of enemies; lest, despising their paucity, we should be more remiss to encounter them, or, expecting sometimes an intermission of hostility, should indulge ourselves in idleness. But when one Satan or devil is frequently mentioned in the singular number, it denotes that principality of wickedness which opposes the kingdom of righteousness. For as the Church and society of saints have Christ as their head, so the faction of the impious, and impiety itself, are represented to us with their prince, who exercises the supreme power among them; which is the meaning of that sentence, "Depart, ye cursed, into everlasting fire, prepared for the devil and his angels." (*r*)

XV. It also ought to stimulate us to a perpetual war with the devil, that he is every where called God's adversary and ours. For, if we feel the concern which we ought to feel for the glory of God, we shall exert all our power against him who attempts the extinction of it. If we are animated by a becoming zeal for defending the kingdom of Christ, we must necessarily have an irreconcilable war with him who conspires its ruin. On the other hand, if we are solicitous for our salvation, we ought to make neither peace nor truce with him who assiduously plots its destruction. Now, such is the description given of him in the third chapter of Genesis, where

(*o*) Mark xvi. 9. (*q*) Luke viii. 30.
(*p*) Matt. xii. 43—45. (*r*) Matt. xxv. 41.

he seduces man from the obedience owed by him to God, so that he at once robs God of his just honour, and precipitates man into ruin. Such, also, is he described in the Evangelists, where he is called an enemy, and said to sow tares in order to corrupt the seed of eternal life. (s) In short, the testimony of Christ concerning him, that he was a murderer and a liar from the beginning, (t) we find verified in all his actions. For he opposes Divine truth with lies; obscures the light with shades of darkness; involves the minds of men in errors; stirs up animosities, and kindles contentions and wars; — and all for the purpose of subverting the kingdom of God, and plunging mankind with himself into eternal destruction. Whence it is evident, that he is naturally depraved, vicious, malignant, and mischievous. For there must be extreme depravity in that mind which is bent on opposing the glory of God and the salvation of men. And this is suggested by John in his Epistle, when he says, that " he sinneth from the beginning." For he intends, that he is the author, conductor, and principal contriver of all wickedness and iniquity.

XVI. But since the devil was created by God, we must remark, that this wickedness which we attribute to his nature is not from creation, but from corruption. For whatever evil quality he has, he has acquired by his defection and fall. And of this the Scripture apprizes us; lest, believing him to have come from God, just as he now is, we should ascribe to God himself that which is in direct opposition to him. For this reason Christ declares, that Satan, " when he speaketh a lie, speaketh of his own ; " (v) and adds the reason — " because he abode not in the truth." When he says that he abode not in the truth, he certainly implies that he had once been in it; and when he calls him the father of a lie, he precludes his imputing to God the depravity of his nature, which originated wholly from himself. Though these things are delivered in a brief and rather obscure manner, yet they are abundantly sufficient to vindicate the majesty of God from every calumny. And what does it concern us to know, respecting devils, either more particulars, or for any other purpose? Some persons are displeased that the Scripture does not give us, in various places, a distinct and detailed account of their fall, with its cause, manner, time, and nature. But, these things being nothing to us, it was better for them, if not to be passed over in total silence, yet certainly to be touched on but lightly; because it would ill comport with the dignity of the Holy Spirit to feed curiosity with vain and unprofitable histories; and we perceive it to have been the design of the Lord, to deliver nothing in his sacred

(s) Matt. xiii. 25, 28.   (t) John viii. 44.   (v) John viii. 44.

oracles, which we might not learn to our edification. That we ourselves, therefore, may not dwell upon unprofitable subjects, let us be content with this concise information respecting the nature of devils; that at their creation they were originally angels of God, but by degenerating have ruined themselves, and become the instruments of perdition to others. This being useful to be known, it is clearly stated by Peter and Jude. "God," say they, "spared not the angels that sinned, and kept not their first estate, but left their own habitation." (*x*) And Paul, mentioning the elect angels, (*y*) without doubt tacitly implies that there are reprobate ones.

XVII. The discord and contention, which we say Satan maintains against God, ought to be understood in a manner consistent with a firm persuasion, that he can do nothing without God's will and consent. For we read in the history of Job, that he presented himself before God to receive his commands, and dared not to undertake any enterprise without having obtained his permission. (*z*) Thus, also, when Ahab was to be deceived, he undertook to be a lying spirit in the mouth of all the prophets; and, being commissioned by God, he performed it. (*a*) For this reason he is also called the "evil spirit from the Lord," who tormented Saul, (*b*) because he was employed as a scourge to punish the sins of that impious monarch. And elsewhere it is recorded, that the plagues were inflicted on the Egyptians by the "evil angels." (*c*) According to these particular examples, Paul declares generally, that the blinding of unbelievers is the work of God, (*d*) whereas he had before called it the operation of Satan. It appears, then, that Satan is subject to the power of God, and so governed by his control, that he is compelled to render obedience to him. Now, when we say that Satan resists God, and that his works are contrary to the works of God, we at the same time assert that this repugnance and contention depend on the Divine permission. I speak now, not of the will or the endeavour, but only of the effect. For the devil, being naturally wicked, has not the least inclination towards obedience to the Divine will, but is wholly bent on insolence and rebellion. It therefore arises from himself and his wickedness, that he opposes God with all his desires and purposes. This depravity stimulates him to attempt those things which he thinks the most opposed to God. But since God holds him tied and bound with the bridle of his power, he executes only those things which are divinely permitted; and thus, whether he

(*x*) 2 Peter ii. 4. Jude, ver. 6.
(*y*) 1 Tim. v. 21.
(*z*) Job i. 6; ii. 1.
(*a*) 1 Kings xxii. 20, &c.
(*b*) 1 Sam. xvi. 14; xviii. 10.
(*c*) Psalm lxxviii. 49.
(*d*) 2 Thess. ii. 9, 11.

will or not, he obeys his Creator, being constrained to fulfil any service to which he impels him.

XVIII. While God directs the courses of unclean spirits hither and thither at his pleasure, he regulates this government in such a manner, that they exercise the faithful with fighting, attack them in ambuscades, harass them with incursions, push them in battles, and frequently fatigue them, throw them into confusion, terrify them, and sometimes wound them, yet never conquer or overwhelm them; but subdue and lead captive the impious, tyrannize over their souls and bodies, and abuse them like slaves by employing them in the perpetration of every enormity. The faithful, in consequence of being harassed by such enemies, are addressed with the following, and other similar exhortations: "Give not place to the devil." (*e*) "Your adversary the devil, as a roaring lion, walketh about, seeking whom he may devour; whom resist, steadfast in the faith." (*f*) Paul confesses that he himself was not free from this kind of warfare, when he declares that, as a remedy to subdue pride, "the messenger of Satan was given to him to buffet him." (*g*) This exercise, then, is common to all the children of God. But, as the promise respecting the breaking of the head of Satan (*h*) belongs to Christ and all his members in common, I therefore deny that the faithful can ever be conquered or overwhelmed by him. They are frequently filled with consternation, but recover themselves again; they fall by the violence of his blows, but are raised up again; they are wounded, but not mortally; finally, they labour through their whole lives in such a manner, as at last to obtain the victory. This, however, is not to be restricted to each single action. For we know that, by the righteous vengeance of God, David was for a time delivered to Satan, that by his instigation he might number the people; (*i*) nor is it without reason that Paul admits a hope of pardon even for those who may have been entangled in the snares of the devil. (*k*) Therefore the same Apostle shows, in another place, that the promise before cited is begun in this life, where we must engage in the conflict; and that after the termination of the conflict it will be completed. "And the God of peace," he says, "shall bruise Satan under your feet shortly." (*l*) In our Head this victory, indeed, has always been complete, because the prince of this world had nothing in him: (*m*) in us, who are his members, it yet appears only in part, but will be completed when we shall have put off our flesh, which makes us still subject to infirm-

(*e*) Ephes. iv. 27.
(*f*) 1 Peter v. 8.
(*g*) 2 Cor. xii. 7.
(*h*) Gen. iii. 15.
(*i*) 2 Sam. xxiv. 1. 1 Chron. xxi. 1.
(*k*) 2 Tim. ii. 26.
(*l*) Rom. xvi. 20.
(*m*) John xiv. 30.

ities, and shall be full of the power of the Holy Spirit. In this manner, when the kingdom of Christ is erected, Satan and his power must fall; as the Lord himself says, "I beheld Satan as lightning falling from heaven." (*n*) For by this answer he confirms what the Apostles had reported concerning the power of his preaching. Again: "When a strong man armed keepeth his palace, his goods are in peace; but when a stronger than he shall come upon him and overcome him," &c. (*o*) And to this end Christ by his death overcame Satan, who had the power of death, and triumphed over all his forces, that they might not be able to hurt the Church; for otherwise it would be in hourly danger of destruction. For such is our imbecility, and such the strength of his fury, how could we stand even for a moment against his various and unceasing attacks, without being supported by the victory of our Captain? Therefore God permits not Satan to exercise any power over the souls of the faithful, but abandons to his government only the impious and unbelieving, whom he designs not to number among his own flock. For he is said to have the undisturbed possession of this world, till he is expelled by Christ. (*p*) He is said also to blind all who believe not the Gospel, (*q*) and to work in the children of disobedience; (*r*) and this justly, for all the impious are vessels of wrath. (*s*) To whom, therefore, should they be subjected, but to the minister of the Divine vengeance? Finally, they are said to be of their father the devil; (*t*) because, as the faithful are known to be the children of God from their bearing his image, (*v*) so the impious, from the image of Satan into which they have degenerated, are properly considered as his children.

XIX. But as we have already confuted that nugatory philosophy concerning the holy angels, which teaches that they are nothing but inspirations, or good motions, excited by God in the minds of men, so in this place we must refute those who pretend that devils are nothing but evil affections or perturbations, which our flesh obtrudes on our minds. But this may be easily done, and that because the testimonies of Scripture on this subject are numerous and clear. First, when they are called unclean spirits and apostate angels, (*w*) who have degenerated from their original condition, the very names sufficiently express, not mental emotions or affections, but rather in reality what are called minds, or spirits endued with perception and intelligence. Likewise, when the children of God are compared with the children of the devil, both by Christ and by John, (*x*) would not the comparison be absurd, if noth-

(*n*) Luke x. 18. (*p*) John xii. 31. (*r*) Eph. ii. 2. (*t*) John viii. 44.
(*o*) Luke xi. 21. (*q*) 2 Cor. iv. 4. (*s*) Rom. ix. 22. (*v*) 1 John iii. 10.
(*w*) Matt. xii. 43. Jude 6. (*x*) John viii. 44. 1 John iii. 10.

ing were intended by the word *devil* but evil inspirations? And John adds something still plainer, that the devil sins from the beginning. Likewise, when Jude introduces Michael the archangel contending with the devil, (y) he certainly opposes to the good angel an evil and rebellious one; to which agrees what is recorded in the history of Job, that Satan appeared with the holy angels before God. (z) But the clearest of all are those passages, which mention the punishment which they begin to feel from the judgment of God, and are to feel much more at the resurrection: "Thou Son of God, art thou come hither to torment us before the time?" (a) Also, "Depart, ye cursed, into everlasting fire, prepared for the devil and his angels." (b) Again, "If God spared not the angels that sinned, but cast them down to hell, and delivered them into chains of darkness, to be reserved unto judgment," &c. (c) How unmeaning were these expressions, that the devils are appointed to eternal judgment; that fire is prepared for them; that they are now tormented and vexed by the glory of Christ, if there were no devils at all! But since this point is not a subject of dispute with those who give credit to the word of the Lord, but with those vain speculators who are pleased with nothing but novelty, little good can be effected by testimonies of Scripture. I consider myself as having done what I intended, which was to fortify the pious mind against such a species of errors, with which restless men disturb themselves and others that are more simple. But it was requisite to touch on it, lest any persons involved in that error, under a supposition that they have no adversary, should become more slothful and incautious to resist him.

XX. Yet let us not disdain to receive a pious delight from the works of God, which every where present themselves to view in this very beautiful theatre of the world. For this, as I have elsewhere observed, though not the principal, is yet, in the order of nature, the first lesson of faith, to remember that, whithersoever we turn our eyes, all the things which we behold are the works of God; and at the same time to consider, with pious meditation, for what end God created them. Therefore to apprehend, by a true faith, what it is for our benefit to know concerning God, we must first of all understand the history of the creation of the world, as it is briefly related by Moses, and afterwards more copiously illustrated by holy men, particularly by Basil and Ambrose. Thence we shall learn that God, by the power of his Word and Spirit, created out of nothing the heaven and the earth; that from them he produced all things, animate and inanimate; distinguished by an admirable

(y) Jude 9.   (z) Job i. 6; ii. 1.   (a) Matt. viii. 29.
(b) Matt. xxv. 41.   (c) 2 Peter ii. 4

gradation the innumerable variety of things; to every species gave its proper nature, assigned its offices, and appointed its places and stations; and since all things are subject to corruption, has, nevertheless, provided for the preservation of every species till the last day; that he therefore nourishes some by methods concealed from us, from time to time infusing, as it were, new vigour into them; that on some he has conferred the power of propagation, in order that the whole species may not be extinct at their death; that he has thus wonderfully adorned heaven and earth with the utmost possible abundance, variety, and beauty, like a large and splendid mansion, most exquisitely and copiously furnished; lastly, that, by creating man, and distinguishing him with such splendid beauty, and with such numerous and great privileges, he has exhibited in him a most excellent specimen of all his works. But since it is not my design to treat at large of the creation of the world, let it suffice to have again dropped these few hints by the way. For it is better, as I have just advised the reader, to seek for fuller information on this subject from Moses, and others who have faithfully and diligently recorded the history of the world.

XXI. It is useless to enter into a prolix disputation respecting the right tendency and legitimate design of a consideration of the works of God, since this question has been, in a great measure, determined in another place, and, as much as concerns our present purpose, may be despatched in few words. Indeed, if we wished to explain how the inestimable wisdom, power, justice, and goodness, of God are manifested in the formation of the world, no splendour or ornament of diction will equal the magnitude of so great a subject. And it is undoubtedly the will of the Lord, that we should be continually employed in this holy meditation; that, while we contemplate in all the creatures, as in so many mirrors, the infinite riches of his wisdom, justice, goodness, and power, we might not only take a transient and cursory view of them, but might long dwell on the idea, seriously and faithfully revolve it in our minds, and frequently recall it to our memory. But, this being a didactic treatise, we must omit those topics which require long declamations. To be brief, therefore, let the readers know, that they have then truly apprehended by faith what is meant by God being the Creator of heaven and earth, if they, in the first place, follow this universal rule, not to pass over, with ungrateful inattention or oblivion, those glorious perfections which God manifests in his creatures; and, secondly, learn to make such an application to themselves as thoroughly to affect their hearts. The first point is exemplified, when we consider how great must have been the Artist who disposed that multitude of stars, which adorn the heaven, in such a regular order, that it is impossible to imagine any thing more beautiful to behold; who fixed some in their stations, so that they cannot be moved; who granted to others a freer course, but so that they never travel beyond their appointed limits; who so regulates the motions of all, that they measure days and nights, months, years, and seasons of the year; and also reduces the inequality of days, which we constantly witness, to such a medium that it occasions no confusion. So, also, when we observe his power in sustaining so great a mass, in governing the rapid revolutions of the celestial machine, and the like. For these few examples sufficiently declare, what it is to recognize the perfections of God in the creation of the world. Otherwise, were I desirous of pursuing the subject to its full extent, there would be no end; since there are as many miracles of Divine power, as many monuments of Divine goodness, as many proofs of Divine wisdom, as there are species of things in the world, and even as there are individual things, either great or small.

XXII. There remains the other point, which approaches more nearly to faith; that, while we observe how God has appointed all things for our benefit and safety, and at the same time perceive his power and grace in ourselves, and the great benefits which he has conferred on us, we may thence excite ourselves to confide in him, to invoke him, to praise him, and to love him. Now, as I have just before suggested, God himself has demonstrated, by the very order of creation, that he made all things for the sake of man. For it was not without reason that he distributed the making of the world into six days; though it would have been no more difficult for him to complete the whole work, in all its parts, at once, in a single moment, than to arrive at its completion by such progressive advances. But in this he has been pleased to display his providence and paternal solicitude towards us, since, before he would make man, he prepared every thing which he foresaw would be useful or beneficial to him. How great would be, now, the ingratitude to doubt whether we are regarded by this best of fathers, whom we perceive to have been solicitous on our account before we existed! How impious would it be to tremble with diffidence, lest at any time his benignity should desert us in our necessities, which we see was displayed in the greatest affluence of all blessings provided for us while we were yet unborn! Besides, we are told by Moses, (*d*) that his liberality has subjected to us all that is contained in the whole world. He certainly has not made this declaration in order to tantalize us with the empty name of such a donation. Therefore we never shall be destitute of any thing which will conduce to

---

(*d*) Gen. i. 28; ix. 2.

our welfare. Finally, to conclude, whenever we call God the Creator of heaven and earth, let us at the same time reflect, that the dispensation of all those things which he has made is in his own power, and that we are his children, whom he has received into his charge and custody, to be supported and educated; so that we may expect every blessing from him alone, and cherish a certain hope that he will never suffer us to want those things which are necessary to our well-being, that our hope may depend on no other; that, whatever we need or desire, our prayers may be directed to him, and that, from whatever quarter we receive any advantage, we may acknowledge it to be his benefit, and confess it with thanksgiving; that, being allured with such great sweetness of goodness and beneficence, we may study to love and worship him with all our hearts.

CHAPTER XV.

THE STATE OF MAN AT HIS CREATION, THE FACULTIES OF THE SOUL, THE DIVINE IMAGE, FREE WILL, AND THE ORIGINAL PURITY OF HIS NATURE.

We must now treat of the creation of man, not only because he exhibits the most noble and remarkable specimen of the Divine justice, wisdom, and goodness, among all the works of God, but because, as we observed in the beginning, we cannot attain to a clear and solid knowledge of God, without a mutual acquaintance with ourselves. But though this is twofold, — the knowledge of the condition in which we were originally created, and of that into which we entered after the fall of Adam, (for indeed we should derive but little advantage from a knowledge of our creation, unless in the lamentable ruin which has befallen us we discovered the corruption and deformity of our nature,) — yet we shall content ourselves at present with a description of human nature in its primitive integrity. And, indeed, before we proceed to the miserable condition in which man is now involved, it is necessary to understand the state in which he was first created. For we must beware lest, in precisely pointing out the natural evils of man, we seem to refer them to the Author of nature; since impious men suppose that this pretext affords them a sufficient defence, if they can plead that whatever defect or fault they have, proceeds in some measure from God; nor do they hesitate, if reproved, to litigate with God himself, and transfer to him the crime of which they are justly accused. And those who would be thought to speak with more reverence concerning the Deity, yet readily endeavour to excuse their depravity from nature, not considering that they also, though in a more obscure manner, are guilty of defaming the character of God; to whose dishonour it would redound, if nature could be proved to have had any innate depravity at its formation. Since we see the flesh, therefore, eagerly catching at every subterfuge, by which it supposes that the blame of its evils may by any means be transferred from itself to any other, we must diligently oppose this perverseness. The calamity of mankind must be treated in such a manner as to preclude all tergiversation, and to vindicate the Divine justice from every accusation. We shall afterwards, in the proper place, see how far men are fallen from that purity which was bestowed upon Adam. And first let it be understood, that, by his being made of earth and clay, a restraint was laid upon pride; since nothing is more absurd than for creatures to glory in their excellence, who not only inhabit a cottage of clay, but who are themselves composed partly of dust and ashes. (*e*) But as God not only deigned to animate the earthen vessel, but chose to make it the residence of an immortal spirit, Adam might justly glory in so great an instance of the liberality of his Maker.

II. That man consists of soul and body, ought not to be controverted. By the "soul" I understand an immortal, yet created essence, which is the nobler part of him. Sometimes it is called a "spirit;" for though, when these names are connected, they have a different signification, yet when "spirit" is used separately, it means the same as "soul;" as when Solomon, speaking of death, says that "then the spirit shall return unto God, who gave it." (*f*) And Christ commending his spirit to the Father, (*g*) and Stephen his to Christ, (*h*) intend no other than that, when the soul is liberated from the prison of the flesh, God is its perpetual keeper. Those who imagine that the soul is called a spirit, because it is a breath or faculty divinely infused into the body, but destitute of any essence, are proved to be in a gross error by the thing itself, and by the whole tenor of Scripture. It is true, indeed, that, while men are immoderately attached to the earth, they become stupid, and, being alienated from the Father of lights, are immersed in darkness, so that they consider not that they shall survive after death; yet in the mean time, the light is not so entirely extinguished by the darkness, but that they are affected with some sense of their immortality. Surely the conscience, which, discerning between good and evil, answers to the judgment of

(*e*) Gen. ii. 7; iii. 19, 23. (*g*) Luke xxiii. 46.
(*f*) Eccles. xii. 7. (*h*) Acts vii. 59.

God, is an indubitable proof of an immortal spirit. For how could an affection or emotion, without any essence, penetrate to the tribunal of God, and inspire itself with terror on account of its guilt? For the body is not affected by a fear of spiritual punishment; that falls only on the soul; whence it follows, that it is possessed of an essence. Now, the very knowledge of God sufficiently proves the immortality of the soul, which rises above the world, since an evanescent breath or inspiration could not arrive at the fountain of life. Lastly, the many noble faculties with which the human mind is adorned, and which loudly proclaim that something Divine is inscribed on it, are so many testimonies of its immortal essence. For the sense which the brutes have, extends not beyond the body, or at most not beyond the objects near it. But the agility of the human mind, looking through heaven and earth, and the secrets of nature, and comprehending in its intellect and memory all ages, digesting every thing in proper order, and concluding future events from those which are past, clearly demonstrates that there is concealed within man something distinct from the body. In our minds we form conceptions of the invisible God and of angels, to which the body is not at all competent. We apprehend what is right, just, and honest, which is concealed from the corporeal senses. The spirit, therefore, must be the seat of this intelligence. Even sleep itself, which, stupefying man, seems to divest him even of life, is no obscure proof of immortality; since it not only suggests to us ideas of things which never happened, but also presages of future events. I briefly touch those things which even profane writers magnificently extol in a more splendid and ornamented diction; but with the pious reader the simple mention of them will be sufficient. Now, unless the soul were something essentially distinct from the body, the Scripture would not inform us that we dwell in houses of clay, (*i*) and at death quit the tabernacle of the flesh; (*k*) that we put off the corruptible, (*l*) to receive a reward at the last day, according to the respective conduct of each individual in the body. (*m*) For certainly these and similar passages, which often occur, not only manifestly distinguish the soul from the body, but, by transferring to it the name of "man," indicate that it is the principal part of our nature. When Paul exhorts the faithful to cleanse themselves from all filthiness of the flesh and of the spirit, (*n*) he points out two parts in which the defilement of sin resides. Peter also, when he called Christ the Shepherd and Bishop of souls, (*o*) would have spoken improperly, if there were no souls over whom he could exercise that office. Nor would there be any

(*i*) Job iv. 19. (*l*) 2 Peter i. 13, 14. (*n*) 2 Cor. vii. 1.
(*k*) 2 Cor. v. 4. (*m*) 2 Cor. v. 10. (*o*) 1 Peter ii. 25.

consistency in what he says concerning the eternal salvation of souls, or in his injunction to purify the souls, or in his assertion that fleshly lusts war against the soul, (*p*) or in what the author of the Epistle to the Hebrews says, that pastors watch to give an account of our souls, (*q*) unless souls had a proper essence. To the same purpose is the place where Paul "calls God for a record upon his soul," (*r*) because it could not be amenable to God, if it were not capable of punishment; which is also more clearly expressed in the words of Christ, where he commands us to fear him, who, after having killed the body, is able to cast the soul into hell. (*s*) Where the author of the Epistle to the Hebrews distinguishes between the fathers of our flesh, and God, who is the only Father of spirits, (*t*) he could not assert the essence or existence of the soul in more express terms. Besides, unless the soul survived after its liberation from the prison of the body, it was absurd for Christ to represent the soul of Lazarus as enjoying happiness in the bosom of Abraham, and the soul of the rich man as condemned to dreadful torments. (*u*) Paul confirms the same point, by informing us that we are absent from God as long as we dwell in the body, but that when absent from the body we are present with the Lord. (*v*) Not to be too prolix on a subject of so little obscurity, I shall only add this from Luke, that it is reckoned among the errors of the Sadducees, that they believed not the existence of angels or of spirits. (*w*)

III. A solid proof of this point may also be gathered from man being said to be created in the image of God. (*x*) For though the glory of God is displayed in his external form, yet there is no doubt that the proper seat of his image is in the soul. I admit that external form, as it distinguishes us from brutes, also exalts us more nearly to God; nor will I too vehemently contend with any one who would understand, by the image of God, that

> "—— while the mute creation downward bend
> Their sight, and to their earthly mother tend,
> Man looks aloft, and with erected eyes
> Beholds his own hereditary skies." (*y*)

Only let it be decided that the image of God, which appears or sparkles in these external characters, is spiritual. For Osiander, whose perverse ingenuity in futile notions is proved by his writings, extending the image of God promiscuously to the body as well as to the soul, confounds heaven and earth together. He says, that the Father, and Son, and Holy Spirit, fixed their

---

(*p*) 1 Peter i. 9, 22; ii. 11. (*s*) Matt. x. 28. Luke xii. 4, 5. (*v*) 2 Cor. v. 6, 8
(*q*) Heb. xiii. 17. (*t*) Heb. xii. 9. (*w*) Acts xxiii. 8.
(*r*) 2 Cor. i. 23. (*u*) Luke xvi. 22. (*x*) Gen. i 27.
(*y*) Ovid's Metam. lib. 1. Dryden's Translation.

image in man, because, even if Adam had remained in his integrity, Christ would, nevertheless, have become man. Thus, according to him, the body which had been destined for Christ was the exemplar and type of that corporeal figure which was then formed. But where will he find that Christ is the image of the Spirit? I grant, indeed, that the glory of the whole Deity shines in the person of the Mediator; but how shall the eternal Word be called the image of the Spirit, whom he precedes in order? Lastly, it subverts the distinction between the Son and Spirit, if the former be denominated the image of the latter. Besides, I could wish to be informed by him, how Christ, in the body which he has assumed, resembles the Spirit, and by what characters or lineaments his similitude is expressed. And since that speech, "Let us make man in our own image," (z) belongs also to the person of the Son, it follows that he is the image of himself; which is altogether repugnant to reason. Moreover, if the notion of Osiander be received, man was formed only to the type or exemplar of the humanity of Christ; and the idea from which Adam was taken was Christ, as about to be clothed in flesh; whereas the Scripture teaches, in a very different sense, that man was "created in the image of God." There is more plausibility in the subtlety of those who maintain that Adam was created in the image of God, because he was conformed to Christ, who is the only image of God. But this also is destitute of solidity. There is no small controversy concerning "image" and "likeness" among expositors who seek for a difference, whereas in reality there is none, between the two words; "likeness" being only added by way of explanation. In the first place, we know that it is the custom of the Hebrews to use repetitions, in which they express one thing twice. In the next place, as to the thing itself, there is no doubt but man is called the image of God, on account of his likeness to God. Hence it appears that those persons make themselves ridiculous who display more subtlety in criticising on these terms, whether they confine *zelem*, that is, "image," to the substance of the soul, and *demuth*, that is, "likeness," to its qualities, or whether they bring forward any different interpretation. Because, when God determined to create man in his own image, that expression being rather obscure, he repeats the same idea in this explanatory phrase, "after our likeness;" as though he had said that he was about to make man, in whom, as in an image, he would give a representation of himself by the characters of resemblance which he would impress upon him. Therefore Moses, a little after, reciting the same thing, introduces the image of God, but makes no mention of his likeness. The objection of Osiander is quite frivolous, that it is not a

(z) Gen. i. 26.

part of man, or the soul with its faculties, that is called the image of God, but the whole Adam, who received his name from the earth whence he was taken; it will be deemed frivolous, I say, by every rational reader. For when the whole man is called mortal, the soul is not therefore made subject to death; nor, on the other hand, when man is called a rational animal, does reason or intelligence therefore belong to the body. Though the soul, therefore, is not the whole man, yet there is no absurdity in calling him the image of God with relation to the soul; although I retain the principle which I have just laid down, that the image of God includes all the excellence in which the nature of man surpasses all the other species of animals. This term, therefore, denotes the integrity which Adam possessed, when he was endued with a right understanding, when he had affections regulated by reason, and all his senses governed in proper order, and when, in the excellency of his nature, he truly resembled the excellence of his Creator. And though the principal seat of the Divine image was in the mind and heart, or in the soul and its faculties, yet there was no part of man, not even the body, which was not adorned with some rays of its glory. It is certain that the lineaments of the Divine glory are conspicuous in every part of the world; whence it may be concluded, that where the image of God is said to be in man, there is implied a tacit antithesis, which exalts man above all the other creatures, and as it were separates him from the vulgar herd. It is not to be denied that angels were created in the similitude of God, since our highest perfection will consist, according to the declaration of Christ, in being like them. (a) But it is not in vain that Moses celebrates the favour of God towards us by this peculiar title; especially as he compares man only to visible creatures.

IV. No complete definition of this image, however, appears yet to be given, unless it be more clearly specified in what faculties man excels, and in what respects he ought to be accounted a mirror of the Divine glory. But that cannot be better known from any thing, than from the reparation of his corrupted nature. There is no doubt that Adam, when he fell from his dignity, was by this defection alienated from God. Wherefore, although we allow that the Divine image was not utterly annihilated and effaced in him, yet it was so corrupted that whatever remains is but horrible deformity. And therefore the beginning of our recovery and salvation is the restoration which we obtain through Christ, who on this account is called the second Adam; because he restores us to true and perfect integrity. For although Paul, opposing the quickening Spirit received by the faithful from Christ, to the living soul in

(a) Matt. xxii. 30

which Adam was created, (*b*) celebrates the degree of grace displayed in regeneration as superior to that manifested in creation, yet he contradicts not that other capital point, that this is the end of regeneration, that Christ may form us anew in the image of God. Therefore he elsewhere informs us, that "the new man is renewed in knowledge after the image of him that created him." (*c*) With which corresponds the following exhortation — "Put on the new man, which after God is created in righteousness and true holiness." (*d*) Now, we may see what Paul comprehends in this renovation. In the first place, he mentions knowledge, and in the next place, sincere righteousness and holiness; whence we infer, that in the beginning the image of God was conspicuous in the light of the mind, in the rectitude of the heart, and in the soundness of all the parts of our nature. For though I grant that the forms of expression are synecdochical, signifying the whole by a part, yet this is an axiom which cannot be overturned, that what holds the principal place in the renovation of the Divine image, must also have held the same place in the creation of it at first. To the same purpose is another passage of the Apostle, that "we, with open face beholding the glory of Christ, are changed into the same image." (*e*) We see, now, how Christ is the most perfect image of God, to which being conformed, we are so restored that we bear the Divine image in true piety, righteousness, purity, and understanding. This position being established, the imagination of Osiander, about the figure of the body, immediately vanishes of itself. The passage where Paul calls the man "the image and glory of God," (*f*) to the exclusion of the woman from that degree of honour, appears from the context to be confined to political subordination. But that the image which has been mentioned comprehended whatever relates to spiritual and eternal life, has now, I think, been sufficiently proved. John confirms the same in other words, by asserting that "the life" which was from the beginning in the eternal Word of God, "was the light of men." (*g*) For as he intended to praise the singular favour of God which exalts man above all the other animals; to separate him from the common number, because he has attained no vulgar life, but a life connected with the light of intelligence and reason, — he at the same time shows how he was made after the image of God. Therefore, since the image of God is the uncorrupted excellence of human nature, which shone in Adam before his defection, but was afterwards so corrupted, and almost obliterated, that nothing remains from the ruin but what is confused, mutilated, and defiled, — it is now

(*b*) 1 Cor. xv. 45.
(*c*) Col. iii. 10.
(*d*) Eph. iv. 24.
(*e*) 2 Cor. iii. 18.
(*f*) 1 Cor. xi. 7.
(*g*) John i. 4.

partly visible in the elect, inasmuch as they are regenerated by the Spirit, but it will obtain its full glory in heaven. But that we may know the parts of which it consists, it is necessary to treat of the faculties of the soul. For that speculation of Augustine is far from being solid, that the soul is a mirror of the Trinity, because it contains understanding, will, and memory. Nor is there any probability in the opinion which places the similitude of God in the dominion committed to man; as though he resembled God only in this character, that he was constituted heir and possessor of all things, whereas it must properly be sought *in* him, not *without* him; it is an internal excellence of the soul.

V. But, before I proceed any further, it is necessary to combat the Manichæan error, which Servetus has attempted to revive and propagate in the present age. Because God is said to have breathed into man the breath of life, (*h*) they supposed that the soul was an emanation from the substance of God; as though some portion of the infinite Deity had been conveyed into man. But it may be easily and briefly shown how many shameful and gross absurdities are the necessary consequences of this diabolical error. For if the soul of man be an emanation from the essence of God, it will follow that the Divine nature is not only mutable and subject to passions, but also to ignorance, desires, and vices of every kind. Nothing is more inconstant than man, because his soul is agitated and variously distracted by contrary motions; he frequently mistakes through ignorance; he is vanquished by some of the smallest temptations; we know that the soul is the receptacle of every kind of impurity;—all which we must ascribe to the Divine nature, if we believe the soul to be part of the essence of God, or a secret influx of the Deity. Who would not dread such a monstrous tenet? It is a certain truth, quoted by Paul from Aratus, that "we are the offspring of God," but in quality, not in substance; forasmuch as he has adorned us with Divine endowments. (*i*) But to divide the essence of the Creator, that every creature may possess a part of it, indicates extreme madness. It must therefore be concluded beyond all doubt, notwithstanding the Divine image is impressed on the souls of men, that they were no less created than the angels. And creation is not a transfusion, but an origination of existence from nothing. Nor, because the spirit is given by God, and returns to him on its departure from the body, is it immediately to be asserted, that it was plucked off like a branch from his essence. And on this point also Osiander, while he is elated with his own illusions, has involved himself in an impious error, not ac-

(*h*) Gen. ii. 7. (*i*) Acts xvii. 23.

knowledging the image of God in man without his essential righteousness, as though God could not, by the inconceivable power of his Spirit, render us conformable to himself, unless Christ were to transfuse himself substantially into us. However some persons may attempt to gloss over these delusions, they will never so far blind the eyes of sensible readers, as to prevent their perceiving that they savour of the error of the Manichæans. And where Paul treats of the restoration of this image, we may readily conclude from his words, that man was conformed to God not by an influx of his substance, but by the grace and power of his Spirit. For he says that, by beholding the glory of Christ, we are transformed into the same image as by the Spirit of the Lord; (*k*) who certainly operates in us not in such a manner as to render us consubstantial with God.

VI. It would be folly to seek for a definition of the soul from the heathen philosophers, of whom Plato is almost the only one who has plainly asserted it to be an immortal substance. Others indeed, the disciples of Socrates, hint at it, but with great doubts; no one clearly teaches that of which he was not persuaded himself. The sentiment of Plato, therefore, is more correct, because he considers the image of God as being in the soul. The other sects so confine its powers and faculties to the present life, that they leave it nothing beyond the body. But we have before stated from the Scripture, that it is an incorporeal substance; now we shall add, that although it is not properly contained in any place, yet, being put into the body, it inhabits it as its dwelling, not only to animate all its parts, and render the organs fit and useful for their respective operations, but also to hold the supremacy in the government of human life; and that not only in the concerns of the terrestrial life, but likewise to excite to the worship of God. Though this last point is not so evident in the state of corruption, yet there remain some relics of it impressed even on our very vices. For whence proceeds the great concern of men about their reputation, but from shame? but whence proceeds shame, unless from a respect for virtue? The principle and cause of which is, that they understand themselves to have been born for the cultivation of righteousness; and in which are included the seeds of religion. But as, without controversy, man was created to aspire to a heavenly life, so it is certain that the knowledge of it was impressed on his soul. And, indeed, man would be deprived of the principal use of his understanding, if he were ignorant of his felicity, the perfection of which consists in being united to God. Thus the chief opera-

---

(*k*) 2 Cor. iii. 18.

tion of the soul is to aspire after it ; and, therefore, the more a man studies to approach to God, the more he proves himself a rational creature. Some maintain that in man there are more souls than one, a sensitive and a rational one ; but notwithstanding some appearance of probability in what they adduce, yet, as there is nothing solid in their arguments, we must reject them, unless we are fond of tormenting ourselves with frivolous and useless things. They say that there is a great repugnancy between the organic motions and the rational part of the soul ; as though reason were not also at variance with itself, and some of its counsels were not in opposition to others, like hostile armies. But as this confusion proceeds from the depravity of nature, it affords no ground for concluding that there are two souls, because the faculties are not sufficiently harmonious with each other. But all curious discussion respecting the faculties themselves I leave to the philosophers; a simple definition will suffice us for the edification of piety. I confess, indeed, that the things which they teach are true, and not only entertaining to be known, but useful and well digested by them; nor do I prohibit those who are desirous of learning from the study of them. I admit, then, in the first place, that there are five senses, which Plato would rather call organs, by which all objects are conveyed into a common sensory, as into a general repository ; that next follows the fancy or imagination, which discerns the objects apprehended by the common sensory ; next reason, to which belongs universal judgment ; lastly, the understanding, which steadily and quietly contemplates the objects revolved and considered by reason. And thus to the understanding, reason, and imagination, the three intellectual faculties of the soul, correspond also the three appetitive ones — the will, whose place it is to choose those things which the understanding and reason propose to it; the irascible faculty, which embraces the things offered to it by reason and imagination ; and the concupiscible faculty, which apprehends the objects presented by the imagination and sensation. Though these things are true, or at least probable, yet, since I fear that they will involve us in their obscurity rather than assist us, I think they ought to be omitted. If any one chooses to make a different distribution of the powers of the soul, so as to call one appetitive, which, though void of reason in itself, obeys reason, if it be under the guidance of any other faculty; and to call another intellective, which is itself a partaker of reason ; I shall not much oppose it. Nor have I any wish to combat the sentiment of Aristotle, that there are three principles of action — sense, intellect, and appetite. But let us rather choose a division placed within the comprehension of all, and which certainly cannot be sought in the philosophers.

For when they wish to speak with the greatest simplicity, they divide the soul into appetite and intellect, and make both these twofold. The latter, they say, is sometimes contemplative, being content merely with knowledge, and having no tendency to action, — which Cicero thinks is designated by the word *ingenium*, — and sometimes practical, variously influencing the will with the apprehension of good or evil. This division comprehends the science of living in a just and virtuous manner. The latter, that is, appetite, they divide into will and concupiscence; they call it "will," whenever appetite obeys reason; but when, shaking off the yoke of reason, it runs into intemperance, they give it the name of "concupiscence." Thus they imagine that man is always possessed of reason sufficient for the proper government of himself.

VII. We are constrained to depart a little from this mode of instruction, because the philosophers, being ignorant of the corruption of nature proceeding from the punishment of the fall, improperly confound two very different states of mankind. Let us, therefore, submit the following division — that the human soul has two faculties which relate to our present design, the understanding and the will. Now, let it be the office of the understanding to discriminate between objects, as they shall respectively appear deserving of approbation or disapprobation; but of the will, to choose and follow what the understanding shall have pronounced to be good; to abhor and avoid what it shall have condemned. Here let us not stay to discuss those subtleties of Aristotle, that the mind has no motion of itself, but that it is moved by the choice, which he also calls the appetitive intellect. Without perplexing ourselves with unnecessary questions, it should be sufficient for us to know that the understanding is, as it were, the guide and governor of the soul; that the will always respects its authority, and waits for its judgment in its desires. For which reason Aristotle himself truly observed, that avoidance and pursuit in the appetite, bear a resemblance to affirmation and negation in the mind. How certain the government of the understanding is in the direction of the will, we shall see in another part of this work. Here we only intend to show that no power can be found in the soul, which may not properly be referred to one or the other of those two members. But in this manner we comprehend the sense in the understanding, which some distinguish thus: sense, they say, inclines to pleasure, whereas the understanding follows what is good; that thence it happens that the appetite of sense becomes concupiscence and lust, and the affection of the understanding becomes will. But instead of the word "appetite," which they prefer, I use the word "will," which is more common.

VIII. God has furnished the soul of man, therefore, with a mind capable of discerning good from evil, and just from unjust; and of discovering, by the light of reason, what ought to be pursued or avoided; whence the philosophers called this directing faculty το ἡγεμονικον, the principal or governing part. To this he has annexed the will, on which depends the choice. The primitive condition of man was ennobled with those eminent faculties; he possessed reason, understanding, prudence, and judgment, not only for the government of his life on earth, but to enable him to ascend even to God and eternal felicity. To these was added choice, to direct the appetites, and regulate all the organic motions; so that the will should be entirely conformed to the government of reason. In this integrity man was endued with free will, by which, if he had chosen, he might have obtained eternal life. For here it would be unreasonable to introduce the question respecting the secret predestination of God, because we are not discussing what might possibly have happened or not, but what was the real nature of man. Adam, therefore, could have stood if he would, since he fell merely by his own will; but because his will was flexible to either side, and he was not endued with constancy to persevere, therefore he so easily fell. Yet his choice of good and evil was free; and not only so, but his mind and will were possessed of consummate rectitude, and all his organic parts were rightly disposed to obedience, till, destroying himself, he corrupted all his excellencies. Hence proceeded the darkness which overspread the minds of the philosophers, because they sought for a complete edifice among ruins, and for beautiful order in the midst of confusion. They held this principle, that man would not be a rational animal, unless he were endued with a free choice of good or evil; they conceived also that otherwise all difference between virtue and vice would be destroyed, unless man regulated his life according to his own inclination. Thus far it had been well, if there had been no change in man, of which as they were ignorant, it is not to be wondered at if they confound heaven and earth together. But those who profess themselves to be disciples of Christ, and yet seek for free will in man, now lost and overwhelmed in spiritual ruin, in striking out a middle path between the opinions of the philosophers and the doctrine of heaven, are evidently deceived, so that they touch neither heaven nor earth. But these things will be better introduced in the proper place. At present be it only remembered, that man, at his first creation, was very different from all his posterity, who, deriving their original from him in his corrupted state, have contracted an hereditary defilement. For all the parts of his soul were formed with the utmost rectitude; he enjoyed soundness of mind, and a will free to the choice of good. If any object, that he was placed in a dangerous situation on account of the imbecility of this faculty, I reply, that the station in which he was placed was sufficient to deprive him of all excuse. For it would have been unreasonable that God should be confined to this condition, to make man so as to be altogether incapable either of choosing or of committing any sin. It is true that such a nature would have been more excellent; but to expostulate with God as though he had been under any obligation to bestow this upon man, were unreasonable and unjust in the extreme; since it was at his choice to bestow as little as he pleased. But why he did not sustain him with the power of perseverance, remains concealed in his mind; but it is our duty to restrain our investigations within the limits of sobriety. He had received the power, indeed, if he chose to exert it; but he had not the will to use that power; for the consequence of this will would have been perseverance. Yet there is no excuse for him; he received so much, that he was the voluntary procurer of his own destruction; but God was under no necessity to give him any other than an indifferent and mutable will, that from his fall he might educe matter for his own glory.

CHAPTER XVI.

GOD'S PRESERVATION AND SUPPORT OF THE WORLD BY HIS POWER, AND HIS GOVERNMENT OF EVERY PART OF IT BY HIS PROVIDENCE.

To represent God as a Creator only for a moment, who entirely finished all his work at once, were frigid and jejune; and in this it behoves us especially to differ from the heathen, that the presence of the Divine power may appear to us no less in the perpetual state of the world than in its first origin. For although the minds even of impious men, by the mere contemplation of earth and heaven, are constrained to rise to the Creator, yet faith has a way peculiar to itself to assign to God the whole praise of creation. To which purpose is that assertion of an Apostle before cited, that it is only "through faith that we understand the worlds were framed by the word of God;" (*l*) because, unless we proceed to his providence, we have no correct conception of the meaning of this article, "that

(*l*) Hebrews xi. 3.

God is the Creator;" however we may appear to comprehend it in our minds, and to confess it with our tongues. The carnal sense, when it has once viewed the power of God in the creation, stops there; and when it proceeds the furthest, it only examines and considers the wisdom, and power, and goodness, of the Author in producing such a work, which spontaneously present themselves to the view even of those who are unwilling to observe them. In the next place, it conceives of some general operation of God in preserving and governing it, on which the power of motion depends. Lastly, it supposes that the vigour originally infused by God into all things is sufficient for their sustentation. But faith ought to penetrate further. When it has learned that he is the Creator of all things, it should immediately conclude that he is also their perpetual governor and preserver; and that not by a certain universal motion, actuating the whole machine of the world, and all its respective parts, but by a particular providence sustaining, nourishing, and providing for every thing which he has made. (*m*) Thus David, having briefly premised that the world was made by God, immediately descends to the continual course of his providence: "By the word of the Lord were the heavens made; and all the host of them by the breath of his mouth." (*n*) He afterwards adds, "The Lord beholdeth all the sons of men;" (*o*) and subjoins more to the same purpose. For though all men argue not so skilfully, yet, since it would not be credible that God was concerned about human affairs, if he were not the Maker of the world, and no one seriously believes that the world was made by God, who is not persuaded that he takes care of his own works, it is not without reason that David conducts us by a most excellent series from one to the other. In general, indeed, both philosophers teach, and the minds of men conceive, that all the parts of the world are quickened by the secret inspiration of God. But they go not so far as David, who is followed by all the pious, when he says, "These all wait upon thee; that thou mayest give them their meat in due season. That thou givest them, they gather; thou openest thine hand, they are filled with good. Thou hidest thy face, they are troubled; thou takest away their breath, they die, and return to their dust. Thou sendest forth thy Spirit, they are created; and thou renewest the face of the earth." (*p*) Though they subscribe to the assertion of Paul, that in God "we live, and move, and have our being," (*q*) yet they are very far from a serious sense of his favour, celebrated by the Apostle; because they have no apprehension

(*m*) Matt. vi. 26; x. 29.   (*n*) Psalm xxxiii. 6.   (*o*) Psalm xxxiii. 13.
(*p*) Psalm civ. 27—30.   (*q*) Acts xvii. 28.

of the special care of God, from which alone his paternal favour is known.

II. For the clearer manifestation of this difference, it must be observed that the providence of God, as it is taught in Scripture, is opposed to fortune and fortuitous accidents. Now, since it has been the common persuasion in all ages, and is also in the present day almost the universal opinion, that all things happen fortuitously, it is certain that every correct sentiment concerning providence is not only obscured, but almost buried in oblivion by this erroneous notion. If any one falls into the hands of robbers, or meets with wild beasts; if by a sudden storm he is shipwrecked on the ocean; if he is killed by the fall of a house or a tree; if another, wandering through deserts, finds relief for his penury, or, after having been tossed about by the waves, reaches the port, and escapes, as it were, but a hair's-breadth from death,—carnal reason will ascribe all these occurrences, both prosperous and adverse, to fortune. But whoever has been taught from the mouth of Christ, that the hairs of his head are all numbered, (*r*) will seek further for a cause, and conclude that all events are governed by the secret counsel of God. And respecting things inanimate, it must be admitted, that, though they are all naturally endued with their peculiar properties, yet they exert not their power, any further than as they are directed by the present hand of God. They are, therefore, no other than instruments into which God infuses as much efficacy as he pleases, bending and turning them to any actions, according to his will. There is no power among all the creatures more wonderful or illustrious, than that of the sun. For, besides his illumination of the whole world by his splendour, how astonishing it is that he cherishes and enlivens all animals with his heat; with his rays inspires fecundity into the earth; from the seeds, genially warmed in her bosom, produces a green herbage, which, being supported by fresh nourishment, he increases and strengthens till it rises into stalks; feeds them with perpetual exhalations, till they grow into blossoms, and from blossoms to fruit, which he then by his influences brings to maturity; that trees, likewise, and vines, by his genial warmth, first put forth leaves, then blossoms, and from the blossoms produce their fruit! But the Lord, to reserve the praise of all these things entirely to himself, was pleased that the light should exist, and the earth abound in every kind of herbs and fruits, before he created the sun. A pious man, therefore, will not make the sun either a principal or necessary cause of those things which existed before the creation of the sun, but only an instrument which God

(*r*) Matt. x. 30.

uses, because it is his pleasure so to do; whereas he would find no more difficulty in acting by himself without that luminary. Lastly, as we read that the sun remained in one situation for two days at the prayer of Joshua, (s) and that his shadow made a retrograde motion of ten degrees for the sake of king Hezekiah, (t) God has declared by these few miracles, that the daily rising and setting of the sun is not from a blind instinct of nature, but that he himself governs his course, to renew the memory of his paternal favour towards us. Nothing is more natural than the succession of spring to winter, of summer to spring, and of autumn to summer. But there is so great a diversity and inequality discovered in this series, that it is obvious that every year, month, and day, is governed by a new and particular providence of God.

III. And, indeed, God asserts his possession of omnipotence, and claims our acknowledgment of this attribute; not such as is imagined by sophists, vain, idle, and almost asleep, but vigilant, efficacious, operative, and engaged in continual action; not a mere general principle of confused motion, as if he should command a river to flow through the channels once made for it, but a power constantly exerted on every distinct and particular movement. For he is accounted omnipotent, not because he is able to act, yet sits down in idleness, or continues by a general instinct the order of nature originally appointed by him; but because he governs heaven and earth by his providence, and regulates all things in such a manner that nothing happens but according to his counsel. For when it is said in the Psalms, that he does whatsoever he pleases, (v) it denotes his certain and deliberate will. For it would be quite insipid to expound the words of the Prophet in the philosophical manner, that God is the prime agent, because he is the principle and cause of all motion; whereas the faithful should rather encourage themselves in adversity with this consolation, that they suffer no affliction, but by the ordination and command of God, because they are under his hand. But if the government of God be thus extended to all his works, it is a puerile cavil to limit it to the influence and course of nature. And they not only defraud God of his glory, but themselves of a very useful doctrine, who confine the Divine providence within such narrow bounds, as though he permitted all things to proceed in an uncontrolled course, according to a perpetual law of nature; for nothing would exceed the misery of man, if he were exposed to all the motions of the heaven, air, earth, and waters. Besides, this notion would shamefully diminish the singular goodness of God towards every individual. David exclaims, that infants yet

(s) Joshua x. 13.   (t) 2 Kings xx. 11.   (v) Psalm cxv. 3.

hanging on the breasts of their mothers are sufficiently eloquent to celebrate the glory of God; (*w*) because, as soon as they are born, they find aliment prepared for them by his heavenly care. This, indeed, is generally true; yet it cannot escape the observation of our eyes and senses, being evidently proved by experience, that some mothers have breasts full and copious, but others almost dry; as it pleases God to provide more liberally for one, but more sparingly for another. But they who ascribe just praise to the Divine omnipotence, receive from this a double advantage. In the first place, he must have ample ability to bless them, who possesses heaven and earth, and whose will all the creatures regard so as to devote themselves to his service. And, secondly, they may securely repose in his protection, to whose will are subject all those evils which can be feared from any quarter; by whose power Satan is restrained, with all his furies, and all his machinations; on whose will depends all that is inimical to our safety; nor is there any thing else by which those immoderate and superstitious fears, which we frequently feel on the sight of dangers, can be corrected or appeased. We are superstitiously timid, I say, if, whenever creatures menace or terrify us, we are frightened, as though they had of themselves the power to hurt us, or could fortuitously injure us; or as if against their injuries God were unable to afford us sufficient aid. For example, the Prophet forbids the children of God to fear the stars and signs of heaven, (*x*) as is the custom of unbelievers. He certainly condemns not every kind of fear. But when infidels transfer the government of the world from God to the stars, pretending that their happiness or misery depends on the decrees and presages of the stars, and not on the will of God, the consequence is, that their fear is withdrawn from him, whom alone they ought to regard, and is placed on stars and comets. Whoever, then, desires to avoid this infidelity, let him constantly remember, that in the creatures there is no erratic power, or action, or motion; but that they are so governed by the secret counsel of God, that nothing can happen but what is subject to his knowledge, and decreed by his will.

IV. First, then, let the readers know that what is called providence describes God, not as idly beholding from heaven the transactions which happen in the world, but as holding the helm of the universe, and regulating all events. Thus it belongs no less to his hands than to his eyes. When Abraham said to his son, "God will provide," (*y*) he intended not only to assert his prescience of a future event, but to leave the care of a thing unknown to the will of him who frequently puts an end to circumstances of perplexity and confusion. Whence it fol-

(*w*) Psalm viii. 2.   (*x*) Jer. x. 2.   (*y*) Gen. xxii. 8.

lows, that providence consists in action; for it is ignorant trifling to talk of mere prescience. Not quite so gross is the error of those who attribute to God a government, as I have observed, of a confused and promiscuous kind; acknowledging that God revolves and impels the machine of the world, with all its parts, by a general motion, without peculiarly directing the action of each individual creature. Yet even this error is not to be tolerated. For they maintain that this providence, which they call universal, is no impediment either to all the creatures being actuated contingently, or to man turning himself hither or thither at the free choice of his own will. And they make the following partition between God and man; that God by his power inspires him with motions, enabling him to act according to the tendency of the nature with which he is endued; but that man governs his actions by his own voluntary choice. In short, they conceive, that the world, human affairs, and men themselves, are governed by the power of God, but not by his appointment. I speak not of the Epicureans, who have always infested the world, who dream of a god absorbed in sloth and inactivity; and of others no less erroneous, who formerly pretended that the dominion of God extended over the middle region of the air, but that he left inferior things to fortune; since the mute creatures themselves sufficiently exclaim against such evident stupidity. My present design is to refute that opinion, which has almost generally prevailed, which, conceding to God a sort of blind and uncertain motion, deprives him of the principal thing, which is his directing and disposing, by his incomprehensible wisdom, all things to their proper end; and thus, robbing God of the government of the world, it makes him the ruler of it in name only, and not in reality. For, pray, what is governing, but presiding in such a manner, as to rule, by fixed decrees, those over whom you preside? Yet I reject not altogether what they assert concerning universal providence, provided they, on their part admit that God governs the world, not merely because he preserves the order of nature fixed by himself, but because he exercises a peculiar care over every one of his works. It is true that all things are actuated by a secret instinct of nature, as though they obeyed the eternal command of God, and that what God has once appointed, appears to proceed from voluntary inclination in the creatures. And to this may be referred the declaration of Christ, that his Father and himself had always been working, even from the beginning; (z) and the assertion of Paul, that "in him we live, and move, and have our being;" (a) and also what is observed by the author of the

(z) John v. 17.   (a) Acts xvii. 28.

Epistle to the Hebrews, with a design to prove the Divinity of Christ, that all things are sustained by the word of his power. (*b*) But they act very improperly in concealing and obscuring, by this pretext, the doctrine of a particular providence, which is asserted in such plain and clear testimonies of Scripture, that it is surprising how any one could entertain a doubt concerning it. And, certainly, they who conceal it with this veil which I have mentioned, are obliged to correct themselves by adding, that many things happen through the peculiar care of God; but this they erroneously restrict to some particular acts. Wherefore we have to prove, that God attends to the government of particular events, and that they all proceed from his determinate counsel, in such a manner that there can be no such thing as fortuitous contingence.

V. If we grant that the principle of motion originates from God, but that all things are spontaneously or accidentally carried whither the bias of nature impels them, the mutual vicissitudes of day and night, of winter and summer, will be the work of God, inasmuch as he has distributed to each its respective parts, and prescribed to them a certain law; that is, this would be the case if with even tenor they always observed the same measure, days succeeding to nights, months to months, and years to years. But sometimes excessive heats and drought parch and burn the fruits of the earth; sometimes unseasonable rains injure the crops of corn, and sudden calamities are occasioned by showers of hail and storms: this will not be the work of God; unless, perhaps, as either clouds or serene weather, or cold or heat, derive their origin from the opposition of the stars and other natural causes. But this representation leaves no room for God to display or exercise his paternal favour, or his judgments. If they say that God is sufficiently beneficent to man, because he infuses into heaven and earth an ordinary power, by which they supply him with food, it is a very flimsy and profane notion; as though the fecundity of one year were not the singular benediction of God, and as though penury and famine were not his malediction and vengeance. But as it would be tedious to collect all the reasons for rejecting this error, let us be content with the authority of God himself. In the law and in the prophets he frequently declares, that whenever he moistens the earth with dew or with rain, he affords a testimony of his favour; and that, on the contrary, when, at his command, heaven becomes hard as iron, when the crops of corn are blasted and otherwise destroyed, and when showers of hail and storms molest the fields, he gives a proof of his certain and special vengeance. If we believe these things, it is certain that not a drop of rain falls but at the ex-

(*b*) Heb. i. 3.

press command of God. David indeed praises the general providence of God, because "he giveth food to the young ravens which cry;"(c) but when God himself threatens animals with famine, does he not plainly declare, that he feeds all living creatures, sometimes with a smaller allowance, sometimes with a larger, as he pleases? It is puerile, as I have already observed, to restrain this to particular acts; whereas Christ says, without any exception, that not a sparrow of the least value falls to the ground without the will of the Father.(d) Certainly, if the flight of birds be directed by the unerring counsel of God, we must be constrained to confess with the Prophet, that, though "he dwelleth on high," yet "he humbleth himself to behold the things which are in heaven and in the earth."(e)

VI. But as we know that the world was made chiefly for the sake of mankind, we must also observe this end in the government of it. The Prophet Jeremiah exclaims, "I know that the way of man is not in himself: it is not in man that walketh to direct his steps."(f) And Solomon: "Man's goings are of the Lord: how can a man then understand his own way?"(g) Now, let them say that man is actuated by God according to the bias of his nature, but that he directs that influence according to his own pleasure. If this could be asserted with truth, man would have the free choice of his own ways. That, perhaps, they will deny, because he can do nothing independently of the power of God. But since it is evident that both the Prophet and Solomon ascribe to God choice and appointment, as well as power, this by no means extricates them from the difficulty. But Solomon, in another place, beautifully reproves this temerity of men, who predetermine on an end for themselves, without regard to God, as though they were not led by his hand: "The preparation of the heart in man," says he, "and the answer of the tongue, is from the Lord."(h) It is, indeed, a ridiculous madness for miserable men to resolve on undertaking any work independently of God, whilst they cannot even speak a word but what he chooses. Moreover, the Scripture, more fully to express that nothing is transacted in the world but according to his destination, shows that those things are subject to him which appear most fortuitous. For what would you be more ready to attribute to chance, than when a limb broken off from a tree kills a passing traveller? But very different is the decision of the Lord, who acknowledges that he has delivered him into the hand of the slayer.(i) Who, likewise, does not leave lots to the blindness of fortune? Yet the Lord leaves

(c) Psalm cxlvii. 9 (e) Psalm cxiii. 5, 6. (g) Prov. xx. 24. (i) Exod. xxi. 13.
(d) Matt. x. 29.   (f) Jer. x. 23.   (h) Prov. xvi. 1.

them not, but claims the disposal of them himself. He teaches us that it is not by any power of their own that lots are cast into the lap (*k*) and drawn out; but the only thing which could be ascribed to chance, he declares to belong to himself. To the same purpose is another passage from Solomon: "The poor and the deceitful man meet together: the Lord enlighteneth the eyes of them both." (*l*) For although the poor and the rich are blended together in the world, yet, as their respective conditions are assigned to them by Divine appointment, he suggests that God, who enlightens all, is not blind, and thus exhorts the poor to patience; because those who are discontented with their lot, are endeavouring to shake off the burden imposed on them by God. Thus also another Prophet rebukes profane persons, who attribute it to human industry, or to fortune, that some men remain in obscurity, and others rise to honours: "Promotion cometh neither from the east, nor from the west, nor from the south. But God is the Judge; he putteth down one, and setteth up another." (*m*) Since God cannot divest himself of the office of a judge, hence he reasons, that it is from the secret counsel of God, that some rise to promotion, and others remain in contempt.

VII. Moreover, particular events are in general proofs of the special providence of God. God raised in the desert a south wind, to convey to the people a large flock of birds. (*n*) When he would have Jonah thrown into the sea, he sent forth a wind to raise a tempest. (*o*) It will be said by them who suppose God not to hold the helm of the world, that this was a deviation from the common course of things. But the conclusion which I deduce from it is, that no wind ever rises or blows but by the special command of God. For otherwise it would not be true that he makes the winds his messengers, and a flame of fire his ministers, that he makes the clouds his chariot, and rides on the wings of the wind, (*p*) unless he directed at his pleasure the course both of the clouds and of the winds, and displayed in them the singular presence of his power. Thus also we are elsewhere taught, that, whenever the sea is blown into a tempest by the winds, those commotions prove the special presence of God. "He commandeth and raiseth the stormy wind, which lifteth up the waves" of the sea. "Then he maketh the storm a calm, so that the waves thereof are still;" (*q*) as in another place he proclaims, that he scourged the people with parching winds. (*r*) Thus, whilst men are naturally endued with a power of generation, yet God will have it acknowledged as the effect of his special

(*k*) Prov. xvi. 33.
(*l*) Prov. xxix. 13.
(*m*) Psalm lxxv. 6, 7.
(*n*) Exod. xvi. 13. Num. xi. 31.
(*o*) Jonah i. 4.
(*p*) Psalm civ. 3, 4.
(*q*) Psalm cvii. 25, 29.
(*r*) Amos iv. 9. Haggai i. 6—11.

favour, that he leaves some without any posterity, and bestows children on others; for "the fruit of the womb is his reward." (s) Therefore Jacob said to his wife, "Am I in God's stead, who hath withheld from thee the fruit of the womb?" (t) But to conclude; there is nothing more common in nature, than for us to be nourished with bread. But the Spirit declares, not only that the produce of the earth is the special gift of God, but that men do not live by bread alone; (v) because they are supported not by the abundance of their food, but by the secret benediction of God; as, on the contrary, he threatens that he will break "the stay of bread." (w) Nor, indeed, could we otherwise seriously offer a prayer for daily bread, if God did not supply us with food from his fatherly hand. The Prophet, therefore, to convince the faithful that in feeding them God acts the part of an excellent father of a family, informs us, that he "giveth food to all flesh." (x) Lastly, when we hear, on the one hand, that "the eyes of the Lord are upon the righteous, and his ears are open unto their cry," and, on the other, that "the face of the Lord is against them that do evil, to cut off the remembrance of them from the earth," (y) we may be assured that all creatures, above and below, are ready for his service, that he may apply them to any use that he pleases. Hence we conclude, not only that there is a general providence of God over the creatures, to continue the order of nature, but that, by his wonderful counsel, they are all directed to some specific and proper end.

VIII. Those who wish to bring an odium on this doctrine, calumniate it as the same with the opinion of the Stoics concerning fate, with which Augustine also was formerly reproached. Though we are averse to all contentious about words, yet we admit not the term *fate;* both because it is of that novel and profane kind which Paul teaches us to avoid, and because they endeavour to load the truth of God with the odium attached to it. But that dogma is falsely and maliciously charged upon us. For we do not, with the Stoics, imagine a necessity arising from a perpetual concatenation and intricate series of causes, contained in nature; but we make God the Arbiter and Governor of all things, who, in his own wisdom, has, from the remotest eternity, decreed what he would do, and now, by his own power, executes what he has decreed. Whence we assert, that not only the heaven and the earth, and inanimate creatures, but also the deliberations and volitions of men, are so governed by his providence, as to be directed to the end appointed by it. What then? you will say; does

(s) Psalm cxxvii. 3.
(t) Gen. xxx. 2.
(v) Deut. viii. 3.
(w) Isaiah iii. 1.
(x) Psalm cxxxvi. 25.
(y) Psalm xxxiv. 15, 16.

nothing happen fortuitously or contingently? I answer, that it was truly observed by Basil the Great, that *fortune* and *chance* are words of the heathen, with the signification of which the minds of the pious ought not to be occupied. For if all success be the benediction of God, and calamity and adversity his malediction, there is no room left in human affairs for fortune or chance. And we should attend to this declaration of Augustine: "I am not pleased with myself," says he, "for having, in my treatises against the Academics, so frequently mentioned *fortune*, although I have not intended by that word any goddess, but a fortuitous occurrence of external things, either good or evil. Hence also such words, the use of which no religion prohibits, as *perhaps*, *perchance*, *peradventure*, which, nevertheless, must be entirely referred to the Divine providence. And on this I have not been silent, remarking that perhaps what is commonly termed *fortune* is regulated by a secret order, and that what we call *chance* is only that, with the reason and cause of which we are not acquainted. Thus, indeed, I have expressed myself; but I repent of having mentioned *fortune* in this manner, since I see that men are habituated to a very sinful custom: when they ought to say, 'This was the will of God,' they say, 'This was the will of Fortune.'" Finally, he every where maintains, that if any thing be left to fortune, the world revolves at random. And though he elsewhere decides, that all things are conducted partly by the free will of man, partly by the providence of God, yet he just after shows that men are subject to it and governed by it, assuming as a principle that nothing could be more absurd, than for any thing to happen independently of the ordination of God; because it would happen at random. By this reasoning he excludes also any contingence dependent on the human will; and immediately after more expressly asserts that we ought not to inquire for any cause of the will of God. But in what sense *permission* ought to be understood, whenever it is mentioned by him, will appear from one passage; where he proves that the will of God is the supreme and first cause of all things, because nothing happens but by his command or permission. He certainly does not suppose God to remain an idle spectator, determining to permit any thing; there is an intervention of actual volition, if I may be allowed the expression, which otherwise could never be considered as a cause.

IX. Yet, since the dulness of our minds is very much below the sublimity of the Divine providence, let us endeavour to assist them by a distinction. I say, then, that, notwithstanding the ordination of all things by the certain purpose and direction of God, yet to us they are fortuitous: not that we suppose fortune holds any dominion over the world and mankind, and whirls about all things at random, for such folly ought to be far from the breast of a Christian; but because the order, reason, end, and necessity of events are chiefly concealed in the purpose of God, and not comprehended by the mind of man, those things are in some measure fortuitous, which must certainly happen according to the Divine will. For they present no other appearance, whether they are considered in their own nature, or are estimated according to our knowledge and judgment. Let us suppose, for example, that a merchant, having entered a wood in the company of honest men, imprudently wanders from his companions, and, pursuing a wrong course, falls into the hands of robbers, and is murdered. His death was not only foreseen by God, but also decreed by him. For it is said, not that he has foreseen to what limits the life of every man would extend, but that he "hath appointed bounds which he cannot pass." (z) Yet, as far as our minds are capable of comprehending, all these circumstances appear fortuitous. What opinion shall a Christian form on this case? He will consider all the circumstances of such a death as in their nature fortuitous; yet he will not doubt that the providence of God presided, and directed fortune to that end. The same reasoning will apply to future contingencies. All future things being uncertain to us, we hold them in suspense, as though they might happen either one way or another. Yet this remains a fixed principle in our hearts, that there will be no event which God has not ordained. In this sense the word *chance* is frequently repeated in the book of Ecclesiastes; because, on the first view, men penetrate not to the first cause, which lies deeply concealed. And yet the doctrine of the Scripture respecting the secret providence of God, has never been so far obliterated from the hearts of men, but that some sparks of it always shone in the darkness. Thus the Philistine sorcerers, though they fluctuated in uncertainty, ascribed adverse accidents partly to God, partly to fortune. "If the ark," say they, "goeth up by that way, we shall know that God hath done us this great evil; but if not, it was a chance that happened to us." (a) They betrayed great folly, indeed, after having been deceived by divination, to have recourse to fortune; yet at the same time, we see them restrained, so that they cannot dare to suppose the affliction which had befallen them was fortuitous. But how God, by the reins of his providence, directs all events according to his own pleasure, will appear by an eminent example. At the very same instant of time when David had been overtaken in the wilderness of Maon, behold, the Philis-

(z) Job xiv. 5. (a) 1 Sam. vi. 9.

tines made an irruption into the land, and Saul was compelled to depart. If God, consulting the safety of his servant, laid this impediment in the way of Saul, then, surely, though the Philistines might have taken up arms suddenly, and contrary to human expectation, yet we will not say that this happened by chance; but what to us seems a contingency, faith will acknowledge to have been a secret impulse of God. It is not always, indeed, that there appears a similar reason; but it should be considered as indubitably certain, that all the revolutions visible in the world proceed from the secret exertion of the Divine power. What God decrees, must necessarily come to pass; yet it is not by absolute or natural necessity. We find a familiar example in respect to the bones of Christ. Since he possessed a body like ours, no reasonable man will deny that his bones were capable of being broken; yet that they should be broken was impossible. Hence, again, we perceive that the distinctions of relative and absolute necessity, as well as necessity of consequent and of consequence, were not without reason invented in the schools; since God made the bones of his Son capable of being broken, which, however, he had exempted from being actually broken, and thus prevented, by the necessity of his purpose, what might naturally have come to pass.

CHAPTER XVII.

THE PROPER APPLICATION OF THIS DOCTRINE TO RENDER IT USEFUL TO US.

As the minds of men are prone to vain subtleties, there is the greatest danger that those who know not the right use of this doctrine will embarrass themselves with intricate perplexities. It will therefore be necessary to touch in a brief manner on the end and design of the Scripture doctrine of the Divine ordination of all things. And here let it be remarked, in the first place, that the providence of God is to be considered as well in regard to futurity, as in reference to that which is past; secondly, that it governs all things in such a manner as to operate sometimes by the intervention of means, sometimes without means, and sometimes in opposition to all means; lastly, that it tends to show the care of God for the whole human race, and especially his vigilance in the government of the Church, which he favours with more particular attention. It must also be observed, that, although the paternal favour and beneficence of God, or the severity of his justice, is frequently conspicuous in the whole course of his providence, yet sometimes the causes of events are concealed, so that a suspicion intrudes itself, that the revolutions of human affairs are conducted by the blind impetuosity of fortune; or the flesh solicits us to murmur, as though God amused himself with tossing men about like tennis-balls. It is true, indeed, if we were ready to learn with quiet and sober minds, that the final issue sufficiently proves the counsels of God to be directed by the best of reasons; that he designs either to teach his people the exercise of patience, or to correct their corrupt affections and subdue the licentiousness of their appetites, or to constrain them to the practice of self-denial, or to arouse them from their indolence; and, on the other hand, to abase the proud, to disappoint the cunning of the wicked, and to confound their machinations. Yet, however the causes may be concealed from us, or escape our observation, we must admit it as a certain truth, that they are hidden with him; and must therefore exclaim with David, "Many, O Lord my God, are thy wonderful works which thou hast done, and thy thoughts which are to us-ward: they cannot be reckoned up in order unto thee: if I would declare and speak of them, they are more than can be numbered." (*b*) For, though our miseries ought always to remind us of our sins, that the punishment itself may urge us to repentance, yet we see that Christ ascribes more sovereignty to the secret purpose of the Father in afflicting men, than to require him to punish every individual according to his demerits. For concerning him who was born blind, he says, "Neither hath this man sinned, nor his parents; but that the works of God should be made manifest in him." (*c*) For here sense murmurs, when calamity precedes the very birth, as though it were a detraction from the Divine clemency thus to afflict the innocent. But Christ declares that the glory of his Father is manifested in this instance, provided our eyes are clear to behold it. But we must proceed with modesty, cautious that we call not God to an account at our tribunal; but that we entertain such reverence for his secret judgments, as to esteem his will the most righteous cause of every thing that he does. When thick clouds obscure the heavens, and a violent tempest arises, because a gloomy mist is before our eyes, and thunder strikes our ears, and terror stupefies all our faculties, all things seem to us to be blended in confusion; yet during the whole time the heavens remain in the same quiet serenity. So it must be concluded, that while the turbulent state of the world deprives us of our judgment, God, by the pure light of his own righteousness and wisdom, regulates all those commotions in the most exact order, and directs them to their proper end. And

(*b*) Psalm xl. 5.   (*c*) John ix. 3.

certainly the madness of many in this respect is monstrous, who dare to arraign the works of God, to scrutinize his secret counsels, and even to pass a precipitate sentence on things unknown, with greater freedom than on the actions of mortal men. For what is more preposterous than towards our equals to observe such modesty, as rather to suspend our judgment than to incur the imputation of temerity, but impudently to insult the mysterious judgments of God, which we ought to hold in admiration and reverence?

II. None, therefore, will attain just and profitable views of the providence of God, but he who considers that he has to do with his Maker and the Creator of the world, and submits himself to fear and reverence with all becoming humility. Hence it happens that so many worthless characters in the present day virulently oppose this doctrine, because they will admit nothing to be lawful for God, but what agrees with the dictates of their own reason. They revile us with the utmost possible impudence, because, not content with the precepts of the law, which comprehend the will of God, we say that the world is governed also by his secret counsels; as though, indeed, what we assert were only an invention of our own brain, and the Holy Spirit did not every where plainly announce the same, and repeat it in innumerable forms of expression. But as they are restrained by some degree of shame from daring to discharge their blasphemies against heaven, in order to indulge their extravagance with greater freedom, they pretend that they are contending with us. But unless they admit, that whatever comes to pass in the world is governed by the incomprehensible counsel of God, let them answer, to what purpose is it said in the Scripture that his "judgments are a great deep"? (*d*) For since Moses proclaims, that the will of God is not to be sought far off, in the clouds or in the deep, (*e*) because it is familiarly explained in the law, it follows that there is another secret will, which is compared to a profound abyss; concerning which Paul also says, "O the depth of the riches both of the wisdom and knowledge of God; how unsearchable are his judgments, and his ways past finding out! For who hath known the mind of the Lord, or who hath been his counsellor?" (*f*) It is true, that the law and the Gospel contain mysteries which far transcend our capacities; but since God illuminates the minds of his people with the spirit of understanding, to apprehend these mysteries which he has condescended to reveal in his word, there we have now no abyss, but a way in which we may safely walk, and a lamp for the direction of our feet, the light of life, and the school of certain and evident truth. But his admirable method of governing

---

(*d*) Psalm xxxvi. 6.   (*e*) Deut. xxx. 12—14. Rom. x. 6, 7.
(*f*) Rom. xi. 33, 34.

the world is justly called a "great deep," because, while it is concealed from our view, it ought to be the object of our profound adoration. Moses has beautifully expressed both in a few words. "The secret things," says he, "belong unto the Lord our God; but those things which are revealed belong unto us and to our children." (g) We see how he enjoins us, not only to devote our attention to meditations on the law of God, but to look up with reverence to his mysterious providence. This sublime doctrine is declared in the book of Job, for the purpose of humbling our minds. For the author concludes a general view of the machine of the world, and a magnificent dissertation on the works of God, in these words: "Lo, these are parts of his ways; but how little a portion is heard of him!" (h) For which reason, in another place he distinguishes between the wisdom which resides in God, and the method of attaining wisdom which he has prescribed to men. For, after discoursing concerning the secrets of nature, he says, that wisdom is known only to God, and " is hid from the eyes of all living." But a little after he subjoins, that it is published in order to be investigated, because it is said to men, "Behold the fear of the Lord, that is wisdom." (i) To the same purpose is this observation of Augustine: "Because we know not all that God does concerning us by an excellent order we act according to the law in a good will only, but in other respects are actuated according to it; because his providence is an immutable law." Therefore, since God claims a power unknown to us of governing the world, let this be to us the law of sobriety and modesty, to acquiesce in his supreme dominion, to account his will the only rule of righteousness, and most righteous cause of all things. Not, indeed, that absolute will which is the subject of the declamation of sophists, impiously and profanely separating his justice from his power, but that providence which governs all things, from which originates nothing but what is right, although the reasons of it may be concealed from us.

III. Those who have learned this modesty, will neither murmur against God on account of past adversities, nor charge him with the guilt of their crimes, like Agamemnon, in Homer, who says, "The blame belongs not to me, but to Jupiter and Fate." Nor will they, as if hurried away by the Fates, under the influence of despair, put an end to their own lives, like the young man whom Plautus introduces as saying, "The condition of our affairs is inconstant; men are governed by the caprice of the Fates; I will betake myself to a precipice, and there destroy my life and every thing at once." Nor will they

(g) Deut. xxix. 29. (h) Job xxvi. 14. (i) Job xxviii. 21, 23.

excuse their flagitious actions by ascribing them to God, after the example of another young man introduced by the same poet, who says, "God was the cause: I believe it was the Divine will. For had it not been so, I know it would not have happened." But they will rather search the Scripture, to learn what is pleasing to God, that by the guidance of the Spirit they may strive to attain it; and at the same time, being prepared to follow God whithersoever he calls them, they will exhibit proofs in their conduct that nothing is more useful than a knowledge of this doctrine. Some profane men foolishly raise such a tumult with their absurdities, as almost, according to a common expression, to confound heaven and earth together. They argue in this manner: If God has fixed the moment of our death, we cannot avoid it; therefore all caution against it will be but lost labour. One man dares not venture himself in a way which he hears is dangerous, lest he should be assassinated by robbers; another sends for physicians, and wearies himself with medicines, to preserve his life; another abstains from the grosser kinds of food, lest he should injure his valetudinary constitution; another dreads to inhabit a ruinous house; and men in general exert all their faculties in devising and executing methods by which they may attain the object of their desires. Now, either all these things are vain remedies employed to correct the will of God, or life and death, health and disease, peace and war, and other things which, according to their desires or aversions, men industriously study to obtain or to avoid, are not determined by his certain decree. Moreover they conclude, that the prayers of the faithful are not only superfluous, but perverse, which contain petitions that the Lord will provide for those things which he has already decreed from eternity. In short, they supersede all deliberations respecting futurity, as opposed to the providence of God, who, without consulting men, has decreed whatever he pleased. And what has already happened they impute to the Divine providence in such a manner as to overlook the person, who is known to have committed any particular act. Has an assassin murdered a worthy citizen? they say he has executed the counsel of God. Has any one been guilty of theft or fornication? because he has done what was foreseen and ordained by the Lord, he is the minister of his providence. Has a son, neglecting all remedies, carelessly waited the death of his father? it was impossible for him to resist God, who had decreed this event from eternity. Thus by these persons all crimes are denominated virtues, because they are subservient to the ordination of God.

IV. But in reference to future things, Solomon easily reconciles the deliberations of men with the providence of God.

For as he ridicules the folly of those who presumptuously undertake any thing without the Lord, as though they were not subject to his government, so in another place he says, "A man's heart deviseth his way; but the Lord directeth his steps;(*k*) signifying that the eternal decrees of God form no impediment to our providing for ourselves, and disposing all our concerns in subservience to his will. The reason of this is manifest. For he who has fixed the limits of our life, has also intrusted us with the care of it; has furnished us with means and supplies for its preservation; has also made us provident of dangers; and, that they may not oppress us unawares, has furnished us with cautions and remedies. Now, it is evident what is our duty. If God has committed to us the preservation of our life, we should preserve it; if he offers supplies, we should use them; if he forewarns us of dangers, we should not rashly run into them; if he furnishes remedies, we ought not to neglect them. But it will be objected, no danger can hurt, unless it has been ordained that it shall hurt us, and then no remedies can avert it. But what if dangers are therefore not fatal, because God has assigned you remedies to repulse and overcome them? Examine whether your reasoning agrees with the order of the Divine providence. You conclude that it is unnecessary to guard against danger, because, if it be not fatal, we shall escape it without caution; but, on the contrary, the Lord enjoins you to use caution, because he intends it not to be fatal to you. These madmen overlook what is obvious to every observer — that the arts of deliberation and caution in men proceed from the inspiration of God, and that they subserve the designs of his providence in the preservation of their own lives; as, on the contrary, by neglect and slothfulness, they procure to themselves the evils which he has appointed for them. For how does it happen, that a prudent man, consulting his own welfare, averts from himself impending evils, and a fool is ruined by his inconsiderate temerity, unless folly and prudence are in both cases instruments of the Divine dispensation? Therefore it has pleased God to conceal from us all future events, that we may meet them as doubtful contingencies, and not cease to oppose to them the remedies with which we are provided, till they shall have been surmounted, or shall have overcome all our diligence. Therefore I have before suggested, that the providence of God ought not always to be contemplated abstractedly by itself, but in connection with the means which he employs.

V. The same persons inconsiderately and erroneously ascribe all past events to the absolute providence of God. For since all things which come to pass are dependent upon it, therefore,

(*k*) Prov. xvi. 9.

say they, neither thefts, nor adulteries, nor homicides, are perpetrated without the intervention of the Divine will. Why, therefore, they ask, shall a thief be punished for having pillaged him whom it has pleased the Lord to chastise with poverty? Why shall a homicide be punished for having slain him whose life the Lord had terminated? If all such characters are subservient to the Divine will, why shall they be punished? But I deny that they serve the will of God. For we cannot say, that he who is influenced by a wicked heart, acts in obedience to the commands of God, while he is only gratifying his own malignant passions. That man obeys God, who, being instructed in his will, hastens whither God calls him. Where can we learn his will, but in his word? Therefore in our actions we ought to regard the will of God, which is declared in his word. God only requires of us conformity to his precepts. If we do any thing contrary to them, it is not obedience, but contumacy and transgression. But it is said, if he would not permit it, we should not do it. This I grant. But do we perform evil actions with the design of pleasing him? He gives us no such command. We precipitate ourselves into them, not considering what is his will, but inflamed with the violence of our passions, so that we deliberately strive to oppose him. In this manner even by criminal actions we subserve his righteous ordination; because, in the infinite greatness of his wisdom, he well knows how to use evil instruments for the accomplishment of good purposes. Now, observe the absurdity of their reasoning: they wish the authors of crimes to escape with impunity, because crimes are not perpetrated but by the ordination of God. I admit more than this; even that thieves, and homicides, and other malefactors, are instruments of Divine providence, whom the Lord uses for the execution of the judgments which he has appointed. But I deny that this ought to afford any excuse for their crimes. For will they either implicate God in the same iniquity with themselves, or cover their depravity with his righteousness? They can do neither. They are prevented from exculpating themselves, by the reproofs of their own consciences; and they can lay no blame upon God, for they find in themselves nothing but evil, and in him only a legitimate use of their wickedness. But it is alleged that he operates by their means. And whence, I ask, proceeds the fetid smell of a carcass, which has been putrefied and disclosed by the heat of the sun? It is visible to all that it is excited by the solar rays; yet no person on this account attributes to those rays an offensive smell. So, when the matter and guilt of evil resides in a bad man, why should God be supposed to contract any defilement, if he uses his service according to his own pleasure? Let us dismiss this petulance, therefore, which may rail against the justice of God from a distance, but can never reach that Divine attribute.

VI. But these cavils, or rather extravagancies of frenzy, will easily be dispelled by the pious and holy contemplation of providence, which the rule of piety dictates to us, so that we may derive from it the greatest pleasure and advantage. The mind of a Christian, therefore, when it is certainly persuaded that all things happen by the ordination of God, and that there is nothing fortuitously contingent, will always direct its views to him as the supreme cause of all things, and will also consider inferior causes in their proper order. He will not doubt that the particular providence of God is watchful for his preservation, never permitting any event which it will not overrule for his advantage and safety. But, since he is concerned in the first place with men, and in the next place with the other creatures, he will assure himself, as to both, that the providence of God reigns over all. With respect to men, whether good or evil, he will acknowledge that their deliberations, wills, endeavours, and powers, are under his control, so that it is at his option to direct them whithersoever he pleases, and to restrain them as often as he pleases. The vigilance of the particular providence of God for the safety of the faithful is attested by numerous and very remarkable promises: "Cast thy burden upon the Lord, and he shall sustain thee: he shall never suffer the righteous to be moved. (*l*) He that dwelleth in the secret place of the Most High shall abide under the shadow of the Almighty. (*m*) He that toucheth you, toucheth the apple of his eye. We have a strong city: salvation will God appoint for walls and bulwarks. (*n*) Though a woman forget her sucking child, yet will I not forget thee." (*o*) Moreover, this is the principal scope of the Biblical histories, to teach us that the Lord so sedulously defends the ways of the saints, that they may not even "dash their foot against a stone." (*p*) Therefore, as we have a little before justly exploded the opinion of those who hold a universal providence of God, which descends not to the care of every creature in particular, so it is principally necessary and useful to contemplate this special care towards ourselves. For this reason, Christ, after having asserted that not the meanest sparrow falls to the ground without the will of the Father, (*q*) immediately makes the following application — that the more we exceed the value of sparrows, the greater care we should consider God as exercising over us; and he carries this to such an extent, that we may be confident that the hairs of our head are numbered. What more can we

(*l*) Psalm lv. 22.   1 Peter v. 7.   (*n*) Zech. ii. 8.   (*p*) Psalm xci. 12.
(*m*) Psalm xci. 1.   (*o*) Isaiah xxvi. 1; xlix. 15.   (*q*) Matt. x. 29, 30.

desire for ourselves, if not a single hair can fall from our head, but according to his will? I speak not exclusively of the human race; but since God has chosen the Church for his habitation, there is no doubt but he particularly displays his paternal care in the government of it.

VII. The servant of God, encouraged by these promises and examples, will add the testimonies, which inform us that all men are subject to his power, either to conciliate their minds in our favour, or to restrain their malice from being injurious. For it is the Lord who gives us favour, not only with our friends, but also in the eyes of the Egyptians; (r) and he knows how to subdue, by various methods, the fury of our enemies. Sometimes he deprives them of understanding, so that they can form no sober or prudent plans; as he sent Satan to fill the mouths of all the prophets with falsehood, in order to deceive Ahab: (s) he infatuated Rehoboam by the counsel of the young men, that through his own folly he might be spoiled of his kingdom. (t) Sometimes, when he grants them understanding, he so terrifies and dispirits them, that they can neither determine nor undertake what they have conceived. Sometimes, also, when he has permitted them to attempt what their rage and passion prompted, he opportunely breaks their impetuosity, not suffering them to proceed to the accomplishment of their designs. Thus he prematurely defeated the counsel of Ahithophel, which would have been fatal to David. (u) Thus, also, he takes care to govern all creatures for the benefit and safety of his people, even the devil himself, who, we see, dared not to attempt any thing against Job, without his permission and command. (r) The necessary consequences of this knowledge are, gratitude in prosperity, patience in adversity, and a wonderful security respecting the future. Every prosperous and pleasing event, therefore, the pious man will ascribe entirely to God, whether his beneficence be received through the ministry of men, or by the assistance of inanimate creatures. For this will be the reflection of his mind: "It is certainly the Lord that has inclined their hearts to favour me, that has united them to me to be the instruments of his benignity towards me." In an abundance of the fruits of the earth, he will consider, that it is the Lord who regards the heaven, that the heaven may regard the earth, that the earth, also, may regard its own productions: in other things he will not doubt that it is the Divine benediction alone which is the cause of all prosperity; nor will he bear to be ungrateful after so many admonitions.

VIII. If any adversity befall him, in this case, also, he will

(r) Exod. iii. 21.   (s) 1 Kings xxii. 22.   (t) 1 Kings xii. 10—15.
(u) 2 Sam. xvii. 7, 14.   (r) Job i. 12.

immediately lift up his heart to God, whose hand is most capable of impressing us with patience and placid moderation of mind. If Joseph had dwelt on a review of the perfidy of his brethren, he never could have recovered his fraternal affection for them. But as he turned his mind to the Lord, he forgot their injuries, and was so inclined to mildness and clemency, as even voluntarily to administer consolation to them, saying, "It was not you that sent me hither, but God did send me before you to save your lives. Ye thought evil against me; but God meant it unto good." (*w*) If Job had regarded the Chaldeans, by whom he was molested, he had been inflamed to revenge; but recognizing the event at the same time as the work of the Lord, he consoled himself with this very beautiful observation: "The Lord gave, and the Lord hath taken away; blessed be the name of the Lord." (*x*) Thus David, when assailed by Shimei with reproachful language and with stones, if he had confined his views to man, would have animated his soldiers to retaliate the injury; but understanding that it was not done without the instigation of the Lord, he rather appeases them: "Let him curse," says he, "because the Lord hath said unto him, Curse David." (*y*) In another place he imposes the same restraint on the intemperance of his grief: "I was dumb," says he, "I opened not my mouth; because thou didst it." (*z*) If there be no more efficacious remedy for anger and impatience, surely that man has made no small proficiency, who has learned in this case to meditate on the Divine providence, that he may be able at all times to recall his mind to this consideration: "It is the will of the Lord, therefore it must be endured; not only because resistance is unlawful and vain, but because he wills nothing but what is both just and expedient.,, The conclusion of the whole is this — that, when we suffer injuries from men, forgetting their malice, which would only exasperate our grief and instigate our minds to revenge, we should remember to ascend to God, and learn to account it a certain truth, that whatever our enemies have criminally committed against us, has been permitted and directed by his righteous dispensation. To restrain us from retaliating injuries, Paul prudently admonishes us that our contention is not with flesh and blood, but with a spiritual enemy, the devil, (*a*) in order that we may prepare ourselves for the contest. But this admonition is the most useful in appeasing all the sallies of resentment, that God arms for the conflict both the devil and all wicked men, and sits himself as the arbiter of the combat, to exercise our patience.

(*w*) Gen. xlv. 7, 8; l. 20.   (*x*) Job i. 21.   (*y*) 2 Sam. xvi. 10.
(*z*) Psalm xxxix. 9.   (*a*) Eph. vi. 12.

But if the calamities and miseries which oppress us happen without the interposition of men, let us recollect the doctrine of the law, that every prosperous event proceeds from the benediction of God, but that all adverse ones are his maledictions; (*b*) and let us tremble at that awful denunciation, "If ye will walk contrary unto me, then will I also walk contrary unto you;" (*c*) language which reproves our stupidity, while, according to the common apprehensions of the flesh, esteeming every event, both prosperous and adverse, to be fortuitous, we are neither animated to the worship of God by his benefits, nor stimulated to repentance by his corrections. This is the reason of the sharp expostulations of Jeremiah and of Amos, (*d*) because the Jews supposed that both good and evil events came to pass without any appointment of God. To the same purpose is this passage of Isaiah: "I form the light, and create darkness: I make peace, and create evil: I the Lord do all these things." (*e*)

IX. Yet at the same time a pious man will not overlook inferior causes. Nor, because he accounts those from whom he has received any benefit, the ministers of the Divine goodness, will he therefore pass them by unnoticed, as though they deserved no thanks for their kindness; but will feel, and readily acknowledge, his obligation to them, and study to return it as ability and opportunity may permit. Finally, he will reverence and praise God as the principal Author of benefits received, but will honour men as his ministers; and will understand, what, indeed, is the fact, that the will of God has laid him under obligations to those persons by whose means the Lord has been pleased to communicate his benefits. If he suffer any loss either through negligence or through imprudence, he will conclude that it happened according to the Divine will, but will also impute the blame of it to himself. If any one be removed by disease, whom, while it was his duty to take care of him, he has treated with neglect,—though he cannot be ignorant that that person had reached those limits which it was impossible for him to pass, yet he will not make this a plea to extenuate his guilt; but, because he has not faithfully performed his duty towards him, will consider him as having perished through his criminal negligence. Much less, when fraud and preconceived malice appear in the perpetration either of murder or of theft, will he excuse those enormities under the pretext of the Divine providence: in the same crime he will distinctly contemplate the righteousness of God and the iniquity of man, as they respectively discover themselves.

(*b*) Deut. xxviii. 1, &c.
(*c*) Lev. xxvi. 23, 24.
(*d*) Lam. iii. 37, 38. Amos iii. 6.
(*e*) Isaiah xlv. 7.

But it is principally in regard to things future that he will direct his attention to inferior causes of this kind. For he will rank it among the blessings of the Lord, not to be destitute of human aids which he may use for his own safety; he will neither be remiss, therefore, in taking the advice, nor negligent in imploring the help, of those whom he perceives to be capable of affording him assistance; but, considering all the creatures, that can in any respect be serviceable to him, as so many gifts from the Lord, he will use them as the legitimate instruments of the Divine providence. And as he is uncertain respecting the issue of his undertakings, except that he knows that the Lord will in all things provide for his good, he studiously aims at what, according to the best judgment he can form, will be for his advantage. Nor, in conducting his deliberations, will he be carried away by his own opinion, but will recommend and resign himself to the wisdom of God, that he may be directed by its guidance to the right end. But he will not place his confidence in external helps to such a degree as, if possessed of them, securely to rely on them, or, if destitute of them, to tremble with despair. For his mind will always be fixed solely on the Divine providence, nor will he suffer himself to be seduced from a steady contemplation of it, by any consideration of present things. Thus Joab, though he acknowledges the event of battle to depend on the will and the power of God, yet surrenders not himself to inactivity, but sedulously executes all the duties of his office, and leaves the event to the Divine decision. "Let us play the men," says he, "for our people, and for the cities of our God; and the Lord do that which seemeth him good." (*f*) This knowledge will divest us of temerity and false confidence, and excite us to continual invocations of God; it will also support our minds with a good hope, that without hesitation we may securely and magnanimously despise all the dangers which surround us.

X. Herein is discovered the inestimable felicity of the pious mind. Human life is beset by innumerable evils, and threatened with a thousand deaths. Not to go beyond ourselves,—since our body is the receptacle of a thousand diseases, and even contains and fosters the causes of diseases, a man must unavoidably carry about with him destruction in unnumbered forms, and protract a life which is, as it were, involved in death. For what else can you say of it, when neither cold nor heat in any considerable degree can be endured without danger? Now, whithersoever you turn, all the objects around you are not only unworthy of your confidence, but almost openly menace you, and seem to threaten immediate death. Embark in a ship; there is but a single step between you and death.

(*f*) 2 Sam. x. 12.

Mount a horse; the slipping of one foot endangers your life. Walk through the streets of a city; you are liable to as many dangers as there are tiles on the roofs. If there be a sharp weapon in your hand, or that of your friend, the mischief is manifest. All the ferocious animals you see are armed for your destruction. If you endeavour to shut yourself in a garden surrounded with a good fence, and exhibiting nothing but what is delightful, even there sometimes lurks a serpent. Your house, perpetually liable to fire, menaces you by day with poverty, and by night with falling on your head. Your land, exposed to hail, frost, drought, and various tempests, threatens you with sterility, and with its attendant, famine. I omit poison, treachery, robbery, and open violence, which partly beset us at home, and partly pursue us abroad. Amidst these difficulties, must not man be most miserable, who is half dead while he lives, and is dispirited and alarmed as though he had a sword perpetually applied to his neck? You will say that these things happen seldom, or certainly not always, nor to every man, but never all at once. I grant it; but as we are admonished by the examples of others, that it is possible for them to happen also to us, and that we have no more claim to exemption from them than others, we must unavoidably dread them as events that we may expect. What can you imagine more calamitous than such a dread? Besides, it is an insult to God to say that he has exposed man, the noblest of his creatures, to the blindness and temerity of fortune. But here I intend to speak only of the misery which man must feel, if he be subject to the dominion of fortune.

XI. On the contrary, when this light of Divine providence has once shined on a pious man, he is relieved and delivered not only from the extreme anxiety and dread with which he was previously oppressed, but also from all care. For, as he justly dreads fortune, so he ventures securely to commit himself to God. This, I say, is his consolation, to apprehend that his heavenly Father restrains all things by his power, governs all things by his will, and regulates all things by his wisdom, in such a manner, that nothing can happen but by his appointment; moreover, that God has taken him under his protection, and committed him to the care of angels, so that he can sustain no injury from water, or fire, or sword, any further than the Divine Governor may be pleased to permit. For thus sings the Psalmist: "Surely he shall deliver thee from the snare of the fowler, and from the noisome pestilence. He shall cover thee with his feathers, and under his wings shalt thou trust: his truth shall be thy shield and buckler. Thou shalt not be afraid for the terror by night; nor for the arrow that flieth by day; nor for the pestilence that walketh in darkness; nor for the destruction that wasteth at noonday." (*g*) Hence also proceeds that confidence of glorying in the saints: "The Lord is on my side; I will not fear what man can do unto me. The Lord is the strength of my life; of whom shall I be afraid? Though a host should encamp against me — though I walk through the valley of the shadow of death, I will fear no evil." (*h*) How is it that their security remains unshaken, while the world appears to be revolving at random, but because they know that the Lord is universally operative, and confide in his operations as beneficial to them? Now, when their safety is attacked, either by the devil or by wicked men, if they were not supported by the recollection and contemplation of providence, they must necessarily and immediately faint. But when they recollect, that the devil and the whole army of the wicked are in every respect so restrained by the Divine power, that they can neither conceive of any hostility against us, nor, after having conceived it, form a plan for its accomplishment, nor even move a finger towards the execution of such plan, any further than he has permitted, and even commanded them; and that they are not only bound by his chains, but also compelled to do him service, — they have an abundant source of consolation. For as it belongs to the Lord to arm their fury, and to direct it to whatever objects he pleases, so it also belongs to him to fix its limits, that they may not enjoy an unbounded triumph according to their own wills. Established in this persuasion, Paul determined his journey in one place by the permission of God, which in another he had declared was prevented by Satan. (*i*) If he had only said that Satan was the obstacle, he would have appeared to attribute too much power to him, as though he were able to subvert the purposes of God; but when he states God to be the arbiter, on whose permission all journeys depend, he at the same time shows, that Satan, with all his machinations, can effect nothing but by his permission. For the same reason, David, on account of the various and constant vicissitudes of life, betakes himself to this asylum: "My times are in thy hand." (*j*) He might have mentioned either the course of life, or *time*, in the singular number; but by the word *times* he intended to express, that, however unstable the condition of men may be, all the vicissitudes which take place are under the government of God. For which reason Rezin and the king of Israel, when, after the junction of their forces for the destruction of Judah, they resembled firebrands kindled to consume and ruin the land, are called by the Prophet

(*g*) Psalm xci. 3—6.
(*h*) Psalm cxviii. 6; xxvii. 1, 3; xxiii. 4.
(*i*) 1 Cor. xvi. 7. 1 Thes. ii. 18.
(*j*) Psalm xxxi. 15.

"smoking firebrands," (*k*) which can do nothing but emit a little smoke. Thus Pharaoh, when his riches, his strength, and the multitude of his forces, rendered him formidable to all, is himself compared to a sea-monster, and his forces to fishes. (*l*) Therefore God denounces that he will take both the captain and his army with his hook, and draw them whither he pleases. Finally, to dwell no longer on this part of the subject, you will easily perceive, on examination, that ignorance of providence is the greatest of miseries, but that the knowledge of it is attended with the highest felicity.

XII. On the doctrine of Divine providence, as far as it may conduce to the solid instruction and consolation of the faithful, (for to satisfy a vain curiosity is neither possible nor desirable,) enough would now have been said, were it not for a difficulty arising from a few passages, which apparently imply, in opposition to what has been stated, that the counsel of God is not firm and stable, but liable to change according to the situation of sublunary affairs. In the first place, there are several instances in which repentance is attributed to God; as, that he repented of having created man, (*m*) and of having exalted Saul to the kingdom; (*n*) and that he will repent of the evil which he had determined to inflict on his people, as soon as he shall have perceived their conversion. (*o*) In the next place, we read of the abrogation of some of his decrees. By Jonah he declared to the Ninevites, (*p*) that, after the lapse of forty days, Nineveh should be destroyed; but their penitence afterwards obtained from him a more merciful sentence. By the mouth of Isaiah he denounced death to Hezekiah; (*q*) which the prayers and tears of that monarch moved him to defer. (*r*) Hence many persons argue, that God has not fixed the affairs of men by an eternal decree; but that every year, day, and hour, he decrees one thing or another, according to the respective merits of each individual, or to his own ideas of equity and justice. With regard to repentance, we must not admit that it can happen to God, any more than ignorance, or error, or impotence. For if no man knowingly and willingly lays himself under the necessity of repentance, we cannot attribute repentance to God, without saying either that he is ignorant of the future, or that he cannot avoid it, or that he precipitately and inconsiderately adopts a resolution, of which he immediately repents. But that is so far from the meaning of the Holy Spirit, that in the very mention of repentance, he denies that it can belong to God, because " he is not a man, that he should repent." (*s*) And it must be remarked, that

(*k*) Isaiah vii. 4.
(*l*) Ezek. xxix. 3, 4.
(*m*) Gen. vi. 6.
(*n*) 1 Sam. xv. 11.
(*o*) Jer. xviii. 8.
(*p*) Jonah iii. 4, 10.
(*q*) Isaiah xxxviii. 1, 5.
(*r*) 2 Kings xx. 1, 5.
(*s*) 1 Sam. xv. 29.

both these points are so connected in the same chapter, that a comparison fully reconciles the apparent inconsistency. Where it is said that God repented of having created Saul king, the change declared to have taken place is figurative. It is almost immediately added, that "The strength of Israel will not lie nor repent; for he is not a man, that he should repent;"(*t*) in which, without any figure, his immutability is plainly asserted. It is certain, therefore, that the ordination of God in the administration of human affairs, is perpetual, and superior to all repentance. And to place his constancy beyond all doubt, even his adversaries have been constrained to attest it. For Balaam, notwithstanding his reluctance, was obliged to break out into the following exclamation: "God is not a man, that he should lie; neither the son of man, that he should repent: hath he said, and shall he not do it? or hath he spoken, and shall he not make it good?"(*u*)

XIII. How, then, it will be inquired, is the term *repentance* to be understood, when attributed to God? I reply, in the same manner as all the other forms of expression, which describe God to us after the manner of men. For, since our infirmity cannot reach his sublimity, the description of him which is given to us, in order that we may understand it, must be lowered to the level of our capacity. His method of lowering it, is to represent himself to us, not as he is in himself, but according to our perception of him. Though he is free from all perturbation of mind, he declares that he is angry with sinners. (*v*) As, therefore, when we hear that God is angry, we ought not to imagine any commotion in him, but rather to consider this expression as borrowed from our perception, because God carries the appearance of one who is very angry, whenever he executes judgment,—so neither by the term *repentance* ought we to understand any thing but a change of actions; because men are accustomed to express their dissatisfaction with themselves by changing their actions. Since every change among men, therefore, is a correction of that which displeases them, and correction proceeds from repentance, therefore the term *repentance* is used to signify that God makes a change in his works. Yet, at the same time, there is no alteration in his counsel or his will, nor any change in his affections; but how sudden soever the variation may appear to the eyes of men, he perpetually and regularly prosecutes what he has foreseen, approved, and decreed from eternity.

XIV. Nor does the Sacred History, when it records the remission of the destruction which had just been denounced against the Ninevites, and the prolongation of the life of Hezekiah

(*t*) 1 Sam. xv. 29.   (*u*) Numb. xxiii. 19.   (*v*) Psalm vii. 11.

after he had been threatened with death, prove that there was any abrogation of the Divine decrees. Persons who thus understand it, are deceived in their ideas of the threatenings; which, though expressed in the form of simple declarations, yet, as the event shows, contain in them a tacit condition. For why did God send Jonah to the Ninevites, to predict the ruin of their city? Why did he, by the mouth of Isaiah, warn Hezekiah of death? He could have destroyed both them and him, without previously announcing their end. He had some other object in view, therefore, than to forewarn them of their death, and to give them a distant prospect of its approach. And that was not to destroy them, but to reform them, that they might not be destroyed. Therefore the prediction of Jonah, that after forty days Nineveh should fall, was uttered to prevent its fall. Hezekiah was deprived of the hope of a longer life, in order that he might obtain a prolongation of it in answer to his prayers. Now, who does not see, that the Lord, by such denunciations as these, intended to arouse to repentance the persons whom he thus alarmed, that they might escape the judgment which their sins had deserved? If this be admitted, the nature of the circumstances leads to the conclusion, that we must understand a tacit condition implied in the simple denunciation. This is also confirmed by similar examples. The Lord, reprehending king Abimelech for having deprived Abraham of his wife, uses these words: — "Behold, thou art but a dead man, for the woman which thou hast taken; for she is a man's wife." But after Abimelech has excused himself, the Lord speaks in this manner: "Restore the man his wife; for he is a prophet, and he shall pray for thee, and thou shalt live; and if thou restore her not, know thou that thou shalt surely die, thou, and all that are thine." (*w*) You see how, by the first declaration, God terrifies his mind, to dispose him to make satisfaction: but in the next, he makes an explicit declaration of his will. Since other passages are to be explained in a similar manner, you must not infer that there is any abrogation of a prior purpose of the Lord, because he may have annulled some former declarations. For God rather prepares the way for his eternal ordination, when, by a denunciation of punishment, he calls to repentance those whom he designs to spare, than makes any variation in his will, or even in his declarations, except that he does not syllabically express what, nevertheless, is easily understood. For that assertion of Isaiah must remain true: "The Lord of hosts hath purposed, and who shall disannul it? and his hand is stretched out, and who shall turn it back?" (*x*)

(*w*) Gen. xx. 3, 7. (*x*) Isaiah xiv. 27.

CHAPTER XVIII.

GOD USES THE AGENCY OF THE IMPIOUS, AND INCLINES THEIR MINDS TO EXECUTE HIS JUDGMENTS, YET WITHOUT THE LEAST STAIN OF HIS PERFECT PURITY.

A QUESTION of greater difficulty arises from other passages, where God is said to incline or draw, according to his own pleasure, Satan himself and all the reprobate. For the carnal understanding scarcely comprehends how he, acting by their means, contracts no defilement from their criminality, and, even in operations common to himself and them, is free from every fault, and yet righteously condemns those whose ministry he uses. Hence was invented the distinction between *doing* and *permitting*; because to many persons this has appeared an inexplicable difficulty, that Satan and all the impious are subject to the power and government of God, so that he directs their malice to whatever end he pleases, and uses their crimes for the execution of his judgments. The modesty of those who are alarmed at the appearance of absurdity, might perhaps be excusable, if they did not attempt to vindicate the Divine justice from all accusation by a pretence utterly destitute of any foundation in truth. They consider it absurd that a man should be blinded by the will and command of God, and afterwards be punished for his blindness. They therefore evade the difficulty, by alleging that it happens only by the permission, and not by the will of God; but God himself, by the most unequivocal declarations, rejects this subterfuge. That men, however, can effect nothing but by the secret will of God, and can deliberate on nothing but what he has previously decreed, and determines by his secret direction, is proved by express and innumerable testimonies. What we have before cited from the Psalmist, that "God hath done whatsoever he hath pleased," (*y*) undoubtedly pertains to all the actions of men. If God be the certain arbiter of war and peace, as is there affirmed, and that without any exception, who will venture to assert, that he remains ignorant and unconcerned respecting men, while they are actuated by the blind influence of chance? But this subject will be better elucidated by particular examples. From the first chapter of Job we know that Satan presents himself before God to receive his commands, as well as the angels, who yield a spontaneous obedience. It is, indeed,

(*y*) Psalm cxv. 3.

in a different manner, and for a different end; yet he cannot attempt any thing but by the Divine will. Although he seems to obtain only a bare permission to afflict that holy man, yet, since this sentence is true, "The Lord gave, and the Lord hath taken away,"(z) we conclude that God was the author of that trial, of which Satan and mischievous robbers and assassins were the immediate agents. Satan endeavours to drive him by desperation into madness. The Sabeans, in a predatory incursion, cruelly and wickedly seize upon property not their own. Job acknowledges that he was stripped of all his wealth, and reduced to poverty, because such was the will of God. Therefore, whatever is attempted by men, or by Satan himself, God still holds the helm, to direct all their attempts to the execution of his judgments. God intends the deception of that perfidious king Ahab; the devil offers his service for that purpose; he is sent with a positive commission to be a lying spirit in the mouth of all the prophets.(a) If the blinding and infatuation of Ahab be a Divine judgment, the pretence of bare permission disappears. For it would be ridiculous for a judge merely to permit, without decreeing what should be done, and commanding his officers to execute it. The Jews designed to destroy Christ; Pilate and his soldiers complied with their outrageous violence; yet the disciples, in a solemn prayer, confess that all the impious did nothing but what "the hand and the counsel of God determined before to be done;"(b) agreeably to what Peter had already preached, that he was "delivered by the determinate counsel and foreknowledge of God," that he might be "crucified and slain."(c) As though he had said that God, who saw every thing from the beginning, with a clear knowledge and determined will, appointed what the Jews executed; as he mentions in another place: "Those things which God before had showed by the mouth of all his prophets, that Christ should suffer, he hath so fulfilled."(d) Absalom, defiling his father's bed with incest, perpetrated a detestable crime; yet God pronounces that this was his work; for his words are, "Thou didst it secretly; but I will do this thing before all Israel, and before the sun."(e) Whatever cruelty the Chaldeans exercised in Judea, Jeremiah pronounces to be the work of God;(f) for which reason Nebuchadnezzar is called the servant of God. God frequently proclaims, that the impious are excited to war by his hissing, by the sound of his trumpet, by his influence, and by his command: he calls the Assyrian the rod of his anger, and the staff which he moves with his hand. The destruction

(z) Job i. 21. (a) 1 Kings xxii. 20—23. (b) Acts iv. 28. (c) Acts ii. 23
(d) Acts iii. 18. (e) 2 Sam. xii. 12; xvi. 22. (f) Jer. l. 25.

of the holy city and the ruin of the temple he calls his own work. (*g*) David, not murmuring against God, but acknowledging him to be a righteous Judge, confesses the maledictions of Shimei to proceed from his command. "The Lord," says he, "hath said unto him, Curse." (*h*) It often occurs in the Sacred History, that whatever comes to pass proceeds from the Lord; as the defection of the ten tribes, (*i*) the death of the sons of Eli, (*j*) and many events of a similar kind. Those who are but moderately acquainted with the Scriptures will perceive that, for the sake of brevity, out of a great number of testimonies, I have produced only a few; which, nevertheless, abundantly evince how nugatory and insipid it is, instead of the providence of God, to substitute a bare permission; as though God were sitting in a watchtower, expecting fortuitous events, and so his decisions were dependent on the will of men.

II. With respect to his secret influences, the declaration of Solomon concerning the heart of a king, that it is inclined hither or thither according to the Divine will, (*k*) certainly extends to the whole human race, and is as much as though he had said, that whatever conceptions we form in our minds, they are directed by the secret inspiration of God. And certainly, if he did not operate internally on the human mind, there would be no propriety in asserting, that he causes "the wisdom of the wise to perish, and the understanding of the prudent to be hid; that he poureth contempt upon princes, and causeth them to wander in the wilderness, where there is no way." (*l*) And to this alludes, what we frequently read, that men are timorous, as their hearts are possessed with his fear. (*m*) Thus David departed from the camp of Saul, without the knowledge of any one; "because a deep sleep from the Lord was fallen upon them all." (*n*) But nothing can be desired more explicit than his frequent declarations, that he blinds the minds of men, strikes them with giddiness, inebriates them with the spirit of slumber, fills them with infatuation, and hardens their hearts. (*o*) These passages also many persons refer to permission, as though, in abandoning the reprobate, God permitted them to be blinded by Satan. But that solution is too frivolous, since the Holy Spirit expressly declares that their blindness and infatuation are inflicted by the righteous judgment of God. He is said to have caused the obduracy of Pharaoh's heart, and also to have aggravated and confirmed it. Some elude the force of these expressions with

---

(*g*) Isaiah v. 26; x. 5; xix. 25.   (*h*) 2 Sam. xvi. 10.   (*i*) 1 Kings xi. 31.
(*j*) 1 Sam. ii. 34.   (*k*) Prov. xxi. 1.
(*l*) Isaiah xxix. 14. Psalm cvii. 40. Ezek. vii. 26.   (*m*) Lev. xxvi. 36.
(*n*) 1 Sam. xxvi. 12.   (*o*) Rom. i. 28; xi. 8. Exod. viii. 15.

a foolish cavil — that, since Pharaoh himself is elsewhere said to have hardened his own heart, his own will is stated as the cause of his obduracy; as though these two things were at all incompatible with each other, that man should be actuated by God, and yet at the same time be active himself. But I retort on them their own objection; for if *hardening* denotes a bare permission, Pharaoh cannot properly be charged with being the cause of his own obstinacy. Now, how weak and insipid would be such an interpretation, as though Pharaoh only permitted himself to be hardened! Besides, the Scripture cuts off all occasion for such cavils. God says, " I will harden his heart." (*p*) So, also, Moses says, concerning the inhabitants of Canaan, that they marched forth to battle, because the Lord had hardened their hearts; (*q*) which is likewise repeated by another Prophet — " He turned their hearts to hate his people." (*r*) Thus, also, in Isaiah, he declares he will " send the Assyrian against a hypocritical nation, and will give him a charge to take the spoil, and to take the prey;" (*s*) not that he meant to teach impious and refractory men a voluntary obedience, but because he would incline them to execute his judgments, just as if they had his commands engraven on their minds. Hence it appears that they were impelled by the positive appointment of God. I grant, indeed, that God often actuates the reprobate by the interposition of Satan; but in such a manner that Satan himself acts his part by the Divine impulse, and proceeds to the extent of the Divine appointment. Saul was disturbed by an evil spirit; but it is said to be " from the Lord;" (*t*) to teach us that Saul's madness proceeded from the righteous vengeance of God. Satan is also said to blind " the minds of them which believe not;" (*u*) but the strength of the delusion proceeds from God himself, " that they should believe a lie, who believe not the truth." (*v*) According to one view of the subject, it is said, " If the prophet be deceived when he hath spoken a thing, I the Lord have deceived that prophet." (*w*) But, according to another, God is said himself to " give men over to a reprobate mind," (*x*) and to the vilest lusts; because he is the principal author of his own righteous vengeance, and Satan is only the dispenser of it. But as we must discuss this subject again in the second book, where we shall treat of the freedom or slavery of the human will, I think I have now said, in a brief manner, as much as the occasion required. The whole may be summed up thus; that, as the will of God is said to be the cause of all things, his providence is established as the governor in all the counsels and works of

(*p*) Exod. iv. 21.
(*q*) Deut. ii. 30. Joshua xi. 20.
(*r*) Psalm cv. 25.
(*s*) Isaiah x. 6.
(*t*) 1 Sam. xvi. 14.
(*u*) 2 Cor. iv. 4.
(*v*) 2 Thess. ii. 10—12
(*w*) Ezek. xiv. 9.
(*x*) Rom. i. 28.

men, so that it not only exerts its power in the elect, who are influenced by the Holy Spirit, but also compels the compliance of the reprobate.

III. But, as I have hitherto only recited such things as are delivered without any obscurity or ambiguity in the Scriptures, let persons who hesitate not to brand with ignominy those oracles of heaven, beware what kind of opposition they make. For, if they pretend ignorance, with a desire to be commended for their modesty, what greater instance of pride can be conceived, than to oppose one little word to the authority of God! as, "It appears otherwise to me," or, "I would rather not meddle with this subject." But if they openly censure, what will they gain by their puny attempts against heaven? Their petulance, indeed, is no novelty; for in all ages there have been impious and profane men, who have virulently opposed this doctrine. But they shall feel the truth of what the Spirit long ago declared by the mouth of David, that God " is clear when he judgeth." (*y*) David obliquely hints at the madness of men who display such excessive presumption amidst their insignificance, as not only to dispute against God, but to arrogate to themselves the power of condemning him. In the mean time, he briefly suggests, that God is unaffected by all the blasphemies which they discharge against heaven, but that he dissipates the mists of calumny, and illustriously displays his righteousness; our faith, also, being founded on the Divine word, (*z*) and therefore, superior to all the world, from its exaltation looks down with contempt upon those mists. For their first objection, that, if nothing happens but by the will of God, he has in him two contrary wills, because he decrees in his secret counsel what he has publicly prohibited in his law, is easily refuted. But before I reply, I wish the reader again to be apprized, that this cavil is directed, not against me, but against the Holy Spirit, who dictated to the pious Job this confession, that what had befallen him had happened according to the Divine will: when he had been plundered by banditti, he acknowledged in their injuries the righteous scourge of God. (*a*) What says the Scripture in another case? "They," the sons of Eli, "hearkened not unto the voice of their father, because the Lord would slay them." (*b*) The Psalmist also exclaims, that "God," who "is in the heavens, hath done whatsoever he hath pleased." (*c*) And now I have sufficiently proved, that God is called the author of all those things, which, according to the system of these censors, happen only by his uninfluential permission. He declares that he

(*y*) Psalm li. 4. (*z*) 1 John v. 4. (*a*) Job i. 21.
(*b*) 1 Sam. ii. 25. (*c*) Psalm cxv. 3.

creates light and darkness, that he forms good and evil, (*d*) and that no evil occurs, which he has not performed. Let them say, then, whether he exercises his judgments voluntarily or involuntarily. But as Moses suggests, that he who is killed by the fortuitous fall of an axe, is delivered by God to the stroke, (*e*) so in the Acts, the whole church asserts that Herod and Pilate conspired to do what the hand and the counsel of God had predetermined. (*f*) And indeed, unless the crucifixion of Christ was according to the will of God, what becomes of our redemption? Yet the will of God is neither repugnant to itself, nor subject to change, nor chargeable with pretending to dislike what it approves; but whilst in him it is uniform and simple, it wears to us the appearance of variety; because the weakness of our understanding comprehends not how the same thing may be in different respects both agreeable to his will, and contrary to it. Paul, after having said that the vocation of the Gentiles was a hidden mystery, adds, that it contained a manifestation of the manifold wisdom of God. (*g*) Now, because, through the dulness of our capacity, the Divine wisdom appears to us manifold, (or multiform, as it has been translated by an ancient interpreter,) shall we therefore dream of any vanity in God himself, as though his counsels were mutable, or his thoughts contradictory to each other? Rather, while we comprehend not how God intends that to be done, the doing of which he forbids, let us remember our imbecility, and at the same time consider, that the light which he inhabits, is justly called inaccessible, (*h*) because it is overspread with impenetrable darkness. Therefore all pious and modest men will easily acquiesce in this opinion of Augustine: "That a man may sometimes choose, with a good intention, that which is not agreeable to the will of God; as, if a good son wishes his father to live, whilst God determines that he shall die. It is also possible for a man to will with a bad design, what God wills with a good one; as, if a bad son wishes his father to die, which is also the will of God. Now, the former wishes what is not agreeable, the latter what is agreeable to the Divine will. And yet the filial affection of the former is more consonant to the righteous will of God, than the want of natural affection in the latter, though it accords with his secret design. So great is the difference between what belongs to the human will, and what to the Divine, and between the ends to which the will of every one is to be referred, for approbation or censure. For God fulfils his righteous will by the wicked wills of wicked men." This writer had just before said, that the apostate angels, and all

---

(*d*) Isaiah xlv. 7. Amos iii. 6. (*e*) Deut. xix. 5. (*f*) Acts iv. 28.
(*g*) Ephes. iii. 9, 10. (*h*) 1 Tim. vi. 16.

the reprobate, in their defection, acted, as far as respected themselves, in direct opposition to the Divine will; but that this was not possible with respect to the Divine omnipotence; because, while they are opposing the will of God, his will is accomplished concerning them. Whence he exclaims, "The works of the Lord are great, prepared according to all his determinations;" (*i*) so that, in a wonderful and ineffable manner, that is not done without his will which yet is contrary to his will; because it would not be done if he did not permit it; and this permission is not involuntary, but voluntary; nor would his goodness permit the perpetration of any evil, unless his omnipotence were able even from that evil to educe good."

IV. In the same manner we answer, or rather annihilate, another objection — that, if God not only uses the agency of the impious, but governs their designs and affections, he is the author of all crimes; and therefore men are undeservedly condemned, if they execute what God has decreed, because they obey his will. For his will is improperly confounded with his precept, between which innumerable examples evince the difference to be very great. For although, when Absalom defiled the wives of his father, it was the will of God by this disgrace to punish the adultery of David, (*k*) he did not therefore command that abandoned son to commit incest, unless perhaps with respect to David, as he speaks of the reproaches of Shimei. (*l*) For when he confesses Shimei's maledictions to proceed from the Divine command, he by no means commends his obedience, as though that impudent and worthless man were fulfilling a Divine precept; but acknowledging his tongue as the scourge of God, he patiently submits to the chastisement. Let it be remembered, that whilst God by means of the impious fulfils his secret decrees, they are not excusable, as though they were obedient to his precepts, which they wantonly and intentionally violate. The direction of the perverse actions of men, by the secret providence of God, is illustriously exemplified in the election of Jeroboam to the regal dignity. (*m*) The temerity and infatuation of the people in this proceeding are severely condemned, (*n*) because they perverted the order established by God, and perfidiously revolted from the family of David; and yet we know that this event was agreeable to the Divine will. Whence there is an appearance of contradiction also in the language of Hosea; for in one place God complains that the erection of that kingdom was without his knowledge and against his will; but in another declares that he gave Jeroboam to be a king in his anger. (*o*) How can these things be reconciled, that Jeroboam

(*i*) Psalm cxi. 2. (*l*) 2 Sam. xvi. 10. (*n*) Hosea viii. 4.
(*k*) 2 Sam. xvi. 22. (*m*) 1 Kings xii. 20. (*o*) Hosea xiii. 11.

did not reign by the will of God, and yet that God appointed him to be king? Why, thus: because neither could the people revolt from the family of David, without shaking off the yoke which God had imposed upon them; nor yet was God deprived of the liberty of thus punishing the ingratitude of Solomon. We see, then, how God, while he hates perfidy, yet righteously and with a different design decrees the defection; whence also Jeroboam is, beyond all expectation, constrained by the holy unction to assume the regal office. In the same manner, the Sacred History relates, that God raised up an enemy, to deprive the son of Solomon of part of the kingdom. (*p*) Let the reader diligently consider both these things: because it had pleased God that the people should be under the government of one king, their division into two parts was contrary to his will; and yet from his will the schism first originated. For certainly since a Prophet, both by a prediction and by the ceremony of unction, excited a hope of succeeding to the kingdom, in the mind of Jeroboam, who before entertained not a thought of such an event, this could not be done, either without the knowledge, or against the will, of God, who commanded it to be done; and yet the rebellion of the people is justly condemned, because, in opposition to the Divine will, they revolted from the posterity of David. Thus, also, it is afterwards subjoined, that "the cause" of the haughty contempt of the people manifested by Rehoboam "was of God, that the Lord might perform his word, which he spake by the hand of Ahijah" his servant. (*q*) See how the sacred union is divided, in opposition to the will of God, and yet by his will the ten tribes are alienated from the son of Solomon. Let us add another similar example, where, with the consent, and even by the assistance of the people, the sons of Ahab are massacred, and all his posterity exterminated. (*r*) Jehu, indeed, truly observed that "there had fallen unto the earth nothing of the word of the Lord," but that he had "done that which he spake by his servant Elijah." And yet he justly reprehends the citizens of Samaria for having lent their assistance. "Are ye righteous?" says he; "behold, I conspired against my master, and slew him; but who slew all these?" If I am not deceived, I have now clearly explained how the same act displays the criminality of men and the justice of God. And to modest minds this answer of Augustine will always be sufficient: "Since God delivered Christ, and Christ delivered his own body, and Judas delivered the Lord, why, in this delivery, is God righteous and man guilty? Because in the same act, they acted not from

(*p*) 1 Kings xi. 23.   (*q*) 1 Kings xii. 15. 2 Chron. x. 15.
(*r*) 2 Kings x. 7, 8, 9, 10.

the same cause." But if any persons find greater difficulty in what we now assert, that there is no consent between God and man, in cases where man by his righteous influence commits unlawful actions, let them remember what is advanced by Augustine in another place: "Who can but tremble at those judgments, when God does even in the hearts of the wicked whatsoever he pleases, and yet renders to them according to their demerits?" And certainly it would no more be right to attribute to God the blame of the perfidy of Judas, because he decreed the delivery of his Son, and actually delivered him to death, than to transfer to Judas the praise of redemption. Therefore the same writer elsewhere informs us, that in this scrutiny God inquires, not what men could have done, nor what they have done, but what they intended to do, that he may take cognizance of their design and their will. Let those to whom there appears any harshness in this procedure, consider a little how far their obstinacy is tolerable, while they reject a truth which is attested by plain testimonies of Scripture, because it exceeds their comprehension, and condemn the publication of those things which God, unless he had known that the knowledge of them would be useful, would never have commanded to be taught by his Prophets and Apostles. For our wisdom ought to consist in embracing with gentle docility, and without any exception, all that is delivered in the sacred Scriptures. But those who oppose this doctrine with less modesty and greater violence, since it is evident that their opposition is against God, are unworthy of a longer refutation.

INSTITUTES

OF THE

CHRISTIAN RELIGION.

BOOK II.

ON THE KNOWLEDGE OF GOD THE REDEEMER IN CHRIST, WHICH WAS REVEALED FIRST TO THE FATHERS UNDER THE LAW, AND SINCE TO US IN THE GOSPEL.

ARGUMENT.

The discussion of the first part of the Apostolic Creed, on the knowledge of God the Creator, being finished, is followed by another, on the knowledge of God the Redeemer in Christ, which is the subject of this Second Book.

It treats, first, of the occasion of redemption, that is, the fall of Adam; secondly, of the redemption itself. The former of these subjects occupies the first five chapters; the remaining ones are assigned to the latter.

On the occasion of redemption, it treats, not only of the fall in general, but also of its effects in particular; that is, of original sin, the slavery of the will, the universal corruption of human nature, the operation of God in the hearts of men—Chap. I.—IV., to which is subjoined a refutation of the objections commonly adduced in defence of free will—Chap. V.

The discourse on redemption may be divided into five principal parts. It shows,

1. In whom salvation must be sought by lost man, that is, in Christ—Chap. VI.

2. How Christ has been manifested to the world; which has been in

two ways; first, under the law (which introduces an explanation of the Decalogue, and a discussion of some other things relative to the Law)—Chap. VII. VIII.; secondly, under the Gospel, which leads to a statement of the similarity and difference of the two Testaments —Chap. IX.—XI.

3. What kind of a being it was necessary for Christ to be, in order to his fulfilment of the office of a Mediator; that is, God and man in one person—Chap. XII.—XIV.

4. The end of his mission from the Father into the world—Chap. XV., which explains his prophetical, regal, and sacerdotal offices.

5. The methods or steps by which he fulfilled the part of a Redeemer, to procure our salvation—Chap. XVI.; which discusses the articles relating to his crucifixion, death, burial, descent into hell, resurrection, ascension to heaven, session at the right hand of the Father, and the benefits arising from this doctrine. Then follows Chap. XVII., a solution of the question, Whether Christ merited for us the grace of God and salvation.

CHAPTER I.

THE FALL AND DEFECTION OF ADAM THE CAUSE OF THE CURSE INFLICTED ON ALL MANKIND, AND OF THEIR DEGENERACY FROM THEIR PRIMITIVE CONDITION. THE DOCTRINE OF ORIGINAL SIN.

There is much reason in the old adage, which so strongly recommends to man the knowledge of himself. For if it be thought disgraceful to be ignorant of whatever relates to the conduct of human life, ignorance of ourselves is much more shameful, which causes us, in deliberating on subjects of importance, to grope our way in miserable obscurity, or even in total darkness. But in proportion to the utility of this precept ought to be our caution not to make a preposterous use of it; as we see some philosophers have done. For while they exhort man to the knowledge of himself, the end they propose is, that he may not remain ignorant of his own dignity and excellence: nor do they wish him to contemplate in himself any thing but what may swell him with vain confidence, and inflate him with pride. But the knowledge of ourselves consists, first, in considering what was bestowed on us at our creation, and the favours we continually receive from the Divine benignity, that we may know how great the excellence of our nature would have been, if it had retained its integrity; yet, at the same time, recollecting that we have nothing properly our own, may feel our precarious tenure of all that God has conferred on us, so as always to place our dependence upon him. Secondly, we should contemplate our miserable condition since the fall of Adam, the sense of which tends to destroy all boasting and confidence, to overwhelm us with shame, and to fill us with real humility. For as God, at the beginning, formed us after his own image, that he might elevate our minds both to the practice of virtue, and to the contemplation of eternal life, so, to prevent the great excellence of our species, which distinguishes us from the brutes, from being buried in sottish indolence, it is worthy of observation, that the design of our being endued with reason and intelligence is, that, leading a holy and virtuous life, we may aspire to the mark set before us of a blessed immortality. But we cannot think upon that primeval dignity, without having our attention immediately called to the melancholy spectacle of our disgrace and ignominy, since in the person of the first man we are fallen from our original condition. Hence arise disapprobation and abhorrence of ourselves, and real humility; and we are inflamed with fresh ardour to seek after God, to recover in him those excellences of which we find ourselves utterly destitute.

II. This is what the truth of God directs us to seek in the examination of ourselves: it requires a knowledge that will abstract us from all confidence in our own ability, deprive us of every cause of boasting, and reduce us to submission. We must observe this rule, if we wish to reach the proper point of knowledge and action. I am aware of the superior plausibility of that opinion, which invites us rather to a consideration of our goodness, than to a view of our miserable poverty and ignominy, which ought to overwhelm us with shame. For there is nothing more desired by the human mind than soothing flatteries; and therefore, it listens with extreme credulity, to hear its excellences magnified. Wherefore it is the less wonderful that the majority of mankind have fallen into such a pernicious error. For, an immoderate self-love being innate in all men, they readily persuade themselves that there is nothing in them which justly deserves to be an object of aversion. Thus, without any extraneous support, this very false opinion, that man has in himself sufficient ability to insure his own virtue and happiness, generally prevails. But if some prefer more modest sentiments, though they concede something to God, in order to avoid the appearance of arrogating every thing to themselves, yet they make such a distribution, that the principal cause of boasting and confidence always remains with them. If they hear any discourse that flatters the pride already operating spontaneously in their hearts, nothing can gratify them more. Therefore every one who in his preaching has kindly extolled the excellence of human nature, has received great applause from almost all ages. But such a commendation of human excellence as teaches man to be satisfied with himself, only enamours him of his own amiableness, and thus produces an illusion which involves those who assent to it in most dreadful perdition. For to what purpose is it for us, relying on every vain confidence, to deliberate, to determine, and to attempt things which we think tend to our advantage, and in our first efforts, to find ourselves destitute of sound understanding and true virtue, yet securely to proceed, till we fall into destruction? But this must be the fate of all who confide in the efficacy of their own virtue. Whosoever, therefore, attends to such teachers as amuse us with a mere exhibition of our virtues, will make no progress in the knowledge of himself, but will be absorbed in the most pernicious ignorance.

III. Therefore, whilst the truth of God agrees in this point with the common consent of all mankind, that the second branch of wisdom consists in the knowledge of ourselves, yet with respect to the knowledge itself there is no small disagreement. For, according to carnal apprehension, a man is thought to be well acquainted with himself, when, confiding in his own understanding and integrity, he assumes a presumptuous boldness, incites himself to the duties of virtue, and, declaring war against vice, uses his most strenuous endeavours to adhere to what is fair and honourable. But he, who inspects and examines himself by the rule of the Divine judgment, finds nothing that can raise his mind to a genuine confidence; and the more fully he has examined himself, the greater is his dejection; till, entirely discarding all confidence, he leaves himself no ability for the proper conduct of his life. Yet it is not the will of God that we should forget the primitive dignity conferred by him on our father Adam, which ought justly to awaken us to the pursuit of righteousness and goodness. For we cannot reflect on our original condition, and on the end of our creation, without being excited to meditate on immortality, and to aspire after the kingdom of God. But this reflection is so far from elating us with pride, that it rather produces humility. For what is that original condition? That from which we are fallen. What is that end of our creation? That from which we are wholly departed; so that we should lament the miseries of our present state, and in the midst of our lamentation, aspire after the dignity which we have lost.

Now, when we say that man should behold in himself nothing that might elate him with pride, we mean that there is nothing in him in the confidence of which he ought to be proud. Wherefore we may divide the knowledge man ought to have of himself into these two parts. First, he should consider the end of his being created and endued with such estimable gifts; a reflection which may excite him to the consideration of Divine worship, and of a future life. Secondly, he should examine his own ability, or rather his want of ability, the view of which may confound and almost annihilate him. The former consideration is adapted to acquaint him with his duty, the latter with his power to perform it. We shall treat of them both in regular order.

IV. But, since it could not have been a trivial offence, but must have been a detestable crime, that was so severely punished by God, we must consider the nature of Adam's sin, which kindled the dreadful flame of Divine wrath against the whole human race. The vulgar opinion concerning the intemperance of gluttony is quite puerile; as though the sum and substance of all virtues consisted in an abstinence from one particular kind of fruit, when there were diffused on every side all the delights which could possibly be desired, and the happy fecundity of the earth afforded an abundance and variety of dainties. We must therefore look further, because the prohibition of the tree of knowledge of good and evil was a test of obedience, that Adam might prove his willing submission to the Divine government. And the name itself shows that the precept was given for no other purpose than that he might be contented with his condition, and not aim with criminal cupidity at any higher. But the promise which authorized him to expect eternal life, as long as he should eat of the tree of life, and, on the other hand, the dreadful denunciation of death, as soon as he should taste of the tree of knowledge of good and evil, were calculated for the probation and exercise of his faith. Hence it is easy to infer by what means Adam provoked the wrath of God against him. Augustine, indeed, properly observes, that pride was the first of all evils; because, if ambition had not elated man beyond what was lawful and right, he might have continued in his honourable situation. But we may obtain a more complete definition from the nature of the temptation as described by Moses. For as the woman, by the subtlety of the serpent, was seduced to discredit the word of God, it is evident that the fall commenced in disobedience. This is also confirmed by Paul, who states that all men were ruined by the disobedience of one. (*s*) But it is also to be observed, that when the first man rebelled against the government of God, he

(*s*) Rom. v. 19.

not only was ensnared by the allurements of Satan, but despised the truth, and turned aside to falsehood. And there certainly can be no reverence of God left, where his word is contemned; for we preserve a sense of his majesty and the purity of his worship, no longer than we implicitly attend to his voice. Infidelity, therefore, was the root of that defection. But hence sprang ambition, pride, and ingratitude, since Adam, by coveting more than was granted, offered an indignity to the Divine goodness, which had so greatly enriched him. Now, it was monstrous impiety, that a son of the earth should not be satisfied with being made after the similitude of God, unless he could also be equal to him. If apostasy, which consists in revolting from the government of the Creator, and petulantly rejecting his authority, be a base and execrable crime, it is a vain attempt to extenuate the sin of Adam. Though the transgression of our first parents was not simple apostasy; they were also guilty of vile reproaches against God, in consenting to the calumnies of Satan, who accused God of falsehood, envy, and malignity. Finally, infidelity opened the gate to ambition, and ambition produced obstinacy, so that they cast off the fear of God, and precipitated themselves whithersoever they were led by their lawless desires. With propriety, therefore, Bernard teaches that the gate of salvation is opened to us, when in the present day we receive the Gospel with our ears, as death was once admitted at the same doors when they lay open to Satan. For Adam had never dared to resist the authority of God, if he had not discredited his word. This was certainly the best check for a due regulation of all the affections, that the chief good consists in the practice of righteousness, in obedience to the commands of God; and that the ultimate end of a happy life is to be beloved by him. Being seduced, therefore, by the blasphemies of the devil, he did all that was in his power towards a total annihilation of the glory of God.

V. As the spiritual life of Adam consisted in a union to his Maker, so an alienation from him was the death of his soul. Nor is it surprising that he ruined his posterity by his defection, which has perverted the whole order of nature in heaven and earth. "The creatures groan," says Paul, "being made subject to vanity, not willingly." (*t*) If the cause be inquired, it is undoubtedly that they sustain part of the punishment due to the demerits of man, for whose use they were created. And his guilt being the origin of that curse which extends to every part of the world, it is reasonable to conclude its propagation to all his offspring. Therefore, when the Divine image in him was obliterated, and he was punished with the loss of wisdom, strength, sanctity, truth, and

(*t*) Rom. viii. 20, 22.

righteousness, with which he had been adorned, but which were succeeded by the dreadful pests of ignorance, impotence, impurity, vanity, and iniquity, he suffered not alone, but involved all his posterity with him, and plunged them into the same miseries. This is that hereditary corruption which the fathers called *original sin;* meaning by sin, the depravation of a nature previously good and pure; on which subject they had much contention, nothing being more remote from natural reason, than that all should be criminated on account of the guilt of one, and thus his sin become common; which seems to have been the reason why the most ancient doctors of the Church did but obscurely glance at this point, or at least explained it with less perspicuity than it required. Yet this timidity could not prevent Pelagius from arising, who profanely pretended, that the sin of Adam only ruined himself, and did not injure his descendants. By concealing the disease with this delusion, Satan attempted to render it incurable. But when it was evinced by the plain testimony of the Scripture, that sin was communicated from the first man to all his posterity, he sophistically urged that it was communicated by imitation, not by propagation. Therefore good men, and beyond all others Augustine, have laboured to demonstrate that we are not corrupted by any adventitious means, but that we derive an innate depravity from our very birth. The denial of this was an instance of consummate impudence. But the temerity of the Pelagians and Celestians will not appear surprising to him who perceives from the writings of Augustine, what a want of modesty they discover in every thing else. There is certainly no ambiguity in the confession of David, that he was shapen in iniquity, and in sin his mother conceived him. (*v*) He is not there exposing the sins of his mother or of his father; but to enhance his commendations of the Divine goodness towards him, he commences the confession of his depravity from the time of his conception. As it is evident that this was not peculiar to David, it is fairly concluded, that his case exemplifies the common condition of mankind. Every descendant, therefore, from the impure source, is born infected with the contagion of sin; and even before we behold the light of life, we are in the sight of God defiled and polluted. For " who can bring a clean thing out of an unclean?" The book of Job tells us, " Not one." (*w*)

VI. We have heard that the impurity of the parents is so transmitted to the children, that all, without a single exception, are polluted as soon as they exist. But we shall not find the origin of this pollution, unless we ascend to the first parent of us all, as to the fountain which sends forth all the streams.

(*v*) Psalm li. 5. (*w*) Job xiv. 4.

Thus it is certain that Adam was not only the progenitor, but as it were the root of mankind, and therefore that all the race were necessarily vitiated in his corruption. The Apostle explains this by a comparison between him and Christ: "As," says he, "by one man sin entered into the world, and death by sin, and so death passed upon all men, for that all have sinned," (*x*) so, by the grace of Christ, righteousness and life have been restored to us. What cavil will the Pelagians raise here? That the sin of Adam was propagated by imitation? Do we then receive no other advantage from the righteousness of Christ than the proposal of an example for our imitation? Who can bear such blasphemy? But if it cannot be controverted that the righteousness of Christ is ours by communication, and life as its consequence, it is equally evident that both were lost in Adam, in the same manner in which they were recovered in Christ, and that sin and death were introduced by Adam, in the same manner in which they are abolished by Christ. There is no obscurity in the declaration that many are made righteous by the obedience of Christ, (*y*) as they had been made sinners by the disobedience of Adam. And, therefore, between these two persons there is this relation, that the one ruined us by involving us in his destruction, the other by his grace has restored us to salvation. Any more prolix or tedious proof of a truth supported by such clear evidence must, I think, be unnecessary. Thus also in the First Epistle to the Corinthians, with a view to confirm the pious in a confidence of the resurrection, he shows, that the life which had been lost in Adam, was recovered in Christ. (*z*) He, who pronounces that we were all dead in Adam, does also at the same time plainly declare, that we were implicated in the guilt of his sin. For no condemnation could reach those who were perfectly clear from all charge of iniquity. But his meaning cannot be better understood than from the relation of the other member of the sentence, where he informs us that the hope of life is restored in Christ. But that is well known to be accomplished, only when Christ, by a wonderful communication, transfuses into us the virtue of his righteousness; as it is elsewhere said, "The Spirit is life, because of righteousness." (*a*) No other explanation therefore can be given of our being said to be dead in Adam, than that his transgression not only procured misery and ruin for himself, but also precipitated our nature into similar destruction. And that not by his personal guilt as an individual, which pertains not to us, but because he infected all his descendants with the corruption into which he had fallen. Otherwise there would be no truth in the assertion of Paul, that all are by nature children of wrath, (*b*)

(*x*) Rom. v. 12.   (*y*) Rom. v. 19.   (*z*) 1 Cor. xv. 22.
(*a*) Rom. viii. 10.   (*b*) Ephes. ii. 3.

if they had not been already under the curse even before their birth. Now, it is easily inferred that our nature is there characterized, not as it was created by God, but as it was vitiated in Adam; because it would be unreasonable to make God the author of death. Adam, therefore, corrupted himself in such a manner, that the contagion has been communicated from him to all his offspring. And Christ himself, the heavenly Judge, declares, in the most unequivocal terms, that all are born in a state of pravity and corruption, when he teaches, that "whatsoever is born of the flesh is flesh," (c) and that, therefore, the gate of life is closed against all who have not been regenerated.

VII. Nor, to enable us to understand this subject, have we any need to enter on that tedious dispute, with which the fathers were not a little perplexed, whether the soul of a son proceeds by derivation or transmission from the soul of the father, because the soul is the principal seat of the pollution. We ought to be satisfied with this, that the Lord deposited with Adam the endowments he chose to confer on the human nature; and therefore that when he lost the favours he had received, he lost them not only for himself, but for us all. Who will be solicitous about a transmission of the soul, when he hears that Adam received the ornaments that he lost, no less for us than for himself? that they were given, not to one man only, but to the whole human nature? There is nothing absurd therefore, if, in consequence of his being spoiled of his dignities, that nature be destitute and poor; if, in consequence of his being polluted with sin, the whole nature be infected with the contagion. From a putrefied root, therefore, have sprung putrid branches, which have transmitted their putrescence to remoter ramifications. For the children were so vitiated in their parent, that they became contagious to their descendants: there was in Adam such a spring of corruption, that it is transfused from parents to children in a perpetual stream. But the cause of the contagion is not in the substance of the body or of the soul; but because it was ordained by God, that the gifts which he conferred on the first man should by him be preserved or lost both for himself and for all his posterity. But the cavil of the Pelagians, that it is improbable that children should derive corruption from pious parents, whereas they ought rather to be sanctified by their purity, is easily refuted. For they descend from their carnal generation, not from their spiritual generation. Therefore, as Augustine says, "Neither the guilty unbeliever, nor the justified believer, generates innocent, but guilty children, because the generation of both is from corrupted nature." If they in some measure participate of the sanctity of their parents, that is the peculiar benediction of the people of God, which su-

(c) John iii. 5, 6.

persedes not the first and universal curse previously denounced on the human nature. For their guilt is from nature, but their sanctification from supernatural grace.

VIII. To remove all uncertainty and misunderstanding on this subject, let us define original sin. It is not my intention to discuss all the definitions given by writers; I shall only produce one, which I think perfectly consistent with the truth. Original sin, therefore, appears to be an hereditary pravity and corruption of our nature, diffused through all the parts of the soul, rendering us obnoxious to the Divine wrath, and producing in us those works which the Scripture calls "works of the flesh." (d) And this is indeed what Paul frequently denominates *sin*. The works which proceed thence, such as adulteries, fornications, thefts, hatreds, murders, revellings, he calls in the same manner "fruits of sin;" although they are also called "sins" in many passages of Scripture, and even by himself. These two things therefore should be distinctly observed: first, that our nature being so totally vitiated and depraved, we are, on account of this very corruption, considered as convicted and justly condemned in the sight of God, to whom nothing is acceptable but righteousness, innocence, and purity. And this liableness to punishment arises not from the delinquency of another; for when it is said that the sin of Adam renders us obnoxious to the Divine judgment, it is not to be understood as if we, though innocent, were undeservedly loaded with the guilt of his sin; but, because we are all subject to a curse, in consequence of his transgression, he is therefore said to have involved us in guilt. Nevertheless we derive from him, not only the punishment, but also the pollution to which the punishment is justly due. Wherefore Augustine, though he frequently calls it the sin of another, the more clearly to indicate its transmission to us by propagation, yet, at the same time, also asserts it properly to belong to every individual. And the Apostle himself expressly declares, that "death has therefore passed upon all men, for that all have sinned;" (e) that is, have been involved in original sin, and defiled with its blemishes. And therefore infants themselves, as they bring their condemnation into the world with them, are rendered obnoxious to punishment by their own sinfulness, not by the sinfulness of another. For though they have not yet produced the fruits of their iniquity, yet they have the seed of it within them: even their whole nature is as it were a seed of sin, and therefore cannot but be odious and abominable to God. Whence it follows, that it is properly accounted sin in the sight of God, because there could be no guilt without crime. The other thing

---

(d) Gal. v. 19.   (e) Rom. v. 12.

to be remarked is, that this depravity never ceases in us, but is perpetually producing new fruits, those works of the flesh, which we have before described, like the emission of flame and sparks from a heated furnace, or like the streams of water from a never failing spring. Wherefore those who have defined original sin as a privation of the original righteousness, which we ought to possess, though they comprise the whole of the subject, yet have not used language sufficiently expressive of its operation and influence. For our nature is not only destitute of all good, but is so fertile in all evils that it cannot remain inactive. Those who have called it *concupiscence* have used an expression not improper, if it were only added, which is far from being conceded by most persons, that every thing in man, the understanding and will, the soul and body, is polluted and engrossed by this concupiscence; or, to express it more briefly, that man is of himself nothing else but concupiscence.

IX. Wherefore I have asserted that sin has possessed all the powers of the soul, since Adam departed from the fountain of righteousness. For man has not only been ensnared by the inferior appetites, but abominable impiety has seized the very citadel of his mind, and pride has penetrated into the inmost recesses of his heart; so that it is weak and foolish to restrict the corruption which has proceeded thence, to what are called the sensual affections, or to call it an incentive which allures, excites, and attracts to sin, only what they style the sensual part. In this the grossest ignorance has been discovered by Peter Lombard, who, when investigating the seat of it, says that it is in the flesh, according to the testimony of Paul, (*f*) not indeed exclusively, but because it principally appears in the flesh; as though Paul designated only a part of the soul, and not the whole of our nature, which is opposed to supernatural grace. Now, Paul removes every doubt by informing us that the corruption resides not in one part only, but that there is nothing pure and uncontaminated by its mortal infection. For, when arguing respecting corrupt nature, he not only condemns the inordinate motions of the appetites, but principally insists on the blindness of the mind, and the depravity of the heart; (*g*) and the third chapter of his Epistle to the Romans is nothing but a description of original sin. This appears more evident from our renovation. For "the Spirit," which is opposed to "the old man" and "the flesh," not only denotes the grace, which corrects the inferior or sensual part of the soul, but comprehends a complete reformation of all its powers. And therefore Paul not only enjoins us to mortify our sensual appetites, but exhorts us to be renewed in the spirit of our mind; (*h*) and in

(*f*) Rom. vii. 18. (*g*) Ephes. iv. 17, 13. (*h*) Ephes. iv. 23.

another place he directs us to be transformed by the renewing of our mind. (*i*) Whence it follows, that that part, which principally displays the excellence and dignity of the soul, is not only wounded, but so corrupted, that it requires not merely to be healed, but to receive a new nature. How far sin occupies both the mind and the heart, we shall presently see. My intention here was only to hint, in a brief way, that man is so totally overwhelmed, as with a deluge, that no part is free from sin; and therefore that whatever proceeds from him is accounted sin; as Paul says that all the affections or thoughts of the flesh are enmity against God, and therefore death. (*k*)

X. Now, let us dismiss those who dare to charge God with their corruptions, because we say that men are naturally corrupt. They err in seeking for the work of God in their own pollution, whereas they should rather seek it in the nature of Adam while yet innocent and uncorrupted. Our perdition therefore proceeds from the sinfulness of our flesh, not from God; it being only a consequence of our degenerating from our primitive condition. And let no one murmur that God might have made a better provision for our safety, by preventing the fall of Adam. For such an objection ought to be abominated, as too presumptuously curious, by all pious minds; and it also belongs to the mystery of predestination, which shall afterwards be treated in its proper place. Wherefore let us remember, that our ruin must be imputed to the corruption of our nature, that we may not bring an accusation against God himself, the author of nature. That this fatal wound is inherent in our nature, is indeed a truth; but it is an important question, whether it was in it originally, or was derived from any extraneous cause. But it is evident that it was occasioned by sin. We have therefore no reason to complain, but of ourselves; which in the Scripture is distinctly remarked. For the Preacher says, "This only have I found, that God hath made man upright; but they have sought out many inventions." (*l*) It is clear that the misery of man must be ascribed solely to himself, since he was favoured with rectitude by the Divine goodness, but has lapsed into vanity through his own folly.

XI. We say, therefore, that man is corrupted by a natural depravity, but which did not originate from nature. We deny that it proceeded from nature, to signify that it is rather an adventitious quality or accident, than a substantial property originally innate. Yet we call it natural, that no one may suppose it to be contracted by every individual from corrupt habit, whereas it prevails over all by hereditary right. Nor is this representation of ours without authority. For the same reason the

(*i*) Rom. xii. 2.   (*k*) Rom. viii. 6, 7.   (*l*) Eccles. vii. 29.

Apostle says, that we are all by nature the children of wrath. (*m*) How could God, who is pleased with all his meanest works, be angry with the noblest of all his creatures? But he is angry rather with the corruption of his work, than with his work itself. Therefore, if, on account of the corruption of human nature, man be justly said to be naturally abominable to God, he may also be truly said to be naturally depraved and corrupt; as Augustine, in consequence of the corruption of nature, hesitates not to call those sins natural, which necessarily predominate in our flesh, where they are not prevented by the grace of God. Thus vanishes the foolish and nugatory system of the Manichæans, who, having imagined in man a substantial wickedness, presumed to invent for him a new creator, that they might not appear to assign the cause and origin of evil to a righteous God.

CHAPTER II.

MAN, IN HIS PRESENT STATE, DESPOILED OF FREEDOM OF WILL, AND SUBJECTED TO A MISERABLE SLAVERY.

SINCE we have seen that the domination of sin, from the time of its subjugation of the first man, not only extends over the whole race, but also exclusively possesses every soul, it now remains to be more closely investigated, whether we are despoiled of all freedom, and, if any particle of it yet remain, how far its power extends. But, that we may the more easily discover the truth of this question, I will first set up by the way a mark, by which our whole course must be regulated. The best method of guarding against error is to consider the dangers which threaten us on every side. For when man is declared to be destitute of all rectitude, he immediately makes it an occasion of slothfulness; and because he is said to have no power of himself for the pursuit of righteousness, he totally neglects it, as though it did not at all concern him. On the other hand, he cannot arrogate any thing to himself, be it ever so little, without God being robbed of his honour, and himself being endangered by presumptuous temerity. Therefore, to avoid striking on either of these rocks, this will be the course to be pursued — that man, being taught that he has nothing good left in his possession, and being surrounded on every side with the most

(*m*) Ephes. ii. 3.

miserable necessity, should, nevertheless, be instructed to aspire to the good of which he is destitute, and to the liberty of which he is deprived; and should be roused from indolence with more earnestness, than if he were supposed to be possessed of the greatest strength. The necessity of the latter is obvious to every one. The former, I perceive, is doubted by more than it ought to be. For this being placed beyond all controversy, that man must not be deprived of any thing that properly belongs to him, it ought also to be manifest how important it is that he should be prevented from false boasting. For if he was not even then permitted to glory in himself, when by the Divine beneficence he was decorated with the noblest ornaments, how much ought he now to be humbled, when, on account of his ingratitude, he has been hurled from the summit of glory to the abyss of ignominy! At that time, I say, when he was exalted to the most honourable eminence, the Scripture attributes nothing to him, but that he was created after the image of God; which certainly implies that his happiness consisted not in any goodness of his own, but in a participation of God. What, then, remains for him now, deprived of all glory, but that he acknowledge God, to whose beneficence he could not be thankful, when he abounded in the riches of his favour? and that he now, at least, by a confession of his poverty, glorify him, whom he glorified not by an acknowledgment of his blessings? It is also no less conducive to our interests than to the Divine glory, that all the praise of wisdom and strength be taken away from us; so that they join sacrilege to our fall, who ascribe to us any thing more than truly belongs to us. For what else is the consequence, when we are taught to contend in our own strength, but that we are lifted into the air on a reed, which being soon broken, we fall to the ground. Though our strength is placed in too favourable a point of view, when it is compared to a reed. For it is nothing but smoke, whatever vain men have imagined and pretend concerning it. Wherefore it is not without reason, that that remarkable sentence is so frequently repeated by Augustine, that free will is rather overthrown than established even by its own advocates. It was necessary to premise these things for the sake of some, who, when they hear that human power is completely subverted in order that the power of God may be established in man, inveterately hate this whole argument, as dangerous and unprofitable; which yet appears to be highly useful to us, and essential to true religion.

II. As we have just before said that the faculties of the soul consist in the mind and the heart, let us now consider the ability of each. The philosophers, indeed, with general consent, pretend, that in the mind presides Reason, which like a lamp illuminates with its counsels, and like a queen governs the will; for that it is so irradiated with Divine light as to be able to give the best counsels, and endued with such vigour as to be qualified to govern in the most excellent manner; that Sense, on the contrary, is torpid and afflicted with weakness of sight, so that it always creeps on the ground, and is absorbed in the grossest objects, nor ever elevates itself to a view of the truth; that Appetite, if it can submit to the obedience of reason, and resist the attractions of sense, is inclined to the practice of virtues, travels the path of rectitude, and is formed into will; but that, if it be devoted to the servitude of sense, it is thereby so corrupted and depraved as to degenerate into lust. And as, according to their opinion, there reside in the soul those faculties which I have before mentioned, understanding, sense, and appetite, or will, — which appellation is now more commonly used, — they assert that the understanding is endued with reason, that most excellent guide to a good and a happy life, provided it only maintains itself in its own excellence, and exerts its innate power; but that the inferior affection of the soul, which is called *sense*, and by which it is seduced into error, is of such a nature that it may be tamed and gradually conquered by the rod of reason. They place the will in the middle station between reason and sense, as perfectly at liberty, whether it chooses to obey reason, or to submit to the violence of sense.

III. Sometimes, indeed, being convinced by the testimony of experience, they admit how extremely difficult it is for a man to establish within him the kingdom of reason; while he is exposed at one time to the solicitations of alluring pleasures, at another to the delusions of pretended blessings, and at others to the violent agitations of immoderate passions, compared by Plato to so many cords dragging him in various directions. For which reason Cicero says that the sparks kindled by nature are soon extinguished by corrupt opinions and evil manners. But when such maladies have once taken possession of the human mind, they acknowledge their progress to be too violent to be easily restrained; nor do they hesitate to compare them to fierce horses, who, having rejected reason, like horses that have thrown off the charioteer, indulge themselves in every extravagance, without the least restraint. But they consider it as beyond all controversy, that virtue and vice are in our own power; for if it be at our election, they say, to do this or that, therefore it must also be, to abstain from doing it. And, on the other hand, if we are free to abstain from it, we must also be free to do it. But we appear freely and voluntarily to do those things which we do, and to abstain from those things from which we abstain; therefore, if we do any good action, when we please we may omit it; if we perpetrate any evil, that also we may avoid. Moreover, some of them have advanced to such a degree of presumption, as to boast, that we are indebted to the gods for our life, but for a virtuous and religious one to ourselves; whence also that assertion of Cicero, in the person of Cotta, that, since every man acquires virtue for himself, none of the wise men have ever thanked God for it. "For," says he, "we are praised for virtue, and in virtue we glory; which would not be the case, if it were a gift of God, and did not originate from ourselves." And a little after: "This is the judgment of all men, that fortune must be asked of God, but that wisdom must be derived from ourselves." This, then, is the substance of the opinion of all the philosophers, that the reason of the human understanding is sufficient for its proper government; that the will, being subject to it, is indeed solicited by sense to evil objects, but, as it has a free choice, there can be no impediment to its following reason as its guide in all things.

IV. Among the ecclesiastical writers, though there has not been one who would not acknowledge both that human reason is grievously wounded by sin, and that the will is very much embarrassed by corrupt affections, yet many of them have followed the philosophers far beyond what is right. The early fathers appear to me to have thus extolled human power from a fear lest, if they openly confessed its impotence, they might, in the first place, incur the derision of the philosophers, with whom they were then contending; and, in the next place, might administer to the flesh, of itself naturally too torpid to all that is good, a fresh occasion of slothfulness. To avoid delivering any principle deemed absurd in the common opinion of mankind, they made it their study, therefore, to compromise between the doctrine of the Scripture and the dogmas of the philosophers. Yet it appears from their language, that they principally regarded the latter consideration, that they might leave no room for slothfulness. Chrysostom says, "Since God has placed good and evil things in our power, he has given us freedom of choice; and he constrains not the unwilling, but embraces the willing." Again: "Oftentimes a bad man, if he will, is changed into a good one; and a good one falls into inactivity, and becomes bad; because God has given us naturally a free will, and imposes no necessity upon us, but, having provided suitable remedies, permits the event to depend entirely on the mind of the patient." Again: "As without the assistance of Divine grace we can never do any thing aright, so unless we bring what is our own, we shall never be able to gain the favour of heaven." He had before said, "That it may not be entirely of the Divine assistance, it behoves us also to bring something." And this is an expression very familiar with him: "Let us bring what is ours; God will supply the rest." Agreeably to which Jerome says, 'That it belongs to us to begin, and to God to complete; that it is ours to offer what we can, but his to supply our deficiencies." In these sentences you see they certainly attributed to man more than could justly be attributed to him towards the pursuit of virtue; because they supposed it impossible to awaken our innate torpor, otherwise than by arguing that this alone constitutes our guilt; but with what great dexterity they did it, we shall see in the course of our work. That the passages which we have recited are exceedingly erroneous, will be shortly proved. Although the Greeks, beyond all others, and among them particularly Chrysostom, have exceeded all bounds in extolling the ability of the human will, yet such are the variations, fluctuations, or obscurities of all the fathers, except Augustine, on this subject, that scarcely any thing certain can be concluded from their writings. Therefore we shall not scrupulously enumerate the particular opinions of them all, but shall at times select from one and another so much as the explication of the argument shall appear to require. Succeeding writers, being every one for himself ambitious of the praise of subtlety in the defence of human nature, gradually and successively fell into opinions more and more erroneous; till at length man was commonly supposed to be corrupted only in his sensual part, but to have his will in a great measure, and his reason entirely, unimpaired. In the mean time, it was proclaimed by every tongue, that the natural talents in men were corrupted, but the supernatural taken away — an expression of Augustine, of the import of which scarcely one man in a hundred had the slightest idea. For myself, if I meant clearly to state wherein the corruption of nature consists, I could easily content myself with this language. But it is of great importance to examine with attention what ability is retained by man in his present state, corrupted in all the parts of his nature, and deprived of supernatural gifts. This subject, therefore, has been treated in too philosophical a manner by those who gloried in being the disciples of Christ. For the Latins have always retained the term *free will*, as though man still remained in his primitive integrity. And the Greeks have not been ashamed to use an expression much more arrogant; for they called it αυτεξουσιον, denoting that man possesses sovereign power over himself. Since all men, therefore, even the vulgar, are tinctured with this principle, that man is endued with free will, and some of those who would be thought intelligent know not how far this freedom extends, — let us first examine the meaning of the term, and then let us describe, according to the simplicity of the Scripture, the power which man naturally possesses to do either good or evil. What *free will* is, though the expression frequently occurs in all writers, few have defined. Yet Origen appears to have advanced a position to which they all assented, when he calls it a power of *reason* to discern good and evil, of *will* to choose either. Nor does Augustine differ from him, when he teaches that it is a power of reason and will, by which good is chosen when grace assists; and evil, when grace is wanting. Bernard, while he affects greater subtlety, has expressed himself with more obscurity: he says, it is a consent on account of the liberty of will, which cannot be lost, and the judgment of reason, which cannot be avoided. The definition of Anselm is not sufficiently plain, who states it to be a power of preserving rectitude for its own sake. Therefore Peter Lombard and the schoolmen have rather adopted the definition of Augustine, because it was more explicit, and did not exclude the grace of God, without which they perceived that the will had no power of itself. But they also make such additions of their own, as they conceived to be either better, or conducive to further explication. First, they agree that the word *arbitrium, will* or *choice*, should rather be referred to reason, whose office it is to discern between good and evil; and that the epithet *free* belongs properly to the faculty of the will, which is capable of being inclined to either. Wherefore, since liberty belongs properly to the will, Thomas Aquinas says, that it would be a very good definition, if free will were called *an elective power*, which, being composed of understanding and appetite, inclines rather to appetite. We see where they represent the power of free will to be placed; that is, in the reason and will. It now remains briefly to inquire how much they attribute respectively to each.

V. Common and external things, which do not pertain to the kingdom of God, they generally consider as subject to the free determination of man; but true righteousness they refer to the special grace of God and spiritual regeneration. With a view to support this notion, the author of the treatise "On the Vocation of the Gentiles" enumerates three kinds of will — the first a sensitive, the second an animal, and the third a spiritual one; the two former of which he states to be freely exercised by us, and the last to be the work of the Holy Spirit in us. The truth or falsehood of this shall be discussed in the proper place; for my design at present is briefly to recite the opinions of others, not to refute them. Hence, when writers treat of free will, their first inquiry respects not its ability in civil or external actions, but its power to obey the Divine law. Though I confess the latter to be the principal question, yet I think the other ought not to be wholly neglected; and for this opinion I hope to give a very good reason. But a distinction has prevailed in the schools, which enumerates three kinds of liberty — the first, freedom from necessity, the second, freedom from sin, the third, freedom from misery; of which the first is naturally inherent in man, so that nothing can ever deprive him of it: the other two are lost by sin. This distinction I readily admit, except that it improperly confounds necessity with coaction. And the wide difference between these things, with the necessity of its being considered, will appear in another place.

VI. This being admitted will place it beyond all doubt, that man is not possessed of free will for good works, unless he be assisted by grace, and that special grace which is bestowed on the elect alone in regeneration. For I stop not to notice those fanatics, who pretend that grace is offered equally and promiscuously to all. But it does not yet appear, whether he is altogether deprived of power to do good, or whether he yet possesses some power, though small and feeble; which of itself can do nothing, but by the assistance of grace does also perform its part. Lombard, in order to establish this notion, informs us that two sorts of grace are necessary to qualify us for the performance of good works. One he calls operative, by which we efficaciously will what is good; the other coöperative, which attends as auxiliary to a good will. This division I dislike, because, while he attributes an efficacious desire of what is good to the grace of God, he insinuates that man has of his own nature antecedent, though ineffectual, desires after what is good; as Bernard asserts that a good will is the work of God, but yet allows that man is self-impelled to desire such a good will. But this is very remote from the meaning of Augustine, from whom, however, Lombard would be thought to have borrowed this division. The second part of it offends me by its ambiguity, which has produced a very erroneous interpretation. For they have supposed that we coöperate with the second sort of Divine grace, because we have it in our power either to frustrate the first sort by rejecting it, or to confirm it by our obedience to it. The author of the treatise "On the Vocation of the Gentiles" expresses it thus — that those who have the use of reason and judgment are at liberty to depart from grace, that they may be rewarded for not having departed, and that what is impossible without the coöperation of the Spirit, may be imputed to their merits, by whose will it might have been prevented. These two things I have thought proper to notice as I proceed, that the reader may perceive how much I dissent from the sounder schoolmen. For I differ considerably more from the later sophists, as they have departed much further from the judgment of antiquity. However, we understand from this division, in what sense they have ascribed free will to man. For Lombard at length pronounces, that we are not therefore possessed of free will, because we have an equal power to do or to think either good or evil, but only because we are free from constraint. And this liberty is not diminished, although we are corrupt, and the slaves of sin, and capable of doing nothing but sin.

VII. Then man will be said to possess free will in this sense, not that he has an equally free election of good and evil, but because he does evil voluntarily, and not by constraint. That, indeed, is very true; but what end could it answer to decorate a thing so diminutive with a title so superb? Egregious liberty indeed, if man be not compelled to serve sin, but yet is such a willing slave, that his will is held in bondage by the fetters of sin. I really abominate contentions about words, which disturb the Church without producing any good effect; but I think that we ought religiously to avoid words which signify any absurdity, particularly when they lead to a pernicious error. How few are there, pray, who, when they hear free will attributed to man, do not immediately conceive, that he has the sovereignty over his own mind and will, and is able by his innate power to incline himself to whatever he pleases? But it will be said, all danger from these expressions will be removed, if the people are carefully apprized of their signification. But, on the contrary, the human mind is naturally so prone to falsehood, that it will sooner imbibe error from one single expression, than truth from a prolix oration; of which we have a more certain experiment than could be wished in this very word. For neglecting that explanation of the fathers, almost all their successors have been drawn into a fatal self-confidence, by adhering to the original and proper signification of the word.

VIII. But if we regard the authority of the fathers — though they have the term continually in their mouths, they at the same time declare with what extent of signification they use it. First of all, Augustine, who hesitates not to call the will a slave. He expresses his displeasure in one place against those who deny free will; but he declares the principal reason for it, when he says, "Only let no man dare so to deny the freedom of the will, as to desire to excuse sin." Elsewhere he plainly confesses, that the human will is not free without the Spirit, since it is subject to its lusts, by which it is conquered and bound. Again: that when the will was overcome by the sin into which it fell, nature began to be destitute of liberty. Again: that man, having made a wrong use of his free will, lost both it and himself. Again: that free will is in a state of captivity, so that it can do nothing towards righteousness. Again: that the will cannot be free, which has not been liberated by Divine grace. Again: that the Divine justice is not fulfilled, while the law commands, and man acts from his own strength; but when the Spirit assists, and the human will obeys, not as being free, but as liberated by God. And he briefly assigns the cause of all this, when, in another place, he tells us, that man at his creation received great strength of free will, but lost it by sin. Therefore, having shown that free will is the result of grace, he sharply inveighs against those who arrogate it to themselves without grace. "How, then," says he, "do miserable men dare to be proud of free will, before they are liberated, or of their own strength, if they have been liberated?" Nor do they consider that the term *free will* signifies liberty. But "where the Spirit of the Lord is, there is liberty." (*n*) If, therefore, they are the slaves of sin, why do they boast of free will? "For of whom a man is overcome, of the same is he brought in bondage." (*o*) But if they have been liberated, why do they boast as of their own work? Are they so much at liberty as to refuse to be the servants of him who says, "Without me ye can do nothing"? (*p*) Besides, in another place, also, he seems to discountenance the use of that expression, when he says that the will is free, but not liberated; free from righteousness, enslaved to sin. This sentiment he also repeats and applies in another place, where he maintains that man is not free from righteousness, but by the choice of his will, and that he is not made free from sin, but by the grace of the Saviour. He who declares that human liberty is nothing but an emancipation or manumission from righteousness, evidently exposes it to ridicule as an unmeaning term. Therefore, if any man allows himself the use of this term without any erroneous signification, he will not be troubled by me on that account: but because I think that it cannot be retained without great danger, and that, on the contrary, its abolition would be very beneficial to the Church, I would neither use it myself, nor wish it to be used by others who may consult my opinion.

IX. Perhaps I may be thought to have raised a great prejudice against myself, by confessing that all the ecclesiastical writers, except Augustine, have treated this subject with such ambiguities or variations, that nothing certain can be learned from their writings. For some will interpret this, as though I intended to deprive them of the right of giving their suffrages, because their opinions are all adverse to mine. But I have had no other object in view than simply and faithfully to consult the benefit of pious minds, who, if they wait to discover the sentiments of the fathers on this subject, will fluctuate in perpetual uncertainty. At one time they teach man, despoiled

---

(*n*) 2 Cor. iii. 17.   (*o*) 2 Peter ii. 19.   (*p*) John xv. 5.

of all strength of free will, to have recourse to grace alone; at another, they either furnish, or appear to furnish, him with armour naturally his own. Yet that, amidst all this ambiguity of expression, esteeming the strength of man as little or nothing, they have ascribed the praise of every thing that is good entirely to the Holy Spirit, is not difficult to prove, if I introduce some passages from them, in which this sentiment is clearly maintained. For what is the meaning of that assertion of Cyprian, so frequently celebrated by Augustine, "That we ought to glory in nothing, because we have nothing of our own;" but that man, completely impoverished in himself, should learn to depend entirely on God? What is the meaning of that observation of Augustine and Eucherius, when they represent Christ as the tree of life, to whom whosoever shall have stretched forth his hand shall live; and free will as the tree of knowledge of good and evil, and say that whosoever forsakes the grace of God and tastes of it shall die? What is the meaning of that assertion of Chrysostom, that every man by nature is not only a sinner, but altogether sin? If we have not one good quality, if from his head to his feet man be entirely sin, if it be wrong even to try how far the power of the will extends,—how, then, can it be right to divide the praise of a good work between God and man? I could introduce many such passages from other fathers; but lest any one should cavil, that I select only those things which favour my own cause, but artfully omit those which oppose it, I refrain from such a recital. I venture to affirm, however, that though they sometimes too highly extol free will, yet their design was to teach man to discard all reliance on his own power, and to consider all his strength as residing in God alone. I now proceed to a simple explication of the truth in considering the nature of man.

X. But I am obliged to repeat here, what I premised in the beginning of this chapter—that he who feels the most consternation, from a consciousness of his own calamity, poverty, nakedness, and ignominy, has made the greatest proficiency in the knowledge of himself. For there is no danger that man will divest himself of too much, provided he learns that what is wanting in him may be recovered in God. But he cannot assume to himself even the least particle beyond his just right, without ruining himself with vain confidence, and incurring the guilt of enormous sacrilege, by transferring to himself the honour which belongs to God. And whenever our minds are pestered with this cupidity, to desire to have something of our own, which may reside in ourselves rather than in God, we may know that this idea is suggested by the same counsellor, who excited in our first parents the desire of resembling "gods, knowing good and evil." (*q*) If that term be diabolical, which exalts man in his own opinion, let us not admit it, unless we wish to take the counsel of an enemy. It is pleasant, indeed, to have so much innate strength as to confide in and be satisfied with ourselves. But from being allured into this vain confidence, let us be deterred by the many awful sentences which severely humble us to the dust; such as "Cursed be the man that trusteth in man, and maketh flesh his arm." (*r*) Again: "God delighteth not in the strength of the horse; he taketh not pleasure in the legs of a man. The Lord taketh pleasure in them that fear him, in those that hope in his mercy." (*s*) Again: "He giveth power to the faint; and to them that have no might he increaseth strength. Even the youths shall faint and be weary, and the young men shall utterly fall; but they that wait upon the Lord shall renew their strength." (*t*) The tendency of all which is to prevent us from depending, in the smallest degree, on our own strength, if we wish God to be propitious to us, who "resisteth the proud, but giveth grace unto the humble." (*v*) Then let us remember these promises; "I will pour water upon him that is thirsty, and floods upon the dry ground:" (*w*) again; "Ho! every one that thirsteth, come ye to the waters:" (*x*) which declare, that none are admitted to a participation of the blessings of God, but those who are pining away with a sense of their own poverty. Nor should such promises as this of Isaiah be overlooked: "The sun shall be no more thy light by day; neither for brightness shall the moon give light unto thee; but the Lord shall be unto thee an everlasting light." (*y*) The Lord certainly does not deprive his servants of the splendour of the sun or of the moon; but because he will appear exclusively glorious in them, he calls off their confidence to a great distance, even from those things which in their opinion are the most excellent.

XI. I have always, indeed, been exceedingly pleased with this observation of Chrysostom, that humility is the foundation of our philosophy; but still more with this of Augustine. "As a rhetorician," says he, "on being interrogated what was the first thing in the rules of eloquence, replied, ' Pronunciation;' and on being separately interrogated what was the second, and what was the third, gave the same reply; so, should any one interrogate me concerning the rules of the Christian religion, the first, second, and third, I would always reply, Humility." Now, he does not consider it as humility, when a man, conscious to himself of some little power, abstains

---

(*q*) Gen. iii. 5.
(*r*) Jer. xvii. 5.
(*s*) Psalm cxlvii. 10.
(*t*) Isaiah xl. 29—31.
(*v*) James iv. 6.
(*w*) Isaiah xliv. 3.
(*x*) Isaiah lv. 1.
(*y*) Isaiah lx. 16.

from pride and haughtiness; but when he truly feels his condition to be such that he has no refuge but in humility, as he elsewhere declares. "Let no man," says he, "flatter himself: of himself he is a devil: every blessing he enjoys is only from God. For what have you that is your own, but sin? Take to yourself sin, which is your own; for righteousness belongs to God." Again: "Why do men so presume on the ability of nature? It is wounded, maimed, distressed, and ruined. It needs a true confession, not a false defence." Again: "When every one knows, that in himself he is nothing, and that he cannot assist himself, the arms are broken within him, and the contentions are subsided." But it is necessary that all the weapons of impiety should be broken in pieces and consumed, that you may remain unarmed, and have no help in yourself. The greater your weakness is in yourself, so much the more the Lord assists you. So in the seventieth Psalm he forbids us to remember our own righteousness, that we may know the righteousness of God; and shows that God so recommends his grace to us, that we may know that we are nothing, and are solely dependent on the Divine mercy, being of ourselves altogether evil. Here, then, let us not contend with God concerning our right, as though what is attributed to him were deducted from our welfare. For as our humility is his exaltation, so the confession of our humility has an immediate remedy in his commiseration. Now, I do not expect that a man unconvinced should voluntarily submit, and, if he has any strength, withdraw his attention from it to be reduced to true humility; but I require, that, discarding the malady of self-love and love of strife, which blinds him, and leads him to entertain too high an opinion of himself, he should seriously contemplate himself in the faithful mirror of the Scripture.

XII. And, indeed, I much approve of that common observation which has been borrowed from Augustine, that the natural talents in man have been corrupted by sin, but that of the supernatural ones he has been wholly deprived. For by the latter are intended, both the light of faith and righteousness, which would be sufficient for the attainment of a heavenly life and eternal felicity. Therefore, when he revolted from the Divine government, he was at the same time deprived of those supernatural endowments, which had been given him for the hope of eternal salvation. Hence it follows, that he is exiled from the kingdom of God, in such a manner, that all the affections relating to the happy life of the soul, are also extinguished in him, till he recovers them by the grace of regeneration. Such are faith, love to God, charity towards our neighbours, and an attachment to holiness and righteousness. All these things, being restored by Christ, are esteemed adventitious and preternatural; and therefore we conclude that they had been lost. Again, soundness of mind and rectitude of heart were also destroyed; and this is the corruption of the natural talents. For although we retain some portion of understanding and judgment together with the will, yet we cannot say that our mind is perfect and sound, which is oppressed with debility and immersed in profound darkness; and the depravity of our will is sufficiently known. Reason, therefore, by which man distinguishes between good and evil, by which he understands and judges, being a natural talent, could not be totally destroyed, but is partly debilitated, partly vitiated, so that it exhibits nothing but deformity and ruin. In this sense John says, that "the light" still "shineth in darkness," but that "the darkness comprehendeth it not." (z) In this passage both these ideas are clearly expressed — that some sparks continue to shine in the nature of man, even in its corrupt and degenerate state, which prove him to be a rational creature, and different from the brutes, because he is endued with understanding; and yet that this light is smothered by so much ignorance, that it cannot act with any degree of efficacy. So the will, being inseparable from the nature of man, is not annihilated; but it is fettered by depraved and inordinate desires, so that it cannot aspire after any thing that is good. This, indeed, is a complete definition, but requires more diffuse explication. Therefore, that the order of our discourse may proceed according to the distinction we have stated, in which we divided the soul into understanding and will, let us first examine the power of the understanding. To condemn it to perpetual blindness, so as to leave it no intelligence in any thing, is repugnant, not only to the Divine word, but also to the experience of common sense. For we perceive in the mind of man some desire of investigating truth, towards which he would have no inclination, but from some relish of it previously possessed. It therefore indicates some perspicuity in the human understanding, that it is attracted with a love of truth; the neglect of which in the brutes argues gross sense without reason; although this desire, small as it is, faints even before its entrance on its course, because it immediately terminates in vanity. For the dulness of the human mind renders it incapable of pursuing the right way of investigating the truth; it wanders through a variety of errors, and groping, as it were, in the shades of darkness, often stumbles, till at length it is lost in its wanderings; thus, in its search after truth, it betrays its incapacity to seek and find it. It also labours under another grievous malady, frequently not discerning what those things are, the true knowledge of which it would be proper to attain,

(z) John i. 5.

and therefore torments itself with a ridiculous curiosity in fruitless and unimportant inquiries. To things most necessary to be known it either never adverts, or contemptuously and rarely digresses; but scarcely ever studies them with serious application. This depravity being a common subject of complaint with heathen writers, all men are clearly proved to have been implicated in it. Wherefore Solomon, in his Ecclesiastes, after having enumerated those pursuits in which men consider themselves as displaying superior wisdom, concludes with pronouncing them to be vain and frivolous.

XIII. Yet its attempts are not always so fruitless, but that it makes some discoveries, particularly when it applies itself to inferior things. Nor is it so stupid, as to be without some slender notion also of superior ones, however negligently it attends to the investigation of them; but it possesses not an equal ability for both. For it is when it goes beyond the limits of the present life, that it is chiefly convinced of its own imbecility. Wherefore, that we may better perceive how far it proceeds in every case according to the degrees of its ability, it will be useful for us to propose the following distinction; that there is one understanding for terrestrial things, and another for celestial ones. I call those things terrestrial which do not pertain to God and his kingdom, to true righteousness, or to the blessedness of a future life; but which relate entirely to the present life, and are in some sense confined within the limits of it. Celestial things are the pure knowledge of God, the method of true righteousness, and the mysteries of the heavenly kingdom. In the first class are included civil polity, domestic economy, all the mechanical arts and liberal sciences; in the second, the knowledge of God and of the Divine will, and the rule for conformity to it in our lives. Now, in regard to the first class, it must be confessed, that as man is naturally a creature inclined to society, he has also by nature an instinctive propensity to cherish and preserve that society; and therefore we perceive in the minds of all men general impressions of civil probity and order. Hence it is that not a person can be found who does not understand, that all associations of men ought to be governed by laws, or who does not conceive in his mind the principles of those laws. Hence that perpetual consent of all nations, as well as all individuals, to the laws, because the seeds of them are innate in all mankind, without any instructor or legislator. I regard not the dissensions and contests which afterwards arise, while some desire to invert all justice and propriety, to break down the barriers of the laws, and to substitute mere cupidity in the room of justice, as is the case with thieves and robbers. Others — which is a fault more common — think that unjust which legislators have sanctioned as just; and, on the contrary, pronounce that to be laudable which they have forbidden. For the former of these hate not the laws from an ignorance that they are good and sacred; but, inflamed with the violence of their passions, manifestly contend against reason, and under the influence of their lawless desires, execrate that which their judgments approve. The controversy of the latter of these is by no means repugnant to that original idea of equity which we have mentioned; for when men dispute with each other on the comparative merits of different laws, it implies their consent to some general rule of equity. This clearly argues the debility of the human mind, which halts and staggers even when it appears to follow the right way. Yet it is certainly true, that some seeds of political order are sown in the minds of all. And this is a powerful argument, that in the constitution of this life no man is destitute of the light of reason.

XIV. Next follow the arts, both liberal and manual; for learning which, as there is in all of us a certain aptitude, they also discover the strength of human ingenuity. But though all men are not capable of learning every art, yet it is a very sufficient proof of the common energy, that scarcely an individual can be found, whose sagacity does not exert itself in some particular art. Nor have they an energy and facility only in learning, but also in inventing something new in every art, or in amplifying and improving what they have learned from their predecessors. Though this excited Plato erroneously to assert that such an apprehension is only a recollection of what the soul knew in its preëxistent state, before it came into the body, it constrains us, by the most cogent reasons, to acknowledge that the principle of it is innate in the human mind. These instances, therefore, plainly prove, that men are endued with a general apprehension of reason and understanding. Yet it is such a universal blessing, that every one for himself ought to acknowledge it as the peculiar favour of God. To this gratitude the Author of nature himself abundantly excites us, by his creation of idiots, in whom he represents the state of the human soul without his illumination, which, though natural to all, is nevertheless a gratuitous gift of his beneficence towards every individual. But the invention and methodical teaching of these arts, and the more intimate and excellent knowledge of them, which is peculiar to a few, are no solid argument of general perspicacity; yet, belonging to both the pious and the impious, they are justly numbered among the natural talents.

XV. Whenever, therefore, we meet with heathen writers, let us learn from that light of truth which is admirably displayed in their works, that the human mind, fallen as it is, and corrupted from its integrity, is yet invested and adorned by God with excellent talents. If we believe that the Spirit of God is the only fountain of truth, we shall neither reject nor despise the truth itself, wherever it shall appear, unless we wish to insult the Spirit of God; for the gifts of the Spirit cannot be undervalued without offering contempt and reproach to the Spirit himself. Now, shall we deny the light of truth to the ancient lawyers, who have delivered such just principles of civil order and polity? Shall we say that the philosophers were blind in their exquisite contemplation and in their scientific description of nature? Shall we say that those, who by the art of logic have taught us to speak in a manner consistent with reason, were destitute of understanding themselves? Shall we accuse those of insanity, who by the study of medicine have been exercising their industry for our advantage? What shall we say of all the mathematics? Shall we esteem them the delirious ravings of madmen? On the contrary, we shall not be able even to read the writings of the ancients on these subjects without great admiration; we shall admire them, because we shall be constrained to acknowledge them to be truly excellent. And shall we esteem any thing laudable or excellent, which we do not recognize as proceeding from God? Let us, then, be ashamed of such great ingratitude, which was not to be charged on the heathen poets, who confessed that philosophy, and legislation, and useful arts, were the inventions of their gods. Therefore, since it appears that those whom the Scripture styles "natural men," ψυχικους, have discovered such acuteness and perspicacity in the investigation of sublunary things, let us learn from such examples, how many good qualities the Lord has left to the nature of man, since it has been despoiled of what is truly good.

XVI. Yet let us not forget that these are most excellent gifts of the Divine Spirit, which for the common benefit of mankind he dispenses to whomsoever he pleases. For if it was necessary that the Spirit of God should infuse into Bezaleel and Aholiab the understanding and skill requisite for the construction of the tabernacle, (a) we need not wonder if the knowledge of those things, which are most excellent in human life, is said to be communicated to us by the Spirit of God. Nor is there any reason for inquiring, what intercourse with the Spirit is enjoyed by the impious who are entirely alienated from God. For when the Spirit of God is said to dwell only in the faithful, that is to be understood of the Spirit of sanctification, by whom we are consecrated as temples to God himself. Yet it is equally by the energy of the same Spirit, that

---

(a) Exod. xxxi. 2—11; xxxv. 30—35

God replenishes, actuates, and quickens all creatures, and that, according to the property of each species which he has given it by the law of creation. Now, if it has pleased the Lord that we should be assisted in physics, logic, mathematics, and other arts and sciences, by the labour and ministry of the impious, let us make use of them; lest, if we neglect to use the blessings therein freely offered to us by God, we suffer the just punishment of our negligence. But, lest any one should suppose a man to be truly happy, when he is admitted to possess such powerful energies for the discovery of truth relating to the elements of this world, it must likewise be added, that all that faculty of understanding, and the understanding which is the consequence of it, is, in the sight of God, a fleeting and transitory thing, where there is not a solid foundation of truth. For the sentiment of Augustine, with whom, as we have observed, the Master of the Sentences and the Schoolmen have been constrained to coincide, is strictly true — that as the gratuitous or supernatural gifts were taken away from man after the fall, so these natural ones which remained have been corrupted; not that they can be defiled in themselves as proceeding from God, but because they have ceased to be pure to polluted man, so that he can obtain no praise from them.

XVII. Let us conclude, therefore, that it is evident in all mankind, that reason is a peculiar property of our nature, which distinguishes us from the brute animals, as sense constitutes the difference between them and things inanimate. For whereas some are born fools and idiots, that defect obscures not the general goodness of God. Such a spectacle should rather teach us that what we retain ought justly to be ascribed to his indulgence; because, had it not been for his mercy to us, our defection would have been followed by the total destruction of our nature. But whereas some excel in penetration, others possess superior judgment, and others have a greater aptitude to learn this or that art, in this variety God displays his goodness to us, that no one may arrogate to himself as his own what proceeds merely from the Divine liberality. For whence is it that one is more excellent than another, unless it be to exalt in our common nature the special goodness of God, which in the preterition of many, proclaims that it is under an obligation to none? Moreover, God inspires particular motions according to the vocation of each individual; of which many examples occur in the book of the Judges, where the Spirit of the Lord is said to "come upon" those whom he called to govern the people. (*b*) Finally, in all important actions there is a special instinct; for which reason it is said that Saul was followed

---

(*b*) Judges vi. 34; xv. 14.

by valiant men, "whose hearts God had touched." (c) And Samuel, when he predicts his inauguration into the kingdom, thus expresses himself: "The Spirit of the Lord will come upon thee, and thou shalt be turned into another man." (d) And this is extended to the whole course of his government; as it is afterwards narrated concerning David, that "the Spirit of the Lord came upon him from that day forward." (e) But the same expression is used in other places in reference to particular impulses. Even in Homer, men are said to excel in abilities, not only as Jupiter has distributed to every one, but according as he guides him from day to day. And experience clearly shows, since the most ingenious and sagacious of mankind frequently stand still in profound astonishment, that the minds of men are subject to the power and will of God to govern them every moment; for which reason it is said, that "he taketh away the heart of the chief people of the earth, and causeth them to wander in a wilderness where there is no way." (f) Yet in this diversity we perceive some remaining marks of the Divine image, which distinguish the human race in general from all the other creatures.

XVIII. We now proceed to show what human reason can discover, when it comes to the kingdom of God, and to that spiritual wisdom, which consists chiefly in three things — to know God, his paternal favour towards us, on which depends our salvation, and the method of regulating our lives according to the rule of the law. In the two first points, but especially in the second, the most sagacious of mankind are blinder than moles. I do not deny that some judicious and apposite observations concerning God may be found scattered in the writings of the philosophers; but they always betray a confused imagination. The Lord afforded them, as we have before observed, some slight sense of his Divinity, that they might not be able to plead ignorance as an excuse for impiety, and sometimes impelled them to utter things, by the confession of which they might themselves be convinced. But they saw the objects presented to their view in such a manner, that by the sight they were not even directed to the truth, much less did they arrive at it; just as a man, who is travelling by night across a field, sees the coruscations of lightning extending for a moment far and wide, but with such an evanescent view, that so far from being assisted by them in proceeding on his journey, he is re-absorbed in the darkness of the night before he can advance a single step. Besides, those few truths, with which they, as it were, fortuitously besprinkle their books, with what numerous and monstrous falsehoods are they defiled! Lastly,

(c) 1 Sam. x. 26.
(d) 1 Sam. x. 6.
(e) 1 Sam. xvi. 13.
(f) Job xii. 24. Psalm cvii. 40.

they never had the smallest idea of that certainty of the Divine benevolence towards us, without which the human understanding must necessarily be full of immense confusion. Human reason, then, neither approaches, nor tends, nor directs its views towards this truth, to understand who is the true God, or in what character he will manifest himself to us.

XIX. But because, from our being intoxicated with a false opinion of our own perspicacity, we do not without great difficulty suffer ourselves to be persuaded, that in Divine things our reason is totally blind and stupid, it will be better, I think, to confirm it by testimonies of Scripture, than to support it by arguments. This is beautifully taught by John, in that passage which I lately cited, where he says that, from the beginning, "in God was life, and the life was the light of men. And the light shineth in darkness; and the darkness comprehended it not." (g) He indicates, indeed, that the soul of man is irradiated with a beam of Divine light, so that it is never wholly destitute either of some little flame, or at least of a spark of it; but he likewise suggests that it cannot comprehend God by that illumination. And this because all his sagacity, as far as respects the knowledge of God, is mere blindness. For when the Spirit calls men "darkness," he at once totally despoils them of the faculty of spiritual understanding. Wherefore he asserts that believers, who receive Christ, are "born not of blood, nor of the will of the flesh, nor of the will of man, but of God;" (h) as though he had said that the flesh is not capable of such sublime wisdom as to conceive of God and Divine things, without being illuminated by the Spirit of God; as Christ testified that his being known by Peter was owing to a special revelation of the Father. (i)

XX. If we were firmly persuaded of what, indeed, ought not to be questioned, that our nature is destitute of all those things which our heavenly Father confers on his elect through the Spirit of regeneration, here would be no cause of hesitation. For this is the language of the faithful by the mouth of the Prophet: "With thee is the fountain of life; in thy light we shall see light." (k) The Apostle confirms the same, when he says that "no man can say that Jesus is Lord, but by the Holy Ghost." (l) And John the Baptist, perceiving the stupidity of his disciples, exclaims, that "a man can receive nothing except it be given him from above." (m) That by "gift" he intends a special illumination, not a common faculty of nature, is evident from the complaint which he makes of the inefficacy of the many discourses in which he had recommended Christ to his disciples. "I see that words are unavailing to instruct the

(g) John i. 4. (i) Matt. xvi. 17. (l) 1 Cor. xii. 3.
(h) John i. 13. (k) Psalm xxxvi. 9. (m) John iii. 27.

minds of men in Divine things, unless God give them understanding by his Spirit." And Moses also, when he reproaches the people for their forgetfulness, yet at the same time remarks, that they cannot be wise in the mysteries of God but by the Divine favour. He says, "Thine eyes have seen the signs and those great miracles; yet the Lord hath not given you a heart to perceive, and eyes to see, and ears to hear." (*n*) What more would he express, if he had called them blockheads, destitute of all understanding in the consideration of the works of God? Whence the Lord, by the Prophet, promises, as an instance of peculiar grace, that he will give the Israelites "a heart to know" him; (*o*) plainly suggesting that the mind of man has no spiritual wisdom any further than as it is enlightened by him. Christ also has clearly confirmed this by his own declaration, that no man can come to him, except the Father draw him. (*p*) What! is he not himself the lively image of the Father, representing to us all "the brightness of his glory"? (*q*) Therefore, he could not better manifest the extent of our capacity for the knowledge of God, than when he affirms that we have no eyes to behold his image where it is so plainly exhibited. What! did he not descend to the earth in order to discover to men the will of the Father? And did he not faithfully fulfil the object of his mission? He certainly did; but his preaching is not at all efficacious, unless the way to the heart be laid open by the internal teaching of the Spirit. Therefore, none come to him but they who have heard and learned of the Father. What is the nature of this hearing and learning? It is when the Spirit, by a wonderful and peculiar power, forms the ears to hear and the mind to understand. And lest this should appear strange, he cites the prophecy of Isaiah, where, predicting the restoration of the Church, he says, that all those who shall be saved "shall be taught of the Lord." If God there predicts something peculiar concerning his elect, it is evident that he speaks not of that kind of instruction which is common also to the impious and profane. It must be concluded, therefore, that there is no admission into the kingdom of God, but for him whose mind has been renewed by the illumination of the Holy Spirit. But Paul expresses himself more clearly than all the others. Having professedly entered upon this argument, after he has condemned all human wisdom as folly and vanity, and even reduced it to nothing, he comes to this conclusion: "The natural man receiveth not the things of the Spirit of God; for they are foolishness unto him; neither can he know them, because they are spiritually discerned." (*r*) Whom does he call the natural man?

(*n*) Deut. xxix. 3, 4. (*o*) Jer. xxiv. 7. (*p*) John vi. 44.
(*q*) Heb. i. 3. (*r*) 1 Cor. ii. 14.

him who depends on the light of nature. He, I say, has no apprehension of the mysteries of God. Why so? because through slothfulness he neglects them? Nay, even his utmost endeavours can avail nothing, "because they are spiritually discerned." This implies, that being entirely concealed from human perspicacity, they are discovered only by the revelation of the Spirit; so that where the illumination of the Spirit is not enjoyed, they are deemed foolishness itself. He had before extolled "the things which God hath prepared for them that love him" (s) above the capacity of our eyes, our ears, and our minds; he had even asserted that human wisdom was a kind of veil, by which the mind is prevented from a discovery of God. What do we want more? The Apostle pronounces that "God hath made foolish the wisdom of this world;" (t) and shall we ascribe to it such a degree of sagacity, as would enable it to penetrate to God, and to the most secret recesses of the heavenly kingdom? Far be from us such extreme stupidity.

XXI. That which he here detracts from men, he in another place ascribes exclusively to God. Praying for the Ephesians, he says, "May God, the Father of glory, give unto you the Spirit of wisdom and revelation." (v) You hear now that all wisdom and revelation is the gift of God. What follows? "The eyes of your understanding being enlightened." If they need a new revelation, they are certainly blind of themselves. It follows, "that ye may know what is the hope of your calling," &c. He confesses, then, that the minds of men are not naturally capable of so great knowledge, as to know their own calling. Nor let any Pelagian here object, that God assists this stupidity or ignorance, when, by the teaching of his word, he directs the human understanding to that which, without a guide, it never could have attained. For David had the law, in which all desirable wisdom was comprised: yet, not content with this, he requested that his eyes might be opened to consider the mysteries of that law. (w) By this expression he clearly signifies, that the sun arises on the earth, where the word of God shines on mankind; but that they derive little advantage from it, till he himself either gives them eyes or opens them, who is therefore called "the Father of lights;" (x) because wherever he shines not by his Spirit, every thing is covered with darkness. Thus also the Apostles were rightly and abundantly taught by the best of all teachers: yet, if they had not needed the Spirit of truth (y) to instruct their minds in that very doctrine which they had previously heard, they would not have been commanded to expect him. If, in imploring any favour of God, we confess our need,

(s) 1 Cor. ii. 9.   (v) Eph. i. 17.   (x) James i. 17.
(t) 1 Cor. i. 20.   (w) Psalm cxix. 18.   (y) John xvi. 14.

and if his promising it argues our poverty, let no man hesitate to acknowledge, that he is incapable of understanding the mysteries of God, any further than he has been illuminated by Divine grace. He who attributes to himself more understanding, is so much the blinder, because he does not perceive and acknowledge his blindness.

XXII. It remains for us to notice the third branch of knowledge, relating to the rule for the proper regulation of our life, which we truly denominate the knowledge of works of righteousness; in which the human mind discovers somewhat more acuteness than in the two former particulars. For the Apostle declares, that " when the Gentiles, which have not the law, do by nature the things contained in the law, these, having not the law, are a law unto themselves; which show the work of the law written in their hearts, their conscience also bearing witness, and their thoughts the mean while accusing or else excusing one another." (z) If the Gentiles have naturally the righteousness of the law engraven on their minds, we certainly cannot say that they are altogether ignorant how they ought to live. And no sentiment is more commonly admitted, than that man is sufficiently instructed in a right rule of life by that natural law of which the Apostle there speaks. But let us examine for what purpose this knowledge of the law was given to men; and then it will appear how far it can conduct them towards the mark of reason and truth. This is evident also from the words of Paul, if we observe the connection of the passage. He had just before said, "As many as have sinned without law, shall also perish without law; and as many as have sinned in the law, shall be judged by the law." Because it might appear absurd that the Gentiles should perish without any previous knowledge, he immediately subjoins that their conscience supplies the place of a law to them, and is therefore sufficient for their just condemnation. The end of the law of nature, therefore, is, that man may be rendered inexcusable. Nor will it be improperly defined in this manner — That it is a sentiment of the conscience sufficiently discerning between good and evil, to deprive men of the pretext of ignorance, while they are convicted even by their own testimony. Such is the indulgence of man to himself, that in the perpetration of evil actions he always gladly diverts his mind as much as he possibly can from all sense of sin; which seems to have induced Plato to suppose, that no sin is committed but through ignorance. This remark of his would be correct, if the hypocrisy of men could go so far in the concealment of their vices, as that the mind would have no consciousness of its guilt

(z) Rom. ii. 14, 15.

before God. But since the sinner, though he endeavours to evade the knowledge of good and evil imprinted on his mind, is frequently brought back to it, and so is not permitted to shut his eyes, but compelled, whether he will or not, sometimes to open them, there is no truth in the assertion, that he sins only through ignorance.

XXIII. Themistius, another philosopher, with more truth, teaches that the human understanding is very rarely deceived in the universal definition, or in the essence of a thing; but that it falls into error, when it proceeds further, and descends to the consideration of particular cases. There is no man, who, if he be interrogated in a general way, will not affirm homicide to be criminal; but he who conspires the death of his enemy, deliberates on it as a good action. The adulterer will condemn adultery in general; but will privately flatter himself in his own. Here lies the ignorance — when a man, proceeding to a particular case, forgets the rule which he had just fixed as a general position. This subject is very excellently treated by Augustine, in his exposition of the first verse of the fifty-seventh Psalm. The observation of Themistius, however, is not applicable to all cases; for sometimes the turpitude of the crime so oppresses the conscience of the sinner, that, no longer imposing on himself under the false image of virtue, he rushes into evil with the knowledge of his mind and the consent of his will. This state of mind produced these expressions, which we find in a heathen poet: "I see the better path, and approve it; I pursue the worse." Wherefore the distinction of Aristotle between incontinence and intemperance appears to me to be highly judicious. Where incontinence predominates, he says, that by the perturbation of the affections or passions, the mind is deprived of particular knowledge, so that in its own evil actions it observes not that criminality which it generally discovers in similar actions committed by other persons; and that when the perturbation has subsided, penitence immediately succeeds; that intemperance is not extinguished or broken by a sense of sin, but, on the contrary, obstinately persists in the choice of evil which it has made.

XXIV. Now, when you hear of a universal judgment in man to discriminate between good and evil, you must not imagine that it is every where sound and perfect. For if the hearts of men be furnished with a capacity of discriminating what is just and unjust, only that they may not excuse themselves with the plea of ignorance, it is not at all necessary for them to discover the truth in every point; it is quite sufficient if they understand so much that they can avail themselves of no subterfuge, but being convicted by the testimony of their own conscience, even now begin to tremble at the tribunal of

God. And if we will examine our reason by the Divine law, which is the rule of perfect righteousness, we shall find in how many respects it is blind. It certainly is far from reaching the principal points in the first table; such as relate to trust in God, ascribing to him the praise of goodness and righteousness, the invocation of his name, and the true observation of the Sabbath. What mind, relying on its natural powers, ever imagined that the legitimate worship of God consisted in these and similar things? For when profane men intend to worship God, though they are recalled a hundred times from their vain and nugatory fancies, yet they are always relapsing into them again. They deny that sacrifices are pleasing to God, unaccompanied with sincerity of heart; thereby testifying that they have some ideas concerning the spiritual worship of God, which, nevertheless, they immediately corrupt by their false inventions. For it is impossible ever to persuade them that every thing is true which the law prescribes concerning it. Shall I say that the mind of man excels in discernment, which can neither understand of itself, nor hearken to good instructions? Of the precepts of the second table it has a little clearer understanding, since they are more intimately connected with the preservation of civil society among men. Though even here it is sometimes found to be deficient; for to every noble mind it appears very absurd to submit to an unjust and imperious despotism, if it be possible by any means to resist it. A uniform decision of human reason is, that it is the mark of a servile and abject disposition patiently to bear it, and of an honest and ingenuous mind to shake it off. Nor is the revenging of injuries esteemed a vice among the philosophers. But the Lord, condemning such excessive haughtiness of mind, prescribes to his people that patience which is deemed dishonourable among men. But in the universal observation of the law, the censure of concupiscence wholly escapes our notice. For the natural man cannot be brought to acknowledge the disorders of his inward affections. The light of nature is smothered, before it approaches the first entrance of this abyss. For when the philosophers represent the inordinate affections of the mind as vices, they intend those which appear and manifest themselves in the grosser external actions; but those corrupt desires which more secretly stimulate the mind, they consider as nothing.

XXV. Wherefore, as Plato has before been deservedly censured for imputing all sins to ignorance, so also we must reject the opinion of those who maintain that all sins proceed from deliberate malice and pravity. For we too much experience how frequently we fall into error even when our intention is good. Our reason is overwhelmed with deceptions in so many forms, is obnoxious to so many errors, stumbles at so many impediments, and is embarrassed in so many difficulties, that it is very far from being a certain guide. Paul shows its deficiency in the sight of the Lord in every part of our life, when he denies "that we are sufficient of ourselves to think any thing as of ourselves." (a) He does not speak of the will or of the affections, but he also divests us of every good thought, that we may not suppose it possible for our minds to conceive how any action may be rightly performed. Are all our industry, perspicacity, understanding, and care so depraved, that we cannot conceive or meditate any thing that is right in the sight of God? To us, who do not contentedly submit to be stripped of the acuteness of our reason, which we esteem our most valuable endowment, this appears too harsh; but in the estimation of the Holy Spirit, who knows that all the thoughts of the wisest of men are vain, (b) and who plainly pronounces every imagination of the human heart to be only evil, (c) such a representation is consistent with the strictest truth. If whatever our mind conceives, agitates, undertakes, and performs, be invariably evil, how can we entertain a thought of undertaking any thing acceptable to God, by whom nothing is accepted but holiness and righteousness? Thus it is evident that the reason of our mind, whithersoever it turns, is unhappily obnoxious to vanity. David was conscious to himself of this imbecility, when he prayed that understanding might be given him, to enable him rightly to learn the commandments of the Lord. (d) For his desire to obtain a new understanding implies the total insufficiency of his own. And this he does not once, but almost ten times in one Psalm he repeats the same petition — a repetition indicating the greatness of the necessity which urges him thus to pray. What David requests for himself alone, Paul frequently supplicates for the churches at large. "We do not cease to pray for you," says he, "and to desire, that ye might be filled with the knowledge of his will in all wisdom and spiritual understanding; that ye might walk worthy of the Lord unto all pleasing." (e) Whenever he represents that as a blessing of God, we should remember that he thereby testifies it to be placed beyond the ability of man. Augustine so far acknowledges this defect of reason in understanding the things of God, that he thinks the grace of illumination no less necessary to our minds than the light of the sun to our eyes. And not content with this, he subjoins the following correction — that we ourselves open our eyes to behold the light, but that the eyes of our minds remain shut, unless they are opened

(a) 2 Cor. iii. 5.   (b) Psalm xciv. 11.   (c) Gen. vi. 5; viii. 21.
(d) Psalm cxix. 34.   (e) Col. i. 9. Phil. i. 4.

by the Lord. Nor does the Scripture teach us that our minds are illuminated only on one day, so as to enable them to see afterwards without further assistance; for the passage just quoted from Paul (*f*) relates to continual advances and improvements. And this is clearly expressed by David in these words: "With my whole heart have I sought thee; O let me not wander from thy commandments." For after having been regenerated, and made a more than common progress in true piety, he still confesses his need of perpetual direction every moment, lest he should decline from that knowledge which he possessed. Therefore, in another place, he prays for the renewal of a right spirit, which he had lost by his sin; (*g*) because it belongs to the same God to restore that which he originally bestowed, but of which we have been for a time deprived.

XXVI. We must now proceed to the examination of the will, to which principally belongs the liberty of choice; for we have before seen that election belongs rather to the will than to the understanding. In the first place, that the opinion advanced by philosophers, and received by general consent, that all things, by a natural instinct, desire what is good, may not be supposed to prove the rectitude of the human will, let us observe, that the power of free choice is not to be contemplated in that kind of appetite, which proceeds rather from the inclination of the nature than from the deliberation of the mind. For even the schoolmen confess that there is no action of free choice, but when reason sees and considers the rival objects presented to it; meaning that the object of appetite must be such as is the subject of choice, and that deliberation precedes and introduces choice. And in fact, if you examine the desire of good which is natural to man, you will find that he has it in common with the brutes. For they also desire to be happy, and pursue every agreeable appearance which attracts their senses. But man neither rationally chooses as the object of his pursuit that which is truly good for him, according to the excellency of his immortal nature, nor takes the advice of reason, nor duly exerts his understanding; but without reason, without reflection, follows his natural inclination, like the herds of the field. It is therefore no argument for the liberty of the will, that man is led by natural instinct to desire that which is good; but it is necessary that he discern what is good according to right reason; that as soon as he knows it, he choose it; and as soon as he has chosen it, he pursue it. To remove every difficulty, we must advert to two instances of false argumentation. For the desire here intended is not a

(*f*) Col. i. 9.   (*g*) Psalm li. 10.

proper motion of the will, but a natural inclination; and the good in question relates not to virtue or righteousness, but to condition; as when we say a man is well or in good health. Lastly, though man has the strongest desire after what is good, yet he does not pursue it. There is no man to whom eternal felicity is unwelcome, yet no man aspires to it without the influence of the Spirit. Since, therefore, the desire of happiness natural to man furnishes no argument for the liberty of the will, any more than a tendency in metals and stones towards the perfection of their nature argues liberty in them, let us consider, in some other particulars, whether the will be in every part so entirely vitiated and depraved that it can produce nothing but what is evil; or whether it retain any small part uninjured which may be the source of good desires.

XXVII. Those who attribute it to the first grace of God, that we are able to will effectually, seem, on the contrary, to imply that the soul has a faculty of spontaneously aspiring to what is good, but that it is too weak to rise into a solid affection, or to excite any endeavour. And there is no doubt that the schoolmen have in general embraced this opinion, which was borrowed from Origen and some of the fathers, since they frequently consider man in things purely natural, as they express themselves, according to the description given by the Apostle in these words: "The good that I would, I do not; but the evil which I would not, that I do. To will is present with me; but how to perform that which is good, I find not." (*h*) But this is a miserable and complete perversion of the argument which Paul is pursuing in that passage. For he is treating of the Christian conflict, which he more briefly hints at to the Galatians; the conflict which the faithful perpetually experience within themselves in the contention between the flesh and the spirit. Now, the spirit is not from nature, but from regeneration. But that the Apostle speaks concerning the regenerate, is evident from his assertion, that in himself dwelt nothing good, being immediately followed by an explanation that he meant it of his flesh. And therefore he affirms that it is not he that does evil, but sin that dwells in him. What is the meaning of this correction, "in me, that is, in my flesh?" It is as if he had expressed himself in the following manner: No good resides in me originating from myself, for in my flesh can be found nothing that is good. Hence follows that form of exculpation: "I do no evil, but sin that dwelleth in me;" (*i*) which is inapplicable to any but the regenerate, who, with the prevailing bias

(*h*) Rom. vii. 18, 19. (*i*) Rom. vii. 20.

of their souls, aim at what is good. Now, the conclusion which is subjoined places all this in a clear point of view: "I delight," says he, "in the law of God after the inward man; but I see another law in my members, warring against the law of my mind." (*k*) Who has such a dissension in himself, but he who, being regenerated by the Divine Spirit, carries about with him the relics of his flesh? Therefore Augustine, though he had at one time supposed that discourse to relate to the natural state of man, retracted his interpretation, as false and inconsistent. And, indeed, if we allow that men destitute of grace have some motions towards true goodness, though ever so feeble, what answer shall we give to the Apostle, who denies that we are sufficient of ourselves to entertain even a good thought? (*l*) What reply shall we make to the Lord, who pronounces, by the mouth of Moses, that every imagination of the human heart is only evil? (*m*) Since they have stumbled on a false interpretation of one passage, therefore, there is no reason why we should dwell on their opinion. Rather let us receive this declaration of Christ, "Whosoever committeth sin is the servant of sin." (*n*) We are all sinners by nature; therefore we are all held under the yoke of sin. Now, if the whole man be subject to the dominion of sin, the will, which is the principal seat of it, must necessarily be bound with the firmest bonds. Nor would there otherwise be any consistency in the assertion of Paul, "that it is God that worketh in us to will," (*o*) if any will preceded the grace of the Spirit. Farewell, then, all the idle observations of many writers concerning preparation; for although the faithful sometimes petition that their hearts may be conformed to the Divine law, as David does in many places, (*p*) yet it should be remarked that even this desire of praying originates from God. This we may gather from the language of David; for when he wishes a clean heart to be created within him, (*q*) he certainly does not arrogate to himself the beginning of such a creation. Let us rather, therefore, attend to this advice of Augustine: "God will prevent you in all things: do you also sometimes prevent his wrath." How? "Confess that you have all those things from God; that whatever good you have, it is from him; but whatever evil, from yourself." And a little after, "Nothing is ours, but sin."

(*k*) Rom. vii. 22, 23.   (*l*) 2 Cor. iii. 5.   (*m*) Gen. viii. 21.   (*n*) John viii. 34.
(*o*) Phil. ii. 13.   (*p*) Psalm cxix.   (*q*) Psalm li. 10.

CHAPTER III.

EVERY THING THAT PROCEEDS FROM THE CORRUPT NATURE OF MAN WORTHY OF CONDEMNATION.

But man cannot be better known in either faculty of his soul, than when he is represented in those characters by which the Scripture has distinguished him. If he be completely described in these words of Christ, "That which is born of the flesh is flesh," (r) as it is easy to prove, it is evident that he is a very miserable creature. For, according to the testimony of the Apostle, "to be carnally minded is death, because the carnal mind is enmity against God; for it is not subject to the law of God, neither indeed can be." (s) Is the flesh so perverse, that, with all its affections, it entertains a secret hatred against God? that it cannot consent to the righteousness of the Divine law? in a word, that it can produce nothing but what tends to death? Now, grant, that in the nature of man there is nothing but flesh, and elicit any good from it, if you can. But the name of flesh, it will be said, pertains only to the sensual, and not to the superior faculties of the soul. This is abundantly refuted by the words of Christ and of the Apostle. For the argument of our Lord is, that man must be born again, because he is flesh. He does not teach a new birth in regard to the body. Now, a new birth of the soul requires not a correction of some portion of it, but an entire renovation. And this is confirmed by the antithesis in both places; for there is such a comparison between the flesh and the spirit, that there is no medium left. Therefore, every thing in man that is not spiritual, is, according to this mode of reasoning, denominated carnal. But we have nothing of the spirit, except by regeneration. Whatever, therefore, we have from nature is carnal. But if on that point there could otherwise be any doubt, we have it removed by Paul, when, after a description of the old man, which he had asserted to be "corrupt according to the deceitful lusts," (t) he directs us to "be renewed in the spirit of our mind." You see that he places unlawful and corrupt affections not only in the sensitive part, but also in the mind itself, and, therefore, requires a renovation of it. And, indeed, he had just before drawn such a picture of human nature, as showed us to be in every part corrupted and depraved. For his description of all the Gentiles, as "walking in the vanity

(r) John iii. 6.   (s) Rom. viii. 6, 7.   (t) Eph. iv. 22. 23.

of their mind, having the understanding darkened, being alienated from the life of God through the ignorance that is in them, because of the blindness of their heart," (v) is undoubtedly applicable to all those whom the Lord has not yet renewed to the rectitude of his wisdom and righteousness. This is still more evident from the comparison soon after introduced, where he reminds the faithful, that they "have not so learned Christ." For from these words we conclude, that the grace of Christ is the only remedy, by which we can be liberated from that blindness, and from the evils consequent upon it. And this is what Isaiah had prophesied concerning the kingdom of Christ, when he predicted that the Lord would be "an everlasting light" to his Church, whilst at the same time "darkness covered the earth, and gross darkness the people." (w) When he declares, that the light of God will only arise upon the Church, beyond the limits of the Church he certainly leaves nothing but darkness and blindness. I will not particularly recite all the passages which are to be found, especially in the Psalms and in the Prophets, concerning the vanity of man. It is a striking observation of David, that "to be laid in the balance, they are altogether lighter than vanity." (x) It is a severe condemnation of his understanding, when all the thoughts which proceed from it are derided as foolish, frivolous, mad, and perverse.

II. Equally severe is the condemnation of the heart, when it is called "deceitful above all things, and desperately wicked." (y) But as I study brevity, I shall be content with citing a single passage, which, however, will resemble a very lucid mirror, in which we may behold at full length the image of our nature. For the Apostle, when he wishes to demolish the arrogance of mankind, does it by these testimonies: "There is none righteous, no, not one; there is none that understandeth, there is none that seeketh after God. They are all gone out of the way, they are together become unprofitable; there is none that doeth good, no, not one. Their throat is an open sepulchre; with their tongues they have used deceit; the poison of asps is under their lips; whose mouth is full of cursing and bitterness; their feet are swift to shed blood; destruction and misery are in their ways; there is no fear of God before their eyes." (z) In this terrible manner he inveighs, not against particular individuals, but against all the posterity of Adam. He does not declaim against the depraved manners of one or another age, but accuses the perpetual corruption of our nature. For his design in that passage is not simply to rebuke men, in

(v) Ephes. iv. 17, 18. (w) Isaiah lx. 1, &c. (x) Psalm lxii. 9.
(y) Jer. xvii. 9. (z) Rom. iii. 10—18.

order that they may repent, but rather to teach us that all men are overwhelmed with an inevitable calamity, from which they can never emerge unless they are extricated by the mercy of God. As this could not be proved unless it were evinced by the ruin and destruction of our nature, he has adduced these testimonies, which demonstrate our nature to be totally ruined. Let this, then, be admitted, that men are such as they are here described, not only by corrupt habits, but also by a depravity of nature; for otherwise the reasoning of the Apostle could not be supported, "that there is no salvation for man but from the mercy of God; since in himself he is in a ruined and desperate condition." Here I shall not attempt to establish the application of the testimonies, to preclude the appearance of their being improperly introduced. I shall treat them just as if they had been originally uttered by Paul, and not quoted from the Prophets. He divests man first of righteousness, that is, integrity and purity, and then of understanding. Defect of understanding is proved by apostasy from God, the seeking of whom is the first step in the path of wisdom; but this loss must necessarily befall those who have revolted from God. He adds, that all have gone out of the way, and are become altogether corrupt, that there is not one that does good. Then he subjoins the flagitious crimes, with which they, who are once abandoned to iniquity, contaminate all the members of their bodies. Lastly, he declares them to be destitute of the fear of God, the rule by which all our steps ought to be directed. If these are the hereditary characters of mankind, in vain do we seek in our nature for any thing that is good. I grant, indeed, that all these crimes are not exhibited in every individual; yet it cannot be denied that this monster lurks in the hearts of all. For as the body, which already contains within itself the cause and matter of a disease, although it has yet no sensation of pain, cannot be said to enjoy good health, neither can the soul be esteemed healthy, while it is full of such moral maladies; although this similitude will not correspond in every particular; for in the body, however diseased, there remains the vigour of life; but the soul, immersed in this gulf of iniquity, is not only the subject of vices, but totally destitute of every thing that is good.

III. A question, nearly the same as we have already answered, here presents itself to us again. For in all ages there have been some persons, who, from the mere dictates of nature, have devoted their whole lives to the pursuit of virtue. And though many errors might perhaps be discovered in their conduct, yet by their pursuit of virtue they afforded a proof, that there was some degree of purity in their nature. The value attached to virtues of such a description before God, we shall more fully discuss when we come to treat of the merits of works; yet it must be stated also in this place, so far as is necessary for the elucidation of the present subject. These examples, then, seem to teach us that we should not consider human nature to be totally corrupted; since, from its instinctive bias, some men have not only been eminent for noble actions, but have uniformly conducted themselves in a most virtuous manner through the whole course of their lives. But here we ought to remember, that amidst this corruption of nature there is some room for Divine grace, not to purify it, but internally to restrain its operations. For should the Lord permit the minds of all men to give up the reins to every lawless passion, there certainly would not be an individual in the world, whose actions would not evince all the crimes, for which Paul condemns human nature in general, to be most truly applicable to him. For can you except yourself from the number of those whose feet are swift to shed blood, whose hands are polluted with rapine and murder, whose throats are like open sepulchres, whose tongues are deceitful, whose lips are envenomed, whose works are useless, iniquitous, corrupt, and deadly, whose souls are estranged from God, the inmost recesses of whose hearts are full of pravity, whose eyes are insidiously employed, whose minds are elated with insolence — in a word, all whose powers are prepared for the commission of atrocious and innumerable crimes? If every soul be subject to all these monstrous vices, as the Apostle fearlessly pronounces, we clearly see what would be the consequence, if the Lord should suffer the human passions to go all the lengths to which they are inclined. There is no furious beast, that would be agitated with such ungovernable rage; there is no river, though ever so rapid and violent, that would overflow its boundaries with such impetuosity. In his elect, the Lord heals these maladies by a method which we shall hereafter describe. In others, he restrains them, only to prevent their ebullitions so far as he sees to be necessary for the preservation of the universe. Hence some by shame, and some by fear of the laws, are prevented from running into many kinds of pollutions, though they cannot in any great degree dissemble their impurity; others, because they think that a virtuous course of life is advantageous, entertain some languid desires after it; others go further, and display more than common excellence, that by their majesty they may confine the vulgar to their duty. Thus God by his providence restrains the perverseness of our nature from breaking out into external acts, but does not purify it within.

IV. But it may be said, the difficulty is not yet removed. For either we must esteem Camillus to be exactly similar to

Catiline, or in Camillus we shall have an example that nature, if it be studiously cultivated, is not altogether destitute of goodness. I grant, indeed, that the virtues displayed in Camillus were gifts of God, and if considered in themselves, appear justly worthy of commendation: but how will they be proofs of any natural goodness in him? To establish this, must we not recur to the heart, and argue, that if a natural man was eminent for such integrity of manners, human nature is not destitute of ability for the pursuit of virtue? But what if his heart was depraved and perverted, and followed any thing rather than the path of rectitude? And that it was such, if you concede that he was a natural man, is beyond all doubt. What ability, then, will you attribute to human nature for the pursuit of virtue, if, with the greatest appearance of integrity, it is discovered to be always tending to corruption? Therefore, as you will not commend a man for virtue, whose vices have only counterfeited the external form of virtue, so you must not attribute to the human will a power of desiring what is right, as long as it continues fixed in its perverseness. The most certain and easy solution of this question, however, is, that those virtues are not the common properties of nature, but the peculiar graces of God, which he dispenses in great variety, and in a certain degree to men that are otherwise profane. For which reason we hesitate not, in common speech, to call the nature of one man good, and of another depraved. Yet we still include both in the universal state of human depravity; but we signify what peculiar grace God has conferred on the one, with which he has not deigned to favour the other. When he determined to exalt Saul to the kingdom, he made him, as it were, a new man; and this is the reason why Plato, alluding to the fable of Homer, says, that the sons of kings are formed with some distinguishing singularity of character; because God, consulting the benefit of mankind, frequently furnishes with an heroic nature those whom he destines to hold the reins of empire; and from this source have proceeded all the exploits of great heroes which are celebrated in history. The same judgment must be formed concerning those also who are in a private station. But because every one who has risen to great eminence has been impelled by his ambition, which defiles all virtues, and deprives them of all excellence in the Divine view, whatever may be apparently laudable in ungodly men, ought not to be esteemed at all meritorious. Besides, the chief branch of rectitude is wanting, where there is no concern to display the glory of God: of this principle all are destitute whom he has not regenerated by his Spirit. Nor is it in vain that Isaiah says, that "the spirit of the fear of the Lord shall rest upon" Christ; (*a*) which teaches us, that all

(*a*) Isaiah xi. 2.

who are alienated from Christ are destitute of that " fear of the Lord " which is " the beginning of wisdom." (*b*) The virtues which deceive us by their vain and specious appearance, will be applauded in civil courts, and in the common estimation of mankind; but before the celestial tribunal they will possess no value to merit the reward of righteousness.

V. The will, therefore, is so bound by the slavery of sin, that it cannot excite itself, much less devote itself to any thing good; for such a disposition is the beginning of a conversion to God, which in the Scriptures is attributed solely to Divine grace. Thus Jeremiah prays to the Lord to convert or turn him, if he would have him to be turned. (*c*) Whence the Prophet, in the same chapter, describing the spiritual redemption of the faithful, says, "The Lord hath redeemed Jacob, and ransomed him from the hand of him that was stronger than he;" (*d*) alluding to the strong fetters with which the sinner is bound as long as he is deserted by the Lord, and continues under the yoke of the devil. Nevertheless there still remains the faculty of will, which with the strongest propensity is inclined to and rushes into sin; for when man subjected himself to this necessity, he was not deprived of his will, but of soundness of will. Bernard properly observes, that we all have a power to will; but that to will what is good, is an advantage; to will what is evil, a defect. Therefore simply to will belongs to man; to will what is evil, to corrupt nature; to will what is good, to grace. Now, when I assert that the will, being deprived of its liberty, is necessarily drawn or led into evil, I should wonder, if any one considered it as a harsh expression, since it has nothing in it absurd, nor is it unsanctioned by the custom of good men. It offends those who know not how to distinguish between necessity and compulsion. But if any one should ask them, whether God is not necessarily good, and whether the devil is not necessarily evil, — what answer will they make? For there is such a close connection between the goodness of God and his Deity, that his being God is not more necessary than his being good. But the devil is by his fall so alienated from communion with all that is good, that he can do nothing but what is evil. But if any one should sacrilegiously object, that little praise is due to God for his goodness, which he is constrained to preserve, — shall we not readily reply, that his inability to do evil arises from his infinite goodness, and not from the impulse of violence? Therefore, if a necessity of doing well impairs not the liberty of the Divine will in doing well; if the devil, who cannot but do evil, nevertheless sins voluntarily; who then will assert

(*b*) Psalm cxi. 10.   (*c*) Jer. xxxi. 18.   (*d*) Jer. xxxi. 11.

that man sins less voluntarily, because he is under a necessity of sinning? This necessity Augustine every where maintains; and even when he was pressed with the cavils of Celestius, who tried to throw an odium on this doctrine, he confidently expressed himself in these terms: "By means of liberty it came to pass that man fell into sin; but now the penal depravity consequent on it, instead of liberty, has introduced necessity." And whenever the mention of this subject occurs, he hesitates not to speak in this manner of the necessary servitude of sin. We must therefore observe this grand point of distinction, that man, having been corrupted by his fall, sins voluntarily, not with reluctance or constraint; with the strongest propensity of disposition, not with violent coercion; with the bias of his own passions, and not with external compulsion: yet such is the pravity of his nature, that he cannot be excited and biassed to any thing but what is evil. If this be true, there is no impropriety in affirming, that he is under a necessity of sinning. Bernard, subscribing to what is said by Augustine, thus expresses himself: "Among all the animals, man alone is free; and yet, by the intervention of sin, he also suffers a species of violence; but from the will, not from nature, so that he is not thereby deprived of his innate liberty." For what is voluntary is also free. And a little after: "The will being, by I know not what corrupt and surprising means, changed for the worse, is itself the author of the necessity to which it is subject; so that neither necessity, being voluntary, can excuse the will, nor the will, being fascinated, can exclude necessity." For this necessity is in some measure voluntary. Afterwards he says, that we are oppressed with a yoke, but no other than that of a voluntary servitude; that therefore our servitude renders us miserable, and our will renders us inexcusable; because the will, when it was free, made itself the slave of sin. At length he concludes, "Thus the soul, in a certain strange and evil manner, under this kind of voluntary and free yet pernicious necessity, is both enslaved and free; enslaved by necessity, free by its will; and, what is more wonderful and more miserable, it is guilty, because free; and enslaved wherein it is guilty; and so therein enslaved wherein it is free." From these passages the reader clearly perceives that I am teaching no novel doctrine, but what was long ago advanced by Augustine, with the universal consent of pious men, and which for nearly a thousand years after was confined to the cloisters of monks. But Lombard, for want of knowing how to distinguish necessity from coaction, gave rise to a pernicious error.

VI. It is necessary, on the other hand, to consider the remedy of Divine grace, by which the depravity of nature is corrected and healed. For since the Lord, in the assistance which he affords us, bestows on us that which we need, an exhibition of the nature of his work in us will immediately discover the nature of our necessity. When the Apostle tells the Philippians, that he is "confident that he which hath begun a good work in them will perform it until the day of Jesus Christ;" (e) by the beginning of a good work he undoubtedly designs the commencement of conversion, which takes place in the will. Therefore God begins the good work in us by exciting in our hearts a love, desire, and ardent pursuit of righteousness; or, to speak more properly, by bending, forming, and directing our hearts towards righteousness; but he completes it, by confirming us to perseverance. That no one may cavil, that the good work is begun by the Lord, inasmuch as the will, which is weak of itself, is assisted by him, the Spirit declares in another place how far the ability of the will reaches, when left to itself. "A new heart also," says he, "will I give you, and a new spirit will I put within you; and I will take away the stony heart out of your flesh, and I will give you a heart of flesh. And I will put my Spirit within you, and cause you to walk in my statutes." (f) Who will assert that the infirmity of the human will is only strengthened by assistance, to enable it efficaciously to aspire to the choice of that which is good, when it actually needs a total transformation and renovation? If there be in a stone any softness, which, by some application, being made more tender, would be flexible in every direction, then I will not deny the flexibility of the human heart to the obedience of rectitude, provided its imperfections are supplied by the grace of God. But if, by this similitude, the Lord intended to show that no good will ever be extracted from our hearts, unless they are entirely renewed, let us not divide between him and us, what he claims exclusively to himself. If, therefore, when God converts us to the pursuit of rectitude, this change is like the transformation of a stone into flesh, it follows, that whatever belongs to our own will is removed, and what succeeds to it is entirely from God. The will, I say, is removed, not considered as the will; because, in the conversion of man, the properties of our original nature remain entire. I assert also, that it is created anew, not that the will then begins to exist, but that it is then converted from an evil into a good one. This I affirm to be done entirely by God, because, according to the testimony of the same Apostle, "we are not sufficient" even "to think." (g) Therefore he elsewhere declares, not merely that God assists the infirmity of our will, or corrects its depravity, but that he "worketh in us to will." (h) Whence

(e) Phil. i. 6.   (f) Ezek. xxxvi. 26, 27.   (g) 2 Cor. iii. 5.   (h) Phil. ii. 13.

it is easy to infer what I have already remarked, that whatever good is in the human will, is the work of pure grace. In the same sense he elsewhere pronounces that it is "God which worketh all in all." (*i*) For in that place he is not discussing the government of the universe, but asserting that the praise of all the excellences found in the faithful belongs to God alone. And by using the word "all," he certainly makes God the author of spiritual life from its commencement even to its termination. This is the same as he had before taught in other words, declaring that the faithful are "of God in Christ;" (*k*) where he evidently intends the new creation, by which what belonged to our common nature is abolished. For we must here understand an implied contrast between Adam and Christ, which he states more plainly in another place, where he teaches that "we are the workmanship of God, created in Christ Jesus unto good works, which God hath before ordained that we should walk in them." (*l*) For by this argument he designs to prove that our salvation is gratuitous, because the beginning of all good is from the second creation, which we obtain in Christ. Now, if we possessed any ability, though ever so small, we should also have some portion of merit. But to annihilate all our pretensions, he argues that we have merited nothing, because "we are created in Christ Jesus unto good works, which God hath before ordained;" in which expressions he again signifies that all the parts of good works, even from the first inclination of the mind, are entirely from God. For this reason the Psalmist, after having said that "he (God) hath made us," that there may be no division of the work, immediately subjoins, "and not we ourselves." (*m*) That he speaks of regeneration, which is the commencement of the spiritual life, is evident from the context, where it follows immediately after, that "we are his people, and the sheep of his pasture." We see, then, that not content with having simply attributed to God the praise of our salvation, he expressly excludes us from all fellowship with him; as though he would say, that man has not even the smallest particle remaining in which he can glory, because all is of God.

VII. But there may be some, who will concede that the will, being, of its own spontaneous inclination, averse to what is good, is converted solely by the power of the Lord; yet in such a manner, that being previously prepared, it has also its own share in the work; that grace, as Augustine teaches, precedes every good work, the will following grace, not leading it, being its companion, not its guide. This unobjectionable observation of that holy man, Peter Lombard preposterously

(*i*) 1 Cor. xii. 6.   (*k*) 1 Cor. i. 30.   (*l*) Eph. ii. 10.   (*m*) Psalm c. 3.

wrests to an erroneous meaning. Now, I contend that both in the words of the Prophet which I have cited, and in other passages, these two things are clearly signified, that the Lord corrects our depraved will, or rather removes it, and of himself introduces a good one in its place. As it is preceded by grace, I allow you to style it an attendant; but since its reformation is the work of the Lord, it is wrong to attribute to man a voluntary obedience in following the guidance of grace. Therefore it is not a proper expression of Chrysostom, that grace is able to effect nothing without the will, nor the will without grace; as if grace did not produce the will itself, as we have just seen from Paul. Nor was it the intention of Augustine, when he called the human will the companion of grace, to assign to it any secondary office next to grace in the good work; but with a view to refute the nefarious dogma broached by Pelagius, who made the prime cause of salvation to consist in human merit, he contends, what was sufficient for his present argument, that grace is prior to all merit; omitting, at this time, the other question concerning the perpetual efficiency of grace, which is admirably treated by him on other occasions. For when he frequently says, that the Lord precedes the unwilling that he may will, and follows the willing that he may not will in vain, he makes him the sole author of the good work. His language on this subject is too explicit to require much argument. "Men labour," says he, "to discover in our will something that is our own, and not derived from God; and how any such discovery can be made, I know not." In his first book against Pelagius and Celestius, where he explains that declaration of Christ, "Every man that hath heard of the Father cometh unto me," (*n*) he says, that "the will is assisted so as to enable it not only to know its duty, but what it knows, also to do." And thus when God teaches not by the letter of the law, but by the grace of the Spirit, he teaches in such a manner, that whatever each one has learned, he not only sees in knowing it, but desires in willing, and performs in doing.

VIII. And as we are now engaged on the principal point of the argument, let us give the reader a summary of the doctrine, and prove it by a few very clear testimonies of Scripture; and then, that no one may accuse us of perverting the Scripture, let us also show that the truth which we assert to be deduced from the Scripture is not destitute of the support of this holy man; I mean Augustine. For I conceive it is unnecessary to recite in regular order all the passages which might be adduced from the Scriptures in confirmation of our opinion; provided

(*n*) John vi. 45.

that the selection, which shall be made, prepares a way to the understanding of all the rest, which are frequently to be found. Nor do I think that there will be any impropriety in evincing my agreement with that man, to whose authority the consent of the pious pays a great and merited deference. The origin of all good clearly appears, from a plain and certain reason, to be from no other than from God alone; for no propensity of the will to any thing good can be found but in the elect. But the cause of election must not be sought in men. Whence we may conclude, that man has not a good will from himself, but that it proceeds from the same decree by which we were elected before the creation of the world. There is also another reason, not dissimilar. For since good volitions and good actions both arise from faith, we must see whence faith itself originates. Now, since the Scripture uniformly proclaims it to be the gratuitous gift of God, it follows that it is the effect of mere grace, when we, who are naturally and completely prone to evil, begin to will any thing that is good. Therefore the Lord, when he mentions these two things in the conversion of his people, that he takes away from them their stony heart, and gives them a heart of flesh, plainly declares, that what originates from ourselves must be removed, that we may be converted to righteousness; and that whatever succeeds in its place proceeds from himself. Nor is it only in one passage that he announces this; for he says in Jeremiah, "I will give them one heart and one way, that they may fear me for ever." (o) And a little after, "I will put my fear in their hearts, that they shall not depart from me." Again in Ezekiel, "I will give them one heart, and will put a new spirit within you; and I will take the stony heart out of their flesh, and will give them a heart of flesh." (p) He could not more evidently claim to himself and take from us all that is good and upright in our will, than when he declares our conversion to be the creation of a new spirit and of a new heart. For it always follows, that nothing good proceeds from our will till it be renovated; and that after its renovation, as far as it is good, it is from God, and not from ourselves.

IX. And we find the saints have made this the subject of their prayers. Solomon prayed, "May the Lord incline our hearts unto him to keep his commandments." (q) He shows the stubbornness of our heart, which, unless a new bias be given to it, naturally indulges itself in rebellion against the Divine law. The same petition is offered by the Psalmist: "Incline my heart unto thy testimonies." (r) For we should always remark the opposition between the perverse bias of the

(o) Jer. xxxii. 39.
(p) Ezek. xi. 19.
(q) 1 Kings viii. 56.
(r) Psalm cxix. 36.

heart, which inclines it to rebellion, and this correction, which constrains it to obedience. But when David, perceiving himself to be for a time deprived of the direction of grace, prays that God would "create in" him "a clean heart, and renew a right spirit within" him, (s) does he not acknowledge that all the parts of his heart are full of impurity, and his spirit warped by a depraved obliquity? and by calling the purity which he earnestly implores, the creation of God, does he not ascribe it entirely to him? If any one object, that the petition itself is a proof of a pious and holy affection, the answer is easy, that although David had already partly repented, yet he compares his former state with that melancholy fall, which he had experienced. Assuming the character, therefore, of a man alienated from God, he properly requests for himself all those things which God confers on his elect in regeneration. Resembling a dead man, therefore, he prays to be created anew, that, instead of being the slave of Satan, he may become the instrument of the Holy Spirit. Truly wonderful and monstrous is the extravagance of our pride. God requires of us nothing more severe than that we most religiously observe his sabbath, by resting from our own works; but there is nothing which we find more difficult, or to which we are more reluctant, than to bid farewell to our own works, in order to give the works of God their proper place. If there were no obstacle arising from our folly, Christ has given a testimony to his graces, sufficiently clear to prevent them from being wickedly suppressed. "I am the vine," says he, "ye are the branches. My Father is the husbandman. As the branch cannot bear fruit of itself, except it abide in the vine, no more can ye, except ye abide in me. For without me ye can do nothing." (t) If we cannot bear fruit of ourselves, any more than a branch can bud after it is torn up from the ground, and deprived of moisture, we must no longer seek for any aptitude in our nature to that which is good. There is no ambiguity in this conclusion, "Without me ye can do nothing." He does not say that we are too weak to be sufficient for ourselves, but reducing us to nothing, excludes every idea of ability, however diminutive. If, being engrafted into Christ, we bear fruit like a vine, which derives the energy of vegetation from the moisture of the earth, from the dew of heaven, and from the benign influences of the sun, I see nothing of our own remaining in any good work, if we preserve entire to God the honour which belongs to him. It is in vain to urge that frivolous subtlety, that the branch already possesses sap, and a fructifying power, and that therefore it does not derive all from the earth, or from the original root,

(s) Psalm li. 10. (t) John xv. 1, 4, 5.

because it contributes something of its own. For the meaning of Christ is clearly that we are as a dry and worthless log, when separated from him; because, independently of him, we have no ability to do good, as he says also in another place: "Every plant, which my heavenly Father has not planted, shall be rooted up." (*v*) Wherefore the Apostle ascribes all the praise to him in the place already cited. "It is God," says he, "which worketh in you both to will and to do." (*w*) The first part of a good work is volition, the next an effectual endeavour to perform it; God is the author of both. Therefore we rob the Lord, if we arrogate any thing to ourselves either in volition or in execution. If God were said to assist the infirmity of our will, then there would be something left to us; but since he is said to produce the will, all the good that is in it, is placed without us. And because the good will is still oppressed by the burden of our flesh, so that it cannot extricate itself, he has added, that in struggling with the difficulties of that conflict, we are supplied with constancy of exertion to carry our volitions into effect. For otherwise there would be no truth in what he elsewhere teaches, that "it is the same God which worketh all in all," (*x*) which we have before shown comprehends the whole course of the spiritual life. For which reason David, after having prayed that the way of God may be discovered to him, that he may walk in his truth, immediately adds, "Unite my heart to fear thy name." (*y*) In these words he intimates, that even good men are subject to so many distractions of mind, that they soon wander and fall, unless they are strengthened to persevere. For the same reason, in another passage, having prayed that his steps might be ordered in the word of the Lord, he likewise implores strength for a warfare: "Let not any iniquity have dominion over me." (*z*) In this manner, therefore, the Lord both begins and completes the good work in us; that it may be owing to him, that the will conceives a love for what is right, that it is inclined to desire it, and is excited and impelled to endeavour to attain it; and then that the choice, desire, and endeavour do not fail, but proceed even to the completion of the desired effect; lastly, that a man proceeds with constancy in them, and perseveres even to the end.

X. And he moves the will, not according to the system maintained and believed for many ages, in such a manner that it would afterwards be at our option either to obey the impulse or to resist it, but by an efficacious influence. The observation, therefore, so frequently repeated by Chrysostom, that "Whom God draws, he draws willing," we are obliged to

(*v*) Matt. xv. 13.   (*w*) Phil. ii. 13.   (*x*) 1 Cor. xii. 6.
(*y*) Psalm lxxxvi. 11.   (*z*) Psalm cxix. 133.

reject, being an insinuation that God only waits for us with his hand extended, if we choose to accept his assistance. We grant that such was the primitive condition of man during his state of integrity, that he could incline to the one side or the other; but since Adam has taught us by his own example how miserable free will is, unless God give us both will and power, what will become of us if he impart his grace to us in that small proportion? Nay, we obscure and diminish his grace by our ingratitude. For the Apostle does not teach that the grace of a good will is offered to us for our acceptance, but that he "worketh in us to will;" which is equivalent to saying, that the Lord, by his Spirit, directs, inclines, and governs our heart, and reigns in it as in his own possession. Nor does he promise by Ezekiel that he will give to the elect a new spirit, only that they may be able to walk, but that they may actually walk, in his precepts. (*a*) Nor can the declaration of Christ, " Every man that hath heard of the Father cometh unto me," (*b*) be understood in any other sense than as a proof of the positive efficacy of Divine grace; as Augustine also contends. This grace the Lord deigns not to give to any person promiscuously, according to the observation commonly attributed, if I mistake not, to Occam, that it is denied to no man who does what he can. Men are to be taught, indeed, that the Divine benignity is free to all who seek it, without any exception; but since none begin to seek it, but those who have been inspired by heavenly grace, not even this diminutive portion ought to be taken from his praise. This is the privilege of the elect, that, being regenerated by the Spirit of God, they are led and governed by his direction. Wherefore Augustine as justly ridicules those who arrogate to themselves any part of a good volition, as he reprehends others, who suppose that to be given promiscuously to all, which is the special evidence of gratuitous election. "Nature," says he, "is common to all men, but not grace." He calls it "a transparent subtlety, which shines merely with vanity, when that is extended generally to all, which God confers on whom he chooses." But elsewhere, "How have you come? by believing. Be afraid, lest while you arrogate to yourself the discovery of the way of righteousness, you perish from the way of righteousness. I am come, you say, by free will; I am come through my own choice. Why are you inflated with pride? Will you know that this also is given to you? Hear him proclaiming, 'No man can come to me, except the Father which hath sent me draw him.'" (*c*) And it incontrovertibly follows, from the words of John, that the hearts of the pious are divinely governed with such effect, that they follow with an af-

---

(*a*) Ezek. xi. 19, 20; xxxvi. 27.   (*b*) John vi. 45.   (*c*) John vi. 44.

fection which nothing can alter. "Whosoever is born of God," he says, "cannot sin; for his seed remaineth in him." (d) For we see that the neutral, inefficacious impulse imagined by the sophists, which every one would be at liberty to obey or resist, is evidently excluded, where it is asserted that God gives a constancy that is effectual to perseverance.

XI. Concerning perseverance there would have been no doubt that it ought to be esteemed the gratuitous gift of God, had it not been for the prevalence of a pestilent error, that it is dispensed according to the merit of men, in proportion to the gratitude which each person has discovered for the grace bestowed on him. But as that opinion arose from the supposition that it was at our own option to reject or accept the offered grace of God, this notion being exploded, the other falls of course. Though here is a double error; for beside teaching that our gratitude for the grace first bestowed on us, and our legitimate use of that grace, are remunerated by subsequent blessings, they add also, that now grace does not operate alone in us, but only coöperates with us. On the first point, we must admit that the Lord, while he daily enriches and loads his servants with new communications of his grace, perceiving the work which he has begun in them grateful and acceptable, discovers something in them which he blesses with still greater degrees of grace. And this is implied in the following declarations: "Unto every one that hath, shall be given." And, "Well done, good and faithful servant; thou hast been faithful over a few things, I will make thee ruler over many things." (e) But here two errors must be avoided; the legitimate use of the grace first bestowed must not be said to be rewarded with subsequent degrees of grace, as though man, by his own industry, rendered the grace of God efficacious; nor must it be accounted a remuneration in such a sense as to cease to be esteemed the free favour of God. I grant, then, that this Divine benediction is to be expected by the faithful, that the better they have used the former measures of grace, they shall afterwards be enriched with proportionably greater degrees of it. But I assert that this use also is from the Lord, and that this remuneration proceeds from his gratuitous benevolence. They are equally awkward and unhappy in their use of the trite distinction of operating and coöperating grace. Augustine has used it indeed, but softens it by a suitable definition; that God in coöperating completes what in operating he begins, and that it is the same grace, but derives its name from the different mode of its efficiency. Whence it follows, that he makes no partition of the work between God and us, as though there

(d) 1 John iii. 9. (e) Matt. xxv. 23, 29. Luke xix. 17, 26.

were a mutual concurrence from the respective exertions of each; but that he only designates the multiplication of grace. To the same purpose is what he elsewhere asserts, that the good will of man precedes many of the gifts of God, but is itself one of their number. Whence it follows, that he leaves nothing for it to arrogate to itself. This is also particularly expressed by Paul. For having said that "it is God which worketh in us both to will and to do," (*f*) he immediately adds, that he does both "of his own good pleasure," signifying by this expression that these are acts of gratuitous benignity. Now, to their wonted assertion, that after we have admitted the first grace, our own endeavours coöperate with the grace which follows, I reply, if they mean that, after having been once subdued by the Divine power to the obedience of righteousness, we voluntarily advance, and are disposed to follow the guidance of grace, I make no objection. For it is very certain, that where the grace of God reigns, there is such a promptitude of obedience. But whence does this arise but from the Spirit of God, who, uniformly consistent with himself, cherishes and strengthens to a constancy of perseverance that disposition of obedience which he first originated? But if they mean that man derives from himself an ability to coöperate with the grace of God, they are involved in a most pestilent error.

XII. And to this purpose they falsely and ignorantly pervert that observation of the Apostle, "I laboured more abundantly than they all; yet not I, but the grace of God which was with me." (*g*) For they understand it in this manner; that because his preference of himself to all others might appear rather too arrogant, he corrects it by referring the praise to the grace of God; but yet so as to denominate himself a coöperator with grace. It is surprising that so many men, not otherwise erroneous, have stumbled at this imaginary difficulty. For the Apostle does not say that the grace of God laboured with him, to make himself a partner in the labour; but rather by that correction ascribes the whole praise of the labour to grace alone. "It is not I," says he, "that have laboured, but the grace of God which was with me." They have been deceived by an ambiguity of expression; but still more by a preposterous translation, in which the force of the Greek article is omitted. For if you translate it literally, he says, not that grace was coöperative with him, but that the grace which was with him was the author of all. And the same is maintained by Augustine, though briefly, yet without obscurity, when he thus expresses himself: "The good will of man precedes many of the gifts of God, but not all. But of those which it

(*f*) Phil. ii. 13.   (*g*) 1 Cor. xv. 10.

precedes it is itself one." Then follows this reason; because it is written, "The God of my mercy shall prevent me." (*h*) And, "Mercy shall follow me." (*i*) It prevents the unwilling, that he may will; it follows the willing, that he may not will in vain." With this agrees Bernard, who introduces the Church, saying, "Draw me unwilling, to make me willing; draw me inactive, to make me run."

XIII. Now, let us hear Augustine speak in his own words, lest the sophists of the Sorbonne, those Pelagians of the present age, according to their usual custom, accuse us of opposing the whole current of antiquity. In this they imitate their father Pelagius, by whom Augustine was formerly obliged to enter into the same field of controversy. In his treatise *De Corr. et Grat.*, addressed to Valentine, he treats very much at large what I shall recite briefly, but in his own words: "That to Adam was given the grace of persevering in good if he chose; that grace is given to us to will, and by willing to overcome concupiscence. That Adam therefore had the power if he had the will, but not the will that he might have the power; but that it is given to us to have both the will and the power. That the primitive liberty was a power to abstain from sin, but that ours is much greater, being an inability to commit sin." And lest he should be supposed to speak of the perfection to be enjoyed after the attainment of a state of immortality, as Lombard misinterprets his meaning, he presently removes this difficulty. For he says, "the will of the saints is so inflamed by the Holy Spirit, that they therefore have an ability, because they have such a will; and that their having such a will proceeds from the operations of God." For if, amidst such great weakness, which still requires "strength" to be "made perfect" (*k*) for the repressing of pride, they were left to their own will, so as to have ability, through the Divine assistance, if they were willing, and God did not operate in them to produce that will; among so many temptations and infirmities their will would fail, and therefore they could not possibly persevere. The infirmity of the human will, then, is succoured, that it may be invariably and inseparably actuated by Divine grace, and so, notwithstanding all its weakness, may not fail. He afterwards discusses more at large how our hearts necessarily follow the impulse of God; and he asserts that the Lord draws men with their own wills, but that those wills are such as he himself has formed. Now, we have a testimony from the mouth of Augustine to the point which we are principally endeavouring to establish; that grace is not merely offered by the Lord to be either received or rejected, according to the free

(*h*) Psalm lix. 10. (*i*) Psalm xxiii. 6. (*k*) 2 Cor. xii. 9.

choice of each individual, but that it is grace which produces both the choice and the will in the heart; so that every subsequent good work is the fruit and effect of it, and that it is obeyed by no other will but that which it has produced. For this is his language also in another place — that it is grace alone which performs every good work in us.

XIV. When he observes that the will is not taken away by grace, but only changed from a bad one into a good one, and when it is good, assisted; he only intends that man is not drawn in such a manner as to be carried away by an external impulse, without any inclination of his mind; but that he is internally so disposed as to obey from his very heart. That grace is specially and gratuitously given to the elect, he maintains in an epistle to Boniface, in the following language: "We know that the grace of God is not given to all men; and that to them to whom it is given, it is given neither according to the merits of works, nor according to the merits of will, but by gratuitous favour; and to those to whom it is not given, we know that it is not given by the righteous judgment of God." And in the same epistle, he strenuously combats that opinion, which supposes that subsequent grace is given to the merits of men, because by not rejecting the first grace they showed themselves worthy of it. For he wishes Pelagius to allow that grace is necessary to us for every one of our actions, and is not a retribution of our works, that it may be acknowledged to be pure grace. But the subject cannot be comprised in a more concise summary than in the eighth chapter of his treatise addressed to Valentine; where he teaches, that the human will obtains, not grace by liberty, but liberty by grace; that being impressed by the same grace with a disposition of delight, it is formed for perpetuity; that it is strengthened with invincible fortitude; that while grace reigns, it never falls, but, deserted by grace, falls immediately; that by the gratuitous mercy of the Lord, it is converted to what is good, and, being converted, perseveres in it; that the first direction of the human will to that which is good, and its subsequent constancy, depend solely on the will of God, and not on any merit of man. Thus there is left to man such a free will, if we choose to give it that appellation, as he describes in another place, that he can neither be converted to God nor continue in God but by grace; and that all the ability which he has is derived from grace.

CHAPTER IV.

THE OPERATION OF GOD IN THE HEARTS OF MEN.

It has now, I apprehend, been sufficiently proved, that man is so enslaved by sin, as to be of his own nature incapable of an effort, or even an aspiration, towards that which is good. We have also laid down a distinction between coaction and necessity, from which it appears that while he sins necessarily, he nevertheless sins voluntarily. But since, while he is devoted to the servitude of the devil, he seems to be actuated by his will, rather than by his own, it remains for us to explain the nature of both kinds of influence. There is also this question to be resolved, whether any thing is to be attributed to God in evil actions, in which the Scripture intimates that some influence of his is concerned. Augustine somewhere compares the human will to a horse, obedient to the direction of his rider; and God and the devil he compares to riders. "If God rides it, he, like a sober and skilful rider, manages it in a graceful manner; stimulates its tardiness; restrains its immoderate celerity; represses its wantonness and wildness; tames its perverseness, and conducts it into the right way. But if the devil has taken possession of it, he, like a foolish and wanton rider, forces it through pathless places, hurries it into ditches, drives it down over precipices, and excites it to obstinacy and ferocity." With this similitude, as no better occurs, we will at present be content. When the will of a natural man is said to be subject to the power of the devil, so as to be directed by it, the meaning is, not that it resists and is compelled to a reluctant submission, as masters compel slaves to an unwilling performance of their commands, but that, being fascinated by the fallacies of Satan, it necessarily submits itself to all his directions. For those whom the Lord does not favour with the government of his Spirit, he abandons, in righteous judgment, to the influence of Satan. Wherefore the Apostle says, that "the god of this world hath blinded the minds of them which believe not," who are destined to destruction, "lest the light of the gospel should shine unto them." (*l*) And in another place, that he "worketh in the children of disobedience." (*m*) The blinding of the wicked, and all those enormities which attend it, are called the works of Satan; the cause of which must nevertheless be sought

---

(*l*) 2 Cor. iv. 4.   (*m*) Eph. ii. 2.

only in the human will, from which proceeds the root of evil, and in which rests the foundation of the kingdom of Satan, that is, sin.

II. Very different, in such instances, is the method of the Divine operation. And that we may have a clearer view of it, let us take as an example the calamity which holy Job suffered from the Chaldeans. (*n*) The Chaldeans massacred his shepherds, and committed hostile depredations on his flock. Now, the wickedness of their procedure is evident; yet in these transactions Satan was not unconcerned; for with him the history states the whole affair to have originated. But Job himself recognizes in it the work of the Lord, whom he asserts to have taken from him those things of which he had been plundered by the Chaldeans. How can we refer the same action to God, to Satan, and to man, as being each the author of it, without either excusing Satan by associating him with God, or making God the author of evil? Very easily, if we examine, first, the end for which the action was designed, and secondly, the manner in which it was effected. The design of the Lord is to exercise the patience of his servant by adversity; Satan endeavours to drive him to despair: the Chaldeans, in defiance of law and justice, desire to enrich themselves by the property of another. So great a diversity of design makes a great distinction in the action. There is no less difference in the manner. The Lord permits his servant to be afflicted by Satan: the Chaldeans, whom he commissions to execute his purpose, he permits and resigns to be impelled by Satan: Satan, with his envenomed stings, instigates the minds of the Chaldeans, otherwise very depraved, to perpetrate the crime: they furiously rush into the act of injustice, and overwhelm themselves in criminality. Satan therefore is properly said to work in the reprobate, in whom he exercises his dominion; that is, the kingdom of iniquity. God also is said to work in a way proper to himself, because Satan, being the instrument of his wrath, turns himself hither and thither at his appointment and command, to execute his righteous judgments. Here I allude not to the universal influence of God, by which all creatures are sustained, and from which they derive an ability to perform whatever they do. I speak only of that special influence which appears in every particular act. We see, then, that the same action is without absurdity ascribed to God, to Satan, and to man; but the variety in the end and in the manner, causes the righteousness of God to shine without the least blemish, and the iniquity of Satan and of man to betray itself to its own disgrace.

(*n*) Job i.

III. The fathers are sometimes too scrupulous on this subject, and afraid of a simple confession of the truth, lest they should afford an occasion to impiety to speak irreverently and reproachfully of the works of God. Though I highly approve this sobriety, yet I think we are in no danger, if we simply maintain what the Scripture delivers. Even Augustine at one time was not free from this scrupulosity; as when he says that hardening and blinding belong not to the operation, but to the prescience of God. But these subtleties are inconsistent with numerous expressions of the Scripture, which evidently import some intervention of God beyond mere foreknowledge. And Augustine himself, in his fifth book against Julian, contends very largely, that sins proceed not only from the permission or the prescience, but from the power of God, in order that former sins may thereby be punished. So also what they advance concerning permission is too weak to be supported. God is very frequently said to blind and harden the reprobate, and to turn, incline, and influence their hearts, as I have elsewhere more fully stated. But it affords no explication of the nature of this influence to resort to prescience or permission. We answer, therefore, that it operates in two ways. For, since, when his light is removed, nothing remains but darkness and blindness; since, when his Spirit is withdrawn, our hearts harden into stones; since, when his direction ceases, they are warped into obliquity; he is properly said to blind, harden, and incline those whom he deprives of the power of seeing, obeying, and acting aright. The second way, which is much more consistent with strict propriety of language, is, when, for the execution of his judgments, he, by means of Satan, the minister of his wrath, directs their counsels to what he pleases, and excites their wills and strengthens their efforts. Thus, when Moses relates that Sihon the king would not grant a free passage to the people, because God had "hardened his spirit, and made his heart obstinate," he immediately subjoins the end of God's design: "That he might deliver him into thy hand." (o) Since God willed his destruction, the obduration of his heart, therefore, was the Divine preparation for his ruin.

IV. The following expressions seem to relate to the former method: "He removeth away the speech of the trusty, and taketh away the understanding of the aged. He taketh away the heart of the chief people of the earth, and causeth them to wander in a wilderness where there is no way." (p) Again: "O Lord, why hast thou made us to err from thy ways, and hardened our heart from thy fear?" (q) For these passages rather indicate what God makes men by deserting them, than show

(o) Deut. ii. 30. (p) Job xii. 20, 24. (q) Isaiah lxiii. 17.

how he performs his operations within them. But there are other testimonies, which go further; as those which relate to the hardening of Pharaoh: "I will harden his (Pharaoh's) heart, that he shall not let the people go." (r) Afterwards the Lord says, "I have hardened his heart." (s) Did he harden it by not mollifying it? That is true; but he did somewhat more, for he delivered his heart to Satan to be confirmed in obstinacy; whence he had before said, "I will harden his heart." The people march out of Egypt; the inhabitants of the country meet them in a hostile manner: by whom were they excited? Moses expressly declared to the people, that it was the Lord who had hardened their hearts. (t) The Psalmist, reciting the same history, says, "He turned their heart to hate his people." (v) Now, it cannot be said that they fell in consequence of being deprived of the counsel of God. For if they are "hardened" and "turned," they are positively inclined to that point. Besides, whenever it has pleased him to punish the transgressions of his people, how has he executed his work by means of the reprobate? In such a manner that any one may see, that the efficacy of the action proceeded from him, and that they were only the ministers of his will. Wherefore he threatened sometimes that he would call them forth by hissing, (w) sometimes that he would use them as a net (x) to entangle, sometimes as a hammer (y) to strike the people of Israel. But he particularly declared himself to be operative in them, when he called Sennacherib an axe, (z) which was both directed and driven by his hand. Augustine somewhere makes the following correct distinction: "that they sin, proceeds from themselves; that in sinning they perform this or that particular action, is from the power of God, who divides the darkness according to his pleasure."

V. Now that the ministry of Satan is concerned in instigating the reprobate, whenever the Lord directs them hither or thither by his providence, may be sufficiently proved even from one passage. For it is frequently asserted in Samuel that an evil spirit of the Lord, and an evil spirit from the Lord, either agitated or quitted Saul. (a) To refer this to the Holy Spirit were impious. An impure spirit, therefore, is called a spirit of God, because it acts according to his command and by his power, being rather an instrument in the performance of the action, than itself the author of it. We must add, also, what is advanced by Paul, that "God shall send strong delusion, that they who believed not the truth should believe a lie." (b) Yet

(r) Exod. iv. 21.   (s) Exod. vii. 3.   (t) Deut. ii. 30.
(v) Psalm cv. 25.   (w) Isaiah v. 26; vii. 18.
(x) Ezek. xii. 13; xvii. 20.   (y) Jer. l. 23.   (z) Isaiah x. 15.
(a) 1 Sam. xvi. 14; xviii. 10; xix. 19.   (b) 2 Thess. ii. 11, 12.

there is always a wide difference, even in the same work, between the operation of God and the attempts of Satan and wicked men. He makes the evil instruments, which he has in his hand, and can turn as he pleases, to be subservient to his justice. They, as they are evil, produce the iniquity which the depravity of their nature has conceived. The other arguments, which tend to vindicate the majesty of God from every calumny, and to obviate the cavils of the impious, have already been advanced in the chapter concerning Providence. For, at present, I only intend briefly to show how Satan reigns in the reprobate man, and how the Lord operates in them both.

VI. But what liberty man possesses in those actions which in themselves are neither righteous nor wicked, and pertain rather to the corporeal than to the spiritual life, although we have before hinted, has not yet been explicitly stated. Some have admitted him in such things to possess a free choice; rather, as I suppose, from a reluctance to dispute on a subject of no importance, than from an intention of positively asserting that which they concede. Now, though I grant that they who believe themselves to be possessed of no power to justify themselves, believe what is principally necessary to be known in order to salvation, yet I think that this point also should not be neglected, that we may know it to be owing to the special favour of God, whenever our mind is disposed to choose that which is advantageous for us; whenever our will inclines to it; and, on the other hand, whenever our mind and understanding avoid what would otherwise hurt us. And the power of the providence of God extends so far, as not only to cause those events to succeed which he foresees will be best, but also to incline the wills of men to the same objects. Indeed, if we view the administration of external things with our own reason, we shall not doubt their subjection to the human will; but if we listen to the numerous testimonies, which proclaim that in these things also the hearts of men are governed by the Lord, they will constrain us to submit the will itself to the special influence of God. Who conciliated the minds of the Egyptians towards the Israelites, (*c*) so as to induce them to lend them the most valuable of their furniture? They would never have been induced to do this of their own accord. It follows, therefore, that their hearts were guided by the Lord rather than by an inclination of their own. And Jacob, if he had not been persuaded that God infuses various dispositions into men according to his pleasure, would not have said concerning his son Joseph, whom he thought to be some profane Egyptian, "God Almighty give you mercy before the man." (*d*)

(*c*) Exod. xi. 3.   (*d*) Gen. xliii. 14.

As the whole Church confesses in the Psalms, that, when God chose to compassionate her, he softened the hearts of the cruel nations into clemency. (*e*) Again, when Saul was so inflamed with rage, as to prepare himself for war, it is expressly mentioned as the cause, that he was impelled by the Spirit of God. (*f*) Who diverted the mind of Absalom from adopting the counsel of Ahithophel, which used to be esteemed as an oracle? (*g*) Who inclined Rehoboam to be persuaded by the counsel of the young men? (*h*) Who caused the nations, that before were very valiant, to feel terror at the approach of the Israelites? Rahab the harlot confessed that this was the work of God. Who, on the other hand, dejected the minds of the Israelites with fear and terror, but he who had threatened in the law that he would "send a faintness into their hearts?" (*i*)

VII. Some one will object, that these are peculiar examples, to the rule of which, things ought by no means universally to be reduced. But I maintain, that they are sufficient to prove that for which I contend; that God, whenever he designs to prepare the way for his providence, inclines and moves the wills of men even in external things, and that their choice is not so free, but that its liberty is subject to the will of God. That your mind depends more on the influence of God, than on the liberty of your own choice, you must be constrained to conclude, whether you are willing or not, from this daily experience, that in affairs of no perplexity your judgment and understanding frequently fail; that in undertakings not arduous your spirits languish; on the other hand, in things the most obscure, suitable advice is immediately offered; in things great and perilous, your mind proves superior to every difficulty. And thus I explain the observation of Solomon, "The hearing ear, and the seeing eye, the Lord hath made even both of them." (*k*) For he appears to me to speak, not of their creation, but of the peculiar favour of God displayed in their performing their functions. When he says, that "the king's heart is in the hand of the Lord; as the rivers of water, he turneth it whithersoever he will;" (*l*) under one species he clearly comprehends the whole genus. For if the will of any man be free from all subjection, that privilege belongs eminently to the will of a king, which exercises a government in some measure over the wills of others; but if the will of the king be subject to the power of God, ours cannot be exempted from the same authority. Augustine has a remarkable passage on this subject: "The Scripture, if it be diligently examined, shows, not only that the good wills of men, which he turns from evil into good, and directs to good actions and to eternal

(*e*) Psalm cvi. 46.   (*f*) 1 Sam. xi. 6.   (*g*) 2 Sam. xvii. 14.   (*h*) 1 Kings xii. 10.
(*i*) Lev. xxvi. 36.   (*k*) Prov. xx. 12.   (*l*) Prov. xxi. 1.

life, but also that those wills which relate to the present life, are subject to the power of God, so that he, by a most secret, but yet a most righteous judgment, causes them to be inclined whither he pleases, and when he pleases, either for the communication of benefits, or for the infliction of punishments."

VIII. Here let the reader remember, that the ability of the human will is not to be estimated from the event of things, as some ignorant men are preposterously accustomed to do. For they conceive themselves fully and ingeniously to establish the servitude of the human will, because even the most exalted monarchs have not all their desires fulfilled. But this ability, of which we speak, is to be considered within man, and not to be measured by external success. For in the dispute concerning free will, the question is not, whether a man, notwithstanding external impediments, can perform and execute whatever he may have resolved in his mind, but whether in every case his judgment exerts freedom of choice, and his will freedom of inclination. If men possess both these, then Attilius Regulus, when confined to the small extent of a cask stuck round with nails, will possess as much free will as Augustus Cæsar, when governing a great part of the world with his nod.

CHAPTER V.

A REFUTATION OF THE OBJECTIONS COMMONLY URGED IN SUPPORT OF FREE WILL.

ENOUGH might appear to have been already said on the servitude of the human will, did not they, who endeavour to overthrow it with a false notion of liberty, allege, on the contrary, certain reasons in opposition to our sentiments. First, they collect together some absurdities, in order to render it odious, as if it were abhorrent to common sense; and then they attack it with testimonies of Scripture. Both these weapons we will repel in order. If sin, say they, be necessary, then it ceases to be sin; if it be voluntary, then it may be avoided. These were also the weapons used by Pelagius in his attacks on Augustine; with whose authority, however, we wish not to urge them, till we shall have given some satisfaction on the subject itself. I deny, then, that sin is the less criminal, because it is necessary; I deny also the other consequence, which they infer, that it is avoidable because it is voluntary. For, if any one wish to dispute with God, and to escape his judgment by the pretext of having been incapable of acting otherwise, he is prepared with an answer, which we have elsewhere advanced, that it arises not from creation, but from the corruption of nature, that men, being enslaved by sin, can will nothing but what is evil. For whence proceeded that impotence, of which the ungodly would gladly avail themselves, but from Adam voluntarily devoting himself to the tyranny of the devil? Hence, therefore, the corruption with which we are firmly bound. It originated in the revolt of the first man from his Maker. If all men are justly accounted guilty of this rebellion, let them not suppose themselves excused by necessity, in which very thing they have a most evident cause of their condemnation. And this I have before clearly explained, and have given an example in the devil himself, which shows, that he who sins necessarily, sins no less voluntarily; and also in the elect angels, whose will, though it cannot swerve from what is good, ceases not to be a will. Bernard also judiciously inculcates the same doctrine, that we are, therefore, the more miserable because our necessity is voluntary; which yet constrains us to be so devoted to it, that we are, as we have already observed, the slaves of sin. The second branch of their argument is erroneous; because it makes an improper transition from what is voluntary to what is free; but we have before evinced, that a thing may be done voluntarily, which yet is not the subject of free choice.

II. They add, that unless both virtues and vices proceed from the free choice of the will, it is not reasonable either that punishments should be inflicted, or that rewards should be conferred on man. This argument, though first advanced by Aristotle, yet I grant is used on some occasions by Chrysostom and Jerome. That it was familiar to the Pelagians, however, Jerome himself does not dissemble, but even relates their own words: "If the grace of God operates in us, then the crown will be given to grace, not to us who labour." In regard to punishments, I reply, that they are justly inflicted on us, from whom the guilt of sin proceeds. For of what importance is it, whether sin be committed with a judgment free or enslaved, so it be committed with the voluntary bias of the passions; especially as man is proved to be a sinner, because he is subject to the servitude of sin? With respect to rewards of righteousness, where is the great absurdity, if we confess that they depend rather on the Divine benignity than on our own merits? How often does this recur in Augustine, "that God crowns not our merits, but his own gifts; and that they are called rewards, not as though they were due to our merits, but because they are retributions to the graces already conferred on us!" They discover great acuteness in this observation, that there remains no room for merits, if they originate not from free will; but in their opinion of the erroneousness of our sentiment they are greatly mistaken. For Augustine hesitates not on all occasions to inculcate as certain, what they think it impious to acknowledge; as where he says, "What are the merits of any man? When he comes not with a merited reward, but with free grace, he alone being free and a deliverer from sins, finds all men sinners." Again: "If you receive what is your due, you must be punished. What then is done? God has given you not merited punishment, but unmerited grace. If you wish to be excluded from grace, boast your merits." Again: "You are nothing of yourself; sins are yours, merits belong to God; you deserve punishment; and when you come to be rewarded, he will crown his own gifts, not your merits." In the same sense he elsewhere teaches that grace proceeds not from merit, but merit from grace. And a little after he concludes, that God with his gifts precedes all merits, that thence he may elicit his other merits, and gives altogether freely, because he discovers nothing as a cause of salvation. But what necessity is there for further quotations, when his writings are full of such passages? But the Apostle will even better deliver them from this error, if they will hear from what origin he deduces the glory of the saints. " Whom he did predestinate, them he also called; and whom he called, them he also justified; and whom he justified, them he also glorified." (*m*) Why, then, according to the Apostle, are the faithful crowned? Because by the mercy of the Lord, and not by their own industry, they are elected, and called, and justified. Farewell, then, this vain fear, that there will be an end of all merits if free will be overturned. For it is a proof of extreme folly, to be terrified and to fly from that to which the Scripture calls us. "If," says he, "thou didst receive it, why dost thou glory, as if thou hadst not received it?" (*n*) You see that he divests free will of every thing, with the express design of leaving no room for merits. But yet, the beneficence and liberality of God being inexhaustible and various, those graces which he confers on us, because he makes them ours, he rewards, just as if they were our own virtues.

III. They further allege what may appear to be borrowed from Chrysostom, that if our will has not this ability to choose good or evil, the partakers of the same nature must be either all evil or all good. And not very far from this is the writer, whoever he was, of the treatise *On the Calling of the Gentiles*, which is circulated under the name of Ambrose, when he argues, that no man would ever recede from the faith, unless

(*m*) Rom. viii. 20. (*n*) 1 Cor. iv. 7.

the grace of God left us the condition of mutability. In which it is surprising that such great men were so inconsistent with themselves. For how did it not occur to Chrysostom, that it is the election of God, which makes this difference between men? We are not afraid to allow, what Paul very strenuously asserts, that all, without exception, are depraved and addicted to wickedness; but with him we add, that the mercy of God does not permit all to remain in depravity. Therefore, since we all naturally labour under the same disease, they alone recover to whom the Lord has been pleased to apply his healing hand. The rest, whom he passes by in righteous judgment, putrefy in their corruption till they are entirely consumed. And it is from the same cause, that some persevere to the end, and others decline and fall in the midst of their course. For perseverance itself also is a gift of God, which he bestows not on all men promiscuously, but imparts to whom he pleases. If we inquire the cause of the difference, why some persevere with constancy, and others fail through instability, no other can be found, but that God sustains the former by his power, that they perish not, and does not communicate the same strength to the latter, that they may be examples of inconstancy.

IV. They urge further, that exhortations are given in vain, that the use of admonitions is superfluous, and that reproofs are ridiculous, if it be not in the power of the sinner to obey. When similar objections were formerly made to Augustine, he was obliged to write his treatise *On Correction and Grace;* in which, though he copiously refutes them, he calls his adversaries to this conclusion: "O man, in the commandment learn what is your duty: in correction learn, that through your own fault you have it not: in prayer learn whence you may receive what you wish to enjoy." There is nearly the same argument in the treatise *On the Spirit and Letter*, in which he maintains that God does not regulate the precepts of his law by the ability of men, but when he has commanded what is right, freely gives to his elect ability to perform it. This is not a subject that requires a prolix discussion. First, we are not alone in this cause, but have the support of Christ and all the Apostles. Let our opponents consider how they can obtain the superiority in a contest with such antagonists. Does Christ, who declares that without him we can do nothing, (*o*) on that account the less reprehend and punish those who without him do what is evil? Does he therefore relax in his exhortations to every man to practise good works? How severely does Paul censure the Corinthians for their neglect of charity! (*p*) Yet he earnestly prays that charity may be given them by the Lord. In his

(*o*) John xv. 5.   (*p*) 1 Cor. iii. 3.

Epistle to the Romans he declares that "it is not of him that willeth, nor of him that runneth, but of God that showeth mercy:" (q) yet afterwards he refrains not from the use of admonition, exhortation, and reproof. Why do they not, therefore, remonstrate with the Lord, not to lose his labour in such a manner, by requiring of men those things which he alone can bestow, and punishing those things which are committed for want of his grace? Why do they not admonish Paul to spare those who are unable to will or run without the previous mercy of God, of which they are now destitute? As though truly the Lord has not the best reason for his doctrine, which readily presents itself to those who religiously seek it. Paul clearly shows how far doctrine, exhortation, and reproof, can of themselves avail towards producing a change of heart, when he says that "neither is he that planteth any thing, neither he that watereth; but" that the efficacy is solely from "God that giveth the increase." (r) Thus we see that Moses severely sanctions the precepts of the law, and the Prophets earnestly urge and threaten transgressors; whilst, nevertheless, they acknowledge, that men never begin to be wise till a heart is given them to understand; that it is the peculiar work of God to circumcise the heart, and instead of a stony heart to give a heart of flesh; to inscribe his law in men's minds; in a word, to render his doctrine effectual by a renovation of the soul.

V. What, then, it will be inquired, is the use of exhortations? I reply, If the impious despise them with obstinate hearts, they will serve for a testimony against them, when they shall come to the tribunal of the Lord; and even in the present state they wound their consciences; for however the most audacious person may deride them, he cannot disapprove of them in his heart. But it will be said, What can a miserable sinner do, if the softness of heart, which is necessary to obedience, be denied him? I ask, What excuse can he plead, seeing that he cannot impute the hardness of his heart to any one but himself? The impious, therefore, who are ready, if possible, to ridicule the Divine precepts and exhortations, are, in spite of their own inclinations, confounded by their power. But the principal utility should be considered in regard to the faithful, in whom as the Lord performs all things by his Spirit, so he neglects not the instrumentality of his word, but uses it with great efficacy. Let it be allowed, then, as it ought to be, that all the strength of the pious consists in the grace of God, according to this expression of the Prophet: "I will give them a new heart, that they may walk in my statutes." (s) But you will object, Why are they admonished of their duty, and not

(q) Rom. ix. 16.   (r) 1 Cor. iii. 7.   (s) Ezek. xi. 19, 20.

rather left to the direction of the Spirit? Why are they importuned with exhortations, when they cannot make more haste than is produced by the impulse of the Spirit? Why are they chastised, if they have ever deviated from the right way, seeing that they erred through the necessary infirmity of the flesh? I reply, Who art thou, O man, that wouldest impose laws upon God? If it be his will to prepare us by exhortation for the reception of this grace, by which obedience to the exhortation is produced, what have you to censure in this economy? If exhortations and reproofs were of no other advantage to the pious, than to convince them of sin, they ought not on that account to be esteemed wholly useless. Now, since, by the internal operation of the Spirit, they are most effectual to inflame the heart with a love of righteousness, to shake off sloth, to destroy the pleasure and poisonous sweetness of iniquity, and, on the contrary, to render it hateful and burdensome, who can dare to reject them as superfluous? If any one would desire a plainer answer, let him take it thus: The operations of God on his elect are twofold — internally, by his Spirit, externally, by his word. By his Spirit illuminating their minds and forming their hearts to the love and cultivation of righteousness, he makes them new creatures. By his word he excites them to desire, seek, and obtain the same renovation. In both he displays the efficacy of his power, according to the mode of his dispensation. When he addresses the same word to the reprobate, though it produces not their correction, yet he makes it effectual for another purpose, that they may be confounded by the testimony of their consciences now, and be rendered more inexcusable at the day of judgment. Thus Christ, though he pronounces that "no man can come to him, except the Father draw him," and that the elect come when they have "heard and learned of the Father," (t) yet himself neglects not the office of a teacher, but with his own mouth sedulously invites those who need the internal teachings of the Holy Spirit to enable them to derive any benefit from his instructions. With respect to the reprobate, Paul suggests that teaching is not useless, because it is to them "the savour of death unto death," but "a sweet savour unto God." (v)

VI. Our adversaries are very laborious in collecting testimonies of Scripture; and this with a view, since they cannot refute us with their weight, to overwhelm us with their number. But as in battles, when armies come to close combat, the weak multitude, whatever pomp and ostentation they may display, are soon defeated and routed, so it will be very easy for us to vanquish them, with all their multitude. For as all

---

(t) John vi. 44, 45. (v) 2 Cor. ii. 16.

the passages, which they abuse in their opposition to us, when properly classed and distributed, centre in a very few topics, one answer will be sufficient for many of them; it will not be necessary to dwell on a particular explication of each. Their principal argument they derive from the precepts; which they suppose to be so proportioned to our ability, that whatever they can be proved to require, it necessarily follows we are capable of performing. They proceed, therefore, to a particular detail of them, and by them measure the extent of our strength. Either, say they, God mocks us, when he commands holiness, piety, obedience, chastity, love, and meekness, and when he forbids impurity, idolatry, unchastity, anger, robbery, pride, and the like; or he requires only such things as we have power to perform. Now, almost all the precepts which they collect, may be distributed into three classes. Some require the first conversion to God; others simply relate to the observation of the law; others enjoin perseverance in the grace of God already received. Let us first speak of them all in general, and then proceed to the particulars. To represent the ability of man as coëxtensive with the precepts of the Divine law, has indeed for a long time not been unusual, and has some appearance of plausibility; but it has proceeded from the grossest ignorance of the law. For those who think it an enormous crime to say that the observation of the law is impossible, insist on this very cogent argument, that otherwise the law was given in vain. For they argue just as if Paul had never said any thing concerning the law. But, pray, what is the meaning of these expressions — "The law was added because of transgressions;" "by the law is the knowledge of sin;" "the law worketh wrath;" "the law entered that the offence might abound?" (*w*) Do they imply a necessity of its being limited to our ability, that it might not be given in vain? Do they not rather show that it was placed far beyond our ability, in order to convince us of our impotence? According to the definition of the same Apostle, "the end of the commandment is charity."(*x*) But when he wishes the minds of the Thessalonians to "abound in love," (*y*) he plainly acknowledges that the law sounds in our ears in vain, unless God inspire the principles of it into our hearts.

VII. Indeed, if the Scripture taught only that the law is the rule of life, to which our conduct ought to be conformed, I would immediately accede to their opinion. But since it carefully and perspicuously states to us various uses of the law, it will be best to consider the operation of the law in man according to that exposition. As far as relates to the present argument,

(*w*) Gal. iii. 19. Rom. iii. 20; iv. 15; v. 20.
(*x*) 1 Tim. i. 5. (*y*) 1 Thess. iii. 12.

when it has prescribed any thing to be performed by us, it teaches that the power of obedience proceeds from the goodness of God, and therefore invites us to pray that it may be given us. If there were only a commandment, and no promise, there would be a trial of the sufficiency of our strength to obey the commandment; but since the commands are connected with promises, which declare that we must derive not only subsidiary power, but our whole strength, from the assistance of Divine grace, they furnish abundant evidence that we are not only unequal to the observation of the law, but altogether incapable of it. Wherefore let them no more urge the proportion of our ability to the precepts of the law, as though the Lord had regulated the standard of righteousness, which he designed to give in the law, according to the measure of our imbecility. It should rather be concluded from the promises, how unprepared we are of ourselves, since we stand in such universal need of his grace. But will it, say they, be credited by any, that the Lord addressed his law to stocks and stones? I reply, that no one will attempt to inculcate such a notion. For neither are the impious stocks or stones, when they are taught by the law the contrariety of their dispositions to God, and are convicted of guilt by the testimony of their own minds; nor the pious, when, admonished of their own impotence, they have recourse to the grace of God. To this purpose are the following passages from Augustine: "God gives commands which we cannot perform, that we may know what we ought to request of him. The utility of the precepts is great, if only so much be given to free will, that the grace of God may receive the greater honour. Faith obtains what the law commands; and the law therefore commands, that faith may obtain that which is commanded by the law: moreover God requires faith itself of us, and finds not what he requires, unless he has given what he finds." Again: "Let God give what he enjoins, and let him enjoin what he pleases."

VIII. This will more clearly appear in an examination of the three kinds of precepts which we have already mentioned. The Lord, both in the law and in the prophets, frequently commands us to be converted to him; (z) but the Prophet, on the other hand, says, "Turn thou me, and I shall be turned." "After that I was turned, I repented," &c. (a) He commands us to circumcise our hearts; but he announces by Moses, that this circumcision is the work of his own hand. (b) He frequently requires newness of heart; but elsewhere declares that this is his own gift. (c) "What God promises," Augustine says, "we do not perform ourselves through free will or nature; but

(z) Joel ii. 12.
(a) Jer. xxxi. 18, 19.
(b) Deut. x. 16, and xxx. 6.
(c) Jer. iv. 4. Ezek. xxxvi. 26.

he does it himself by his grace." And this is the observation to which he himself assigns the fifth place in his enumeration of Ticonius's rules of Christian doctrine; that we should make a proper distinction between the law and the promises, or between the commandments and grace. This may suffice, in answer to those who from the precepts infer an ability in man to obey them, that they may destroy the grace of God, by which those very precepts are fulfilled. The precepts of the second class are simple, enjoining on us the worship of God, constant submission to his will, observance of his commands, and adherence to his doctrine. But there are innumerable passages, which prove that the highest degree of righteousness, sanctity, piety, and purity, capable of being attained, is his own gift. Of the third class is that exhortation of Paul and Barnabas to the faithful, mentioned by Luke, "to continue in the grace of God." (*d*) But whence the grace of perseverance should be sought, the same Apostle informs us, when he says, "Finally, my brethren, be strong in the Lord." (*e*) In another place he cautions us to "grieve not the Holy Spirit of God, whereby we are sealed unto the day of redemption." (*f*) But because what he there requires could not be performed by men, he prays for the Thessalonians, "that our God would count them worthy of this calling, and fulfil all the good pleasure of his goodness, and the work of faith with power." (*g*) Thus, also, in the Second Epistle to the Corinthians, treating of alms, he frequently commends their benevolent and pious disposition; (*h*) yet a little after he gives thanks to God for having inclined the heart of Titus to "accept" or undertake "the exhortation." If Titus could not even use his own tongue to exhort others without having been prompted by God, how should others have been inclined to act, unless God himself had directed their hearts?

IX. Our more subtle adversaries cavil at all these testimonies, because there is no impediment, they say, that prevents our exerting our own ability, and God assisting our weak efforts. They adduce also passages from the Prophets, where the accomplishment of our conversion seems to be divided equally between God and us. "Turn ye unto me, and I will turn unto you." (*i*) What assistance we receive from the Lord has already been shown, and needs not to be repeated here. I wish only this single point to be conceded to me, that it is in vain to infer our possession of ability to fulfil the law from God's command to us to obey it; since it is evident, that for the performance of all the Divine precepts, the grace of the

(*d*) Acts xiii. 43. (*f*) Eph. iv. 30. (*h*) 2 Cor. viii. 1, &c.
(*e*) Eph. vi. 10. (*g*) 2 Thess. i. 11. (*i*) Zech. i. 3.

Legislator is both necessary for us, and promised to us; and hence it follows, that at least more is required of us than we are capable of performing. Nor is it possible for any cavils to explain away that passage of Jeremiah, which assures us, that the covenant of God, made with his ancient people, was frustrated because it was merely a literal one; (*k*) and that it can only be confirmed by the influence of the Spirit, who forms the heart to obedience. Nor does their error derive any support from this passage: "Turn ye unto me, and I will turn unto you." For this denotes, not that turning of God in which he renovates our hearts to repentance, but that in which he declares his benevolence and kindness by external prosperity; as by adversity he sometimes manifests his displeasure. When the people of Israel, therefore, after having been harassed with miseries and calamities under various forms, complained that God was departed from them, he replies that his benignity will not fail them if they return to rectitude of life, and to himself, who is the standard of righteousness. The passage, then, is miserably perverted, when it is made to represent the work of conversion as divided between God and men. We have observed the greater brevity on these points, because it will be a more suitable place for this argument when we treat of the Law.

X. The second description of arguments is nearly allied to the first. They allege the promises, in which God covenants with our will; such as, "Seek good, and not evil, that ye may live." "If ye be willing and obedient, ye shall eat the good of the land; but if ye refuse and rebel, ye shall be devoured with the sword; for the mouth of the Lord hath spoken it." (*l*) Again: "If thou wilt put away thine abominations out of my sight, then shalt thou not remove." "If thou shalt hearken diligently unto the voice of the Lord thy God, to observe and to do all his commandments which I command thee this day, the Lord thy God will set thee on high above all nations of the earth;" (*m*) and other similar passages. They consider it an absurdity and mockery, that the benefits which the Lord offers in the promises are referred to our will, unless it be in our power either to confirm or to frustrate them. And truly it is very easy to amplify this subject with eloquent complaints, that we are cruelly mocked by the Lord, when he announces that his benignity depends on our will, if that will be not in our own power; that this would be egregious liberality in God, to present his benefits to us in such a manner, that we should have no power to enjoy them; and that there must be a strange certainty in his promises, if they depend on a thing impossible, so that they can never be fulfilled. Concerning

(*k*) Jer. xxxi. 32. (*l*) Amos v. 14. Isaiah i. 19, 20.
(*m*) Jer. iv. 1. Deut. xxviii. 1.

promises of this kind, to which a condition is annexed, we shall speak in another place, and evince that there is no absurdity in the impossibility of their completion. With respect to the present question, I deny that God is cruel or insincere to us, when he invites us to merit his favours, though he knows us to be altogether incapable of doing this. For as the promises are offered equally to the faithful and to the impious, they have their use with them both. As by the precepts God disturbs the consciences of the impious, that they may not enjoy too much pleasure in sin without any recollection of his judgments, so in the promises he calls them to attest how unworthy they are of his kindness. For who can deny that it is most equitable and proper for the Lord to bless those who worship him, and severely to punish the despisers of his majesty? God acts, therefore, in a right and orderly manner, when, addressing the impious, who are bound with the fetters of sin, he adds to the promises this condition, that when they shall have departed from their wickedness, they shall then, and not till then, enjoy his favours; even for this sole reason, that they may know that they are deservedly excluded from those benefits which belong to the worshippers of the true God. On the other hand, since he designs by all means to stimulate the faithful to implore his grace, it will not be at all strange, if he tries in his promises also, what we have shown he does with considerable effect in his precepts. Being instructed by the precepts concerning the will of God, we are apprized of our misery, in having our hearts so completely averse to it; and are at the same time excited to invoke his Spirit, that we may be directed by him into the right way. But because our sluggishness is not sufficiently roused by the precepts, God adds his promises, to allure us by their sweetness to the love of his commands. Now, in proportion to our increased love of righteousness will be the increase of our fervour in seeking the grace of God. See how, in these addresses, "If ye be willing," "If ye be obedient," the Lord neither attributes to us an unlimited power to will and to obey, nor yet mocks us on account of our impotence.

XI. The third class of arguments also has a great affinity with the preceding. For they produce passages in which God reproaches an ungrateful people, that it was wholly owing to their own fault that they did not receive blessings of all kinds from his indulgent hand. Of this kind are the following passages: "The Amalekites and the Canaanites are there before you, and ye shall fall by the sword; because ye are turned away from the Lord." (*n*) "Because I called you, but ye answered not, therefore will I do unto this house as I have done

(*n*) Numb. xiv. 43.

to Shiloh." (o)   Again: "This is a nation that obeyeth not
the voice of the Lord their God, nor receiveth correction: the
Lord hath rejected and forsaken the generation of his wrath." (p)
Again: "They obeyed not thy voice, neither walked in thy
law; they have done nothing of all that thou commandedst
them to do: therefore thou hast caused all this evil to come
upon them." (q)   How, say they, could such reproaches be applicable to those who might immediately reply, It is true that
we desired prosperity and dreaded adversity; but our not obeying the Lord, or hearkening to his voice, in order to obtain
good and to avoid evil, has been owing to our want of liberty,
and subjection to the dominion of sin. It is in vain, therefore,
to reproach us with evils, which we had no power to avoid.
In answer to this, leaving the pretext of necessity, which is
but a weak and futile plea, I ask whether they can exculpate
themselves from all guilt. For if they are convicted of any
fault, the Lord justly reproaches them with their perverseness,
as the cause of their not having experienced the advantage of
his clemency. Let them answer, then, if they can deny that
their own perverse will was the cause of their obstinacy. If
they find the source of the evil within themselves, why do
they so earnestly inquire after extraneous causes, that they
may not appear to have been the authors of their own ruin?
But if it be true that sinners are deprived of the favours of God,
and chastised with his punishments, for their own sin, and
only for their own, there is great reason why they should hear
those reproaches from his mouth; that if they obstinately persist in their crimes, they may learn in their calamities rather to
accuse and detest their iniquity, than to charge God with unrighteous cruelty; that if they have not cast off all docility,
they may become weary of their sins, the demerits of which
they see to be misery and ruin, and may return into the good
way, acknowledging in a serious confession the very thing for
which the Lord rebukes them. And that those reproofs, which
are quoted from the Prophets, have produced this beneficial
effect on the faithful, is evident from the solemn prayer of
Daniel, given us in his ninth chapter. Of the former use of
them we find an example in the Jews, to whom Jeremiah is
commanded to declare the cause of their miseries; though
nothing could befall them, otherwise than the Lord had foretold.
"Thou shalt speak all these words unto them; but they will not
hearken to thee: thou shalt also call unto them; but they will
not answer thee." (r)   For what purpose, then, it will be asked,
did they speak to persons that were deaf? It was in order
that, in spite of their disinclination and aversion, they might

(o) Jer. vii. 13, 14.   (p) Jer. vii. 28, 29.   (q) Jer. xxxii. 23.   (r) Jer. vii. 27.

know what was declared to them to be true; that it was an abominable sacrilege to transfer to God the guilt of their crimes, which belonged solely to themselves. With these few solutions, we may very easily despatch the immense multitude of testimonies, which the enemies of the grace of God are accustomed to collect, both from the precepts of the law, and from the expostulations directed to transgressors of it, in order to establish the idol of free will. In one psalm the Jews are stigmatized as "a stubborn and rebellious generation, a generation that set not their heart aright." (s) In another, the Psalmist exhorts the men of his age to " harden not their hearts;" (t) which implies, that all the guilt of rebellion lies in the perverseness of men. But it is absurd to infer from this passage that the heart is equally flexible to either side; whereas "the preparation" of it is "from the Lord." (v) The Psalmist says, "I have inclined my heart to perform thy statutes;" (w) because he had devoted himself to the service of God without any reluctance, but with a cheerful readiness of mind. Yet he boasts not of being himself the author of this inclination, which in the same psalm he acknowledges to be the gift of God. (x) We should remember, therefore, the admonition of Paul, when he commands the faithful to " work out" their " own salvation with fear and trembling; for it is God which worketh in" them " both to will and to do." (y) He assigns them a part to perform, that they may not indulge themselves in carnal negligence; but by inculcating "fear and trembling," he humbles them, and reminds them that this very thing, which they are commanded to do, is the peculiar work of God. In this he plainly suggests that the faithful act, if I may be allowed the expression, passively, inasmuch as they are furnished with strength from heaven, that they may arrogate nothing at all to themselves. Wherefore, when Peter exhorts us to "add to" our "faith, virtue," (z) he does not allot us an under part to be performed, as though we could do any thing separately, of ourselves; he only arouses the indolence of the flesh, by which faith itself is frequently extinguished. To the same purpose is the exhortation of Paul: "Quench not the Spirit;" (a) for slothfulness gradually prevails over the faithful, unless it be corrected. But if any one should infer from this, that it is at his own option to cherish the light offered him, his ignorance will easily be refuted; since this diligence which Paul requires, proceeds only from God. For we are also frequently commanded to "cleanse ourselves from all filthiness," (b) whilst the Spirit claims the office of sanctifying us exclusively to himself. In short, that

---

(s) Psalm lxxviii. 8.
(t) Psalm xcv. 8.
(v) Prov. xvi. 1.
(w) Psalm cxix. 112.
(x) Psalm cxix. 33—40.
(y) Phil. ii. 12.
(z) 2 Peter i. 5.
(a) 1 Thess. v. 19.
(b) 2 Cor. vii. 1.

what properly belongs to God is, by concession, transferred to us, is plain from the words of John: "He that is begotten of God, keepeth himself." (c) The preachers of free will lay hold of this expression, as though we were saved partly by the Divine power, partly by our own; as though we did not receive from heaven this very preservation which the Apostle mentions. Wherefore also Christ prays that his Father would "keep" us "from evil;" (d) and we know that the pious, in their warfare against Satan, obtain the victory by no other arms than those which are furnished by God. Therefore Peter, having enjoined us to "purify" our "souls, in obeying the truth," immediately adds, as a correction, "through the Spirit." (e) Finally, the impotence of all human strength in the spiritual conflict is briefly demonstrated by John when he says, "Whosoever is born of God cannot sin; for his seed remaineth in him:" (f) and in another place he adds the reason, that "this is the victory that overcometh the world, even our faith." (g)

XII. There is also a testimony cited from the law of Moses, which appears directly repugnant to our solution. For, after having published the law, he makes the following solemn declaration to the people: "This commandment, which I command thee this day, it is not hidden from thee, neither is it far off: it is not in heaven: but the word is very nigh unto thee, in thy mouth, and in thy heart, that thou mayest do it." (h) If these expressions be understood merely of the precepts, I grant that they have much weight in the present argument. For although we might easily elude their force, by saying that they treat of the facility and promptitude, not of observance, but of knowledge, yet still perhaps they might leave some doubt. But the Apostle, in whose expositions there is no ambiguity, removes all our doubts, by affirming that Moses here spake of the doctrine of the gospel. (i) But if any one should obstinately contend, that Paul has violently perverted the passage from its genuine meaning, by applying it to the gospel, although his presumption could not be acquitted of impiety, yet there is enough to refute him, independently of the authority of the Apostle. For, if Moses spoke only of the precepts, he was deceiving the people with the vainest confidence. For would they not have precipitated themselves into ruin, if they had attempted the observance of the law in their own strength, as a thing of no difficulty? What, then, becomes of the very obvious facility with which the law may be observed, when there appears no access to it but over a fatal precipice? Where-

(c) 1 John v. 18.
(d) John xvii. 15.
(e) 1 Peter i. 22.
(f) 1 John iii. 9.
(g) 1 John v. 4.
(h) Deut. xxx. 11—14.
(i) Rom. x. 8.

fore nothing is more certain, than that Moses in these words comprehended the covenant of mercy, which he had promulgated together with the precepts of the law. For in a preceding verse he had taught that our hearts must be circumcised by God, in order that we may love him. (*k*) Therefore he placed this facility, of which he afterwards speaks, not in the strength of man, but in the assistance and protection of the Holy Spirit, who powerfully accomplishes his work in our infirmity. However, the passage is not to be understood simply of the precepts, but rather of the promises of the gospel, which are so far from maintaining an ability in us to obtain righteousness, that they prove us to be utterly destitute of it. Paul, considering the same, proves by this testimony that salvation is proposed to us in the gospel, not under that hard, difficult, and impossible condition, prescribed to us in the law, which pronounces it attainable only by those who have fulfilled all the commandments, but under a condition easily and readily to be performed. Therefore this testimony contributes nothing to support the liberty of the human will.

XIII. Some other passages also are frequently objected, which show that God sometimes tries men by withdrawing the assistance of his grace, and waits to see what course they will pursue; as in Hosea: "I will go and return to my place, till they acknowledge their offence, and seek my face." (*l*) It would be ridiculous, they say, for the Lord to consider, whether Israel would seek his face, unless their minds were flexible, capable of inclining either way, according to their own pleasure; as if it were not very common for God, in the Prophets, to represent himself as despising and rejecting his people, till they should amend their lives. But what will our adversaries infer from such threats? If they maintain, that those who are deserted by God, are capable of converting themselves, they oppose the uniform declarations of Scripture. If they acknowledge that the grace of God is necessary to conversion, what is their controversy with us? But they will reply, that they concede its necessity in such a sense as to maintain that man still retains some power. How do they prove it? Certainly not from this or any similar passages. For it is one thing to depart from a man, to observe what he will do when forsaken and left to himself, and another to assist his little strength in proportion to his imbecility. What, then, it will be inquired, is implied in such forms of expression? I reply, that the import of them is just as if God had said, Since admonitions, exhortations, and reproofs, produce no good effect on this rebellious people, I will withdraw myself for a little while, and silently

(*k*) Deut. xxx. 6. (*l*) Hos. v. 15.

leave them to affliction. I will see whether, at some future period, after a series of calamities, they will remember me, and seek my face. The departure of the Lord signifies the removal of his word. His observing what men will do, signifies his concealing himself in silence, and exercising them for a season with various afflictions. He does both to humble us the more; for we should sooner be confounded than corrected with the scourges of adversity, unless he rendered us docile by his Spirit. Now, when the Lord, offended, and, as it were, wearied by our extreme obstinacy, leaves us for a time, by the removal of his word, in which he is accustomed to manifest his presence with us, and makes the experiment, what we shall do in his absence, — it is falsely inferred from this, that there is some power of free will, which he observes and proves; since he acts in this manner with no other design than to bring us to a sense and acknowledgment of our own nothingness.

XIV. They argue also from the manner of expression which is invariably observed, both in the Scripture and in the common conversation of mankind. For good actions are called our own, and we are said to perform what is holy and pleasing to the Lord, as well as to commit sins. But if sins be justly imputed to us, as proceeding from ourselves, certainly some share ought to be, for the same reason, assigned to us also in works of righteousness. For it would be absurd that we should be said to do those things, to the performance of which, being incapable of any exertion of our own, we were impelled by God, as so many stones. Wherefore, though we allow the grace of God the preëminence, yet these expressions indicate that our own endeavours hold at least the second place. If it were only alleged, that good works are called our own, I would reply, that the bread which we pray to God to give us, is called ours. What will they prove by this term, but that what otherwise by no means belongs to us, becomes ours through the benignity and gratuitous munificence of God? Therefore let them either ridicule the same absurdity in the Lord's prayer, or no longer esteem it ridiculous, that good works are denominated ours, in which we have no propriety but from the liberality of God. But there is rather more force in what follows; that the Scripture frequently affirms that we ourselves worship God, work righteousness, obey the law, and perform good works. These being the proper offices of the understanding and will, how could they justly be referred to the Spirit, and at the same time be attributed to us, if there were not some union of our exertions with the grace of God? We shall easily extricate ourselves from these objections, if we properly consider the manner in which the Spirit of the Lord operates in the saints. The similitude with which they try to cast an odium on our sentiments, is quite foreign to the subject; for who is so senseless as to suppose that there is no difference between impelling a man, and throwing a stone? Nor does any such consequence follow from our doctrine. We rank among the natural powers of man, approving, rejecting; willing, nilling; attempting, resisting; that is, a power to approve vanity, and to reject true excellence; to will what is evil, to refuse what is good; to attempt iniquity, and to resist righteousness. What concern has the Lord in this? If it be his will to use this depravity as an instrument of his wrath, he directs and appoints it according to his pleasure, in order to execute his good work by means of a wicked hand. Shall we, then, compare a wicked man who is thus subservient to the Divine power, while he only studies to gratify his own corrupt inclination, to a stone which is hurled by an extrinsic impulse, and driven along without any motion, sense, or will of its own? We perceive what a vast difference there is. But how does the Lord operate in good men, to whom the question principally relates? When he erects his kingdom within them, he by his Spirit restrains their will, that it may not be hurried away by unsteady and violent passions, according to the propensity of nature; that it may be inclined to holiness and righteousness, he bends, composes, forms, and directs it according to the rule of his own righteousness; that it may not stagger or fall, he establishes and confirms it by the power of his Spirit. For which reason Augustine says, " You will reply to me, Then we are actuated; we do not act. Yes, you both act and are actuated; and you act well, when you are actuated by that which is good. The Spirit of God, who actuates you, assists those who act, and calls himself a helper, because you also perform something." In the first clause he inculcates that the agency of man is not destroyed by the influence of the Spirit; because the will, which is guided to aspire to what is good, belongs to his nature. But the inference which he immediately subjoins, from the term *help*, that we also perform something, we should not understand in such a sense, as though he attributed any thing to us independently; but in order to avoid encouraging us in indolence, he reconciles the Divine agency with ours in this way; that to will is from nature, to will what is good is from grace. Therefore he had just before said, " Without the assistance of God, we shall be not only unable to conquer, but even to contend."

XV. Hence it appears that the grace of God, in the sense in which this word is used when we treat of regeneration, is the rule of the Spirit for directing and governing the human will. He cannot govern it unless he correct, reform, and renovate it; whence we say that the commencement of regeneration is an abolition of what is from ourselves; nor unless he also excite, actuate, impel, support, and restrain it; whence we truly assert, that all the actions which proceed from this are entirely of the Spirit. At the same time, we fully admit the truth of what Augustine teaches, that the will is not destroyed by grace, but rather repaired; for these two things are perfectly consistent — that the human will may be said to be repaired, when, by the correction of its depravity and perverseness, it is directed according to the true standard of righteousness; and also that a new will may be said to be created in man, because the natural will is so vitiated and corrupted, that it needs to be formed entirely anew. Now, there is no reason why we may not justly be said to perform that which the Spirit of God performs in us, although our own will contributes nothing of itself, independently of his grace. And, therefore, we should remember what we have before cited from Augustine, that many persons labour in vain to find in the human will some good, properly its own. For whatever mixture men study to add from the power of free will to the grace of God, is only a corruption of it; just as if any one should dilute good wine with dirty or bitter water. But although whatever good there is in the human will, proceeds wholly from the internal influence of the Spirit, yet because we have a natural faculty of willing, we are, not without reason, said to do those things, the praise of which God justly claims to himself; first, because whatever God does in us, becomes ours by his benignity, provided we do not apprehend it to originate from ourselves; secondly, because the understanding is ours, the will is ours, and the effort is ours, which are all directed by him to that which is good.

XVI. The other testimonies, which they rake together from every quarter, will not much embarrass even persons of moderate capacities, who have well digested the answers already given. They quote this passage from Genesis: "Unto thee shall be his desire, and thou shalt rule over him;" (m) or, as they would translate the words, "Subject to thee shall be its appetite, and thou shalt rule over it;" which they explain to relate to sin, as though the Lord promised Cain, that the power of sin should not obtain dominion over his mind, if he would labour to overcome it. But we say that it is more agreeable to the tenor of the context, to understand it to be spoken concerning Abel. For the design of God in it is to prove the iniquity of that envy, which Cain had conceived against his brother. This he does by two reasons: first, that

(m) Gen. iv. 7.

it was in vain for him to meditate crimes in order to excel his brother in the sight of God, with whom no honour is given but to righteousness; secondly, that he was extremely ungrateful for the favours God had already conferred on him, since he could not bear his brother, even though subject to his authority. But that we may not appear to adopt this explanation, merely because the other is unfavourable to our tenets, let us admit that God spake concerning sin. If it be so, then what the Lord there declares, is either promised or commanded by him. If it be a command, we have already demonstrated that it affords no proof of the power of men: if it be a promise, where is the completion of the promise, seeing that Cain fell under the dominion of sin, over which he ought to have prevailed? They will say, that the promise includes a tacit condition, as though it had been declared to him that he should obtain the victory if he would contend for it; but who can admit these subterfuges? For if this dominion be referred to sin, the speech is doubtless a command, expressive, not of our ability, but of our duty, which remains our duty even though it exceed our ability. But the subject itself, and grammatical propriety, require a comparison to be made between Cain and Abel; in which the elder brother would not have been placed below the younger, if he had not degraded himself by his own wickedness.

XVII. They adduce also the testimony of the Apostle, who says, that "it is not of him that willeth, nor of him that runneth, but of God that showeth mercy; " (n) whence they conclude, that there is something in the will and endeavour, which, though ineffectual of itself, is rendered successful by the assistance of the Divine mercy. But if they would soberly examine the subject there treated by Paul, they would not so inconsiderately pervert this passage. I know that they can allege the suffrages of Origen and Jerome in defence of their exposition; and in opposition to them, I could produce that of Augustine. But their opinions are of no importance to us if we can ascertain what was the meaning of Paul. He is there teaching, that salvation is provided for them alone, whom the Lord favours with his mercy; but that ruin and perdition await all those whom he has not chosen. He had shown, by the example of Pharaoh, the condition of the reprobate; and had confirmed the certainty of gratuitous election by the testimony of Moses: "I will have mercy on whom I will have mercy." His conclusion is, that "it is not of him that willeth, nor of him that runneth, but of God that showeth mercy." If this be understood to imply that our will and endeavour are

(n) Rom. ix. 16.

not sufficient, because they are not equal to so great a work, Paul has expressed himself with great impropriety. Away, therefore, with these sophisms: "It is not of him that willeth, nor of him that runneth;" therefore there is some willing and some running. For the meaning of Paul is more simple — It is neither our willing nor our running, which procures for us a way of salvation, but solely the mercy of God. For he expresses here the same sentiment as he does to Titus, when he says, "that the kindness and love of God towards man appeared, not by works of righteousness which we have done, but according to his mercy." (o) The very persons, who argue that Paul, in denying that it is of him that willeth or of him that runneth, implies that there is some willing and some running, would not allow me to use the same mode of reasoning, that we have done some good works, because Paul denies that we have obtained the favour of God by any works which we have done. But if they perceive a flaw in this argumentation, let them open their eyes, and they will perceive a similar fallacy in their own. For the argument on which Augustine rests the dispute is unanswerable: "If it be said, that it is not of him that willeth, nor of him that runneth, merely because neither our willing nor our running is sufficient, it may, on the contrary, be retorted, that it is not of the mercy of God, because that does not act alone." (p) The latter position being absurd, Augustine justly concludes the meaning of this passage to be, that there is no good will in man, unless it be prepared by the Lord; not but that we ought to will and to run, but because God works in us both the one and the other. With similar want of judgment, some pervert this declaration of Paul, "We are labourers together with God;" (q) which, without doubt, is restricted solely to ministers, who are denominated "workers with him," not that they contribute any thing of themselves, but because God makes use of their agency, after he has qualified them and furnished them with the necessary talents.

XVIII. They produce a passage from Ecclesiasticus, which is well known to be a book of doubtful authority. But though we should not reject it, which, nevertheless, if we chose, we might justly do, what testimony does it afford in support of free will? The writer says, that man, as soon as he was created, was left in the power of his own will; that precepts were given to him, which if he kept, he should also be kept by them; that he had life and death, good and evil, set before him; and that whatever he desired, would be given him. (r) Let it be granted, that man at his creation was endowed with a power of choosing life or death. What if we reply, that he

(o) Tit. iii. 4, 5.
(p) Epist. 107, ad Vital.
(q) 1 Cor. iii. 9.
(r) Ecclus. xv. 14.

has lost it? I certainly do not intend to contradict Solomon, who asserts that "God hath made man upright; but they have sought out many inventions." (s) But man, by his degeneracy, having shipwrecked both himself and all his excellences, whatever is attributed to his primitive state, it does not immediately follow that it belongs to his vitiated and degenerated nature. Therefore I reply, not only to them, but also to Ecclesiasticus himself, whoever he be: If you design to teach man to seek within himself a power to attain salvation, your authority is not so great in our estimation as to obtain even the smallest degree of credit, in opposition to the undoubted word of God. But if you only aim to repress the malignity of the flesh, which vainly attempts to vindicate itself by transferring its crimes to God, and you therefore reply, that man was originally endued with rectitude, from which it is evident that he was the cause of his own ruin, I readily assent to it; provided we also agree in this, that through his own guilt he is now despoiled of those ornaments with which God invested him at the beginning; and so unite in confessing, that in his present situation he needs not an advocate, but a physician.

XIX. But there is nothing which our adversaries have more frequently in their mouths, than the parable of Christ concerning the traveller, who was left by robbers in the road half dead. (t) I know it is the common opinion of almost all writers, that the calamity of the human race is represented under the type of this traveller. Hence they argue, that man is not so mutilated by the violence of sin and the devil, but that he still retains some relics of his former excellences, since he is said to have been left only half dead; for what becomes of the remaining portion of life, unless there remain some rectitude both of reason and will? In the first place, what could they say, if I refused to admit their allegory? For there is no doubt but that this interpretation, invented by the fathers, is foreign to the genuine sense of our Lord's discourse. Allegories ought to be extended no further than they are supported by the authority of Scripture; for they are far from affording of themselves a sufficient foundation for any doctrines. Nor is there any want of arguments by which, if I chose, I could completely confute this erroneous notion; for the word of God does not leave man in the possession of a proportion of life, but teaches, that as far as respects happiness of life, he is wholly dead. Paul, when speaking of our redemption, says, not that we were recovered when half dead, but that "even when we were dead, we were raised up." He calls not on the half dead, but on those who are in the grave, sleeping the

(s) Eccles. vii. 29.   (t) Luke x. 30.

sleep of death, to receive the illumination of Christ. (*u*) And the Lord himself speaks in a similar manner, when he says, that "the hour is coming, and now is, when the dead shall hear the voice of the Son of God; and they that hear shall live." (*w*) With what face can they oppose a slight allusion against so many positive expressions? Yet let this allegory even be admitted as a clear testimony; what will it enable them to extort from us? Man, they will say, is but half dead; therefore he has some faculty remaining entire. I grant that he has a mind capable of understanding, though it attains not to heavenly and spiritual wisdom; he has some idea of virtue; he has some sense of the Deity, though he acquires not the true knowledge of God. But what is to be concluded from all this? It certainly does not disprove the assertion of Augustine, which has received the general approbation even of the schools, that man, since his fall, has been deprived of the gifts of grace on which salvation depends; but that the natural ones are corrupted and polluted. Let us hold this, then, as an undoubted truth, which no opposition can ever shake — that the mind of man is so completely alienated from the righteousness of God, that it conceives, desires, and undertakes every thing that is impious, perverse, base, impure, and flagitious; that his heart is so thoroughly infected by the poison of sin, that it cannot produce any thing but what is corrupt; and that if at any time men do any thing apparently good, yet the mind always remains involved in hypocrisy and fallacious obliquity, and the heart enslaved by its inward perverseness.

CHAPTER VI.

REDEMPTION FOR LOST MAN TO BE SOUGHT IN CHRIST.

The whole human race having perished in the person of Adam, our original excellence and dignity, which we have noticed, so far from being advantageous to us, only involves us in greater ignominy, till God, who does not acknowledge the pollution and corruption of man by sin to be his work, appears as a Redeemer in the person of his only begotten Son. Therefore, since we are fallen from life into death, all that knowledge of God as a Creator, of which we have been treating, would be useless, unless it were succeeded by faith exhibiting God to

(*u*) Eph. ii. 5; v. 14.   (*w*) John v. 25.

us as a Father in Christ. This, indeed, was the genuine order of nature, that the fabric of the world should be a school in which we might learn piety, and thence be conducted to eternal life and perfect felicity. But since the fall, whithersoever we turn our eyes, the curse of God meets us on every side, which, whilst it seizes innocent creatures and involves them in our guilt, must necessarily overwhelm our souls with despair. For though God is pleased still to manifest his paternal kindness to us in various ways, yet we cannot, from a contemplation of the world, conclude that he is our Father, when our conscience disturbs us within, and convinces us that our sins afford a just reason why God should abandon us, and no longer esteem us as his children. We are also chargeable with stupidity and ingratitude; for our minds, being blinded, do not perceive the truth; and all our senses being corrupted, we wickedly defraud God of his glory. We must therefore subscribe to the declaration of Paul: "For after that in the wisdom of God, the world by wisdom knew not God, it pleased God by the foolishness of preaching to save them that believe." (*x*) What he denominates the wisdom of God, is this magnificent theatre of heaven and earth, which is replete with innumerable miracles, and from the contemplation of which we ought wisely to acquire the knowledge of God. But because we have made so little improvement in this way, he recalls us to the faith of Christ, which is despised by unbelievers on account of its apparent folly. Wherefore, though the preaching of the cross is not agreeable to human reason, we ought, nevertheless, to embrace it with all humility, if we desire to return to God our Creator, from whom we have been alienated, and to have him reassume the character of our Father. Since the fall of the first man, no knowledge of God, without the Mediator, has been available to salvation. For Christ speaks not of his own time only, but comprehends all ages, when he says that "this is life eternal, to know thee, the only true God, and Jesus Christ, whom thou hast sent." (*y*) And this aggravates the stupidity of those who set open the gate of heaven to all unbelievers and profane persons, without the grace of Christ, whom the Scripture universally represents as the only door of entrance into salvation. But if any man would restrict this declaration of Christ to the period of the first promulgation of the gospel, we are prepared with a refutation. For it has been a common opinion, in all ages and nations, that those who are alienated from God, and pronounced accursed, and children of wrath, cannot please him without a reconciliation. Here add the answer of Christ to the woman of Samaria: "Ye

(*x*) 1 Cor. i. 21. (*y*) John xvii. 3.

worship ye know not what: we know what we worship; for salvation is of the Jews." (z) In these words he at once condemns all the religions of the Gentiles as false, and assigns a reason for it; because under the law the Redeemer was promised only to the chosen people; whence it follows that no worship has ever been acceptable to God, unless it had respect to Christ. Hence also Paul affirms that all the Gentiles were without God, and destitute of the hope of life. (a) Now, as John teaches us that life was from the beginning in Christ, and that the whole world are fallen from it, (b) it is necessary to return to that fountain; and therefore Christ asserts himself to be the life, as he is the author of the propitiation. And, indeed, the celestial inheritance belongs exclusively to the children of God. But it is very unreasonable that they should be considered in the place and order of his children, who have not been engrafted into the body of his only begotten Son. And John plainly declares that "they who believe in his name become the sons of God." (c) But as it is not my design in this place to treat professedly of faith in Christ, these cursory hints shall at present suffice.

II. Therefore God never showed himself propitious to his ancient people, nor afforded them any hope of his favour, without a Mediator. I forbear to speak of the legal sacrifices, by which the faithful were plainly and publicly instructed that salvation was to be sought solely in that expiation, which has been accomplished by Christ alone. I only assert, that the happiness of the Church has always been founded on the person of Christ. For though God comprehended in his covenant all the posterity of Abraham, yet Paul judiciously reasons, that Christ is in reality that Seed in whom all the nations were to be blessed; (d) since we know that the natural descendants of that patriarch were not reckoned as his seed. For, to say nothing of Ishmael and others, what was the cause, that of the two sons of Isaac, the twin-brothers Esau and Jacob, even when they were yet unborn, one should be chosen and the other rejected? How came it to pass that the first-born was rejected, and that the younger obtained his birthright? How came the majority of the people to be disinherited? It is evident, therefore, that the seed of Abraham is reckoned principally in one person, and that the promised salvation was not manifested till the coming of Christ, whose office it is to collect what had been scattered abroad. The first adoption, therefore, of the chosen people, depended on the grace of the Mediator; which, though it is not so plainly expressed by

(z) John iv. 22.   (a) Ephes. ii. 12.   (b) John i. 4.
   (c) John i. 12.   (d) Gal. iii. 16.

Moses, yet appears to have been generally well known to all the pious. For before the appointment of any king in the nation, Hannah, the mother of Samuel, speaking of the felicity of the faithful, thus expressed herself in her song: "The Lord shall give strength unto his king, and exalt the horn of his anointed." (*e*) Her meaning in these words is, that God will bless his Church. And to this agrees the oracle, which is soon after introduced: "I will raise me up a faithful priest, and he shall walk before mine anointed." And there is no doubt that it was the design of the heavenly Father to exhibit in David and his posterity a lively image of Christ. With a design to exhort the pious, therefore, to the fear of God, he enjoins them to "kiss the Son;" (*f*) which agrees with this declaration of the gospel: "He that honoureth not the Son honoureth not the Father." (*g*) Therefore, though the kingdom was weakened by the revolt of the ten tribes, yet the covenant, which God had made with David and his successors, could not but stand, as he also declared by the Prophets: "I will not rend away all the kingdom, but will give one tribe to thy son, for David my servant's sake, and for Jerusalem's sake which I have chosen." (*h*) This is repeated again and again. It is also expressly added, "I will for this afflict the seed of David, but not for ever." (*i*) At a little distance of time it is said, "For David's sake did the Lord his God give him a lamp in Jerusalem, to set up his son after him, and to establish Jerusalem." (*k*) Even when the state was come to the verge of ruin, it was again said, "The Lord would not destroy Judah, for David his servant's sake, as he promised him to give him alway a light, and to his children." (*l*) The sum of the whole is this — that David alone was chosen, to the rejection of all others, as the perpetual object of the Divine favour; as it is said, in another place, "He forsook the tabernacle of Shiloh; he refused the tabernacle of Joseph, and chose not the tribe of Ephraim; but chose the tribe of Judah, the mount Zion, which he loved. He chose David also his servant, to feed Jacob his people, and Israel his inheritance." (*m*) Finally, it pleased God to preserve his Church in such a way, that its security and salvation should depend on that head. David therefore exclaims, "The Lord is their strength, and he is the saving strength of his anointed;" (*n*) and immediately adds this petition: "Save thy people, and bless thine inheritance;" signifying that the state of the Church is inseparably connected with the government of Christ. In the same sense he elsewhere says, "Save, Lord; let the king hear us when

(*e*) 1 Sam. ii. 10. (*f*) Psalm ii. 12. (*g*) John v. 24.
(*h*) 1 Kings xi. 13. (*i*) 1 Kings xi. 39.
(*k*) 1 Kings xv. 4. (*l*) 2 Kings viii. 19. (*m*) Psalm lxxviii. 60, 67, 68, 70, 71.
(*n*) Psalm xxviii. 8.

we call." (o) In these words he clearly teaches us that the faithful resort to God for assistance, with no other confidence than because they are sheltered under the protection of the king. This is to be inferred from another psalm: "Save, O Lord! Blessed be he that cometh in the name of the Lord;" (p) where it is sufficiently evident that the faithful are invited to Christ, that they may hope to be saved by the power of God. The same thing is alluded to in another prayer, where the whole Church implores the mercy of God: "Let thy hand be upon the man of thy right hand, upon the Son of man whom thou madest strong for thyself." (q) For though the author of the psalm deplores the dissipation of all the people, yet he ardently prays for their restoration in their head alone. But when Jeremiah, after the people were driven into exile, the land laid waste, and all things apparently ruined, bewails the miseries of the Church, he principally laments that by the subversion of the kingdom, the hope of the faithful was cut off. "The breath of our nostrils, the anointed of the Lord, was taken in their pits, of whom we said, Under his shadow we shall live among the heathen." (r) Hence it is sufficiently evident, that since God cannot be propitious to mankind but through the Mediator, Christ was always exhibited to the holy fathers under the law, as the object to which they should direct their faith.

III. Now, when consolation is promised in affliction, but especially when the deliverance of the Church is described, the standard of confidence and hope is erected in Christ alone. "Thou wentest forth for the salvation of thy people, even for salvation with thine anointed," (s) says Habakkuk. And whenever the Prophets mention the restoration of the Church, they recall the people to the promise given to David concerning the perpetuity of his kingdom. Nor is this to be wondered at; for otherwise there would be no stability in the covenant. To this refers the memorable answer of Isaiah. For when he saw that his declaration concerning the raising of the siege, and the present deliverance of Jerusalem, was rejected by that unbelieving king, Ahaz, he makes rather an abrupt transition to the Messiah: "Behold, a virgin shall conceive, and bear a son;" (t) indirectly suggesting, that although the king and the people, in their perverseness, rejected the promise which had been given them, as though they would purposely labour to invalidate the truth of God, yet that his covenant would not be frustrated, but that the Redeemer should come at his appointed time. Finally, all the Prophets, in order to display

(o) Psalm xx. 9. (q) Psalm lxxx. 17. (s) Hab. iii. 13.
(p) Psalm cxviii. 25, 26. (r) Lam. iv. 20. (t) Isaiah vii. 14.

the Divine mercy, were constantly careful to exhibit to view that kingdom of David, from which redemption and eternal salvation were to proceed. Thus Isaiah: "I will make an everlasting covenant with you, even the sure mercies of David. Behold, I have given him for a witness to the people;" (v) because in desperate circumstances the faithful could have no hope, any otherwise than by his interposition as a witness, that God would be merciful to them. Thus also Jeremiah, to comfort them who were in despair, says, "Behold, the days come, saith the Lord, that I will raise unto David a righteous Branch. In his days Judah shall be saved, and Israel shall dwell safely." (w) And Ezekiel: "I will set up one Shepherd over them, and he shall feed them, even my servant David. And I the Lord will be their God, and my servant David a prince among them; and I will make with them a covenant of peace." (x) Again, in another place, having treated of their incredible renovation, he says, "David my servant shall be king over them; and they all shall have one Shepherd. Moreover I will make a covenant of peace with them; it shall be an everlasting covenant with them." (y) I select a few passages out of many, because I only wish to apprize the reader, that the hope of the pious has never been placed any where but in Christ. All the other Prophets also uniformly speak the same language. As Hosea: "Then shall the children of Judah and the children of Israel be gathered together, and appoint themselves one head." (z) And in a subsequent chapter he is still more explicit: "The children of Israel shall return, and seek the Lord their God, and David their king." (a) Micah also, discoursing on the return of the people, expressly declares, "their king shall pass before them, and the Lord on the head of them." (b) Thus Amos, intending to predict the restoration of the people, says, "In that day I will raise up the tabernacle of David that is fallen, and close up the breaches thereof; and I will raise up his ruins." (c) This implies that the only standard of salvation was the restoration of the regal dignity in the family of David, which was accomplished in Christ. Zechariah, therefore, living nearer to the time of the manifestation of Christ, more openly exclaims, "Rejoice greatly, O daughter of Zion; shout, O daughter of Jerusalem: behold, thy King cometh unto thee: he is just, and having salvation." (d) This corresponds with a passage from a psalm, already cited: "The Lord is the saving strength of his anointed. Save thy people;" (e) where salvation is extended from the head to the whole body.

(v) Isaiah lv. 3.   (w) Jer. xxiii. 5, 6.   (x) Ezek. xxxiv. 23—25.
(y) Ezek. xxxvii. 24, 26.   (z) Hos. i. 11.
(a) Hos. iii. 5.   (b) Mic. ii. 13.   (c) Amos ix. 11.
(d) Zech. ix. 9.   (e) Psalm xxviii. 8, 9.

IV. It was the will of God that the Jews should be instructed by these prophecies, so that they might direct their eyes to Christ whenever they wanted deliverance. Nor, indeed, notwithstanding their shameful degeneracy, could the memory of this general principle ever be obliterated — that God would be the deliverer of the Church by the hand of Christ, according to his promise to David; and that in this manner the covenant of grace, in which God had adopted his elect, would at length be confirmed. Hence it came to pass, that when Christ, a little before his death, entered into Jerusalem, that song was heard from the mouths of children, "Hosanna to the Son of David." (*f*) For the subject of their song appears to have been derived from a sentiment generally received and avowed by the people, that there remained to them no other pledge of the mercy of God, but in the advent of the Redeemer. For this reason Christ commands his disciples to believe in him, that they may distinctly and perfectly believe in God: "Ye believe in God, believe also in me." (*g*) For though, strictly speaking, faith ascends from Christ to the Father, yet he suggests, that though it were even fixed on God, yet it would gradually decline, unless he interposed, to preserve its stability. The majesty of God is otherwise far above the reach of mortals, who are like worms crawling upon the earth. Wherefore, though I do not reject that common observation that God is the object of faith, yet I consider it as requiring some correction. For it is not without reason that Christ is called "the image of the invisible God;" (*h*) but by this appellation we are reminded, that unless God reveal himself to us in Christ, we cannot have that knowledge of him which is necessary to salvation. For although among the Jews the scribes had by false glosses obscured the declarations of the Prophets concerning the Redeemer, yet Christ assumed it for granted, as if allowed by common consent, that there was no other remedy for the confusion into which the Jews had fallen, nor any other mode of deliverance for the Church, but the exhibition of the Mediator. There was not, indeed, such a general knowledge as there ought to have been, of the principle taught by Paul, that "Christ is the end of the law;" (*i*) but the truth and certainty of this evidently appears both from the law itself and from the Prophets. I am not yet treating of faith; there will be a more suitable place for that subject in another part of the work. Only let this be well fixed in the mind of the reader; that the first step to piety is to know that God is our Father, to protect, govern, and support us till he gathers us into the eternal inheritance of his

(*f*) Matt. xxi. 9.   (*g*) John xiv. 1.   (*h*) Col. i. 15.   (*i*) Rom. x. 4

kingdom; that hence it is plain, as we have before asserted, that there can be no saving knowledge of God without Christ; and consequently that from the beginning of the world he has always been manifested to all the elect, that they might look to him, and repose all their confidence in him. In this sense Irenæus says that the Father, who is infinite in himself, becomes finite in the Son; because he has accommodated himself to our capacity, that he may not overwhelm our minds with the infinity of his glory. (*k*) And fanatics, not considering this, pervert a useful observation into an impious reverie, as though there were in Christ merely a portion of Deity, an emanation from the infinite perfection; whereas the sole meaning of that writer is, that God is apprehended in Christ, and in him alone. The assertion of John has been verified in all ages, " Whosoever denieth the Son, the same hath not the Father." (*l*) For though many in ancient times gloried in being worshippers of the Supreme Deity, the Creator of heaven and earth, yet, because they had no Mediator, it was impossible for them to have any real acquaintance with the mercy of God, or persuasion that he was their Father. Therefore, as they did not hold the head, that is, Christ, all their knowledge of God was obscure and unsettled; whence it came to pass, that degenerating at length into gross and vile superstitions, they betrayed their ignorance, like the Turks in modern times; who, though they boast of having the Creator of heaven and earth for their God, yet only substitute an idol instead of the true God as long as they remain enemies to Christ.

CHAPTER VII.

THE LAW GIVEN, NOT TO CONFINE THE ANCIENT PEOPLE TO ITSELF, BUT TO ENCOURAGE THEIR HOPE OF SALVATION IN CHRIST, TILL THE TIME OF HIS COMING.

From the deduction we have made, it may easily be inferred, that the law was superadded about four hundred years after the death of Abraham, not to draw away the attention of the chosen people from Christ, but rather to keep their minds waiting for his advent, to inflame their desires and confirm their expectations, that they might not be discouraged by so

---

(*k*) Lib. 4, c. 8. (*l*) 1 John ii. 23.

long a delay. By the word *law*, I intend, not only the decalogue, which prescribes the rule of a pious and righteous life, but the form of religion delivered from God by the hands of Moses. For Moses was not made a legislator to abolish the blessing promised to the seed of Abraham; on the contrary, we see him on every occasion reminding the Jews of that gracious covenant made with their fathers, to which they were heirs; as though the object of his mission had been to renew it. It was very clearly manifested in the ceremonies. For what could be more vain or frivolous than for men to offer the fetid stench arising from the fat of cattle, in order to reconcile themselves to God? or to resort to any aspersion of water or of blood, to cleanse themselves from pollution? In short, the whole legal worship, if it be considered in itself, and contain no shadows and figures of correspondent truths, will appear perfectly ridiculous. Wherefore it is not without reason, that both in the speech of Stephen and in the Epistle to the Hebrews, that passage is so carefully stated, in which God commands Moses to make all things pertaining to the tabernacle "according to the pattern showed to him in the mount." (*m*) For unless there had been some spiritual design, to which they were directed, the Jews would have laboured to no purpose in these observances, as the Gentiles did in their mummeries. Profane men, who have never seriously devoted themselves to the pursuit of piety, have not patience to hear of such various rites: they not only wonder why God should weary his ancient people with such a mass of ceremonies, but they even despise and deride them as puerile and ludicrous. This arises from inattention to the end of the legal figures, from which if those figures be separated, they must be condemned as vain and useless. But the "pattern," which is mentioned, shows that God commanded the sacrifices, not with a design to occupy his worshippers in terrestrial exercises, but rather that he might elevate their minds to sublimer objects. This may be likewise evinced by his nature; for as he is a Spirit, he is pleased with none but spiritual worship. Testimonies of this truth may be found in the numerous passages of the Prophets, in which they reprove the stupidity of the Jews for supposing that sacrifices possess any real value in the sight of God. Do they mean to derogate from the law? Not at all; but being true interpreters of it, they designed by this method to direct the eyes of the people to that point from which the multitude were wandering. Now, from the grace offered to the Jews, it is inferred as a certain truth, that the law was not irrespective of Christ; for Moses mentioned to

(*m*) Acts vii. 44. Heb. viii. 5. Ex. xxv. 40.

them this end of their adoption, that they might "be unto God a kingdom of priests;" (*n*) which could not be attained without a greater and more excellent reconciliation than could arise from the blood of beasts. For what is more improbable than that the sons of Adam, who by hereditary contagion are all born the slaves of sin, should be exalted to regal dignity, and thus become partakers of the glory of God, unless such an eminent blessing proceeded from some other source than themselves? How also could the right of the priesthood remain among them, the pollution of whose crimes rendered them abominable to God, unless they had been consecrated in a holy head? Wherefore Peter makes a beautiful application of this observation of Moses, suggesting that the plenitude of that grace, of which the Jews enjoyed a taste under the law, is exhibited in Christ. "Ye are," says he, "a chosen generation, a royal priesthood." (*o*) This application of the words tends to show, that they, to whom Christ has appeared under the gospel, have obtained more than their forefathers; because they are all invested with sacerdotal and regal honours, that in a dependence on their Mediator they may venture to come boldly into the presence of God.

II. And here it must be remarked, by the way, that the kingdom, which at length was erected in the family of David, is a part of the law, and comprised under the ministry of Moses; whence it follows, that both in the posterity of David, and in the whole Levitical tribe, as in a twofold mirror, Christ was exhibited to the view of his ancient people. For, as I have just observed, it was otherwise impossible that in the Divine view they should be kings and priests, who were the slaves of sin and death, and polluted by their own corruptions. Hence appears the truth of the assertion of Paul, that the Jews were subject, as it were, to the authority of a schoolmaster, till the advent of that seed, for whose sake the promise was given. (*p*) For Christ being not yet familiarly discovered, they were like children, whose imbecility could not yet bear the full knowledge of heavenly things. But how they were led to Christ by the ceremonies, has been already stated, and may be better learned from the testimonies of the Prophets. For although they were obliged every day to approach God with new sacrifices, in order to appease him, yet Isaiah promises them the expiation of all their transgressions by a single sacrifice, (*q*) which is confirmed by Daniel. (*r*) The priests chosen from the tribe of Levi, used to enter into the sanctuary; but concerning that one priest it was once said, that he was

(*n*) Exod. xix. 6. (*o*) 1 Peter ii. 9. (*p*) Gal. iii. 24.
(*q*) Isaiah liii. 5, &c. (*r*) Dan. ix. 26, &c.

divinely chosen with an oath, to be "a priest for ever after the order of Melchisedec." (s) There was, then, an unction of visible oil; but Daniel, from his vision, foretells an unction of a different kind. But not to insist on many proofs, the author of the Epistle to the Hebrews, from the fourth chapter to the eleventh, demonstrates in a manner sufficiently copious and clear, that, irrespective of Christ, all the ceremonies of the law are worthless and vain. And in regard to the decalogue, we should attend to the declaration of Paul, that "Christ is the end of the law for righteousness to every one that believeth;" (t) and also that Christ is "the Spirit," who gives "life" to the otherwise dead letter. (v) For in the former passage he signifies that righteousness is taught in vain by the precepts, till Christ bestows it both by a gratuitous imputation, and by the Spirit of regeneration. Wherefore he justly denominates Christ the completion or end of the law; for we should derive no benefit from a knowledge of what God requires of us, unless we were succoured by Christ when labouring and oppressed under its yoke and intolerable burden. In another place, he states that "the law was added because of transgressions;" (w) that is, to humble men, by convicting them of being the causes of their own condemnation. Now, this being the true and only preparation for seeking Christ, the various declarations which he makes are in perfect unison with each other. But as he was then engaged in a controversy with erroneous teachers, who pretended that we merit righteousness by the works of the law, — in order to refute their error, he was sometimes obliged to use the term *law* in a more restricted sense, as merely preceptive, although it was otherwise connected with the covenant of gratuitous adoption.

III. But it is worthy of a little inquiry, how we are rendered more inexcusable by the instructions of the moral law, in order that a sense of our guilt may excite us to supplicate for pardon. If it be true that the law displays a perfection of righteousness, it also follows that the complete observation of it, is in the sight of God a perfect righteousness, in which a man would be esteemed and reputed righteous at the tribunal of heaven. Wherefore Moses, when he had promulgated the law, hesitated not to "call heaven and earth to record" (x) that he had proposed to the Israelites life and death, good and evil. Nor can we deny that the reward of eternal life awaits a righteous obedience to the law, according to the Divine promise. But, on the other hand, it is proper to examine whether we perform that obedience, the merit of which can warrant

(s) Psalm cx. 4.   (t) Rom. x. 4.   (v) 2 Cor. iii 17.
(w) Gal. iii. 19.   (x) Deut. xxx. 15, 19.

our confident expectation of that reward. For how unimportant is it, to discover that the reward of eternal life depends on the observance of the law, unless we also ascertain whether it be possible for us to arrive at eternal life in that way! But in this point the weakness of the law is manifest. For as none of us are found to observe the law, we are excluded from the promises of life, and fall entirely under the curse. I am now showing, not only what does happen, but what necessarily must happen. For the doctrine of the law being far above human ability, man may view the promises, indeed, from a distance, but cannot gather any fruit from them. It only remains for him, from their goodness to form a truer estimate of his own misery, while he reflects that all hope of salvation is cut off, and that he is in imminent danger of death. On the other hand, we are urged with terrible sanctions, which bind, not a few of us, but every individual of mankind; they urge, I say, and pursue us with inexorable rigour, so that in the law we see nothing but present death.

IV. Therefore, if we direct our views exclusively to the law, the effects upon our minds will only be despondency, confusion, and despair, since it condemns and curses us all, and keeps us far from that blessedness which it proposes to them who observe it. Does the Lord, then, you will say, in this case do nothing but mock us? For how little does it differ from mockery, to exhibit a hope of felicity, to invite and exhort to it, to declare that it is ready for our reception, whilst the way to it is closed and inaccessible! I reply, although the promises of the law, being conditional, depend on a perfect obedience to the law, which can nowhere be found, yet they have not been given in vain. For when we have learned that they will be vain and inefficacious to us, unless God embrace us with his gratuitous goodness, without any regard to our works, and unless we have also embraced by faith that goodness, as exhibited to us in the gospel,—then these promises are not without their use, even with the condition annexed to them. For then he gratuitously confers every thing upon us, so that he adds this also to the number of his favours, that not rejecting our imperfect obedience, but pardoning its deficiencies, he gives us to enjoy the benefit of the legal promises, just as if we had fulfilled the condition ourselves. But as we shall more fully discuss this question when we treat of the justification of faith, we shall pursue it no further at present.

V. Our assertion, respecting the impossibility of observing the law, must be briefly explained and proved; for it is generally esteemed a very absurd sentiment, so that Jerome has not scrupled to denounce it as accursed. What was the opinion of

Jerome, I regard not; let us inquire what is truth. I shall not here enter into a long discussion of the various species of possibility; I call that impossible which has never happened yet, and which is prevented by the ordination and decree of God from ever happening in future. If we inquire from the remotest period of antiquity, I assert that there never has existed a saint, who, surrounded with a body of death, could attain to such a degree of love, as to love God with all his heart, with all his soul, and with all his mind; and, moreover, that there never has been one, who was not the subject of some inordinate desire. Who can deny this? I know, indeed, what sort of saints the folly of superstition imagines to itself, such as almost excel even the angels of heaven in purity; but such an imagination is repugnant both to Scripture and to the dictates of experience. I assert also that no man, who shall exist in future, will reach the standard of true perfection, unless released from the burden of the body. This is established by clear testimonies of Scripture: Solomon says, "There is not a just man upon earth, that doeth good and sinneth not." (*y*) David; "In thy sight shall no man living be justified." (*z*) Job in many passages affirms the same thing; (*a*) but Paul most plainly of all, that "the flesh lusteth against the Spirit, and the Spirit against the flesh." (*b*) Nor does he prove, that "as many as are of the works of the law are under the curse," by any other reason but because "it is written, Cursed is every one that continueth not in all things which are written in the book of the law to do them;" (*c*) evidently suggesting, and even taking it for granted, that no one can continue in them. Now, whatever is predicted in the Scriptures, must be considered as perpetual, and even as necessary. With a similar fallacy Augustine used to be teased by the Pelagians, who maintained that it is an injury to God, to say that he commands more than the faithful through his grace are able to perform. To avoid their cavil, he admitted that the Lord might, if he chose, exalt a mortal man to the purity of angels; but that he neither had ever done it, nor would ever do it, because he had declared otherwise in the Scriptures. (*d*) This I do not deny; but I add that it is absurd to dispute concerning the power of God, in opposition to his veracity; and that, therefore, it affords no room for cavilling, when any one maintains that to be impossible, which the Scriptures declare will never happen. But if the dispute be about the term, the Lord, in reply to an inquiry of his disciples, "Who, then, can be saved?" says, "With men this is impossible; but with God all things are

(*y*) Eccles. vii. 20.   (*z*) Psalm cxliii. 2.   (*a*) Job iv. 17; ix. 2; xv. 14; xxv 4.
(*b*) Gal. v. 17.   (*c*) Gal. iii. 10.   (*d*) Lib. de Nat. et Grat.

possible." (e) Augustine contends, with a very powerful argument, that in this flesh we never render to God the legitimate love which we owe to him. "Love," says he, "is an effect of knowledge, so that no man can perfectly love God, who has not first a complete knowledge of his goodness. During our pilgrimage in this world, we see through an obscure medium; the consequence of this, then, is, that our love is imperfect." It ought, therefore, to be admitted without controversy, that it is impossible in this carnal state to fulfil the law, if we consider the impotence of our nature, as will elsewhere be proved also from Paul. (f)

VI. But for the better elucidation of the subject, let us state, in a compendious order, the office and use of what is called the moral law. It is contained, as far as I understand it, in these three points. The first is, that while it discovers the righteousness of God, that is, the only righteousness which is acceptable to God, it warns every one of his own unrighteousness, places it beyond all doubt, convicts, and condemns him. For it is necessary that man, blinded and inebriated with self-love, should thus be driven into a knowledge of himself, and a confession of his own imbecility and impurity. Since, unless his vanity be evidently reproved, he is inflated with a foolish confidence in his strength, and can never be brought to perceive its feebleness as long as he measures it by the rule of his own fancy. But as soon as he begins to compare it to the difficulty of the law, he finds his insolence and pride immediately abate. For how great soever his preconceived opinion of it, he perceives it immediately pant under so heavy a load, and then totter, and at length fall. Thus, being instructed under the tuition of the law, he lays aside that arrogance with which he was previously blinded. He must also be cured of the other disease, of pride, with which, we have observed, he is afflicted. As long as he is permitted to stand in his own judgment, he substitutes hypocrisy instead of righteousness; contented with which, he rises up with I know not what pretended righteousnesses, in opposition to the grace of God. But when he is constrained to examine his life according to the rules of the law, he no longer presumes on his counterfeit righteousness, but perceives that he is at an infinite distance from holiness; and also that he abounds with innumerable vices, from which he before supposed himself to be pure. For the evils of concupiscence are concealed in such deep and intricate recesses, as easily to elude the view of man. And it is not without cause that the Apostle says, "I had not known lust, except the law had said, Thou shalt not covet;" (g) because, unless it be stripped of its

(e) Matt. xix. 25, 26.   (f) Rom. viii. 3, &c.   (g) Rom. vii. 7.

disguises, and brought to light by the law, it destroys the miserable man in so secret a manner, that he does not perceive its fatal dart.

VII. Thus the law is like a mirror, in which we behold, first, our impotence; secondly, our iniquity, which proceeds from it; and lastly, the consequence of both, our obnoxiousness to the curse; just as a mirror represents to us the spots on our face. For when a man is destitute of power to practise righteousness, he must necessarily fall into the habits of sin. And sin is immediately followed by the curse. Therefore the greater the transgression of which the law convicts us, the more severe is the judgment with which it condemns us. This appears from the observation of the Apostle, that "by the law is the knowledge of sin." (*h*) For he there speaks only of the first office of the law, which is experienced in sinners not yet regenerated. The same sentiment is conveyed in the following passages: that "the law entered, that the offence might abound;" (*i*) and that it is therefore "the ministration of death, which worketh wrath and slayeth." (*k*) For iniquity undoubtedly increases more and more, in proportion to the clearness of that sense of sin which strikes the conscience; because to transgression of the law, there is then added contumacy against the lawgiver. It remains, therefore, that the law arm the Divine wrath against the sinner; for of itself it can only accuse, condemn, and destroy. And, as Augustine says, if we have not the Spirit of grace, the law serves only to convict and slay us. But this assertion neither reflects dishonour on the law, nor at all derogates from its excellence. Certainly, if our will were wholly conformed to the law, and disposed to obey it, the mere knowledge of it would evidently be sufficient to salvation. But since our carnal and corrupt nature is in a state of hostility against the spirituality of the Divine law, and not amended by its discipline, it follows that the law, which was given for salvation, if it could have found adequate attention, becomes an occasion of sin and death. For since we are all convicted of having transgressed it, the more clearly it displays the righteousness of God, so, on the contrary, the more it detects our iniquity, and the more certainly it confirms the reward of life and salvation reserved for the righteous, so much the more certain it makes the perdition of the wicked. These expressions, therefore, are so far from being dishonourable to the law, that they serve more illustriously to recommend the Divine goodness. For hence it really appears, that our iniquity and depravity prevent us from enjoying that blessed life which is revealed to all men in the law. Hence the grace of God, which

(*h*) Rom. iii. 20.   (*i*) Rom. v. 20.   (*k*) 2 Cor. iii. 7. Rom. iv. 15.

succours us without the assistance of the law, is rendered sweeter; and his mercy, which confers it on us, more amiable; from which we learn that he is never wearied with repeating his blessings and loading us with new favours.

VIII. But though the iniquity and condemnation of us all are confirmed by the testimony of the law, this is not done (at least if we properly profit by it) in order to make us sink into despair, and fall over the precipice of despondency. It is true that the wicked are thus confounded by it, but this is occasioned by the obstinacy of their hearts. With the children of God, its instructions must terminate in a different manner. The Apostle indeed declares that we are all condemned by the sentence of the law, "that every mouth may be stopped, and all the world may become guilty before God." (*l*) Yet the same Apostle elsewhere informs us, that "God hath concluded them all in unbelief," not that he might destroy or suffer all to perish, but "that he might have mercy upon all;" (*m*) that is, that leaving their foolish opinion of their own strength, they may know that they stand and are supported only by the power of God; that being naked and destitute, they may resort for assistance to his mercy, recline themselves wholly upon it, hide themselves entirely in it, and embrace it alone for righteousness and merits, since it is offered in Christ to all who with true faith implore it and expect it. For in the precepts of the law, God appears only, on the one hand, as the rewarder of perfect righteousness, of which we are all destitute; and on the other, as the severe judge of transgressions. But in Christ, his face shines with a plenitude of grace and lenity, even towards miserable and unworthy sinners.

IX. Of making use of the law to implore the assistance of God, Augustine frequently treats; as when he writes to Hilary: "The law gives commands, in order that, endeavouring to perform them, and being wearied through our infirmity under the law, we may learn to pray for the assistance of grace." Also to Asellius: "The utility of the law is to convince man of his own infirmity, and to compel him to pray for the gracious remedy provided in Christ." Also to Innocentius Romanus: "The law commands: grace furnishes strength for the performance." Again, to Valentine: "God commands what we cannot perform, that we may know for what blessings we ought to supplicate him." Again: "The law was given to convict you; that being convicted you might fear, that fearing you might pray for pardon, and not presume on your own strength." Again: "The end for which the law was given, was to diminish that which was great, to demonstrate that you

(*l*) Rom. iii. 19.   (*m*) Rom. xi. 32.

have of yourself no ability to work righteousness, that thus, being poor, indigent, and destitute, you might have recourse to grace for relief." Afterwards he addresses himself to God: "Thus do, O Lord! thus do, O merciful Lord! command that which cannot be performed: even command that which cannot be performed without thy grace: that when men cannot perform it in their own strength, every mouth may be stopped, and no man appear great in his own estimation. Let all men be mean, and let all the world be proved guilty before God." But I am not wise in collecting so many testimonies, when this holy man has written a treatise expressly on this subject, which he has entitled *De Spiritu et Litera*, On the Spirit and Letter. The second use of the law he does not so clearly describe, either because he knew that it depends on the first, or because he did not so fully understand it, or because he wanted words to explain it with distinctness and perspicuity adequate to his ideas of it. Yet this first office of the law is not confined to the pious, but extends also to the reprobate. For though they do not, with the children of God, advance so far as, after the mortification of the flesh, to be renewed, and to flourish again in the inner man, but, confounded with the first horrors of conscience, remain in despair, yet they contribute to manifest the equity of the Divine judgment, by their consciences being agitated with such violent emotions. For they are always desirous of cavilling against the judgment of God; but now, while it is not yet manifested, they are, nevertheless, so confounded with the testimony of the law and of their own conscience, that they betray in themselves what they have deserved.

X. The second office of the law is, to cause those who, unless constrained, feel no concern for justice and rectitude, when they hear its terrible sanctions, to be at least restrained by a fear of its penalties. And they are restrained, not because it internally influences or affects their minds, but because, being chained, as it were, they refrain from external acts, and repress their depravity within them, which otherwise they would have wantonly discharged. This makes them neither better nor more righteous in the Divine view. For although, being prevented either by fear or by shame, they dare not execute what their minds have contrived, nor openly discover the fury of their passions, yet their hearts are not disposed to fear and obey God; and the more they restrain themselves, the more violently they are inflamed within; they ferment, they boil, ready to break out into any external acts, if they were not prevented by this dread of the law. And not only so, they also inveterately hate the law itself, and execrate God the lawgiver, so that, if they could, they would wish to annihilate him whom they cannot bear, either in commanding that which is right, or in punishing the despisers of his majesty. In some, indeed, this state of mind is more evident, in others more concealed; but it is really the case of all who are yet unregenerate, that they are induced to attend to the law, not by a voluntary submission, but with reluctance and resistance, only by the violence of fear. But yet this constrained and extorted righteousness is necessary to the community, whose public tranquillity is provided for by God in this instance, while he prevents all things being involved in confusion, which would certainly be the case, if all men were permitted to pursue their own inclinations. Moreover, it is useful even to the children of God, to be exercised by its discipline before their vocation, while they are destitute of the Spirit of sanctification, and are absorbed in carnal folly. For when the dread of Divine vengeance restrains them even from external licentiousness, although, their minds being not yet subdued, they make but a slow progress at present, yet they are in some measure accustomed to bear the yoke of righteousness; so that when they are called, they may not be entirely unaccustomed to its discipline, as a thing altogether unknown. To this office of the law the Apostle appears particularly to have referred, when he says, "that the law is not made for a righteous man, but for the lawless and disobedient; for the ungodly and for sinners; for unholy and profane; for murderers of fathers and murderers of mothers; for manslayers, for whoremongers, for them that defile themselves with mankind, for men-stealers, for liars, for perjured persons, and if there be any other thing that is contrary to sound doctrine." (*n*) For he here signifies that it restrains the violence of the carnal desires, which would otherwise indulge themselves in the most unbounded licentiousness.

XI. But we may apply to both what he elsewhere asserts, that to the Jews "the law was a schoolmaster to bring them to Christ;" (*o*) for there are two kinds of persons who are led to Christ by its discipline. Some, whom we mentioned in the first place, from too much confidence either in their own strength or in their own righteousness, are unfit to receive the grace of Christ, till they have first been stripped of every thing. The law, therefore, reduces them to humility by a knowledge of their own misery, that thus they may be prepared to pray for that of which they before supposed themselves not destitute. Others need a bridle to restrain them, lest they abandon themselves to carnal licentiousness, to such a degree as wholly to depart from all practice of righteousness. For where the Spirit does not yet reign, there is sometimes such a violent ebullition of the passions, as to occasion great danger of the soul that is under their influence being swallowed up in forget-

(*n*) 1 Tim. i. 9, 10.   (*o*) Gal. iii. 24.

fulness and contempt of God; which would certainly be the case, if the Lord did not provide this remedy against it. Those, therefore, whom he has destined to the inheritance of his kingdom, if he do not immediately regenerate them, he keeps under fear by the works of the law till the time of his visitation; not that chaste and pure fear which ought to be felt by his children, but a fear which is, nevertheless, useful to train them, according to their capacity, to true piety. Of this we have so many proofs, that there is no need to adduce any example. For all who have lived for a considerable time in ignorance of God will confess it to have been their experience, that they were constrained by the law to a certain kind of fear and reverence of God, till, being regenerated by his Spirit, they began to love him from their hearts.

XII. The third use of the law, which is the principal one, and which is more nearly connected with the proper end of it, relates to the faithful, in whose hearts the Spirit of God already lives and reigns. For although the law is inscribed and engraven on their hearts by the finger of God,—that is, although they are so excited and animated by the direction of the Spirit, that they desire to obey God,—yet they derive a twofold advantage from the law. For they find it an excellent instrument to give them, from day to day, a better and more certain understanding of the Divine will to which they aspire, and to confirm them in the knowledge of it. As, though a servant be already influenced by the strongest desire of gaining the approbation of his master, yet it is necessary for him carefully to inquire and observe the orders of his master, in order to conform to them. Nor let any one of us exempt himself from this necessity; for no man has already acquired so much wisdom, that he could not by the daily instruction of the law make new advances into a purer knowledge of the Divine will. In the next place, as we need not only instruction, but also exhortation, the servant of God will derive this further advantage from the law; by frequent meditation on it he will be excited to obedience, he will be confirmed in it, and restrained from the slippery path of transgression. For in this manner should the saints stimulate themselves, because, with whatever alacrity they labour for the righteousness of God according to the Spirit, yet they are always burdened with the indolence of the flesh, which prevents their proceeding with due promptitude. To this flesh the law serves as a whip, urging it, like a dull and tardy animal, forwards to its work; and even to the spiritual man, who is not yet delivered from the burden of the flesh, it will be a perpetual spur, that will not permit him to loiter. To this use of the law David referred, when he celebrated it in such remarkable encomiums as these: "The law of the Lord is perfect, converting the soul: the statutes of the Lord are right, rejoicing the heart: the commandment of the Lord is pure, enlightening the eyes," &c. (*p*) Again: "Thy word is a lamp unto my feet, and a light unto my path;" (*q*) and many others, which he introduces in every part of this psalm. Nor are these assertions repugnant to those of Paul, in which he shows, not what service the law renders to the regenerate, but what it can bestow upon man merely of itself; whereas the Psalmist in these passages celebrates the great advantage derived, through the Divine teaching, from the reading of the law, by those whom God inspires with an inward promptitude to obedience. And he adverts not only to the precepts, but to the promise of grace annexed to their performance, which alone causes that which is bitter to become sweet. For what would be less amiable than the law, if by demands and threats it only distressed the mind with fear, and harassed it with terror? But David particularly shows, that in the law he discovered the Mediator, without whom there is nothing pleasant or delightful.

XIII. Some unskilful men, being unable to discern this distinction, rashly explode Moses altogether, and discard the two tables of the law; because they consider it improper for Christians to adhere to a doctrine which contains the administration of death. Far from us be this profane opinion; for Moses has abundantly taught us, that the law, which in sinners can only produce death, ought to have a better and more excellent use in the saints. For just before his death he thus addressed the people: "Set your hearts unto all the words which I testify among you this day, which ye shall command your children to observe, to do all the words of this law. For it is not a vain thing for you; because it is your life." (*r*) But if no one can deny that the law exhibits a perfect model of righteousness, either we ought to have no rule for an upright and just life, or it is criminal for us to deviate from it. For there are not many rules of life, but one, which is perpetually and immutably the same. Wherefore, when David represents the life of a righteous man as spent in continual meditations on the law, (*s*) we must not refer it to one period of time only, because it is very suitable for all ages, even to the end of the world. Let us neither be deterred, therefore, nor fly from its instructions, because it prescribes a holiness far more complete than we shall attain, as long as we remain in the prison of the body. For it no longer exercises towards us the part of a rigorous exactor, only to be satisfied by the perfect performance of every injunction; but in this perfection,

(*p*) Psalm xix. 7, 8.   (*r*) Deut. xxxii. 46, 47.
(*q*) Psalm cxix. 105.   (*s*) Psalm i. 2.

to which it exhorts us, it shows us a goal, to aim at which, during the whole of our lives, would be equally conducive to our interest and consistent with our duty; in which attempt it is happy for us if we fail not. For the whole of this life is a course, which when we have completed, the Lord will grant us to reach that goal, towards which at so great a distance our efforts are now vigorously directed.

XIV. Now, because the law, in regard to the faithful, has the force of an exhortation, not to bind their consciences with a curse, but by its frequent admonitions to arouse their indolence, and reprove their imperfection, — many persons, when they design to express this liberation from its curse, say that the law (I still speak of the moral law) is abrogated to the faithful; not that it no longer enjoins upon them that which is right, but only that it ceases to be to them what it was before, no longer terrifying and confounding their consciences, condemning and destroying them. And such an abrogation of the law is clearly taught by Paul. It appears also to have been preached by our Lord, since he would not have refuted the opinion concerning his abolishing the law, unless it had prevailed among the Jews. Now, as this opinion could not prevail without any pretext, it is probable that it proceeded from a false interpretation of his doctrine; in the same manner as almost all errors have usually taken some colour from the truth. But lest we ourselves fall into the same error, let us accurately distinguish what is abrogated in the law, and what still remains in force. When the Lord declares that he came "not to destroy the law, but to fulfil it," and that "till heaven and earth shall pass, one jot or one tittle shall in no wise pass from the law, till all be fulfilled," (*t*) he sufficiently proves that his advent would detract nothing from the observance of the law. And with sufficient reason, since the express end of his advent was to heal the transgressions of it. The doctrine of the law remains, therefore, through Christ, inviolable; which by tuition, admonition, reproof, and correction, forms and prepares us for every good work.

XV. The assertions of Paul respecting the abrogation of the law evidently relate, not to the instruction itself, but to the power of binding the conscience. For the law not only teaches, but authoritatively requires, obedience to its commands. If this obedience be not yielded, and even if there be any partial deficiency of duty, it hurls the thunderbolt of its curse. For this reason the Apostle says, that "as many as are of the works of the law are under the curse; for it is written, Cursed is every one that continueth not in all things." (*u*) Now, he affirms those to be "of the works of the law," who place not their righteousness

---

(*t*) Matt. v. 17, 18. (*u*) Gal. iii. 10.

in the remission of sins, by which we are released from the rigour of the law. He teaches us, therefore, that we must be released from the bondage of the law, unless we would perish in misery under it. But what bondage? the bondage of that austere and rigid exaction, which remits nothing from its strictest requirements, and permits no transgression to pass with impunity; I say, Christ, in order to redeem us from this curse, was "made a curse for us. For it is written, Cursed is every one that hangeth on a tree." (*w*) In the following chapter, indeed, he tells us, that Christ was "made under the law, to redeem them that were under the law;" but in the same sense; for he immediately adds, "that we might receive the adoption of sons." (*x*) What is this? that we might not be oppressed with a perpetual servitude, which would keep our consciences in continual distress with the dread of death. At the same time this truth remains for ever unshaken, that the law has sustained no diminution of its authority, but ought always to receive from us the same veneration and obedience.

XVI. The case of ceremonies, which have been abrogated, not as to their effect, but only as to their use, is very different. Their having been abolished by the advent of Christ, is so far from derogating from their sanctity, that it rather recommends and renders it more illustrious. For as they must have exhibited to the people, in ancient times, a vain spectacle, unless they had discovered the virtue of the death and resurrection of Christ, so, if they had not ceased, we should, in the present age, have been unable to discern for what purpose they were instituted. To prove, therefore, that the observance of them is not only needless, but even injurious, Paul teaches us that they were shadows, the body of which we have in Christ. (*y*) We see, then, that the truth shines with greater splendour in their abolition, than if they still continued to give a distant and obscure representation of Christ, who has openly appeared. For this reason, at the death of Christ, "the veil of the temple was rent in twain from the top to the bottom;" (*z*) because, according to the author of the Epistle to the Hebrews, the living and express image of the heavenly blessings, which before had been only sketched in obscure lineaments, was now clearly revealed. The same truth is conveyed in the declaration of Christ, that "the law and the prophets were until John; since that time the kingdom of God is preached." (*a*) Not that the holy fathers had been destitute of that preaching which contains the hope of salvation, and of eternal life, but because they saw only at a distance, and under shadows, what we now contemplate in open day. But the reason, why it was neces-

(*w*) Gal. iii. 13. (*x*) Gal. iv. 4, 5. (*y*) Col. ii. 17.
(*z*) Matt. xxvii. 51. (*a*) Luke xvi. 16.

sary for the Church of God to ascend from those rudiments to sublimer heights, is explained by John the Baptist: "the law was given by Moses, but grace and truth came by Jesus Christ." (*b*) For although expiation of sin was truly promised in the ancient sacrifices, and the ark of the covenant was a certain pledge of the paternal favour of God, all these would have been mere shadows, if they had not been founded in the grace of Christ, where alone we may find true and eternal stability. Let us firmly maintain, then, that though the legal rites have ceased to be observed, yet their very discontinuance gives us a better knowledge of their great utility before the advent of Christ, who, abolishing the observance of them, confirmed their virtue and efficacy in his death.

XVII. The reasoning of Paul is attended with more difficulty: "And you, being dead in your sins, and the uncircumcision of your flesh, hath he quickened together with him, having forgiven you all trespasses; blotting out the handwriting of ordinances that was against us, which was contrary to us, and took it out of the way, nailing it to his cross," &c. (*c*) For it seems to extend the abolition of the law somewhat further, as though we had now no concern with its "ordinances." For they are in an error who understand it simply of the moral law, the abolition of which they, nevertheless, explain to relate to its inexorable severity, rather than to its precepts. Others, more acutely and carefully considering the words of Paul, perceive that they belong particularly to the ceremonial law; and prove that the word "ordinances" is more than once used by Paul in that signification. For he thus expresses himself to the Ephesians: "He is our peace, who hath made both one; having abolished the law of commandments contained in ordinances; for to make in himself of twain one new man." (*d*) That he there speaks of the ceremonies, is very evident; for he calls the law "the middle wall of partition," by which the Jews were separated from the Gentiles. Wherefore I allow that the former commentators are justly censured by these; but even these do not appear to me clearly to explain the meaning of the Apostle. For to compare these two passages as in all respects similar, is what I by no means approve. When he designs to assure the Ephesians of their admission into fellowship with the Israelites, he informs them, that the impediment which formerly prevented it is now removed. That consisted in ceremonies. For the rites of ablutions and sacrifices, by which the Jews were consecrated to the Lord, caused a separation between them and the Gentiles. But in the Epistle to the Co-

(*b*) John i. 17.   (*c*) Col. ii. 13, 14.   (*d*) Ephes. ii. 14, 15.

lossians he treats of a sublimer mystery. The controversy there relates to the Mosaic observances, to which the false Apostles were strenuously attempting to subject the Christians. But as in the Epistle to the Galatians he goes to the depth of that controversy, and reduces it to its source, so also in this place. For if in the rites you contemplate nothing but the necessity of performing them, to what purpose were they called a "hand-writing that was against us"? and almost the whole of our redemption made to consist in its being "blotted out?" Wherefore it is evident, that here is something to be considered beside the external ceremonies. And I am persuaded that I have discovered the genuine meaning, at least if that be conceded to me as a truth, which Augustine somewhere very truly asserts, and which he has even borrowed from the positive expressions of an Apostle, (*e*) that in the Jewish ceremonies there was rather a confession of sins than an expiation of them. For what did they do in offering sacrifices, but confess themselves worthy of death, since they substituted victims to be slain in their stead? What were their purifications, but confessions that they were themselves impure? Thus the hand-writing both of their sin and of their impurity was frequently renewed by them; but that confession afforded no deliverance. For which reason the Apostle says that the death of Christ effected "the redemption of the transgressions that were under the first testament." (*f*) The Apostle, therefore, justly denominates the ceremonies "a hand-writing against those who observe them;" because by them they publicly attested their condemnation and impurity. Nor does any objection arise from their having been also partakers of the same grace with us. For this they obtained in Christ, not in the ceremonies, which the Apostle there distinguishes from Christ; for being practised at that time after the introduction of the gospel, they obscured the glory of Christ. We find, then, that the ceremonies, considered by themselves, are beautifully and appositely called a "hand-writing that was against" the salvation of men; because they were solemn instruments testifying their guilt. When the false Apostles wished to bring the Church back to the observance of them, the Apostle deeply investigated their signification, and very justly admonished the Colossians into what circumstances they would relapse, if they should suffer themselves to be thus enslaved by them. For they would at the same time be deprived of the benefit of Christ; since, by the eternal expiation that he has once effected, he has abolished those daily observances, which could only attest their sins, but could never cancel them.

(*e*) Heb. x. 3—14.   (*f*) Heb. ix. 15.

CHAPTER VIII.

AN EXPOSITION OF THE MORAL LAW.

Here I think it will not be foreign to our subject to introduce the ten precepts of the law, with a brief exposition of them. For this will more clearly evince what I have suggested, that the service which God has once prescribed always remains in full force; and will also furnish us with a confirmation of the second remark, that the Jews not only learned from it the nature of true piety, but when they saw their inability to observe it, were led by the fear of its sentence, though not without reluctance, to the Mediator. Now, in giving a summary of those things which are requisite to the true knowledge of God, we have shown that we can form no conceptions of his greatness, but his majesty immediately discovers itself to us, to constrain us to worship him. In the knowledge of ourselves, we have laid down this as a principal article, that being divested of all opinion of our own strength, and confidence in our own righteousness, and, on the other hand, discouraged and depressed by a consciousness of our poverty, we should learn true humility and self-dejection. The Lord accomplishes both these things in his law, where, in the first place, claiming to himself the legitimate authority to command, he calls us to revere his Divinity, and prescribes the parts of which this reverence consists; and in the next place, promulgating the rule of his righteousness, (the rectitude of which, our nature, being depraved and perverted, perpetually opposes; and from the perfection of which, our ability, through its indolence and imbecility towards that which is good, is at a great distance,) he convicts us both of impotence and of unrighteousness. Moreover, the internal law, which has before been said to be inscribed and as it were engraven on the hearts of all men, suggests to us in some measure the same things which are to be learned from the two tables. For our conscience does not permit us to sleep in perpetual insensibility, but is an internal witness and monitor of the duties we owe to God, shows us the difference between good and evil, and so accuses us when we deviate from our duty. But man, involved as he is in a cloud of errors, scarcely obtains from this law of nature the smallest idea of what worship is accepted by God; but is certainly at an immense distance from a right understanding of it. Besides, he is so elated with arrogance and ambition, and so blinded with self-love, that he cannot yet take a view of himself, and as it were retire within, that he may learn to submit and humble himself, and to confess his misery. Since it was necessary, therefore, both for our dulness and obstinacy, the Lord gave us a written law; to declare with greater certainty what in the law of nature was too obscure, and by arousing our indolence, to make a deeper impression on our understanding and memory.

II. Now, it is easy to perceive, what we are to learn from the law; namely, that God, as he is our Creator, justly sustains towards us the character of a Father and of a Lord; and that on this account we owe to him glory and reverence, love and fear. Moreover, that we are not at liberty to follow every thing to which the violence of our passions may incite us; but that we ought to be attentive to his will, and to practise nothing but what is pleasing to him. In the next place, that righteousness and rectitude are a delight, but iniquity an abomination to him; and that, therefore, unless we will with impious ingratitude rebel against our Maker, we must necessarily spend our whole lives in the practice of righteousness. For if we manifest a becoming reverence for him, only when we prefer his will to our own, it follows that there is no other legitimate worship of him, but the observance of righteousness, sanctity, and purity. Nor can we pretend to excuse ourselves by a want of ability, like insolvent debtors. For it is improper for us to measure the glory of God by our ability; for whatever may be our characters, he ever remains like himself, the friend of righteousness, the enemy of iniquity. Whatever he requires of us, since he can require nothing but what is right, we are under a natural obligation to obey; but our inability is our own fault. For if we are bound by our own passions, which are under the government of sin, so that we are not at liberty to obey our Father, there is no reason why we should plead this necessity in our defence, the criminality of which is within ourselves, and must be imputed to us.

III. When we have made such a proficiency as this by means of the instruction of the law, we ought, under the same teacher, to retire within ourselves; from which we may learn two things: First, by comparing our life with the righteousness of the law, we shall find, that we are very far from acting agreeably to the will of God, and are therefore unworthy to retain a place among his creatures, much less to be numbered among his children. Secondly, by examining our strength, we shall see, that it is not only unequal to the observance of the law, but a mere nullity. The necessary consequence of this will be a diffidence in our own strength, and an anxiety and trepidation of mind. For the conscience cannot sustain the load of iniquity, without an immediate discovery of the

Divine judgment. And the Divine judgment cannot be perceived, without inspiring a dread of death. Compelled also by proofs of its impotence, it cannot avoid falling into an absolute despair of its own strength. Both these dispositions produce humility and dejection. The result of all this is, that the man terrified with the apprehension of eternal death, which he sees justly impending over him for his unrighteousness, betakes himself entirely to the Divine mercy, as to the only port of salvation; and perceiving his inability to fulfil the commands of the law, and feeling nothing but despair in himself, he implores and expects assistance from another quarter.

IV. But not contented with having conciliated a reverence for his righteousness, the Lord has also subjoined promises and threatenings, in order that our hearts might imbibe a love for him, and at the same time a hatred to iniquity. For since the eyes of our mind are too dim to be attracted with the mere beauty of virtue, our most merciful Father has been graciously pleased to allure us to the love and worship of himself by the sweetness of his rewards. He announces, therefore, that he has reserved rewards for virtue, and that the person who obeys his commandments shall not labour in vain. He proclaims, on the contrary, not only that unrighteousness is execrable in his sight, but also that it shall not escape with impunity; but that he will avenge himself on all the despisers of his majesty. And to urge us by all possible motives, he promises also the blessings of the present life, as well as eternal felicity, to the obedience of those who keep his commandments, the transgressors of which he threatens not only with present calamities, but with the torments of eternal death. For that promise, "these if a man do, he shall live in them," (*g*) and this correspondent threatening, "the soul that sinneth, it shall die," (*h*) undoubtedly relate to a future and endless immortality or death. Wherever we read of the Divine benevolence or wrath, the former comprehends eternal life, the latter eternal destruction. Now, of present blessings and curses, the law contains a long catalogue. The penal sanctions display the consummate purity of God, which cannot tolerate iniquity; while the promises not only manifest his perfect love of righteousness, which he cannot defraud of its reward, but likewise illustrate his wonderful goodness. For since we, with all that belongs to us, are indebted to his majesty, whatever he requires of us, he most justly demands as the payment of a debt; but the payment of a debt is not entitled to remuneration. Therefore he recedes from the strictness of his claims, when he proposes a reward to our obedience, which is not performed spontaneously,

(*g*) Lev. xviii. 5.   (*h*) Ezek. xviii. 4.

as if it were not a duty. But the effect of those promises on us has partly been mentioned already, and will hereafter more clearly appear in its proper place. Suffice it at present, if we remember and consider that the promises of the law contain no mean recommendation of righteousness, to make it more evident how much God is pleased with the observance of it; and that the penal sanctions are annexed, to render unrighteousness more execrable, lest the sinner, amidst the fascinations of sin, should forget that the judgment of the Legislator awaits him.

V. Now, since the Lord, when about to deliver a rule of perfect righteousness, referred all the parts of it to his own will, this shows that nothing is more acceptable to him than obedience. This is worthy of the most diligent observation, since the licentiousness of the human mind is so inclined to the frequent invention of various services in order to merit his favour. For this irreligious affectation of religion, which is a principle innate in the human mind, has betrayed itself in all ages, and betrays itself even in the present day; for men always take a pleasure in contriving some way of attaining righteousness, which is not agreeable to the Divine word. Hence, among those which are commonly esteemed good works, the precepts of the law hold a very contracted station, the numberless multitude of human inventions occupying almost the whole space. But what was the design of Moses, unless it was to repress such an unwarrantable license, when, after the promulgation of the law, he addressed the people in the following manner! "Observe and hear all these words which I command thee, that it may go well with thee, and with thy children after thee for ever, when thou doest that which is good and right in the sight of the Lord thy God. What thing soever I command you, observe to do it: thou shalt not add thereto, nor diminish from it." (*i*) And before, when he had declared that this was their wisdom and their understanding in the sight of other nations, that they had received statutes, and judgments, and ceremonies, from the Lord, he had added, "Take heed to thyself, and keep thy soul diligently, lest thou forget the things which thine eyes have seen, and lest they depart from thy heart all the days of thy life." (*k*) Foreseeing that the Israelites would not rest, but, even after the reception of the law, would labour to produce new species of righteousness, foreign from what the law requires, unless they should be rigorously restrained, God pronounces that his word comprehends the perfection of righteousness; and yet, though this ought most effectually to have prevented them, they were guilty of that very presumption which was so expressly forbidden. But

(*i*) Deut. xii. 28, 32.   (*k*) Deut. iv. 5, 6, 9.

what is this to us? We are certainly bound by the same declaration; for the claims of the Lord on behalf of his law, that it contains the doctrine of perfect righteousness, beyond all doubt remain perpetually the same; yet not contented with it, we are wonderfully laborious in inventing and performing other good works, one after another. The best remedy for this fault will be a constant attention to this reflection; that the law was given to us from heaven to teach us a perfect righteousness; that in it no righteousness is taught, but that which is conformable to the decrees of the Divine will; that it is therefore vain to attempt new species of works in order to merit the favour of God, whose legitimate worship consists solely in obedience, but that any pursuit of good works deviating from the law of God is an intolerable profanation of the Divine and real righteousness. There is much truth also in the observation of Augustine, who calls obedience to God sometimes the parent and guardian, and sometimes the origin of all virtues.

VI. But when we have given an exposition of the Divine law, we shall then more suitably and profitably confirm what has been already advanced concerning its office and use. Before we enter, however, on the discussion of each article separately, it will be useful to premise some things which may contribute to a general knowledge of it. First, let it be understood, that the law inculcates a conformity of life, not only to external probity, but also to internal and spiritual righteousness. Now, though none can deny this, yet very few persons pay proper attention to it. This arises from their not considering the Legislator, by whose nature we ought to estimate also the nature of the law. If a king prohibit, by an edict, adultery, murder, or theft, no man, I confess, will be liable to the penalty of such a law, who has only conceived in his mind a desire to commit adultery, murder, or theft, but has not perpetrated any of them. Because the superintendence of a mortal legislator extends only to the external conduct, and his prohibitions are not violated unless the crimes be actually committed. But God, whose eye nothing escapes, and who esteems not so much the external appearance as the purity of the heart, in the prohibition of adultery, murder, and theft, comprises a prohibition of lust, wrath, hatred, coveting what belongs to another, fraud, and every similar vice. For, being a spiritual Legislator, he addresses himself to the soul as much as to the body. Now, the murder of the soul is wrath and hatred; the theft of the soul is evil concupiscence and avarice; the adultery of the soul is lust. But it will be said, that human laws also relate to designs and intentions, and not to fortuitous events. This I grant; but they relate to such designs and intentions as have been manifested in outward actions. They examine and consider with what intention every act has been performed; but do not scrutinize the secret thoughts. Human laws therefore are satisfied, when a man abstains from external transgression. But, on the contrary, the Divine law being given to our minds, the proper regulation of them is the principal requisite to a righteous observance of it. But men in general, even while they resolutely dissemble their contempt of the law, dispose their eyes, their feet, their hands, and all the parts of their body, to some kind of observance of it, while at the same time their hearts are entirely alienated from all obedience to it, and they suppose that they have discharged their duty, if they have concealed from man what they practise in the sight of God. They hear the commands, Thou shalt not kill, Thou shalt not commit adultery, Thou shalt not steal. They draw not the sword to commit murder; they never associate with harlots; they lay no violent hands on the property of others. All these things thus far are well; but in their whole souls they breathe after murders, they kindle into lust, they look with dishonest eyes on the property of others, and in their cupidity they devour it. Now, then, they are destitute of the principal requisite of the law. Whence arises such gross stupidity, but from discarding the Legislator, and accommodating a righteousness to their own inclination? These persons Paul strongly opposes, when he affirms that "the law is spiritual;" (*l*) signifying that it requires not only the obedience of the soul, the understanding, and the will, but even an angelic purity, which, being cleansed from all the pollution of the flesh, may savour entirely of the Spirit.

VII. When we say that this is the sense of the law, we are not introducing a novel interpretation of our own, but following Christ, who is the best interpreter of it. For the people having imbibed from the Pharisees the corrupt opinion, that he, who has perpetrated no external act of disobedience to the law, is an observer of the law, he confutes this very dangerous error, and pronounces an unchaste look at a woman to be adultery; he declares them to be murderers, who hate a brother; he makes them "in danger of the judgment," who have only conceived resentment in their hearts; them "in danger of the council," who in murmuring or quarrelling have discovered any sign of an angry mind; and them "in danger of hell fire," who with opprobrious and slanderous language have broken forth into open rage. (*m*) Persons who have not perceived these things, have pretended that Christ was another Moses, the giver of an evangelical law, which supplied the deficiencies of the law of Moses. Whence that common max-

(*l*) Rom. vii. 14.   (*m*) Matt. v. 22, 28

im, concerning the perfection of the evangelical law, that it is far superior to the old law — a maxim in many respects very pernicious. For when we introduce a summary of the commandments, it will appear from Moses himself what an indignity this fixes on the Divine law. It certainly insinuates that all the sanctity of the fathers under the Old Testament, was not very remote from hypocrisy, and draws us aside from that one perpetual rule of righteousness. But there is not the least difficulty in the confutation of this error; for they have supposed that Christ made additions to the law, whereas he only restored it to its genuine purity, by clearing it from the obscurities and blemishes which it had contracted from the falsehoods and the leaven of the Pharisees.

VIII. It must be observed, in the second place, that the commands and prohibitions always imply more than the words express; but this must be so restricted, that we may not make it a Lesbian rule, by the assistance of which the Scripture may be licentiously perverted, and any sense be extorted at pleasure from any passage. For some people, by this immoderate and excursive liberty, cause one person to despise the authority of the law, and another to despair of understanding it. Therefore, if it be possible, we must find some way that may lead us by a straight and steady course to the will of God. We must inquire, I say, how far our interpretation ought to exceed the limits of the expressions; that it may evidently appear, not to be an appendix of human glosses annexed to the Divine law, but a faithful explanation of the pure and genuine sense of the legislator. Indeed, in all the commandments, the figure synecdoche, by which a part is expressed instead of the whole, is so conspicuous, that he may justly be the object of ridicule, who would restrict the sense of the law within the narrow limits of the words. It is plain, then, that a sober exposition of the law goes beyond the words of it; but how far, remains doubtful, unless some rule be laid down. The best rule, then, I conceive will be, that the exposition be directed to the design of the precept; that in regard to every precept it should be considered for what end it was given. For example, every precept is either imperative or prohibitory. The true meaning of both these kinds of precepts will immediately occur to us, if we consider the design or the end of them; as the end of the fifth commandment is, that honour may be given to them to whom God assigns it. The substance of this precept, then, is, that it is right, and pleasing to God, that we should honour those on whom he has conferred any excellence, and that contemptuous and contumacious conduct towards them is an abomination to him. The design of the first commandment is, that God alone may be worshipped. The substance of this precept, then, will be, that true piety, that is, the worship of his majesty, is pleasing to God, and that he abominates impiety. Thus in every commandment we should first examine the subject of it; in the next place we should inquire the end of it, till we discover what the Legislator really declares in it to be either pleasing or displeasing to him. Lastly, we must draw an argument from this commandment to the opposite of it, in this manner: — If this please God, the contrary must displease him; if this displease him, the contrary must please him; if he enjoin this, he forbids the contrary; if he forbid this, he enjoins the contrary.

IX. What we now rather obscurely hint at, will be fully and practically elucidated in our exposition of the commandments. Wherefore it is sufficient to have suggested it; only the last position, which otherwise might not be understood, or, if understood, might seem unreasonable, requires to be briefly established by suitable proof. It needs no proof, that an injunction of any thing good is a prohibition of the opposite evil; for every man will concede it. And common sense will easily admit, that a prohibition of crimes is a command to practise the contrary duties. It is commonly considered as a commendation of virtues, when censure is passed on the opposite vices. But we require somewhat more than is commonly intended by those forms of expression. For men generally understand the virtue which is opposite to any vice to be an abstinence from that vice; but we affirm that it goes further, even to the actual performance of the opposite duty. Therefore, in this precept, "Thou shalt not kill," the common sense of mankind will perceive nothing more than that we ought to abstain from all acts of injury to others, and from all desire to commit any such acts. I maintain that it also implies, that we should do every thing that we possibly can towards the preservation of the life of our neighbour. And not to speak without reason, I prove it in the following manner: God forbids us to injure the safety of our brother, because he wishes his life to be dear and precious to us: he therefore at the same time requires of us all those offices of love which may contribute to the preservation of it. Thus we perceive, that the end of the precept will always discover to us whatever it enjoins or forbids us to do.

X. Many reasons are frequently given, why God has, as it were, in incomplete precepts, rather partially intimated his will than positively expressed it; but the reason which affords me more satisfaction than all others is the following. Because the flesh always endeavours to extenuate, and by specious pretexts to conceal the turpitude of sin, unless it be exceedingly palpable, he has proposed, by way of example, in every kind of transgression, that which is most atrocious and detestable, and the mention of which inspires us with horror, in order that our minds might be impressed with the greater detestation of every sin. This often deceives us in forming an opinion of vices; if they be private, we extenuate them. The Lord destroys these subterfuges, when he accustoms us to refer the whole multitude of vices to these general heads, which best represent the abominable nature of every species of transgressions. For example, anger and hatred are not supposed to be such execrable crimes when they are mentioned under their own proper appellations; but when they are forbidden to us under the name of murder, we have a clearer perception how abominable they are in the view of God, by whose word they are classed under such a flagitious and horrible species of crimes; and being influenced by his judgment, we accustom ourselves more seriously to consider the atrociousness of those offences which we previously accounted trivial.

XI. In the third place, let it be considered, what is intended by the division of the Divine law into two tables; the frequent and solemn mention of which all wise men will judge not to be without some particular design. And we have a reason at hand, which removes all ambiguity on this subject. For God has divided his law into two parts, which comprise the perfection of righteousness, so that he has assigned the first part to the duties of religion, which peculiarly belongs to the worship of his majesty, and the second to those duties of charity, which respect men. The first foundation of righteousness is certainly the worship of God; and if this be destroyed, all the other branches of righteousness, like the parts of a disjointed and falling edifice, are torn asunder and scattered. For what kind of righteousness will you pretend to, because you refrain from harassing men by acts of theft and rapine, if at the same time you atrociously and sacrilegiously defraud the majesty of God of the glory which is due to him?—because you do not pollute your body with fornication, if you blasphemously profane the sacred name of God?—because you murder no man, if you strive to destroy and extinguish all memory of God? It is in vain, therefore, to boast of righteousness without religion; as well might the trunk of a body be exhibited as a beautiful object, after the head has been cut off. Nor is religion only the head of righteousness, but the very soul of it, constituting all its life and vigour; for without the fear of God, men preserve no equity and love among themselves. We therefore call the worship of God the principle and foundation of righteousness, because, if that be wanting, whatever equity, continence, and temperance men may practise among themselves, it is all vain and frivolous in the sight of God. We assert also that it is the source and soul of righteousness; because men are taught by it to live temperately and justly with one another, if they venerate God as the judge of right and wrong. In the first table, therefore, he instructs us in piety and the proper duties of religion, in which his majesty is to be worshipped; in the second he prescribes the duties which the fear of his name should excite us to practise in society. For this reason our Lord, as the evangelists inform us, (*n*) summarily comprised the whole law in two principal points — that we love God with all our heart, with all our soul, and with all our strength; and that we love our neighbour as ourselves. Of the two parts in which he comprehends the whole law, we see how he directs one towards God, and assigns the other to men.

XII. But, although the whole law is contained in these two principal points, yet our God, in order to remove every pretext of excuse, has been pleased in the ten commandments more diffusely and explicitly to declare, as well those things which relate to our honour, love, and fear of him, as those which pertain to that charity, which he commands us for his sake to exercise towards men. Nor is it a useless study to examine into the division of the commandments; provided you remember it is a subject of such a nature, that every man ought to be at liberty to judge of it, and that we ought not contentiously to oppose any who may differ from us respecting it. But we are under a necessity of touching on this topic, lest the reader should despise or wonder at the division that we shall adopt, as a novel invention. That the law is divided into ten precepts, is beyond all controversy, being frequently established by the authority of God himself. The question, therefore, is not concerning the number of the precepts, but concerning the manner of dividing them. Those who divide them, so as to assign three precepts to the first table, and leave the remaining seven to the second, expunge from the number the precept concerning images, or at least conceal it under the first; whereas it is undoubtedly delivered by the Lord as a distinct commandment. But the tenth, against coveting the property of our neighbour, they improperly divide into two. We shall see presently that such a method of division was unknown in purer ages. Others reckon with us four articles in the first table; but the first commandment they consider as a simple promise, without a precept. Now, I understand the "ten words" mentioned by Moses to be ten precepts; and I think I see that number disposed in the most beautiful order. And therefore, unless I am convinced by clear argument, leaving

(*n*) Matt. xxii. 37—40. Luke x. 27.

them in possession of their opinion, I shall follow what appears to me to be preferable; that is, that what they make the first precept is a preface to the whole law; that it is followed by the precepts, four belonging to the first table and six to the second, in the order in which they will now be recited. Origen has mentioned this division as if it were universally received in his time without any controversy. Augustine also coincides with us; for in enumerating them to Boniface, he observes this order: That God alone be religiously worshipped; that no adoration be paid to an idol; that the name of the Lord be not taken in vain. He had before spoken separately of the shadowy precept of the sabbath. It is true, that in another passage he expresses his approbation of the former division, but for a most trivial reason; namely, that if the first table be digested into three precepts, the trinal number will be a more conspicuous exhibition of the mystery of the Trinity. In the same place, however, he does not conceal that in other respects he prefers our division. Beside these writers, the author of the unfinished treatise on Matthew is of the same opinion with us. Josephus, doubtless according to the common opinion of his time, assigns five precepts to each table. This is repugnant to reason, because it confounds the distinction between religion and charity; and is also refuted by the authority of our Lord, who in Matthew places the precept concerning honour to parents in the second table. Now let us hear God himself speaking in his own words.

THE FIRST COMMANDMENT.

I am the Lord thy God, which have brought thee out of the land of Egypt, out of the house of bondage. Thou shalt have no other gods before me.

XIII. Whether you make the first sentence a part of the first commandment, or read it separately, is a matter of indifference to me, provided you allow it to be a preface to the whole law. The first object of attention in making laws is to guard against their being abrogated by contempt. Therefore God in the first place provides, that the majesty of the law, which he is about to deliver, may never fall into contempt; and to sanction it he uses a threefold argument. He asserts his authority and right of giving commands, and thereby lays his chosen people under a necessity of obeying them. He exhibits a promise of grace, to allure them by its charms to the pursuit of holiness. He reminds the Israelites of his favour, to convict them of ingratitude if they do not conduct themselves in a manner correspondent to his goodness. The name Lord, or Jehovah, designates his authority and legitimate dominion. For if all things be of him, and if in him all things consist, it is reasonable that all things be referred to him, agreeably to the observation of Paul. (*o*) Therefore by this word alone we are brought into complete subjection to the power of the Divine majesty; for it would be monstrous for us to desire to remove ourselves from his jurisdiction, out of whom we cannot exist.

XIV. After having shown that he has a right to command, and that obedience is his just due, — that he may not appear to constrain us by necessity alone, he sweetly allures us by pronouncing himself the God of the Church. For the expression implies the mutual relation which is contained in that promise, "I will be their God, and they shall be my people." (*p*) Whence Christ proves the immortality of Abraham, Isaac, and Jacob, from the declaration of the Lord, that he is their God. (*q*) Wherefore it is the same as if he had said, I have chosen you as my people, not only to bless you in the present life, but to bestow upon you abundant felicity in the life to come. The design of this favour is remarked in various places in the law; for when the Lord in mercy condescends to number us among the society of his people, "He chooseth us," says Moses, "to be a peculiar people unto himself, a holy people, to keep his commandments." (*r*) Hence that exhortation, "Ye shall be holy, for I am holy." (*s*) Now, from these two considerations is derived the remonstrance of the Lord by the Prophet: "A son honoureth his father, and a servant his master; if then I be a father, where is mine honour? and if I be a master, where is my fear?" (*t*)

XV. Next follows a recital of his kindness, which ought to produce a most powerful effect upon our minds, in proportion to the detestable guilt of ingratitude, even among men. He reminded the Israelites, indeed, of a favour which they had recently experienced, but which, on account of its magnitude and concomitant miracles, being worthy of everlasting remembrance, might also have an influence on succeeding generations. Besides, it was particularly suitable to the present occasion, when the law was about to be published; for the Lord suggests that they were liberated from a miserable slavery in order that they might serve the author of their liberty with a promptitude of reverence and obedience. To retain us in the true and exclusive worship of himself, he generally distinguishes himself by certain epithets, by which he discriminates his sacred name from all idols and fictitious deities. For, as I have

(*o*) Rom. xi. 36.
(*p*) Jer. xxxi. 33.
(*q*) Matt. xxii. 32.
(*r*) Deut. vii. 6; xiv. 2; xxvi. 18.
(*s*) Lev. xi. 44.
(*t*) Mal. i. 6.

before observed, such is our proneness to vanity and presumption, that as soon as God is mentioned, our mind is unable to guard itself from falling into some vain imagination. Therefore, when God intends to apply a remedy to this evil, he adorns his majesty with certain titles, and thus circumscribes us with barriers, that we may not run into various follies, and presumptuously invent to ourselves some new deity, discarding the living God, and setting up an idol in his stead. For this reason the Prophets, whenever they intend a proper designation of him, invest him, and as it were surround him, with those characters under which he had manifested himself to the people of Israel. Yet, when he is called "the God of Abraham," or "the God of Israel," when he is said to reside "between the cherubim," "in the temple," "at Jerusalem," (*v*) these and similar forms of expression do not confine him to one place, or to one nation; they are only used to fix the thoughts of the pious on that God, who, in the covenant which he has made with Israel, has given such a representation of himself, that it is not proper to deviate in the smallest instance from such a model. Nevertheless, let it be concluded, that the deliverance of the Jews is mentioned to induce them to devote themselves with more alacrity to the service of God, who justly claims a right to their obedience. But, that we may not suppose this to have no relation to us, it behoves us to consider, that the servitude of Israel in Egypt was a type of the spiritual captivity, in which we are all detained, till our celestial Deliverer extricates us by the power of his arm, and introduces us into the kingdom of liberty. As formerly, therefore, when he designed to restore the dispersed Israelites to the worship of his name, he rescued them from the intolerable tyranny of Pharaoh, by which they were oppressed, so now he delivers all those, whose God he declares himself to be, from the fatal dominion of Satan, which was represented by that corporeal captivity. Wherefore there is no one, whose mind ought not to be excited to listen to the law, which he is informed came from the King of kings; from whom as all creatures derive their origin, so it is reasonable that they should regard him as their end in all things. Every man, I say, ought to welcome the Legislator; to observe whose commands he is taught that he is particularly chosen; from whose benignity he expects an abundance of temporal blessings, and a life of immortality and glory; by whose wonderful power and mercy he knows himself to be delivered from the jaws of death.

XVI. Having firmly established the authority of his law, he publishes the first commandment, "That we should have

(*v*) Exod. iii. 6. Amos i. 2. Hab. ii. 20. Psalm lxxx. 1; xcix. 1. Isaiah xxxvii. 16.

no other gods before him." The end of this precept is, that God chooses to have the sole preëminence, and to enjoy undiminished his authority among his people. To produce this end, he enjoins us to keep at a distance from all impiety and superstition, by which we should either diminish or obscure the glory of his Deity; and for the same reason he directs us to worship and adore him in the exercise of true piety. The simplicity of the language almost expresses this; for we cannot "have" God without at the same time comprising all that belongs to him. Therefore, when he forbids us to "have" any other gods, he implies, that we must not transfer to another what belongs to him. But although the duties we owe to God are innumerable, yet they may not improperly be classed under four general heads — adoration, a necessary branch of which is the spiritual obedience of the conscience; trust; invocation; and thanksgiving. By adoration I mean the reverence and worship which he receives from every one of us who has submitted to his majesty. Wherefore it is not without reason that I make it partly to consist in a subjection of our consciences to his law; [for it is a spiritual homage which is rendered to him, as to a sovereign King possessed of all power over our souls.] Trust is a secure dependence on him arising from a knowledge of his perfections; when ascribing to him all wisdom, righteousness, power, truth, and goodness, we esteem ourselves happy only in communications from him. Invocation is the application of our minds, under every pressure of necessity, resorting to his fidelity, faithfulness, and assistance, as its only defence. Thanksgiving is gratitude, which ascribes to him the praise of all blessings. As the Lord permits no portion of these duties to be transferred to another, so he commands them to be wholly given to himself. Nor will it be sufficient for you to refrain from worshipping any other god, unless you also refrain from imitating certain nefarious despisers, who take the compendious method of treating all religions with contempt. But the observance of this precept must be preceded by true religion, leading our minds to the living God; that being endued with the knowledge of him, they may aspire to admire, fear, and worship his majesty, to receive his communication of blessings, to request his aid upon all occasions, to acknowledge and celebrate the magnificence of his works, as the sole end in all the actions of our lives. We must also beware of corrupt superstition, by which those whose minds are diverted from the true God, are carried about after various deities. Therefore, if we be contented with one God, let us remember what has before been observed, that all fictitious deities must be driven far away, and that we must not divide that worship which he claims exclusively to himself. For it is criminal to detract even the smallest portion from his glory; he must be left in possession of all that belongs to him. The following clause, "before me," aggravates the atrociousness of the offence; for God is provoked to jealousy whenever we substitute the figments of our own minds instead of him; just as an immodest woman, by openly introducing an adulterer into the presence of her husband, would inflame his mind with the greater resentment. When God, therefore, by the presence of his power and grace, gave a proof of his regard to the people whom he had chosen, — in order the more forcibly to deter them from the crime of rebellion against him, he warns them of the impossibility of introducing new deities without his being a witness and spectator of the sacrilege. For this presumption rises to the highest degree of impiety, when man imagines that he can elude the observation of God in his acts of rebellion. God, on the contrary, proclaims, that whatever we devise, whatever we attempt, whatever we perform, is present to his view. Our conscience must therefore be pure even from the most latent thoughts of apostasy, if we wish our religion to obtain the approbation of the Lord. For he requires from us the glory due to his Divinity undiminished and uncorrupted, not only in external confession, but in his own eyes, which penetrate the inmost recesses of our hearts.

THE SECOND COMMANDMENT.

Thou shalt not make unto thee any graven image, or any likeness of any thing that is in heaven above, or that is in the earth beneath, or that is in the water under the earth. Thou shalt not bow down thyself to them, nor serve them.

XVII. As in the preceding commandment the Lord has declared himself to be the one God, besides whom no other deities ought to be imagined or worshipped, so in this he more clearly reveals his nature, and the kind of worship with which he ought to be honoured, that we may not dare to form any carnal conceptions of him. The end, therefore, of this precept is, that he will not have his legitimate worship profaned with superstitious rites. Wherefore, in a word, he calls us off, and wholly abstracts us from carnal observances, which our foolish minds are accustomed to devise, when they conceive of God according to the grossness of their own apprehensions; and therefore he calls us to the service which rightfully belongs to him; that is, the spiritual worship which he has instituted. He marks what is the grossest transgression of this kind; that is, external idolatry. And this precept consists of two parts. The first restrains us from licentiously daring to make God, who is incomprehensible, the subject of our senses, or to represent him under any visible form. The second prohibits us from paying religious adoration to any images. He likewise briefly enumerates all the forms, in which he used to be represented by profane and superstitious nations. By those things which are in heaven, he means the sun, the moon, and the other stars, and perhaps birds; as, when he explains his meaning in the fourth chapter of Deuteronomy, he mentions birds as well as the stars. (*w*) This I should not have remarked, had I not known some persons injudiciously refer this clause to angels. I omit the other particulars, as needing no explanation. And in the first book (*x*) we have already sufficiently proved that whatever visible representations of God are invented by man, are diametrically opposite to his nature; and that, therefore, as soon as ever idols are introduced, true religion is immediately corrupted and adulterated.

XVIII. The penal sanction which is annexed ought to have no small influence in arousing us from our lethargy. He thus threatens:

For I the Lord thy God am a jealous God, visiting the iniquity of the fathers upon the children unto the third and fourth generation of them that hate me; and showing mercy unto thousands of them that love me, and keep my commandments.

This is equivalent to a declaration that it is to him alone that we ought to adhere. And to urge us to it, he announces his power, which he permits none with impunity to despise or undervalue. For the Hebrew word *El*, which is here used for God, is expressive of strength. In the second place, he calls himself "a jealous God," who can bear no rival. Thirdly, he declares that he will avenge his majesty and glory on those who transfer it to creatures or to graven images; and that not with the transient punishment of the original transgressors only, but of their posterity to the third and fourth generation; that is, of those who shall imitate the impiety of their fathers; as he also permanently displays his mercy and goodness, through a long line of posterity, to those who love him and keep his law. It is very common for God to assume the character of a husband to us; for the union, in which he connects us with himself, when he receives us into the bosom of his Church, bears a resemblance to the sacred conjugal relation, which requires to be supported by mutual fidelity. As he performs towards us all the duties of a true and faithful husband, so he demands from us the reciprocal duties of conjugal love and chastity; that

(*w*) Deut. iv. 17.   (*x*) Cap. xi. xii.

is, that we do not prostitute our souls to Satan, to lust, and to the impurity of the carnal appetites. Wherefore, when he reproves the apostasy of the Jews, he complains that they had discarded chastity, and were polluted with adulteries. (*y*) Therefore, as a husband, in proportion to the superiority of his purity and chastity, is the more grievously incensed, if he perceive the affection of his wife inclining to a rival, so the Lord, who has in truth espoused us to himself, declares that he feels the most ardent jealousy, whenever we neglect the sacred purity of his conjugal relation to us, and defile ourselves with criminal lusts, but especially when we transfer to any other, or adulterate with any superstition, the worship of his majesty, which ought to be preserved in the most consummate perfection; since by such conduct we not only violate the faith pledged in our nuptials, but even pollute our souls with spiritual adultery.

XIX. Let us inquire what he intends by his threatening to "visit the iniquity of the fathers upon the children to the third and fourth generation." For besides that it is inconsistent with the equity of the Divine justice to inflict upon an innocent person the punishment due to the offences of another, God himself declares that "the son shall not bear the iniquity of the father." (*z*) But this expression is repeated more than once, concerning a deferring to future generations of the punishments of crimes committed by their ancestors. For Moses frequently speaks of "the Lord visiting the iniquity of the fathers upon the children unto the third and fourth generation." (*a*) In like manner Jeremiah: "Thou showest loving-kindness unto thousands, and recompensest the iniquity of the fathers into the bosom of their children after them." (*b*) Some, who labour very hard to solve this difficulty, are of opinion that its meaning is to be confined to temporal punishments; which if children sustain through the sins of their parents, there is nothing absurd in it; because they frequently conduce to the salvation of those on whom they are inflicted. This is certainly true. For Isaiah denounced to Hezekiah, that on account of the sin which he had committed, his sons should be despoiled of the kingdom and carried away into exile. (*c*) The families of Pharaoh and Abimelech are afflicted on account of the injury sustained by Abraham. (*d*) But when this is adduced as a solution of these questions, it is rather an evasion of it, than a proper explanation. For in this and in similar places the Lord threatens a punishment too great to be terminated by the limits of the present life. It must therefore

(*y*) Jer. iii. 1, 2. Hos. ii. 2. (*a*) Num. xiv. 18. (*c*) Isaiah xxxix. 7.
(*z*) Ezek. xviii. 20. (*b*) Jer. xxxii. 18. (*d*) Gen. xii. 17; xx. 3.

be understood as a declaration that the curse of the Lord righteously rests, not only on the person of an impious man, but also on his whole family. Where it has rested, what can be expected, but that the father, being destitute of the Spirit of God, will lead a most flagitious life; and that the son, experiencing, in consequence of the iniquity of his father, a similar dereliction by the Lord, will pursue the same path to perdition; and that the grandson and the great grandson, the execrable posterity of detestable men, will run headlong after them down the same precipice of destruction?

XX. First let us inquire, whether such punishment be inconsistent with the Divine justice. If the whole nature of man be worthy of condemnation, we know that destruction awaits those who are not favoured by the Lord with the communication of his grace. Nevertheless, they perish through their own iniquity, and not through the unjust hatred of God. Nor is there any room left for expostulation, why they are not assisted by Divine grace to obtain salvation as well as others. Since it is a punishment, therefore, inflicted on the impious and flagitious, in consequence of their transgressions, that their families remain destitute of Divine grace for many generations, who can bring any accusation against God for this most righteous instance of his vengeance? But it will be said, the Lord declares, on the contrary, that the punishment of the sin of the father shall not be transferred to the son. Observe the subject that is treated of in that place. The Israelites, after they had been long harassed by numerous and unceasing calamities, began to use this proverb, "The fathers have eaten sour grapes, and the children's teeth are set on edge;" (e) by which they insinuated, that sins had been committed by their parents, the punishment of which was inflicted on them who were otherwise righteous and innocent, more through the implacable wrath of God, than through a just severity. The Prophet announces to them that this is not the case, but that they are punished for their own transgressions, and that it is incompatible with the Divine justice to punish a righteous son for the iniquity of a wicked father. Nor is this to be found in the penal sanction now under consideration. For if the visitation, of which we are treating, be fulfilled, when God removes from the family of the impious his grace, the light of his truth, and the other means of salvation, the very circumstance of children blinded and abandoned by him being found treading in the footsteps of their fathers, is an instance of their bearing the curse in consequence of the crimes of their parents. But their being the subjects of temporal miseries, and at length of eternal perdition, are punishments from

---

(e) Ezek. xviii. 2.

the righteous judgment of God, not for the sins of others, but on account of their own iniquity.

XXI. On the other hand, God gives a promise to extend his mercy to a thousand generations; which also frequently occurs in the Scripture, and is inserted in the solemn covenant with the Church: "I will be a God unto thee, and to thy seed after thee."(*f*) In allusion to this, Solomon says, that "the children of the just man are blessed after him;" (*g*) not only as the effect of a religious education, which is of no small importance, but also in consequence of the blessing promised in the covenant, that the grace of God shall perpetually remain in the families of the pious. This is a source of peculiar consolation to the faithful, but to the impious of great terror; for if, even after death, the memory of righteousness and iniquity has so much influence with God, that the curse of the one and the blessing of the other will redound to posterity, much more will it remain on the persons of the actors themselves. Now, it is no objection to our argument, that the descendants of the impious sometimes grow better, while those of the faithful degenerate; since the Legislator never intended to establish in this case such an invariable rule, as would derogate from his own free choice. For it is sufficient for the consolation of the righteous and the terror of the sinner, that the denunciation is not vain or inefficacious, although it be not always executed. For as the temporal punishments inflicted on a few wicked men are testimonies of the Divine wrath against sin, and of the judgment that will hereafter be pronounced on all sinners, though many escape with impunity even to the end of their lives, so, when the Lord exhibits one example of this blessing, in manifesting his mercy and goodness to the son for the sake of his father, he affords a proof of his constant and perpetual favour to his worshippers; and when, in any one instance, he pursues the iniquity of the father in the son, he shows what a judgment awaits all the reprobate on account of their own transgressions; the certainty of which was what he principally designed in this passage. He also gives us a cursory intimation of the greatness of his mercy, which he extends to a thousand generations, while he has assigned only four generations to his vengeance.

THE THIRD COMMANDMENT.

Thou shalt not take the name of the Lord thy God in vain.

XXII. The end of this precept is, that the Lord will have the majesty of his name to be held inviolably sacred by us.

(*f*) Gen. xvii. 7.   (*g*) Prov. xx. 7.

The substance of the command therefore is, that we ought not to profane that name by a contemptuous or irreverent use of it. This prohibition necessarily implies an injunction, that we studiously and carefully treat it with religious veneration. Therefore it becomes us to regulate our thoughts and words in such a manner that we may not think or speak any thing concerning God and his mysteries, but with the greatest sobriety and reverence; that in meditating on his works we may form no opinion that is dishonourable to him. These three things, I say, we ought most carefully to observe — first, that whatever we think, and whatever we say of him, should savour of his excellence, correspond to the sacred sublimity of his name, and tend to the exaltation of his magnificence. Secondly, we should not rashly and preposterously abuse his holy word and adorable mysteries to the purposes of ambition, of avarice, or of amusement; but as they bear an impression of the dignity of his name, they should always receive from us the honour and esteem which belong to them. Lastly, we should not injure his works by obloquy or detraction, as some miserable mortals are accustomed to do; but whenever we mention any thing done by him, we should celebrate it with encomiums of wisdom, justice, and goodness. This is "sanctifying" the name of God. In every other case, it is violated by a vain and criminal abuse, because it is carried beyond the limits of that legitimate use, to which alone it is consecrated; and though no other consequence ensue, it is deprived of its dignity, and by degrees rendered contemptible. But if it be so criminal thus rashly and unseasonably to introduce the name of God on every occasion, much more so must it be to apply it to such nefarious uses as they do, who make it subservient to the superstitions of necromancy, to horrible imprecations, to unlawful exorcisms, and to other impious incantations. But an oath is the thing principally contemplated in the command, as the most detestable instance of the perverse abuse of the Divine name; and this is done to inspire us with the greater horror of every species of profanation of it. That this precept relates to the worship of God and the reverence of his name, and not to the equity that ought to be observed among mankind, appears from this — that the subsequent condemnation, in the second table, of perjury and false witness, by which society is injured, would be a needless repetition, if the present precept related to a civil duty. Besides, the division of the law requires this; for, as we have already observed, it is not in vain that God has distributed the law into two tables. Whence we conclude, that in this command he vindicates his just claims, and guards the sanctity of his name, but does not teach the duties which men owe to each other.

XXIII. In the first place, we have to explain what an oath is. It consists in calling upon God as a witness, to confirm the truth of any declaration that we make. For execrations, which contain manifest reproaches against God, are not worthy to be mentioned among oaths. That such an attestation, when rightly performed, is a species of Divine worship, is evident from many places of Scripture; as when Isaiah prophesies of the vocation of the Assyrians and Egyptians to participate in the covenant with Israel. "They shall speak," says he, "the language of Canaan, and swear to the Lord of hosts." (*h*) By "swearing to the Lord" here is intended making a profession of religion. Again, when he speaks of the extension of his kingdom: "He who blesseth himself in the earth shall bless himself in the God of truth; and he that sweareth in the earth shall swear by the God of truth." (*i*) Jeremiah says, "If they will diligently learn the ways of my people, to swear by my name, The Lord liveth; as they taught my people to swear by Baal, then shall they be built in the midst of my people." (*k*) And we are justly said to profess our religion to the Lord, when we invoke his name to bear witness to us. For thereby we confess that he is truth itself, eternal and immutable; whom we call not only as a witness of the truth, excelling all others, but also as the only defender of it, who is able to bring to light things which are concealed, and in a word, as the searcher of all hearts. For where human testimonies are wanting, we resort for refuge to the testimony of God; and particularly when any thing is to be affirmed, which is hidden in the conscience. For which reason the Lord is extremely angry with them who swear by strange gods, and interprets that species of swearing as a proof of manifest defection from him. "Thy children have forsaken me, and sworn by them that are no gods." (*l*) And he declares the atrociousness of this crime by his denunciation of punishment: "I will cut off them that swear by the Lord, and that swear by Malcham." (*m*)

XXIV. Now, since we understand it to be the will of the Lord, that we should reverence his name in our oaths, we ought to use so much the more caution, lest, instead of reverence, they betray dishonour or contempt of it. It is no trifling insult to him, when perjury is committed in his name; and therefore the law calls it a profanation. (*n*) But what remains to the Lord, when he is despoiled of his truth? he will then cease to be God. But he is certainly despoiled of it, when he is made an abettor and approver of a falsehood. Wherefore, when Joshua would induce Achan to a confession of the truth,

(*h*) Isaiah xix. 18. (*k*) Jer. xii. 16. (*m*) Zeph. i. 4, 5.
(*i*) Isaiah lxv. 16. (*l*) Jer. v. 7. (*n*) Lev. xix. 12.

he says, " My son, give, I pray thee, glory to the Lord God of Israel ; " (*o*) implying in this that the Lord is grievously dishonoured, if perjury be committed in his name. Nor is this strange ; for in such a case we do all that is in our power to brand his sacred name with a falsehood. And that this form of expression was customary among the Jews, whenever any man was called to take an oath, appears from a similar adjuration used by the Pharisees in the Gospel of John. (*p*) To this caution we are accustomed by the forms of oaths which are used in the Scriptures : " The Lord liveth ; " (*q*) " God do so and more also to me ; " (*r*) " I call God for a record upon my soul ; " (*s*) which imply, that we cannot invoke God to be a witness to our declarations, without imprecating his vengeance upon us if we be guilty of perjury.

XXV. The name of God is rendered vile and contemptible, when it is used in unnecessarily swearing even to what is true ; for in this instance also it is taken in vain. Wherefore it will not be sufficient to abstain from perjury ; unless we also remember, that swearing is permitted and appointed, not for the sake of our pleasure or caprice, but from necessity ; and that the lawful use of it, therefore, is transgressed by those who apply it to cases where it is not necessary. Now, no other necessity can be pretended, but when we want to serve either religion or charity. This crime, in the present day, is carried to a very great extent ; and it is so much the more intolerable, since by its frequency it has ceased to be considered as a crime, though before the Divine tribunal it is deemed no trivial offence. For the name of God is universally profaned without concern in trifling conversations ; and it is not considered as sinful, because this presumptuous wickedness has been so long practised with impunity. But the Divine command remains valid ; the sanction remains firm ; and a future day will witness the completion of that part of it which denounces a particular punishment against those who take his name in vain. This precept is violated also in another way. If in our oaths we substitute the servants of God in the place of God himself, we are guilty of manifest impiety ; because we thereby transfer to them the glory due to the Deity. Nor is it without reason, that God, by a special command, enjoins us to swear by his name, (*t*) and by a special prohibition interdicts us from swearing by any strange gods. (*v*) And the Apostle evidently attests the same, when he says, that " men swear by the greater, but that God, because he could swear by no greater, sware by himself." (*w*)

(*o*) Joshua vii. 19.   (*p*) John ix. 24.   (*q*) 1 Sam. xiv. 45.
(*r*) 2 Kings vi. 31.   (*s*) 2 Cor. i. 23.
(*t*) Deut. vi. 13.   (*v*) Exod. xxiii. 13.   (*w*) Heb. vi. 13, 16.

XXVI. The Anabaptists, not satisfied with this limitation of oaths, condemn all oaths without exception; because the prohibition of Christ is general: "I say unto you, Swear not at all. But let your communication be, Yea, yea; Nay, nay: for whatsoever is more than these cometh of evil." (*x*) But by this mode of interpretation they set Christ in opposition to the Father, as though he descended into this world to abrogate the Father's decrees. For in the law the eternal God not only permits an oath, as a lawful thing, which would be sufficient to justify the use of it, but in cases of necessity commands it. (*y*) Now, Christ asserts, that "he and his Father are one," that "he acts only according to the commands of the Father," that "his doctrine is not of himself," &c. (*z*) What then? Will they make God to contradict himself, by prohibiting and condemning in our conduct that which he has before approved and enjoined? But as the words of Christ involve some difficulty, let us enter on a brief examination of them. Here we shall never arrive at the truth, unless we attend to the design of Christ, and advert to the subject of which he is there treating. His design is not to relax or to restrict the law, but to reduce it to its true and genuine meaning, which had been very much corrupted by the false comments of the scribes and Pharisees. If we bear this in our minds, we shall not be of opinion that Christ condemned all oaths, but only those which transgress the rule of the law. It appears to have been the custom of the people at that time to avoid nothing but perjuries; whereas the law forbids not only perjuries, but likewise all vain and superfluous oaths. Our Lord, therefore, that infallible expositor of the law, apprizes them that it is sinful, not only to perjure themselves, but even to swear. To swear in what manner? In vain. But the oaths which are sanctioned in the law he leaves without any objection. They consider themselves as urging a very powerful argument, when they violently insist on the particle *at all;* which, nevertheless, refers not to the word *swear*, but to the forms of oaths that are there subjoined. For the error there condemned consisted, partly, in a supposition that in swearing by heaven and earth, there was no interference with the name of God. Therefore, after the principal instance of transgression, the Lord goes on to destroy all their subterfuges, that they may not imagine themselves to have escaped by suppressing the name of God, and calling heaven and earth to witness for them. For here, by the way, it must be remarked, that men indirectly swear by God, though his name is not expressed; as when they swear by the light of life, by the bread which they eat, by their

---

(*x*) Matt. v. 34. (*y*) Exod. xxii. 11. (*z*) John x. 30, 18; vii. 16.

baptism, or by any other blessings which they have received from the Divine munificence. Nor does Christ in that place prohibit them from swearing by heaven, and earth, and Jerusalem, in order to correct superstition, as some falsely imagine; but rather to confute the sophistical subtlety of persons who thought there was no crime in the foolish use of indirect oaths, as though they were not chargeable with profaning the sacred name of God, which is engraven, however, on all his benefits. But the case is different, where any mortal man, or one that is dead, or an angel, is substituted in the place of God; as, among idolatrous nations, adulation invented that odious form of swearing by the life or genius of a king; because in such cases the deification of a creature obscures and diminishes the glory of the only true God. But when we mean nothing but to derive a confirmation to our assertions from the sacred name of God, although it be done in an indirect manner, yet all such frivolous oaths are offensive to his majesty. Christ deprives this licentious practice of every vain excuse, by his prohibition of swearing at all. James also aims at the same point, (*a*) where he uses the language of Christ, which I have cited; because this presumption has always been prevalent in the world, notwithstanding it is a profanation of the name of God. For if you refer the particle *at all* to the substance of swearing, as though every oath, without exception, were unlawful, what means the explanation which is immediately annexed, "Neither by heaven, neither by earth," &c., language evidently used in refutation of those cavils, which the Jews considered as furnishing an excuse for their sin.

XXVII. It can no longer be doubtful, therefore, to persons of sound judgment, that the Lord, in that passage, only condemns those oaths which had been forbidden by the law. For even he, who exhibited in his life an example of the perfection which he inculcated, hesitated not to make use of oaths whenever occasion required; and his disciples, who, we doubt not, were obedient to their master in all things, followed the same example. Who can dare to assert, that Paul would have sworn, if all oaths had been prohibited? But when the occasion requires it, he swears without any scruple, and sometimes even adds an imprecation. The question, however, is not yet decided; for it is the opinion of some persons, that public oaths are the only exceptions from this prohibition; such as we take when required by a magistrate; such also as princes are accustomed to use in ratifying treaties; or subjects, when they swear allegiance to their princes; or soldiers, as a military test; and others of a similar kind. To this class also they

(*a*) James v. 12.

justly refer those oaths which we find used by Paul in assertion of the dignity of the gospel; because the Apostles, in the exercise of their functions, were not private persons, but public ministers of God. And indeed I will not deny that these are the safest oaths; because they are sanctioned by the strongest testimonies of Scripture. A magistrate is directed, in a dubious case, to put a witness to his oath, and the witness, on the other hand, is required to answer on his oath; and the Apostle says, that human controversies are adjusted by this expedient. (*b*) In this precept both parties are furnished with a complete justification of their conduct. Moreover we may observe, that among the ancient heathen a public and solemn oath was held in great reverence; but that common ones, which they used in their ordinary intercourse, were not esteemed of any, or of much importance, because they imagined that these were not regarded by the Divine majesty. But it would be too dangerous to condemn private oaths, which are taken, in cases of necessity, with sobriety, integrity, and reverence, since they are supported both by reason and by scriptural examples. For if it be lawful for private persons in an important and serious affair to appeal to God as a judge between them, much more must it be allowable to invoke him as a witness. Your brother will accuse you of perfidy; you endeavour to exculpate yourself; he will not permit himself by any means to be satisfied. If your reputation be endangered by his obstinate malignity, you may, without any offence, appeal to the judgment of God, that in his own time he will manifest your innocence. If the words be strictly examined, it is a less thing to appeal to him as a witness than as a judge. I see not, therefore, why we should assert such an appeal to him to be unlawful. There are not wanting numerous examples of it. If the oath of Abraham and Isaac with Abimelech be alleged to have been taken in a public capacity, certainly Jacob and Laban were private persons, and yet they confirmed the covenant between them by a mutual oath. (*c*) Boaz was a private person, who confirmed in the same manner his promise of marriage to Ruth. (*d*) Obadiah was a private person, a righteous man, and one that feared the Lord, who declared with an oath the fact of which he wished to convince Elijah. (*e*) I can find, therefore, no better rule, than that we regulate our oaths in such a manner, that they be not rash or inconsiderate, wanton or frivolous, but used in cases of real necessity, as for vindicating the glory of the Lord, or promoting the edification of our brother; which is the end of this commandment of the law.

(*b*) Heb. vi. 16.
(*c*) Gen. xxi. 24; xxvi. 31; xxxi. 53.
(*d*) Ruth iii. 13.
(*e*) 1 Kings xviii. 10.

THE FOURTH COMMANDMENT.

Remember the sabbath day, to keep it holy. Six days shalt thou labour, and do all thy work ; but the seventh day is the sabbath of the Lord thy God ; in it thou shalt not do any work, &c.

XXVIII. The end of this precept is, that, being dead to our own affections and works, we should meditate on the kingdom of God, and be exercised in that meditation in the observance of his institutions. But, as it has an aspect peculiar and distinct from the others, it requires a little different kind of exposition. The fathers frequently call it a *shadowy commandment*, because it contains the external observance of the day, which was abolished with the rest of the figures at the advent of Christ. And there is much truth in their observation; but it reaches only half of the subject. Wherefore it is necessary to seek further for an exposition, and to consider three causes, on which I think I have observed this commandment to rest. For it was the design of the heavenly Lawgiver, under the rest of the seventh day, to give the people of Israel a figure of the spiritual rest, by which the faithful ought to refrain from their own works, in order to leave God to work within them. His design was, secondly, that there should be a stated day, on which they might assemble together to hear the law and perform the ceremonies, or at least which they might especially devote to meditations on his works ; that by this recollection they might be led to the exercises of piety. Thirdly, he thought it right that servants, and persons living under the jurisdiction of others, should be indulged with a day of rest, that they might enjoy some remission from their labour.

XXIX. Yet we are taught in many places that this adumbration of the spiritual rest was the principal design of the sabbath. For the Lord is hardly so strict in his requisitions of obedience to any other precept. (*f*) When he means to intimate, in the Prophets, that religion is totally subverted, he complains that his sabbaths are polluted, violated, neglected, and profaned; (*g*) as though, in case of that duty being neglected, there remained no other way in which he could be honoured. On the other hand, he notices the observance of it with singular encomiums. Wherefore also, among the other Divine communications, the faithful used very highly to esteem the revelation of the sabbath. For this is the language of the Levites in a solemn assembly, recorded by Nehemiah : " Thou

---

(*f*) Numb. xiii. 22. Ezek. xx. 12; xxii. 8; xxiii. 38.
(*g*) Jer. xvii. 21, 22, 27. Isaiah lvi. 2.

madest known unto our fathers thy holy sabbath, and commandedst them precepts, statutes, and laws, by the hand of Moses." (*h*) We see the singular estimation in which it is held above all the commandments of the law. All these things tend to display the dignity of the mystery, which is beautifully expressed by Moses and Ezekiel. In Exodus we read as follows: "Verily my sabbaths ye shall keep; for it is a sign between me and you throughout your generations; that ye may know that I am the Lord that doth sanctify you. Ye shall keep the sabbath therefore; for it is holy unto you. The children of Israel shall keep the sabbath, to observe the sabbath throughout their generations, for a perpetual covenant. It is a sign between me and the children of Israel for ever." (*i*) This is more fully expressed by Ezekiel; but the substance of what he says is, that the sabbath was a sign by which the Israelites might know that God was their sanctifier. (*k*) If our sanctification consists properly in the mortification of our own will, there is a very natural analogy between the external sign and the internal thing which it represents. We must rest altogether, that God may operate within us; we must recede from our own will, resign our own heart, and renounce all our carnal affections; in short, we must cease from all the efforts of our own understanding, that having God operating within us, we may enjoy rest in him, as we are also taught by the Apostle. (*l*)

XXX. This perpetual cessation was represented to the Jews by the observance of one day in seven, which the Lord, in order that it might be the more religiously kept, recommended by his own example. For it is no small stimulus to any action, for a man to know that he is imitating his Creator. If any one inquire after a hidden signification in the septenary number, it is probable, that because in Scripture it is the number of perfection, it is here selected to denote perpetual duration. This is confirmed also by the circumstance, that Moses, with that day in which he narrates that the Lord rested from his works, concludes his description of the succession of days and nights. We may also adduce another probable conjecture respecting this number — that the Lord intended to signify that the sabbath would never be completed until the arrival of the last day. For in it we begin that blessed rest, in which we make new advances from day to day. But because we are still engaged in a perpetual warfare with the flesh, it will not be consummated before the completion of that prediction of Isaiah, "It shall come to pass, that from one new moon to another, and from one sabbath to another, shall all

---

(*h*) Neh. ix. 14.
(*i*) Exod. xxxi. 13, 14, 16, 17.
(*k*) Ezek. xx. 12.
(*l*) Heb. iv. 9.

flesh come to worship before me, saith the Lord;" (*m*) that is, when God shall be "all in all." (*n*) The Lord may be considered, therefore, as having delineated to his people, in the seventh day, the future perfection of his sabbath in the last day, that, by a continual meditation on the sabbath during their whole life, they might be aspiring towards this perfection.

XXXI. If any one disapprove of this observation on the number, as too curious, I object not to its being understood in a more simple manner; that the Lord ordained a certain day, that the people under the discipline of the law might be exercised in continual meditations on the spiritual rest; that he appointed the seventh day, either because he foresaw it would be sufficient, or in order that the proposal of a resemblance to his own example might operate as a stronger stimulus to the people, or at least to apprize them that the only end of the sabbath was to promote their conformity to their Creator. For this is of little importance, provided we retain the mystery, which is principally exhibited, of a perpetual rest from our own works. To the contemplation of this, the Prophets used frequently to recall the Jews, that they might not suppose themselves to have discharged their duty merely by a cessation from manual labours. Beside the passages already cited, we have the following in Isaiah: "If thou turn away thy foot from the sabbath, from doing thy pleasure on my holy day; and call the sabbath a delight, the holy of the Lord, honourable; and shalt honour him, not doing thine own ways, nor finding thine own pleasure, nor speaking thine own words; then shalt thou delight thyself in the Lord," &c. (*o*) But all that it contained of a ceremonial nature was without doubt abolished by the advent of the Lord Christ. For he is the truth, at whose presence all figures disappear; the body, at the sight of which all the shadows are relinquished. He, I say, is the true fulfilment of the sabbath. Having been "buried with him by baptism, we have been planted together in the likeness of his death, that being partakers of his resurrection, we may walk in newness of life." (*p*) Therefore the Apostle says in another place, that "the sabbath was a shadow of things to come; but the *body* is of Christ;" (*q*) that is, the real substance of the truth, which he has beautifully explained in that passage. This is contained not in one day, but in the whole course of our life, till, being wholly dead to ourselves, we be filled with the life of God. Christians therefore ought to depart from all superstitious observance of days.

XXXII. As the two latter causes, however, ought not to be

(*m*) Isaiah lxvi. 23.   (*n*) 1 Cor. xv. 28.   (*o*) Isaiah lviii. 13, 14.
(*p*) Rom. vi. 4, &c.   (*q*) Col. ii. 16, 17.

numbered among the ancient shadows, but are equally suitable to all ages,—though the sabbath is abrogated, yet it is still customary among us to assemble on stated days for hearing the word, for breaking the mystic bread, and for public prayers; and also to allow servants and labourers a remission from their labour. That in commanding the sabbath, the Lord had regard to both these things, cannot be doubted. The first is abundantly confirmed even by the practice of the Jews. The second is proved by Moses, in Deuteronomy, in these words: "that thy man-servant and thy maid-servant may rest as well as thou. And remember that thou wast a servant in the land of Egypt." (r) Also, in Exodus: "that thine ox and thine ass may rest, and the son of thy handmaid, and the stranger, may be refreshed." (s) Who can deny that both these things are as proper for us as for the Jews? Assemblies of the Church are enjoined in the Divine word, and the necessity of them is sufficiently known even from the experience of life. Unless there be stated days appointed for them, how can they be held? According to the direction of the Apostle, "all things" are to "be done decently and in order" among us. (t) But so far is it from being possible to preserve order and decorum without this regulation, that, if it were abolished, the Church would be in imminent danger of immediate convulsion and ruin. But if we feel the same necessity, to relieve which the Lord enjoined the sabbath upon the Jews, let no one plead that it does not belong to us. For our most provident and indulgent Father has been no less attentive to provide for our necessity than for that of the Jews. But why, it may be asked, do we not rather assemble on every day, that so all distinction of days may be removed? I sincerely wish that this were practised; and truly spiritual wisdom would be well worthy of some portion of time being daily allotted to it; but if the infirmity of many persons will not admit of daily assemblies, and charity does not permit us to require more of them, why should we not obey the rule which we have imposed upon us by the will of God?

XXXIII. I am obliged to be rather more diffuse on this point, because, in the present age, some unquiet spirits have been raising noisy contentions respecting the Lord's day. They complain that Christians are tinctured with Judaism, because they retain any observance of days. But I reply, that the Lord's day is not observed by us upon the principles of Judaism; because in this respect the difference between us and the Jews is very great. For we celebrate it not with scrupulous rigour, as a ceremony which we conceive to be a

(r) Deut. v. 14, 15. (s) Exod. xxiii. 12. (t) 1 Cor. xiv. 40.

figure of some spiritual mystery, but only use it as a remedy necessary to the preservation of order in the Church. But they say, Paul teaches that Christians are not to be judged in the observance of it, because it is a shadow of something future. (*v*) Therefore he is "afraid lest" he has "bestowed" on the Galatians "labour in vain," because they continued to "observe days." (*w*) And in the Epistle to the Romans, he asserts him to be "weak in the faith," who "esteemeth one day above another." (*x*) But who, these furious zealots only excepted, does not see what observance the apostle intends? For they did not observe them for the sake of political and ecclesiastical order; but when they retained them as shadows of spiritual things, they were so far guilty of obscuring the glory of Christ and the light of the gospel. They did not, therefore, rest from their manual labours, as from employments which would divert them from sacred studies and meditations; but from a principle of superstition, imagining their cessation from labour to be still an expression of reverence for the mysteries formerly represented by it. This preposterous distinction of days the Apostle strenuously opposes; and not that legitimate difference which promotes the peace of the Christian Church. For in the churches which he founded, the sabbath was retained for this purpose. He prescribes the same day to the Corinthians, for making collections for the relief of the brethren at Jerusalem. If superstition be an object of fear, there was more danger in the holy days of the Jews, than in the Lord's days now observed by Christians. Now, whereas it was expedient for the destruction of superstition, the day which the Jews kept holy was abolished; and it being necessary for the preservation of decorum, order, and peace, in the Christian Church, another day was appointed for the same use.

XXXIV. However, the ancients have not without sufficient reason substituted what we call the Lord's day in the room of the sabbath. For since the resurrection of the Lord is the end and consummation of that true rest, which was adumbrated by the ancient sabbath, the same day which put an end to the shadows, admonishes Christians not to adhere to a shadowy ceremony. Yet I do not lay so much stress on the septenary number, that I would oblige the Church to an invariable adherence to it; nor will I condemn those churches which have other solemn days for their assemblies, provided they keep at a distance from superstition. And this will be the case, if they be only designed for the observance of discipline and well-regulated order. Let us sum up the whole in the following manner: As the truth was delivered to the Jews under a figure, so

(*v*) Col. ii. 16, 17.   (*w*) Gal. iv. 10, 11.   (*x*) Rom. xiv. 5.

it is given to us without any shadows; first, in order that during our whole life we should meditate on a perpetual rest from our own works, that the Lord may operate within us by his Spirit; secondly, that every man, whenever he has leisure, should diligently exercise himself in private in pious reflections on the works of God, and also that we should at the same time observe the legitimate order of the Church, appointed for the hearing of the word, for the administration of the sacraments, and for public prayer; thirdly, that we should not unkindly oppress those who are subject to us. Thus vanish all the dreams of false prophets, who in past ages have infected the people with a Jewish notion, affirming that nothing but the ceremonial part of this commandment, which, according to them, is the appointment of the seventh day, has been abrogated, but that the moral part of it, that is, the observance of one day in seven, still remains. But this is only changing the day in contempt of the Jews, while they retain the same opinion of the holiness of a day; for on this principle the same mysterious signification would still be attributed to particular days, which they formerly obtained among the Jews. And indeed we see what advantages have arisen from such a sentiment. For those who adhere to it, far exceed the Jews in a gross, carnal, and superstitious observance of the sabbath; so that the reproofs, which we find in Isaiah, are equally applicable to them in the present age, as to those whom the Prophet reproved in his time. But the principal thing to be remembered is the general doctrine; that, lest religion decay or languish among us, sacred assemblies ought diligently to be held, and that we ought to use those external means which are adapted to support the worship of God.

THE FIFTH COMMANDMENT.

Honour thy father and thy mother; that thy days may be long upon the land which the Lord thy God giveth thee.

XXXV. The end of this precept is, that since the Lord God desires the preservation of the order he has appointed, the degrees of preëminence fixed by him ought to be inviolably preserved. The sum of it, therefore, will be, that we should reverence them whom God has exalted to any authority over us, and should render them honour, obedience, and gratitude. Whence follows a prohibition to derogate from their dignity by contempt, obstinacy, or ingratitude. For in the Scripture the word "honour" has an extensive signification; as, when the Apostle directs that "the elders who rule well be counted worthy of double honour," (y) he means not only that they

---

(y) 1 Tim. v. 17.

are entitled to reverence, but likewise such a remuneration as their ministry deserves. But as this precept, which enjoins subjection to superiors, is exceedingly repugnant to the depravity of human nature, whose ardent desire of exaltation will scarcely admit of subjection, it has therefore proposed as an example that kind of superiority which is naturally most amiable and least invidious; because that might the more easily mollify and incline our minds to a habit of submission. By that subjection, therefore, which is most easy to be borne, the Lord accustoms us by degrees to every kind of legitimate obedience; because the reason of all is the same. For to those, to whom he gives any preëminence, he communicates his own authority, as far as is necessary for the preservation of that preëminence. The titles of Father, God, and Lord, are so eminently applicable to him, that, whenever we hear either of them mentioned, our minds cannot but be strongly affected with a sense of his majesty. Those, therefore, on whom he bestows these titles, he illuminates with a ray of his splendour, to render them all honourable in their respective stations. Thus in a father we ought to recognize something Divine; for it is not without reason that he bears one of the titles of the Deity. Our prince, or our lord, enjoys an honour somewhat similar to that which is given to God.

XXXVI. Wherefore it ought not to be doubted that God here lays down a universal rule for our conduct; namely, that to every one, whom we know to be placed in authority over us by his appointment, we should render reverence, obedience, gratitude, and all the other services in our power. Nor does it make any difference, whether they are worthy of this honour, or not. For whatever be their characters, yet it is not without the appointment of the Divine providence, that they have attained that station, on account of which the supreme Legislator has commanded them to be honoured. He has particularly enjoined reverence to our parents, who have brought us into this life; which nature itself ought to teach us. For those who violate the parental authority by contempt or rebellion, are not men, but monsters. Therefore the Lord commands all those, who are disobedient to their parents, to be put to death, as having rendered themselves unworthy to enjoy the light, by their disregard of those by whose means they were introduced to it. And various appendices to the law evince the truth of our observation, that the honour here intended consists in reverence, obedience, and gratitude. The first the Lord confirms, when he commands him to be slain who has cursed his father or mother; (z) for in that case he punishes contempt. He confirms the second, when he denounces the punishment

(z) Exod. xxi. 17.

of death against disobedient and rebellious children. (*a*) The third is supported by Christ, who says, "God commanded, saying, Honour thy father and mother;" and, "He that curseth father or mother, let him die the death. But ye say, Whosoever shall say to his father or his mother, It is a gift, by whatsoever thou mightest be profited by me; and honour not his father or his mother, he shall be free. Thus have ye made the commandment of God of none effect by your tradition." (*b*) And whenever Paul mentions this commandment, he explains it as a requisition of obedience. (*c*)

XXXVII. In order to recommend it, a promise is annexed, which is a further intimation how acceptable to God that submission is which is here enjoined. Paul employs that stimulus to arouse our inattention, when he says, " This is the first commandment with promise." For the preceding promise, in the first table, was not particularly confined to one commandment, but extended to the whole law. Now, the true explanation of this promise is, that the Lord spake particularly to the Israelites concerning the land which he had promised them as an inheritance. If the possession of that land therefore was a pledge of the Divine goodness, we need not wonder, if it was the Lord's will to manifest his favour by bestowing length of life, in order to prolong the enjoyment of the blessing conferred by him. The meaning of it therefore is, Honour thy father and thy mother, that through the space of a long life thou mayest enjoy the possession of the land, which will be to thee a testimony of my favour. But, as the whole earth is blessed to the faithful, we justly place the present life among the blessings we receive from God. Wherefore this promise belongs likewise to us, inasmuch as the continuance of the present life affords us a proof of the Divine benevolence. For neither is it promised to us, nor was it promised to the Jews, as though it contained any blessedness in itself; but because to the pious it is generally a token of the Divine favour. Therefore, if a son, that is obedient to his parents, happen to be removed out of life before the age of maturity, — which is a case of frequent occurrence, — the Lord, nevertheless, perseveres with as much punctuality in the completion of his promise, as if he were to reward a person with a hundred acres of land to whom he had only promised one. The whole consists in this: We should consider that long life is promised to us so far as it is the blessing of God; but that it is a blessing, only as it is a proof of the favour of God, which he infinitely more richly and substantially testifies and actually demonstrates to his servants in their death.

(*a*) Deut. xxi. 18—21. (*b*) Matt. xv. 4—6. (*c*) Eph. vi. 1. Col. iii. 20.

XXXVIII. Moreover, when the Lord promises the blessing of the present life to those children who honour their parents with proper reverence, he at the same time implies that a certain curse impends over all those who are disobedient and perverse. And that it might not fail of being executed, he pronounces them in his law to be liable to the sentence of death, and commands that punishment to be inflicted on them. If they escape that, he punishes them himself in some other way. For we see what great numbers of persons of this character fall in battles and in private quarrels; others are afflicted in unusual ways; and almost all of them are proofs of the truth of this threatening. But if any arrive at an extreme age, being deprived of the Divine blessing, they only languish in misery in this life, and are reserved to greater punishments hereafter; and consequently they are far from participating in the blessing promised to dutiful children. But it must be remarked by the way, that we are commanded to obey them only "in the Lord;" and this is evident from the foundation before laid; for they preside in that station to which the Lord has exalted them by communicating to them a portion of his honour. Wherefore the submission exercised towards them ought to be a step towards honouring the Supreme Father. Therefore, if they instigate us to any transgression of the law, we may justly consider them not as parents, but as strangers, who attempt to seduce us from obedience to our real Father. The same observation is applicable to princes, lords, and superiors of every description. For it is infamous and absurd, that their eminence should avail to depreciate the preëminence of God, upon which it depends, and to which it ought to conduct us.

THE SIXTH COMMANDMENT.

Thou shalt not kill.

XXXIX. The end of this precept is, that since God has connected mankind together in a kind of unity, every man ought to consider himself as charged with the safety of all. In short, then, all violence and injustice, and every kind of mischief, which may injure the body of our neighbour, are forbidden to us. And therefore we are enjoined, if it be in our power, to assist in protecting the lives of our neighbours; to exert ourselves with fidelity for this purpose; to procure those things which conduce to their tranquillity; to be vigilant in shielding them from injuries; and in cases of danger to afford them our assistance. If we remember that this is the language of the Divine Legislator, we should consider, at the same time, that he intends this rule to govern the soul. For it were ridiculous, that he who beholds the thoughts of the heart, and principally insists on them, should content himself with forming only the body to true righteousness. Mental homicide, therefore, is likewise prohibited, and an internal disposition to preserve the life of our brother is commanded in this law. The hand, indeed, accomplishes the homicide, but it is conceived by the mind under the influence of anger and hatred. Examine whether you can be angry with your brother, without being inflamed with a desire of doing him some injury. If you cannot be angry with him, then you cannot hate him; for hatred is nothing more than inveterate anger. However you may dissemble, and endeavour to extricate yourself by vain subterfuges, whenever there is either anger or hatred, there is also a disposition to do injury. If you persist in your evasions, it is already pronounced by the Holy Spirit, that " Whosoever hateth his brother is a murderer." (d) It is declared by the Lord Christ, " that whosoever is angry with his brother without a cause shall be in danger of the judgment; and whosoever shall say to his brother, Raca, shall be in danger of the council; but whosoever shall say, Thou fool, shall be in danger of hell fire." (e)

XL. Now, the Scripture states two reasons on which this precept is founded; the first, that man is the image of God; the second, that he is our own flesh. Wherefore, unless we would violate the image of God, we ought to hold the personal safety of our neighbour inviolably sacred; and unless we would divest ourselves of humanity, we ought to cherish him as our own flesh. The motives which are derived from the redemption and grace of Christ will be treated in another place. These two characters, which are inseparable from the nature of man, God requires us to consider as motives to our exertions for his security; so that we may reverence his image impressed on him, and show an affectionate regard for our own flesh. That person, therefore, is not innocent of the crime of murder, who has merely restrained himself from the effusion of blood. If you perpetrate, if you attempt, if you only conceive in your mind any thing inimical to the safety of another, you stand guilty of murder. Unless you also endeavour to defend him to the utmost of your ability and opportunity, you are guilty of the same inhuman transgression of the law. But if so much concern be discovered for the safety of the body, we may conclude, how much care and attention should be devoted to the safety of the soul, which, in the sight of God, is of infinitely superior value.

(d) 1 John iii. 15. (e) Matt. v. 22.

THE SEVENTH COMMANDMENT.

Thou shalt not commit adultery.

XLI. The end of this precept is, that because God loves chastity and purity, we ought to depart from all uncleanness. The sum of it therefore is, that we ought not to be polluted by any carnal impurity, or libidinous intemperance. To this prohibition corresponds the affirmative injunction, that every part of our lives ought to be regulated by chastity and continence. But he expressly forbids adultery, to which all incontinence tends; in order that by the turpitude of that which is very gross and palpable, being an infamous pollution of the body, he may lead us to abominate every unlawful passion. Since man was created in such a state as not to live a solitary life, but to be united to a help-meet; and moreover since the curse of sin has increased this necessity, — the Lord has afforded us ample assistance in this case by the institution of marriage — a connection which he has not only originated by his authority, but also sanctified by his blessing. Whence it appears, that every other union, but that of marriage, is cursed in his sight; and that the conjugal union itself is appointed as a remedy for our necessity, that we may not break out into unrestrained licentiousness. Let us not flatter ourselves, therefore, since we hear that there can be no cohabitation of male and female, except in marriage, without the curse of God.

XLII. Now, since the original constitution of human nature, and the violence of the passions consequent upon the fall, have rendered a union of the sexes doubly necessary, except to those whom God has exempted from that necessity by peculiar grace, let every one carefully examine what is given to him. Virginity, I acknowledge, is a virtue not to be despised. But as this is denied to some, and to others is granted only for a season, let those who are troubled with incontinence, and cannot succeed in resisting it, avail themselves of the help of marriage, that they may preserve their chastity according to the degree of their calling. For persons who " cannot receive this saying," (*f*) if they do not assist their frailty by the remedy offered and granted to them, oppose God and resist his ordinance. Here let no one object, as many do in the present day, that with the help of God he can do all things. For the assistance of God is granted only to them who walk in his ways, that is, in their calling; which is deserted by all those who neglect the means which God has afforded them, and strive to over-

---

(*f*) Matt. xix. 11.

come their necessities by vain presumption. That continence is a peculiar gift of God, and of that kind which is not imparted promiscuously, or to the whole body of the Church, but only conferred on a few of its members, is affirmed by our Lord. For he mentions a certain class of men who "have made themselves eunuchs for the kingdom of heaven's sake;" (*g*) that is, that they might be more at liberty to devote their attention to the affairs of the kingdom of heaven. But that no one might suppose this to be in the power of man, he had already declared that "all men cannot receive this saying, save they to whom it is given." And he concludes, "He that is able to receive it, let him receive it." Paul is still more explicit, when he says, that "every man hath his proper gift of God, one after this manner, and another after that." (*h*)

XLIII. Since we are so expressly apprized that it is not in the power of every one to preserve chastity in celibacy, even with the most strenuous efforts for that purpose, and that it is a peculiar grace, which the Lord confers only on particular persons, that he may have them more ready for his service, do we not resist God, and strive against the nature instituted by him, unless we accommodate our manner of life to the measure of our ability? In this commandment the Lord prohibits adultery: therefore he requires of us purity and chastity. The only way of preserving this is, that every one should measure himself by his own capacity. Let no one rashly despise marriage as a thing useless or unnecessary to him; let no one prefer celibacy, unless he can dispense with a wife. And in that state let him not consult his carnal tranquillity or advantage, but only that, being exempted from this restraint, he may be the more prompt and ready for all the duties of piety. Moreover, as this benefit is conferred upon many persons only for a season, let every one refrain from marriage as long as he shall be capable of supporting a life of celibacy. When his strength fails to overcome his passions, let him consider that the Lord has laid him under a necessity of marrying. This is evident from the direction of the Apostle: "To avoid fornication, let every man have his own wife, and let every woman have her own husband." Again: "If they cannot contain, let them marry." (*i*) Here, in the first place, he signifies that the majority of men are subject to the vice of incontinence; in the next place, of those who are subject to it, he makes no exception, but enjoins them all to have recourse to that sole remedy which obviates unchastity. Those who are incontinent, therefore, if they neglect this method of curing their infirmity, are guilty of sin, in not obeying this injunction of the Apostle. And let not him who refrains from actual for-

(*g*) Matt. xix. 12.   (*h*) 1 Cor. vii. 7.   (*i*) 1 Cor. vii. 2, 9.

nication, flatter himself, as though he could not be charged with unchastity, while his heart at the same time is inflamed with libidinous desire. For Paul defines chastity to consist in sanctity of mind connected with purity of body. "The unmarried woman," he says, "careth for the things of the Lord, that she may be holy both in body and in spirit." (*k*) Therefore, when he gives a reason to confirm the preceding injunction, he does not content himself with saying that it is better for a man to marry than to pollute himself with the society of a harlot, but affirms that "it is better to marry than to burn." (*l*)

XLIV. Now, if married persons are satisfied that their society is attended with the blessing of the Lord, they are thereby admonished that it must not be contaminated by libidinous and dissolute intemperance. For if the honour of marriage conceals the shame of incontinence, it ought not on that account to be made an incitement to it. Wherefore let it not be supposed by married persons that all things are lawful to them. Every man should observe sobriety towards his wife, and every wife, reciprocally, towards her husband; conducting themselves in such a manner as to do nothing unbecoming the decorum and temperance of marriage. For thus ought marriage contracted in the Lord to be regulated by moderation and modesty, and not to break out into the vilest lasciviousness. Such sensuality has been stigmatized by Ambrose with a severe, but not unmerited censure, when he calls those who in their conjugal intercourse have no regard to modesty or decorum, the adulterers of their own wives. Lastly, let us consider who the Legislator is, by whom adultery is here condemned. It is no other than he who ought to have the entire possession of us, and justly requires the whole of our spirit, soul, and body. Therefore, when he prohibits us from committing adultery, he at the same time forbids us, either by lasciviously ornamenting our persons, or by obscene gesticulations, or by impure expressions, insidiously to attack the chastity of others. For there is much reason in the address of Archelaus to a young man clothed in an immoderately effeminate and delicate manner, that it was immaterial in what part he was immodest, with respect to God, who abominates all contamination, in whatever part it may discover itself, either of soul or of body. And that there may be no doubt on the subject, let us remember that God here recommends chastity. If the Lord requires chastity of us, he condemns every thing contrary to it. Wherefore, if we aspire to obedience, neither let our mind internally burn with depraved concupiscence, nor let our eyes wanton into corrupt affections,

(*k*) 1 Cor. vii. 34.   (*l*) 1 Cor. vii. 9.

nor let our body be adorned for purposes of seduction, nor let our tongue with impure speeches allure our mind to similar thoughts, nor let us inflame ourselves with intemperance. For all these vices are stains, by which the purity of chastity is defiled.

THE EIGHTH COMMANDMENT.

Thou shalt not steal.

XLV. The end of this precept is, that, as injustice is an abomination to God, every man may possess what belongs to him. The sum of it, then, is, that we are forbidden to covet the property of others, and are therefore enjoined faithfully to use our endeavours to preserve to every man what justly belongs to him. For we ought to consider, that what a man possesses has fallen to his lot, not by a fortuitous contingency, but by the distribution of the supreme Lord of all ; and that therefore no man can be deprived of his possessions by criminal methods, without an injury being done to the Divine dispenser of them. But the species of theft are numerous. One consists in violence ; when the property of any person is plundered by force and predatory license. Another consists in malicious imposture ; when it is taken away in a fraudulent manner. Another consists in more secret cunning ; where any one is deprived of his property under the mask of justice. Another consists in flatteries ; where we are cheated under the pretence of a donation. But not to dwell too long on the recital of the different species of theft, let us remember that all artifices by which the possessions and wealth of our neighbours are transferred to us, whenever they deviate from sincere love into a desire of deceiving, or doing any kind of injury, are to be esteemed acts of theft. This is the only view in which God considers them, even though the property may be gained by a suit at law. For he sees the tedious manœuvres with which the designing man begins to decoy his more simple neighbour, till at length he entangles him in his snares. He sees the cruel and inhuman laws, by which the more powerful man oppresses and ruins him that is weaker. He sees the baits with which the more crafty trepan the imprudent. All which things are concealed from the judgment of man, nor ever come to his knowledge. And this kind of injury relates not only to money, or to goods, or to lands, but to whatever each individual is justly entitled to ; for we defraud our neighbours of their property, if we deny them those kind offices, which it is our duty to perform to them. If an idle agent or steward devour the substance of his master, and be inattentive to the care of his domestic affairs; if he either improperly waste, or squander with a luxurious profusion, the property intrusted to him; if a servant deride his master, if he divulge his secrets, if by any means he betray either his life or his property; and if, on the other hand, a master inhumanly oppress his family, — God holds him guilty of theft. For the property of others is withheld and misapplied by him, who does not perform towards them those offices which the duty of his situation requires of him.

XLVI. We shall rightly obey this commandment therefore, if, contented with our own lot, we seek no gain but in an honest and lawful way; if we neither desire to enrich ourselves by injustice, nor attempt to ruin the fortune of our neighbour, in order to increase our own; if we do not labour to accumulate wealth by cruelty, and at the expense of the blood of others; if we do not greedily scrape together from every quarter, regardless of right or wrong, whatever may conduce to satiate our avarice or support our prodigality. On the contrary, it should be our constant aim, as far as possible, faithfully to assist all by our advice and our property in preserving what belongs to them; but if we are concerned with perfidious and fallacious men, let us be prepared rather to recede a little from our just right than to contend with them. Moreover, let us communicate to the necessities, and according to our ability alleviate the poverty, of those whom we perceive to be pressed by any embarrassment of their circumstances. Lastly, let every man examine what obligations his duty lays him under to others, and let him faithfully discharge the duties which he owes them. For this reason the people should honour their governors, patiently submit to their authority, obey their laws and mandates, and resist nothing, to which they can submit consistently with the Divine will. On the other hand, let governors take care of their people, preserve the public peace, protect the good, punish the wicked, and administer all things in such a manner, as becomes those who must render an account of their office to God the supreme Judge. Let the ministers of churches faithfully devote themselves to the ministry of the word, and let them never adulterate the doctrine of salvation, but deliver it pure and uncontaminated to the people of God. Let them teach, not only by their doctrine, but by the example of their lives; in a word, let them preside as good shepherds over the sheep. Let the people, on their part, receive them as the messengers and apostles of God, render to them that honour to which the supreme Master has exalted them, and furnish them with the necessaries of life. Let parents undertake the support, government, and instruction of their children, as committed by God to their care; nor let them exasperate their minds and alienate their affections from them by cruelty, but cherish and embrace them with the lenity and indulgence becoming their character. And that obedience is due to them from their children has been before observed. Let juniors revere old age, since the Lord has designed that age to be honourable. Let old men, by their prudence and superior experience, guide the imbecility of youth; not teasing them with sharp and clamorous invectives, but tempering severity with mildness and affability. Let servants show themselves obedient and diligent in the service of their masters; and that not only in appearance, but from the heart, as serving God himself. Neither let masters behave morosely and perversely to their servants, harassing them with excessive asperity, or treating them with contempt; but rather acknowledge them as their brethren and companions in the service of the heavenly Master, entitled to be regarded with mutual affection, and to receive kind treatment. In this manner, I say, let every man consider what duties he owes to his neighbours, according to the relations he sustains; and those duties let him discharge. Moreover, our attention should always be directed to the Legislator; to remind us that this law is ordained for our hearts as much as for our hands, in order that men may study both to protect the property and to promote the interests of others.

THE NINTH COMMANDMENT.

Thou shalt not bear false witness against thy neighbour.

XLVII. The end of this precept is, that because God, who is truth itself, execrates a lie, we ought to preserve the truth without the least disguise. The sum of it therefore is, that we neither violate the character of any man, either by calumnies or by false accusations, nor distress him in his property by falsehood, nor injure him by detraction or impertinence. This prohibition is connected with an injunction to do all the service we can to every man, by affirming the truth for the protection of his reputation and his property. The Lord seems to have intended the following words as an exposition of this command: "Thou shalt not raise a false report: put not thine hand with the wicked to be an unrighteous witness." Again: "Keep thee far from a false matter." (*m*) In another place also he not only forbids us to practise backbiting and tale-bearing among the people, but prohibits every man from deceiving his brother; (*n*) for he cautions us against both in distinct commandments. Indeed there is no doubt but that, as, in the preceding precepts, he has prohibited cruelty, impurity, and

(*m*) Exod. xxiii. 1, 7.   (*n*) Lev. xix. 16.

avarice, so in this he forbids falsehood; of which there are two branches, as we have before observed. For either we transgress against the reputation of our neighbours by malignity and perverse detraction, or by falsehood and sometimes by obloquy we injure their interests. It is immaterial whether we suppose the testimony here designed to be solemn and judicial, or a common one, which is delivered in private conversations. For we must always recur to this maxim — that, of each of the separate kinds of vices, one species is proposed as an example, to which the rest may be referred; and that, in general, the species selected is that in which the turpitude of the vice is most conspicuous. It is proper, however, to extend it more generally to calumnies and detraction, by which our neighbours are unjustly harassed; because falsehood in a forensic testimony is always attended with perjury. But perjury, being a profanation and violation of the name of God, has already been sufficiently condemned in the third commandment. Wherefore the legitimate observance of this precept is, that our tongue, by asserting the truth, ought to serve both the reputation and the profit of our neighbours. The equity of this is self-evident. For if a good name be more precious than any treasures whatever, a man sustains as great an injury when he is deprived of the integrity of his character, as when he is despoiled of his wealth. And in plundering his substance, there is sometimes as much effected by false testimony, as by the hands of violence.

XLVIII. Nevertheless, it is wonderful with what supine security this precept is generally transgressed, so that few persons can be found, who are not notoriously subject to this malady; we are so fascinated with the malignant pleasure of examining and detecting the faults of others. Nor should we suppose it to be a sufficient excuse, that in many cases we cannot be charged with falsehood. For he who forbids the character of our brother to be bespattered with falsehood, wills also that as far as the truth will permit, it be preserved immaculate. For although he only guards it against falsehood, he thereby suggests that it is committed to his charge. But this should be sufficient to induce us to defend the fair character of our neighbour — that God concerns himself in its protection. Wherefore detraction is, without doubt, universally condemned. Now, by detraction we mean, not reproof, which is given from a motive of correction; not accusation or judicial denunciation, by which recompense is demanded for an injury; not public reprehension, which tends to strike terror into other offenders; not a discovery to them whose safety depends on their being previously warned, that they may not be endangered through ignorance; but odious crimination, which arises from malice, and a violent propensity to detraction. This commandment also extends so far as to forbid us to affect a pleasantry tinctured with scurrilous and bitter sarcasms, severely lashing the faults of others under the appearance of sport; which is the practice of some who aim at the praise of raillery, to the prejudice of the modesty and feelings of others; for such wantonness sometimes fixes a lasting stigma on the characters of our brethren. Now, if we turn our eyes to the Legislator whose proper right it is to rule our ears and our minds, as much as our tongues, it will certainly appear that an avidity of hearing detraction, and an unreasonable propensity to unfavourable opinions respecting others, are equally prohibited. For it would be ridiculous for any one to suppose that God hates slander in the tongue, and does not reprobate malice in the heart. Wherefore, if we possess the true fear and love of God, let us make it our study, that as far as is practicable and expedient, and consistent with charity, we devote neither our tongues nor our ears to opprobrious and malicious raillery, nor inadvertently attend to unfavourable suspicions; but that, putting fair constructions on every man's words and actions, we regulate our hearts, our ears, and our tongues, with a view to preserve the reputation of all around us.

THE TENTH COMMANDMENT.

Thou shalt not covet thy neighbour's house, thou shalt not covet thy neighbour's wife, nor his man-servant, nor his maid-servant, nor his ox, nor his ass, nor any thing that is thy neighbour's.

XLIX. The end of this precept is, that, since it is the will of God that our whole soul should be under the influence of love, every desire inconsistent with charity ought to be expelled from our minds. The sum, then, will be, that no thought should obtrude itself upon us, which would excite in our minds any desire that is noxious, and tends to the detriment of another. To which corresponds the affirmative precept, that all our conceptions, deliberations, resolutions, and undertakings, ought to be consistent with the benefit and advantage of our neighbours. But here we meet with what appears to be a great and perplexing difficulty. For if our previous assertions be true, that the terms *adultery* and *theft* comprehend the licentious desire, and the injurious and criminal intention, this may be thought to have superseded the necessity of a separate command being afterwards introduced, forbidding us to covet the possessions of others. But we shall easily solve this difficulty by a distinction between intention and concupiscence. For an intention, as we have before observed in explaining the former commandments, is a deliberate consent of the will, when the mind has been enslaved by any unlawful desire. Concupiscence may exist without such deliberation or consent, when the mind is only attracted and stimulated by vain and corrupt objects. As the Lord, therefore, has hitherto commanded our wills, efforts, and actions to be subject to the law of love, so now he directs that the conceptions of our minds be subject to the same regulation, lest any of them be corrupt and perverted, and give our hearts an improper impulse. As he has forbidden our minds to be inclined and persuaded to anger, hatred, adultery, rapine, and falsehood, so now he prohibits them from being instigated to these vices.

L. Nor is it without cause that he requires such consummate rectitude. For who can deny that it is reasonable for all the powers of our souls to be under the influence of love? But if any one deviate from the path of love, who can deny that that soul is in an unhealthy state? Now, whence is it, that your mind conceives desires prejudicial to your neighbour, but that, neglecting his interest, you consult nothing but your own? For if your heart were full of love, there would be no part of it exposed to such imaginations. It must therefore be destitute of love, so far as it is the seat of concupiscence. Some one will object, that it is unreasonable, that imaginations, which without reflection flutter about in the mind, and then vanish away, should be condemned as symptoms of concupiscence, which has its seat in the heart. I reply, that the present question relates to that kind of imaginations, which, when they are presented to our understandings, at the same time strike our hearts, and inflame them with cupidity; since the mind never entertains a wish for any thing after which the heart is not excited to pant. Therefore God enjoins a wonderful ardour of love, which he will not allow to be interrupted even by the smallest degree of concupiscence. He requires a heart admirably well regulated, which he permits not to be disturbed with the least emotion contrary to the law of love. Do not imagine that this doctrine is unsupported by any great authority; for I derived the first idea of it from Augustine. Now, though the design of the Lord was to prohibit us from all corrupt desires, yet he has exhibited, as examples, those objects which most generally deceive us with a fallacious appearance of pleasure; that he might not leave any thing to concupiscence, after having driven it from those objects towards which it is most violently inclined. Behold, then, the second table of the law, which sufficiently instructs us in the duties we owe to men for the sake of God, on regard to whom the whole rule of love depends. The duties taught in this second table, therefore, we shall inculcate in vain, unless our instruction be founded on the fear and reverence of God. To divide the prohibition of concupiscence into two precepts, the discerning reader, without any comment of mine, will pronounce to be a corrupt and violent separation of what is but one. Nor is the repetition of this phrase, "Thou shalt not covet," any objection against us; because, having mentioned the house or family, God enumerates the different parts of it, beginning with the wife. Hence it clearly appears that it ought to be read, as it is correctly read by the Hebrews, in one continued connection; and in short, that God commands, that all that every man possesses remain safe and entire, not only from any actual injury or fraudulent intention, but even from the least emotion of cupidity that can solicit our hearts.

LI. But what is the tendency of the whole law, will not now be difficult to judge: it is to a perfection of righteousness, that it may form the life of man after the example of the Divine purity. For God has so delineated his own character in it, that the man who exemplifies in his actions the precepts it contains, will exhibit in his life, as it were, an image of God. Wherefore, when Moses would recall the substance of it to the remembrance of the Israelites, he said, "And now, Israel, what doth the Lord thy God require of thee, but to fear the Lord thy God, to walk in all his ways, and to love him, and to serve the Lord thy God with all thy heart, and with all thy soul, to keep the commandments of the Lord?" (o) Nor did he cease to reiterate the same things to them, whenever he intended to point out the end of the law. The tendency of the doctrine of the law is to connect man with his God, and, as Moses elsewhere expresses it, to make him cleave to the Lord in sanctity of life. (p) Now, the perfection of this sanctity consists in two principal points, already recited — "that we love the Lord our God with all our heart, and with all our soul, and with all our strength, and with all our mind; and our neighbour as ourselves." (q) And the first is, that our souls be completely filled with the love of God. From this the love of our neighbour will naturally follow; as the Apostle signifies, when he says, that "the end of the commandment is charity out of a pure heart, and of a good conscience, and of faith unfeigned." (r) Here we find a good conscience and faith unfeigned, that is, in a word, true piety, stated to be the grand source from which charity is derived. He is deceived, therefore, who supposes that the law teaches nothing but certain rudiments and first principles of righteousness, by which men are introduced to the commencement, but are not directed to the true goal of good

(o) Deut. x. 12, 13.
(p) Deut. xi. 22.
(q) Luke x. 27.
(r) 1 Tim. i. 5.

works; since beyond the former sentence of Moses, and the latter of Paul, nothing further can be wanted to the highest perfection. For how far will he wish to proceed, who will not be content with this instruction, by which man is directed to the fear of God, to the spiritual worship of him, to the observance of his commands, to persevering rectitude in the way of the Lord, to purity of conscience, and sincere faith and love? Hence we derive a confirmation of the foregoing exposition of the law, which traces and finds in its precepts all the duties of piety and love. For they who attend merely to dry and barren elements, as though it taught them but half of the Divine will, are declared by the Apostle to have no knowledge of its end.

LII. But because Christ and his Apostles, in reciting the substance of the law, sometimes omit the first table, (s) many persons are deceived in this point, who wish to extend their expressions to both tables. In the Gospel of Matthew, Christ calls judgment, mercy, and faith, "the weightier matters of the law." By the word *faith* it is evident to me that he intends truth or fidelity towards men. Some, however, in order to extend the passage to the whole law, take the word *faith* to mean religion towards God. But for this there is no foundation; for Christ is treating of those works by which man ought to prove himself to be righteous. If we attend to this observation, we shall cease also to wonder, why, in another place, to the inquiry of a young man, what those commandments are by the observance of which we enter into life, he only returns the following answer: "Thou shalt do no murder, Thou shalt not commit adultery, Thou shalt not steal, Thou shalt not bear false witness, Honour thy father and thy mother; and, Thou shalt love thy neighbour as thyself." (t) For obedience to the first table consisted chiefly either in the disposition of the heart, or in ceremonies. The disposition of the heart was not visible, and the ceremonies were diligently performed by hypocrites; but the works of charity are such as enable us to give a certain evidence of righteousness. But the same occurs in the Prophets so frequently, that it must be familiar to the reader who is but tolerably conversant with them. For in almost all cases when they exhort to repentance, they omit the first table, and insist on faith, judgment, mercy, and equity. Nor do they by this method neglect the fear of God, but require substantial proof of it from those marks. It is well known that when they treat of the observation of the law, they generally insist on the second table; because it is in it that the love of righteousness and integrity is principally discovered. It is unnecessary to quote the passages, as every person will of himself easily remark what I have stated.

(s) Matt. xxiii. 23.   (t) Matt. xix. 18, 19.

LIII. Is it, then, it will be asked, of more importance towards the attainment of righteousness to live innocently with men, than piously towards God? By no means. But because no man fulfils all the duties of charity, unless he really fear God, we derive from those duties a proof of his piety. Besides, the Lord, well knowing that he can receive no benefit from us, which he also declares by the Psalmist, (v) requires not our services for himself, but employs us in good works towards our neighbour. It is not without reason, then, that the Apostle makes all the perfection of the saints to consist in love; (w) which in another place he very justly styles "the fulfilling of the law;" adding, that "he that loveth another hath fulfilled the law." (x) Again: that "all the law is fulfilled in one word, even in this, Thou shalt love thy neighbour as thyself." (y) For he teaches nothing different from what is taught by Christ himself, when he says, "All things whatsoever ye would that men should do to you, do ye even so to them; for this is the law and the prophets." (z) It is certain that in the law and the prophets, faith, and all that pertains to the legitimate worship of God, hold the principal place, and that love occupies an inferior station; but our Lord intends that the observance of justice and equity among men is only prescribed to us in the law, that our pious fear of him, if we really possess any, may be proved by our actions.

LIV. Here, then, we must rest, that our life will then be governed according to the will of God, and the prescriptions of his law, when it is in all respects most beneficial to our brethren. But we do not find in the whole law one syllable, that lays down any rule for a man respecting those things which he should practise or omit for his carnal convenience. And surely, since men are born in such a state, that they are entirely governed by an immoderate self-love, — a passion which, how great soever their departure from the truth, they always retain, — there was no need of a law which would inflame that love, already of itself too violent. Whence it plainly appears, that the observance of the commandments consists not in the love of ourselves, but in the love of God and of our neighbour; that his is the best and most holy life, who lives as little as possible to himself; and that no man leads a worse or more iniquitous life, than he who lives exclusively to himself, and makes his own interest the sole object of his thoughts and pursuits. Moreover, the Lord, in order to give us the best expression of the strength of that love which we ought to exercise towards our neighbours, has regulated it by the standard of our self-love, because there was no stronger or more vehement af-

(v) Psalm xvi. 2.   (w) Ephes. iii. 17.   (x) Rom. xiii. 8.
(y) Gal. v. 14.   (z) Matt. vii. 12.

fection. And the force of the expression must be carefully examined; for he does not, according to the foolish dreams of some sophists, concede the first place to self-love, and assign the second to the love of our neighbour; but rather transfers to others that affection of love which we naturally restrict to ourselves. Whence the Apostle asserts that "charity seeketh not her own." (a) Nor is their argument, that every thing regulated by any standard is inferior to the standard by which it is regulated, worthy of the least attention. For God does not appoint our self-love as the rule, to which our love to others should be subordinate; but whereas, through our natural depravity, our love used to terminate in ourselves, he shows that it ought now to be diffused abroad; that we may be ready to do any service to our neighbour with as much alacrity, ardour, and solicitude, as to ourselves.

LV. Now, since Christ has demonstrated, in the parable of the Samaritan, that the word "neighbour" comprehends every man, even the greatest stranger, we have no reason to limit the commandment of love to our own relations or friends. I do not deny, that the more closely any person is united to us, the greater claim he has to the assistance of our kind offices. For the condition of humanity requires, that men should perform more acts of kindness to each other, in proportion to the closeness of the bonds by which they are connected, whether of relationship, or acquaintance, or vicinity; and this without any offence to God, by whose providence we are constrained to it. But I assert, that the whole human race, without any exception, should be comprehended in the same affection of love, and that in this respect there is no difference between the barbarian and the Grecian, the worthy and unworthy, the friend and the foe; for they are to be considered in God, and not in themselves, and whenever we deviate from this view of the subject, it is no wonder if we fall into many errors. Wherefore, if we wish to adhere to the true law of love, our eyes must chiefly be directed, not to man, the prospect of whom would impress us with hatred more frequently than with love, but to God, who commands that our love to him be diffused among all mankind; so that this must always be a fundamental maxim with us, that whatever be the character of a man, yet we ought to love him because we love God.

LVI. Wherefore the schoolmen have discovered either their ignorance or their wickedness in a most pestilent manner, when, treating of the precepts prohibiting the desire of revenge, and enjoining the love of our enemies, which were anciently delivered to all the Jews, and afterwards equally to all

(a) 1 Cor. xiii. 5.

Christians, they have made them to be counsels which we are at liberty to obey or not to obey, and have confined the necessary observance of them to the monks, who, on account of this very circumstance, would be more righteous than plain Christians, because they voluntarily bound themselves to observe these counsels. The reason which they assign for not receiving them as laws, is, that they appear too burdensome and grievous, especially to Christians who are under the law of grace. Do they presume in this manner to disannul the eternal law of God respecting the love of our neighbour? Is such a distinction to be found in any page of the law? On the contrary, does it not abound with commandments most strictly enjoining the love of our enemies? For what is the meaning of the injunction to feed our neighbour when he is hungry? (b) to direct into the right way his oxen or his asses when they are going astray, and to help them when sinking under a burden? (c) Shall we do good to his cattle for his sake, and feel no benevolence to his person? What! is not the word of the Lord eternal? "Vengeance is mine, I will repay:" (d) which is expressed in another passage still more explicitly: "Thou shalt not avenge, nor bear any grudge against the children of thy people." (e) Let them either obliterate these passages from the law, or acknowledge that the Lord was a Legislator, and no longer falsely pretend that he was only a counsellor.

LVII. And what is the meaning of the following expressions, which they have presumed to abuse by the absurdity of their comment? "Love your enemies, bless them that curse you, do good to them that hate you, and pray for them which despitefully use you, and persecute you; that ye may be the children of your Father which is in heaven." (f) Here, who would not argue with Chrysostom, that the allegation of such a necessary cause clearly proves these to be, not exhortations, but commandments? What have we left us, after being expunged from the number of the children of God? But according to them, the monks will be the only sons of the heavenly Father; they alone will venture to invoke God as their Father. What will now become of the Church? Upon the same principle it will be confined to heathen and publicans. For Christ says, "If ye love them which love you, what reward have ye? do not even the publicans the same?" (g) Shall not we be in a happy situation, if they leave us the title of Christians, but deprive us of the inheritance of the kingdom of heaven? The argument of Augustine is equally strong. When the Lord, says he, prohibits adultery, he forbids you to violate the

(b) Prov. xxv. 21.
(c) Exod. xxiii. 4, 5.
(d) Rom. xii. 19.
(e) Lev. xix. 18.
(f) Matt. v. 44, 45.
(g) Matt. v. 46.

wife of your enemy no less than of your friend: when he prohibits theft, he permits you not to steal from any one, whether he be a friend or an enemy. Now, Paul reduces these two prohibitions of theft and adultery to the rule of love, and even teaches that they are "briefly comprehended in this saying, namely, Thou shalt love thy neighbour as thyself." (*h*) Either, then, Paul must have been an erroneous expositor of the law, or it necessarily follows from this, that we are commanded to love, not only our friends, but also our enemies. Those, therefore, who so licentiously shake off the yoke common to the children of God, evidently betray themselves to be the sons of Satan. It is doubtful whether they have discovered greater stupidity or impudence in the publication of this dogma. For all the fathers decidedly pronounce that these are mere precepts. That no doubt was entertained on the subject in the time of Gregory, appears from his positive assertions; for he treats them as precepts, as though it had never been controverted. And how foolishly do they argue! They would be a burden, say they, too grievous for Christians; as though truly any thing could be conceived more difficult, than to love God with all our heart, with all our soul, and with all our strength. Compared with this law, every thing must be accounted easy, whether it be to love an enemy, or to banish from the mind all desire of revenge. To our imbecility, indeed, every thing is arduous and difficult, even the smallest point in the law. It is the Lord in whom we find strength: let him give what he commands, and let him command what he pleases. The being Christians under the law of grace consists not in unbounded license uncontrolled by any law, but in being ingrafted into Christ, by whose grace they are delivered from the curse of the law, and by whose Spirit they have the law inscribed on their hearts. This grace Paul has figuratively denominated a law, in allusion to the law of God, to which he was comparing and contrasting it. Their dispute concerning the word *law* is a dispute about nothing.

LVIII. Of the same nature is what they have called venial sin — a term which they apply to secret impiety, which is a breach of the first table, and to the direct transgression of the last commandment. For this is their definition, that "it is evil desire without any deliberate assent, and without any long continuance in the heart." Now, I assert that evil desire cannot enter the heart, except through a deficiency of those things which the law requires. We are forbidden to have any strange gods. When the mind, assaulted by mistrust, looks around to some other quarter; when it is stimulated by a sud-

(*h*) Rom. xiii. 9.

den desire of transferring its happiness from God to some other being; whence proceed these emotions, however transient, but from the existence of some vacant space in the soul to receive such temptations? And not to protract this argument to greater length, we are commanded to love God with all our heart, with all our mind, and with all our soul: therefore, unless all the powers of our soul be intensely engaged in the love of God, we have already departed from the obedience required by the law; for that the dominion of God is not well established in our conscience, is evident, from the enemies that there rebel against his government, and interrupt the execution of his commands. That the last commandment properly belongs to this point, has been already demonstrated. Have we felt any evil desire in our heart? we are already guilty of concupiscence, and are become at once transgressors of the law; because the Lord forbids us, not only to plan and attempt any thing that would prove detrimental to another, but even to be stimulated and agitated with concupiscence. Now, the curse of God always rests on the transgression of the law. We have no reason, therefore, to exempt even the most trivial emotions of concupiscence from the sentence of death. "In determining the nature of different sins," says Augustine, "let us not use deceitful balances, to weigh what we please and how we please, according to our own humour, saying, This is heavy, — This is light; but let us borrow the Divine balance from the Holy Scriptures, as from the treasury of the Lord, and therein weigh what is heavy; or rather let us weigh nothing ourselves, but acknowledge the weights already determined by the Lord." And what says the Scripture? The assertion of Paul, that "the wages of sin is death," (*i*) sufficiently demonstrates this groundless distinction to have been unknown to him. As we have already too strong a propensity to hypocrisy, this opiate ought by no means to have been added, to lull our consciences into greater insensibility.

LIX. I wish these persons would consider the meaning of this declaration of Christ: "Whosoever shall break one of these least commandments, and shall teach men so, he shall be called the least in the kingdom of heaven." (*k*) Are not they of this number, who thus presume to extenuate the transgression of the law, as though it were not worthy of death? But they ought to consider, not merely what is commanded, but who it is that gives the commands; because the smallest transgression of the law, which he has given, is a derogation from his authority. Is the violation of the Divine majesty in any case a trivial thing in their estimation? Lastly, if God has de-

(*i*) Rom. vi. 23.   (*k*) Matt. v. 19.

clared his will in the law, whatever is contrary to the law displeases him. Will they pretend that the wrath of God is so debilitated and disarmed, that the punishment of death cannot immediately follow ? He has unequivocally declared, if they could induce themselves to listen to his voice, rather than obscure the plain truth with their frivolous subtleties, "The soul that sinneth, it shall die ; "(*l*) and, which I have before cited, "The wages of sin is death." (*m*) They acknowledge it to be sin, because it is impossible to deny it ; yet they contend that it is not *mortal* sin. But, as they have hitherto too much resigned themselves to infatuation, they should at length learn to return to the exercise of their reason. If they persevere in their dreams, we will take our leave of them. Let the children of God know that all sin is *mortal;* because it is a rebellion against the will of God, which necessarily provokes his wrath ; because it is a transgression of the law, against which the Divine judgment is universally denounced ; and that the offences of the saints are *venial*, not of their own nature, but because they obtain pardon through the mercy of God.

CHAPTER IX.

CHRIST, THOUGH KNOWN TO THE JEWS UNDER THE LAW, YET CLEARLY REVEALED ONLY IN THE GOSPEL.

As it was not without reason, or without effect, that God was pleased, in ancient times, to manifest himself as a Father by means of expiations and sacrifices, and that he consecrated to himself a chosen people, there is no doubt that he was known, even then, in the same image in which he now appears to us with meridian splendour. Therefore Malachi, after having enjoined the Jews to attend to the law of Moses, and to persevere in the observance of it, (because after his death there was to be an interruption of the prophetical office,) immediately announces, that "the Sun of righteousness shall arise." (*n*) In this language he suggests, that the law tended to excite in the pious an expectation of the Messiah that was to come, and that at his advent there was reason to hope for a much greater degree of light. For this reason Peter says that "the Prophets have inquired and searched diligently concerning the salvation," which is now manifested in the gospel ; and that "it was re-

(*l*) Ezek. xviii. 20.   (*m*) Rom. vi. 23.   (*n*) Mal. iv. 2.

vealed to them, that not unto themselves, but unto us, they did minister the things which are now reported unto you by them that have preached the gospel unto you." (*o*) Not that their instructions were useless to the ancient people, or unprofitable to themselves, but because they did not enjoy the treasure, which God through their hands has transmitted to us. For in the present day, the grace, which was the subject of their testimony, is familiarly exhibited before our eyes; and whereas they had but a small taste, we have offered to us a more copious fruition of it. Therefore Christ, who asserts that " Moses wrote of him," (*p*) nevertheless extols that measure of grace in which we excel the Jews. Addressing his disciples, he says, " Blessed are your eyes, for they see ; and your ears, for they hear." (*q*) " For I tell you, that many prophets and kings have desired to see those things which ye see, and have not seen them ; and to hear those things which ye hear, and have not heard them." (*r*) This is no small recommendation of the evangelical revelation, that God has preferred us to those holy fathers who were eminent for singular piety. To this declaration that other passage is not at all repugnant, where Christ says, " Abraham saw my day, and was glad." (*s*) For though his prospect of a thing so very remote was attended with much obscurity, yet there was nothing wanting to the certainty of a well founded hope; and hence that joy which accompanied the holy patriarch even to his death. Neither does this assertion of John the Baptist, " No man hath seen God at any time; the only begotten Son, which is in the bosom of the Father, he hath declared him," (*t*) exclude the pious, who had died before his time, from a participation of the understanding and light which shine in the person of Christ; but, comparing their condition with ours, it teaches us that we have a clear manifestation of those mysteries, of which they had only an obscure prospect through the medium of shadows; as the author of the Epistle to the Hebrews more copiously and excellently shows, that " God, who at sundry times, and in divers manners, spake in time past unto the fathers by the prophets, hath in these last days spoken unto us by his Son." (*v*) Therefore, though the only begotten Son, who is now to us " the brightness of the glory, and the express image of the person," (*w*) of God the Father, was formerly known to the Jews, as we have elsewhere shown by a quotation from Paul, that he was the leader of their ancient deliverance from Egypt; yet this also is a truth, which is asserted by the same Paul in another place, that " God, who commanded the light to shine out of darkness, hath shined in

(*o*) 1 Peter i. 10—12.   (*q*) Matt. xiii. 16.   (*s*) John viii. 56.   (*v*) Heb. i. 1, 2
(*p*) John v. 46.   (*r*) Luke x. 24.   (*t*) John i. 18.   (*w*) Heb. i. 3.

our hearts, to give the light of the knowledge of the glory of God in the face of Jesus Christ." (*x*) For when he appeared in this his image, he made himself visible, as it were, in comparison with the obscure and shadowy representation of him which had been given before. This renders the ingratitude and obstinacy of those, who shut their eyes amid this meridian blaze, so much the more vile and detestable. And therefore Paul says that Satan, "the god of this world, hath blinded their minds, lest the light of the glorious gospel of Christ should shine unto them." (*y*)

II. Now, I understand the gospel to be a clear manifestation of the mystery of Christ. I grant indeed, since Paul styles the gospel *the doctrine of faith*, (*z*) that whatever promises we find in the law concerning the gracious remission of sins, by which God reconciles men to himself, are accounted parts of it. For he opposes faith to those terrors which torment and harass the conscience, if salvation is to be sought by works. Whence it follows, that taking the word *gospel* in a large sense, it comprehends all those testimonies, which God formerly gave to the fathers, of his mercy and paternal favour; but it is more eminently applicable to the promulgation of the grace exhibited in Christ. This acceptation is not only sanctioned by common use, but supported by the authority of Christ and the Apostles. Whence it is properly said of him, that he "preached the gospel of the kingdom." (*a*) And Mark introduces himself with this preface: "The beginning of the gospel of Jesus Christ." But it is needless to collect more passages to prove a thing sufficiently known. Christ, then, by his advent, "hath brought life and immortality to light through the gospel." (*b*) By these expressions Paul means, not that the fathers were immerged in the shades of death, till the Son of God became incarnate; but, claiming for the gospel this honourable prerogative, he teaches that it is a new and unusual kind of legation, in which God has performed those things that he had promised, that the truth of the promises might appear in the person of his Son. For though the faithful have always experienced the truth of the assertion of Paul, that "all the promises of God in him are Yea, and in him Amen," (*c*) because they have been sealed in their hearts, yet, since he has completed in his body all the parts of our salvation, the lively exhibition of those things has justly obtained new and singular praise. Hence this declaration of Christ: "Hereafter ye shall see heaven open, and the angels of God ascending and descending upon the Son of man." (*d*) For though he seems to allude to the ladder which

(*x*) 2 Cor. iv. 6.   (*y*) 2 Cor. iv. 4.   (*z*) 1 Tim. iv. 6.
(*a*) Matt. ix. 35.   (*b*) 2 Tim. i. 10.   (*c*) 2 Cor. i. 20.   (*d*) John i. 51.

the patriarch Jacob saw in a vision, yet he displays the superior excellence of his advent by this character — that he has opened the gate of heaven to give us free admittance into it.

III. Nevertheless, we must beware of the diabolical imagination of Servetus, who, while he designs to extol the magnitude of the grace of Christ, or at least professes such a design, totally abolishes all the promises, as though they were terminated together with the law. He pretends, that by faith in the gospel we receive the completion of all the promises; as though there were no distinction between us and Christ. I have just observed, that Christ left nothing incomplete of all that was essential to our salvation; but it is not a fair inference, that we already enjoy the benefits procured by him; for this would contradict the declaration of Paul, that "hope is laid up for us." (e) I grant, indeed, that when we believe in Christ, we at the same time pass from death to life; but we should also remember the observation of John, that though "we are now the sons of God, it doth not yet appear what we shall be; but we know that, when he shall appear, we shall be like him; for we shall see him as he is." (f) Though Christ, therefore, offers us in the gospel a present plenitude of spiritual blessings, yet the fruition of them is concealed under the custody of hope, till we are divested of our corruptible body, and transfigured into the glory of him who has gone before us. In the mean time, the Holy Spirit commands us to rely on the promises; and his authority we ought to consider sufficient to silence all the clamours of Servetus. For according to the testimony of Paul, "godliness hath promise of the life that now is, and of that which is to come;" (g) and therefore he boasts of being an Apostle of Christ, "according to the promise of life which is in Christ Jesus." (h) In another place he apprizes us that we have the same promises which were given to the saints in former times. (i) Finally, he represents it as the summit of felicity, that we are sealed with the Holy Spirit of promise. (k) Nor, indeed, have we otherwise any enjoyment of Christ, any further than as we embrace him invested with his promises. Hence it is, that he dwells in our hearts, and yet we live like pilgrims at a distance from him; because "we walk by faith, and not by sight." Nor is there any contrariety in these two positions, that we possess in Christ all that belongs to the perfection of the life of heaven, and yet that faith is a vision of invisible blessings. Only there is a difference to be observed in the nature or quality of the promises; because the gospel affords a clear discovery of that which the law has represented in shadows and types.

(e) Col. i. 5. (g) 1 Tim. iv. 8. (i) 2 Cor. vii. 1.
(f) 1 John iii. 2. (h) 2 Tim. i. 1. (k) Ephes. i. 13.

IV. This likewise evinces the error of those who never make any other comparison between the Law and the Gospel, than between the merit of works and the gratuitous imputation of righteousness. This antithesis, I grant, is by no means to be rejected; because Paul by the word *law* frequently intends the rule of a righteous life, in which God requires of us what we owe to him, affording us no hope of life, unless we fulfil every part of it, and, on the contrary, annexing a curse if we are guilty of the smallest transgression. This is the sense in which he uses it in those passages, where he argues that we are accepted by God through grace, and are accounted righteous through his pardon of our sins, because the observance of the law, to which the reward is promised, is not to be found in any man. Paul, therefore, justly represents the righteousness of the law and that of the gospel as opposed to each other. But the gospel has not superseded the whole law, so as to introduce a different way of salvation; but rather to confirm and ratify the promises of the law, and to connect the body with the shadows. For when Christ says that "the law and the prophets were until John," he does not abandon the fathers to the curse which the slaves of the law cannot escape; he rather implies that they were only initiated in the rudiments of religion, so that they remained far below the sublimity of the evangelical doctrine. Wherefore, when Paul calls the gospel "the power of God unto salvation to every one that believeth," he afterwards adds that it is "witnessed by the law and the prophets." (*l*) But at the end of the same Epistle, although he asserts that the preaching of Jesus Christ is " the revelation of the mystery which was kept secret since the world began," he qualifies this sentiment with the following explication — that it "is now made manifest, and by the Scriptures of the prophets made known to all nations." (*m*) Hence we conclude, that when mention is made of the whole law, the gospel differs from it only with respect to a clear manifestation; but on account of the inestimable plenitude of grace, which has been displayed to us in Christ, the celestial kingdom of God is justly said to have been erected in the earth at his advent.

V. Now, John was placed between the Law and the Gospel, holding an intermediate office connected with both. For though, in calling Christ "the Lamb of God" and "the victim for the expiation of sins," (*n*) he preached the substance of the gospel; yet, because he did not clearly express that incomparable power and glory which afterwards appeared in his resurrection, Christ affirms that he is not equal to the Apostles. This is his meaning in the following words: "Among them

(*l*) Rom. i. 16; iii. 21.   (*m*) Rom. xvi. 25, 26.   (*n*) John i. 29.

that are born of women, there hath not risen a greater than John the Baptist: notwithstanding, he that is least in the kingdom of heaven is greater than he."(*o*) For he is not there commending the persons of men, but after having preferred John to all the prophets, he allots the highest degree of honour to the preaching of the gospel, which we have elsewhere seen is signified by " the kingdom of heaven." When John himself said that he was only a "voice,"(*p*) as though he were inferior to the prophets, this declaration proceeded not from a pretended humility; he meant to signify that he was not intrusted with a proper embassy, but acted merely in the capacity of a herald, according to the prediction of Malachi: " Behold, I will send you Elijah the prophet before the coming of the great and dreadful day of the Lord."(*q*) Nor indeed, through the whole course of his ministry, did he aim at any thing but procuring disciples for Christ, which he also proves from Isaiah to have been the commission given him by God. In this sense he was called by Christ "a burning and a shining light," (*r*) because the full day had not yet arrived. Yet this is no reason why he should not be numbered among the preachers of the gospel, as he used the same baptism which was afterwards delivered to the apostles. But it was not till after Christ was received into the celestial glory, that the more free and rapid progress of the apostles completed what John had begun.

CHAPTER X.

THE SIMILARITY OF THE OLD AND NEW TESTAMENTS.

From the preceding observations it may now be evident, that all those persons, from the beginning of the world, whom God has adopted into the society of his people, have been federally connected with him by the same law and the same doctrine which are in force among us: but because it is of no small importance that this point be established, I shall show, by way of appendix, since the fathers were partakers with us of the same inheritance, and hoped for the same salvation through the grace of our common Mediator, how far their condition in this connection was different from ours. For though the testimonies we have collected from the law and the prophets in proof of this, render it sufficiently evident that the people

(*o*) Matt. xi. 11.   (*p*) John i. 23.   (*q*) Mal. iv. 5.   (*r*) John v. 35.

of God have never had any other rule of religion and piety, yet because some writers have raised many disputes concerning the difference of the Old and New Testaments, which may occasion doubts in the mind of an undiscerning reader, we shall assign a particular chapter for the better and more accurate discussion of this subject. Moreover, what would otherwise have been very useful, has now been rendered necessary for us by Servetus and some madmen of the sect of the Anabaptists, who entertain no other ideas of the Israelitish nation, than of a herd of swine, whom they pretend to have been pampered by the Lord in this world, without the least hope of a future immortality in heaven. To defend the pious mind, therefore, from this pestilent error, and at the same time to remove all difficulties which may arise from the mention of a diversity between the Old and New Testaments, let us, as we proceed, examine what similarity there is between them, and what difference; what covenant the Lord made with the Israelites, in ancient times, before the advent of Christ, and what he has entered into with us since his manifestation in the flesh.

II. And, indeed, both these topics may be despatched in one word. The covenant of all the fathers is so far from differing substantially from ours, that it is the very same; it only varies in the administration. But as such extreme brevity would not convey to any man a clear understanding of the subject, it is necessary, if we would do any good, to proceed to a more diffuse explication of it. But in showing their similarity, or rather unity, it will be needless to recapitulate all the particulars which have already been mentioned, and unseasonable to introduce those things which remain to be discussed in some other place. We must here insist chiefly on three principal points. We have to maintain, First, that carnal opulence and felicity were not proposed to the Jews as the mark towards which they should ultimately aspire, but that they were adopted to the hope of immortality, and that the truth of this adoption was certified to them by oracles, by the law, and by the prophets. Secondly, that the covenant, by which they were united to the Lord, was founded, not on any merits of theirs, but on the mere mercy of God who called them. Thirdly, that they both possessed and knew Christ as the Mediator, by whom they were united to God, and became partakers of his promises. The second of these points, as perhaps it is not yet sufficiently known, shall be demonstrated at large in its proper place. For we shall prove by numerous and explicit testimonies of the prophets, that whatever blessing the Lord ever gave or promised to his people, proceeded from his indulgent goodness. The third point has been clearly demonstrated in several places. And we have not wholly neglected the first.

III. In discussing the first point, therefore, because it principally belongs to the present argument, and is the grand subject of their controversy against us, we will use the more diligent application; yet in such a manner, that if any thing be wanting to the explication of the others, it may be supplied as we proceed, or added afterwards in a suitable place. Indeed, the apostle removes every doubt respecting all these points, when he says, that God the Father "promised afore by his prophets in the holy Scriptures, the gospel concerning his Son," (s) which he promulgated in the appointed time: and again, that the righteousness of faith, which is revealed in the gospel, is " witnessed by the law and the prophets." (t) For the gospel does not detain men in the joy of the present life, but elevates them to the hope of immortality; does not fasten them to terrestrial delights, but announcing to them a hope reserved in heaven, does as it were transport them thither. For this is the description which he gives in another place: "In whom also after that ye believed, ye were sealed with that Holy Spirit of promise, which is the earnest of our inheritance until the redemption of the purchased possession." (v) Again: " We heard of your faith in Christ Jesus, and of the love which ye have to all the saints, for the hope which is laid up for you in heaven, whereof ye heard before in the word of the truth of the gospel." (w) Again: "He called you by our gospel, to the obtaining of the glory of our Lord Jesus Christ." (x) Whence it is called "the word of salvation," and " the power of God to the salvation of believers," and " the kingdom of heaven." Now, if the doctrine of the gospel be spiritual, and open a way to the possession of an immortal life, let us not suppose that they, to whom it was promised and announced, were totally negligent and careless of their souls, and stupefied in the pursuit of corporeal pleasures. Nor let any one here cavil, that the promises which are recorded in the law and the prophets, respecting the gospel, were not designed for the Jews. For just after having spoken of the gospel being promised in the law, he adds, " that what things soever the law saith, it saith to them who are under the law." (y) This was in another argument, I grant; but when he said that whatever the law inculcates truly belonged to the Jews, he was not so forgetful as not to remember what he had affirmed, a few verses before, concerning the gospel promised in the law. By declaring that the Old Testament contained evangelical promises, therefore, the apostle most clearly demonstrates that it principally related to a future life.

IV. For the same reason it follows, that it was founded on

(s) Rom. i. 1—3 (v) Ephes. i. 13, 14. (x) 2 Thess. ii. 14.
(t) Rom. iii. 21 (w) Col. i. 4, 5. (y) Rom. iii. 19.

the free mercy of God, and confirmed by the mediation of Christ. For even the preaching of the gospel only announces, that sinners are justified by the paternal goodness of God, independently of any merit of their own; and the whole substance of it terminates in Christ. Who, then, dares to represent the Jews as destitute of Christ,—them with whom we are informed the evangelical covenant was made, of which Christ is the sole foundation? Who dares to represent them as strangers to the benefit of a free salvation, to whom we are informed the doctrine of the righteousness of faith was communicated? But not to be prolix in disputing on a clear point, we have a remarkable expression of the Lord: " Abraham rejoiced to see my day; and he saw it, and was glad." (z) And what Christ there declares concerning Abraham, the apostle shows to have been universal among the faithful, when he says that Christ remains "the same yesterday, and to-day, and for ever." (a) For he there speaks, not only of the eternal Divinity of Christ, but of his power, which has been perpetually manifested to the faithful. Wherefore both the blessed Virgin and Zachariah declare, in their songs, that the salvation revealed in Christ is a performance of the promises which the Lord had made to Abraham and the patriarchs. (b) If the Lord, in the manifestation of Christ, faithfully performed his ancient oath, it cannot be denied that the end of the Old Testament was always in Christ and eternal life.

V. Moreover the apostle makes the Israelites equal to us, not only in the grace of the covenant, but also in the signification of the sacraments. For when he means to adduce examples of the punishments with which the Scripture states them to have been formerly chastised, in order to deter the Corinthians from running into similar crimes, he begins by premising, that we have no reason to arrogate any preëminence to ourselves, which can deliver us from the Divine vengeance inflicted on them; since the Lord not only favoured them with the same benefits, but illustrated his grace among them by the same symbols; (c) as though he had said, If ye confide in being beyond the reach of danger, because both baptism by which you have been sealed, and the supper which you daily receive, have excellent promises, while at the same time you despise the Divine goodness, and live licentious lives,—know ye, that the Jews also were not destitute of such symbols, though the Lord inflicted on them his severest judgments. They were baptized in their passage through the sea, and in the cloud by which they were protected from the fervour of the sun. Our opponents maintain that passage to have been a carnal baptism,

(z) John viii. 56.   (a) Heb. xiii. 8.   (b) Luke i. 54, 72.   (c) 1 Cor. x. 1—11.

corresponding in some degree to our spiritual one. But if that were admitted, the apostle's argument would not proceed; for his design here is to prevent Christians from supposing that they excel the Jews in the privilege of baptism. Nor is what immediately follows, that they "did all eat the same spiritual meat, and did all drink the same spiritual drink," which he interprets of Christ, liable to this cavil.

VI. To invalidate this declaration of Paul, they object the assertion of Christ, "Your fathers did eat manna in the wilderness, and are dead. If any man eat of this bread, (that is, my flesh,) he shall live for ever." (d) But the two passages are reconciled without any difficulty. The Lord, because he was addressing auditors who only sought to be satisfied with corporeal sustenance, but were unconcerned about food for the soul, accommodates his discourse in some measure to their capacity, and institutes a comparison between manna and his own body, particularly to strike their senses. They demand that in order to acquire authority to himself, he should prove his power by some miracle, such as Moses performed in the desert, when he obtained manna from heaven. In the manna, however, they had no idea of any thing but a remedy for corporeal hunger, with which the people were then afflicted. They did not penetrate to that sublimer mystery of which Paul treats. Christ, therefore, to demonstrate the superiority of the blessing they ought to expect from him, to that which they said their fathers had received from Moses, makes this comparison: If it be in your opinion a great and memorable miracle, that the Lord, to prevent his people from perishing in the wilderness, supplied them, by means of Moses, with heavenly food, which served them as a temporary sustenance, — hence conclude how much more excellent that food must be, which communicates immortality. We see, then, why the Lord omitted the principal thing designed by the manna, and only remarked the lowest advantage that resulted from it. It was because the Jews, as if with an intention of reproaching him, contrasted him with Moses, who had supplied the necessities of the people with manna. He replies, that he is the dispenser of a far superior favour, in comparison with which the corporeal sustenance of the people, the sole object of their great admiration, deserves to be considered as nothing. Knowing that the Lord, when he rained manna from heaven, not only poured it down for the support of their bodies, but likewise dispersed it as a spiritual mystery, to typify that spiritual vivification which is experienced in Christ, Paul does not neglect that view of the subject which is most deserving of consideration. Wherefore

(d) John vi. 49, 51.

it is certainly and clearly proved, that the same promises of an eternal and heavenly life, with which the Lord now favours us, were not only communicated to the Jews, but even sealed and confirmed by sacraments truly spiritual. This subject is argued at length by Augustine against Faustus the Manichæan.

VII. But if the reader would prefer a recital of testimonies from the law and the prophets, to show him that the spiritual covenant was common also to the fathers, as we have heard from Christ and his apostles,—I will attend to this wish, and that with the greater readiness, because our adversaries will thereby be more decisively confuted, and will have no pretence for any future cavil. I will begin with that demonstration, which, though I know the Anabaptists will superciliously deem it futile and almost ridiculous, yet will have considerable weight with persons of docility and good understanding. And I take it for granted, that there is such a vital efficacy in the Divine word as to quicken the souls of all those whom God favours with a participation of it. For the assertion of Peter has ever been true, that it is " an incorruptible seed, which abideth for ever;" (*e*) as he also concludes from the words of Isaiah. (*f*) Now, when God anciently united the Jews with himself in this sacred bond, there is no doubt that he separated them to the hope of eternal life. For when I say, that they embraced the word which was to connect them more closely with God, I advert not to that general species of communication with him, which is diffused through heaven and earth, and all the creatures in the universe, which although it animates all things according to their respective natures, yet does not deliver from the necessity of corruption. I refer to that particular species of communication, by which the minds of the pious are enlightened into the knowledge of God, and in some measure united to him. Since Adam, Abel, Noah, Abraham, and the other patriarchs, were attached to God by such an illumination of his word, I maintain, there can be no doubt that they had an entrance into his immortal kingdom. For it was a real participation of God, which cannot be separated from the blessing of eternal life.

VIII. If the subject still appear involved in any obscurity, let us proceed to the very form of the covenant; which will not only satisfy sober minds, but will abundantly prove the ignorance of those who endeavour to oppose it. For the Lord has always made this covenant with his servants: " I will be your God, and ye shall be my people." (*g*) These expressions, according to the common explanation of the prophets, comprehend life, and salvation, and consummate felicity. For it is not

(*e*) 1 Peter i. 23, 25.   (*f*) Isaiah xl. 8.   (*g*) Lev. xxvi. 12.

without reason that David frequently pronounces, how "blessed is the nation whose God is the Lord; and the people whom he hath chosen for his own inheritance;" (*h*) and that not on account of any earthly felicity, but because he delivers from death, perpetually preserves, and attends with everlasting mercy, those whom he has taken for his people. As it is expressed in the other prophets, "Art thou not from everlasting, O Lord my God, mine Holy One? we shall not die." (*i*) "The Lord is our Lawgiver, the Lord is our King; he will save us." (*k*) "Happy art thou, O Israel: who is like unto thee, O people saved by the Lord?" (*l*) But not to labour much on a point which does not require it, we are frequently reminded, in reading the prophets, that we shall have a plenitude of all blessings, and even a certainty of salvation, provided the Lord be our God. And that on good ground; for if his face, as soon as it has begun to shine, be a present pledge of salvation, will God manifest himself to any man without opening the treasures of salvation to him? For God is our God, on the express condition of his "walking in the midst of us," as he declared by Moses. (*m*) But this presence of his cannot be obtained without the possession of life. And though nothing further had been expressed, they had a promise of spiritual life sufficiently clear in these words: "I am the Lord your God." (*n*) For he announced that he would be a God, not only to their bodies, but chiefly to their souls; for the soul, unless united to God by righteousness, remains alienated from him at death. But let that union take place, and it will be attended with eternal salvation.

IX. Moreover, he not only declared himself to be their God, but promised to continue so for ever; in order that their hope, not contented with present blessings, might be extended to eternity. And that the use of the future tense conveyed this idea to them, appears from many expressions, where the faithful console themselves not only amidst present evils, but for futurity, that God will never desert them. But in regard to the second part of the promise, he still more plainly encouraged them concerning the extension of the Divine blessing to them beyond the limits of the present life: "I will be a God to thy seed after thee." (*o*) For if he intended to declare his benevolence to them after they were dead, by blessing their posterity, much more would he not fail of manifesting his favour towards themselves. For God is not like men, who transfer their love to the children of their friends, because death takes away their opportunity of performing kind offices to those who were ob-

(*h*) Psalm cxliv. 15; xxxiii. 12.   (*i*) Hab. i. 12.   (*k*) Isaiah xxxiii. 22.
(*l*) Deut. xxxiii. 29.   (*m*) Lev. xxvi. 12.   (*n*) Exod. vi. 7.   (*o*) Gen. xvii. 7

jects of their regard. But God, whose beneficence is not interrupted by death, deprives not the dead of the blessings of his mercy, which for their sakes he diffuses through a thousand generations. The design of the Lord, therefore, was to show them, by a clear proof, the magnitude and abundance of his goodness which they should experience after death, when he described its exuberance as reaching to all their posterity. (*p*) Now, the Lord sealed the truth, and, as it were, exhibited the completion of this promise, when he called himself the God of Abraham, Isaac, and Jacob, long after they were dead. (*q*) For what is implied in it? Would it not have been a ridiculous appellation, if they had perished? It would have been just as if he had said, I am the God of those who have no existence. Wherefore, the evangelists relate, that with this single argument the Sadducees were so embarrassed by Christ, (*r*) as to be unable to deny that Moses had given a testimony in favour of the resurrection of the dead; for they had learned from Moses himself, that "all his saints are in his hand." (*s*) Whence it was easy to infer, that death had not annihilated those whom he, who is the arbiter of life and death, had received into his guardianship and protection.

X. Now, to come to the principal point on which this controversy turns, let us examine, whether the faithful themselves were not so instructed by the Lord, as to be sensible that they had a better life in another world, and to meditate on that to the neglect of the present. In the first place, the course of life which was divinely enjoined them was a perpetual exercise, by which they were reminded that they were the most miserable of all mankind, if they had no happiness but in the present life. Adam, rendered most unhappy by the mere remembrance of his lost felicity, finds great difficulty in supplying his wants by anxious toils. (*v*) Nor does the Divine malediction confine itself to his manual labours; he experiences the bitterest sorrow from that which was his only remaining consolation. Of his two sons, he is deprived of one by the parricidal hands of his brother; the survivor is deservedly the object of his detestation and abhorrence. (*w*) Abel, cruelly assassinated in the flower of his age, exhibits an example of human calamity. Noah, while the whole world securely abandons itself to sensual delights, consumes a valuable part of his life with excessive fatigue in building the ark. (*x*) His escape from death was attended with greater distress than if he had died a hundred times. For besides that the ark was, as it were, a sepulchre to him for ten months, (*y*) nothing could be

(*p*) Exod. xx. 6.   (*q*) Exod. iii. 6.   (*r*) Matt. xxii. 32—34. Luke xx. 37—40.
(*s*) Deut. xxxiii. 3.   (*v*) Gen. iii. 17—19.
(*w*) Gen. iv. 8, 14.   (*x*) Gen. vi. 14—21.   (*y*) Gen. vii. 11; viii. 13.

more disagreeable than to be detained for so long a period almost immersed in the ordure of animals. After having escaped from such great difficulties, he meets with a fresh occasion of grief. He sees himself ridiculed by his own son, and is constrained to pronounce a curse with his own mouth upon him, whom by the great goodness of God he had received safe from the deluge. (*z*)

XI. Abraham is one who ought to be deemed equal to a host, if we consider his faith, which is proposed to us as the best standard of believing, so that we must be numbered in his family, in order to be the children of God. Now, what would be more absurd, than that Abraham should be the father of all the faithful, and not possess even the lowest place among them? But he cannot be excluded from the number, nor even from the most honourable station, without the destruction of the whole Church. Now, with respect to the circumstances of his life;—when he is first called, he is torn by the Divine command from his country, his parents, and his friends, the enjoyment of whom is supposed to give life its principal relish; as though God positively intended to deprive him of all the pleasures of life. (*a*) As soon as he has entered the land in which he is commanded to reside, he is driven from it by a famine. He removes, in search of relief, to a place where, for the preservation of his own safety, he finds it necessary to disown his wife, which would probably be more afflictive to him than many deaths. (*b*) After having returned to the country of his residence, he is again expelled from it by famine. What kind of felicity is it to dwell in such a country, where he must so frequently experience hunger, and even perish for want of sustenance, unless he leaves it? In the country of Abimelech, he is again driven to the same necessity of purchasing his own personal safety with the loss of his wife. (*c*) While he wanders hither and thither for many years in an unsettled state, he is compelled, by the continual quarrels of his servants, to send away his nephew, whom he regarded as a son. (*d*) There is no doubt that he bore this separation just as he would the amputation of one of his limbs. Soon after he is informed that enemies have carried him away captive. (*e*) Whithersoever he directs his course, he finds himself surrounded by savage barbarians, who will not even permit him to drink the water of wells which with immense labour he has himself digged. For he could not have bought the use of them from the king of Gerar, if it had not been previously prohibited. (*f*) When he arrives to old age, beyond the time of having children, he experiences

---

(*z*) Gen. ix. 24, 25.   (*a*) Gen. xii. 1.   (*b*) Gen. xii. 10—15.   (*c*) Gen. xx. 1, 2.
(*d*) Gen. xiii. 7—11.   (*e*) Gen. xiv. 12, 13.   (*f*) Gen. xxi. 25—30.

the most disagreeable and painful circumstance with which that age is attended. (*g*) He sees himself destitute of posterity, till, beyond all expectation, he begets Ishmael; whose birth he purchases at a dear rate, while he is wearied with the reproaches of Sarah, just as if he encouraged the contumacy of his maid-servant, and so were himself the cause of the domestic disturbance. (*h*) At length Isaac is born; but his birth is attended with this condition, that Ishmael the first-born must be banished from the family, and abandoned like an enemy. (*i*) When Isaac is left alone to solace the good man in his declining years, he is soon after commanded to sacrifice him. (*k*) What can the human mind imagine more calamitous, than for a father to become the executioner of his own son? If he had been taken away by sickness, every one would have thought the aged parent unhappy in the extreme, as having had a son given him in mockery, at the loss of whom, his former grief on account of his being destitute of children would certainly be redoubled. If he had been massacred by some stranger, the calamity would have been greatly increased by the horrible nature of his end; but to be slain by his father's own hand exceeds all the other instances of distress. In short, through the whole course of his life, Abraham was so driven about and afflicted, that if any one wished to give an example of a life full of calamity, he could not find one more suitable. Nor let it be objected, that he was not entirely miserable, because he had at length a prosperous deliverance from such numerous and extreme dangers. For we cannot pronounce his to be a happy life, who for a long period struggles through an infinity of difficulties; but his, who is exempted from afflictions, and favoured with the peaceful enjoyment of present blessings.

XII. Isaac, though afflicted with fewer calamities, yet scarcely ever enjoys the smallest taste of pleasure. He also experiences those vexations which permit not a man to be happy in the world. Famine drives him from the land of Canaan; his wife is torn from his bosom; his neighbours frequently harass him, and take every method of distressing him, so that he also is constrained to contend with them about water. (*l*) In his own family he suffers much uneasiness from Esau's wives; (*m*) he is distressed by the discord of his sons, and unable to remedy that great evil, but by the exile of him to whom he had given the blessing. (*n*) With respect to Jacob, he is an eminent example of nothing but extreme infelicity. He passes his childhood at home, amidst the menaces and terrors of his elder brother, to which he is at length constrained

(*g*) Gen. xv. 2. (*h*) Gen. xvi. 1—15.
(*i*) Gen. xxi. 2, 3, 10—14. (*k*) Gen. xxii. 2. (*l*) Gen. xxvi. 1, 7, 20, 21.
(*m*) Gen. xxvi. 34, 35. (*n*) Gen. xxviii. 5.

to give way. (*o*) A fugitive from his parents and his native soil, in addition to the bitterness of exile, he is treated with unkindness by his uncle Laban. It is not sufficient for him to endure a most hard and severe servitude of seven years, but he is fraudulently deceived in a wife. (*p*) For the sake of another wife he must enter on a new servitude, (*q*) in which, as he himself complains, he is scorched all the day by the fervid rays of the sun, and through the wakeful night benumbed by the icy cold. (*r*) During twenty years, which he spends in such extreme hardships, he is daily afflicted with fresh injuries from his father-in-law. Nor does he enjoy tranquillity in his own family, which he sees distracted and almost torn asunder by the animosities, contentions, and rivalship of his wives. (*s*) When he is commanded to return to his own country, he is obliged to depart in a manner resembling an ignominious flight. Nor even then can he escape the iniquity of his father-in-law, but is harassed with his reproaches and insults in the midst of his journey. (*t*) Immediately after, he falls into a much greater difficulty. For as he advances towards his brother, he has death before his eyes in as many forms as a cruel and inveterate enemy can possibly contrive. He is exceedingly tormented and distracted with dreadful terrors, while he is expecting the approach of his brother; when he sees him, he falls at his feet like a person half dead, till he finds him more reconciled than he could have ventured to hope. (*v*) Moreover, on his first entrance into the land, he is deprived of Rachel, his dearly beloved wife. (*w*) Afterwards he hears that the son whom he had by her, and whom, therefore, he loved above the rest, is torn asunder by wild beasts. The severity of his grief on account of his death is expressed by himself, when, after many days of mourning, he obstinately refuses all consolation, saying, "I will go down into the grave unto my son mourning." (*x*) In the mean time, the rape and violation of his daughter, and the rashness of his sons in revenging it, which not only made him an object of abhorrence to all the inhabitants of the country, but put him in immediate danger of being massacred; what abundant sources were these of anxiety, grief, and vexation! (*y*) Then follows the horrible crime of Reuben, his first-born, than which no greater affliction could befall him. For if the pollution of a man's wife be numbered among the greatest miseries, what shall we say of it, when the crime is perpetrated by his own son? (*z*) Not long after, his family is contaminated with incest; (*a*) so that such a number of dis-

---

(*o*) Gen. xxvii. 41—45.
(*p*) Gen. xxix. 20, 23, 25.
(*q*) Gen. xxix. 27.
(*r*) Gen. xxxi. 40, 41.
(*s*) Gen. xxx. 1.
(*t*) Gen. xxxi. 25, 36.
(*v*) Gen. xxxii. xxxiii.
(*w*) Gen. xxxv. 19.
(*x*) Gen. xxxvii. 32—35.
(*y*) Gen. xxxiv.
(*z*) Gen. xxxv. 22.
(*a*) Gen. xxxviii. 13—18.

graceful occurrences may be expected to break a heart otherwise very firm and unbroken by calamities. Towards the end of life, when he is seeking sustenance for himself and family in a season of famine, his ears are wounded by the report of a new calamity, which informs him that one of his sons is detained in prison; and in order to recover him he is obliged to intrust his darling Benjamin to the care of the rest. (*b*) Who can suppose that in such an accumulation of distresses he had a single moment of respite? He himself, who is best able to give a testimony respecting himself, declares to Pharaoh, that his days on the earth have been few and evil. (*c*) By affirming that he has lived in continual miseries, he denies that he has enjoyed that prosperity which the Lord had promised him. Therefore either Jacob formed an improper and ungrateful estimate of the favour of God, or he spake the truth in asserting that he had been miserable on the earth. If his affirmation was true, it follows that his hope was not fixed on terrestrial things.

XIII. If these holy fathers expected, as undoubtedly they did expect, a life of happiness from the hand of God, they both knew and contemplated a different kind of blessedness from that of this terrestrial life. This the apostle very beautifully shows, when he says, "By faith Abraham sojourned in the land of promise, as in a strange country, dwelling in tabernacles with Isaac and Jacob, the heirs with him of the same promise; for he looked for a city which hath foundations, whose builder and maker is God. These all died in faith, not having received the promises, but having seen them afar off, and were persuaded of them, and embraced them and confessed that they were strangers and pilgrims on the earth. For they that say such things declare plainly that they seek a country. And truly if they had been mindful of that country from whence they came out, they might have had opportunity to have returned. But now they desire a better country, that is, a heavenly; wherefore God is not ashamed to be called their God; for he hath prepared for them a city." (*d*) For they would have been stupid beyond all comparison, so steadily to follow promises, of which there appeared no hope on earth, unless they had expected the completion of them in another world. But the apostle, with great force, principally insists on this — that they called the present life a *pilgrimage*, as is also stated by Moses. (*e*) For if they were strangers and sojourners in the land of Canaan, what became of the Divine promise, by which they had been appointed heirs of it? This manifestly implies, therefore, that the promise, which the Lord had given them concern-

(*b*) Gen. xlii.   (*c*) Gen. xlvii 9.   (*d*) Heb. xi. 9, &c.   (*e*) Gen. xlvii. 9.

ing the possession of it, related to something more remote. Wherefore they never acquired a foot of land in Canaan, except for a sepulchre; by which they testified that they had no hope of enjoying the benefit of the promise till after death. And this is the reason why Jacob thought it so exceedingly desirable to be buried there, that he made his son Joseph promise it to him by oath; (*f*) and why Joseph commanded that his bones should be removed thither, even several ages after his death, when they would have been long reduced to ashes. (*g*)

XIV. In short, it evidently appears, that in all the pursuits of life they kept in view the blessedness of the future state. For why should Jacob have so eagerly desired, and exposed himself to such danger in endeavouring to obtain, the primogeniture, which would occasion his exile, and almost his rejection from his family, but from which he could derive no possible benefit, unless he had his views fixed on a nobler blessing? And that such was his view he declared in these words, which he uttered with his expiring breath: "I have waited for thy salvation, O Lord." (*h*) What salvation could he expect, when he felt himself about to expire, unless he had seen in death the commencement of a new life? But why do we argue concerning the saints and children of God, when even one, who in other respects endeavoured to oppose the truth, was not entirely destitute of such a knowledge? For what was the meaning of Balaam, when he said, "Let me die the death of the righteous, and let my last end be like his," (*i*) but the same which David afterwards expressed in the following words? "Precious in the sight of the Lord is the death of his saints." (*k*) "Evil shall slay the wicked." (*l*) If death were the ultimate bound of human existence, no difference could be observed in it between the righteous and the impious; the distinction between them consists in the different destinies which await them after death.

XV. We have not yet proceeded beyond Moses; whose only office, our opponents allege, was to persuade a carnal people to the worship of God by the fertility of the land, and an abundance of all things: and yet, unless any one wilfully rejects the evidence presented to him, we already discover a clear declaration of a spiritual covenant. But if we come down to the prophets, there we have the fullest revelation both of eternal life and of the kingdom of Christ. And first, with what perspicuity and certainty does David direct all his writings to this end; though, as he was prior to the rest in point

(*f*) Gen. xlvii. 30.
(*g*) Gen. l. 25.
(*h*) Gen. xlix. 18.
(*i*) Numb. xxiii. 10.
(*k*) Psalm cxvi. 15.
(*l*) Psalm xxxiv. 21.

of time, so, according to the order of the Divine dispensation, he shadowed forth the heavenly mysteries more obscurely than they did! What estimate he formed of his terrestrial habitation, the following passage declares: "I am a stranger with thee, and a sojourner, as all my fathers were. Verily, every man at his best estate is altogether vanity. Surely every man walketh in a vain show. And now, Lord, what wait I for? my hope is in thee." (*m*) He who, after having confessed that there is nothing substantial or permanent on earth, still retains the constancy of his hope in God, certainly contemplates the felicity reserved for him in another world. To this contemplation he frequently recalls the faithful, whenever he wishes to afford them true consolation. For in another place, after having spoken of the brevity and the transitory nature of human life, he adds, "But the mercy of the Lord is from everlasting to everlasting upon them that fear him." (*n*) Similar to which is the following: "Of old hast thou laid the foundations of the earth; and the heavens are the work of thy hands. They shall perish, but thou shalt endure; yea, all of them shall wax old like a garment; as a vesture shalt thou change them, and they shall be changed; but thou art the same, and thy years shall have no end. The children of thy servants shall continue, and their seed shall be established before thee." (*o*) If, notwithstanding the destruction of heaven and earth, the pious cease not to be established before the Lord, it follows that their salvation is connected with his eternity. But this hope cannot be at all supported, unless it rest on the promise which we find in Isaiah: "The heavens," saith the Lord, "shall vanish away like smoke, and the earth shall wax old like a garment, and they that dwell therein shall die in like manner; but my salvation shall be for ever, and my righteousness shall not be abolished;" (*p*) where perpetuity is ascribed to righteousness and salvation, considered not as resident in God, but as experienced by men.

XVI. Nor can what he frequently says concerning the prosperity of the faithful be understood in any other sense than as referring to the manifestation of the glory of heaven. Such are the following passages: "The Lord preserveth the souls of his saints; he delivereth them out of the hand of the wicked. Light is sown for the righteous, and gladness for the upright in heart." (*q*) Again: "The righteousness of the righteous endureth for ever; his horn shall be exalted with honour. The desire of the wicked shall perish." (*r*) Again: "Surely the righteous shall give thanks unto thy name; the upright

(*m*) Psalm xxxix. 12, 5, 6, 7. (*o*) Psalm cii. 25—28. (*q*) Psalm xcvii. 10, 11.
(*n*) Psalm ciii. 17. (*p*) Isaiah li. 6. (*r*) Psalm cxii. 9, 10.

shall dwell in thy presence."(s) Again: "The righteous shall be had in everlasting remembrance."(t) Again: "The Lord redeemeth the soul of his servants."(v) For the Lord frequently leaves his servants to the rage of the impious, not only to be harassed, but to be torn asunder and ruined; he suffers good men to languish in obscurity and meanness, while the impious are almost as glorious as the stars; nor does he exhilarate the faithful with the light of his countenance, so that they can enjoy any lasting pleasure. Wherefore David does not dissemble that, if the faithful fix their eyes on the present state of things, they will be most grievously tempted with an apprehension lest innocence should obtain from God neither favour nor reward. So much does impiety in most cases prosper and flourish, while the pious are oppressed with ignominy, poverty, contempt, and distress of every kind. "My feet," says he, "were almost gone; my steps had well nigh slipped. For I was envious at the foolish, when I saw the prosperity of the wicked."(w) At length he concludes his account of them: "When I thought to know this, it was too painful for me; until I went into the sanctuary of God; then understood I their end."(x)

XVII. We may learn, then, even from this confession of David, that the holy fathers under the Old Testament were not ignorant, that God rarely or never in this world gives his servants those things which he promises them, and that, therefore, they elevated their minds to the sanctuary of God, where they had a treasure in reserve which is not visible amid the shadows of the present life. This sanctuary was the last judgment, which, not being discernible by their eyes, they were contented to apprehend by faith. Relying on this confidence, whatever events might befall them in the world, they, nevertheless, had no doubt that there would come a time when the Divine promises would be fulfilled. This is evident from the following passages: "I will behold thy face in righteousness: I shall be satisfied, when I awake, with thy likeness."(y) Again: "I am like a green olive-tree in the house of God."(z) Again: "The righteous shall flourish like the palm-tree: he shall grow like a cedar in Lebanon. Those that be planted in the house of the Lord shall flourish in the courts of our God. They shall still bring forth fruit in old age; they shall be fat and flourishing." He had just before said, "O Lord, how great are thy works! and thy thoughts are very deep. When the wicked spring as the grass, and when all the workers of iniquity do flourish, it is that they shall be destroyed for ever."(a) Where can this

(s) Psalm cxl. 13.   (w) Psalm lxxiii. 2.   (z) Psalm lii. 8.
(t) Psalm cxii. 6.   (x) Psalm lxxiii. 16, 17.   (a) Psalm xcii. 12–14, 5, 7.
(v) Psalm xxxiv. 22.   (y) Psalm xvii. 15.

beauty and gracefulness of the faithful be found, but where the appearance of this world has been reversed by the manifestation of the kingdom of God? When they could turn their eyes towards that eternity, despising the momentary rigour of present calamities, they securely broke forth into the following expressions: "The Lord shall never suffer the righteous to be moved. But thou, O God, shalt bring them" (wicked men) "down into the pit of destruction." (b) Where, in this world, is the pit of destruction, to absorb the wicked, as an instance of whose felicity it is mentioned in another place that without languishing for any long time "they go down to the grave in a moment?" (c) Where is that great stability of the saints, whom David himself, in the language of complaint, frequently represents as not only troubled, but oppressed and consumed? He certainly had in view, not any thing that results from the agitations of the world, which are even more tumultuous than those of the sea, but what will be accomplished by the Lord, when he shall one day sit in judgment to fix the everlasting destiny of heaven and earth. This appears from another psalm, in which he gives the following beautiful description: "They that trust in their wealth, and boast themselves in the multitude of their riches; none of them can by any means redeem his brother, nor give to God a ransom for him. For he seeth that wise men die, likewise the fool and the brutish person perish, and leave their wealth to others. Their inward thought is, that their houses shall continue for ever, and their dwelling-places to all generations; they call their lands after their own names. Nevertheless man being in honour abideth not: he is like the beasts that perish. This their way is their folly: yet their posterity approve their sayings. Like sheep they are laid in the grave; death shall feed on them; and the upright shall have dominion over them in the morning; and their beauty shall consume in the grave from their dwelling." (d) In the first place, this derision of fools, for placing their dependence on the mutable and transitory blessings of the world, shows that the wise ought to seek a very different felicity. But he more evidently discloses the mystery of the resurrection, when he establishes the reign of the pious after the ruin and destruction of the wicked. For what shall we understand by "the morning" which he mentions, but the revelation of a new life commencing after the conclusion of the present?

XVIII. Hence arose that reflection, which served the faithful as a consolation under their miseries, and a remedy for their sufferings: "The anger of the Lord endureth but a moment;

(b) Psalm lv. 22, 23.   (c) Job xxi. 13.   (d) Psalm xlix. 6, &c.

in his favour is life." (e) How did they limit their afflictions to a moment, who were afflicted all their lifetime? When did they perceive so long a duration of the Divine goodness, of which they had scarcely the smallest taste? If their views had been confined to the earth, they could have made no such discovery; but as they directed their eyes towards heaven, they perceived, that the afflictions with which the Lord exercises his saints are but "for a small moment," and that the "mercies" with which he "gathers" them are "everlasting." (f) On the other hand, they foresaw the eternal and never-ending perdition of the impious, who had been happy, as in a dream, for a single day. Hence the following sentiments: "The memory of the just is blessed; but the name of the wicked shall rot." (g) "Precious in the sight of the Lord is the death of his saints." (h) Also in Samuel: "The Lord will keep the feet of his saints, and the wicked shall be silent in darkness." (i) These expressions suggest to us, that they well knew, that whatever vicissitudes may befall the saints, yet their last end will be life and salvation; and that the prosperity of the impious is a pleasant path, which gradually leads to the gulf of everlasting death. Therefore they called the death of such the "destruction of the uncircumcised," (k) as of those from whom all hope of resurrection had been cut off. Wherefore David could not conceive a more grievous imprecation than this: "Let them be blotted out of the book of the living, and not be written with the righteous." (l)

XIX. But the following declaration of Job is remarkable beyond all others: "I know that my Redeemer liveth, and that he shall stand at the latter day upon the earth; and though after my skin, worms destroy this body, yet in my flesh shall I see God; whom I shall see for myself, and mine eyes shall behold, and not another." (m) Some, who wish to display their critical sagacity, cavil that this is not to be understood of the final resurrection, but even of the first day on which Job expected God to be more propitious to him. Though we partly concede this, we shall extort an acknowledgment from them, whether they are willing or not, that Job could never have attained to such an enlarged hope, if his thoughts had been confined to the earth. We must, therefore, be obliged to confess that he, who saw that his Redeemer would be present with him even when lying in the sepulchre, must have elevated his views to a future immortality. For to them, who think only of the present life, death is a source of extreme despair, which, however, could not annihilate his hope. "Though he

(e) Psalm xxx. 5.
(f) Isaiah liv. 7, 8.
(g) Prov. x. 7.
(h) Psalm cxvi. 15.
(i) 1 Sam. ii. 9.
(k) Ezek. xxviii. 10; xxxi. 18.
(l) Psalm lxix. 28.
(m) Job xix. 25, &c.

slay me," said he, "yet will I trust in him." (*n*) Nor let any trifler here object, that these were the expressions of a few persons, and are far from furnishing proof that such a doctrine was current among the Jews. I will immediately reply, that these few persons did not in these declarations reveal any recondite wisdom, in which only superior understandings were separately and privately instructed; but that the Holy Spirit having constituted them teachers of the people, they publicly promulgated the Divine mysteries which were to be generally received, and to be the principles of the popular religion. When we hear the public oracles of the Holy Spirit, therefore, in which he has so clearly and evidently spoken of the spiritual life in the Jewish church, it would be intolerable perverseness to apply them entirely to the carnal covenant, in which no mention is made but of the earth and earthly opulence.

XX. If we descend to the later prophets, there we may freely expatiate as quite at home. For if it was not difficult to prove our point from David, Job, and Samuel, we shall do it there with much greater facility. For this is the order and economy which God observed in dispensing the covenant of his mercy, that as the course of time accelerated the period of its full exhibition, he illustrated it from day to day with additional revelations. Therefore, in the beginning, when the first promise was given to Adam, it was like the kindling of some feeble sparks. Subsequent accessions caused a considerable enlargement of the light, which continued to increase more and more, and diffused its splendour through a wide extent, till at length, every cloud being dissipated, Christ, the Sun of Righteousness, completely illuminated the whole world. There is no reason to fear, therefore, if we want the suffrages of the prophets in support of our cause, that they will fail us. But as I perceive it would be a very extensive field, which would engross more of our attention than the nature of our design will admit, — for it would furnish matter for a large volume, — and as I also think that by what has been already said, I have prepared the way even for a reader of small penetration to proceed without any difficulties, I shall abstain from a prolixity which at present is not very necessary. I shall only caution the reader to advance with the clew which we have put into his hand; namely, that whenever the prophets mention the blessedness of the faithful, scarcely any vestiges of which are discernible in the present life, he should recur to this distinction; that in order to the better elucidation of the Divine goodness, the prophets represented it to the people in a figurative manner; but that they gave such a representation of it as

(*n*) Job xiii. 15.

would withdraw the mind from earth and time, and the elements of this world, all which must ere long perish, and would necessarily excite to a contemplation of the felicity of the future spiritual life.

XXI. We will content ourselves with one example. When the Israelites, after being carried to Babylon, perceived how very much their dispersion resembled a death, they could scarcely be convinced that the prophecy of Ezekiel concerning their restitution (*o*) was not a mere fable; for they considered it in the same light, as if he had announced, that putrid carcasses would be restored to life. The Lord, in order to show that even that difficulty would not prevent him from displaying his beneficence, gave the prophet a vision of a field full of dry bones, which he instantaneously restored to life and vigour solely by the power of his word. The vision served indeed to correct the existing incredulity; but at the same time it reminded the Jews, how far the power of the Lord extended beyond the restoration of the people, since the mere expression of his will so easily reanimated the dry and dispersed bones. Wherefore you may properly compare that passage with another of Isaiah: "Thy dead men shall live; together with my dead body shall they arise. Awake and sing, ye that dwell in dust; for thy dew is as the dew of herbs, and the earth shall cast out the dead. Come, my people, enter thou into thy chambers, and shut thy doors about thee: hide thyself as it were for a little moment, until the indignation be overpast. For, behold, the Lord cometh out of his place to punish the inhabitants of the earth for their iniquity: the earth also shall disclose her blood, and shall no more cover her slain." (*p*)

XXII. It would be absurd, however, to attempt to reduce every passage to such a canon of interpretation. For there are some places, which show without any disguise the future immortality which awaits the faithful in the kingdom of God. Such are some which we have recited, and such are many others, but particularly these two; one in Isaiah: "As the new heavens and the new earth which I will make, shall remain before me, saith the Lord, so shall your seed and your name remain. And it shall come to pass, that from one new moon to another, and from one sabbath to another, shall all flesh come to worship before me, saith the Lord. And they shall go forth, and look upon the carcasses of the men that have transgressed against me; for their worm shall not die, neither shall their fire be quenched." (*q*) And another in Daniel: "At that time shall Michael stand up, the great prince which standeth for the children of thy people; and there shall be a time of trouble

---

(*o*) Ezek. xxxvii.   (*p*) Isaiah xxvi. 19—21.   (*q*) Isaiah lxvi. 22—24.

such as never was since there was a nation even to that same time; and at that time thy people shall be delivered, every one that shall be found written in the book. And many of them that sleep in the dust of the earth shall awake, some to everlasting life, and some to shame and everlasting contempt." (r)

XXIII. Now, the two remaining points, that the fathers had Christ as the pledge of their covenant, and that they reposed in him all their confidence of the blessing, being less controvertible and more plain, I shall take no pains to prove them. We may safely conclude, therefore, what all the machinations of the devil can never subvert, that the Old Testament, or covenant which the Lord made with the Israelitish nation, was not limited to terrestrial things, but contained a promise of spiritual and eternal life; the expectation of which must have been impressed on the minds of all who truly consented to the covenant. Then let us drive far away from us this absurd and pernicious notion, either that the Lord proposed nothing else to the Jews, or that the Jews sought nothing else, but an abundance of food, carnal delights, flourishing wealth, external power, a numerous offspring, and whatever is esteemed valuable by a natural man. For under the present dispensation, Christ promises to his people no other kingdom of heaven, than where they may sit down with Abraham, Isaac, and Jacob; (s) and Peter asserted the Jews of his time to be heirs of the grace of the gospel, when he said that "they were the children of the prophets, and of the covenant which God made with their fathers." (t) And that this might not only be testified in words, the Lord also proved it by a matter of fact. For on the day in which he rose from the dead, he honoured many of the saints with a participation of his resurrection, and caused them to appear in the city; (u) thus furnishing a certain assurance that whatever he did and suffered for the acquisition of eternal salvation, belonged to the faithful of the Old Testament as much as to us. For, as Peter declares, they also were endued with the same Spirit, who is the author of our regeneration to life. (w) When we are informed that the same Spirit, which is as it were a spark of immortality in us, and is therefore called in one place "the earnest of our inheritance," (x) dwelt in a similar manner in them, how can we dare to deprive them of the inheritance of eternal life? It is therefore the more surprising, that the Sadducees formerly fell into such stupidity as to deny the resurrection, and the immortality of the soul, since they had proofs of these points from such clear testimonies of Scripture. And the folly of the whole nation of the Jews in the present age, in

(r) Dan. xii. 1, 2. (t) Acts iii. 25. (w) Acts xv. 8.
(s) Matt. viii. 11. (u) Matt. xxvii. 52. (x) Eph. i. 14.

expecting an earthly kingdom of the Messiah, would be equally extraordinary, had not the Scriptures long before predicted that they would thus be punished for their rejection of the gospel. For it was consistent with the righteous judgment of God to strike with blindness the minds of those, who, rejecting the light of heaven when presented to them, kept themselves in voluntary darkness. Therefore they read Moses, and assiduously turn over his pages, but are prevented by an interposing veil from perceiving the light which beams in his countenance; (*y*) and thus it will remain covered and concealed to them, till they are converted to Christ, from whom they now endeavour as much as they can to withdraw and divert it.

CHAPTER XI.

THE DIFFERENCE OF THE TWO TESTAMENTS.

WHAT, then, it will be said, will there be no difference left between the Old Testament and the New? and what becomes of all those passages of Scripture, where they are compared together as things that are very different? I readily admit the differences which are mentioned in the Scripture, but I maintain that they derogate nothing from the unity already established; as will be seen when we have discussed them in proper order. But the principal differences, as far as my observation or memory extends, are four in number; to which if any one choose to add a fifth, I shall not make the least objection. I assert, and engage to demonstrate, that all these are such as pertain rather to the mode of administration, than to the substance. In this view, they will not prevent the promises of the Old and New Testament from remaining the same, and the promises of both Testaments from having in Christ the same foundation. Now, the first difference is, that although it was always the will of the Lord that the minds of his people should be directed, and their hearts elevated, towards the celestial inheritance, yet, in order that they might be the better encouraged to hope for it, he anciently exhibited it for their contemplation and partial enjoyment under the figures of terrestrial blessings Now, having by the gospel more clearly and explicitly revealed the grace of the future life, he leaves the inferior mode of instruction which he used with the Israelites, and directs

(*y*) 2 Cor. iii. 14—16.

our minds to the immediate contemplation of it. Those who overlook this design of God, suppose that the ancients ascended no higher than the corporeal blessings which were promised them; they so frequently hear the land of Canaan mentioned as the eminent, and indeed the only, reward for the observers of the Divine law. They hear that God threatens the transgressors of this law with nothing more severe than being expelled from the possession of that country, and dispersed into foreign lands. They see this to be nearly the whole substance of all the blessings and of all the curses pronounced by Moses. Hence they confidently conclude, that the Jews were separated from other nations, not for their own sakes, but for ours, that the Christian Church might have an image, in whose external form they could discern examples of spiritual things. But since the Scripture frequently shows, that God himself appointed the terrestrial advantages with which he favoured them for the express purpose of leading them to the hope of celestial blessings, it argued extreme inexperience, not to say stupidity, not to consider such a dispensation. The point of controversy between us and these persons, is this: they maintain that the possession of the land of Canaan was accounted by the Israelites their supreme and ultimate blessedness, but that to us, since the revelation of Christ, it is a figure of the heavenly inheritance. We, on the contrary, contend, that in the earthly possession which they enjoyed, they contemplated, as in a mirror, the future inheritance which they believed to be prepared for them in heaven.

II. This will more fully appear from the similitude which Paul has used in his Epistle to the Galatians. (*z*) He compares the Jewish nation to a young heir, who, being yet incapable of governing himself, follows the dictates of a tutor or a governor, to whose charge he has been committed. His application of this similitude chiefly to the ceremonies, is no objection against the propriety of its application to our present purpose. The same inheritance was destined for them as for us; but they were not of a sufficient age to be capable of entering on the possession and management of it. The Church among them was the same as among us; but it was yet in a state of childhood. Therefore the Lord kept them under this tuition, that he might give them the spiritual promises, not open and unconcealed, but veiled under terrestrial figures. Therefore, when he admitted Abraham, Isaac, and Jacob, with their posterity, to the hope of immortality, he promised them the land of Canaan as their inheritance; not that their hopes might terminate in that land, but that in the prospect of it they might

(*z*) Gal. iv.

exercise and confirm themselves in the hope of that true inheritance which was not yet visible. And that they might not be deceived, a superior promise was given them, which proved that country not to be the highest blessing which God would bestow. Thus Abraham is not permitted to grow indolent after having received a promise of the land, but a greater promise elevates his mind to the Lord. For he hears him saying, "Abram, I am thy shield, and thy exceeding great reward." (*a*) Here we see that the Lord proposes himself to Abraham as his ultimate reward, that he may not seek an uncertain and transitory one in the elements of this world, but may consider that which can never fade away. God afterwards annexes a promise of the land, merely as a symbol of his benevolence, and a type of the heavenly inheritance. And that this was the opinion of the saints, is plain from their own language. Thus David rises from temporary blessings to that consummate and ultimate felicity. "My soul longeth, yea, even fainteth, for the courts of the Lord." (*b*) "God is my portion for ever." (*c*) Again: "The Lord is the portion of mine inheritance and of my cup: thou maintainest my lot." (*d*) Again: "I cried unto thee, O Lord: I said, Thou art my refuge and my portion in the land of the living." (*e*) Persons who venture to express themselves thus, certainly profess that in their hopes they rise above the world and all present blessings. Nevertheless the prophets frequently describe this blessedness of the future world under the type which the Lord had given them. In this sense we must understand the following passages: "The righteous shall inherit the land;" (*f*) "But the wicked shall be cut off from the earth;" (*g*) and various predictions of Isaiah, which foretell the future prosperity of Jerusalem, and the abundance that will be enjoyed in Zion. We see that all these things are inapplicable to the land of our pilgrimage, or to the earthly Jerusalem, but that they belong to the true country of the faithful, and to that celestial city, where "the Lord commanded the blessing, even life for evermore." (*h*)

III. This is the reason why the saints, under the Old Testament, are represented as holding this mortal life with its blessings in higher estimation than becomes us now. For although they well knew that they ought not to rest in it as the end of their course, yet when they recollected what characters of his grace the Lord had impressed on it, in order to instruct them in a manner suitable to their tender state, they felt a greater degree of pleasure in it than if they had considered it merely in itself. But as the Lord, in declaring his benevolence

(*a*) Gen. xv. 1.   (*b*) Psalm lxxxiv. 2.   (*c*) Psalm lxxiii. 26.
(*d*) Psalm xvi. 5.   (*e*) Psalm cxlii. 5.
(*f*) Psalm xxxvii. 29.   (*g*) Prov. ii. 22.   (*h*) Psalm cxxxiii. 3.

to the faithful by present blessings, gave them, under these types and symbols, a figurative exhibition of spiritual felicity, so, on the other hand, in corporal punishments he exemplified his judgment against the reprobate. Therefore, as the favours of God were more conspicuous in earthly things, so also were his punishments. Injudicious persons, not considering this analogy and harmony (so to speak) between the punishments and rewards, wonder at so great a variety in God, that in ancient times he was ready to avenge all the transgressions of men by the immediate infliction of severe and dreadful punishments, but now, as if he had laid aside his ancient wrath, punishes with far less severity and frequency; and on this account they almost adopt the notion of the Manichæans, that the God of the Old Testament is a different being from the God of the New. But we shall easily get rid of such difficulties, if we direct our attention to that dispensation of God, which I have observed; namely, that during that period, in which he gave the Israelites his covenant involved in some degree of obscurity, he intended to signify and prefigure the grace of future and eternal felicity by terrestrial blessings, and the grievousness of spiritual death by corporal punishments.

IV. Another difference between the Old Testament and the New consists in figures, because the former, in the absence of the truth, displayed merely an image and shadow instead of the body; but the latter exhibits the present truth and the substantial body. (*i*) And this is generally mentioned wherever the New Testament is opposed to the Old, but is treated more at large in the Epistle to the Hebrews than in any other place. (*k*) The apostle is there disputing against those who supposed that the observance of the Mosaic law could not be abolished, without being followed by the total ruin of religion. To refute this error, he adduces the prediction of the psalmist concerning the priesthood of Christ; (*l*) for since he has an eternal priesthood committed to him, we may argue the certain abolition of that priesthood, in which new priests daily succeeded each other. (*m*) But he proves the superiority of the appointment of this new Priest, because it is confirmed with an oath. (*n*) He afterwards adds that this transfer of the priesthood implies also a change of the covenant. (*o*) And he proves that this change was necessary, because such was the imbecility of the law, that it could bring nothing to perfection. (*p*) Then he proceeds to state the nature of this imbecility; namely, that the law prescribed external righteousnesses, consisting in carnal ordinances, which could not make the ob-

---

(*i*) Col. ii. 17. (*k*) Heb. x. 1, &c. (*l*) Heb. vii. 17. Psalm cx. 4.
(*m*) Heb. vii. 23, 24. (*n*) Heb. vii. 20, 21. (*o*) Heb. vii. 12. (*p*) Heb. vii. 19.

servers of them "perfect as pertaining to the conscience," that by animal victims it could neither expiate sins nor procure true holiness. (q) He concludes, therefore, that it contained "a shadow of good things to come, but not the very image of the things;" (r) and that consequently it had no other office, but to serve as an introduction to "a better hope," (s) which is exhibited in the gospel. Here we have to inquire in what respect the Legal covenant is compared with the Evangelical, the ministry of Christ with the ministry of Moses. For if the comparison related to the substance of the promises, there would be a great discordance between the two testaments; but as the state of the question leads us to a different point, we must attend to the scope of the apostle, in order to discover the truth. Let us, then, bring forward the covenant, which God has once made, which is eternal, and never to be abolished. The accomplishment, whence it derives its establishment and ratification, is Christ. While such a confirmation was waited for, the Lord by Moses prescribed ceremonies, to serve as solemn symbols of the confirmation. It came to be a subject of contention, whether the ceremonies ordained in the law ought to cease and give place to Christ. Now, though these ceremonies were only accidents or concomitants of the covenant, yet being the instruments of its administration, they bear the name of the covenant; as it is common to give to other sacraments the names of the things they represent. In a word, therefore, what is here called the Old Testament is a solemn method of confirming the covenant, consisting of ceremonies and sacrifices. Since it contains nothing substantial, unless we proceed further, the apostle contends that it ought to be repealed and abrogated, in order to make way for Christ, the Surety and Mediator of a better testament, (t) by whom eternal sanctification has been at once procured for the elect, and those transgressions obliterated, which remained under the law. Or, if you prefer it, take the following statement of it; that the Old Testament of the Lord was that which was delivered to the Jews, involved in a shadowy and inefficacious observance of ceremonies, and that it was therefore temporary, because it remained as it were in suspense, till it was supported by a firm and substantial confirmation; but that it was made new and eternal, when it was consecrated and established by the blood of Christ. Whence Christ calls the cup which he gives to his disciples in the supper, "the cup of the New Testament in his blood;" (u) to signify that when the testament of God is sealed with his blood, the truth of it is then accomplished, and thus it is made new and eternal.

(q) Heb. ix. 13, 14; x. 4.   (r) Heb. x. 1.   (s) Heb. vii. 19.
(t) Heb. vii. 22.   (u) Matt. xxvi 23.

V. Hence it appears in what sense the apostle said, that the Jews were conducted to Christ by the tuition of the law, before he was manifested in the flesh. (*w*) He confesses also that they were children and heirs of God, but such as, on account of their age, required to be kept under the care of a tutor. (*x*) For it was reasonable that before the Sun of Righteousness was risen, there should be neither such a full blaze of revelation, nor such great clearness of understanding. Therefore the Lord dispensed the light of his word to them in such a manner, that they had yet only a distant and obscure prospect of it. Paul describes this slenderness of understanding as a state of childhood, which it was the Lord's will to exercise in the elements of this world and in external observances, as rules of puerile discipline, till the manifestation of Christ, by whom the knowledge of the faithful was to grow to maturity. Christ himself alluded to this distinction, when he said, "The law and the prophets were until John: since that time the kingdom of God is preached." (*y*) What discoveries did Moses and the prophets make to their contemporaries? They afforded them some taste of that wisdom which was in after times to be clearly manifested, and gave them a distant prospect of its future splendour. But when Christ could be plainly pointed out, the kingdom of God was revealed. For in him are discovered "all the treasures of wisdom and knowledge," (*z*) by which we penetrate almost into the furthest recesses of heaven.

VI. Nor is it any objection to our argument, that scarcely a person can be found in the Christian Church, who is to be compared with Abraham in the excellency of his faith; or that the prophets were distinguished by such energy of the Spirit as, even at this day, is sufficient to illuminate the whole world. For our present inquiry is, not what grace the Lord has conferred on a few, but what is the ordinary method which he has pursued in the instruction of his people; such as is found even among the prophets themselves, who were endued with peculiar knowledge above others. For their preaching is obscure, as relating to things very distant, and is comprehended in types. Besides, notwithstanding their wonderful eminence in knowledge, yet because they were under a necessity of submitting to the same tuition as the rest of the people, they are considered as sustaining the character of children as well as others. Finally, none of them possessed knowledge so clear as not to partake more or less of the obscurity of the age. Whence this observation of Christ: "Many prophets and kings have desired to see those things which ye see, and have

(*w*) Gal. iii. 24.   (*x*) Gal. iv. 1, &c.   (*y*) Luke xvi. 16.   (*z*) Col. ii. 3.

not seen them; and to hear those things which ye hear, and have not heard them." (a) "Blessed are your eyes, for they see; and your ears, for they hear." (b) And, indeed, it is reasonable that the presence of Christ should be distinguished by the prerogative of introducing a clearer revelation of the mysteries of heaven. To the same purpose also is the passage, which we have before cited from the First Epistle of Peter, that it was revealed to them, that the principal advantage of their labours would be experienced in our times. (c)

VII. I come now to the third difference, which is taken from Jeremiah, whose words are these: "Behold, the days come, saith the Lord, that I will make a new covenant with the house of Israel, and with the house of Judah; not according to the covenant that I made with their fathers in the day that I took them by the hand to bring them out of the land of Egypt; which my covenant they brake, although I was a husband to them, saith the Lord; but this shall be the covenant that I will make with the house of Israel. After those days, saith the Lord, I will put my law in their inward parts, and write it in their hearts; and will be their God, and they shall be my people. And they shall teach no more every man his neighbour, and every man his brother, saying, Know the Lord; for they shall all know me, from the least of them unto the greatest of them, saith the Lord; for I will forgive their iniquity, and I will remember their sin no more." (d) From this passage the apostle took occasion to institute the following comparison between the law and the gospel: he calls the former a literal, the latter a spiritual doctrine; the former, he says, was engraven on tables of stone, but the latter is inscribed on the heart; (e) the former was the preaching of death, but the latter of life; the former was the ministration of condemnation, but the latter of righteousness; the former is abolished, but the latter remains. As the design of the apostle was to express the sense of the prophet, it will be sufficient for us to consider the language of one of them, in order to discover the meaning of both. There is, however, some difference between them. For the apostle speaks of the law in less honourable terms than the prophet does; and that not simply with respect to the law itself, but, because there were some disturbers, who were full of improper zeal for the law, and by their perverse attachment to the ceremonies obscured the glory of the gospel, he disputes concerning the nature of the law with reference to their error and foolish affection for it. This peculiarity in Paul, therefore, will be worthy of our obser-

(a) Luke x. 24.   (b) Matt. xiii. 16.   (c) 1 Peter i. 12.
(d) Jer. xxxi. 31, &c.   (e) 2 Cor. iii. 6, &c.

vation. Both of them, as they contrast the Old and New Testaments with each other, consider nothing in the law, but what properly belongs to it. For example, the law contains frequent promises of mercy; but as they are borrowed from another dispensation, they are not considered as part of the law, when the mere nature of the law is the subject of discussion. All that they attribute to it is, that it enjoins what is right, and prohibits crimes; that it proclaims a reward for the followers of righteousness, and denounces punishments against transgressors; but that it neither changes nor corrects the depravity of heart which is natural to all men.

VIII. Now, let us explain the comparison of the apostle in all its branches. In the first place, the Old Testament is literal, because it was promulgated without the efficacy of the Spirit; the New is spiritual, because the Lord has engraven it in a spiritual manner on the hearts of men. The second contrast, therefore, serves as an elucidation of the first. The Old Testament is the revelation of death, because it can only involve all mankind in a curse; the New is the instrument of life, because it delivers us from the curse, and restores us to favour with God. The former is the ministry of condemnation, because it convicts all the children of Adam of unrighteousness; the latter is the ministry of righteousness, because it reveals the mercy of God, by which we are made righteous. The last contrast must be referred to the legal ceremonies. The law having an image of things that were at a distance, it was necessary that in time it should be abolished and disappear. The gospel, exhibiting the body itself, retains a firm and perpetual stability. Jeremiah calls even the moral law a weak and frail covenant, but for another reason; namely, because it was soon broken by the sudden defection of an ungrateful people. But as such a violation arises from the fault of the people, it cannot be properly attributed to the Testament. The ceremonies, however, which at the advent of Christ were abolished by their own weakness, contained in themselves the cause of their abrogation. Now, this difference between the "letter" and the "spirit" is not to be understood as if the Lord had given his law to the Jews without any beneficial result, without one of them being converted to him; but it is used in a way of comparison, to display the plenitude of grace with which the same Legislator, assuming as it were a new character, has honoured the preaching of the gospel. For if we survey the multitude of those, from among all nations, whom, by the influence of his Spirit in the preaching of the gospel, the Lord has regenerated and gathered into communion with his Church, we shall say that those of the ancient Israelites, who cordially and sincerely embraced the covenant of the Lord, were extremely few; though, if estimated by themselves without any comparison, they amounted to a considerable number.

IX. The fourth difference arises out of the third. For the Scripture calls the Old Testament a covenant of bondage, because it produces fear in the mind; but the New it describes as a covenant of liberty, because it leads the heart to confidence and security. Thus Paul, in the eighth chapter of his Epistle to the Romans, says, "Ye have not received the spirit of bondage again to fear; but ye have received the Spirit of adoption, whereby we cry, Abba, Father." (*f*) To the same purpose is that passage in the Epistle to the Hebrews, that the faithful now "are not come unto the mount that might be touched, and that burned with fire, nor unto blackness, and darkness, and tempest," where nothing can be either heard or seen, but what must strike terror into the mind; so that even Moses himself is exceedingly afraid at the sound of the terrible voice, which they all pray that they may hear no more; but that now the faithful "are come unto mount Sion, and unto the city of the living God, the heavenly Jerusalem," (*g*) &c. What Paul briefly touches in the passage which we have adduced from the Epistle to the Romans, he explains more at large in his Epistle to the Galatians, when he allegorizes the two sons of Abraham in the following manner — that Agar, the bond-woman, is a type of mount Sinai, where the people of Israel received the law; that Sarah, the free-woman, is a figure of the celestial Jerusalem, whence proceeds the gospel. That as the son of Agar is born in bondage, and can never attain to the inheritance, and the son of Sarah is born free, and has a right to the inheritance, (*h*) so by the law we were devoted to slavery, but by the gospel alone are regenerated to liberty. Now, the whole may be summed up thus — that the Old Testament filled men's consciences with fear and trembling; but that by the benefit of the New Testament, they are delivered, and enabled to rejoice. The former kept their consciences under a yoke of severe bondage; but by the liberality of the latter they are emancipated and admitted to liberty. If any one object to us the case of the holy fathers of the Israelitish people, that as they were clearly possessed of the same spirit of faith as we are, they must consequently have been partakers of the same liberty and joy, we reply, that neither of these originated from the law; but that, when they felt themselves, by means of the law, oppressed with their servile condition, and wearied with disquietude of conscience, they fled for refuge to the gospel; and that therefore it was a peculiar advantage

(*f*) Rom. viii. 15.   (*g*) Heb. xii. 18, &c.   (*h*) Gal. iv. 22, &c.

of the New Testament, that they enjoyed an exception from the common law of the Old Testament, and were exempted from those evils. Besides, we shall deny that they were favoured with the spirit of liberty and security, to such a degree as not to experience from the law some measure both of fear and of servitude. For notwithstanding their enjoyment of that privilege, which they obtained by the grace of the gospel, yet they were subject to the same observances and burdens as the people in general. As they were obliged, therefore, to a diligent observance of these ceremonies, which were emblems of the state of pupilage similar to bondage, and the hand-writing, by which they confessed themselves guilty of sin, did not release them from the obligation, they may justly be said, in comparison with us, to have been under a testament of bondage and fear, when we consider the common mode of procedure which the Lord then pursued with the Israelitish nation.

X. The three last comparisons which we have mentioned are between the law and the gospel. In these, therefore, "the Old Testament" denotes *the law;* and "the New Testament," *the gospel.* The first comparison extends further, for it comprehends also the promises, which were given before the law. When Augustine denied that they ought to be considered as part of the Old Testament, he gave a very proper opinion, and intended the same that we now teach; for he had in view those passages of Jeremiah and Paul, in which the Old Testament is distinguished from the word of grace and mercy. He very judiciously adds also in the same place, that the children of the promise, from the beginning of the world, who have been regenerated by God, and, under the influence of faith working by love, have obeyed his commands, belong to the New Testament; and *that,* in hope, not of carnal, terrestrial, and temporal things, but of spiritual, celestial, and eternal blessings; especially believing in the Mediator, through whom they doubted not that the Spirit was dispensed to them to enable them to do their duty, and that whenever they sinned they were pardoned. For this is the very same thing which I meant to assert: That all the saints, whom, from the beginning of the world, the Scripture mentions as having been peculiarly chosen by God, have been partakers of the same blessing with us to eternal salvation. Between our distinction and that of Augustine there is this difference — that ours (according to this declaration of Christ, "the law and the prophets were until John; since that time the kingdom of God is preached;")(*i*) distinguishes between the clearness of the gospel and the more obscure dispensation of the word which preceded it; whilst the other merely

(*i*) Luke xvi. 16.

discriminates the weakness of the law from the stability of the gospel. Here it must also be remarked concerning the holy fathers, that though they lived under the Old Testament, they did not rest satisfied with it, but always aspired after the New, and thus enjoyed a certain participation of it. For all those who contented themselves with present shadows, and did not extend their views to Christ, are condemned by the apostle as blind and under the curse. For, to say nothing on other points, what greater ignorance can be imagined than to hope for an expiation of sin by the sacrifice of an animal? than to seek for the purification of the soul by an external ablution with water? than to wish to appease God with frigid ceremonies, as though they afforded him great pleasure? For all these absurdities are chargeable on those who adhere to the observances of the law, without any reference to Christ.

XI. The fifth difference, which we may add, consists in this — that till the advent of Christ, the Lord selected one nation, to which he would limit the covenant of his grace. Moses says, "When the Most High divided to the nations their inheritance, when he separated the sons of Adam, — the Lord's portion is his people; Jacob is the lot of his inheritance." (*k*) In another place he thus addresses the people: "Behold, the heaven, and the heaven of heavens is the Lord's thy God, the earth also, with all that therein is. Only the Lord had a delight in thy fathers to love them, and he chose their seed after them, even you above all people." (*l*) Therefore he favoured that people with the exclusive knowledge of his name, as though they alone of all mankind belonged to him; he deposited his covenant as it were in their bosom; to them he manifested the presence of his power; he honoured them with every privilege. But to omit the rest of his benefits, the only one that relates to our present argument is, that he united them to himself by the communication of his word, in order that he might be denominated and esteemed their God. In the mean time he suffered other nations, as though they had no business or intercourse with him, to walk in vanity; (*m*) nor did he employ means to prevent their destruction by sending them the only remedy — the preaching of his word. The Israelitish nation, therefore, were then as darling sons; others were strangers: they were known to him, and received under his faithful protection: others were left to their own darkness. they were sanctified by God; others were profane: they were honoured with the Divine presence; others were excluded from approaching it. But when the fulness of the time was come, (*n*) appointed for the restoration of all things, (*o*) and

(*k*) Deut. xxxii. 8, 9.   (*l*) Deut. x. 14.   (*m*) Acts xiv. 16.
(*n*) Gal. iv. 4.   (*o*) Matt. xvii. 11.

the Reconciler of God and men was manifested, (*p*) the barrier was demolished, which had so long confined the Divine mercy within the limits of the Jewish church, and peace was announced to them who were at a distance, and to them who were near, that being both reconciled to God, they might coalesce into one people. Wherefore "there is neither Greek nor Jew, circumcision nor uncircumcision, but Christ is all and in all;" (*q*) "to whom the heathen are given for his inheritance, and the uttermost parts of the earth for his possession;" (*r*) that he may have a universal "dominion from sea to sea, and from the river unto the ends of the earth." (*s*)

XII. The vocation of the Gentiles, therefore, is an eminent illustration of the superior excellence of the New Testament above the Old. It had, indeed, before been most explicitly announced in numerous predictions of the prophets; but so as that the completion of it was deferred to the kingdom of the Messiah. And even Christ himself made no advances towards it at the first commencement of his preaching, but deferred it till he should have completed all the parts of our redemption, finished the time of his humiliation, and received from the Father "a name which is above every name, before which every knee shall bow." (*t*) Wherefore, when this season was not yet arrived, he said to a Canaanitish woman, "I am not sent but unto the lost sheep of the house of Israel:" (*u*) nor did he permit the apostles, in his first mission of them, to exceed these limits. "Go not," says he, "into the way of the Gentiles, and into any city of the Samaritans enter ye not; but go rather to the lost sheep of the house of Israel." (*w*) And though this calling of the Gentiles was announced by so many testimonies, yet when the apostles were about to enter upon it, it appeared to them so novel and strange, that they dreaded it, as if it had been a prodigy: indeed it was with trepidation and reluctance that they at length engaged in it. Nor is this surprising; for it seemed not at all reasonable, that the Lord, who for so many ages had separated the Israelites from the rest of the nations, should, as it were, suddenly change his design, and annihilate this distinction. It had indeed been predicted in the prophecies; but they could not pay such great attention to the prophecies, as to be wholly unmoved with the novelty of the circumstance, which forced itself on their observation. Nor were the specimens, which the Lord had formerly given, of the future vocation of the Gentiles, sufficient to influence them. For besides his having called only very few of them, he had even incorporated them into the family of Abra-

(*p*) Eph. ii. 14. (*q*) Col. iii. 11. (*r*) Psalm ii. 8. (*s*) Psalm lxxii. 8.
(*t*) Phil. ii. 9, 10. (*u*) Matt. xv. 24. (*w*) Matt. x. 5, 6.

ham, that they might be added to his people; but by that public vocation, the Gentiles were not only raised to an equality with the Jews, but appeared to succeed to their places as though they had been dead. Besides, of all the strangers whom God had before incorporated into the Church, none were ever placed on an equality with the Jews. Therefore it is not without reason that Paul so celebrates this "mystery which was hidden from ages and from generations," (*x*) and which he represents as an object of admiration even to angels. (*y*)

XIII. In these four or five points, I think I have given a correct and faithful statement of the whole of the difference between the Old and the New Testament, as far as is sufficient for a simple system of doctrine. But because some persons represent this variety in the government of the Church, these different modes of instruction, and such a considerable alteration of rites and ceremonies, as a great absurdity, we must reply to them, before we proceed to other subjects. And this may be done in a brief manner, since the objections are not so strong as to require a laborious refutation. It is not reasonable, they say, that God, who is perpetually consistent with himself, should undergo so great a change as afterwards to disallow what he had once enjoined and commanded. I reply, that God ought not therefore to be deemed mutable, because he has accommodated different forms to different ages, as he knew would be suitable for each. If the husbandman prescribes different employments to his family in the winter, from those which he allots them in the summer, we must not therefore accuse him of inconstancy, or impute to him a deviation from the proper rules of agriculture, which are connected with the perpetual course of nature. Thus, also, if a father instructs, governs, and manages his children one way in infancy, another in childhood, and another in youth, we must not therefore charge him with being inconstant, or forsaking his own designs. Why, then, do we stigmatize God with the character of inconstancy, because he has made an apt and suitable distinction between different times? The last similitude ought fully to satisfy us. Paul compares the Jews to children, and Christians to youths. (*z*) What impropriety is there in this part of the government of God, that he detained them in the rudiments which were suitable to them on account of their age, but has placed us under a stronger and more manly discipline? It is a proof, therefore, of the constancy of God, that he has delivered the same doctrine in all ages, and perseveres in requiring the same worship of his name which he commanded from the

(*x*) Col. i. 26.   (*y*) Eph. iii. 10.   (*z*) Gal. iv. 1—3.

beginning. By changing the external form and mode, he has discovered no mutability in himself, but has so far accommodated himself to the capacity of men, which is various and mutable.

XIV. But they inquire whence this diversity proceeded, except from the will of God. Could he not, as well from the beginning as since the advent of Christ, give a revelation of eternal life in clear language without any figures, instruct his people by a few plain sacraments, bestow his Holy Spirit, and diffuse his grace through all the world? This is just the same as if they were to quarrel with God, because he created the world at so late a period, whereas he might have done it before; or because he has appointed the alternate vicissitudes of summer and winter, of day and night. But let us not doubt what ought to be believed by all pious men, that whatever is done by God is done wisely and righteously; although we frequently know nothing of the causes which render such transactions necessary. For it would be arrogating too much to ourselves, not to permit God to keep the reasons of his decrees concealed from us. But it is surprising, say they, that he now rejects and abominates the sacrifices of cattle, and all the apparatus of the Levitical priesthood, with which he used to be delighted; as though truly these external and transitory things could afford pleasure to God, or affect him in any way whatever. It has already been observed, that he did none of these things on his own account, but appointed them all for the salvation of men. If a physician cure a young man of any disease by a very excellent method, and afterwards adopt a different mode of cure with the same person when advanced in years, shall we therefore say that he rejects the method of cure which he before approved? We will rather say, that he perseveres in the same system, and considers the difference of age. Thus it was necessary, before the appearance of Christ, that he should be prefigured, and his future advent announced by one kind of emblems; since he has been manifested, it is right that he should be represented by others. But with respect to the Divine vocation, now more widely extended among all nations since the advent of Christ than it was before, and with regard to the more copious effusion of the graces of the Spirit, who can deny, that it is reasonable and just for God to retain under his own power and will the free dispensation of his favours; that he may illuminate what nations he pleases; that wherever he pleases he may introduce the preaching of his word; that he may give to his instruction whatever kind and degree of profit and success he pleases; that wherever he pleases, in any age, he may punish the ingratitude of the world by depriving them of the knowledge of his name, and when he pleases restore it on account of his mercy? We see, therefore, the absurdity of the cavils with which impious men disturb the minds of the simple on this subject, to call in question either the righteousness of God or the truth of the Scripture.

CHAPTER XII.

THE NECESSITY OF CHRIST BECOMING MAN IN ORDER TO FULFIL THE OFFICE OF MEDIATOR.

It was of great importance to our interests, that he, who was to be our Mediator, should be both true God and true man. If an inquiry be made concerning the necessity of this, it was not indeed a simple, or, as we commonly say, an absolute necessity, but such as arose from the heavenly decree, on which the salvation of men depended. But our most merciful Father has appointed that which was best for us. For since our iniquities, like a cloud intervening between us and him, had entirely alienated us from the kingdom of heaven, no one that could not approach to God could be a mediator for the restoration of peace. But who could have approached to him? Could any one of the children of Adam? They, with their parent, all dreaded the Divine presence. Could any one of the angels? They also stood in need of a head, by a connection with whom they might be confirmed in a perfect and unvarying adherence to their God. What, then, could be done? Our situation was truly deplorable, unless the Divine majesty itself would descend to us; for we could not ascend to it. Thus it was necessary that the Son of God should become Immanuel, that is, God with us; and this in order that there might be a mutual union and coalition between his Divinity and the nature of man; for otherwise the proximity could not be sufficiently near, nor could the affinity be sufficiently strong, to authorize us to hope that God would dwell with us. So great was the discordance between our pollution and the perfect purity of God. Although man had remained immaculately innocent, yet his condition would have been too mean for him to approach to God without a Mediator. What, then, can he do, after having been plunged by his fatal fall into death and hell, defiled with so many blemishes, putrefying in his own corruption, and, in a word, overwhelmed with every curse? It is not without reason, therefore, that Paul, when about to exhibit Christ in the character of a Mediator, expressly speaks of him as a man. "There is one Mediator," he says, "between God and man, the man Christ Jesus." (a) He might have called him God, or might indeed have omitted the appellation of man, as well as that of God; but because the Spirit, who spake by him, knew our infirmity, he has provided a very suitable remedy against it, by placing the Son of God familiarly among us, as though he were one of us. Therefore, that no one may distress himself where he is to seek the Mediator, or in what way he may approach him, the apostle, by denominating him a man, apprizes us that he is near, and even close to us, since he is our own flesh. He certainly intends the same as is stated in another place more at large — "that we have not a high priest which cannot be touched with the feeling of our infirmities, but was in all points tempted like as we are, yet without sin." (b)

II. This will still more fully appear, if we consider, that it was no mean part which the Mediator had to perform; namely, to restore us to the Divine favour, so as, of children of men, to make us children of God; of heirs of hell, to make us heirs of the kingdom of heaven. Who could accomplish this, unless the Son of God should become also the Son of man, and thus receive to himself what belongs to us, and transfer to us that which is his, and make that which is his by nature ours by grace? Depending, therefore, on this pledge, we have confidence that we are the children from God, because he, who is the Son of God by nature, has provided himself a body from our body, flesh from our flesh, bones from our bones, (c) that he might be the same with us: he refused not to assume that which was peculiar to us, that we also might obtain that which he had peculiar to him; and that so in common with us he might be both the Son of God and the Son of man. Hence arises that holy fraternity, which he mentions with his own mouth in the following words: "I ascend unto my Father, and your Father; and to my God, and your God." (d) On this account we have a certainty of the inheritance of the kingdom of heaven, because the only Son of God, to whom it exclusively belonged, has adopted us as his brethren; and if we are his brethren, we are consequently co-heirs to the inheritance. (e) Moreover it was highly necessary also for this reason, that he who was to be our Redeemer should be truly both God and man. It was his office to swallow up death; who could do this, but he who was life itself? It was his to overcome sin; who could accomplish this, but righteousness itself? It was his to put to flight the powers of the world and of the air; who could do this, but a power superior both to

(a) 1 Tim. ii. 5. (b) Heb. iv. 15. (c) Eph. v. 30.
(d) John xx. 17. (e) Rom. viii. 17.

the world and to the air? Now, who possesses life or righteousness, or the empire and power of heaven, but God alone? Therefore the most merciful God, when he determined on our redemption, became himself our Redeemer in the person of his only begotten Son!

III. Another branch of our reconciliation with God was this — that man, who had ruined himself by his own disobedience, should remedy his condition by obedience, should satisfy the justice of God, and suffer the punishment of his sin. Our Lord then made his appearance as a real man; he put on the character of Adam, and assumed his name, to act as his substitute in his obedience to the Father, to lay down our flesh as the price of satisfaction to the justice of God; and to suffer the punishment which we had deserved, in the same nature in which the offence had been committed. As it would have been impossible, therefore, for one who was only God to suffer death, or for one who was a mere man to overcome it, he associated the human nature with the Divine, that he might submit the weakness of the former to death, as an atonement for sins; and that with the power of the latter he might contend with death, and obtain a victory on our behalf. Those who despoil Christ, therefore, either of his Divinity or his humanity, either diminish his majesty and glory, or obscure his goodness. Nor are they, on the other hand, less injurious to men, whose faith they weaken and subvert; since it cannot stand any longer than it rests upon this foundation. Moreover, the Redeemer to be expected was that Son of Abraham and David, whom God had promised in the law and the prophets. Hence the minds of the faithful derive another advantage, because from the circumstance of his ancestry being traced to David and to Abraham, they have an additional assurance that this is the Christ, who was celebrated in so many prophecies. But we should particularly remember, what I have just stated — that our common nature is a pledge of our fellowship with the Son of God; that, clothed in our flesh, he vanquished sin and death, in order that the victory and triumph might be ours; that the flesh which he received from us he offered up as a sacrifice, in order to expiate and obliterate our guilt, and appease the just wrath of the Father.

IV. The persons who consider these things, with the diligent attention which they deserve, will easily disregard vague speculations which attract minds that are inconstant and fond of novelty. Such is the notion, that Christ would have become man, even though the human race had needed no redemption. I grant, indeed, that at the original creation, and in the state of integrity, he was exalted as head over angels and men; for which reason Paul calls him " the first-born of every creature;" (*f*) but since the whole Scriptures proclaim, that he was clothed in flesh in order to become a Redeemer, it argues excessive temerity to imagine another cause or another end for it. The end for which Christ was promised from the beginning, is sufficiently known; it was to restore a fallen world, and to succour ruined men. Therefore under the law his image was exhibited in sacrifices, to inspire the faithful with a hope that God would be propitious to them, after he should be reconciled by the expiation of their sins. And as, in all ages, even before the promulgation of the law, the Mediator was never promised without blood, we conclude that he was destined by the eternal decree of God to purify the pollution of men; because the effusion of blood is an emblem of expiation. The prophets proclaimed and foretold him, as the future reconciler of God and men. As a sufficient specimen of all, we refer to that very celebrated testimony of Isaiah, where he predicts, that he should be smitten of God for the transgressions of the people, that the chastisement of their peace might be upon him; and that he should be a priest to offer up himself as a victim; that by his stripes others should be healed; and that because all men had gone astray, and been dispersed like sheep, it had pleased the Lord to afflict him and to lay on him the iniquities of all. (*g*) As we are informed that Christ is particularly appointed by God for the relief of miserable sinners, all who pass these bounds are guilty of indulging a foolish curiosity. When he himself appeared in the world, he declared the design of his advent to be, to appease God and restore us from death to life. The apostles testified the same. Thus John, before he informs us that the Word was made flesh, mentions the defection of man. (*h*) But our principal attention is due to Christ himself speaking of his own office. He says, "God so loved the world, that he gave his only begotten Son, that whosoever believeth in him should not perish, but have everlasting life." (*i*) Again: "The hour is coming, and now is, when the dead shall hear the voice of the Son of God; and they that hear shall live." (*k*) " I am the resurrection and the life; he that believeth in me, though he were dead, yet shall he live." (*l*) Again: "The Son of man is come to save that which was lost." (*m*) Again: "They that be whole need not a physician." (*n*) There would be no end, if I meant to quote all the passages. The apostles with one consent call us back to this principle; for certainly, if he had not come to reconcile God, the honour of his priesthood would have been lost, for a priest is appointed as a Mediator to intercede between God and

---

(*f*) Col. i. 15.   (*g*) Isaiah liii. 4, &c.   (*h*) John i. 9, &c.
              (*i*) John iii. 16.   (*k*) John v. 25.
  (*l*) John xi. 25.   (*m*) Matt. xviii. 11.   (*n*) Matt. ix. 12.

men: (o) he could not have been our righteousness, because he was made a sacrifice for us, that God might not impute sins to us. (p) Finally, he would have been despoiled of all the noble characters under which he is celebrated in the Scripture. This assertion of Paul would have no foundation: "What the law could not do, God, sending his own Son in the likeness of sinful flesh, and for sin, condemned sin in the flesh." (q) Nor would there be any truth in what he teaches in another place, that "the kindness and love of God our Saviour towards man appeared" (r) in the gift of Christ as a Redeemer. To conclude, the Scripture no where assigns any other end, for which the Son of God should choose to become incarnate, and should also receive this command from the Father, than that he might be made a sacrifice to appease the Father on our account. "Thus it is written, and thus it behoved Christ to suffer; and that repentance should be preached in his name." (s) "Therefore doth my Father love me, because I lay down my life. This commandment have I received of my Father." (t) "As Moses lifted up the serpent in the wilderness, even so must the Son of man be lifted up." (u) Again: "Father, save me from this hour; but for this cause came I unto this hour." (w) "Father, glorify thy Son." (x) Where he clearly assigns, as the end of his assumption of human nature, that it was to be an expiatory sacrifice for the abolition of sins. For the same reason, Zacharias pronounces that he is come, according to the promise given to the fathers, "to give light to them that sit in the shadow of death." (y) Let us remember that all these things are spoken of the Son of God, "in whom," according to the testimony of Paul, "are hidden all the treasures of wisdom and knowledge," (z) and besides whom he glories in knowing nothing. (a)

V. If any one object, that it is not evinced by any of these things, that the same Christ, who has redeemed men from condemnation, could not have testified his love to them by assuming their nature, if they had remained in a state of integrity and safety,—we briefly reply, that since the Spirit declares these two things, Christ's becoming our Redeemer, and his participation of the same nature, to have been connected by the eternal decree of God, it is not right to make any further inquiry. For he who feels an eager desire to know something more, not being content with the immutable appointment of God, shows himself also not to be contented with this Christ, who has been given to us as the price of our redemption.

(o) Heb. v. 1.
(p) 2 Cor. v. 19.
(q) Rom. viii. 3.
(r) Titus iii. 4.
(s) Luke xxiv. 46, 47.
(t) John x. 17, 18.
(u) John iii. 14.
(w) John xii. 27.
(x) John xvii. 1.
(y) Luke i. 72, 79.
(z) Col. ii. 3.
(a) 1 Cor. ii. 2.

Paul not only tells us the end of his mission, but ascending to the sublime mystery of predestination, very properly represses all the licentiousness and prurience of the human mind, by declaring, that "the Father hath chosen us in Christ before the foundation of the world, and predestinated us to the adoption of children according to the good pleasure of his will, and made us accepted in his beloved Son, in whom we have redemption through his blood." (b) Here the fall of Adam is certainly not presupposed, as of anterior date; but we have a discovery of what was decreed by God before all ages, when he determined to remedy the misery of mankind. If any adversary object again, that this design of God depended on the fall of man, which he foresaw, it is abundantly sufficient for me, that every man is proceeding with impious presumption to imagine to himself a new Christ, whoever he be that permits himself to inquire, or wishes to know, concerning Christ, any more than God has predestinated in his secret decree. And justly does Paul, after having been thus treating of the peculiar office of Christ, implore, on behalf of the Ephesians, the spirit of understanding, "that they may be able to comprehend what is the breadth, and length, and depth, and height; and to know the love of Christ, which passeth knowledge;" (c) as though he would labour to surround our minds with barriers, that wherever mention is made of Christ, they may not decline in the smallest degree from the grace of reconciliation. Wherefore, since "this is" testified by Paul to be "a faithful saying, that Christ Jesus came into the world to save sinners," (d) I gladly acquiesce in it. And since the same apostle in another place informs us, that "the grace, which is now made manifest by the gospel, was given us in Christ Jesus before the world began," (e) I conclude that I ought to persevere in the same doctrine with constancy to the end. This modesty is unreasonably censured by Osiander, who in the present age has unhappily agitated this question, which a few persons had slightly touched before. He alleges a charge of presumption against those who deny that the Son of God would have appeared in the flesh, if Adam had never fallen, because this tenet is contradicted by no testimony of Scripture; as if Paul laid no restraint on such perverse curiosity, when, after having spoken of the accomplishment of our redemption by Christ, he immediately adds this injunction: "Avoid foolish questions." (f) The frenzy of some, that have been desirous of appearing prodigiously acute, has proceeded to such a length as to question whether the Son of God could assume the nature of an ass.

(b) Eph. i. 4, &c.   (c) Eph. iii. 18, 19.   (d) 1 Tim. i. 15.
(e) 2 Tim. i. 9.   (f) Titus iii. 9.

This monstrous supposition, which all pious persons justly abhor and detest, Osiander excuses under this pretext, that it is nowhere in Scripture expressly condemned; as if, when Paul esteems nothing valuable or worthy of being known but Christ crucified, he would admit an ass to be the author of salvation! Therefore he who in another place declares that Christ was appointed by the eternal decree of the Father as "the head over all," (*g*) would never acknowledge any other who had not been appointed to the office of a Redeemer.

VI. But the principle which he boasts is altogether frivolous. He maintains that man was created in the image of God, because he was formed in the similitude of the future Messiah, that he might resemble him whom the Father had already decreed to clothe with flesh. Whence he concludes that if Adam had never fallen from his primitive integrity, Christ would nevertheless have become man. How nugatory and forced this is, all who possess a sound judgment readily perceive. But he supposes that he has been the first to discover wherein the Divine image consisted; namely, that the glory of God not only shone in those eminent talents with which man was endued, but that God himself essentially resided in him. Now, though I admit that Adam bore the Divine image, inasmuch as he was united to God, which is the true and consummate perfection of dignity, yet I contend that the similitude of God is to be sought only in those characters of excellence, with which God distinguished Adam above the other creatures. And that Christ was even then the image of God, is universally allowed; and therefore whatever excellence was impressed on Adam proceeded from this circumstance, that he approached to the glory of his Maker by means of his only begotten Son. Man, therefore, was made in the image of God, and was designed to be a mirror to display the glory of his Creator. He was exalted to this degree of honour by the favour of the only begotten Son; but I add, that this Son was a common head to angels as well as to men; so that the angels also were entitled to the same dignity which was conferred on man. And when we hear them called the "children of God," (*h*) it would be unreasonable to deny that they have some resemblance to their Father. But if he designed his glory to be represented in angels as well as in men, and to be equally conspicuous in the angelic as in the human nature, Osiander betrays his ignorance and folly in saying that men were preferred to angels, because the latter did not bear the image of Christ. For they could not constantly enjoy the present contemplation of God, unless they were like him. And

(*g*) Eph. i. 22.   (*h*) Psalm lxxxii. 6.

Paul teaches us that men are no otherwise renewed after the image of God, than that if they be associated with angels, they may be united together under one head. (i) Finally, if we give credit to Christ, our ultimate felicity, when we shall be received into heaven, will consist in being conformed to the angels. But if Osiander may infer, that the primary exemplar of the Divine image was taken from the human nature of Christ, with the same justice may any other person contend, that Christ must have been a partaker of the nature of angels, because they likewise possess the image of God.

VII. Osiander, then, has no reason to fear, that God might possibly be proved a liar, unless the decree concerning the incarnation of his Son had been previously and immutably fixed in his mind. Because, though Adam had not fallen from his integrity, yet he would have resembled God just as the angels do; and yet it would not have been necessary on that account for the Son of God to become either a man or an angel. Nor has he any cause to fear this absurdity, that if God had not immutably decreed, before the creation of man, that Christ should be born, not as a Redeemer, but as the first man, he might lose his prerogative; whereas now he would not have become incarnate but for an accidental cause, that is, to restore mankind from ruin; so that he might thence infer, that Christ was created after the image of Adam. For why should he dread, what the Scripture so plainly teaches, that he was made like us in all things, sin excepted? (k) whence also Luke hesitates not in his genealogy to call him "the son of Adam." (l) I would also wish to know why Paul styles Christ "the second Adam," (m) but because he was destined to become man, in order to extricate the posterity of Adam from ruin. If he sustained that capacity before the creation, he ought to have been called "the first Adam." Osiander boldly affirms, that because Christ was already foreknown as man in the Divine mind, therefore men were formed in his likeness. But Paul, by denominating him "the second Adam," places the fall, whence arises the necessity of restoring our nature to its primitive condition, in an intermediate point between the first original of mankind and the restitution which we obtain through Christ; whence it follows that the fall was the cause of the incarnation of the Son of God. Now, Osiander argues unreasonably and impertinently, that while Adam retained his integrity, he would be the image of himself, and not of Christ. On the contrary, I reply, that although the Son of God had never been incarnate, both the body and the soul of man would equally have displayed the image of God; in whose

(i) Col. ii. 10.   (k) Heb. iv. 15.   (l) Luke iii. 38.   (m) 1 Cor. xv. 45, 47.

radiance it always appeared, that Christ was truly the head, possessing the supremacy over all. And thus we destroy that futile subtilty raised by Osiander, that the angels would have been destitute of this head, unless God had decreed to clothe his Son with flesh, even without any transgression of Adam. For he too inconsiderately takes for granted, what no wise man will concede, that Christ has no supremacy over angels, and that he is not their Prince, except in his human nature. But we may easily conclude, from the language of Paul, that, as the eternal Word of God, he is "the first-born of every creature;"(n) not that he was created, or ought to be numbered among creatures, but because the holy state of the world, adorned as it was at the beginning with consummate beauty, had no other author; and that afterwards, as man, he was "the first begotten from the dead." For in one short passage he proposes to our consideration both these points — that all things were created by the Son, that he might have dominion over angels; and that he was made man, that he might become our Redeemer. (o) Another proof of Osiander's ignorance is his assertion, that men would not have had Christ for their King, if he had not been incarnate; as though the kingdom of God could not subsist, if the eternal Son of God, without being invested with humanity, uniting angels and men in the participation of his glorious life, had himself held the supreme dominion! But he is always deceived, or rather bewilders himself, in this false principle, that the Church would have been destitute of a head, if Christ had not been manifested in the flesh; as if, while he was head over angels, he could not likewise by his Divine power preside over men, and by the secret energy of his Spirit animate and support them, like his own body, till they should be exalted to heaven, and enjoy the life of angels! These impertinencies, which I have thus far refuted, Osiander esteems as incontrovertible oracles. Inebriated by the charms of his own speculations, he is accustomed to express himself in the language of ridiculous triumph, without any sufficient cause. But he quotes one passage more, which he asserts to be conclusive beyond all the rest; that is, the prophecy of Adam, who, when he saw his wife, said, "This is now bone of my bone, and flesh of my flesh." (p) But how does he prove this to be a prophecy? Because Christ, according to Matthew, attributes the same language to God; as though every thing that God has spoken by men contained some prophecy! Then Osiander may seek for prophecies in each of the precepts of the law, of which it is evident God was the author. Besides, Christ would have been a low and grovelling expositor, if he had confined himself to the literal

(n) Col. i. 15.   (o) Col. i. 16, 18.   (p) Gen. ii. 23.

sense. Because he is treating, not of the mystical union, with which he has honoured his Church, but only of conjugal fidelity; he informs us, that God had pronounced a husband and wife to be one flesh, that no one might attempt by a divorce to violate that indissoluble bond. If Osiander be displeased with this simplicity, let him censure Christ, because he did not conduct his disciples to a mystery, by a more subtile interpretation of the language of the Father. Nor does his delirious imagination obtain any support from Paul, who, after having said that "we are members of Christ's flesh," immediately adds, "this is a great mystery." (*q*) For the apostle's design was, not to explain the sense in which Adam spoke, but, under the figure and similitude of marriage, to display the sacred union which makes us one with Christ. And this is implied in his very words; for when he apprizes us that he is speaking of Christ and the Church, he introduces a kind of correction to distinguish between the law of marriage and the spiritual union of Christ and the Church. Wherefore this futile notion appears destitute of any solid foundation. Nor do I think there will be any necessity for me to discuss similar subtilties; since the vanity of them all will be discovered from the foregoing very brief refutation. But this sober declaration will be amply sufficient for the solid satisfaction of the children of God; that "when the fulness of the time was come, God sent forth his Son, made of a woman, made under the law, to redeem them that were under the law." (*r*)

CHAPTER XIII.

CHRIST'S ASSUMPTION OF REAL HUMANITY.

The arguments for the Divinity of Christ, which has already been proved by clear and irrefragable testimonies, it would, I conceive, be unnecessary to reiterate. It remains, then, for us to examine, how, after having been invested with our flesh, he has performed the office of a Mediator. Now, the reality of his humanity was anciently opposed by the Manichæans and by the Marcionites. Of whom the latter imagined to themselves a visionary phantom instead of the body of Christ; and the former dreamed that he had a celestial body. But both these notions are contrary to numerous and powerful testimonies of

(*q*) Eph. v. 30, 32.   (*r*) Gal. iv. 4.

Scripture. For the blessing is promised, neither in a heavenly seed, nor in a phantom of a man, but in the seed of Abraham and Jacob; nor is the eternal throne promised to an aërial man, but to the Son of David and the fruit of his loins. (s) Wherefore, on his manifestation in the flesh, he is called the Son of David and of Abraham, not because he was merely born of the virgin after having been formed of some aërial substance; but because, according to Paul, he was "made of the seed of David according to the flesh;" as the same apostle in another place informs us, that "according to the flesh" he descended from the Jews. (t) Wherefore the Lord himself, not content with the appellation of *man*, frequently calls himself also *the Son of Man*—a term which he intended as a more express declaration of his real humanity. As the Holy Spirit has on so many occasions, by so many instruments, and with such great diligence and simplicity, declared a fact by no means abstruse in itself, who could have supposed that any mortals would have such consummate impudence as to dare to obscure it with subtilties? But more testimonies offer themselves, if we wished to multiply them; such as this of Paul, that "God sent forth his Son made of a woman;" (u) and innumerable others, from which he appears to have been liable to hunger, thirst, cold, and other infirmities of our nature. But from the multitude we must chiefly select those, which may conduce to the edification of our minds in true faith; as when it is said, that "he took not on him the nature of angels, but he took on him the seed of Abraham;" that he took flesh and blood, "that through death he might destroy him that had the power of death;" for which cause he is not ashamed to call them brethren; that "in all things it behoved him to be made like unto his brethren, that he might be a merciful and faithful high priest;" that "we have not a high priest which cannot be touched with the feeling of our infirmities;" (x) and the like. To the same purpose is what we have just before mentioned, that it was necessary for the sins of the world to be expiated in our flesh; which is clearly asserted by Paul. (y) And certainly all that the Father has conferred on Christ, belongs to us, because he "is the head, from whom the whole body is fitly joined together, and compacted by that which every joint supplieth." (z) There will otherwise be no propriety in the declaration, "that God giveth the Spirit not by measure unto him, that we may all receive of his fulness;" (a) since nothing would be more absurd, than that God should be en-

---

(s) Gen. xii. 3; xviii. 18; xxii. 18; xxvi. 4. Acts iii. 25; ii. 30. Psalm cxxxii. 11. Matt. i. 1.
(t) Rom. i. 3; ix. 5.   (u) Gal. iv. 4.   (x) Heb. ii. 14, 16, 17; iv. 15.
(y) Rom. viii. 3.   (z) Eph. iv. 15, 16.   (a) John iii. 34; i. 16.

riched in his essence by any adventitious gift. For this reason also Christ himself says in another place, "For their sakes I sanctify myself." (b)

II. The passages which they adduce in confirmation of this error, they most foolishly pervert; nor do their frivolous subtilties at all avail them in their endeavours to obviate the arguments which I have advanced in defence of our sentiments. Marcion imagines that Christ invested himself with a phantom instead of a real body; because he is said to have been "made in the likeness of men," and to have been "found in fashion as a man." (c) But in drawing this conclusion, he totally overlooks the scope of Paul in that passage. For his design is, not to describe the nature of the body which Christ assumed, but to assert that whilst he might have displayed his Divinity, he manifested himself in the condition of an abject and despised man. For, to exhort us to humility by the example of Christ, he shows, that being God, he might have instantaneously made a conspicuous exhibition of his glory to the world; yet that he receded from his right, and voluntarily debased himself, for that he assumed the form of a servant, and content with that humble station, suffered his Divinity to be hidden behind the veil of humanity. The subject of this statement, without doubt, is not the nature of Christ, but his conduct. From the whole context also it is easy to infer, that Christ humbled himself by the assumption of a real human nature. For what is the meaning of this clause, "that he was found in fashion as a man," but that for a time his Divine glory was invisible, and nothing appeared but the human form, in a mean and abject condition? For otherwise there would be no foundation for this assertion of Peter, that he was "put to death in the flesh, but quickened by the Spirit," (d) if the Son of God had not been subject to the infirmities of human nature. This is more plainly expressed by Paul, when he says, that "he was crucified through weakness." (e) The same is confirmed by his exaltation, because he is positively asserted to have obtained a new glory after his humiliation; which could only be applicable to a real man composed of body and soul. Manichæus fabricates for Christ an aërial body; because he is called "the second Adam, the Lord from heaven." (f) But the apostle in that place is not speaking of a celestial corporeal essence, but of a spiritual energy, which, being diffused from Christ, raises us into life. That energy we have already seen that Peter and Paul distinguish from his body. The orthodox doctrine, therefore, concerning the body of Christ, is firmly es-

---

(b) John xvii. 19.   (c) Phil. ii. 7, 8.   (d) 1 Peter iii. 18.
(e) 2 Cor. xiii. 4.   (f) 1 Cor. xv. 47.

tablished by this very passage. For unless Christ had the same corporeal nature with us, there would be no force in the argument which Paul so vehemently urges, that if Christ be risen from the dead, then we also shall rise; that if we rise not, neither is Christ risen. (*g*) Of whatever cavils either the ancient Manichæans, or their modern disciples, endeavour to avail themselves, they cannot succeed. Their nugatory pretence that Christ is called "the Son of man," because he was promised to men, is a vain subterfuge; for it is evident that in the Hebrew idiom, *the Son of man* is a phrase expressive of a real man. And Christ undoubtedly retained the phraseology of his own language. There is no room for disputing what is meant by *the sons of Adam*. And not to go any further, it will be fully sufficient to quote a passage in the eighth psalm which the apostles apply to Christ: "What is man, that thou art mindful of him, or the son of man, that thou visitest him?" This phrase expresses the true humanity of Christ; because, though he was not immediately begotten by a mortal father, yet his descent was derived from Adam. Nor would there otherwise be any truth in what we have just quoted, that Christ became a partaker of flesh and blood, that he might bring many sons to glory — language which clearly styles him to be a partaker of the same common nature with us. In the same sense the apostle says, that "both he that sanctifieth and they who are sanctified are all of one." For the context proves that this refers to a community of nature; because he immediately adds, "for which cause he is not ashamed to call them brethren." (*h*) For if he had already said that the faithful are of God, what reason could Jesus Christ have to be ashamed of such great dignity? But because Christ, of his infinite grace, associates himself with those who are vile and contemptible, it is therefore said that he is not ashamed. It is a vain objection which they make, that on this principle the impious will become the brethren of Christ; because we know that the children of God are born, not of flesh and blood, but of the Spirit through faith; therefore a community of nature alone is not sufficient to constitute a fraternal union. But though it is only to the faithful that the apostle assigns the honour of being one with Christ, yet it does not follow that unbelievers are not, according to the flesh, born of the same original; as, when we say that Christ was made man, to make us children of God, this expression extends not to all men; because faith is the medium by which we are spiritually ingrafted into the body of Christ. They likewise raise a foolish contention respecting the appellation of *first-born*. They plead that Christ ought to

(*g*) 1 Cor. xv. 13, 14.   (*h*) Heb. ii. 10, 11, 14.

have been born at the beginning, immediately of Adam, in order "that he might be the first-born among many brethren." (*i*) But the primogeniture attributed to him refers not to age, but to the degree of honour and the eminence of power which he enjoys. Nor is there any more plausibility in their notion, that Christ is said to have assumed the nature of man, and not of angels, because he received the human race into his favour. For the apostle, to magnify the honour with which Christ has favoured us, compares us with the angels, before whom in this respect we are preferred. (*k*) And if the testimony of Moses be duly considered, where he says that the Seed of the woman shall bruise the head of the serpent, (*l*) it will decide the whole controversy. For that prediction relates not to Christ alone, but to the whole human race. Because the victory was to be gained for us by Christ, God pronounces, in general, that the posterity of the woman should be superior to the devil. Whence it follows, that Christ descended from the human race; because the design of God, in that promise to Eve, was to comfort her with a good hope, that she might not be overcome with sorrow.

III. Those passages, where Christ is called "the seed of Abraham," and "the fruit of the body of David," they with equal folly and wickedness involve in allegories. For if the word *seed* had been used in an allegorical sense, Paul certainly would not have been silent respecting it, where, without any figure, he explicitly affirms, that there are not many sons of Abraham who are Redeemers, but Christ alone. (*m*) Equally unfounded is their notion, that Christ is called the Son of David in no other sense, but because he had been promised, and was at length manifested in due time. For after Paul has declared him to have been "made of the seed of David," the immediate addition of this phrase, "according to the flesh," (*n*) is certainly a designation of nature. Thus also in another place he calls him "God blessed for ever," and distinctly states that he descended from the Jews "as concerning the flesh." (*o*) Now, if he was not really begotten of the seed of David, what is the meaning of this expression, "the fruit of his loins?" (*p*) What becomes of this promise, "Of the fruit of thy body will I set upon thy throne?" (*q*) They likewise trifle in a sophistical manner with the genealogy of Christ, as it is given by Matthew. For though he mentions the parents of Joseph, and not of Mary, yet as he was treating of a thing then generally known, he thought it sufficient to show that Joseph descended from the seed of David, while there could be no doubt that

(*i*) Rom. viii. 29. (*l*) Gen. iii. 15. (*n*) Rom. i. 3. (*p*) Acts ii. 30.
(*k*) Heb. ii. 16. (*m*) Gal. iii. 16. (*o*) Rom. ix. 5. (*q*) Psalm cxxxii. 11.

Mary was of the same family. But Luke goes further, with a view to signify, that the salvation procured by Christ is common to all mankind; since Christ, the author of salvation, is descended from Adam, the common parent of all. I grant, indeed, that from the genealogy it cannot be inferred that Christ is the Son of David, any otherwise than as he was born of the Virgin. But the modern Marcionites, to give a plausibility to their error, that Christ derived his body from nothing, contend that women have no generative semen; and thus they subvert the elements of nature. But as this is not a theological question, and the arguments which they adduce are so futile that there will be no difficulty in repelling them, I shall not meddle with points belonging to philosophy and the medical art. It will be sufficient for me to obviate the objection which they allege from the Scripture, namely, that Aaron and Jehoiada married wives of the tribe of Judah; and thus, if women contain generative semen, the distinction of tribes was confounded. But it is sufficiently known, that, for the purposes of political regulation, the posterity is always reckoned from the father; yet that the superiority of the male sex forms no objection to the coöperation of the female semen in the process of generation. This solution extends to all the genealogies. Frequently, when the Scripture exhibits a catalogue of names, it mentions none but men; is it therefore to be concluded that women are nothing? Even children themselves know that women are comprehended under their husbands. For this reason women are said to bear children to their husbands, because the name of the family always remains with the males. Now, as it is a privilege conceded to the superiority of the male sex, that children should be accounted noble or ignoble, according to the condition of their fathers, so, on the other hand, it is held by the lawyers, that in a state of slavery the offspring follows the condition of the mother. Whence we may infer, that the offspring is produced partly from the seed of the mother; and the common language of all nations implies that mothers have some share in the generation of children. This is in harmony with the Divine law, which otherwise would have no ground for the prohibition of the marriage of an uncle with his sister's daughter; because in that case there would be no consanguinity. It would also be lawful for a man to marry his uterine sister, provided she were begotten by another father. But while I grant that a passive power is ascribed to women, I also maintain that the same that is affirmed of men is indiscriminately predicated of them. Nor is Christ himself said to be "made" by a woman, but "of a woman." (*r*) Some of these persons, casting off all modesty,

(*r*) Gal. iv. 4.

impudently inquire, whether we choose to say that Christ was procreated from the menstrual seed of the Virgin. I will inquire, on the other hand, whether he was not united with the blood of his mother; and this they must be constrained to confess. It is properly inferred, therefore, from the language of Matthew, that inasmuch as Christ was begotten of Mary, (s) he was procreated from her seed; as when Booz is said to have been begotten of Rahab, (t) it denotes a similar generation. Nor is it the design of Matthew here to describe the Virgin as a tube through which Christ passed, but to discriminate this miraculous conception from ordinary generation, in that Jesus Christ was generated of the seed of David by means of a Virgin. In the same sense, and for the same reason that Isaac is said to have been begotten of Abraham, Solomon of David, and Joseph of Jacob, so Christ is said to have been begotten of his mother. For the evangelist has written the whole of his account upon this principle; and to prove that Christ descended from David, he has contented himself with this one fact, that he was begotten of Mary. Whence it follows, that he took for granted the consanguinity of Mary and Joseph.

IV. The absurdities, with which these opponents wish to press us, are replete with puerile cavils. They esteem it mean and dishonourable to Christ, that he should derive his descent from men; because he could not be exempt from the universal law, which concludes all the posterity of Adam, without exception, under sin. (v) But the antithesis, which we find in Paul, easily solves this difficulty: " As by one man sin entered into the world, and death by sin, even so by the righteousness of one, the grace of God hath abounded." (w) To this the following passage corresponds: " The first man is of the earth, earthy; the second man is the Lord from heaven." (x) Therefore the same apostle, in another place, by teaching us that Christ was " sent in the likeness of sinful flesh " (y) to satisfy the law, expressly distinguishes him from the common condition of mankind; so that he is a real man, and yet free from all fault and corruption. They betray their ignorance in arguing that, if Christ is perfectly immaculate, and was begotten of the seed of Mary, by the secret operation of the Spirit, then it follows that there is no impurity in the seed of women, but only in that of men. For we do not represent Christ as perfectly immaculate, merely because he was born of the seed of a woman unconnected with any man, but because he was sanctified by the Spirit, so that his generation was pure and holy, such as it would have been before the fall of Adam. And it

(s) Matt. i. 16. ἐξ ἧς ἐγεννήθη Ἰησοῦς.
(t) Matt. i. 5. Σαλμὼν δὲ ἐγέννησε τὸν Βοὸζ ἐκ τῆς Ῥαχαβ.
(v) Gal. iii. 22. (w) Rom. v. 12, 15, 18. (x) 1 Cor. xv. 47. (y) Rom. viii. 3.

is a fixed maxim with us, that whenever the Scripture mentions the purity of Christ, it relates to a real humanity; because to assert the purity of Deity would be quite unnecessary. The sanctification, also, of which he speaks in the seventeenth chapter of John, (z) could have no reference to the Divine nature. Nor do we, as they pretend, imagine two kinds of seed in Adam, notwithstanding Christ was free from all contagion. For the generation of man is not naturally and originally impure and corrupt, but only accidentally so, in consequence of the fall. Therefore we need not wonder, that Christ, who was to restore our integrity, was exempted from the general corruption. But what they urge on us as an absurdity, that if the Word of God was clothed with flesh, it was therefore confined within the narrow prison of an earthly body, is mere impudence; because, although the infinite essence of the Word is united in one person with the nature of man, yet we have no idea of its incarceration or confinement. For the Son of God miraculously descended from heaven, yet in such a manner that he never left heaven; he chose to be miraculously conceived in the womb of the Virgin, to live on the earth, and to be suspended on the cross; and yet he never ceased to fill the universe, in the same manner as from the beginning.

CHAPTER XIV.

THE UNION OF THE TWO NATURES CONSTITUTING THE PERSON OF THE MEDIATOR.

When it is said that "the Word was made flesh," (a) this is not to be understood as if the Word was transmuted into flesh, or blended with flesh. Choosing from the womb of the Virgin a temple for his residence, he who was the Son of God, became also the Son of man, not by a confusion of substance, but by a unity of person. For we assert such a connection and union of the Divinity with the humanity, that each nature retains its properties entire, and yet both together constitute one Christ. If any thing among men can be found to resemble so great a mystery, man himself appears to furnish the most apposite similitude; being evidently composed of two substances, of which, however, neither is so confounded with the other, as not to retain its distinct nature. For the soul is not

(z) John xvii. 19.   (a) John i. 14.

the body, nor is the body the soul. Wherefore that is predicated separately of the soul, which cannot be at all applied to the body. On the contrary, that is predicated of the body, which is totally incompatible with the soul. And that is predicated of the whole man, which cannot with propriety be understood either of the soul or of the body alone. Lastly, the properties of the soul are transferred to the body, and the properties of the body to the soul; yet he that is composed of these two parts is no more than one man. Such forms of expression signify that there is in man one person composed of two distinct parts; and that there are two different natures united in him to constitute that one person. The Scriptures speak in a similar manner respecting Christ. They attribute to him, sometimes those things which are applicable merely to his humanity; sometimes those things which belong peculiarly to his Divinity; and not unfrequently those things which comprehend both his natures, but are incompatible with either of them alone. And this union of the two natures in Christ they so carefully maintain, that they sometimes attribute to one what belongs to the other — a mode of expression which the ancient writers called a communication of properties.

II. These things might be liable to objection, if the Scripture did not abound with passages, which prove that none of them is of human invention. What Christ asserted concerning himself, "Before Abraham was, I am," (*b*) was very inapplicable to his humanity. I am aware of the cavil with which erroneous spirits would corrupt this passage, — that he was before all ages, because he was even then foreknown as the Redeemer, as well in the decree of the Father, as in the minds of the faithful. But as he clearly distinguishes the day of his manifestation from his eternal essence, and professedly urges his antiquity, in proof of his possessing an authority in which he excels Abraham, there is no doubt that he challenges to himself what is peculiar to the Deity. Paul asserts him to be "the first-born of every creature, that he is before all things, and that by him all things consist:" (*c*) he declares himself, that he "had a glory with the Father before the world was," (*d*) and that he coöperates with the Father. (*e*) These things are equally incompatible with humanity. It is certain that these, and such as these, are peculiar attributes of Divinity. But when he is called the "servant" of the Father; (*f*) when it is stated that he "increased in wisdom and stature, and in favour with God and man;" (*g*) that he seeks not his own glory; that he knows not the last day; that he speaks not of himself; that he does not his own will; that he was

(*b*) John viii. 58.   (*d*) John xvii. 5.   (*f*) Isaiah xlii. 1.
(*c*) Col. i. 15.   (*e*) John v. 17.   (*g*) Luke ii. 52.

seen and handled; (*h*) all this belongs solely to his humanity. For as he is God, he is incapable of any augmentation whatever; he does all things for his own glory, and there is nothing concealed from him; he does all things according to the decision of his own will, and is invisible and intangible. And yet he ascribes these things not to his human nature separately, but to himself, as though they belonged to the person of the Mediator. But the communication of properties is exemplified in the assertion of Paul that "God purchased the Church with his own blood," (*i*) and that "the Lord of glory" was "crucified." (*k*) Also in what John says, that they had "handled the Word of life." (*l*) God has no blood; he is not capable of suffering, or of being touched with hands; but since he, who was at once the true God and the man Christ Jesus, was crucified and shed his blood for us, those things which were performed in his human nature are improperly, yet not without reason, transferred to the Divinity. There is a similar example of this, where John teaches us, that "God laid down his life for us." (*m*) There also the property of the humanity is transferred to the other nature. Again, when Christ, while he still lived on the earth, said, "No man hath ascended up to heaven, but he that came down from heaven, even the Son of man which is in heaven:" (*n*) as man, and in the body which he had assumed, he certainly was not at that time in heaven, but because he was both God and man, on account of the union of both natures, he attributed to one what belonged to the other.

III. But the clearest of all the passages declarative of the true substance of Christ are those which comprehend both the natures together; such as abound in the Gospel of John. For it is not with exclusive reference to the Deity or the humanity, but respecting the complex person composed of both, that we find it there stated; that he has received of the Father power to forgive sins, to raise up whom he will, to bestow righteousness, holiness, and salvation; that he is appointed to be the Judge of the living and the dead, that he may receive the same honour as the Father; (*o*) finally, that he is "the light of the world," "the good shepherd," "the only door," "the true vine." (*p*) For with such prerogatives was the Son of God invested at his manifestation in the flesh; which although he enjoyed with the Father before the creation of the world, yet not in the same manner or on the same account; and which could not be conferred on a mere man. In the same sense also it is reasonable to understand the declaration of Paul, that after the last judgment

(*h*) John viii. 50.   Mark xiii. 32.   John xiv. 10; vi. 38.   Luke xxiv. 39.
(*i*) Acts xx. 28.   (*k*) 1 Cor. ii. 8.   (*l*) 1 John i. 1.   (*m*) 1 John iii. 16.
(*n*) John iii. 13.   (*o*) John i. 29; v. 21—23.   (*p*) John ix. 5; x. 9, 11; xv. 1.

Christ "shall deliver up the kingdom to God, even the Father." (*q*) Now, the kingdom of the Son of God, which had no beginning, will never have any end. But as he concealed himself under the meanness of the flesh, and humbled himself by assuming the form of a servant, and laid aside his external majesty in obedience to the Father, (*r*) and after having undergone this humiliation, was at length crowned with glory and honour, and exalted to supreme dominion, (*s*) that before him "every knee should bow;" (*t*) so he shall then surrender to the Father that name and crown of glory, and all that he has received from the Father, "that God may be all in all." (*u*) For why has power and dominion been given to him, but that the Father may rule us by his hand? In this sense he is also said to sit at the right hand of the Father. But this is only temporary, till we can enjoy the immediate contemplation of the Deity. And here it is impossible to excuse the error of the ancients, who, for want of sufficient attention to the person of the Mediator, obscure the genuine sense of almost all the doctrine which we have in the Gospel of John, and involve themselves in many difficulties. Let this maxim, then, serve us as a key to the true sense, that those things which relate to the office of the Mediator, are not spoken simply of his Divine or of his human nature. Christ therefore will reign, till he comes to judge the world, forasmuch as he connects us with the Father as far as is compatible with our infirmity. But when we shall participate the glory of heaven, and see God as he is, then, having fulfilled the office of Mediator, he will cease to be the ambassador of the Father, and will be content with that glory which he enjoyed before the creation of the world. Nor is the title of Lord peculiarly applied to the person of Christ in any other respect, than as it marks an intermediate station between God and us. This is the meaning of that expression of Paul, "One God, of whom are all things; and one Lord, by whom are all things;" (*w*) namely, to whom the Father has committed a temporary dominion, till we shall be admitted to the immediate presence of his Divine majesty; which will be so far from sustaining any diminution by his surrender of the kingdom to the Father, that it will exhibit itself in far superior splendour. For then also God will cease to be the head of Christ, because the Deity of Christ himself, which is still covered with a veil, will shine forth in all its native effulgence.

' IV. And this observation, if the reader make a judicious application of it, will be of great use towards the solution of many difficulties. For it is surprising how much ignorant

(*q*) 1 Cor. xv. 24.   (*s*) Heb. ii. 7.   (*u*) 1 Cor. xv. 28.
(*r*) Phil. ii. 8.   (*t*) Phil. ii. 10.   (*w*) 1 Cor. viii. 6.

persons, and even some who are not altogether destitute of learning, are perplexed by such forms of expression, as they find attributed to Christ, which are not exactly appropriate either to his Divinity or to his humanity. This is for want of considering that they are applicable to his complex person, consisting of God and man, and to his office of Mediator. And indeed we may see the most beautiful coherence between all these things, if they have only a sober expositor, to examine such great mysteries with becoming reverence. But these furious and frantic spirits throw every thing into confusion. They lay hold of the properties of his humanity, to destroy his Divinity; on the other hand, they catch at the attributes of his Divinity, to destroy his humanity; and by what is spoken of both natures united, but is applicable separately to neither, they attempt to destroy both. Now, what is this but to contend that Christ is not man, because he is God; that he is not God, because he is man; and that he is neither man nor God, because he is at once both man and God? We conclude, therefore, that Christ, as he is God and man, composed of these two natures united, yet not confounded, is our Lord and the true Son of God, even in his humanity; though not on account of his humanity. For we ought carefully to avoid the error of Nestorius, who, attempting rather to divide than to distinguish the two natures, thereby imagined a double Christ. This we find clearly contradicted by the Scripture, where the appellation of "the Son of God" is given to him who was born of the Virgin, and the Virgin herself is called "the mother of our Lord." (*x*) We must also beware of the error of Eutyches, lest while we aim to establish the unity of Christ's person, we destroy the distinction of his two natures. For we have already cited so many testimonies, where his Divinity is distinguished from his humanity, and the Scripture abounds with so many others, that they may silence even the most contentious. I shall shortly subjoin some, in order to a more complete refutation of that notion. At present one passage shall suffice us; for Christ would not have styled his body "a temple," (*y*) if it had not been the residence of the Divinity, and at the same time distinct from it. Wherefore, as Nestorius was justly condemned in the council of Ephesus, so also was Eutyches afterwards in the councils of Constantinople and Chalcedon; for to confound the two natures in Christ, and to separate them, are equally wrong.

V. But in our time also there has arisen a heretic equally pestilent, Michael Servetus, who in the place of the Son of God has substituted an imaginary being composed of the

(*x*) Luke i. 35, 43.   (*y*) John ii. 19.

essence of God, spirit, flesh, and three uncreated elements. In the first place, he denies Christ to be the Son of God, in any other respect than as he was begotten by the Holy Spirit in the womb of the Virgin. But his subtlety tends to subvert the distinction of the two natures, and thereby to represent Christ as something composed of God and man, and yet neither God nor man. For this is the principal point which he constantly endeavours to establish, that before Christ was manifested in the flesh, there were in God only some shadowy figures; the truth or effect of which had no real existence till the Word, who had been destined to this honour, actually began to be the Son of God. Now, we confess that the Mediator, who was born of the Virgin, is properly the Son of God. Nor indeed could the man Christ be a mirror of the inestimable grace of God, if this dignity had not been conferred on him, to be, and to be called, "the only begotten Son of God." The doctrine of the Church, however, remains unshaken, that he is accounted the Son of God, because, being the Word begotten by the Father before all ages, he assumed the human nature in a hypostatical union. By the "hypostatical union" the ancients expressed the combination of two natures constituting one person. It was invented to refute the error of Nestorius, who imagined the Son of God to have dwelt in flesh in such a manner as, notwithstanding that, to have had no real humanity. Servetus falsely accuses us of making two Sons of God, when we say that the eternal Word was the Son of God, before he was clothed with flesh; as though we affirmed any other than that he was manifested in the flesh. For if he was God before he became man, it is not to be inferred that he began to be a new God. There is no more absurdity in affirming that the Son of God appeared in the flesh, who nevertheless was always the Son of God by eternal generation. This is implied in the words of the angel to Mary: "That holy thing which shall be born of thee shall be called the Son of God;" (z) as though he had said, that the name of the Son, which had been in obscurity under the law, was about to be celebrated and universally known. Consistent with this is the representation of Paul; that through Christ we are the sons of God, and may freely and confidently cry, Abba, Father. (a) But were not the holy patriarchs in ancient times numbered among the children of God? Yes; and depending on this claim, they invoked God as their Father. But because, since the introduction of the only begotten Son of God into the world, the celestial paternity has been more clearly revealed, Paul mentions this

(z) Luke i. 35.   (a) Rom. viii. 15. Gal. iv. 5, 6.

as the privilege of the kingdom of Christ. It must, however, be steadily maintained, that God never was a Father, either to angels or to men, but with reference to his only begotten Son; and especially that men, whom their own iniquity renders odious to God, are his sons by gratuitous adoption, because Christ is his Son by nature. Nor is there any force in the cavil of Servetus, that this depends on the filiation which God has decreed in himself; because we are not here treating of figures, as expiation was represented by the blood of the sacrifices: but as they could not be the sons of God in reality, unless their adoption were founded on this head, it is unreasonable to detract from the head, that which is common to all the members. I go further: since the Scripture calls angels "the children of God," (b) whose enjoyment of such high dignity depended not on the future redemption, yet it is necessary that Christ should precede them in order, seeing it is by him that they are connected with the Father. I will briefly repeat this observation, and apply the same to the human race. Since angels and men were originally created in such a condition, that God was the common Father of both, if there be any truth in the assertion of Paul, "that Christ was before all things, the head of the body, and the first-born of every creature, that in all things he might have the preëminence," (c) I conceive I am right in concluding, that he was also the Son of God before the creation of the world.

VI. But if his filiation (so to speak) commenced at the time of his manifestation in the flesh, it will follow that he was the Son also in respect of his human nature. Servetus and other heretics maintain that Christ, who appeared in the flesh, was the Son of God; because out of the flesh he could not be entitled to this appellation. Now, let them answer me, whether he be the Son according to both natures, and in respect of both. So indeed they idly pretend; but Paul teaches us very differently. We confess that Christ is called "the Son" in his human nature, not as the faithful are, merely by adoption and grace, but the true and natural, and therefore the only Son; that by this character he may be distinguished from all others. For we, who are regenerated to a new life, are honoured by God with the title of sons; but the appellation of "his true and only begotten Son" he gives to Christ alone. But among such a multitude of brethren, how can he be the only Son, unless he possess by nature what we have received as a gift? And we extend this honour to the whole person of the Mediator, that he who was born of the Virgin, and offered himself on the cross as a victim to the Father, is truly and properly

(b) Psalm lxxxii. 6.   (c) Col. i. 15—18.

the Son of God; but nevertheless with respect to his Deity, as Paul suggests, when he says that he was "separated unto the gospel of God, which he had promised afore, concerning his Son Jesus Christ our Lord, which was made of the seed of David according to the flesh, and declared to be the Son of God with power." (d) When he distinctly denominates him the Son of David according to the flesh, why should he particularly say that he was declared to be the Son of God with power, unless he intended to suggest that this dignity depended not on that flesh, but on something else? For in the same sense in which he says in another place that "he was crucified through weakness, yet that he liveth by the power of God," so in this passage he introduces the difference between the two natures. They certainly must be constrained to admit, that as he has received of his mother that which causes him to be called the Son of David, so he has from his Father that which constitutes him the Son of God, and that this is something distinct and different from his humanity. The Scripture distinguishes him by two names, calling him sometimes "the Son of God," sometimes "the Son of man." With respect to the latter, it cannot be disputed that he is styled the "Son of man," in conformity to the common idiom of the Hebrew language, because he is one of the posterity of Adam. I contend, on the other hand, that he is denominated "the Son of God" on account of his Deity and eternal existence; because it is equally reasonable that the appellation of "Son of God" should be referred to the Divine nature, as that that of "Son of man" should be referred to the human nature. In short, in the passage which I have cited, "that he, who was made of the seed of David according to the flesh, was declared to be the Son of God with power," Paul intends the same as he teaches us in another place, that "Christ, who as concerning the flesh came of the Jews, is God blessed for ever." But if the distinction of the two natures be expressed in both these passages, by what authority will they deny that he is the Son of God in respect of his Divine nature, who according to the flesh is likewise the Son of man?

VII. They clamorously urge in support of their error that God is said "not to have spared his own Son," (e) and that the angel directed that the very same who was to be born of the Virgin, should be called "the Son of the Highest." (f) But to prevent their glorying in so futile an objection, let them accompany us in a brief examination of the validity of their reasoning. For if it be rightly concluded, that he began to be the Son of God at his conception, because he that is

(d) Rom. i. 1—4.   (e) Rom. viii. 32.   (f) Luke i. 32.

conceived is called his Son, it will follow that he began to be the Word at his manifestation in the flesh, because John tells us that "he declares that, which his hands have handled, of the Word of life."(*g*) So when they read the following address of the prophet, "Thou, Bethlehem Ephratah, though thou be little among the thousands of Judah, yet out of thee shall he come forth unto me that is to be Ruler in Israel, whose goings forth have been from of old, from everlasting, or from the days of eternity,"(*h*) what interpretation will they be obliged to adopt, if they determine to pursue such a mode of argumentation? For I have declared that we by no means coincide with Nestorius, who imagined two Christs. According to our doctrine, Christ has made us the sons of God, together with himself, by the privilege of a fraternal union, because he is, in our nature which he assumed, the only begotten Son of God. And Augustine judiciously apprizes us, "that it is an illustrious mirror of the wonderful and singular grace of God, that Jesus Christ, considered as man, obtained honour which he could not merit." From his very birth, therefore, was Christ adorned, even in his human nature, with the dignity of being the Son of God. Yet in the unity of person we must not imagine such a confusion, as to destroy that which is peculiar to Deity. For it is no more unreasonable, that the eternal Word of God and the man Christ Jesus, the two natures being united into one person, should be called the Son of God in different senses, than that he should be styled, in various respects, sometimes the Son of God, sometimes the Son of man. Nor are we any more embarrassed with the other cavil of Servetus, that before Christ appeared in the flesh, he is no where called the Son of God, but in a figurative sense. For though the description of him then was rather obscure, yet since it has now been clearly proved, that he was the eternal God no otherwise than as he was the Word begotten of the eternal Father, and that this name is applicable to him in the character of Mediator which he has assumed, only because he is God manifested in the flesh; and that God the Father would not have been thus denominated from the beginning, unless there had even then been a mutual relation to the Son, who is the source of all kindred or paternity in heaven and in earth; (*i*) the inference is clear, that even under the law and the prophets he was the Son of God, before this name was commonly used in the Church. If the contention be merely about the word, Solomon, in speaking of the infinite sublimity of God, affirms his Son to be incomprehensible as well as himself: "What is his name," says he, "and what is his Son's name, if thou canst tell?" (*k*) I am aware that this testimony will not have

---

(*g*) 1 John i. 1.   (*h*) Micah v. 2.   (*i*) Eph. iii. 15.   (*k*) Prov. xxx. 4.

sufficient weight with contentious persons, nor indeed do I lay much stress on it, only that it fixes the charge of a malicious cavil on those who deny that Christ is the Son of God, any otherwise than because he has become man. It must also be remarked that all the most ancient writers have with one accord so unequivocally asserted the same doctrine, that it argues impudence equally ridiculous and detestable in those who dare to represent us as opposing Irenæus and Tertullian, who both acknowledge that Jesus Christ, who at length made a visible appearance, was always the invisible Son of God.

VIII. But although Servetus has accumulated many horrible and monstrous notions, to which some of his brethren, perhaps, would refuse to subscribe, yet, whoever they are that acknowledge not Christ to be the Son of God, except in the human nature, if we press them closely, we shall find that this title is admitted by them on no other ground than because he was conceived of the Holy Spirit in the womb of the Virgin; as the Manichæans formerly pretended that man received his soul by emanation from God, because it is said that God breathed into Adam the breath of life. (*l*) For they lay such stress on the name of Son, that they leave no difference between the two natures, but tell us, in a confused manner, that Christ is the Son of God, considered as man, because his human nature was begotten by God. Thus the eternal generation of Wisdom, of which Solomon speaks, (*m*) is destroyed, and no notice is taken of the Deity in the Mediator, or a phantom is substituted instead of his humanity. It might indeed be useful to refute the grosser fallacies of Servetus, with which he has fascinated himself and others, that the pious reader, admonished by this example, may preserve himself within the bounds of sobriety and modesty; yet I conceive this will be unnecessary here, as I have already done it in a separate treatise. The substance of them all is, that the Son of God was from the beginning an ideal existence, and that even then he was predestinated to be a man who was to be the essential image of God. Nor does he acknowledge any other word of God than what consists in an external splendour. His generation he explains thus: that there existed in God from the beginning a will to beget a Son, which was carried into effect by his actual formation. He likewise confounds the Spirit with the Word, by asserting that God distributed the invisible Word and Spirit into body and soul. In short, he puts the prefiguration of Christ in the place of his generation; and affirms that he who was then in external appearance a shadowy Son, was at length begotten by the Word, to which he attributes the properties of seed. Whence it will follow, that the mean-

(*l*) Gen. ii. 7.   (*m*) Prov. viii. 22, &c.

est animals are equally the children of God, because they were created of the original seed of the Word of God. For though he compounds Christ of three uncreated elements, to countenance the assertion that he is begotten of the essence of God, yet he pretends him to have been the first-born among creatures in such a sense, that even inanimate substances, according to their rank, possess the same essential Divinity. And that he may not seem to despoil Christ of his Deity, he asserts that his flesh is coëssential with God, and that the Word was made flesh by a conversion of the humanity into Deity. Thus, while he cannot conceive Christ to be the Son of God, unless his flesh proceeded from the essence of God, and were reconverted into Deity, he annihilates the eternal hypostasis of the Word, and deprives us of the Son of David, the promised Redeemer. He frequently indeed repeats this, that the Son was begotten of God by knowledge and predestination, but that at length he was made man of those materials, which in the beginning appeared with God in the three elements, and which afterwards appeared in the first light of the world, in the cloud, and in the pillar of fire. Now, how shamefully he contradicts himself, it would be too tedious to relate. From this summary the judicious reader will conclude, that by the subtle fallacies of this heretic, the hope of salvation is completely extinguished. For if the body were the Deity itself, it would no longer be the temple of it. Now, we can have no Redeemer, except him who became man, by being really begotten of the seed of Abraham and David according to the flesh. Servetus makes a very improper use of the language of John, that "the word was made flesh;" for while it opposes the error of Nestorius, it is as far from affording the least countenance to this impious notion, which originated with Eutyches. The sole design of the evangelist was, to assert the union of the two natures in one person.

CHAPTER XV.

THE CONSIDERATION OF CHRIST'S THREE OFFICES, PROPHETICAL, REGAL, AND SACERDOTAL, NECESSARY TO OUR KNOWING THE END OF HIS MISSION FROM THE FATHER, AND THE BENEFITS WHICH HE CONFERS ON US.

It is a just observation of Augustine, that although heretics profess the name of Christ, yet he is not a foundation to them in common with the pious, but remains exclusively the foundation of the Church; because, on a diligent consideration of what belongs to Christ, Christ will be found among them only in name, not in reality. Thus the Papists in the present age, although the name of the Son of God, the Redeemer of the world, be frequently in their mouths, yet since they are contented with the mere name, and despoil him of his power and dignity, these words of Paul, "not holding the head," (*n*) are truly applicable to them. Therefore, that faith may find in Christ a solid ground of salvation, and so may rely on him, it is proper for us to establish this principle, that the office which was assigned to him by the Father consists of three parts. For he was given as a Prophet, a King, and a Priest; though we should derive but little benefit from an acquaintance with these names, unaccompanied with a knowledge of their end and use. For they are likewise pronounced among the Papists, but in a frigid and unprofitable manner, while they are ignorant of what is included in each of these titles. We have before observed, that although God sent prophets one after another in a continual succession, and never left his people destitute of useful instruction, such as was sufficient for salvation, yet the minds of the pious were always persuaded, that the full light of understanding was not to be expected till the advent of the Messiah. And that this opinion had even reached the Samaritans, notwithstanding they had never been acquainted with the true religion, appears from the speech of the woman: "When Messias is come, he will tell us all things." (*o*) Nor had the Jews entertained this sentiment without sufficient ground, but believed as they had been taught by infallible oracles. One of the most remarkable is this passage of Isaiah: "Behold, I have given him for a witness to the people, a leader and commander to the people;" (*p*) just as he had before styled him "the Wonderful Counsellor." (*q*) In the same manner the apostle, with a view to display the perfection of the evangelical doctrine, after having said, that "God at sundry times and in divers manners spake unto the fathers by the prophets," adds, that he "hath in these last days spoken unto us by his Son." (*r*) But because it was the office of all the prophets to keep the Church in a state of suspense and expectation, and also to support it till the advent of the Mediator, we therefore find the faithful complaining, in their dispersion, that they were deprived of this ordinary blessing: "We see not our signs: there is no more any prophet: neither is there among us any that knoweth how long." (*s*) At length, when Christ was at no great

(*n*) Col. ii. 19.   (*p*) Isaiah lv. 4.   (*r*) Heb. i. 1, 2.
(*o*) John iv. 25.   (*q*) Isaiah ix. 6.   (*s*) Psalm lxxiv. 9.

distance, a time was prefixed for Daniel to seal up the vision and prophecy, not only to authenticate the prediction it contained, but in order that the faithful might patiently bear for a time the want of prophets, because the plenitude and conclusion of all revelations was near at hand. (*t*)

II. Now, it is to be observed, that the appellation of "Christ" belongs to these three offices. For we know that under the law not only priests and kings, but prophets also, were anointed with holy oil. Hence the celebrated title of "Messiah" was given to the promised Mediator. But though I confess that he was called the Messiah with particular reference to his kingdom, as I have already shown, yet the prophetical and sacerdotal unctions have their respective places, and must not be neglected by us. The former is expressly mentioned by Isaiah in these words: "The Spirit of the Lord God is upon me; because the Lord hath anointed me to preach good tidings unto the meek; he hath sent me to bind up the broken-hearted, to proclaim liberty to the captives, to proclaim the acceptable year of the Lord." (*u*) We see that he was anointed by the Spirit, to be a preacher and witness of the grace of the Father; and that not in a common manner; for he is distinguished from other teachers, who held a similar office. And here again it must be remarked, that he received this unction, not only for himself, that he might perform the office of a teacher, but for his whole body, that the preaching of the gospel might continually be attended with the power of the Spirit. But it remains beyond all doubt, that by this perfection of doctrine which he has introduced, he has put an end to all prophecies; so that they who, not contented with the gospel, make any extraneous addition to it, are guilty of derogating from his authority. For that voice, which thundered from heaven, "This is my beloved Son; hear ye him," (*v*) has exalted him by a peculiar privilege above all others. From the head this unction is afterwards diffused over the members, according to the prediction of Joel: "Your sons and your daughters shall prophesy and see visions." (*w*) But the declarations of Paul, that "he is made unto us wisdom," (*x*) and that "in him are hid all the treasures of wisdom and knowledge," (*y*) have rather a different meaning; namely, that beside him there is nothing useful to be known, and that they who by faith apprehend him as he is, have embraced the whole infinitude of celestial blessings. For which reason he writes in another place, "I determined not to know any thing among you, save Jesus Christ, and him crucified;" (*z*) which is perfectly just, because

(*t*) Dan. ix. 24.   (*u*) Isaiah lxi. 1, 2.   (*v*) Matt. xvii. 5.   (*w*) Joel ii. 28.
(*x*) 1 Cor. i. 30.   (*y*) Col. ii. 3.   (*z*) 1 Cor. ii. 2.

it is unlawful to go beyond the simplicity of the gospel. And the tendency of the prophetic dignity in Christ is, to assure us that all the branches of perfect wisdom are included in the system of doctrine which he has given us.

III. I come now to his kingdom, of which it would be useless to speak, without first apprizing the reader, that it is of a spiritual nature; because thence we may gather what is its use, and what advantage it confers upon us, and in short all its power and eternity. The eternity, which the angel in Daniel ascribes to the person of Christ, the angel in Luke justly applies to the salvation of the people. But this also is twofold, or is to be considered in two points of view; one extending to the whole body of the Church, the other belonging to every individual member. To the former must be referred the following passage in the Psalms: "Once have I sworn by my holiness that I will not lie unto David. His seed shall endure for ever, and his throne as the sun before me. It shall be established for ever as the moon, and as a faithful witness in heaven." (*a*) There is no doubt that God here promises to be the everlasting Governor and Defender of his Church, through the medium of his Son. For the truth of this prophecy will only be found in Christ; since immediately after the death of Solomon, the dignity of the kingdom sustained a considerable degradation, the greater part of it, to the disgrace of the family of David, being transferred to a private man, and afterwards was diminished more and more, till at length it fell in a melancholy and total ruin. The same sentiment is conveyed in this exclamation of Isaiah: "Who shall declare his generation?" (*b*) For when he pronounces that Christ will survive after his death, he connects his members with him. Therefore, whenever we hear that Christ is armed with eternal power, let us remember, that this is the bulwark which supports the perpetuity of the Church; that amidst the turbulent agitations with which it is incessantly harassed, and amidst the painful and formidable commotions which menace it with innumerable calamities, it may still be preserved in safety. Thus, when David derides the presumption of the enemies who attempt to break the yoke of God and of his Christ, and says, that the kings and the people rage in vain, since he that dwelleth in the heavens is sufficiently powerful to repel their violence,—he assures the faithful of the perpetual preservation of the Church, and animates them to entertain a cheerful hope, whenever it happens to be oppressed. (*c*) So, in another place, when, speaking in the name of God, he says, "Sit thou at my right hand, until I make thine enemies thy footstool," (*d*) he apprizes us that though

(*a*) Psalm lxxxix. 35—37.　　(*c*) Psalm ii. 1, &c.
(*b*) Isaiah iii. 8.　　(*d*) Psalm cx. 1.

numerous and powerful enemies conspire to assault the Church, yet they are not strong enough to prevail against that immutable decree of God, by which he has constituted his Son an eternal King. Whence it follows that it is impossible for the devil, with all the assistance of the world, ever to destroy the Church, which is founded on the eternal throne of Christ. Now, with respect to its particular use to each individual, this same eternity ought to encourage our hope of a blessed immortality; for we see that whatever is terrestrial and worldly is temporary and perishable. Therefore, to raise our hope towards heaven, Christ declares that his "kingdom is not of this world." (e) In a word, whenever we hear that the kingdom of Christ is spiritual, excited by this declaration, we ought to penetrate to the hope of a better life, and as we are now protected by the power of Christ, let us expect the full benefit of this grace in the world to come.

IV. The truth of our observation, that it is impossible to perceive the nature and advantages of the kingdom of Christ, unless we know it to be spiritual, is sufficiently evident from a consideration of the hardship and misery of our condition in the state of warfare under the cross, in which we have to continue as long as we live. What advantage, then, could accrue to us from being collected under the government of the heavenly King, if the benefit of it were not to extend beyond the present state? It ought therefore to be known, that whatever felicity is promised us in Christ, consists not in external accommodations, such as a life of joy and tranquillity, abundant wealth, security from every injury, and numerous delights suited to our carnal desires, but that it is peculiar to the heavenly state. As in the world the prosperous and desirable state of a nation consists partly in domestic peace, and an abundance of all blessings, and every good, and partly in strong bulwarks to secure it from external violence, so Christ enriches his people with every thing necessary to the eternal salvation of their souls, and arms them with strength to enable them to stand invincible against all the assaults of their spiritual foes. Whence we infer that he reigns rather for us than for himself, and that both internally and externally; that being replenished, as far as God knows to be necessary for us, with the gifts of the Spirit, of which we are naturally destitute, we may perceive from these first-fruits that we are truly united to God, in order to our perfect happiness; and in the next place, that, depending on the power of the same Spirit, we may not doubt of being always victorious over the devil, the world, and every kind of evil. This is implied in the answer of Christ to

(e) John xviii. 36.

the Pharisees, that as "the kingdom of God is within" us, it "cometh not with observation." (*f*) For it is probable, that in consequence of his having professed himself to be that King, under whom the highest blessing of God was to be expected, they ludicrously desired him to display the insignia of his dignity. But to prevent them, who had otherwise too great a propensity to the world, from directing all their attention to external pomp, he commands them to enter into their own consciences, "for the kingdom of God is righteousness, peace, and joy in the Holy Ghost." (*g*) Here we are briefly taught what advantage results to us from the kingdom of Christ. For since it is not terrestrial or carnal, so as to be liable to corruption, but spiritual, it elevates us even to eternal life, that we may patiently pass through this life in afflictions, hunger, cold, contempt, reproaches, and other disagreeable circumstances; contented with this single assurance, that our King will never desert us, but will assist our necessities, till having completed the term of our warfare, we shall be called to the triumph; for the rule of his government is, to communicate to us whatever he has received of the Father. Now, since he furnishes and arms us with his power, adorns us with his beauty and magnificence, and enriches us with his wealth, hence we derive most abundant cause for glorying, and even confidence, to enable us to contend with intrepidity against the devil, sin, and death. In the last place, since we are clothed with his righteousness, we may boldly rise superior to all the reproaches of the world; and as he liberally replenishes us with his favours, so we ought on our part to bring forth fruit to his glory.

V. His regal unction, therefore, is not represented to us as composed of oil and aromatic perfumes; but he is called "the Christ of God," (*h*) because "the spirit of wisdom and understanding, the spirit of counsel and might, the spirit of knowledge and of the fear of the Lord," (*i*) rested upon him. This is the "oil of gladness," with which the Psalmist declares him to have been "anointed above" his "fellows;" (*k*) because, if he were not possessed of such excellence, we should be all oppressed with poverty and famine. And, as we have observed, he was not enriched on his own private account, but that he might communicate his abundance to them who are hungry and thirsty. For as it is said that the Father "giveth not the Spirit by measure unto him," (*l*) so another passage expresses the reason — "that of his fulness we might all receive, and grace for grace." (*m*) From this source proceeds the munificence mentioned by Paul, by which grace is variously distri-

---

(*f*) Luke xvii. 20, 21.   (*g*) Rom. xiv. 17.   (*h*) Luke ix. 20.
(*i*) Isaiah xi. 2.   (*k*) Psalm xlv. 7.   (*l*) John iii. 34.   (*m*) John i. 16.

buted to the faithful, "according to the measure of the gift of Christ." (n) These passages abundantly confirm what I have said — that the kingdom of Christ consists in the Spirit, not in terrestrial pleasures or pomps; and that, therefore, in order to be partakers of it, we must renounce the world. A visible emblem of this unction was displayed at the baptism of Christ, when the Holy Spirit rested on him in the form of a dove. That the Holy Spirit and his gifts are designated by the word *unction*, ought not to be esteemed either novel or absurd, because we have no other support even for our animal life; but especially as it respects the heavenly life, we have not a particle of vigour in us, but what we have received from the Holy Spirit, who has chosen his residence in Christ, that those heavenly riches, which we so greatly need, may from him be copiously distributed to us. Now, as the faithful stand invincible in the strength of their King, and are enriched with his spiritual blessings, they are justly denominated Christians. But to this eternity, of which we have spoken, there is nothing repugnant in these expressions of Paul: "Then he shall deliver up the kingdom to God, even the Father," and " Then shall the Son himself be subject, that God may be all in all." (o) He only intends, that in that perfect glory the administration of the kingdom will not be the same as it is at present. For the Father has given all power to the Son, that he may guide, nourish, and sustain us by his hand, may guard us by his protection, and aid us in all our necessities. Thus, during the period of our pilgrimage, while we are absent from God, Christ interposes between us, to bring us by degrees to a perfect union with him. His being said to sit at the right hand of the Father, is equivalent to his being called the Father's vicegerent, intrusted with all the power of the government; because it is the will of God to govern and defend his Church through the mediation of his Son. This is the explanation given by Paul to the Ephesians, that he was "set at the right hand of the Father, to be the head over all things to the Church, which is his body." (p) To the same purpose is what he states in another place, that there has been " given him a name which is above every name; that at the name of Jesus every knee should bow; and that every tongue should confess that Jesus Christ is Lord, to the glory of God the Father." (q) For even in these words he displays the order in the kingdom of Christ necessary for our present infirmity. Thus Paul rightly concludes, that God himself will then be the only head of the Church, because the functions of Christ in the preservation and

(n) Eph. iv. 7.
(o) 1 Cor. xv. 24, 28.
(p) Eph. i. 20, 22, 23.
(q) Phil. ii. 9—11.

salvation of the Church will be fully discharged. For the same reason the Scripture often styles him Lord, because the Father has given him authority over us, that he may exercise his own dominion by the agency of his Son. " For though there be " many authorities celebrated in the world, " to us there is but one God, the Father, of whom are all things, and we in him; and one Lord Jesus Christ, by whom are all things, and we by him," (r) says Paul. Whence it may justly be concluded, that he is the same God, who by the mouth of Isaiah has asserted himself to be the King and Lawgiver of his Church. (s) For though he every where ascribes all the authority he possesses to the free gift of the Father, yet he only signifies that he reigns in the majesty and power of God; because he assumed the character of Mediator, in order to approach to us by descending from the bosom and incomprehensible glory of his Father. Wherefore it is the more reasonable that we should all with one consent be ready to obey him, and with the greatest alacrity conform all our services to his will. For as he combines the offices of a King and a Shepherd towards the faithful who yield a voluntary obedience, so, on the contrary, we are informed, that he bears "a rod of iron" to "break" all the stubborn and rebellious, and to "dash them in pieces like a potter's vessel." (t) It is likewise predicted that "he shall judge among the heathen; he shall fill the places with the dead bodies; he shall wound the heads over many countries." (u) Of this there are some instances to be seen in the present state, but the complete accomplishment of it will be at the last judgment, which may also with propriety be considered as the last act of his reign.

VI. Concerning his priesthood, we have briefly to remark, that the end and use of it is, that he may be a Mediator pure from every stain, and by his holiness may render us acceptable to God. But because the righteous curse prevents our access to him, and God in his character of Judge is offended with us,—in order that our Priest may appease the wrath of God, and procure his favour for us, there is a necessity for the intervention of an atonement. Wherefore, that Christ might perform this office, it was necessary for him to appear with a sacrifice. For even under the law the priest was not permitted to enter the sanctuary without blood; that the faithful might know, that notwithstanding the interposition of the Priest as an intercessor, yet it was impossible for God to be propitiated without the expiation of sins. This subject the apostle discusses at large in the Epistle to the Hebrews, from the seventh chapter almost to the end of the tenth. But the sum of the whole

---

(r) 1 Cor. viii. 5, 6.   (s) Isaiah xxxiii. 22.   (t) Psalm ii. 9.   (u) Psalm cx. 6.

is this — that the sacerdotal dignity belongs exclusively to Christ, because, by the sacrifice of his death, he has abolished our guilt, and made satisfaction for our sins. The vast importance of this we are taught by that solemn oath which " the Lord hath sworn, and will not repent; Thou art a priest for ever, after the order of Melchisedec." (v) For there is no doubt that God intended to establish that capital point, which he knew to be the principal hinge on which our salvation turns. And as we have observed, there is no access to God, either for ourselves or our prayers, unless our Priest sanctify us by taking away our sins, and obtain for us that grace from which we are excluded by the pollution of our vices and crimes. Thus, we see, it is necessary to begin with the death of Christ, in order to experience the efficacy and utility of his priesthood. Hence it follows, that he is an eternal intercessor, and that it is by his intervention we obtain favour with God. Hence proceeds not only confidence in prayer, but also tranquillity to the consciences of the faithful; while they recline in safety on the paternal indulgence of God, and are certainly persuaded, that he is pleased with whatever is consecrated to him through the Mediator. Now, as under the law God commanded victims to be offered to him from the flock and the herd, a new and different method has been adopted in the case of Christ, that the sacrifice should be the same with the priest; because it was impossible to find any other adequate satisfaction for sins, or any one worthy of so great an honour as to offer to God his only begotten Son. Besides, Christ sustains the character of a Priest, not only to render the Father favourable and propitious to us by an eternal law of reconciliation, but also to associate us with himself in so great an honour. For we, who are polluted in ourselves, being "made priests" (w) in him, offer ourselves and all our services to God, and enter boldly into the heavenly sanctuary, so that the sacrifices of prayers and praise, which proceed from us, are "acceptable," and "a sweet-smelling savour" (x) in the Divine presence. This is included in the declaration of Christ, "For their sakes I sanctify myself;" (y) for being arrayed in his holiness, he having dedicated us, together with himself, to the Father, we, who are otherwise offensive in his sight, become acceptable to him, as pure, unpolluted, and holy. This is the meaning of the "anointing of the Most Holy," (z) which is mentioned in Daniel. For we must observe the contrast between this unction and that shadowy unction which was then in use; as though the angel had said,

(v) Psalm cx. 4. (w) Rev. i. 6. (x) Eph. v. 2.
(y) John xvii. 19. (z) Dan. ix. 24.

that the shadows would be dissipated, and that there would be a real priesthood in the person of Christ. So much the more detestable is the invention of those, who, not content with the priesthood of Christ, have presumed to take upon themselves the office of sacrificing him; which is daily attempted among the Papists, where the mass is considered as an immolation of Christ.

CHAPTER XVI.

CHRIST'S EXECUTION OF THE OFFICE OF A REDEEMER TO PROCURE OUR SALVATION. HIS DEATH, RESURRECTION, AND ASCENSION TO HEAVEN.

ALL that we have hitherto advanced concerning Christ is to be referred to this point, that being condemned, dead, and ruined in ourselves, we should seek righteousness, deliverance, life, and salvation in him; as we are taught by this remarkable declaration of Peter, that "there is none other name under heaven given among men, whereby we must be saved." (a) The name of JESUS was given him, not rashly or by a fortuitous accident, or by the will of men, but was brought from heaven by the angel, the herald of the supreme decree, and also with this reason annexed to it: "for he shall save his people from their sins;" (b) in which words may be remarked, what we have before hinted, that the office of a Redeemer was assigned to him in order that he might be our Saviour. Nevertheless, the redemption would be incomplete, if he did not by continual advances carry us forward to the ultimate end of salvation. Therefore, as soon as we deviate from him, though but in the smallest degree, we gradually lose sight of salvation, which resides entirely in him; so that those who are not satisfied with him, voluntarily deprive themselves of all grace. And the following observation of Bernard is worthy of recital: "that the name of Jesus is not only light, but also food; that it is likewise oil, without which all the food of the soul is dry: that it is salt, unseasoned by which, whatever is presented to us is insipid; finally, that it is honey in the mouth, melody in the ear, joy in the heart, and medicine to the soul; and that there are no charms in any discourse where his name is not heard." But here we ought diligently to examine how he has procured salvation for us; that we may not only know

(a) Acts iv. 12.   (b) Matt. i. 21.

him to be the author of it, but, embracing those things which are sufficient for the establishment of our faith, may reject every thing capable of drawing us aside to the right hand or to the left. For since no man can descend into himself and seriously consider his own character, without perceiving that God is angry with him and hostile to him, and consequently he must find himself under a necessity of anxiously seeking some way to appease him, which can never be done without a satisfaction, — this is a case in which the strongest assurance is required. For sinners, till they be delivered from guilt, are always subject to the wrath and malediction of God, who, being a righteous Judge, never suffers his law to be violated with impunity, but stands prepared to avenge it.

II. Before we proceed any further, let us examine, by the way, how it could be consistent, that God, who prevents us with his mercy, should be our enemy, till he was reconciled to us by Christ. For how could he have given us a special pledge of his love in his only begotten Son, if he had not previously embraced us in his gratuitous favour? As there is some appearance of contradiction, therefore, in this representation, I shall solve the difficulty. The Spirit speaks in the Scriptures nearly in this manner — That God was an enemy to men, till by the death of Christ they were restored to his favour; (b) that they were under the curse till their iniquity was expiated by his sacrifice; (c) that they were separated from God, till they were restored to union with him by the body of Christ. (d) Such modes of expression are accommodated to our capacity, that we may better understand how miserable and calamitous our condition is, out of Christ. For if it were not clearly expressed, that we are obnoxious to the wrath and vengeance of God, and to eternal death, we should not so fully discover how miserable we must be without the Divine mercy, nor should we so highly estimate the blessing of deliverance. For example; let any man be addressed in the following manner: " If, while you remained a sinner, God had hated you, and rejected you according to your demerits, horrible destruction would have befallen you; but because he has voluntarily, and of his own gratuitous kindness, retained you in his favour, and not permitted you to be alienated from him, he has thus delivered you from that danger;" he will be affected, and will in some measure perceive how much he is indebted to the Divine mercy. But if, on the contrary, he be told, what the Scripture teaches, " that he was alienated from God by sin, an heir of wrath, obnoxious to the punishment of eternal death, excluded from all hope of salvation, a total stranger to the Divine bless-

---

(b) Rom. v. 10.   (c) Gal. iii. 10—13.   (d) Col. i. 21, 22.

ing, a slave to Satan, a captive under the yoke of sin, and, in a word, condemned to, and already involved in, a horrible destruction; that in this situation, Christ interposed as an intercessor; that he has taken upon himself and suffered the punishment which by the righteous judgment of God impended over all sinners; that by his blood he has expiated those crimes which render them odious to God; that by this expiation God the Father has been satisfied and duly atoned; that by this intercessor his wrath has been appeased; that this is the foundation of peace between God and men; that this is the bond of his benevolence towards them;" will he not be the more affected by these things in proportion to the more correct and lively representation of the depth of calamity from which he has been delivered? In short, since it is impossible for the life which is presented by the mercy of God, to be embraced by our hearts with sufficient ardour, or received with becoming gratitude, unless we have been previously terrified and distressed with the fear of the Divine wrath, and the horror of eternal death, we are instructed by the sacred doctrine, that irrespective of Christ we may contemplate God as in some measure incensed against us, and his hand armed for our destruction, and that we may embrace his benevolence and paternal love only in Christ.

III. Now, though this is expressed according to the weakness of our capacity, yet it is strictly true. For God, who is the perfection of righteousness, cannot love iniquity, which he beholds in us all. We all, therefore, have in us that which deserves God's hatred. Wherefore, in respect of our corrupt nature, and the succeeding depravity of our lives, we are all really offensive to God, guilty in his sight, and born to the damnation of hell. But because the Lord will not lose in us that which is his own, he yet discovers something that his goodness may love. For notwithstanding we are sinners through our own fault, yet we are still his creatures; notwithstanding we have brought death upon ourselves, yet he had created us for life. Thus, by a pure and gratuitous love towards us, he is excited to receive us into favour. But if there is a perpetual and irreconcilable opposition between righteousness and iniquity, he cannot receive us entirely, as long as we remain sinners. Therefore, to remove all occasion of enmity, and to reconcile us completely to himself, he abolishes all our guilt, by the expiation exhibited in the death of Christ, that we, who before were polluted and impure, may appear righteous and holy in his sight. The love of God the Father therefore precedes our reconciliation in Christ; or rather it is because he first loves, that he afterwards reconciles us to himself. (*e*)

(*e*) 1 John iv. 19.

But because, till Christ relieves us by his death, we are not freed from that iniquity which deserves the indignation of God, and is accursed and condemned in his sight; we have not a complete and solid union with God, before we are united to him by Christ. And therefore, if we would assure ourselves that God is pacified and propitious to us, we must fix our eyes and hearts on Christ alone, since it is by him only that we really obtain the non-imputation of sins, the imputation of which is connected with the Divine wrath.

IV. For this reason Paul says, that the love which God had for us before the creation of the world, was founded on Christ. (*f*) This doctrine is clear, and consistent with the Scripture, and admirably reconciles the different passages, where it is said, that God manifested his love to us by the gift of his only begotten Son, (*g*) and yet that he was our enemy till he was reconciled by the death of Christ. (*h*) But for a further confirmation of it, to such as require the testimony of the ancient Church, I will cite a passage from Augustine, which expressly maintains the same. "The love of God," says he, "is incomprehensible and immutable. For he did not begin to love us when we were reconciled to him by the blood of his Son, but he loved us before the creation of the world, that we might be his children, together with his only begotten Son, even before we had any existence. Therefore our reconciliation by the death of Christ must not be understood as if he reconciled us to God, that God might begin to love those whom he had before hated; but we are reconciled to him who already loved us, but with whom we were at enmity on account of sin. And whether my assertion be true, let the apostle attest. 'God,' says he, 'commendeth his love toward us, in that, while we were yet sinners, Christ died for us.' (*i*) He loved us, therefore, even when we were in the exercise of enmity against him, and engaged in the practice of iniquity. Wherefore, in a wonderful and Divine manner, he both hated and loved us at the same time. He hated us, as being different from what he had made us; but as our iniquity had not entirely destroyed his work in us, he could at the same time in every one of us hate what we had done, and love what proceeded from himself." This is the language of Augustine.

V. Now, in answer to the inquiry, how Christ, by the abolition of our sins, has destroyed the enmity between God and us, and procured a righteousness to render him favourable and propitious to us, it may be replied in general, that he accomplished it for us by the whole course of his obedience. This is proved by the testimony of Paul. "As by

(*f*) Eph. i. 4, 5.   (*g*) John iii. 16.   (*h*) Rom. v. 10.   (*i*) Rom. v. 8.

one man's disobedience many were made sinners, so by the obedience of one shall many be made righteous." (*k*) And indeed in another place he extends the cause of the pardon, which exempts us from the malediction of the law, to the whole life of Christ. "When the fulness of the time was come, God sent forth his Son, made of a woman, made under the law, to redeem them that were under the law." (*l*) Thus he himself affirmed even his baptism to be a branch of his righteousness, because he acted in obedience to the command of the Father. (*m*) In short, from the time of his assuming the character of a servant, he began to pay the price of our deliverance in order to redeem us. Yet more precisely to define the means of our salvation, the Scripture ascribes this in a peculiar manner to the death of Christ. He himself announces, that he "gives his life a ransom for many." (*n*) Paul teaches that "he died for our sins." (*o*) John the Baptist exclaims, "Behold the Lamb of God, which taketh away the sin of the world!" (*p*) Paul in another place declares, that we are "justified freely by his grace, through the redemption that is in Christ Jesus; whom God hath set forth to be a propitiation through faith in his blood." (*q*) Also that we are "justified by his blood," and "reconciled by his death." (*r*) Again: "He hath made him to be sin for us, who knew no sin; that we might be made the righteousness of God in him." (*s*) I shall not proceed with all the proofs, because the catalogue would be immense, and many of them must hereafter be cited in their proper order. Wherefore, in what is called the Apostles' Creed, there is very properly an immediate transition from the birth of Christ to his death and resurrection, in which the sum of perfect salvation consists. Yet there is no exclusion of the rest of the obedience which he performed in his life; as Paul comprehends the whole of it, from the beginning to the end, when he says, that "he made himself of no reputation, and took upon him the form of a servant, and became obedient unto death, even the death of the cross." (*t*) And indeed his voluntary submission is the principal circumstance even in his death; because the sacrifice, unless freely offered, would have been unavailable to the acquisition of righteousness. Therefore our Lord, after having declared, "I lay down my life for the sheep," expressly adds, "No man taketh it from me." (*v*) In which sense Isaiah says, "As a sheep before her shearers is dumb, so he openeth not his mouth." (*w*) And the evangelical history relates, that he went forth to meet the soldiers, (*x*)

(*k*) Rom. v. 19.
(*l*) Gal. iv. 4, 5.
(*m*) Matt. iii. 15.
(*n*) Matt. xx. 28.
(*o*) 1 Cor. xv. 3.
(*p*) John i. 29.
(*q*) Rom. iii. 24, 25.
(*r*) Rom. v. 9, 10.
(*s*) 2 Cor. v. 21.
(*t*) Phil. ii. 7, 8.
(*v*) John x. 15, 18.
(*w*) Isaiah liii. 7.
(*x*) John xviii. 4.

and that before Pilate he neglected making any defence, and waited to submit to the sentence. (*y*) Nor was this without inward conflict, because he had taken our infirmities, and it was necessary to give this proof of his obedience to his Father. And it was no mean specimen of his incomparable love to us, to contend with horrible fear, and amid those dreadful torments to neglect all care of himself, that he might promote our benefit. Indeed we must admit, that it was impossible for God to be truly appeased in any other way, than by Christ renouncing all concern for himself, and submitting and devoting himself entirely to his will. On this subject the apostle appositely cites the testimony of the Psalmist: "Then said I, Lo, I come; in the volume of the book it is written of me, I delight to do thy will, O my God; yea, thy law is within my heart." (*z*) But since terrified consciences find no rest but in a sacrifice and ablution to expiate their sins, we are properly directed thither, and the death of Christ is exhibited to us as the source of life. Now, because our guilt rendered us liable to a curse at the heavenly tribunal of God, the condemnation of Christ before Pontius Pilate, the governor of Judea, is stated in the first place, that we may know that on this righteous person was inflicted the punishment which belonged to us. We could not escape the terrible judgment of God; to deliver us from it, Christ submitted to be condemned even before a wicked and profane mortal. For the name of the governor is mentioned, not only to establish the credit of the history, but that we may learn, what is taught by Isaiah, that "the chastisement of our peace was upon him; and with his stripes we are healed." (*a*) For to supersede our condemnation it was not sufficient for him to suffer any kind of death; but, to accomplish our redemption, that kind of death was to be chosen, by which, both sustaining our condemnation and atoning for our sins, he might deliver us from both. Had he been assassinated by robbers, or murdered in a popular tumult, in such a death there would have been no appearance of satisfaction. But when he is placed as a criminal before the tribunal, — when he is accused and overpowered by the testimony of witnesses, and by the mouth of the judge is condemned to die, — we understand from these circumstances, that he sustained the character of a malefactor. And we shall remark two things which were foretold in the predictions of the prophets, and afford peculiar consolation and confirmation to our faith. For when we are told, that Christ was sent from the tribunal of the judge to the place of execution, and suspended between two thieves, we see the completion of that prophecy, which is cited by the Evangelist, "He

---

(*y*) Matt. xxvii. 12, 14.   (*z*) Psalm xl. 7, 8.   (*a*) Isaiah liii. 5.

was numbered with the transgressors." (*b*) For what reason? to sustain the character of a sinner, not of a righteous or innocent person. For he died, not for his innocence, but on account of sin. On the contrary, when we hear him absolved by the same mouth by which he was condemned, (for Pilate was constrained repeatedly to give a public testimony of his innocence,) (*c*) let it remind us of what we read in another prophet: "I restored that which I took not away." (*d*) Thus we shall behold Christ sustaining the character of a sinner and malefactor, while from the lustre of his innocence it will at the same time evidently appear, that he was loaded with the guilt of others, but had none of his own. He suffered, then, under Pontius Pilate, after having been condemned as a criminal by the solemn sentence of the governor; yet not in such a manner, but that he was at the same time pronounced to be righteous, by the declaration of the same judge, that he found in him no cause of accusation. This is our absolution, that the guilt, which made us obnoxious to punishment, is transferred to the person of the Son of God. For we ought particularly to remember this satisfaction, that we may not spend our whole lives in terror and anxiety, as though we were pursued by the righteous vengeance of God, which the Son of God has transferred to himself.

VI. Moreover, the species of death which he suffered, is fraught with a peculiar mystery. The cross was accursed, not only in the opinion of men, but by the decree of the Divine law. Therefore, when Christ is lifted up upon it, he renders himself obnoxious to the curse. And this was necessary to be done, that by this transfer we might be delivered from every curse which awaited us, or rather was already inflicted upon us, on account of our iniquities. This was also prefigured in the law. For the victims and expiations offered for sins were called אשמות, a word which properly signifies *sin* itself. By this appellation the Spirit intended to suggest that they were vicarious sacrifices, to receive and sustain the curse due to sin. But that which was figuratively represented in the Mosaic sacrifices, is actually exhibited in Christ, the archetype of the figures. Wherefore, in order to effect a complete expiation, he gave his soul אשם, that is, *an atoning sacrifice for sin,* (*f*) as the prophet says; so that our guilt and punishment being as it were transferred to him, they must cease to be imputed to us. The apostle more explicitly testifies the same, when he says, "He hath made him to be sin for us, who knew no sin; that we might be made the righteousness of God in him." (*g*) For the Son of God, though perfectly free from all sin, nevertheless assumed the disgrace and ignominy of our iniquities, and, on

(*b*) Isaiah liii. 12. Mark xv. 28. (*c*) Matt. xxvii. 18, 23, 24. John xviii. 38.
(*d*) Psalm lxix. 4. (*f*) Isaiah liii. 10. (*g*) 2 Cor. v. 21.

the other hand, arrayed us in his purity. He appears to have intended the same, when he says concerning sin, that it was "condemned in the flesh," (*h*) that is, in Christ. For the Father destroyed the power of sin, when the curse of it was transferred to the body of Christ. This expression therefore indicates, that Christ at his death was offered to the Father as an expiatory sacrifice, in order that, a complete atonement being made by his oblation, we may no longer dread the Divine wrath. Now, it is evident what the prophet meant, when he said, "The Lord hath laid on him the iniquity of us all;" (*i*) namely, that when he was about to expiate our sins, they were transferred to him by imputation. The cross, to which he was fixed, was a symbol of this, as the apostle informs us: "Christ hath redeemed us from the curse of the law, being made a curse for us; for it is written, Cursed is every one that hangeth on a tree; that the blessing of Abraham might come on the Gentiles through Jesus Christ." (*k*) Peter alluded to the same, where he said, "He bare our sins in his own body on the tree;" (*l*) because from the visible symbol of the curse, we more clearly apprehend, that the burden, with which we were oppressed, was imposed on him. Nor must we conceive that he submitted to a curse which overwhelmed him, but, on the contrary, that by sustaining it, he depressed, broke, and destroyed all its power. Wherefore faith apprehends an absolution in the condemnation of Christ, and a benediction in his curse. It is not without reason, therefore, that Paul magnificently proclaims the triumph which Christ gained for himself on the cross; as though the cross, which was full of ignominy, had been converted into a triumphal chariot. For he says, that "he nailed to his cross the hand-writing, which was contrary to us, and having spoiled principalities and powers, he made a show of them openly." (*m*) Nor should this surprise us; for, according to the testimony of another apostle, "Christ offered himself through the eternal Spirit." (*n*) Hence arose that change of the nature of things. But that these things may be deeply rooted and firmly fixed in our hearts, let us always remember his sacrifice and ablution. For we certainly could have no confidence that Christ was our (απολυτρωσις, (*o*) και αντιλυτρον, (*p*) και ιλαστηριον,) (*q*) *redemption, ransom,* and *propitiation,* if he had not been a slaughtered victim. And for this reason it is, that when the Scripture exhibits the method of redemption, it so often makes mention of blood; though the blood shed by Christ has not only served as an atonement to God, but likewise as a laver to purge away our pollutions.

(*h*) Rom. viii. 3.
(*i*) Isaiah liii. 6.
(*k*) Gal. iii. 13, 14.
(*l*) 1 Peter ii. 24.
(*m*) Col. ii. 14, 15.
(*n*) Heb. ix. 14.
(*o*) 1 Cor. i. 30.
(*p*) 1 Tim. ii. 6.
(*q*) Rom. iii. 25.

VII. It follows in the Creed, "that he died and was buried;" in which may be further seen, how in every respect he substituted himself in our room to pay the price of our redemption. Death held us in bondage under his yoke; Christ, to deliver us from it, surrendered himself to his power in our stead. This is the meaning of the apostle, when he says, that "he tasted death for every man." (r) For by his death he prevented us from dying, or, which comes to the same thing, by his death recovered life for us. But in this respect he differed from us — he surrendered himself to death to be, as it were, overcome by it, not that he might be absorbed in its abysses, but rather that he might destroy that, by which we should have been at length devoured; he surrendered himself to death to be subdued, not that he might be overwhelmed by its power, but rather that he might overthrow that which threatened us, which indeed had already overcome us, and was triumphing over us. Lastly, he died, "that he might destroy him that had the power of death, that is, the devil; and deliver them who through fear of death were all their lifetime subject to bondage."(s) This is the first benefit we have received from his death. The second is, that, by a communication of himself, he "mortifies" our "members which are upon the earth," (t) that they may no longer perform their own actions; and slays our old man, that it may not flourish and bear fruit any more. The burial of Christ has the same tendency, namely, that being made partakers of it, we may be buried to sin. For when the apostle teaches us that "we have been planted in the likeness of the death of Christ, and buried with him," (v) to the death of sin; that "by his cross the world is crucified" unto us, and we "unto the world;" (w) and that we "are dead with him;" (x) he not only exhorts us to imitate the example of his death, but declares that it contains such an efficacy, as ought to be conspicuous in all Christians, unless they wish to render that death ineffectual and useless. In the death and burial of Christ, therefore, we have a twofold benefit proposed to our enjoyment — deliverance from the thraldom of death, and the mortification of our flesh.

VIII. But it is not right to omit his "descent into hell," which is of no small importance towards the accomplishment of redemption. For though it appears from the writings of the ancients, that this article of the Creed was not always in common use in the churches, yet in discussing a system of doctrine, it is necessary to introduce it, as containing a mystery highly useful, and by no means to be despised. Indeed, there

(r) Heb. ii. 9.
(s) Heb. ii. 14, 15.
(t) Col. iii. 5.
(v) Rom. vi. 4, 5.
(w) Gal. vi. 14.
(x) Col. iii. 3.

are some of the ancients who do not omit it. Hence we may conjecture that it was inserted a little after the days of the apostles, and was not immediately but gradually received in the churches. This at least cannot be controverted, that it was agreeable to the general opinion of all the faithful; since there is not one of the fathers, who does not mention in his writings the descent of Christ into hell, though they explain it in different senses. But by whom, or at what period, it was first inserted, is of little consequence; it is of more importance that the Creed should present us a full and complete summary of faith, into which nothing should be inserted, but what is taken from God's most holy word. Yet if any morosely refuse to admit it into the Creed, it shall presently be proved to be so necessary to the perfection of our redemption, that the omission of it considerably lessens the benefit of the death of Christ. Some, again, are of opinion, that this clause contains nothing new, but is only a repetition, in other words, of what had before been said respecting his burial; because the word here rendered "hell" is frequently used in the Scriptures to signify the *grave*. I admit the truth of their observation respecting the signification of this word, that it is frequently to be understood of the "grave;" but their opinion is opposed by two reasons, which easily induce me to dissent from them. For what extreme carelessness it would betray, after a plain fact had been stated in the most explicit and familiar manner, to assert it a second time in an obscure combination of words calculated rather to perplex than to elucidate it! For when two phrases expressive of the same thing are connected together, the latter ought to be an explanation of the former. But what an explanation would this be, if one were to express it thus: "When Christ is said to have been buried, the meaning is, that he descended into hell!" Besides, it is not probable that such a superfluous tautology could have found its way into this compendium, in which the principal articles of faith are summarily expressed with the utmost possible brevity. And I doubt not, that all who have considered this point with any attention will easily assent to what I have advanced.

IX. Others give a different interpretation; that Christ descended to the souls of the fathers who had died under the law, for the purpose of announcing the accomplishment of redemption, and liberating them from the prison in which they were confined. To this purpose they pervert a passage in the psalms, that "he hath broken the gates of brass, and cut the bars of iron in sunder;" (*y*) and another in Zechariah, "I have sent forth thy prisoners out of the pit wherein is no

(*y*) Psalm cvii. 16.

water." (z) But since the Psalmist celebrates the liberation of those who are suffering captivity and imprisonment in distant countries; and Zechariah compares the destruction in which the people had been overwhelmed in Babylon, to a dry pit or abyss; and at the same time suggests, that the salvation of the whole Church is a deliverance from the abysses of hell; I know not how it came to pass, that posterity should imagine a subterraneous cavern, to which they have given the name of *Limbus*. But this fable, although it is maintained by great authors, and even in the present age is by many seriously defended as a truth, is after all nothing but a fable. For to confine the souls of the dead in a prison, is quite puerile; but what necessity was there for Christ to descend thither in order to liberate them? I freely confess, indeed, that Christ illuminated them by the power of his Spirit; that they might know that the grace, which they had only tasted by hope, was then exhibited to the world. And probably to this we may accommodate that passage of Peter, where he says, that Christ "went and preached unto the spirits who were keeping watch as in a tower." (a) This is generally rendered "the spirits in prison," but I conceive improperly. The context also gives us to understand, that the faithful who had died before that time, were partakers of the same grace with us. For the apostle amplifies the efficacy of the death of Christ from this consideration, that it penetrated even to the dead; when the souls of the faithful enjoyed the present view of that visitation which they had been anxiously expecting; whilst, on the contrary, it was more clearly discovered to the reprobate, that they were excluded from all salvation. But since Peter has not spoken in this distinct manner of the pious and the impious, we must not understand him as confounding them all together, without any discrimination. He only designs to inform us, that the knowledge of the death of Christ was common to them both.

X. But laying aside all consideration of the Creed, we have to seek for a more certain explanation of the descent of Christ into hell; and we find one in the Divine word, not only holy and pious, but likewise replete with singular consolation. If Christ had merely died a corporeal death, no end would have been accomplished by it; it was requisite, also, that he should feel the severity of the Divine vengeance, in order to appease the wrath of God, and satisfy his justice. Hence it was necessary for him to contend with the powers of hell and the horror of eternal death. We have already stated from the prophet, that "the chastisement of our peace was upon him," that "he was wounded for our transgressions, and bruised for

(z) Zech. ix. 11.   (a) 1 Peter iii. 19.

our iniquities;" (b) the meaning of which is, that he was made a substitute and surety for transgressors, and even treated as a criminal himself, to sustain all the punishments which would have been inflicted on them; only with this exception, that "it was not possible that he should be holden of the pains of death." (c) Therefore it is no wonder, if he be said to have descended into hell, since he suffered that death which the wrath of God inflicts on transgressors. It is a very frivolous and even ridiculous objection to say that by this explanation the order of things is perverted, because it is absurd to make that subsequent to his burial, which really preceded it. For the relation of those sufferings of Christ, which were visible to men, is very properly followed by that invisible and incomprehensible vengeance which he suffered from the hand of God; in order to assure us that not only the body of Christ was given as the price of our redemption, but that there was another greater and more excellent ransom, since he suffered in his soul the dreadful torments of a person condemned and irretrievably lost.

XI. In this sense Peter says, that "God raised him up, having loosed the pains of death; because it was not possible that he should be holden of it." (d) He does not say simply "death;" but tells us, that the Son of God was involved in "the pains of death," which proceed from the Divine wrath and malediction, which is the origin of death. For what a little thing it would have been for Christ to appear in order to suffer death, without any distress or perplexity, and even with pleasure! But this was a true specimen of his infinite mercy, not to evade that death which he so much dreaded. Nor can it be doubted, but the apostle means to suggest the same in the Epistle to the Hebrews, when he says, that Christ "was heard in that he feared." (e) Some, instead of *fear*, translate it *reverence* or *piety;* but how improperly, is evident from the subject itself, and also from the form of expression. Christ, therefore, "when he offered up prayers with strong crying and tears, was heard in that he feared;" not that he might obtain an exemption from death, but that he might not be swallowed up by it as a sinner; for he was then sustaining our character. And it is certainly impossible to imagine any more formidable abyss, than to perceive ourselves forsaken and abandoned by God, and not to be heard when we call upon him, as though he had conspired to destroy us. Now, we see Christ was so deeply dejected, that in the urgency of distress, he was constrained to exclaim, "My God, my God, why hast thou forsaken me?" (f)

(b) Isaiah liii. 5.   (c) Acts ii. 24.   (d) Acts ii. 24.
(e) Heb. v. 7.   (f) Matt. xxvii. 46.

For the idea of some, that he spoke rather according to the opinion of others than from his own feelings, is utterly improbable; since he evidently appears to have spoken from the anguish of his inmost soul. We do not admit that God was ever hostile to him, or angry with him. For how could he be angry with his beloved Son, " in whom his soul delighted ? " (*g*) or how could Christ, by his intercession, appease the Father for others, if the Father were incensed against him ? But we affirm, that he sustained the weight of the Divine severity; since, being "smitten and afflicted of God," (*h*) he experienced from God all the tokens of wrath and vengeance. Wherefore, Hilary argues, that by this descent we have obtained the destruction of death. And in other places he accords with our opinion; as when he says, "The cross, death, and hell, are our life." Again, in another place, "The Son of God is in hell, but man is raised to heaven." But why do I cite the testimony of a private person, when the apostle asserts the same thing, mentioning, as the reward of Christ's victory, the deliverance of them "who, through fear of death, were all their lifetime subject to bondage?" (*i*) It was necessary, therefore, that he should overcome that fear, which naturally and incessantly harasses all men; which he could not do without contending with it. Now, that his was not a common or trivial sorrow, will soon be more clearly evinced. Thus, by contending with the power of the devil, with the dread of death, and with the pains of hell, he obtained the victory, and triumphed over them, that in death we may no longer dread those things which our Prince has destroyed.

XII. Here some contentious, though illiterate men, impelled rather by malice than by ignorance, exclaim against me, that I am guilty of an atrocious injury to Christ; because it is utterly unreasonable that he should have any fear concerning the salvation of his soul. And then they aggravate the cavil, by pretending that I attribute despair to the Son of God, which is contrary to faith. In the first place, it is presumptuous in them to raise a controversy concerning the fear and consternation of Christ, which is so expressly asserted by the evangelists. For, before the approach of his death, he experienced a perturbation of spirit and depression of mind; but, in the actual struggle with it, he began to feel a greater degree of consternation. If they say that this was only pretence, it is a most paltry subterfuge. We ought, therefore, as Ambrose justly advises, fearlessly to acknowledge the sorrow of Christ, unless we are ashamed of his cross. And, indeed, if his soul had experienced no punishment, he would have been only a Redeemer

(*g*) Isaiah xlii. 1. (*h*) Isaiah liii. 4. (*i*) Heb. ii. 15.

for the body. It was necessary for him to combat, in order to raise up those who lay prostrate on the earth; and his heavenly glory is so far from being diminished by this, that his goodness, which is never sufficiently celebrated, is conspicuous in his voluntary and unreluctant assumption of our infirmities. Hence that consolation which the apostle offers us under our anxieties and sorrows, that this Mediator has experienced our infirmities, in order that he might be the more ready to succour the wretched. (*j*) They pretend, that what is intrinsically bad cannot be justly attributed to Christ; as though they were wiser than the Spirit of God, who connects these two things together, that Christ "was in all points tempted like as we are, yet without sin." We have no reason, therefore, to be alarmed by the infirmity of Christ, to which he was not compelled by violence or necessity, but induced merely by his mercy and love for us voluntarily to submit himself. But none of his voluntary sufferings for us have been any diminution of his power. These captious objectors, however, are deceived in one point; they do not perceive that this infirmity in Christ was perfectly free from every stain of guilt, because he always kept himself within the limits of obedience. For, because no moderation can be discovered in the corruption of our nature, where all our passions transgress all bounds with impetuous violence, they erroneously measure the Son of God by this standard. But he being innocent, and free from every defect, all his affections were governed by a moderation which admitted of no excess. Whence it was very possible for him to resemble us in sorrow, fear, and dread, and yet, in this respect, to be very different from us. Refuted here, they proceed to another cavil; that, although Christ was afraid of death, yet he was not afraid of the malediction and wrath of God, from which he knew himself to be safe. But let the pious reader consider how much honour it reflects on Christ, that he was more delicate and timorous than the generality of mankind. Robbers and other malefactors obstinately rush forward to death; many men nobly despise it; others calmly submit to it. But what constancy or magnanimity would the Son of God have discovered, in being astonished and almost struck dead with the fear of it? For it is related of him, what might generally be accounted a prodigy, that through the vehemence of his agonies, drops of blood flowed from his face. Nor did he exhibit this spectacle to the eyes of others; he sent up his groans to his Father, in the secrecy of retirement. And every doubt is removed by the necessity that there was for angels to descend from heaven, to support him with unusual consolation.

(*j*) Heb. iv. 15.

What disgraceful effeminacy, as I have suggested, would this have been, to be so distressed by the fear of a common death, as to be in a bloody sweat, and incapable of being comforted without the presence of angels! What! does not this prayer, which he repeated three times, "O my Father, if it be possible, let this cup pass from me," (k) proceeding from an incredible bitterness of soul, demonstrate that Christ had a more severe and arduous conflict than with a common death? Whence it appears, that those triflers, with whom I am now disputing, presumptuously chatter about things which they know not; because they never seriously considered the nature or the importance of our redemption from the Divine judgment. But it is our wisdom to have a clear understanding how much our salvation cost the Son of God. If any one inquire whether Christ was then descending to hell, when he deprecated death, I reply, that this was the prelude to it; whence we may conclude what dreadful and horrible agonies he must have suffered, while he was conscious of standing at the tribunal of God accused as a criminal on our account. But, although the Divine power of the Spirit concealed itself for a moment, to give place to the infirmity of the flesh, yet we know, that the temptation arising from a sense of grief and fear was such as was not repugnant to faith. And thus was fulfilled what we find in the sermon of Peter, "that it was not possible that he should be holden of the pains of death;" (l) because, when he perceived himself, as it were, deserted by God, still he relaxed not in the least from his confidence in his Father's goodness. This is evident from his celebrated invocation, when, through the vehemence of grief, he exclaimed, "My God, my God, why hast thou forsaken me?" (m) For notwithstanding his extreme agony, yet he continues to call God *his* God, even when he complains that he is forsaken by him. Now, this serves to refute the error of Apollinaris, and also of those who were called Monothelites. Apollinaris pretended that the eternal Spirit supplied the place of a soul in Christ, so that he was but half a man, as though he could expiate our sins without obedience to the Father. But where was the disposition or will, requisite to obedience, but in his soul? which we know was "troubled," (n) in order to dissipate all our fears, and obtain peace and rest for ours. Moreover, in opposition to the Monothelites, we see, that what was contrary to his will as man, was agreeable to his will as God. I say nothing of his overcoming the fear of which we have spoken, by a contrary disposition. For there is a manifest appearance of contrariety when he says, "Father, save me from this hour: but for this

(k) Matt. xxvi. 39.   (l) Acts ii. 24.   (m) Matt. xxvii. 46.   (n) John xii. 27

cause came I unto this hour. Father, glorify thy name." (o) Yet, in this perplexity, there is no such want of moderation as is evident in us, even while we are exerting our most strenuous endeavours to conquer ourselves.

XIII. Next follows his resurrection from the dead, without which all that we have said would be incomplete. For, since there appears nothing but infirmity in the cross, death, and burial of Christ, faith must proceed beyond all these things, to be furnished with sufficient strength. Wherefore, although our salvation is perfectly accomplished by his death, because by that we are reconciled to God, a satisfaction is given to his righteous judgment, the curse is removed, and the punishment sustained, yet we are said to have been "begotten again to a lively hope," not by his death, but "by his resurrection from the dead." (p) For as at his resurrection he appeared the conqueror of death, so it is on his resurrection that our faith principally rests. This is better expressed in the words of Paul, when he says, that Christ "was delivered for our offences, and was raised again for our justification;" (q) as though he had said, that sin was removed by his death, and righteousness renewed and restored by his resurrection. For how was it possible for him by dying to liberate us from death, if he had himself remained under its power? how could he have obtained the victory for us, if he had been vanquished in the contest? Wherefore we ascribe our salvation partly to the death of Christ, and partly to his resurrection; we believe that sin was abolished, and death destroyed, by the former; that righteousness was restored, and life established, by the latter; yet so that the former discovers its power and efficacy in us by means of the latter. Therefore Paul asserts that he was "declared to be the Son of God, by the resurrection from the dead;" (r) because he then displayed his heavenly power, which is both a lucid mirror of his Divinity, and a firm support of our faith. So, in another place, he says, that "he was crucified through weakness, yet he liveth by the power of God." (s) In the same sense, in another place, treating of perfection, he says, "that I may know him, and the power of his resurrection." (t) Yet, immediately after, he adds, "the fellowship of his sufferings, and conformity to his death." In perfect harmony with this, is the following declaration of Peter: "God raised him up from the dead, and gave him glory; that your faith and hope might be in God:" (u) not that faith totters when it rests on his death; but because "the power of God," which "keeps us through faith," (v) chiefly discovers itself in his resurrection.

(o) John xii. 27, 28.
(p) 1 Peter i. 3
(q) Rom. iv. 25.
(r) Rom. i. 4.
(s) 2 Cor. xiii. 4.
(t) Phil. iii. 10.
(u) 1 Peter i. 21.
(v) 1 Peter i. 5.

Let us remember, therefore, that whenever mention is made of his death alone, it comprehends also what strictly belongs to his resurrection; and that the same figure of speech is applied to the word *resurrection*, whenever it is used without any mention of his death, so that it connects with it what is peculiarly applicable to his death. But since it was by rising from the dead that he obtained the palm of victory, to become the resurrection and the life, Paul justly contends, that, "if Christ be not risen, then is" the "preaching" of the gospel "vain, and" our "faith is also vain." (*v*) Therefore, in another place, after having gloried in the death of Christ in opposition to all the fears of condemnation, he adds, by way of amplification, "Yea, rather, that is risen again, who is even at the right hand of God, who also maketh intercession for us." (*w*) Besides, as we have before stated, that the mortification of our flesh depends on communion with his cross, so it must also be understood, that we obtain another benefit, corresponding to that, from his resurrection. The apostle says, "If we have been planted together in the likeness of his death, we shall be also in the likeness of his resurrection: even so we also should walk in newness of life." (*x*) Therefore, in another place, as, from our being dead with Christ, he deduces an argument for the mortification of our members which are upon the earth, (*y*) so also, because we are risen with Christ, he thence infers that we should seek those things which are above, and not those which are on the earth. (*z*) By which expressions we are not only invited to walk in newness of life, after the example of Christ raised from the dead, but are taught that our regeneration to righteousness is effected by his power. We derive also a third benefit from his resurrection, having received, as it were, a pledge to assure us of our own resurrection, of which his clearly affords the most solid foundation and evidence. This subject the apostle discusses more at large in the First Epistle to the Corinthians. (*a*) But it must be remarked by the way, that when he is said to have "risen from the dead," this phrase expresses the reality both of his death and of his resurrection; as though it were said, that he died the same death as other men naturally die, and received immortality in the same body which he had assumed in a mortal state.

XIV. His *resurrection* is properly followed in the Creed by his *ascension to heaven*. For though Christ began to make a more illustrious display of his glory and power at his resurrection, having now laid aside the abject and ignoble condition of this mortal life, and the ignominy of the cross, yet his ascension into heaven was the real commencement of his reign.

(*v*) 1 Cor. xv. 14, 17. (*x*) Rom. vi. 4, 5. (*z*) Col. iii. 1, 2.
(*w*) Rom. viii. 34. (*y*) Col. iii. 5 (*a*) 1 Cor. xv.

This the apostle shows, when he informs us, that he "ascended that he might fill all things." (b) Here, in an apparent contradiction, he suggests to us that there is a beautiful harmony, because Christ departed from us, that his departure might be more useful to us than that presence, which, during his continuance on earth, confined itself within the humble mansion of his body. Therefore John, after having related that remarkable invitation, "If any man thirst, let him come unto me, and drink," subjoins, that " the Holy Ghost was not yet given; because that Jesus was not yet glorified." (c) This the Lord himself also declared to his disciples: "It is expedient for you that I go away; for if I go not away, the Comforter will not come unto you." (d) Now, he proposes a consolation for his corporeal absence, that he "will not leave them comfortless, or orphans, but will come again to them," in a manner invisible indeed, but more desirable; because they were then taught by a more certain experience that the authority which he enjoys, and the power which he exercises, is sufficient for the faithful, not only to procure them a blessed life, but to insure them a happy death. And, indeed, we see how largely he then increased the effusions of his Spirit, how greatly he advanced the magnificence of his reign, and what superior power he exerted both in assisting his friends, and in defeating his enemies. Being received up into heaven, therefore he removed his corporeal presence from our view; not that he might no longer be present with the faithful who were still in a state of pilgrimage on earth, but that he might govern both heaven and earth by a more efficacious energy. Moreover, his promise, that he would be with us till the end of the world, he has performed by this his ascension; by which, as his body was elevated above all heavens, so his power and energy have been diffused and extended beyond all the limits of heaven and earth. In representing this, I would prefer the language of Augustine to my own. "Christ," says he, "was about to go by death to the right hand of the Father, whence he will hereafter come to judge the living and the dead; and this by a corporeal presence, according to the rule of faith and sound doctrine. For in his spiritual presence with them, he was to come soon after his ascension." And elsewhere he treats this subject in a manner still more diffuse and explicit. By his ineffable and invisible grace, Christ has fulfilled his declaration, "Lo, I am with you alway, even unto the end of the world." (e) But with respect to the body which the Word assumed, which was born of the Virgin, which was apprehended by the Jews, which was fixed to the cross, which was taken down from the cross,

(b) Eph. iv. 10.   (c) John vii. 37, 39.   (d) John xvi. 7.   (e) Matt. xxviii. 20

which was folded in linen, which was laid in the sepulchre, which was manifested at the resurrection, there has been an accomplishment of this prediction: "Ye shall not have me always with you." Why? Because in his corporeal presence he conversed with his disciples for forty days, and while they were attending him, seen but not followed by them, he ascended into heaven; and he is not here, for he sits there at the right hand of the Father; and yet he is here, for he has not withdrawn the presence of his majesty. In the presence of his majesty, therefore, we have Christ always with us; but with respect to his corporeal presence, he said with truth to his disciples, "Me ye have not always." For the Church enjoyed his corporeal presence for a few days; now she enjoys him by faith, and does not behold him with her eyes.

XV. Wherefore it is immediately added, *that he is seated at the right hand of the Father;* which is a similitude borrowed from princes, who have their assistants, to whom they depute the exercise of the government. So Christ, in whom the Father determines to be exalted, and by whose medium he chooses to reign, is said to have been received to his right hand; as though it were said, that he had been inaugurated in the government of heaven and earth, and had solemnly entered on the actual administration of the power committed to him; and not only that he has entered on it, but that he continues in it, till he descends to judgment. For so the apostle explains it, in the following words: "The Father hath set him at his own right hand, far above all principality, and power, and might, and dominion, and every name that is named, not only in this world, but also in that which is to come; and hath put all things under his feet, and gave him to be the head over all things to the church," &c. (*g*) We see the end of this session; it is, that all creatures, both celestial and terrestrial, may admire his majesty, be governed by his hand, obey his will, and be subject to his power. And the only design of the apostles in their frequent mention of it, is to teach us that all things are committed to his government. Wherefore they who suppose that nothing but blessedness is signified in this article, are not right in that opinion. It affects not our argument, that Stephen declares that he sees Christ "standing," (*h*) because the present question relates, not to the posture of his body, but to the majesty of his dominion; so that *sitting* signifies no other than presiding at the tribunal of heaven.

XVI. Hence faith receives many advantages. For it perceives, that by his ascension the Lord has opened the way to the kingdom of heaven, which had been stopped by Adam.

(*g*) Eph. i. 20—22.   (*h*) Acts vii. 55, 56.

For since he entered there in our nature, and as it were in our names, it follows that, as the apostle expresses it, we now "sit together" with him "in heavenly places," (*i*) because we not only hope for heaven, but already possess it in our Head. Besides, faith knows that his residence with his Father conduces greatly to our advantage. For being entered into a sanctuary, which is not of human erection, (*k*) he continually appears in the presence of the Father as our advocate and intercessor : (*l*) he attracts the eyes of the Father to his righteousness, so as to avert them from our sins; he reconciles him to us, so as to procure for us, by his intercession, a way of access to his throne, which he replenishes with grace and mercy, but which otherwise would be pregnant with horror to miserable sinners. (*m*) In the third place, faith has an apprehension of his power, in which consists our strength, our fortitude, our wealth, and our triumph over hell. For "when he ascended up on high, he led captivity captive," (*n*) spoiled his enemies, and enriched his people, and daily loads them with spiritual favours. He sits, therefore, on high, that from thence he may shed forth his power upon us, that he may animate us with spiritual life, that he may sanctify us by his Spirit, that he may adorn his Church with a variety of graces, and defend it by his protection from every calamity, that by the strength of his hand he may restrain the ferocious enemies of his cross and of our salvation; finally, that he may retain all power in heaven and in earth; till he shall have overthrown all his enemies, who are also ours, and completed the edification of his Church. And this is the true state of his kingdom, this the power which the Father has conferred on him, till he completes the last act by coming to judge the living and the dead.

XVII. Christ gives his servants unequivocal tokens of the presence of his power; but because on earth his kingdom is in some measure concealed under the meanness of the flesh, faith is, for a very good reason, called to meditate on that visible presence which he will manifest at the last day. For he will descend from heaven in a visible form, in the same manner in which he was seen to ascend; (*o*) and will appear to all with the ineffable majesty of his kingdom, with the splendour of immortality, with the infinite power of Deity, and with a host of angels. (*p*) From thence, therefore, we are commanded to expect him as our Redeemer at the last day, when he will separate the sheep from the goats, the elect from the reprobate ; and there will not be an individual of either the living or the dead that can escape his judgment. For from the most remote

(*i*) Eph. ii. 6.   (*l*) Rom. viii. 34.   (*n*) Eph. iv. 8.
(*k*) Heb. ix. 24.   (*m*) Heb. iv. 16.   (*o*) Acts i. 11.
(*p*) Matt. xxiv. 30; xxv. 31. 1 Thess. iv. 16, 17.

corners of the world they will hear the sound of the trumpet, with which all mankind will be summoned to his tribunal, both those whom that day shall find alive, and those whom death shall previously have removed from the society of the living. There are some who understand the words *quick*, or *living, and dead*, in a different sense. And indeed we find that some of the fathers hesitated respecting the exposition of this clause; but the sense we have given, being plain and clear, is far more consistent with the design of the Creed, which appears to have been composed for the common people. Nor is this repugnant to the assertion of the apostle, that "it is appointed unto men once to die." (*k*) For although they who shall survive in this mortal life till the last judgment, shall not die in a natural manner and order, yet that change, which they shall experience, since it will resemble death, may without impropriety be designated by that appellation. It is certain indeed that "all shall not sleep, but all shall be changed." (*l*) What is that? In one moment their mortal life will be extinguished and absorbed, and will be transformed into a nature entirely new. This extinction of the flesh no man can deny to be death. Nevertheless it remains a truth, that the living and the dead will be summoned to judgment; for "the dead in Christ shall rise first: then they which are alive and remain shall be caught up together with them in the clouds, to meet the Lord in the air." (*m*) And it is very probable that this article was taken from the sermon of Peter, (*n*) and from the solemn charge of Paul to Timothy. (*o*)

XVIII. It is a source of peculiar consolation to hear that he will preside at the judgment, who has already destined us to participate with himself the honour of sitting in judgment with him, so far will he be from ascending the tribunal to condemn us. For how could a most merciful prince destroy his own people? how could a head scatter his own members? how could an advocate condemn his own clients? For if the apostle ventures to exclaim, that no one can condemn us while Christ intercedes for us, (*p*) it is much more certain that Christ himself, our intercessor, will not condemn those whose cause he has undertaken, and whom he has engaged to support. Indeed, it is no inconsiderable security, that we shall stand before no other tribunal than that of our Redeemer, from whom we are to expect salvation; and that he, who by the gospel now promises eternal life, will at the judgment ratify and perform the promise which he has given. The design of the Father in honouring the Son by "committing all judgment to

(*k*) Heb. ix. 27. (*m*) 1 Thess. iv. 16, 17. (*o*) 2 Tim. iv. 1.
(*l*) 1 Cor. xv. 51. (*n*) Acts x. 42. (*p*) Rom. viii. 34.

him," (*q*) was, that he might relieve the consciences of his people from all fear concerning the judgment. Thus far I have followed the order of the Apostles' Creed; because, while it comprises, in a few words, the principal points of redemption, it may serve to give us a distinct and separate view of those particulars respecting Christ which merit our attention. I style it the Apostles' Creed, but am not at all solicitous to know who was the composer of it. The ancient writers agree in ascribing it to the apostles, either from a belief that it was written and published by their common concurrence, or from an opinion that this compendium, being faithfully collected from the doctrine delivered by them, was worthy of being sanctioned by such a title. And whoever was the author of it, I have no doubt that it has been publicly and universally received as a confession of faith from the first origin of the Church, and even from the days of the apostles. Nor is it probable that it was composed by any private individual, since from time immemorial it has evidently been esteemed as of sacred authority by all the pious. But what we ought principally to regard, is beyond all controversy — that it comprehends a complete account of our faith in a concise and distinct order, and that every thing it contains is confirmed by decisive testimonies of Scripture. This being ascertained, it is of no use anxiously to inquire, or to contend with any one, respecting its author, unless it be not sufficient for any one to have the unerring truth of the Holy Spirit, without knowing either by whose mouth it was uttered, or by whose hand it was written.

XIX. Since we see that the whole of our salvation, and all the branches of it, are comprehended in Christ, we must be cautious not to alienate from him the least possible portion of it. If we seek salvation, we are taught by the name of JESUS, that it is in him; if we seek any other gifts of the Spirit, they will be found in his unction; strength, in his dominion; purity, in his conception; indulgence discovers itself in his nativity, by which he was made to resemble us in all things, that he might learn to condole with us; if we seek redemption, it will be found in his passion; absolution, in his condemnation; remission of the curse, in his cross; satisfaction, in his sacrifice; purification, in his blood; reconciliation, in his descent into hell; mortification of the flesh, in his sepulchre; newness of life and immortality, in his resurrection; the inheritance of the celestial kingdom, in his entrance into heaven; protection, security, abundance, and enjoyment of all blessings, in his kingdom; a fearless expectation of the judgment, in the judicial authority committed to him. Finally, blessings of every

---

(*q*) John v. 22.

kind are deposited in him; let us draw from his treasury, and from no other source, till our desires are satisfied. For they who, not content with him alone, are carried hither and thither into a variety of hopes, although they fix their eyes principally on him, nevertheless deviate from the right way in the diversion of any part of their attention to another quarter. This distrust, however, cannot intrude, where the plenitude of his blessings has once been truly known.

CHAPTER XVII.

CHRIST TRULY AND PROPERLY SAID TO HAVE MERITED THE GRACE OF GOD AND SALVATION FOR US.

We must devote an additional Chapter to the solution of this question. For there are some men, more subtle than orthodox, who, though they confess that Christ obtained salvation for us, yet cannot bear the word *merit*, by which they suppose the grace of God is obscured. So they maintain that Christ is only the instrument or minister, not, as he is called by Peter, the Author, or Leader, and "Prince of life." (*q*) I grant, indeed, if any man would oppose Christ simply and alone to the judgment of God, there would be no room for merit; because it is impossible to find in man any excellence which can merit the favour of God; nay, as Augustine most truly observes, "The brightest illustration of predestination and grace is the Saviour himself, the man Christ Jesus, who has acquired this character in his human nature, without any previous merit either of works or of faith. Let any one tell me, how that man merited the honour of being assumed into one person with the Word, who is coëternal with the Father, and so becoming the only begotten Son of God. Thus the fountain of grace appears in our Head, and from him diffuses its streams through all his members according to their respective capacities. Every one, from the commencement of his faith, is made a Christian, by the same grace, by which this man, from the commencement of his existence, was made the Christ." Again, in another treatise, Augustine says, "There is not a more illustrious example of predestination than the Mediator himself. For he who made of the seed of David this righteous man, so that he never was unrighteous, without any previous merit of his

(*q*) Acts iii. 15.

will, converts unrighteous persons into righteous ones, and makes them members of that Head," &c. When we speak of the merit of Christ, therefore, we do not consider him as the origin of it, but we ascend to the ordination of God, which is the first cause; because it was of his mere good pleasure, that God appointed him Mediator to procure salvation for us. And thus it betrays ignorance to oppose the merit of Christ to the mercy of God. For it is a common maxim, that between two things, of which one succeeds or is subordinate to the other, there can be no opposition. There is no reason, therefore, why the justification of men should not be gratuitous from the mere mercy of God, and why at the same time the merit of Christ should not intervene, which is subservient to the mercy of God. But to our works are directly and equally opposed the gratuitous favour of God and the obedience of Christ, each in its respective place. For Christ could merit nothing except by the good pleasure of God, by which he had been predestinated to appease the Divine wrath by his sacrifice, and to abolish our transgressions by his obedience. To conclude, since the merit of Christ depends solely on the grace of God, which appointed this method of salvation for us, therefore his merit and that grace are with equal propriety opposed to all the righteousnesses of men.

II. This distinction is gathered from numerous passages of Scripture. "God so loved the world, that he gave his only begotten Son, that whosoever believeth in him should not perish." (r) We see that the love of God holds the first place, as the supreme and original cause, and that faith in Christ follows as the second and proximate cause. If it be objected, that Christ is only the formal cause, this diminishes his merit more than the words now quoted will bear. For if we obtain righteousness by a faith which relies on him, it is in him we are to seek the cause of our salvation. This is evident from many passages. "Not that we loved God, but that he loved us, and sent his Son to be the propitiation for our sins." (s) These words clearly demonstrate, that to remove every obstacle in the way of his love towards us, God appointed a method of reconciliation in Christ. And there is much contained in the word "propitiation;" for God, in a certain ineffable manner, at the same time that he loved us, was nevertheless angry with us, till he was reconciled in Christ. This is implied in the following passages: "He is the propitiation for our sins." (t) Again: "It pleased the Father, having made peace through the blood of his cross, by him to reconcile all things unto himself." (v) Again: "God was in Christ, reconciling

(r) John iii. 16.   (s) 1 John iv. 10.   (t) 1 John ii. 2.   (v) Col. i. 19, 20.

the world unto himself, not imputing their trespasses unto them." (*w*) Again: "He hath made us accepted in the Beloved." (*x*) Again: "That he might reconcile both unto God in one body by the cross." (*y*) The reason of this mystery may be learned from the first chapter of the Epistle to the Ephesians, where Paul, having taught that we are chosen in Christ, adds at the same time, that we are accepted in him. How did God begin to favour those whom he had loved before the creation of the world, but by the manifestation which he made of his love when he was reconciled by the blood of Christ? For since God is the fountain of all righteousness, he must necessarily be the enemy and judge of every sinner. Wherefore the beginning of his love is the righteousness described by Paul: "He hath made him to be sin for us, who knew no sin; that we may be made the righteousness of God in him." (*z*) For his meaning is, that by the sacrifice of Christ we obtain gratuitous righteousness, so as to be acceptable to God, though by nature we are the children of wrath, and alienated from him by sin. This distinction is indicated also wherever the grace of Christ is connected with the love of God; whence it follows that our Saviour bestows on us what he has purchased; for otherwise it would be inconsistent to ascribe this praise to him distinctly from the Father, that grace is his, and proceeds from him.

III. Now, that Christ by his obedience has really procured and merited grace from the Father for us, is certainly and justly concluded from various passages of Scripture. For I assume this as granted: if Christ has satisfied for our sins; if he has sustained the punishment due to us; if he has appeased God by his obedience; in a word, if he has suffered, the just for the unjust,— then salvation has been obtained for us by his righteousness, which is the same as being merited. But according to the testimony of Paul, "We were reconciled by his death, by whom we have received the atonement," or reconciliation. (*a*) Now, there is no room for reconciliation without a previous offence. The sense therefore is, that God, to whom our sins had rendered us odious, has been appeased by the death of his Son, so as to be propitious to us. And the antithesis, which follows just after, is worthy of careful observation: "As by one man's disobedience many were made sinners, so by the obedience of one shall many be made righteous." (*b*) For the meaning is, that as by the sin of Adam we were alienated from God and devoted to destruction, so by the obedience of Christ we are received into favour, as righteous persons.

(*w*) 2 Cor. v. 19. (*y*) Eph. ii. 16. (*a*) Rom. v. 10, 11.
(*x*) Eph. i. 6. (*z*) 2 Cor. v. 21. (*b*) Rom. v. 19.

Nor does the future tense of the verb exclude present righteousness; as appears from the context. For he had before said, "The free gift is of many offences unto justification." (c)

IV. But when we say that grace is procured for us by the merit of Christ, we intend, that we have been purified by his blood, and that his death was an expiation for sins. "The blood of Jesus Christ cleanseth us from all sin." (d) "This blood is shed for the remission of sins." (e) If the non-imputation of our sins to us be the effect of the blood which he shed, it follows that this was the price of satisfaction to the justice of God. This is confirmed by the declaration of the Baptist: "Behold the Lamb of God, which taketh away the sin of the world." (f) For he opposes Christ to all the sacrifices of the law, to show that what they prefigured was accomplished in him alone. Now we know what Moses frequently says — that an atonement shall be made for sin, and it shall be forgiven. In short, the ancient figures give us a fine exhibition of the power and efficacy of the death of Christ. And the apostle copiously discusses this subject in the Epistle to the Hebrews, judiciously assuming this as a fundamental principle, that "without shedding of blood there is no remission." Whence he infers, that Christ has "once appeared to put away sin by the sacrifice of himself;" and that "he was offered to bear the sins of many." (g) He had already said, that "Not by the blood of goats and calves, but by his own blood; he entered once into the holy place, having obtained eternal redemption." (h) Now, when he argues in this manner, "If the blood of bulls and of goats, and the ashes of a heifer sprinkling the unclean, sanctifieth to the purifying of the flesh, how much more shall the blood of Christ purge your conscience from dead works!" (i) it evidently appears that we too much undervalue the grace of Christ, unless we attribute to his sacrifice an expiatory, placatory, and satisfactory efficacy. Therefore it is immediately added, "He is the mediator of the New Testament, that by means of death, for the redemption of the transgressions that were under the first testament, they which are called might receive the promise of eternal inheritance." (k) But we ought particularly to consider the relation described by Paul, that he was "made a curse for us." (l) For it would be unnecessary, and consequently absurd, for Christ to be loaded with a curse, except in order to discharge the debts due from others, and thereby to obtain a righteousness for them. The testimony of Isaiah likewise is clear, that "the chastisement

(c) Rom. v. 16.
(d) 1 John i. 7.
(e) Matt. xxvi. 28.
(f) John i. 29.
(g) Heb. ix. 22, 26, 28.
(h) Heb. ix. 12.
(i) Heb. ix. 13, 14.
(k) Heb. ix. 15.
(l) Gal. iii. 13.

of our peace was upon him; and with his stripes we are healed." (*o*) For if Christ had not made a satisfaction for our sins, he could not be said to have appeased God by suffering the punishment to which we were exposed. This is confirmed by a subsequent clause: "For the transgression of my people was he stricken." (*p*) Let us add the interpretation of Peter, which will remove all difficulty, that "he bare our sins in his own body on the tree;" (*q*) which imports that the burden of condemnation, from which we have been relieved, was laid upon Christ.

V. The apostles explicitly declare, that he paid a price to redeem us from the sentence of death: "Being justified freely by his grace, through the redemption that is in Christ Jesus; whom God hath set forth to be a propitiation, through faith in his blood." (*r*) Here Paul celebrates the grace of God, because he has given the price of our redemption in the death of Christ; and then enjoins us to betake ourselves to his blood, that we may obtain righteousness, and may stand secure before the judgment of God. Peter confirms the same when he says, "Ye were not redeemed with corruptible things, as silver and gold, but with the precious blood of Christ, as of a lamb without blemish and without spot." (*s*) For there would be no propriety in the comparison, unless this blood had been the price of satisfaction for sin; for which reason Paul says, "Ye are bought with a price." (*t*) Nor would there be any truth in his other assertion, that "there is one Mediator, who gave himself a ransom," (*v*) unless the punishment due to our demerits had been transferred to him. Therefore the same apostle defines "redemption through his blood" to be "the forgiveness of sins;" (*w*) as though he had said, We are justified or acquitted before God, because that blood is a complete satisfaction for us. This is consonant with the following passage, that "he blotted out the hand-writing, which was contrary to us, nailing it to his cross." (*x*) For these words signify the payment or compensation which absolves us from guilt. There is great weight also in these words of Paul: "If righteousness come by the law, then Christ is dead in vain." (*y*) For hence we conclude, that we must seek from Christ what the law would confer upon any one who fulfilled it; or, which is the same, that we obtain by the grace of Christ what God promised in the law to our works; "which" commandments "if a man do, he shall live in them." (*z*) This the apostle confirms with equal perspicuity in his sermon at Antioch, as-

(*o*) Isaiah liii. 5.
(*p*) Isaiah liii. 8.
(*q*) 1 Peter ii. 24.
(*r*) Rom. iii. 24, 25.
(*s*) 1 Peter i. 18, 19.
(*t*) 1 Cor. vi. 20.
(*v*) 1 Tim. ii. 5, 6.
(*w*) Col. i. 14.
(*x*) Col. ii. 14.
(*y*) Gal. ii. 21.
(*z*) Lev. xviii. 5.

serting that "by Christ all that believe are justified from all things, from which they could not be justified by the law of Moses." (a) For if righteousness consist in an observance of the law, who can deny that Christ merited favour for us, when, by bearing this burden himself, he reconciles us to God, just as though we were complete observers of the law ourselves? The same idea is conveyed in what he afterwards writes to the Galatians, that "God sent forth his Son, made under the law, to redeem them that were under the law." (b) For what was the design of that subjection to the law, but to procure a righteousness for us, by undertaking to perform that which we were not able to do? Hence that imputation of righteousness without works, of which Paul treats; (c) because that righteousness which is found in Christ alone is accepted as ours. Nor indeed is the "flesh" of Christ called our "food" (d) for any other reason but because we find in it the substance of life. Now, this virtue proceeds solely from the crucifixion of the Son of God, as the price of our righteousness. Thus Paul says, "Christ hath given himself for us, an offering and a sacrifice to God for a sweet-smelling savour." (e) And in another place, "He was delivered for our offences, and was raised again for our justification." (f) Hence it is inferred, not only that salvation is given us through Christ, but that the Father is now propitious to us for his sake. For it cannot be doubted, but this, which God declares in a figurative way by Isaiah, is perfectly fulfilled in him: "I will" do it "for mine own sake, and for my servant David's sake." (g) Of this the apostle is a sufficient witness, when he says, "Your sins are forgiven you for his name's sake." (h) For although the name of Christ is not expressed, yet John, in his usual manner, designates him by the pronoun αὐτος, *he*. In this sense the Lord declares, "As I live by the Father, so he that eateth me, even he shall live by me." (i) With which corresponds the following declaration of Paul: "Unto you it is given for the love of Christ (ὑπερ Χριστου) not only to believe on him, but also to suffer for his sake." (k)

VI. But the inquiry made by Lombard and the schoolmen, whether Christ merited for himself, discovers as much foolish curiosity, as the assertion does presumption when they affirm it. For what necessity was there for the only begotten Son of God to descend, in order to make any new acquisition for himself? And God by the publication of his own counsel removes every doubt. For it is said, not that the Father con-

---

(a) Acts xiii. 39.
(b) Gal. iv. 4, 5.
(c) Rom. iv. 5.
(d) John vi. 55.
(e) Eph. v. 2.
(f) Rom. iv. 25.
(g) Isaiah xxxvii. 35.
(h) 1 John ii. 12.
(i) John vi. 57.
(k) Phil. i. 29.

sulted the benefit of the Son in his merits, but that he "delivered him to death, and spared him not," (*l*) "because he loved the world." (*m*) And the language of the prophets is worthy of observation: "Unto us a Child is born." (*n*) Again: "Rejoice greatly, O daughter of Zion; behold, thy King cometh unto thee." (*o*) There would otherwise be no force in that confirmation of his love, which Paul celebrates, that he "died for us, while we were enemies." (*p*) For we infer from this, that he had no regard to himself; and this he clearly affirms himself, when he says, "For their sakes I sanctify myself." (*q*) For by transferring the benefit of his sanctity to others, he declares that he makes no acquisition for himself. And it is highly worthy of our observation, that in order to devote himself wholly to our salvation, Christ in a manner forgot himself. To support this notion of theirs, the schoolmen preposterously pervert the following passage of Paul: "Wherefore also God hath highly exalted him, and given him a name which is above every name." (*r*) For, considered as a man, by what merits could he obtain such dignity as to be the Judge of the world and the Head of angels, to enjoy the supreme dominion of God, and to be the residence of that majesty, the thousandth part of which can never be approached by all the abilities of men and of angels? But the solution is easy and complete, that Paul, in that passage, is not treating of the cause of the exaltation of Christ, but only showing the consequence of it, that he might be an example to us; nor did he mean any other than what is declared in another place, that "Christ ought to have suffered, and to enter into his glory." (*s*)

(*l*) Rom. viii. 32. (*n*) Isaiah ix. 6. (*p*) Rom. v. 8, 10. (*r*) Phil. ii. 9.
(*m*) John iii. 16.   (*o*) Zech. ix. 9.   (*q*) John xvii. 19. (*s*) Luke xxiv. 26.

INSTITUTES

OF THE

CHRISTIAN RELIGION.

BOOK III.

ON THE MANNER OF RECEIVING THE GRACE OF CHRIST, THE BENEFITS WHICH WE DERIVE FROM IT, AND THE EFFECTS WHICH FOLLOW IT.

ARGUMENT.

THE two former books relate to God the Creator and Redeemer. This treats of God the Sanctifier, or of the operations of the Holy Spirit towards our salvation, being an accurate exposition of the third part of the Apostles' Creed.

The principal topics of this are seven, relating chiefly to one object, the doctrine of faith.

First. Since our enjoyment of Christ and all his benefits depends on the secret and special operation of the Holy Spirit, it discusses this operation, which is the foundation of faith, of newness of life, and of all holy exercises—Chap. I.

Secondly. Faith being as it were the hand by which we embrace Christ the Redeemer, as offered to us by the Holy Spirit, it next adds a complete description of faith—Chap. II.

Thirdly. To improve our knowledge of this salutary faith, it proceeds to show the effects which necessarily result from it; and contends that true penitence is always the consequence of true faith. But first it proposes the doctrine of repentance in general—Chap. III.; and then treats of Popish penance and its constituent parts—Chap. IV.

—of indulgences and purgatorial fire—Chap. V. But institutes a particular discussion of the two branches of true penitence, the mortification of the flesh, and the vivification of the spirit, or the life of a Christian, which is excellently described—Chap. VI VII. VIII. IX. X.

Fourthly. In order to a clearer display of the advantages and consequences of this faith, it first treats of justification by faith—Chap. XI.—then explains the questions which arise from it—Chap. XII. XIII. XIV. XV. XVI. XVII. XVIII.—and, lastly, proceeds to a dissertation on Christian liberty, which is an appendage to justification—Chap. XIX.

Fifthly. Next follows prayer, the principal exercise of faith, and the medium or instrument by which we daily receive blessings from God—Chap. XX.

Sixthly. But since the communication of Christ offered in the gospel is not embraced by men in general, but only by those whom the Lord has favoured with the efficacy and peculiar grace of his Spirit, it obviates any supposition of absurdity, by subjoining a necessary and appropriate dissertation on the doctrine of Divine election—Chap. XXI. XXII. XXIII. XXIV.

Lastly. Since we are liable to various difficulties and troubles while exercised in the severe warfare which always attends the life of a Christian, it contends that this may be alleviated by meditating on the final resurrection; and therefore adds a discourse on that subject —Chap. XXV.

CHAPTER I.

WHAT IS DECLARED CONCERNING CHRIST RENDERED PROFITABLE TO US BY THE SECRET OPERATION OF THE SPIRIT.

WE are now to examine how we obtain the enjoyment of those blessings which the Father has conferred on his only begotten Son, not for his own private use, but to enrich the poor and needy. And first it must be remarked, that as long as there is a separation between Christ and us, all that he suffered and performed for the salvation of mankind is useless and unavailing to us. To communicate to us what he received from his Father, he must, therefore, become ours, and dwell within us. On this account he is called our "Head," (a) and "the

(a) Ephes. iv. 15.

first-born among many brethren;" (b) and we, on the other hand, are said to be "grafted into him," (c) and to "put him on;" (d) for, as I have observed, whatever he possesses is nothing to us, till we are united to him. But though it be true that we obtain this by faith, yet, since we see that the communication of Christ, offered in the gospel, is not promiscuously embraced by all, reason itself teaches us to proceed further, and to inquire into the secret energy of the Spirit, by which we are introduced to the enjoyment of Christ and all his benefits. I have already treated of the eternal Deity and essence of the Spirit; let us now confine ourselves to this particular point: Christ came thus by water and blood, that the Spirit may testify concerning him, in order that the salvation procured by him may not be lost to us. For as "there are three that bear record in heaven, the Father, the Word, and the Spirit," so also "there are three on earth, the spirit, the water, and the blood." (e) Nor is this a useless repetition of the testimony of the Spirit, which we perceive to be engraven like a seal on our hearts, so that it seals the ablution and sacrifice of Christ. For which reason Peter also says, that believers are "elect through sanctification of the Spirit unto obedience, and sprinkling of the blood of Jesus Christ." (f) This passage suggests to us, that our souls are purified by the secret ablution of the Spirit, that the effusion of that sacred blood may not be in vain. For the same reason also Paul, when speaking of purification and justification, says, we enjoy both "in the name of the Lord Jesus, and by the Spirit of our God." (g) The sum of all is this — that the Holy Spirit is the bond by which Christ efficaciously unites us to himself. And what we have advanced in the last book concerning his unction, tends to establish the same truth.

II. But as a further confirmation of this point, which is highly worthy of being understood, we must remember that Christ was endued with the Holy Spirit in a peculiar manner; in order to separate us from the world, and introduce us into the hope of an eternal inheritance. Hence the Spirit is called "the Spirit of holiness;" (h) not only because he animates and supports us by that general power which is displayed in mankind, and in all other creatures, but because he is the seed and root of a heavenly life within us. The principal topic, therefore, dwelt on by the prophets in celebrating the kingdom of Christ, is, that there would then be a more exuberant effusion of the Spirit. The most remarkable passage is that of Joel: "I will pour out my Spirit upon all flesh in those

(b) Rom. viii. 29.   (c) Rom. xi. 17.   (d) Gal. iii. 27.   (e) 1 John v. 7, 8.
(f) 1 Pet. i. 2.   (g) 1 Cor. vi. 11.   (h) Rom. i. 4.

days." (*i*) For, though the prophet seems to restrict the gifts of the Spirit to the exercise of the prophetic function, yet he signifies, in a figurative way, that God, by the illumination of his Spirit, will make those his disciples, who before were total strangers to the heavenly doctrine. Besides, as God the Father gives us his Holy Spirit for the sake of his Son, and yet has deposited "all fulness" with his Son, that he might be the minister and dispenser of his own goodness,—the Holy Spirit is sometimes called the Spirit of the Father, and sometimes the Spirit of the Son. "Ye (says Paul) are not in the flesh, but in the Spirit, if so be that the Spirit of God dwell in you. Now, if any man have not the Spirit of Christ, he is none of his." (*k*) And thence he inspires a hope of complete renovation, for "he that raised up Christ from the dead, shall also quicken your mortal bodies by his Spirit that dwelleth in you." (*l*) For there is no absurdity in ascribing to the Father the praise of his own gifts, of which he is the author; and also ascribing the same glory to Christ, with whom the gifts of the Spirit are deposited, to be given to his people. Therefore he invites all who thirst to come to him and drink. (*m*) And Paul teaches us, that "unto every one of us is given grace according to the measure of the gift of Christ." (*n*) And it must be remarked, that he is called the Spirit of Christ, not only because the eternal Word of God is united with the same Spirit as the Father, but also with respect to his character of Mediator; for, if he had not been endued with this power, his advent to us would have been altogether in vain. In which sense he is called "the second Adam, the Lord from heaven, a quickening Spirit;" (*o*) where Paul compares the peculiar life with which the Son of God inspires his people, that they may be one with him, to that animal life which is equally common to the reprobate. So, where he wishes to the faithful "the grace of Christ, and the love of God," he adds also "the communion of the Spirit," (*p*) without which there can be no enjoyment of the paternal favour of God, or the beneficence of Christ. As he says also in another place, "the love of God is shed abroad in our hearts by the Holy Ghost, which is given unto us." (*q*)

III. And here it will be proper to notice the titles by which the Scripture distinguishes the Spirit, where it treats of the commencement, progress, and completion of our salvation. First, he is called the "Spirit of adoption," (*r*) because he witnesses to us the gratuitous benevolence of God, with which God the Father has embraced us in his beloved and only begotten

(*i*) Joel ii. 23.
(*k*) Rom. viii. 9.
(*l*) Rom. viii. 11.
(*m*) John vii. 37.
(*n*) Ephes. iv. 7.
(*o*) 1 Cor. xv. 45.
(*p*) 2 Cor. xiii. 14.
(*q*) Rom. v. 5.
(*r*) Rom. viii. 15.

Son, that he might be a father to us; and animates us to pray with confidence, and even dictates expressions, so that we may boldly cry, "Abba, Father." For the same reason, he is said to be "the earnest" and "seal" of our inheritance; because, while we are pilgrims and strangers in the world, and as persons dead, he infuses into us such life from heaven, that we are certain of our salvation being secured by the Divine faithfulness and care. (*s*) Whence he is also said to be "life," because of righteousness. (*t*) Since by his secret showers he makes us fertile in producing the fruits of righteousness, he is frequently called "water;" as in Isaiah: "Ho, every one that thirsteth, come ye to the waters." (*u*) Again: "I will pour water upon him that is thirsty, and floods upon the dry ground." (*w*) To which corresponds the invitation of Christ, just quoted: "If any man thirst, let him come unto me." (*x*) He sometimes, however, receives this appellation from his purifying and cleansing energy; as in Ezekiel, where the Lord promises to sprinkle clean water on his people, to cleanse them from their impurities. (*y*) Because he restores to life and vigour, and continually supports, those whom he has anointed with the oil of his grace, he thence obtains the name of "unction." (*z*) Because he daily consumes the vices of our concupiscence, and inflames our hearts with the love of God and the pursuit of piety, — from these effects he is justly called "fire." (*a*) Lastly, he is described to us as a "fountain," whence we receive all the emanation of heavenly riches; and as "the hand of God," by which he exerts his power; because by the breath of his power he inspires us with Divine life, so that we are not now actuated from ourselves, but directed by his agency and influence; so that if there be any good in us, it is the fruit of his grace, whereas our characters without him are darkness of mind and perverseness of heart. It has, indeed, already been clearly stated, that till our minds are fixed on the Spirit, Christ remains of no value to us; because we look at him as an object of cold speculation without us, and therefore at a great distance from us. But we know that he benefits none but those who have him for their "head" and "elder brother," and who have "put him on." (*b*) This union alone renders his advent in the character of a Saviour available to us. We learn the same truth from that sacred marriage, by which we are made flesh of his flesh and bone of his bone, and therefore one with him. (*c*) It is only by his Spirit that he unites himself with us; and by the grace and power of the same

(*s*) 2 Cor. i. 22. Eph. i. 13, 14. (*t*) Rom. viii. 10. (*u*) Isaiah lv. 1.
(*w*) Isaiah xliv. 3. (*x*) John vii. 37; iv. 14.
(*y*) Ezek. xxxvi. 25. (*z*) 1 John ii. 20. (*a*) Luke iii. 16.
(*b*) Eph. iv. 15. Rom. viii. 29. Gal. iii. 27. (*c*) Eph. v. 30.

Spirit we are made his members; that he may keep us under himself, and we may mutually enjoy him.

IV. But faith, being his principal work, is the object principally referred to in the most frequent expressions of his power and operation; because it is the only medium by which he leads us into the light of the gospel; according to the declaration of John, that "Christ gave power (or privilege) to become the sons of God to them that believed on his name; which were born, not of blood, nor of the will of the flesh, nor of the will of man, but of God;" (*d*) where, opposing God to flesh and blood, he asserts the reception of Christ by faith, by those who would otherwise remain unbelievers, to be a supernatural gift. Similar to which is this answer of Christ: "Flesh and blood hath not revealed it unto thee, but my Father, which is in heaven;" (*e*) which I now merely mention because I have elsewhere treated it at large. Similar also is the assertion of Paul, that the Ephesians "were sealed with that Holy Spirit of promise." (*f*) For this shows, that there is an eternal teacher, by whose agency the promise of salvation, which otherwise would only strike the air, or at most our ears, penetrates into our minds. Similar also is his remark, that the Thessalonians were "chosen by God through sanctification of the Spirit, and belief of the truth;" (*g*) by which connection, he briefly suggests, that faith itself proceeds only from the Spirit. John expresses this in plainer terms: "We know that he abideth in us, by the Spirit which he hath given us." (*h*) Again: "Hereby know we that we dwell in him, and he in us, because he hath given us of his Spirit." (*i*) Therefore Christ promised to send to his disciples "the Spirit of truth, whom the world cannot receive," (*k*) that they might be capable of attaining heavenly wisdom. He ascribes to him the peculiar office of suggesting to their minds all the oral instructions which he had given them. For in vain would the light present itself to the blind, unless this Spirit of understanding would open their mental eyes; so that he may be justly called the key with which the treasures of the kingdom of heaven are unlocked to us; and his illumination constitutes our mental eyes to behold them. It is therefore that Paul so highly commends the ministry of the Spirit; (*l*) because the instructions of preachers would produce no benefit, did not Christ himself, the internal teacher, by his Spirit, draw to him those who were given him by the Father. (*m*) Therefore, as we have stated, that complete salvation is found in the person of Christ, so, to make us

---

(*d*) John i. 12, 13.
(*e*) Matt. xvi. 17.
(*f*) Eph. i. 13.
(*g*) 2 Thess. ii. 13.
(*h*) 1 John iii. 24.
(*i*) 1 John iv. 13.
(*k*) John xiv. 17.
(*l*) 2 Cor. iii. 6.
(*m*) John vi. 44.

partakers of it, he " baptizes us with the Holy Spirit and with fire," (*n*) enlightening us into the faith of his Gospel, regenerating us so that we become new creatures, and, purging us from profane impurities, consecrates us as holy temples to God.

CHAPTER II.

FAITH DEFINED, AND ITS PROPERTIES DESCRIBED.

ALL these things will be easily understood when we have given a clearer definition of faith, that the reader may perceive its nature and importance. But it will be proper to recall to his remembrance, what has been already stated ; that God has given us his law as the rule of our conduct, and that, if we are guilty of even the smallest breach of it, we are exposed to the dreadful punishment of eternal death, which he denounces. Again, that since it is not only difficult, but entirely above our strength, and beyond the utmost extent of our ability, to fulfil the law as he requires, — if we only view ourselves, and consider what we have demerited, we have not the least hope left, but, as persons rejected by God, are on the verge of eternal perdition. In the third place, it has been explained, that there is but one method of deliverance, by which we can be extricated from such a direful calamity ; that is, the appearance of Christ the Redeemer, by whose means our heavenly Father, commiserating us in his infinite goodness and mercy, has been pleased to relieve us, if we embrace this mercy with a sincere faith, and rely on it with a constant hope. But we must now examine the nature of this faith, by which all who are the adopted sons of God enter on the possession of the heavenly kingdom ; since it is certain, that not every opinion, nor even every persuasion, is equal to the accomplishment of so great a work. And we ought to be the more cautious and diligent in our meditations and inquiries on the genuine property of faith, in proportion to the pernicious tendency of the mistakes of multitudes in the present age on this subject. For a great part of the world, when they hear the word *faith*, conceive it to be nothing more than a common assent to the evangelical history. And even the disputes of the schools concerning faith, by simply styling God the object of it, (as I have elsewhere observed,) rather mislead miserable souls by a vain speculation,

(*n*) Luke iii. 16.

than direct them to the proper mark. For, since God "dwelleth in the light, which no man can approach unto," (o) there is a necessity for the interposition of Christ, as the medium of access to him. Whence he calls himself "the light of the world," (p) and in another place, "the way, and the truth, and the life;" because "no man cometh unto the Father," who is the fountain of life, "but by him;" (q) because he alone knows the Father, and reveals him to believers. (r)

For this reason Paul asserts, that he esteemed nothing worthy of being known but Jesus Christ; (s) and in the twentieth chapter of the Acts declares, that he had preached faith in Christ; and in another place, he introduces Christ speaking in the following manner: "I send thee unto the Gentiles, that they may receive forgiveness of sins, and inheritance among them which are sanctified by faith, that is in me." (t) This apostle tells us, that the glory of God is visible to us in his person, or (which conveys the same idea) that "the light of the knowledge of the glory of God" shines "in his face." (u) It is true, that faith relates to the one God; but there must also be added a knowledge of Jesus Christ, whom he has sent. (w) For God himself would be altogether concealed from us, if we were not illuminated by the brightness of Christ. For this purpose the Father has deposited all his treasures with his only begotten Son, that he might reveal himself in him; and that, by such a communication of blessings, he might express a true image of his glory. For as it has been observed, that we require to be drawn by the Spirit, that we may be excited to seek Christ, so we should also be apprized, that the invisible Father is to be sought only in this image. On which subject, Augustine, treating of the object of faith, beautifully remarks, "that we ought to know whither we should go, and in what way;" and immediately after he concludes, "that he who unites Deity and humanity in one person, is the way most secure from all errors; for that it is God towards whom we tend, and man by whom we go; but that both together can be found only in Christ." Nor does Paul, when he speaks of faith in God, intend to subvert what he so frequently inculcates concerning faith, whose stability is wholly in Christ. And Peter most suitably connects them together, when he says, that "by him we believe in God." (x)

II. This evil, then, as well as innumerable others, must be imputed to the schoolmen, who have, as it were, concealed Christ, by drawing a veil over him; whereas, unless our views be immediately and steadily directed to him, we shall

(o) 1 Tim. vi. 16.
(p) John viii. 12.
(q) John xiv. 6.
(r) Luke x. 22.
(s) 1 Cor. ii. 2.
(t) Acts xxvi. 17, 18.
(u) 2 Cor. iv. 6.
(w) John xvii. 3.
(x) 1 Pet. i. 21.

always be wandering through labyrinths without end. They not only, by their obscure definition, diminish, and almost annihilate, all the importance of faith, but have fabricated the notion of implicit faith, a term with which they have honoured the grossest ignorance, and most perniciously deluded the miserable multitude. Indeed, to express the fact more truly and plainly, this notion has not only buried the true faith in oblivion, but has entirely destroyed it. Is this faith — to understand nothing, but obediently to submit our understanding to the Church? Faith consists not in ignorance, but in knowledge; and that not only of God, but also of the Divine will. For we do not obtain salvation by our promptitude to embrace as truth whatever the Church may have prescribed, or by our transferring to her the province of inquiry and of knowledge. But when we know God to be a propitious Father to us, through the reconciliation effected by Christ, and that Christ is given to us for righteousness, sanctification, and life, — by this knowledge, I say, not by renouncing our understanding, we obtain an entrance into the kingdom of heaven. For, when the apostle says, that "with the heart man believeth unto righteousness, and with the mouth confession is made unto salvation," (*y*) he indicates, that it is not sufficient for a man implicitly to credit what he neither understands, nor even examines; but he requires an explicit knowledge of the Divine goodness, in which our righteousness consists.

III. I do not deny (such is the ignorance with which we are enveloped) that many things are very obscure to us at present, and will continue to be so, till we shall have cast off the burden of the flesh, and arrived nearer to the presence of God. On such subjects, nothing would be more proper than a suspension of judgment, and a firm resolution to maintain unity with the Church. But that ignorance combined with humility should, under this pretext, be dignified with the appellation of Faith, is extremely absurd. For faith consists in a knowledge of God and of Christ, (*z*) not in reverence for the Church. And we see what a labyrinth they have fabricated by this notion of theirs, so that the ignorant and inexperienced, without any discrimination, eagerly embrace as oracular every thing obtruded upon them under the name of the Church; sometimes even the most monstrous errors. This inconsiderate credulity, though it be the certain precipice of ruin, is, nevertheless, excused by them on the plea that it credits nothing definitively, but with this condition annexed, If such be the faith of the Church. Thus they pretend that truth is held in error, light in darkness, and true knowledge in ignorance.

(*y*) Rom. x. 10   (*z*) John xvii. 3.

But, not to occupy any more time in refuting them, we only admonish the reader to compare their doctrine with ours; for the perspicuity of the truth will of itself furnish a sufficient refutation. For the question with them is not, whether faith be yet involved in many relics of ignorance, but they positively assert, that persons are possessed of true faith, who are charmed with their ignorance, and even indulge it, provided they assent to the authority and judgment of the Church concerning things unknown; as if the Scripture did not universally inculcate that knowledge is united with faith.

IV. We grant, that during our pilgrimage in the world, our faith is implicit, not only because many things are yet hidden from our view, but because our knowledge of every thing is very imperfect, in consequence of the clouds of error by which we are surrounded. For the greatest wisdom of those who are most perfect, is to improve, and to press forward with patient docility. Therefore Paul exhorts the faithful, if they differ from each other on any subject, to wait for further revelation. (*a*) And experience teaches us, that till we are divested of the flesh, our knowledge falls far short of what might be wished; in reading also, many obscure passages daily occur, which convince us of our ignorance. With this barrier God restrains us within the bounds of modesty, assigning to every one a measure of faith, that even the most learned teacher may be ready to learn. We may observe eminent examples of this implicit faith in the disciples of Christ, before they were fully enlightened. We see with what difficulty they imbibed the first rudiments; how they hesitated even at the most minute particulars; what inconsiderable advances they made even while hanging on the lips of their Master; and when they ran to the grave at the intelligence of the women, his resurrection was like a dream to them. The testimony already borne by Christ to their possession of faith, forbids us to say that they were entirely destitute of it; indeed, if they had not been persuaded that Christ would rise from the dead, they would have felt no further concern about him. The women were not induced by superstition to embalm with spices the body of a deceased man, of whose life there was no hope; but though they credited his declarations, whose veracity they well knew, yet the ignorance, which still occupied their minds, involved their faith in darkness, so that they were almost lost in astonishment. Whence also they are said at length to have believed, when they saw the words of Christ verified by facts; not that their faith then commenced, but the seed of faith, which had been latent, and as it were dead in their hearts, then shot forth

(*a*) Phil. iii. 15.

with additional vigour. They had therefore a true but an implicit faith, because they received Christ with reverence as their only teacher: being taught by him, they were persuaded that he was the author of their salvation; and they believed that he came from heaven, that through the grace of the Father he might assemble all his disciples there. But we need not seek a more familiar proof of this point, than that some portion of unbelief is always mixed with faith in every Christian.

V. We may also style that an implicit faith, which in strict propriety is nothing but a preparation for faith. The evangelists relate that many believed, who, only being filled with admiration at the miracles of Christ, proceeded no further than a persuasion that he was the promised Messiah, although they had little or no knowledge of evangelical doctrine. Such reverence, which induced them cheerfully to submit themselves to Christ, is dignified with the title of faith, of which, however, it was merely the commencement. Thus the nobleman, or courtier, who believed the promise of Christ concerning the healing of his son, when he returned to his house, (*b*) according to the testimony of the evangelist, believed again; that is, first he esteemed as an oracle what he had heard from the lips of Christ; but afterwards he devoted himself to his authority to receive his doctrine. It must be understood, however, that he was docile and ready to learn; that the word *believe*, in the first place, denotes a particular faith; but in the second place, it numbers him among the disciples who had given their names to Christ. John gives us a similar example in the Samaritans, who believed the report of the woman, so as to run with eagerness to Christ; but who, after having heard him, said to the woman, "Now we believe, not because of thy saying; for we have heard him ourselves, and know, that this is indeed the Christ, the Saviour of the world." (*c*) Hence it appears, that persons not yet initiated into the first elements, but only inclined to obedience, are called believers; not, indeed, with strict propriety, but because God, in his goodness, distinguishes that pious disposition with such a great honour. But this docility, connected with a desire of improvement, is very remote from that gross ignorance which stupefies those who are content with such an implicit faith as the Papists have invented. For if Paul severely condemns those who are "ever learning, yet never come to the knowledge of the truth," (*d*) how much greater ignominy do they deserve who make it their study to know nothing!

VI. This, then, is the true knowledge of Christ — to receive

(*b*) John iv. 50—53.   (*c*) John iv. 42.   (*d*) 2 Tim. iii. 7.

him as he is offered by the Father, that is, invested with his gospel; for, as he is appointed to be the object of our faith, so we cannot advance in the right way to him, without the guidance of the gospel. The gospel certainly opens to us those treasures of grace, without which Christ would profit us little. Thus Paul connects faith as an inseparable concomitant with doctrine, where he says, "Ye have not so learned Christ; if so be ye have been taught by him, as the truth is in Jesus." (*e*) Yet I do not so far restrict faith to the gospel, but that I admit Moses and the prophets to have delivered what was sufficient for its establishment; but because the gospel exhibits a fuller manifestation of Christ, it is justly styled by Paul, "the words of faith and of good doctrine." (*f*) For the same reason, in another place, he represents the law as abolished by the coming of faith; (*g*) comprehending under this term the new kind of teaching, by which Christ, since his appearance as our Master, has given a brighter display of the mercy of the Father, and a more explicit testimony concerning our salvation. The more easy and convenient method for us will be, to descend regularly from the genus to the species. In the first place, we must be apprized, that faith has a perpetual relation to the word, and can no more be separated from it, than the rays from the sun, whence they proceed. Therefore God proclaims by Isaiah, "Hear, and your souls shall live." (*h*) And that the word is the fountain of faith, is evident from this language of John: "These are written, that ye might believe." (*i*) The Psalmist also, intending to exhort the people to faith, says, "To-day, if ye will hear his voice;" (*k*) and *to hear*, generally means *to believe*. Lastly, it is not without reason that in Isaiah, God distinguishes the children of the Church from strangers, by this character, that they shall all be his disciples, and be taught by him; (*l*) for, if this were a benefit common to all, why should he address himself to a few? Correspondent with this is the general use of the words "believers," and "disciples," as synonymous, by the evangelists, on all occasions, and by Luke in particular, very frequently in the Acts of the Apostles; in the ninth chapter of which, he extends the latter epithet even to a woman. Wherefore, if faith decline in the smallest degree from this object, towards which it ought to be directed, it no longer retains its own nature, but becomes an uncertain credulity, and an erroneous excursion of the mind. The same Divine word is the foundation by which faith is sustained and supported, from which it cannot be moved without an immediate downfall. Take away the word, then, and there will be no faith left. We are not here

(*e*) Eph. iv. 20, 21.　(*f*) 1 Tim. iv. 6.　(*g*) Gal. iii. 23—25.　(*h*) Isaiah lv. 3.
(*i*) John xx. 31.　(*k*) Psalm xcv. 7.　(*l*) Isaiah liv. 13.

disputing whether the ministry of men be necessary to disseminate the word of God, by which faith is produced, which we shall discuss in another place; but we assert, that the word itself, however it may be conveyed to us, is like a mirror, in which faith may behold God. Whether, therefore, God in this instance use the agency of men, or whether he operate solely by his own power, he always discovers himself by his word to those whom he designs to draw to himself. (*m*) Whence Paul defines faith as an obedience rendered to the gospel, and praises the service of faith. (*n*) For the apprehension of faith is not confined to our knowing that there is a God, but chiefly consists in our understanding what is his disposition towards us. For it is not of so much importance to us to know what he is in himself, as what he is willing to be to us. We find, therefore, that faith is a knowledge of the will of God respecting us, received from his word. And the foundation of this is a previous persuasion of the Divine veracity; any doubt of which being entertained in the mind, the authority of the word will be dubious and weak, or rather it will be of no authority at all. Nor is it sufficient to believe that the veracity of God is incapable of deception or falsehood, unless you also admit, as beyond all doubt, that whatever proceeds from him is sacred and inviolable truth.

VII. But as the human heart is not excited to faith by every word of God, we must further inquire what part of the word it is, with which faith is particularly concerned. God declared to Adam, "Thou shalt surely die;" (*o*) and to Cain, "The voice of thy brother's blood crieth unto me from the ground;" (*p*) but these declarations are so far from being adapted to the establishment of faith, that of themselves they can only shake it. We do not deny that it is the office of faith to subscribe to the truth of God, whatever be the time, the nature, or the manner of his communications; but our present inquiry is only, what faith finds in the Divine word, upon which to rest its dependence and confidence. When our conscience beholds nothing but indignation and vengeance, how shall it not tremble with fear? And if God be the object of its terror, how should it not fly from him? But faith ought to seek God, not to fly from him. It appears, then, that we have not yet a complete definition of faith; since a knowledge of the Divine will indefinitely, ought not to be accounted faith. But suppose, instead of will, — the declaration of which is often productive of fear and sorrow, — we substitute benevolence or mercy. This will certainly bring us nearer to the nature of

(*m*) Rom. i. 5.
(*n*) Phil. ii. 17.
(*o*) Gen. ii. 17.
(*p*) Gen. iv. 10.

faith. For we are allured to seek God, after we have learned that salvation is laid up for us with him; which is confirmed to us by his declaring it to be the object of his care and affection. Therefore we need a promise of grace, to assure us that he is our propitious Father; since we cannot approach to him without it, and it is upon that alone that the human heart can securely depend. For this reason, in the Psalms, mercy and truth are generally united, as being closely connected; because it would be of no avail for us to know the veracity of God, if he did not allure us to himself by his mercy; nor should we embrace his mercy, if he did not offer it with his own mouth. " I have declared thy faithfulness and thy salvation: I have not concealed thy loving-kindness and thy truth. Let thy loving-kindness and thy truth continually preserve me." (*q*) Again: "Thy mercy, O Lord, is in the heavens; and thy faithfulness reacheth unto the clouds." (*r*) Again: "All the paths of the Lord are mercy and truth unto such as keep his covenant." (*s*) Again: "His merciful kindness is great towards us; and the truth of the Lord endureth for ever." (*t*) Again: "I will praise thy name for thy loving-kindness, and for thy truth." (*u*) I forbear to quote what we read in the prophets to the same purport, that God is merciful and faithful in his promises. For it will be temerity to conclude that God is propitious to us, unless he testify concerning himself, and anticipate us by his invitation, that his will respecting us may be neither ambiguous nor obscure. But we have already seen, that Christ is the only pledge of his love, without whom the tokens of his hatred and wrath are manifest both above and below. Now, since the knowledge of the Divine goodness will not be attended with much advantage, unless it lead us to rely upon it, we must exclude that apprehension of it which is mixed with doubts, which is not uniform and steady, but wavering and undecided. Now, the human mind, blinded and darkened as it is, is very far from being able to penetrate and attain to a knowledge of the Divine will; and the heart also, fluctuating in perpetual hesitation, is far from continuing unshaken in that persuasion. Therefore our mind must be illuminated, and our heart established by some exterior power, that the word of God may obtain full credit with us. Now, we shall have a complete definition of faith, if we say, that it is a steady and certain knowledge of the Divine benevolence towards us, which, being founded on the truth of the gratuitous promise in Christ, is both revealed to our minds, and confirmed to our hearts, by the Holy Spirit.

(*q*) Psalm xl. 10, 11.   (*r*) Psalm xxxvi. 5.   (*s*) Psalm xxv. 10.
(*t*) Psalm cxvii. 2.   (*u*) Psalm cxxxviii. 2.

VIII. But before I proceed any further, it will be necessary to make some preliminary observations, for the solution of difficulties, which otherwise might prove obstacles in the way of the reader.

And first, we must refute the nugatory distinction, which prevails in the schools, of formal and informal faith. For they imagine, that such as are not impressed with any fear of God, or with any sense of piety, believe all that is necessary to be known in order to salvation; as though the Holy Spirit, in illuminating our hearts to faith, were not a witness to us of our adoption. Yet, in opposition to the whole tenor of Scripture, they presumptuously dignify such a persuasion, destitute of the fear of God, with the name of faith. We need not contend with this definition any further than by simply describing the nature of faith, as it is represented in the Divine word. And this will clearly evince the ignorance and insipidity of their clamour concerning it. I have treated it in part already, and shall subjoin what remains in its proper place. At present, I affirm, that a greater absurdity than this figment of theirs, cannot possibly be imagined. They maintain faith to be a mere assent, with which every despiser of God may receive as true whatever is contained in the Scripture. But first it should be examined, whether every man acquires faith for himself by his own power, or whether it is by faith that the Holy Spirit becomes the witness of adoption. They betray puerile folly, therefore, in inquiring whether faith, which is formed by the superaddition of a quality, be the same, or whether it be a new and different faith. It clearly appears, that while they have been trifling in this manner, they never thought of the peculiar gift of the Spirit; for the commencement of faith contains in it the reconciliation by which man draws near to God. But, if they would duly consider that declaration of Paul, "With the heart man believeth unto righteousness," (*w*) they would cease their trifling about this superadded quality. If we had only this one reason, it ought to be sufficient to terminate the controversy — that the assent which we give to the Divine word, as I have partly suggested before, and shall again more largely repeat, is from the heart rather than the head, and from the affections rather than the understanding. For which reason it is called "the obedience of faith," (*x*) to which the Lord prefers no other obedience; because nothing is more precious to him than his own truth; which, according to the testimony of John the Baptist, (*y*) believers, as it were, subscribe and seal. As this is by no means a dubious point, we conclude at once, that it is an absurdity to say, that faith is formed by the

(*w*) Rom. x. 10.   (*x*) Rom. i. 5.   (*y*) John iii. 33.

addition of a pious affection to an assent of the mind; whereas, even this assent consists in a pious affection, and is so described in the Scriptures. But another argument offers itself, which is still plainer. Since faith accepts Christ, as he is offered to us by the Father; and he is offered, not only for righteousness, remission of sins, and peace, but also for sanctification and as a fountain of living water; it is certain, that no man can ever know him aright, unless he at the same time receive the sanctification of the Spirit. Or, if any one would wish it to be more clearly expressed, Faith consists in a knowledge of Christ. Christ cannot be known without the sanctification of his Spirit. Consequently, faith is absolutely inseparable from a pious affection.

IX. This passage of Paul, "Though I have all faith, so that I could remove mountains, and have not charity, I am nothing," (z) is generally adduced by them to support the notion of an informal faith unaccompanied with charity; but they overlook the sense in which the apostle uses the word "faith" in this place. For having, in the preceding chapter, treated of the various gifts of the Spirit, among which he has enumerated "divers kinds of tongues, the working of miracles and prophecy," (a) and having exhorted the Corinthians to "covet earnestly the best gifts," from which the greatest benefit and advantage would accrue to the whole body of the Church, he adds, "yet show I unto you a more excellent way;" implying, that all such gifts, whatever be their intrinsic excellence, are yet to be deemed worthless, unless they be subservient to charity; for that, being given for the edification of the Church, if not employed for that purpose, they lose their beauty and value. To prove this, he particularly specifies them, repeating the same gifts, which he had before enumerated, but under other names. He uses the word "faith" to denote what he had before called powers, (δυναμεις, potestates, virtutes,) that is, a power of working miracles. This, then, whether it be called power or faith, being a particular gift of God, which any impious man may both possess and abuse, as the gift of tongues, or prophecy, or other gifts, we need not wonder if it be separated from charity. But the mistake of such persons arises wholly from this — that though the word "faith" is used in many senses, not observing this diversity of signification, they argue as if it had always the same meaning. The passage which they adduce from James in support of the same error, shall be discussed in another place. Now, although, for the sake of instruction, when we design to show the nature of that knowledge of God, which is possessed by the impious, we

(z) 1 Cor. xiii. 2.   (a) 1 Cor. xii. 10—31.

allow that there are various kinds of faith, yet we acknowledge and preach only one faith in the pious, according to the doctrine of the Scripture. Many men certainly believe that there is a God: they admit the evangelical history and the other parts of Scripture to be true; just as we form an opinion of transactions which are narrated as having occurred in former times, or of which we have ourselves been spectators. There are some who go further; esteeming the word of God as an undoubted revelation from heaven, not wholly disregarding its precepts, and being in some measure affected both by its denunciations and by its promises. To such persons, indeed, faith is attributed; but by a catachresis, a tropical or improper form of expression; because they do not with open impiety resist, or reject, or contemn the word of God, but rather exhibit some appearance of obedience to it.

X. But this shadow or image of faith, as it is of no importance, so is unworthy of the name of faith; its great distance from the substantial truth of which, though we shall show more at large hereafter, there can be no objection to its being briefly pointed out here. Simon Magus (b) is said to have believed, who, nevertheless, just after, betrays his unbelief. When faith is attributed to him, we do not apprehend, with some, that he merely pretended to it with his lips, while he had none in his heart; but we rather think, that being overcome with the majesty of the gospel, he did exercise a kind of faith, and perceived Christ to be the author of life and salvation, so as freely to profess himself one of his followers. Thus, in the Gospel of Luke, those persons are said to believe for a time, in whom the seed of the word is prematurely choked before it fructifies, and those in whom it takes no root, but soon dries up and perishes. We doubt not but such persons, being attracted with some taste of the word, receive it with avidity, and begin to perceive something of its Divine power; so that by the fallacious counterfeit of faith, they impose not only on the eyes of men, but even on their own minds. For they persuade themselves, that the reverence which they show for the word of God, is real piety; supposing that there is no impiety but a manifest and acknowledged abuse or contempt of it. But, whatever be the nature of that assent, it penetrates not to the heart, so as to fix its residence there; and though it sometimes appears to have shot forth roots, yet there is no life in them. The heart of man has so many recesses of vanity, and so many retreats of falsehood, and is so enveloped with fraudulent hypocrisy, that it frequently deceives even himself. But let them, who glory in such phantoms of faith, know, that in

(b) Acts viii. 13, 18, 19.

this respect they are not at all superior to devils. Persons of the former description, who hear and understand without any emotion those things, the knowledge of which makes devils tremble, are certainly far inferior to the fallen spirits; and the others are equal to them in this respect — that the sentiments with which they are impressed, finally terminate in terror and consternation. (c)

XI. I know that it appears harsh to some, when faith is attributed to the reprobate; since Paul affirms it to be the fruit of election. But this difficulty is easily solved; for, though none are illuminated to faith, or truly feel the efficacy of the gospel, but such as are preordained to salvation, yet experience shows, that the reprobate are sometimes affected with emotions very similar to those of the elect, so that, in their own opinion, they in no respect differ from the elect. Wherefore, it is not at all absurd, that a taste of heavenly gifts is ascribed to them by the apostle, and a temporary faith by Christ: (d) not that they truly perceive the energy of spiritual grace and clear light of faith, but because the Lord, to render their guilt more manifest and inexcusable, insinuates himself into their minds, as far as his goodness can be enjoyed without the Spirit of adoption. If any one object, that there remains, then, no further evidence by which the faithful can certainly judge of their adoption, I reply, that although there is a great similitude and affinity between the elect of God and those who are endued with a frail and transitory faith, yet the elect possess that confidence, which Paul celebrates, so as boldly to "cry, Abba, Father." (e) Therefore, as God regenerates for ever the elect alone with incorruptible seed, so that the seed of life planted in their hearts never perishes, so he firmly seals within them the grace of his adoption, that it may be confirmed and ratified to their minds. But this by no means prevents that inferior operation of the Spirit from exerting itself even in the reprobate. In the mean time the faithful are taught to examine themselves with solicitude and humility, lest carnal security insinuate itself, instead of the assurance of faith. Besides, the reprobate have only a confused perception of grace, so that they embrace the shadow rather than the substance; because the Spirit properly seals remission of sins in the elect alone, and they apply it by a special faith to their own benefit. Yet the reprobate are justly said to believe that God is propitious to them, because they receive the gift of reconciliation, though in a confused and too indistinct manner: not that they are partakers of the same faith or regeneration with the sons of God, but because they appear, under the disguise of hypocrisy, to

(c) James ii. 19.   (d) Heb. vi. 4.   (e) Gal. iv. 6.

have the principle of faith in common with them. Nor do I deny, that God so far enlightens their minds, that they discover his grace; but he so distinguishes that perception from the peculiar testimony, which he gives to his elect, that they never attain any solid effect and enjoyment. For he does not, therefore, show himself propitious to them, by truly delivering them from death, and receiving them under his protection; but he only manifests to them present mercy. But he vouchsafes to the elect alone, the living root of faith, that they may persevere even to the end. Thus we have refuted the objection, that if God truly discovers his grace, it remains for ever; because nothing prevents God from illuminating some with a present perception of his grace, which afterwards vanishes away.

XII. Moreover, though faith is a knowledge of the benevolence of God towards us, and a certain persuasion of his veracity, yet it is not to be wondered at, that the subjects of these temporary impressions lose the sense of Divine love, which, notwithstanding its affinity to faith, is yet widely different from it. The will of God, I confess, is immutable, and his truth always consistent with itself. But I deny that the reprobate ever go so far as to penetrate to that secret revelation, which the Scripture confines to the elect. I deny, therefore, that they either apprehend the will of God, as it is immutable, or embrace his truth with constancy; because they rest in a fugitive sentiment. Thus a tree, not planted deeply enough to shoot forth living roots, in process of time withers; though for some years it may produce not only leaves and blossoms, but even fruits. Finally, as the defection of the first man was sufficient to obliterate the Divine image from his mind and soul, so we need not wonder if God enlightens the reprobate with some beams of his grace, which he afterwards suffers to be extinguished. Nor does any thing prevent him from slightly tincturing some with the knowledge of his gospel, and thoroughly imbuing others with it. It must, nevertheless, be remembered, that how diminutive and weak soever faith may be in the elect, yet, as the Spirit of God is a certain pledge and seal to them of their adoption, his impression can never be erased from their hearts; but that the reprobate have only a few scattered rays of light, which are afterwards lost; yet that the Spirit is not chargeable with deception, because he infuses no life into the seed which he drops in their hearts, that it may remain for ever incorruptible, as in the elect. I go still further; for since it is evident from the tenor of the Scripture, and from daily experience, that the reprobate are sometimes affected with a sense of Divine grace, some desire of mutual love must necessarily be excited in their hearts. Thus Saul had for a time a pious disposition to love God, from whom experiencing paternal kindness, he was allured by the charms of his goodness. But as the persuasion of the paternal love of God is not radically fixed in the reprobate, so they love him not reciprocally with the sincere affection of children, but are influenced by a mercenary disposition; for the spirit of love was given to Christ alone, that he might instil it into his members. And this observation of Paul certainly extends to none but the elect: "The love of God is shed abroad in our hearts by the Holy Ghost, which is given unto us;" (*f*) the same love, which generates that confidence of invocation which I have before mentioned. Thus, on the contrary, we see that God is wonderfully angry with his children, whom he ceases not to love: not that he really hates them, but because he designs to terrify them with a sense of his wrath, to humble their carnal pride, to shake off their indolence, and to excite them to repentance. Therefore they apprehend him to be both angry with them, or at least with their sins, and propitious to them at the same time; for they sincerely deprecate his wrath, and yet resort to him for succour with tranquillity and confidence. Hence it appears, that faith is not hypocritically counterfeited by some, who nevertheless are destitute of true faith; but, while they are hurried away with a sudden impetuosity of zeal, they deceive themselves by a false opinion. Nor is it to be doubted, that indolence preoccupies them, and prevents them from properly examining their hearts as they ought to do. It is probable that those persons were of this description, to whom, according to John, "Jesus did not commit himself," notwithstanding that they believed in him, "because he knew all men: he knew what was in man." (*g*) If multitudes did not depart from the common faith, (I style it common, because there is a great similitude and affinity between temporary faith and that which is living and perpetual,) Christ would not have said to his disciples, "If ye continue in my word, then are ye my disciples indeed, and ye shall know the truth, and the truth shall make you free." (*h*) For he addresses those who have embraced his doctrine, and exhorts them to an increase of faith, that the light which they have received may not be extinguished by their own supineness. Therefore Paul claims faith as peculiar to the elect, (*i*) indicating that many decay, because they have had no living root. Thus also Christ says in Matthew, "Every plant, which my heavenly Father hath not planted, shall be rooted up." (*k*) There is a grosser deception in others, who are not ashamed to attempt to deceive both God and men. James inveighs against this class

(*f*) Rom. v. 5.   (*g*) John ii. 24, 25.   (*h*) John viii. 31, 32.
(*i*) Titus i. 1.   (*k*) Matt. xv. 13.

of men, who impiously profane faith by hypocritical pretensions to it. (*l*) Nor would Paul require from the children of God, a "faith unfeigned," (*m*) but because multitudes presumptuously arrogate to themselves what they possess not, and with their vain pretences deceive others, and sometimes even themselves. Therefore he compares a good conscience to a vessel in which faith is kept; because many, "having put away a good conscience, concerning faith have made shipwreck." (*n*)

XIII. We must also remember the ambiguous signification of the word *faith*; for frequently faith signifies the sound doctrine of piety, as in the place which we have just cited, and in the same Epistle, where Paul says, that deacons must hold "the mystery of the faith in a pure conscience." (*o*) Also where he predicts the apostasy of some "from the faith." (*p*) But, on the contrary, he says, that Timothy had been "nourished up in the words of faith." (*q*) Again, where he says, "avoiding profane and vain babblings, and oppositions of science, falsely so called; which some professing, have erred concerning the faith;" (*r*) whom in another place he styles "reprobates concerning the faith." (*s*) Thus, also, when he directs Titus to "rebuke them, that they may be sound in the faith," (*t*) by soundness, he means nothing more than that purity of doctrine, which is so liable to be corrupted and to degenerate through the instability of men. Since "all the treasures of wisdom and knowledge are hidden in Christ," (*u*) whom faith possesses, faith is justly extended to the whole summary of heavenly doctrines, with which it is inseparably connected. On the contrary, it is sometimes restricted to a particular object; as when Matthew says, that "Jesus saw their faith," (*w*) who let down the paralytic man through the roof; and when Christ exclaimed respecting the centurion, "I have not found so great faith, no, not in Israel." (*x*) But it is probable, that the centurion was wholly intent on the recovery of his son, a concern for whom wholly occupied his mind; yet, because he was contented with the mere answer of Christ, without being importunate for his corporeal presence, it is on account of this circumstance that his faith is so greatly extolled. And we have lately shown, that Paul uses faith for the gift of miracles; which is possessed by those who are neither regenerated by the Spirit of God, nor serious worshippers of him. In another place, also, he uses it to denote the instruction by which we are edified in the faith; for, when he suggests that faith will be abolished, it must undoubtedly be referred to the ministry of the Church, which is, at present, useful to our infirmity. In

(*l*) James ii. 14.
(*m*) 1 Tim. i. 5.
(*n*) 1 Tim. i. 19.
(*o*) 1 Tim. iii. 9
(*p*) 1 Tim. iv. 1.
(*q*) 1 Tim. iv. 6.
(*r*) 1 Tim. vi. 20, 21.
(*s*) 2 Tim. iii. 8.
(*t*) Titus i. 13.
(*u*) Col. ii. 3.
(*w*) Matt. ix 2. Mark ii. 5
(*x*) Matt. viii. 10.

these forms of expression, however, there is an evident analogy. But when the word "faith" is in an improper sense transferred to a hypocritical profession, or to that which falsely assumes the name, it should not be accounted a harsher catachresis, than when the fear of God is used for a corrupt and perverse worship; as when it is frequently said in the sacred history, that the foreign nations, which had been transplanted to Samaria and its vicinity, feared the fictitious deities and the God of Israel; which is like confounding together heaven and earth. But our present inquiry is, what is that faith by which the children of God are distinguished from unbelievers, by which we invoke God as our Father, by which we pass from death to life, and by which Christ, our eternal life and salvation, dwells in us? The force and nature of it, I conceive, I have concisely and clearly explained.

XIV. Now, let us again examine all the parts of that definition; a careful consideration of which, I think, will leave nothing doubtful remaining. When we call it knowledge, we intend not such a comprehension as men commonly have of those things which fall under the notice of their senses. For it is so superior, that the human mind must exceed and rise above itself, in order to attain to it. Nor does the mind which attains it comprehend what it perceives, but being persuaded of that which it cannot comprehend, it understands more by the certainty of this persuasion, than it would comprehend of any human object by the exercise of its natural capacity. Wherefore Paul beautifully expresses it in these terms: "to comprehend what is the breadth, and length, and depth, and height; and to know the love of Christ, which passeth knowledge." (*y*) For he meant to suggest, that what our mind apprehends by faith is absolutely infinite, and that this kind of knowledge far exceeds all understanding. Yet, because God has revealed to his saints the secret of his will, "which had been hidden from ages and from generations," (*z*) therefore *faith* is in Scripture justly styled "an acknowledgment;" (*a*) and by John, "knowledge," when he asserts, that believers know that they are the sons of God. (*b*) And they have indeed a certain knowledge of it; but are rather confirmed by a persuasion of the veracity of God, than taught by any demonstration of reason. The language of Paul also indicates this: "whilst we are at home in the body, we are absent from the Lord; for we walk by faith, not by sight." By this he shows that the things which we understand through faith, are at a distance from us, and beyond our sight. Whence we conclude, that the knowledge of faith consists more in certainty than in comprehension.

(*y*) Eph. iii. 18.   (*a*) Col. ii. 2.
(*z*) Col. i. 26.   (*b*) 1 John iii. 2.

XV. To express the solid constancy of the persuasion, we further say, that it is a certain and steady knowledge. For, as faith is not content with a dubious and versatile opinion, so neither with an obscure and perplexed conception; but requires a full and fixed certainty, such as is commonly obtained respecting things that have been tried and proved. For unbelief is so deeply rooted in our hearts, and such is our propensity to it, that though all men confess with the tongue, that God is faithful, no man can persuade himself of the truth of it, without the most arduous exertions. Especially when the time of trial comes, the general indecision discloses the fault which was previously concealed. Nor is it without reason that the Holy Spirit asserts the authority of the Divine word in terms of such high commendation, but with a design to remedy the disease which I have mentioned, that the promises of God may obtain full credit with us. "The words of the Lord (says David) are pure words; as silver tried in a furnace of earth purified seven times." (c) Again: "The word of the Lord is tried: he is a buckler to all those that trust in him." (d) And Solomon confirms the same, nearly in the same words: "Every word of God is pure." (e) But, as the hundred and nineteenth Psalm is almost entirely devoted to this subject, it were needless to recite any more testimonies. Whenever God thus recommends his word to us, he, without doubt, obliquely reprehends our unbelief; for the design of those recommendations is no other than to eradicate perverse doubts from our hearts. There are also many, who have such conceptions of the Divine mercy, as to receive but very little consolation from it. For they are at the same time distressed with an unhappy anxiety, doubting whether he will be merciful to them; because they confine within too narrow limits that clemency, of which they suppose themselves to be fully persuaded. For they reflect with themselves thus: that his mercy is large and copious, bestowed upon many, and ready for the acceptance of all; but that it is uncertain whether it will reach them also, or, rather, whether they shall reach it. This thought, since it stops in the midst of its course, is incomplete. Therefore it does not so much confirm the mind with secure tranquillity, as disturb it with restless hesitation. But very different is the meaning of "full assurance," ($\pi\lambda\eta\rho o\phi o\rho\iota\alpha\varsigma$,) which is always attributed to faith in the Scriptures; and which places the goodness of God, that is clearly revealed to us, beyond all doubt. But this cannot take place, unless we have a real sense and experience of its sweetness in ourselves. Wherefore the apostle from faith deduces confidence, and from confidence boldness.

(c) Psalm xii. 6. (d) Psalm xviii. 30. (e) Prov. xxx. 5.

For this is his language: "In Christ we have boldness and access, with confidence by the faith of him." (*f*) These words imply that we have no right faith, but when we can venture with tranquillity into the Divine presence. This boldness arises only from a certain confidence of the Divine benevolence and our salvation; which is so true, that the word "faith" is frequently used for confidence.

XVI. The principal hinge on which faith turns is this — that we must not consider the promises of mercy, which the Lord offers, as true only to others, and not to ourselves; but rather make them our own, by embracing them in our hearts. Hence arises that confidence, which the same apostle in another place calls "peace;" (*g*) unless any one would rather make peace the effect of confidence. It is a security, which makes the conscience calm and serene before the Divine tribunal, and without which it must necessarily be harassed and torn almost asunder with tumultuous trepidation, unless it happen to slumber for a moment in an oblivion of God and itself. And indeed it is but for a moment; for it does not long enjoy that wretched oblivion, but is most dreadfully wounded by the remembrance, which is perpetually recurring, of the Divine judgment. In short, no man is truly a believer, unless he be firmly persuaded, that God is a propitious and benevolent Father to him, and promise himself every thing from his goodness; unless he depend on the promises of the Divine benevolence to him, and feel an undoubted expectation of salvation; as the apostle shows in these words: "If we hold fast the beginning of our confidence steadfast unto the end." (*h*) Here he supposes, that no man has a good hope in the Lord, who does not glory with confidence, in being an heir of the kingdom of heaven. He is no believer, I say, who does not rely on the security of his salvation, and confidently triumph over the devil and death, as Paul teaches us in this remarkable peroration: "I am persuaded (says he) that neither death, nor life, nor angels, nor principalities, nor powers, nor things present, nor things to come, shall be able to separate us from the love of God, which is in Christ Jesus our Lord." (*i*) Thus the same apostle is of opinion, that "the eyes of our understanding" are not truly "enlightened," unless we discover what is the hope of the eternal inheritance, to which we are called. (*k*) And he every where inculcates, that we have no just apprehensions of the Divine goodness, unless we derive from it a considerable degree of assurance.

XVII. But some one will object, that the experience of believers is very different from this; for that, in recognizing the

(*f*) Eph. iii. 12.   (*g*) Rom. v. 1.   (*h*) Heb. iii. 14.
(*i*) Rom. viii. 38.   (*k*) Eph. i. 18.

grace of God towards them, they are not only disturbed with inquietude, (which frequently befalls them,) but sometimes also tremble with the most distressing terrors. The vehemence of temptations, to agitate their minds, is so great, that it appears scarcely compatible with that assurance of faith of which we have been speaking. We must therefore solve this difficulty, if we mean to support the doctrine we have advanced. When we inculcate, that faith ought to be certain and secure, we conceive not of a certainty attended with no doubt, or of a security interrupted by no anxiety; but we rather affirm, that believers have a perpetual conflict with their own diffidence, and are far from placing their consciences in a placid calm, never disturbed by any storms. Yet, on the other hand, we deny, however they may be afflicted, that they ever fall and depart from that certain confidence which they have conceived in the Divine mercy. The Scripture proposes no example of faith more illustrious or memorable than David, especially if you consider the whole course of his life. Yet that his mind was not invariably serene, appears from his innumerable complaints, of which it will be sufficient to select a few. When he rebukes his soul for turbulent emotions, is he not angry with his unbelief? "Why (says he) art thou cast down, O my soul? and why art thou disquieted in me? Hope thou in God." (*l*) And, certainly, that consternation was an evident proof of diffidence, as though he supposed himself to be forsaken by God. In another place, also, we find a more ample confession: "I said, in my haste, I am cut off from before thine eyes." (*m*) In another place, also, he debates with himself in anxious and miserable perplexity, and even raises a dispute concerning the nature of God: "Hath God forgotten to be gracious? Will the Lord cast off for ever?" What follows is still harsher: "And I said, I must fall; these are the changes of the right hand of the Most High." (*n*) For, in a state of despair, he consigns himself to ruin; and not only confesses that he is agitated with doubts, but, as vanquished in the conflict, considers all as lost; because God has deserted him, and turned to his destruction that hand which used to support him. Wherefore it is not without reason that he says, "Return unto thy rest, O my soul;" (*o*) since he had experienced such fluctuations amidst the waves of trouble. And yet, wonderful as it is, amidst these concussions, faith sustains the hearts of the pious, and truly resembles the palm-tree, rising with vigour undiminished by any burdens which may be laid upon it, but which can never retard its growth; as David, when he might appear to be overwhelmed,

(*l*) Psalm xlii. 5.   (*n*) Psalm lxxvii. 7, 9, 10.
(*m*) Psalm xxxi. 22.   (*o*) Psalm cxvi. 7.

yet, chiding himself, ceased not to aspire towards God. Indeed, he who, contending with his own infirmity, strives in his anxieties to exercise faith, is already in a great measure victorious. Which we may infer from such passages as this: "Wait on the Lord: be of good courage, and he shall strengthen thine heart; wait, I say, on the Lord." (*p*) He reproves himself for timidity, and repeating the same twice, confesses himself to be frequently subject to various agitations. In the mean time, he is not only displeased with himself for these faults, but ardently aspires towards the correction of them. Now, if we enter into a close and correct examination of his character and conduct, and compare him with Ahaz, we shall discover a considerable difference. Isaiah is sent to convey consolation to the anxiety of the impious and hypocritical king; he addresses him in these words: "Take heed, and be quiet; fear not," &c. (*q*) But what effect had the message on him? As it had been before said, that "his heart was moved as the trees of the wood are moved with the wind," (*r*) though he heard the promise, he ceased not to tremble. This therefore is the proper reward and punishment of infidelity — so to tremble with fear, that he who opens not the gate to himself by faith, in the time of temptation departs from God; but, on the contrary, believers, whom the weight of temptations bends and almost oppresses, constantly emerge from their distresses, though not without trouble and difficulty. And because they are conscious of their own imbecility, they pray with the Psalmist, "Take not the word of truth utterly out of my mouth." (*s*) By these words we are taught, that they sometimes become dumb, as though their faith were destroyed; yet that they neither fail nor turn their backs, but persevere in their conflict, and arouse their inactivity by prayer, that they may not be stupefied by self-indulgence.

XVIII. To render this intelligible, it is necessary to recur to that division of the flesh and the spirit, which we noticed in another place, and which most clearly discovers itself in this case. The pious heart therefore perceives a division in itself, being partly affected with delight, through a knowledge of the Divine goodness; partly distressed with sorrow, through a sense of its own calamity; partly relying on the promise of the gospel; partly trembling at the evidence of its own iniquity; partly exulting in the apprehension of life; partly alarmed by the fear of death. This variation happens through the imperfection of faith; since we are never so happy, during the present life, as to be cured of all diffidence, and entirely filled and possessed by faith. Hence those conflicts, in which

(*p*) Psalm xxvii. 14.   (*r*) Isaiah vii. 2.
(*q*) Isaiah vii. 4.   (*s*) Psalm cxix. 43.

the diffidence which adheres to the relics of the flesh, rises up in opposition to the faith formed in the heart. But if, in the mind of a believer, assurance be mixed with doubts, do we not always come to this point, that faith consists not in a certain and clear, but only in an obscure and perplexed knowledge of the Divine will respecting us? Not at all. For, if we are distracted by various thoughts, we are not therefore entirely divested of faith; neither, though harassed by the agitations of diffidence, are we therefore immerged in its abyss; nor, if we be shaken, are we therefore overthrown. For the invariable issue of this contest is, that faith at length surmounts those difficulties, from which, while it is encompassed with them, it appears to be in danger.

XIX. Let us sum it up thus: As soon as the smallest particle of grace is infused into our minds, we begin to contemplate the Divine countenance as now placid, serene, and propitious to us: it is indeed a very distant prospect, but so clear, that we know we are not deceived. Afterwards, in proportion as we improve, — for we ought to be continually improving by progressive advances, — we arrive at a nearer, and therefore more certain view of him, and by continual habit he becomes more familiar to us. Thus we see, that a mind illuminated by the knowledge of God, is at first involved in much ignorance, which is removed by slow degrees. Yet it is not prevented either by its ignorance of some things, or by its obscure view of what it beholds, from enjoying a clear knowledge of the Divine will respecting itself, which is the first and principal exercise of faith. For, as a man who is confined in a prison, into which the sun shines only obliquely and partially through a very small window, is deprived of a full view of that luminary, yet clearly perceives its splendour, and experiences its beneficial influence, — thus we, who are bound with terrestrial and corporeal fetters, though surrounded on all sides with great obscurity, are nevertheless illuminated, sufficiently for all the purposes of real security, by the light of God shining ever so feebly to discover his mercy.

XX. The apostle beautifully inculcates both these ideas in various places. For when he says, that "we know in part, and we prophesy in part, and see through a glass darkly," (*t*) he indicates, how very slender a portion of that wisdom which is truly Divine, is conferred upon us in the present life. For although these words imply, not only that faith remains imperfect as long as we groan under the burden of the flesh, but that our imperfection renders it necessary for us to be unremittingly employed in acquiring further knowledge, yet he suggests, that it is impossible for our narrow capacity to comprehend that which is infinite. And this Paul predicates con-

(*t*) 1 Cor. xiii. 9, 12.

cerning the whole Church; though every individual of us is obstructed and retarded, by his own ignorance, from making that progress which might be wished. But what a sure and certain experience, of itself, even the smallest particle of faith gves us, the same apostle shows in another place, where he asserts, that " we, with open face, beholding as in a glass the glory of the Lord, are changed into the same image." (*u*) Such profound ignorance must necessarily involve much doubt and trepidation; especially as our hearts are, by a kind of natural instinct, inclined to unbelief. Besides, temptations, various and innumerable, frequently assail us with great violence. Above all, our own conscience, oppressed by its incumbent load of sin, sometimes complains and groans within itself, sometimes accuses itself, sometimes murmurs in secret, and sometimes is openly disturbed. Whether, therefore, adversity discover the wrath of God, or the conscience find in itself any reason or cause of it, thence unbelief derives weapons to oppose faith, which are perpetually directed to this object, to persuade us, that God is angry with us, and inimical to us; that we may not hope for any assistance from him, but may dread him as our irreconcilable enemy.

XXI. To sustain these attacks, faith arms and defends itself with the word of the Lord. And when such a temptation as this assails us,—that God is our enemy, because he is angry with us,—faith, on the contrary, objects, that he is merciful even when he afflicts, because chastisement proceeds rather from love than from wrath. When it is pressed with this thought, that God is an avenger of iniquities, it opposes the pardon provided for all offences, whenever the sinner makes application to the Divine clemency. Thus the pious mind, how strangely soever it may be agitated and harassed, rises at length superior to all difficulties, nor ever suffers its confidence in the Divine mercy to be shaken. The various disputes which exercise and fatigue it, terminate rather in the confirmation of that confidence. It is a proof of this, that when the saints conceive themselves to feel most the vengeance of God, they still confide their complaints to him, and when there is no appearance of his hearing them, they continue to call upon him. For what end would be answered by addressing complaint to him from whom they expected no consolation? And they would never be disposed to call upon him, unless they believed him to be ready to assist them. (*w*) Thus the disciples, whom Christ reprehends for the weakness of their faith, complained indeed that they were perishing, but still they implored his assistance. Nor, when he chides them on account of their weak faith, does he reject them from the number of his children, or

(*u*) 2 Cor. iii. 18.   (*w*) Matt. viii. 25.

class them with unbelievers; but he excites them to correct that fault. Therefore we repeat the assertion already made, that faith is never eradicated from a pious heart, but continues firmly fixed, however it may be shaken, and seem to bend this way or that; that its light is never so extinguished or smothered, but that it lies at least concealed under embers; and that this is an evident proof, that the word, which is an incorruptible seed, produces fruit similar to itself, whose germ never entirely perishes. For, though it is the last cause of despair that can happen to saints, to perceive, according to their apprehension of present circumstances, the hand of God lifted up for their destruction, yet Job asserts the extent of his hope to be such, that though he should be slain by him, he would continue to trust in him. (*x*) This, then, is the real state of the case: Unbelief is not inwardly predominant in the hearts of the pious, but it assails them from without; nor do its weapons mortally wound them; they only molest them, or at least inflict such wounds as are curable. For faith, according to Paul, serves us as a shield, which, being opposed to hostile weapons, receives their blows, and entirely repels them, or at least breaks their force, so that they penetrate no vital part. When faith is shaken, therefore, it is just as if a soldier, otherwise bold, were constrained, by a violent stroke of a javelin, to change his position and retreat a little; but when faith itself is wounded, it is just as if his shield were broken by a blow, yet not pierced through. For the pious mind will always recover so far as to say, with David, "Though I walk through the valley of the shadow of death, I will fear no evil; for thou art with me." (*y*) To walk in the gloom of death is certainly terrible; and believers, whatever degree of firmness they have, cannot but dread it. But when this thought prevails, that God is present with them, and concerned for their salvation, fear at once gives way to security. But, as Augustine says, whatever powerful engines the devil erects against us, when he possesses not the heart, which is the residence of faith, he is kept at a distance. Thus, if we judge from the event, believers not only escape in safety from every battle, so that, receiving an accession of vigour, they are soon after prepared to enter the field again, but we see the accomplishment of what John says, in his canonical Epistle: "This is the victory that overcometh the world, even our faith." (*z*) For he affirms, that it will be not only victorious in one or in a few battles, or against some particular assault, but that it will overcome the whole world, though it should be attacked a thousand times.

XXII. There is another species of fear and trembling, by

(*x*) Job xiii. 15.   (*y*) Psalm xxiii. 4.   (*z*) 1 John v. 4.

which, nevertheless, the assurance of faith is so far from being impaired, that it is more firmly established. That is, when believers, considering the examples of the Divine vengeance against the impious as lessons given to them, are solicitously cautious not to provoke the wrath of God against themselves by the same crimes; or when, feeling their own misery, they learn to place all their dependence on the Lord, without whom they perceive themselves to be more inconstant and transient than the wind. For when the apostle, by a representation of the punishments which the Lord formerly inflicted on the Israelitish nation, alarms the fears of the Corinthians, lest they should involve themselves in the same calamities, (a) he in no respect weakens their confidence, but shakes off the indolence of the flesh, by which faith is rather impaired than confirmed. Nor when, from the fall of the Jews, he takes an occasion to exhort him that standeth to beware lest he fall, (b) does he direct us to waver, as though we were uncertain of our stability; but only forbids all arrogance and presumptuous, overweening confidence in our own strength, that the Gentiles may not proudly insult over the expelled Jews, into whose place they have been received. (c) In that passage, however, he not only addresses believers, but in his discourse also includes hypocrites, who gloried merely in external appearance. For he admonishes not men individually, but instituting a comparison between the Jews and the Gentiles, after having shown that the rejection of the former was a righteous punishment for their unbelief and ingratitude, he exhorts the latter not to lose, by pride and haughtiness, the grace of adoption recently transferred to them. But as, in the general rejection of the Jews, there remained some of them who fell not from the covenant of adoption, so among the Gentiles there might possibly arise some, who, destitute of true faith, would only be inflated with foolish and carnal confidence, and thus abuse the goodness of God to their own ruin. But though you should understand this to be spoken to the elect and believers, no inconvenience would result from it. For it is one thing to repress the temerity, which from remaining carnality sometimes discovers itself in the saints, that it may not produce vain confidence; and another to strike the conscience with fear, that it may not rely with full security on the mercy of God.

XXIII. Moreover, when he teaches us to "work out our own salvation with fear and trembling," (d) he only requires us to accustom ourselves, with great self-humiliation, to look up to the power of the Lord. For nothing arouses us to repose all confidence and assurance of mind on the Lord, so much as dif-

(a) 1 Cor. x. 11.   (b) 1 Cor. x. 12.   (c) Rom. xi. 10.   (d) Phil. ii. 11.

fidence of ourselves, and anxiety arising from a consciousness of our own misery. In which sense, we must understand this declaration of the Psalmist, "I will come into thy house in the multitude of thy mercy, and in thy fear will I worship." (*e*) Whence he beautifully connects the confidence of faith, which relies on the mercy of God, with that religious fear by which we ought to be affected, whenever we come into the presence of the Divine Majesty, and from its splendour, discover our extreme impurity. Solomon also truly pronounces, "Happy is the man who feareth alway; but he that hardeneth his heart shall fall into mischief." (*f*) But he intends that fear which will render us more cautious, not such as would afflict and ruin us, such as, when the mind, confounded in itself, recovers itself in God; dejected in itself, finds consolation in him; and despairing of itself, revives with confidence in him. Wherefore nothing prevents believers from being distressed with fear, and at the same time enjoying the most serene consolation; as they now turn their eyes towards their own vanity, and now direct the attention of their mind to the truth of God. How can fear and faith, it will be asked, both reside in the same mind? Just as, on the contrary, insensibility and anxiety. For though the impious endeavour to acquire a habit of insensibility, that they may not be disquieted by the fear of God, the judgment of God follows them so closely, that they cannot attain the object of their desires. So nothing prevents God from training his people to humility, that in their valiant warfare they may restrain themselves within the bounds of modesty. And that this was the design of the apostle appears from the context, where, as the cause of fear and trembling, he assigns the good pleasure of God, by which he gives to his people both rightly to will, and strenuously to perform. In the same sense we should understand this prediction: "The children of Israel shall fear the Lord and his goodness;" (*g*) for not only piety produces a reverence of God, but also the sweetness of grace fills a man that is dejected in himself, with fear and admiration; causing him to depend upon God, and humbly submit himself to his power.

XXIV. Yet we give no encouragement to the very pestilent philosophy, begun to be broached by some semi-Papists in the present day. For, being unable to defend that gross notion of faith as a doubtful opinion, which has been taught in the schools, they resort to another invention, and propose a confidence mixed with unbelief. They confess, that whenever we look to Christ, we find in him a sufficient ground of comfortable hope; but because we are always unworthy of all those

(*e*) Psalm v. 7.   (*f*) Prov. xxviii. 14.   (*g*) Hosea iii. 5.

blessings which are offered to us in Christ, they wish us to fluctuate and hesitate in the view of our own unworthiness. In short, they place the conscience in such a state between hope and fear, that it alternately inclines to both. They also connect hope and fear together, so that when the former rises, it depresses the latter, and when the latter lifts its head, the former falls. Thus Satan, finding that those open engines, which he heretofore employed to destroy the assurance of faith, are now no longer of any avail, secretly endeavours to undermine it. But what kind of confidence would that be, which should frequently give way to despair? If you consider Christ, (say they,) salvation is certain; if you return to yourself, condemnation is certain. Diffidence and good hope, therefore, must of necessity alternately prevail in your mind. As though we ought to consider Christ as standing apart from us, and not rather as dwelling within us. For we therefore expect salvation from him, not because he appears to us at a great distance, but because, having ingrafted us into his body, he makes us partakers not only of all his benefits, but also of himself. Wherefore I thus retort their own argument: If you consider yourself, condemnation is certain; but since Christ, with all his benefits, is communicated to you, so that all that he has becomes yours, and you become a member of him, and one with him,—his righteousness covers your sins; his salvation supersedes your condemnation; he interposes with his merit, that your unworthiness may not appear in the Divine presence. Indeed, the truth is, that we ought by no means to separate Christ from us, or ourselves from him; but, with all our might, firmly to retain that fellowship by which he has united us to himself. Thus the apostle teaches us: "The body (says he) is dead because of sin; but the spirit is life because of righteousness." (*h*) According to this frivolous notion of these persons, he ought to have said, Christ indeed has life in himself; but you, being sinners, remain obnoxious to death and condemnation. But he speaks in a very different manner; for he states, that the condemnation which we demerit in ourselves is swallowed up by the salvation of Christ; and in confirmation of this, uses the same argument as I have adduced, that Christ is not without us, but dwells within us; and not only adheres to us by an indissoluble connection of fellowship, but by a certain wonderful communion coalesces daily more and more into one body with us, till he becomes altogether one with us. Nor do I deny, what I have lately said, that some interruptions of faith at times occur, as its imbecility is by the force of violence inclined to this or the other direction.

(*h*) Rom. viii. 10.

Thus, in the thick gloom of temptations, its light is smothered; but, whatever befalls it, it never discontinues its efforts in seeking God.

XXV. Bernard reasons in a similar manner, when he professedly discusses this subject, in the Fifth Homily, on the Dedication of the Temple. "By the goodness of God, meditating sometimes on the soul, I think I discover in it, as it were, two opposite characters. If I view it as it is in itself and of itself, I cannot utter a greater truth concerning it, than that it is reduced to nothing. What need is there at present to enumerate all its miseries, how it is loaded with sins, enveloped in darkness, entangled with allurements, inflamed with inordinate desires, subject to the passions, filled with illusions, always prone to evil, inclined to every vice, and finally full of ignominy and confusion? Now, if even our righteousnesses, when viewed in the light of truth, be found to be 'as filthy rags,'(*i*) what judgment will be formed of our acknowledged unrighteousness? 'If the light that is in' us 'be darkness, how great is that darkness!' (*k*) What then? Man is undoubtedly become like vanity; man is reduced to nothing; man is nothing. Yet how is he entirely nothing, whom God magnifies? How is he nothing, on whom the heart of God is fixed? Brethren, let us revive again. Although we are nothing in our own hearts, perhaps there may be something for us latent in the heart of God. O Father of mercies, O Father of the miserable, how dost thou fix thine heart on us! For thine heart is where thy treasure is. But how are we thy treasure, if we are nothing? All nations are before thee as though they existed not; they must be considered as nothing. That is, before thee; not within thee: thus it is in the judgment of thy truth; but not thus in the affection of thy clemency. Thou callest things which are not, as though they were; and therefore they are not, because thou callest things which are not; yet they are, because thou callest them. For though they are not, with reference to themselves, yet with thee they are; according to this expression of Paul: 'Not of works, but of him that calleth.'"(*l*) After this, Bernard says, that there is a wonderful connection between these two considerations. Things which are connected with each other, certainly do not reciprocally destroy each other; which he also more plainly declares in the following conclusion: "Now, if we diligently examine what we are in both considerations,—how in one view we are nothing, and in the other how we are magnified,—I conceive that our boasting appears to be restrained; but perhaps it is more increased, and indeed established, that we may glory not in

(*i*) Isaiah lxiv. 6.   (*k*) Matt. vi. 23.   (*l*) Rom. ix. 11.

ourselves, but in the Lord. If we reflect, if he has decreed to save us, we shall shortly be delivered; this is sufficient to recover us. But ascending to a loftier and more extensive prospect, let us seek the city of God, let us seek his temple, let us seek his palace, let us seek his spouse. I have not forgotten, but with fear and reverence I say, We are; but in the heart of God. We are; but by his condescending favour, not by our own merit."

XXVI. Now, the fear of the Lord, which is universally ascribed to all the saints, and which is called sometimes "the beginning of wisdom," (*m*) sometimes "wisdom" (*n*) itself, although it be but one, proceeds from a twofold apprehension of him. For God requires the reverence of a Father and of a Master. Therefore he who truly desires to worship him, will study to pay him the obedience of a son and the submission of a servant. The Lord, by the prophet, distinguishes the obedience which is paid to him as a father, by the appellation of honour; and the service which he receives as a master, by that of fear. "A son (says he) honoureth his father, and a servant his master. If, then, I be a father, where is mine honour? And if I be a master, where is my fear?" (*o*) But notwithstanding his distinction between them, you see how he confounds them together. Let the fear of the Lord therefore with us be a reverence mingled with this honour and fear. Nor is it surprising, that the same mind cherishes both these affections; for he who considers what a Father God is to us, has ample reason, even though there were no hell, to dread his displeasure more than any death. But, such is the propensity of our nature to the licentiousness of transgression, that in order to restrain it by every possible method, we should at the same time indulge this reflection, that all iniquity is an abomination to the Lord, under whose power we live, and whose vengeance they will not escape, who provoke his wrath against them by the wickedness of their lives.

XXVII. Now, the assertion of John, that "there is no fear in love, but perfect love casteth out fear, because fear hath torment," (*p*) is not at all repugnant to what we have advanced. For he speaks of the terror of unbelief, between which and the fear of believers there is a wide difference. For the impious fear not God from a dread of incurring his displeasure, if they could do it with impunity; but because they know him to be armed with vindictive power, they tremble with horror at hearing of his wrath. And thus also they fear his wrath, because they apprehend it to be impending over them, because they every moment expect it to fall on their heads. But the

(*m*) Psalm cxi. 10.
(*n*) Prov. i. 7; ix. 10. Job xxviii. 28.
(*o*) Mal. i. 6.
(*p*) 1 John iv. 18.

faithful, as we have observed, fear his displeasure more than punishment, and are not disturbed with the fear of punishment, as though it were impending over them, but are rendered more cautious that they may not incur it. Thus the apostle, when addressing believers, says, "Let no man deceive you with vain words; for, because of these things cometh the wrath of God upon the children of disobedience [or unbelief.]" (*q*) He threatens not its descending on them; but admonishes them to consider the wrath of the Lord prepared for the impious, on account of the crimes which he had enumerated, that they may avoid tempting it. It seldom happens, however, that the reprobate are aroused merely by simple threatenings; but, on the contrary, being already obdurate and insensible, when God thunders from heaven, if it be only in words, they rather harden themselves in rebellion: but when they feel the stroke of his hand, they are compelled to fear him, whether they will or not. This is commonly called a servile fear, in opposition to a filial fear, which is ingenuous and voluntary. Some persons curiously introduce an intermediate species of fear; because that servile and constrained affection sometimes subdues men's minds, so that they voluntarily approach to the fear of God.

XXVIII. Now, in the Divine benevolence, which is affirmed to be the object of faith, we apprehend the possession of salvation and everlasting life to be obtained. For, if no good can be wanting when God is propitious, we have a sufficient certainty of salvation, when he himself assures us of his love. "O God, cause thy face to shine, and we shall be saved," (*r*) says the Psalmist. Hence the Scriptures represent this as the sum of our salvation, that he has "abolished" all "enmity," (*s*) and received us into his favour. In which they imply, that since God is reconciled to us, there remains no danger, but that all things will prosper with us. Wherefore faith, having apprehended the love of God, has promises for the present life and the life to come, and a solid assurance of all blessings; but it is such an assurance as may be derived from the Divine word. For faith certainly promises itself neither longevity, nor honour, nor wealth, in the present state; since the Lord has not been pleased to appoint any of these things for us; but is contented with this assurance, that whatever we may want of the conveniences or necessaries of this life, yet God will never leave us. But its principal security consists in an expectation of the future life, which is placed beyond all doubt by the word of God. For whatever miseries and calamities may on earth await those who are the objects of the love of God, they

(*q*) Eph. v. 6. Col. iii. 6.   (*r*) Psalm lxxx. 3.   (*s*) Eph. ii. 14, 15.

cannot prevent the Divine benevolence from being a source of complete felicity. Therefore, when we meant to express the perfection of blessedness, we have mentioned the grace of God, as the fountain from which every species of blessings flows down to us. And we may generally observe in the Scriptures, that when they treat not only of eternal salvation, but of any blessing we enjoy, our attention is recalled to the love of God. For which reason David says, that "The lovingkindness of God," when experienced in a pious heart, "is better" and more desirable "than life" itself. (t) Finally, if we have an abundance of all things to the extent of our desires, but are uncertain of the love or hatred of God, our prosperity will be cursed, and therefore miserable. But if the paternal countenance of God shine on us, even our miseries will be blessed, because they will be converted into aids of our salvation. (u) Thus Paul, after an enumeration of all possible adversities, glories that they can never separate us from the love of God; and in his prayers, he always begins with the grace of God, from which all prosperity proceeds. David likewise opposes the Divine favour alone against all the terrors which disturb us: "Though I walk through the valley of the shadow of death, (says he,) I will fear no evil, for thou art with me." (w) And we always feel our minds wavering, unless, contented with the grace of God, they seek their peace in it, and are deeply impressed with the sentiment of the Psalmist: "Blessed is the nation whose God is the Lord; and the people whom he hath chosen for his own inheritance." (x)

XXIX. We make the foundation of faith to be the gratuitous promise; for on that faith properly rests. For, although faith admits the veracity of God in all things, whether he command or prohibit, whether he promise or threaten; though it obediently receives his injunctions, carefully observes his prohibitions, and attends to his threatenings, — yet with the promise it properly begins, on that it stands, and in that it ends. For it seeks in God for life, which is found, not in precepts nor in denunciations of punishments, but in the promise of mercy, and in that only which is gratuitous; for a conditional promise, which sends us back to our own works, promises life to us only if we find it in ourselves. Therefore, if we wish our faith not to tremble and waver, we must support it with the promise of salvation, which is voluntarily and liberally offered us by the Lord, rather in consideration of our misery, than in respect of our worthiness. Wherefore the apostle denominates the gospel "the word of faith;" (y) a character which he denies both to the precepts and to the promises of the law; since there is

(t) Psalm lxiii. 3. (u) Rom. viii. 39. (w) Psalm xxiii. 4.
(x) Psalm xxxiii. 12. (y) Rom. x. 8.

nothing that can establish faith, but that liberal embassy by which God reconciles the world to himself. Hence also the same apostle frequently connects faith with the gospel; as when he states, that "the ministry of the gospel was committed to him for obedience to the faith;" that it is "the power of God unto salvation to every one that believeth;" that therein is the "righteousness of God revealed from faith to faith." (z) Nor is this to be wondered at; for the gospel being "the ministry of reconciliation," (a) there is no other sufficient testimony of the Divine benevolence towards us, the knowledge of which is necessary to faith. When we assert, therefore, that faith rests on the gratuitous promise, we deny not that believers embrace and revere every part of the Divine word, but we point out the promise of mercy as the peculiar object of faith. Thus believers ought to acknowledge God as a judge and avenger of crimes; yet they fix their eyes peculiarly on his clemency; described for their contemplation as "gracious and full of compassion; slow to anger, and of great mercy; good to all, and diffusing his tender mercies over all his works." (b)

XXX. Nor do I regard the clamours of Pighius, or any such snarlers, who censure this restriction, as though it divided faith, and comprehended only one branch of it. I grant that, as I have already said, the general object of faith (as they express themselves) is the veracity of God, whether he threaten, or give us a hope of his grace. Wherefore the apostle attributes this to faith, that Noah feared the destruction of the world while it was yet unseen. (c) If the fear of impending punishment was the work of faith, threatenings ought not to be excluded from the definition of it. This indeed is true; but these cavillers unjustly charge us with denying that faith respects every part of the word of God. For we only intend to establish these two points; first, that it never stands firmly till it comes to the gratuitous promise; secondly, that we are reconciled to God only as it unites us to Christ. Both these points are worthy of observation. We are inquiring for a faith which may distinguish the sons of God from the reprobate, and believers from unbelievers. If any man believes the justice of the Divine commands and the truth of the Divine threatenings, must he therefore be called a believer? By no means. Therefore faith can have no stability, unless it be placed on the Divine mercy. Now, to what purpose do we argue concerning faith? Is it not that we may understand the way of salvation? But how is faith saving, but by ingrafting us into

(z) Rom. i. 5, 16, 17.
(a) 2 Cor. v. 18.
(b) Psalm cxlv. 8, 9.
(c) Heb. xi. 7.

the body of Christ? There will be no absurdity, then, if, in the definition of it, we insist on its principal effect, and as a difference, add to the genus that character which separates believers from unbelievers. In a word, these malevolent men have nothing to carp at in this doctrine, without involving in the same reprehension with us, the apostle Paul, who particularly styles the gospel "the word of faith." (*d*)

XXXI. Hence, again, we infer, what has been before stated, that the word is as necessary to faith, as the living root of the tree is to the fruit; because, according to David, none can trust in God but those who know his name. (*e*) But this knowledge proceeds not from every man's own imagination, but from the testimony which God himself gives of his own goodness. This the same Psalmist confirms in another place: "Thy salvation according to thy word." (*f*) Again: "Save me: I hoped in thy word." (*g*) Where we must observe the relation of faith to the word, and that salvation is the consequence of it. Yet we exclude not the Divine power, by a view of which, unless faith be supported, it will never ascribe to God the honour that is due to him. Paul seems to relate a trifling or uninteresting circumstance concerning Abraham, when he says, that he was persuaded that God, who had promised him the blessed seed, "was able also to perform." (*h*) In another place, respecting himself he says, "I know whom I have believed, and am persuaded that he is able to keep that which I have committed unto him against that day." (*i*) But if any one considers, how many doubts respecting the power of God frequently intrude themselves, he will fully acknowledge, that they who magnify it as it deserves, have made no small progress in faith. We shall all confess, that God is able to do whatever he pleases; but whilst the smallest temptation strikes us with consternation and terror, it is evident that we derogate from the Divine power, to which we prefer the menaces of Satan in opposition to the promises of God. This is the reason why Isaiah, when he would impress the hearts of the people with an assurance of salvation, discourses in so magnificent a manner concerning the infinite power of God. He frequently appears, after having begun to treat of the hope of pardon and reconciliation, to digress to another subject, and to wander through prolix and unnecessary circumlocutions, celebrating the wonders of the Divine government in the machine of heaven and earth, and the whole order of nature: yet there is nothing but what is applicable to the present subject; for, unless the omnipotence of God be presented to our eyes,

(*d*) Rom. x. 8.
(*e*) Psalm ix. 10.
(*f*) Psalm cxix. 41.
(*g*) Psalm cxix. 146, 147.
(*h*) Rom. iv. 21.
(*i*) 2 Tim. i. 12.

our ears will not attend to his word, or not esteem it according to its worth. Moreover, the Scripture there speaks of his effectual power; for piety, as we have elsewhere seen, always makes a useful and practical application of the power of God: and particularly proposes to itself those of his works in which he has discovered himself as a father. Hence the frequent mention of redemption in the Scriptures, from which the Israelites might learn, that God, who had once been the author of salvation, would be its everlasting preserver. David also teaches us by his own example, that the private benefits which God has conferred on an individual, conduce to the confirmation of his faith for the future; even when he seems to have deserted us, we ought to extend our views further, so as to derive encouragement from his ancient benefits, as it is said in another psalm: "I remember the days of old; I meditate on all thy works," &c. (*k*) Again: "I will remember the works of the Lord: surely I will remember thy wonders of old." (*l*) But since, without the word, all our conceptions of the power and works of God are unprofitable and transient, we have sufficient reason for asserting, that there can be no faith, without the illumination of Divine grace. But here a question might be raised — What must be thought of Sarah and Rebecca, both of whom, apparently impelled by the zeal of faith, transgressed the limits of the word? Sarah, when she ardently desired the promised son, gave her maid-servant to her husband. That she sinned in many respects, is not to be denied; but I now refer to her error in being carried away by her zeal, and not restraining herself within the bounds of the Divine word. Yet it is certain, that this desire proceeded from faith. Rebecca, having been divinely assured of the election of her son Jacob, procures him the benediction by a sinful artifice; she deceives her husband, the witness and minister of the grace of God; she constrains her son to utter falsehoods; she corrupts the truth of God by various frauds and impostures; finally, by exposing his promise to ridicule, she does all in her power to destroy it. And yet this transaction, however criminal and reprehensible, was not unaccompanied with faith; because she had to overcome many obstacles, that she might aspire earnestly to that which, without any expectation of worldly advantage, was pregnant with great troubles and dangers. So we must not pronounce the holy patriarch Isaac to be entirely destitute of faith, because, after having been divinely apprized of the translation of the honour to his younger son, he nevertheless ceases not to be partial to Esau, his first-born. These examples certainly teach that errors are frequently mixed with faith,

(*k*) Psalm cxliii. 5.   (*l*) Psalm lxxvii. 11.

yet that faith, when real, always retains the preëminence. For, as the particular error of Rebecca did not annul the effect of the benediction, so neither did it destroy the faith which generally predominated in her mind, and was the principle and cause of that action. Nevertheless, Rebecca, in this instance, has discovered how liable the human mind is to error, as soon as it allows itself the smallest license. But though our deficiency or imbecility obscures faith, yet it does not extinguish it: in the mean time it reminds us how solicitously we ought to attend to the declarations of God; and confirms what we have said, that faith decays unless it be supported by the word; as the minds of Sarah, Isaac, and Rebecca, would have been lost in their obliquities, if they had not, by the secret restraint of God, been kept in obedience to the word.

XXXII. Again: it is not without reason that we include all the promises in Christ; (m) as the apostle in the knowledge of him includes the whole gospel; and in another place teaches, that "all the promises of God in him are yea, and in him amen." (n) The reason of this is plain. For, if God promises any thing, he gives a proof of his benevolence; so that there is no promise of his which is not a testimony of his love. Nor does it affect the argument, that the impious, when they are loaded with great and continual benefits from the Divine goodness, render themselves obnoxious to a heavier judgment. For since they neither think nor acknowledge that they receive those things from the hand of the Lord, — or if ever they acknowledge it, yet they never reflect within themselves on his goodness, — they cannot thereby be instructed concerning his mercy, any more than the brutes, who, according to the circumstances of their condition, receive the same effusion of his liberality, but never perceive it. Nor is it any more repugnant to our argument, that by generally rejecting the promises designed for them, they draw down on themselves severer vengeance. For although the efficacy of the promises is manifested only when they have obtained credit with us, yet their force and propriety are never extinguished by our unbelief or ingratitude. Therefore, when the Lord by his promises invites a man not only to receive, but also to meditate on the effects of his goodness, he at the same time gives him a declaration of his love. Whence we must return to this principle, that every promise is an attestation of the Divine love to us. But it is beyond all controversy, that no man is loved by God but in Christ; (o) he is the "beloved Son," in whom the love of the Father perpetually rests, and then from him diffuses itself to us; as Paul says, that we are "accepted in the beloved." (p)

(m) 1 Cor. ii. 2.   (n) 2 Cor. i. 20.   (o) Matt. iii. 17; xvii. 5.   (p) Eph. i. 6.

It must therefore be communicated to us by his mediation. (*q*) Wherefore the apostle, in another place, calls him "our peace," (*r*) and elsewhere represents him as the bond by which God is united to us in his paternal love. It follows, that whenever any promise is presented to us, our eyes must be directed to him; and that Paul is correct in stating, that all the promises of God are confirmed and accomplished in him. (*s*) This is opposed by some examples. For it is not credible that Naaman the Syrian, when he inquired of the prophet respecting the right method of worshipping God, (*t*) was instructed concerning the Mediator; yet his piety is commended. Cornelius, (*u*) a Gentile and Roman, could scarcely be acquainted with what was not universally or clearly known among the Jews; yet his benefactions and prayers were acceptable to God; and the sacrifices of Naaman received the approbation of the prophet, which neither of these persons could have obtained without faith. Similar was the case of the eunuch to whom Philip was conducted; (*w*) who, unless he had been possessed of some faith, would never have incurred the labour and expense of a long and difficult journey, for the sake of worshipping at Jerusalem. Yet we see how, on being interrogated by Philip, he betrayed his ignorance of the Mediator. I confess, indeed, that their faith was in some measure implicit, not only with respect to the person of Christ, but with respect to the power and office assigned him by the Father. At the same time it is certain that they had imbibed principles which afforded them some notion of Christ, however slight; nor should this be thought strange; for the eunuch would not have hastened from a remote country to Jerusalem to adore an unknown God; nor did Cornelius spend so much time, after having once embraced the Jewish religion, without acquainting himself with the rudiments of sound doctrine. With regard to Naaman, it would have been extremely absurd for Elisha, who directed him concerning the minutest particulars, to have been silent on the most important subject. Although their knowledge of Christ, therefore, was obscure, yet to suppose that they had none is unreasonable; because they practised the sacrifices of the law, which must have been distinguished by their end, that is, Christ, from the illegitimate sacrifices of the heathen.

XXXIII. This simple and external demonstration of the Divine word ought, indeed, to be fully sufficient for the production of faith, if it were not obstructed by our blindness and perverseness. But such is our propensity to error, that our

(*q*) Eph. ii. 14.
(*r*) Rom. viii. 3.
(*s*) Rom. xv. 8.
(*t*) 2 Kings v. 17—19.
(*u*) Acts x. 31.
(*w*) Acts viii. 17, 31.

mind can never adhere to Divine truth; such is our dulness, that we can never discern the light of it. Therefore nothing is effected by the word, without the illumination of the Holy Spirit. Whence it appears, that faith is far superior to human intelligence. Nor is it enough for the mind to be illuminated by the Spirit of God, unless the heart also be strengthened and supported by his power. On this point, the schoolmen are altogether erroneous, who, in the discussion of faith, regard it as a simple assent of the understanding, entirely neglecting the confidence and assurance of the heart. Faith, therefore, is a singular gift of God in two respects; both as the mind is enlightened to understand the truth of God, and as the heart is established in it. For the Holy Spirit not only originates faith, but increases it by degrees, till he conducts us by it all the way to the heavenly kingdom. "That good thing," says Paul, " which was committed unto thee, keep, by the Holy Ghost which dwelleth in us." (*x*) If it be urged, that Paul declares the Spirit to be given to us "by the hearing of faith," (*y*) this objection is easily answered. If there were only one gift of the Spirit, it would be absurd to represent the Spirit as the effect of faith, of which he is the author and cause; but when the apostle is treating of the gifts with which God adorns his Church, to lead it, by advancements in faith, forwards to perfection, we need not wonder that he ascribes those gifts to faith, which prepares us for their reception. It is accounted by the world exceedingly paradoxical, when it is affirmed, that no one can believe in Christ, but he to whom it is given. But this is partly for want of considering the depth and sublimity of heavenly wisdom, and the extreme dulness of man in apprehending the mysteries of God, and partly from not regarding that firm and steadfast constancy of heart, which is the principal branch of faith.

XXXIV. But if, as Paul tells us, no one is acquainted with the will of a man but "the spirit of a man which is in him," (*z*) how could man be certain of the will of God? And if we are uncertain respecting the truth of God in those things which are the subjects of our present contemplation, how should we have a greater certainty of it, when the Lord promises such things as no eye sees and no heart conceives? Human sagacity is here so completely lost, that the first step to improvement, in the Divine school, is to forsake it. For, like an interposing veil, (*a*) it prevents us from discovering the mysteries of God, which are revealed only to babes. (*b*) "For flesh and blood hath not revealed," (*c*) and "the natural man receiveth not the

(*x*) 2 Tim. i. 14.
(*y*) Gal. iii. 2.
(*z*) 1 Cor. ii. 11.
(*a*) 2 Cor. iii. 14.
(*b*) Matt. xi. 25.
(*c*) Matt. xvi. 17.

things of the Spirit of God; for they are foolishness unto him; neither can he know them, because they are spiritually discerned." (*d*) The aids of the Spirit therefore are necessary, or rather it is his influence alone that is efficacious here. "Who hath known the mind of the Lord? or who hath been his counsellor?" (*e*) but "the Spirit searcheth all things, yea, the deep things of God;" (*f*) and through him, "we have the mind of Christ." (*g*) "No man can come to me (says he) except the Father, which hath sent me, draw him. Every man therefore that hath heard and hath learned of the Father, cometh unto me. Not that any man hath seen the Father, save he which is of God." Therefore, as we can never come to Christ, unless we are drawn by the Spirit of God, so when we are drawn, we are raised both in mind and in heart above the reach of our own understanding. For illuminated by him, the soul receives, as it were, new eyes for the contemplation of heavenly mysteries, by the splendour of which it was before dazzled. And thus the human intellect, irradiated by the light of the Holy Spirit, then begins to relish those things which pertain to the kingdom of God, for which before it had not the smallest taste. Wherefore Christ's two disciples receive no benefit from his excellent discourse to them on the mysteries of his kingdom, (*h*) till he opens their understanding that they may understand the Scriptures. Thus, though the apostles were taught by his Divine mouth, yet the Spirit of Truth must be sent to them, to instil into their minds the doctrine which they had heard with their ears. (*i*) The word of God is like the sun shining on all to whom it is preached; but without any benefit to the blind. But in this respect we are all blind by nature; therefore it cannot penetrate into our minds, unless the internal teacher, the Spirit, make way for it by his illumination.

XXXV. In a former part of this work, relating to the corruption of nature, we have shown more at large the inability of men to believe; therefore I shall not fatigue the reader by a repetition of the same things. Let it suffice that faith itself, which we possess not by nature, but which is given us by the Spirit, is called by Paul "the spirit of faith." (*k*) Therefore he prays "that God would fulfil," in the Thessalonians, "all the good pleasure of his goodness, and the work of faith with power." (*l*) By calling faith "the work" of God, and "the good pleasure of his goodness," he denies it to be the proper effect of human exertion; and not content with that, he adds that it is a specimen of the Divine power. When he says to

---

(*d*) 1 Cor. ii. 14.   (*f*) 1 Cor. ii. 10.   (*h*) Luke xxiv. 45.   (*k*) 2 Cor. iv. 13.
(*e*) Rom. xi. 34.   (*g*) 1 Cor. ii. 16.   (*i*) John xvi. 13.   (*l*) 2 Thess. i. 11.

the Corinthians, that faith stands "not in the wisdom of men, but in the power of God," (*n*) he speaks indeed of external miracles; but because the reprobate have no eyes to behold them, he comprehends also the inward seal which he elsewhere mentions. And that he may more illustriously display his liberality in so eminent a gift, God deigns not to bestow it promiscuously on all, but by a singular privilege imparts it to whom he will. We have already cited testimonies to prove this point. Augustine, who is a faithful expositor of them, says, "It was in order to teach us that the act of believing is owing to the Divine gift, not to human merit, that our Saviour declared, 'No man can come to me, except the Father which hath sent me draw him; (*o*) and except it were given unto him of my Father.' (*p*) It is wonderful, that two persons hear; one despises, the other ascends. Let him who despises, impute it to himself; let him who ascends, not arrogate it to himself." In another place he says, "Wherefore is it given to one, not to another? I am not ashamed to reply, This is a depth of the cross. From I know not what depth of the Divine judgments, which we cannot scrutinize, proceeds all our ability. That I can, I see; whence I can, I see not; unless that I see thus far, that it is of God. But why one, and not another? It is too much for me; it is an abyss, a depth of the cross. I can exclaim with admiration, but not demonstrate it in disputation." The sum of the whole is this — that Christ, when he illuminates us with faith by the power of his Spirit, at the same time ingrafts us into his body, that we may become partakers of all his benefits.

XXXVI. It next remains, that what the mind has imbibed, be transfused into the heart. For the word of God is not received by faith, if it floats on the surface of the brain; but when it has taken deep root in the heart, so as to become an impregnable fortress to sustain and repel all the assaults of temptation. But if it be true that the right apprehension of the mind proceeds from the illumination of the Spirit, his energy is far more conspicuous in such a confirmation of the heart; the diffidence of the heart being greater than the blindness of the mind; and the furnishing of the heart with assurance being more difficult than the communication of knowledge to the understanding. Therefore the Spirit acts as a seal, to seal on our hearts those very promises, the certainty of which he has previously impressed on our minds, and serves as an earnest to confirm and establish them. "After that ye believed," says the apostle, "ye were sealed with that Holy Spirit of promise, which is the earnest of our inheritance." (*q*)

(*n*) 1 Cor. ii. 5.   (*o*) John vi. 44.   (*p*) John vi. 65.   (*q*) Eph. i. 13.

Do you see how he shows that the hearts of believers are impressed by the Spirit, as by a seal? How, for this reason, he calls him "the Spirit of promise," because he ratifies the gospel to us? So, to the Corinthians, he says, "He which hath anointed us, is God; who hath also sealed us, and given the earnest of the Spirit in our hearts." (r) And in another place, where he speaks of the confidence and boldness of hope, he makes "the earnest of the Spirit" (s) the foundation of it.

XXXVII. I have not forgotten what I have already observed, and the remembrance of which experience incessantly renews, that faith is agitated with various doubts; so that the minds of the pious are seldom at ease, or at best enjoy not a state of perpetual tranquillity. But whatever assaults they may sustain, they either emerge from the very gulf of temptation, or remain firm in their station. This assurance alone nourishes and supports faith, while we are satisfied of what is declared by the Psalmist, "God is our refuge and strength, a very present help in trouble. Therefore will we not fear, though the earth be removed, and the mountains be carried into the midst of the sea." (t) This most delightful repose is celebrated also in another psalm: "I laid me down and slept; I awaked; for the Lord sustained me." (u) Not that David enjoyed a happy cheerfulness of soul perpetually flowing on in one even tenor; but having tasted the grace of God according to the proportion of his faith, he glories in intrepidly despising whatever could disquiet the peace of his mind. Therefore the Scripture, intending to exhort us to faith, commands us to "be quiet." In Isaiah, "In quietness and in confidence shall be your strength." (w) In the Psalms, "Rest in the Lord, and wait patiently for him." (x) With which corresponds the observation of the apostle to the Hebrews, "Ye have need of patience." (y)

XXXVIII. Hence we may judge, how pernicious that dogma of the schoolmen is, that it is impossible to decide concerning the favour of God towards us, any otherwise than from moral conjecture, as every individual may deem himself not unworthy of it. If it must be determined by our works how the Lord is affected towards us, I admit we cannot attain this object even by a very slight conjecture; but as faith ought to correspond to the simple and gratuitous promise, there remains no room for doubting. For with what confidence, pray, shall we be armed, if we reason that God is propitious to us on this condition, provided the purity of our life deserve it? But having determined on a separate discussion of these points, I shall pur-

(r) 2 Cor. i. 21.   (s) 1 Cor. v. 5.   (t) Psalm xlvi. 1, 2.   (u) Psalm iii. 5.
(w) Isaiah xxx. 16.   (x) Psalm xxxvii. 7.   (y) Heb. x. 36.

sue them no further at present; especially since it is manifest that nothing is more opposite to faith than either conjecture or any thing else approaching to doubt. And they very mischievously pervert to this purpose the observation of the Preacher, which is frequently in their mouths: "No man knoweth whether he is worthy of hatred or of love." (z) For not to observe that this passage is falsely rendered in the Vulgate translation, yet the meaning of Solomon, in such expressions, must be clear even to children; it is, that if any one wishes, from the present state of things, to judge who are the objects of Divine love or hatred, he labours in vain, and distresses himself to no good purpose; since "there is one event to the righteous and to the wicked; to him that sacrificeth, and to him that sacrificeth not." (a) Whence it follows that God neither testifies his love to those whom he prospers with success, nor invariably discovers his hatred against those whom he plunges into affliction. And this observation is designed to reprove the vanity of the human understanding; since it is so extremely stupid respecting things most necessary to be known. He had just before said, "That which befalleth the sons of men, befalleth beasts; as the one dieth, so dieth the other; yea, they have all one breath; so that a man hath no preëminence above a beast." (b) If any one would infer from this, that the opinion which we hold of the immortality of the soul rests upon mere conjecture, would he not be deservedly deemed insane? Are those persons, then, in a state of sanity, who conclude that there is no certainty of the favour of God, because it cannot be attained from the carnal contemplation of present things?

XXXIX. But they plead that it is rash presumption in men to arrogate to themselves an undoubted knowledge of the Divine will. This, indeed, I would concede to them, if we pretended to subject the incomprehensible counsel of God to the slenderness of our understanding. But when we simply assert with Paul, that "we have received, not the spirit of the world, but the Spirit which is of God, that we might know the things that are freely given to us of God," (c) what opposition can they make to us, without at the same time insulting the Spirit of God? But if it be a horrible sacrilege to accuse the revelation which proceeds from him either of falsehood, or of uncertainty, or of ambiguity, wherein do we err in affirming its certainty? But they exclaim, that we betray great temerity, in thus presuming to boast of the Spirit of Christ. Who could believe the stupidity of men desirous of being esteemed teachers of the world, to be so extreme as to stumble in this shameful manner at the first elements of religion? It would certainly

(z) Eccl. ix. 1.   (a) Eccl. ix. 2.   (b) Eccl. iii. 19.   (c) 1 Cor. ii. 12.

be incredible to me, if it were not proved by the writings which they have published. Paul pronounces them alone to be the sons of God, who are led by his Spirit : (*d*) these men will have those who are the sons of God to be led by their own spirit, but to be destitute of the Spirit of God. He teaches, that we call God our Father at the suggestion of the Spirit, who "beareth witness with our spirit, that we are the children of God : " (*e*) these men, though they forbid not all invocation of God, yet deprive us of the Spirit, by whose influence alone he can be rightly invoked. He denies them to be the servants of Christ, who are not led by the Spirit of Christ : (*f*) these men invent a sort of Christianity, to which the Spirit of Christ is not necessary. He admits no hope of a happy resurrection, unless we experience the Spirit dwelling in us : (*g*) these men fabricate a hope unattended by such experience. But perhaps they will answer, that they deny not the necessity of our being endued with the Spirit ; but that it is the part of modesty and humility not to acknowledge our possession of him. What, then, is the meaning of the apostle in this exhortation to the Corinthians — " Examine yourselves, whether ye be in the faith ; prove your own selves ; know ye not yourselves, how that Jesus Christ is in you, except ye be reprobates ? " (*h*) But says John, "We know that he abideth in us, by the Spirit which he hath given us." (*i*) And do we not call in question the promises of Christ, when we wish to be accounted the servants of God without the possession of his Spirit, whom he has announced that he will pour out upon all his people ? (*k*) Do we not injure the Holy Spirit, if we separate faith from him, which is his peculiar work ? These being the first rudiments of piety, it is a proof of most miserable blindness, that Christians are censured as arrogant for presuming to glory in the presence of the Holy Spirit, without which glorying Christianity itself cannot exist. But they exemplify the truth of Christ's assertion, " The world knoweth not the Spirit of truth ; but ye know him ; for he dwelleth with you, and shall be in you." (*l*)

XL. Not satisfied with one attempt to destroy the stability of faith, they assail it again from another quarter ; by arguing, that although we may form a judgment concerning the favour of God from the present state of our righteousness, yet the knowledge of final perseverance remains in suspense. Truly we are left in possession of an admirable confidence of salvation, if we can only conclude from mere conjecture that we are in the favour of God at the present instant, but are utterly

---

(*d*) Rom. viii. 14.   (*f*) Rom. viii. 9.   (*h*) 2 Cor. xiii. 5.   (*k*) Isaiah xliv. 3.
(*e*) Rom. viii. 16.   (*g*) Rom. viii. 11.   (*i*) 1 John iii. 24.   (*l*) John xiv. 7.

ignorant what may be our fate to-morrow. The apostle expresses a very different opinion: "I am persuaded (says he) that neither life, nor death, nor angels, nor principalities, nor powers, nor things present, nor things to come, nor height, nor depth, nor any other creature, shall be able to separate us from the love of God, which is in Christ Jesus our Lord." (*m*) They attempt to evade the force of this, by a frivolous pretence that the apostle had it from a particular revelation; but they are too closely pressed to avail themselves of this evasion. For he is there treating of the benefits resulting from faith to all believers in common, not of any which were peculiar to his own experience. But the same apostle, they say, in another place, excites fear in us, by the mention of our imbecility and inconstancy. "Let him (says he) that thinketh he standeth, take heed lest he fall." (*n*) It is true; but not a fear by which we may be thrown into consternation, but from which we may learn to "humble ourselves," as Peter expresses it, "under the mighty hand of God." Besides, how preposterous is it to limit to a moment of time the assurance of faith, whose nature it is to go beyond the bounds of the present life, and reach forward to a future immortality! Since believers, then, ascribe it to the grace of God that they are illuminated by his Spirit, and enjoy through faith a contemplation of the heavenly life, such a glorying is so remote from arrogance, that, if any one be ashamed to confess it, he rather betrays extreme ingratitude by a criminal suppression of the Divine goodness, than gives an evidence of modesty or humility.

XLI. Because we thought that the nature of faith could not be better or more clearly expressed than by the substance of the promise, which is the proper foundation on which it rests, and the removal of which would occasion its fall or annihilation, — it is from the promise, therefore, that we have taken our definition, which, nevertheless, is not at all at variance with that definition, or rather description, of the apostle, which he accommodates to his argument; where he says, that "faith is the substance of things hoped for, the evidence of things not seen." (*o*) For by ὑπόστασις, which is the word he uses, and which is rendered *substance*, he intends a prop, as it were, on which the pious mind rests and reclines; as though he had said, that faith is a certain and secure possession of those things which are promised to us by God. Unless any one would rather understand ὑπόστασις of confidence, to which I shall not object, though I adopt that idea which is the more generally received. Again: to signify that even till the last day, when the books shall be opened, these objects are too sublime to be

(*m*) Rom. viii. 38   (*n*) 1 Cor. x. 12.   (*o*) Heb. xi. 1.

perceived by our senses, seen with our eyes, or handled with our hands; and that, in the mean time, they are enjoyed by us only as we exceed the capacity of our own understanding, extend our views beyond all terrestrial things, and even rise above ourselves; he has added, that this security of possession relates to things which are the objects of hope, and therefore invisible. For "hope that is seen (as Paul observes) is not hope; for what a man seeth, why doth he yet hope for?" (*p*) But when he calls it an evidence, or proof, or (as Augustine has frequently rendered it) a conviction of things not seen, (for the Greek word is ἔλεγχος,) it is just as though he had called it the evidence of things not apparent, the vision of things not seen, the perspicuity of things obscure, the presence of things absent, the demonstration of things concealed. For the mysteries of God, of which description are the things that pertain to our salvation, cannot be discerned in themselves, and in their own nature; we only discover them in his word, of whose veracity we ought to be so firmly persuaded, as to consider all that he speaks as though it were already performed and accomplished. But how can the mind elevate itself to receive such a taste of the Divine goodness, without being all inflamed with mutual love to God? For the plenitude of happiness, which God has reserved for them who fear him, cannot be truly known, but it must at the same time excite a vehement affection. And those whom it has once affected, it draws and elevates towards itself. Therefore we need not wonder if a perverse and malicious heart never feel this affection, which conducts us to heaven itself, and introduces us to the most secret treasures of God and the most sacred recesses of his kingdom, which must not be profaned by the entrance of an impure heart. For what the schoolmen (*q*) advance concerning the priority of charity to faith and hope, is a mere reverie of a distempered imagination, since it is faith alone which first produces charity in us. How much more accurately Bernard speaks! "I believe," says he, "that the testimony of conscience, which Paul calls the rejoicing of the pious, consists in three things. For it is necessary to believe, first of all, that you cannot have remission of sins but through the mercy of God; secondly, that you cannot have any good work, unless he bestow this also; lastly, that you cannot by any works merit eternal life, unless that also be freely given." (*r*) Just after he adds, "that these things are not sufficient, but are a beginning of faith; because in believing that sins can only be forgiven by God, we ought at the same time to consider that they are forgiven us, till we are also persuaded, by the tes-

---

(*p*) Rom. viii. 24.   (*q*) Lombard.   (*r*) Bernard. Serm. 1. in Annunciat.

timony of the Holy Spirit, that salvation is laid up for us; because God forgives sins; he also bestows merits; he likewise confers rewards; it is not possible to remain in this beginning." But these and other things must be treated in the proper places; it may suffice, at present, to ascertain wherein faith itself consists.

XLII. Now, wherever this living faith shall be found, it must necessarily be attended with the hope of eternal salvation as its inseparable concomitant, or rather must originate and produce it; since the want of this hope would prove us to be utterly destitute of faith, however eloquently and beautifully we might discourse concerning it. For if faith be, as has been stated, a certain persuasion of the truth of God, that it can neither lie, nor deceive us, nor be frustrated, — they who have felt this assurance, likewise expect a period to arrive when God will accomplish his promises, which, according to their persuasion, cannot but be true; so that, in short, hope is no other than an expectation of those things which faith has believed to be truly promised by God. Thus faith believes the veracity of God, hope expects the manifestation of it in due time; faith believes him to be our Father, hope expects him always to act towards us in this character; faith believes that eternal life is given to us, hope expects it one day to be revealed; faith is the foundation on which hope rests, hope nourishes and sustains faith. For as no man can have any expectations from God, but he who has first believed his promises, so also the imbecility of our faith must be sustained and cherished by patient hope and expectation, lest it grow weary and faint. For which reason, Paul rightly places our salvation in hope. (s) For hope, while it is silently expecting the Lord, restrains faith, that it may not be too precipitate; it confirms faith, that it may not waver in the Divine promises, or begin to doubt of the truth of them; it refreshes it, that it may not grow weary; it extends it to the farthest goal, that it may not fail in the midst of the course, or even at the entrance of it. Finally, hope, by continually renewing and restoring faith, causes it frequently to persevere with more vigour than hope itself. But in how many cases the assistance of hope is necessary to the establishment of faith, will better appear, if we consider how many species of temptations assail and harass those who have embraced the word of God. First, the Lord, by deferring the execution of his promises, frequently keeps our minds in suspense longer than we wish; here it is the office of hope to obey the injunction of the prophet — " though it tarry, wait for it." (t) Sometimes he not only suffers us to languish, but openly mani-

---

(s) Rom. viii. 24. (t) Heb. ii. 3.

fests his indignation: in this case it is much more necessary to have the assistance of hope, that, according to the language of another prophet, we may "wait upon the Lord that hideth his face from Jacob." (*u*) Scoffers also arise, as Peter says, and inquire, "Where is the promise of his coming? for since the fathers fell asleep, all things continue as they were from the beginning of the creation." (*w*) And the flesh and the world whisper the same things into our ears. Here faith must be supported by the patience of hope, and kept fixed on the contemplation of eternity, that it may consider "a thousand years as one day." (*x*)

XLIII. On account of this union and affinity, the Scripture sometimes uses the words faith and hope without any distinction. For when Peter says that we "are kept by the power of God through faith unto salvation, ready to be revealed," (*y*) he attributes to faith, what was more applicable to hope; and not without reason, since we have already shown, that hope is no other than the nourishment and strength of faith. Sometimes they are joined together, as in a passage of the same Epistle — "that your faith and hope might be in God." (*z*) But Paul, in the Epistle to the Philippians, (*a*) deduces expectation from hope; because in patient hope we suspend our desires till the arrival of God's appointed time. All which may be better understood from the tenth chapter of the Epistle to the Hebrews, (*b*) which I have already cited. In another place, Paul, though with some impropriety of expression, conveys the very same idea in these words: "We, through the Spirit, wait for the hope of righteousness by faith;" (*c*) because, having embraced the testimony of the gospel concerning his gratuitous love, we wait till God openly manifests what is now concealed under hope. Now, it is easy to see the absurdity of Peter Lombard, in laying a twofold foundation of hope; the grace of God, and the merit of works. Hope can have no other object than faith; and the only object of faith, we have very clearly stated to be the mercy of God; to which both its eyes, if I may be allowed the expression, ought to be directed. But it may be proper to hear what kind of a reason he advances. If, says he, you venture to hope for any thing without merits, it must not be called hope, but presumption. Who is there that will not justly detest such teachers, who pronounce a confidence in the veracity of God to be temerity and presumption? For whereas it is the will of the Lord that we should expect every thing from his goodness, they assert that it is presumption to depend and rely upon it. Such a master is

(*u*) Isaiah viii. 17.　　(*y*) 1 Pet. i. 5.　　(*b*) Heb. x. 36.
(*w*) 2 Pet. iii. 4.　　(*z*) 1 Pet. i. 21.　　(*c*) Gal. v. 5.
(*x*) Psalm xc. 4.　2 Pet. iii. 8.　(*a*) Phil. i. 20.

worthy of such disciples as he has found in the schools of wranglers! But, as for us, since we see that sinners are enjoined by the oracles of God to entertain a hope of salvation, let us joyfully presume so far on his veracity as to reject all confidence in our own works, to depend solely on his mercy, and venture to cherish a hope of happiness. He who said, "According to your faith be it unto you," (*d*) will not deceive us.

CHAPTER III.

ON REPENTANCE.

Though we have already shown, in some respect, how faith possesses Christ, and how by means of faith we enjoy his benefits, yet the subject would still be involved in obscurity, unless we were to add a description of the effects which we experience. The substance of the gospel is, not without reason, said to be comprised in "repentance and remission of sins." Therefore, if these two points be omitted, every controversy concerning faith will be jejune and incomplete, and consequently of little use. Now, since both are conferred on us by Christ, and we obtain both by faith, — that is, newness of life and gratuitous reconciliation, — the regular method of instruction requires me, in this place, to enter on the discussion of both. But our immediate transition will be from faith to repentance; because, when this point is well understood, it will better appear how man is justified by faith alone, and mere pardon, and yet that real sanctity of life (so to speak) is not separated from the gratuitous imputation of righteousness. Now, it ought not to be doubted that repentance not only immediately follows faith, but is produced by it. For since pardon, or remission, is offered by the preaching of the gospel, in order that the sinner, liberated from the tyranny of Satan, from the yoke of sin, and the miserable servitude of his vices, may remove into the kingdom of God, — no one can embrace the grace of the gospel, but he must depart from the errors of his former life, enter into the right way, and devote all his attention to the exercise of repentance. Those who imagine that repentance rather precedes faith, than is produced by it, as fruit by a tree, have never been acquainted with its power, and are induced to adopt that sentiment by a very insufficient argument.

(*d*) Matt. ix. 29.

II. They argue that Jesus Christ and John the Baptist, in their preaching, first exhort the people to repentance; and afterwards add, that "the kingdom of heaven is at hand;" (*e*) that thus the apostles were commanded to preach, and that this (according to the account of Luke) (*f*) was the method followed by Paul. But they superstitiously attend to the connection of the syllables, and disregard the sense and coherence of the words. For when Christ and John preach in this manner, "Repent, for the kingdom of heaven is at hand," (*g*) do they not derive an argument for repentance from grace itself, and the promise of salvation? The meaning of their language, therefore, is just as though they had said, Since the kingdom of heaven is at hand, therefore repent. For Matthew, having related that John preached in this manner, informs us, that in him was accomplished the prediction of Isaiah concerning "the voice of one crying in the wilderness, Prepare ye the way of the Lord, make his paths straight." But, in the prophet, that voice is commanded to begin with consolation and glad tidings. (*h*) Yet, when we speak of faith as the origin of repentance, we dream not of any space of time which it employs in producing it; but we intend to signify, that a man cannot truly devote himself to repentance, unless he knows himself to be of God. Now, no man is truly persuaded that he is of God, except he has previously received his grace. But these things will be more clearly discussed as we proceed. This circumstance, perhaps, has deceived them — that many are overcome or led to obedience by terrors of conscience, before they have imbibed a knowledge of grace, or have even tasted it. And this is the initial fear, which some number among the graces, because they perceive it to be nearly connected with true and righteous obedience. But we are not inquiring, at present, in how many ways Christ draws us to himself, or prepares us for the practice of piety: only I assert, that no rectitude can be found but where that Spirit reigns, whom he has received in order to communicate him to his members. In the next place, according to this passage in the Psalms, "There is forgiveness with thee, that thou mayest be feared," (*i*) no man will ever reverence God, but he who confides in his being propitious to him: no man will cheerfully devote himself to the observance of his law, but he who is persuaded that his services are pleasing to him: and this indulgence in pardoning us, and bearing with our faults, is an evidence of his paternal favour. The same also appears from this exhortation of Hosea, "Come, and let us return unto the Lord; for he hath torn, and he will heal

---

(*e*) Matt. iii. 2; iv. 17.   (*f*) Acts xx. 21.   (*g*) Matt. iii. 2, 3.
(*h*) Isaiah xl. 1, 3.   (*i*) Psalm cxxx. 4.

us; he hath smitten, and he will bind us up;" (*k*) because the hope of pardon is added as a stimulus, to prevent them from being stupefied in their sins. But there is not the least appearance of reason in the notion of those who, in order to begin with repentance, prescribe to their young converts certain days, during which they must exercise themselves in repentance; after the expiration of which, they admit them to the communion of evangelical grace. I speak of many of the Anabaptists, especially of those who wonderfully delight in being accounted spiritual; and their companions, the Jesuits, and other such worthless men. Such are the effects produced by that spirit of fanaticism, that it terminates repentance within the limits of a few short days, which a Christian ought to extend throughout his whole life.

III. But concerning repentance, some learned men, in times very remote from the present, desiring to express themselves with simplicity and sincerity according to the rule of the Scripture, have said that it consists of two parts — mortification and vivification. Mortification they explain to be the sorrow of the mind, and the terror experienced from a knowledge of sin and a sense of the Divine judgments. For when any one has been brought to a true knowledge of sin, he then begins truly to hate and abhor it; then he is heartily displeased with himself, confesses himself to be miserable and lost, and wishes that he were another man. Moreover, when he is affected with some sense of the Divine judgment, (for the one immediately follows the other,) then, indeed, he is stricken with consternation, he trembles with humility and dejection, he feels a despondency of mind, he falls into despair. This is the first part of repentance, which they have generally styled contrition. Vivification they explain to be the consolation which is produced by faith; when a man, after having been humbled with a consciousness of sin, and stricken with the fear of God, afterwards contemplates the goodness of God, and the mercy, grace, and salvation bestowed through Christ, rises from his depression, feels himself re-invigorated, recovers his courage, and as it were returns from death to life. These terms, provided they be rightly understood, are sufficiently adapted to express the nature of repentance; but when they explain vivification of that joy which the mind experiences after its perturbations and fears are allayed, I cannot coincide with them; since it should rather signify an ardent desire and endeavour to live a holy and pious life, as though it were said, that a man dies to himself, that he may begin to live to God.

IV. Others, perceiving this word to have various acceptations

(*k*) Hos. vi. 1.

in Scripture, have laid down two kinds of repentance; and, to distinguish them by some character, have called one Legal; in which the sinner, wounded by the envenomed dart of sin, and harassed by the fear of Divine wrath, is involved in deep distress, without the power of extricating himself: the other they style Evangelical; in which the sinner is grievously afflicted in himself, but rises above his distress, and embraces Christ as the medicine for his wound, the consolation of his terrors, and his refuge from all misery. Of legal repentance, they consider Cain, Saul, and Judas, as examples: (*l*) the scriptural account of whose repentance gives us to understand, that from a knowledge of the greatness of their sins they dreaded the Divine wrath, but that considering God only as an avenger and a judge, they perished under that apprehension. Their repentance, therefore, was only, as it were, the antechamber of hell, which having already entered in this life, they began to suffer punishment from the manifestation of the wrath of the Divine Majesty. Evangelical repentance we discover in all who have been distressed by a sense of sin in themselves, but have been raised from their depression, and reinvigorated by a confidence in the Divine mercy, and converted to the Lord. Hezekiah was terrified when he received the message of death; (*m*) but he wept and prayed, and, contemplating the goodness of God, recovered his former confidence. The Ninevites were confounded by the terrible denunciation of destruction; (*n*) but they covered themselves with sackcloth and ashes, and prayed, in hope that the Lord might be appeased, and the fury of his wrath averted. David confessed that he had committed a great sin in numbering the people; but added, "O Lord, take away the iniquity of thy servant." (*o*) He acknowledged his crime of adultery at the rebuke of Nathan, and prostrated himself before the Lord; but at the same time cherished an expectation of pardon. (*p*) Such was the repentance of those who felt compunction of heart at the preaching of Peter, but, confiding in the goodness of God, exclaimed, "Men and brethren, what shall we do?" (*q*) Such also was that of Peter himself, who wept bitterly, but never lost his hope.

V. Though all these observations are true, yet the term *repentance*, as far as I can ascertain from the Scriptures, must have a different acceptation. For to include faith in repentance, is repugnant to what Paul says in the Acts — that he testified "both to the Jews, and also to the Greeks, repentance toward God, and faith toward our Lord Jesus Christ;" (*r*) where he mentions faith and repentance, as two things totally

---

(*l*) Gen. iv. 13.   1 Sam. xv. 30.   Matt. xxvii. 3, 4.
(*m*) 2 Kings xx. 2.   Isaiah xxxviii. 2.   (*n*) Jonah iii. 5.
(*o*) 2 Sam. xxiv. 10.   (*p*) 2 Sam. xii. 13—16.   (*q*) Acts ii. 37.   (*r*) Acts xx. 21.

distinct. What then? Can true repentance exist without faith? Not at all. But though they cannot be separated, yet they ought to be distinguished. As faith exists not without hope, and yet there is a difference between them, so repentance and faith, although they are perpetually and indissolubly united, require to be connected rather than confounded. I am well aware, that under the term *repentance* is comprehended a complete conversion to God, of which faith is one of the principal branches; but in what sense, will best appear from an explication of its nature and properties. The Hebrew word for repentance denotes conversion or return. The Greek word signifies change of mind and intention. Repentance itself corresponds very well with both etymologies, for it comprehends these two things — that, forsaking ourselves, we should turn to God, and laying aside our old mind, should assume a new one. Wherefore I conceive it may be justly defined to be "*a true conversion of our life to God, proceeding from a sincere and serious fear of God, and consisting in the mortification of our flesh and of the old man, and in the vivification of the Spirit.*" In this sense we must understand all the addresses, in which either the prophets in ancient days, or the apostles in a succeeding age, exhorted their contemporaries to repentance. For the point to which they endeavoured to bring them was this — that being confounded by their sins, and penetrated with a fear of the Divine judgment, they might prostrate themselves in humility before him against whom they had offended, and with true penitence return into his right way. Therefore these expressions, "*to repent*" (s) and "*to return to the Lord,*" (t) are promiscuously used by them in the same signification. Hence also the sacred history expresses repentance by *seeking after* and *following God*, when men who have disregarded him, and indulged their criminal propensities, begin to obey his word, and are ready to follow whithersoever he calls them. And John and Paul have spoken of "bringing forth fruits meet for repentance," to signify a life which, in every action, will discover and testify such a repentance.

VI. But before we proceed any further, it will be useful to amplify and explain the definition we have given; in which there are three points to be particularly considered. In the first place, when we call repentance "a conversion of the life to God," we require a transformation, not only in the external actions, but in the soul itself; which, after having put off its old nature, should produce the fruits of actions corresponding to its renovation. The prophet, intending to express this idea,

(s) Matt. iii. 2.   (t) 1 Sam. vii. 3.

commands those whom he calls to repentance, to make themselves a new heart. (*u*) Wherefore Moses, when about to show how the Israelites might repent and be rightly converted to the Lord, frequently teaches them that it must be done with all their heart, and with all their soul; and by speaking of the circumcision of the heart, he enters into the inmost affections of the mind. This mode of expression we find often repeated by the prophets; but there is no passage from which we may obtain clearer ideas of the true nature of repentance, than from the language of God in the fourth chapter of Jeremiah: "If thou wilt return, O Israel, saith the Lord, return unto me. Break up your fallow ground, and sow not among thorns. Circumcise yourselves to the Lord, and take away the foreskins of your heart." (*w*) Observe how he denounces that they shall labour in vain in the pursuit of righteousness, unless impiety be previously eradicated from the bottom of their hearts. And in order to make a deeper impression upon them, he apprizes them that they have to do with God, with whom subterfuges are of no avail, because he abhors all duplicity of heart. For this reason, Isaiah ridicules the preposterous endeavours of hypocrites, who did indeed strenuously attempt an external repentance by the observance of ceremonies, but at the same time were not concerned "to loose the bands of wickedness," (*x*) with which they oppressed the poor. In that passage he also beautifully shows, in what duties unfeigned repentance properly consists.

VII. In the second place, we represented repentance as proceeding from a serious fear of God. For before the mind of a sinner can be inclined to repentance, it must be excited by a knowledge of the Divine judgment. But when this thought has once been deeply impressed, that God will one day ascend his tribunal to exact an account of all words and actions, it will not permit the miserable man to take any interval of rest, or to enjoy even a momentary respite, but perpetually stimulates him to adopt a new course of life, that he may be able to appear with security at that judgment. Wherefore the Scripture, when it exhorts to repentance, frequently introduces a mention of the judgment; as in Jeremiah; "Lest my fury come forth like fire, and burn that none can quench it, because of the evil of your doings:" (*y*) in the address of Paul to the Athenians; "The times of this ignorance God winked at; but now commandeth all men every where to repent; because he hath appointed a day in which he will judge the world in righteousness:" (*z*) and in many other

(*u*) Ezekiel xviii. 31.   (*w*) Jer. iv. 1, 3, 4.   (*x*) Isaiah lviii. 6.
(*y*) Jer. iv. 4.   (*z*) Acts xvii. 30, 31

places. Sometimes, by the punishments already inflicted, it declares that God is a judge; in order that sinners may consider with themselves that worse calamities await them, unless they speedily repent. We have an example of this in the twenty-ninth chapter of Deuteronomy. But since conversion commences with a dread and hatred of sin, therefore the apostle makes godly sorrow the cause of repentance. (a) He calls it godly sorrow when we not only dread punishment, but hate and abhor sin itself, from a knowledge that it is displeasing to God. Nor ought this to be thought strange; for, unless we felt sharp compunction, our carnal sluggishness could never be corrected, and even these distresses of mind would not be sufficient to arouse it from its stupidity and indolence, if God, by the infliction of his chastisements, did not make a deeper impression. Beside this, there is a rebellious obstinacy, which requires violent blows, as it were, to overcome it. The severity, therefore, which God uses in his threatenings, is extorted from him by the depravity of our minds; since it would be in vain for him to address kind and alluring invitations to those who are asleep. I forbear to recite the testimonies with which the Scripture abounds. The fear of God is called the beginning of repentance also for another reason; because though a man's life were perfect in every virtue, if it be not devoted to the worship of God, it may indeed be commended by the world, but in heaven it will be only an abomination; since the principal branch of righteousness consists in rendering to God the honour due to him, of which he is impiously defrauded, when it is not our end and aim to submit ourselves to his government.

VIII. It remains for us, in the third place, to explain our position, that repentance consists of two parts — the mortification of the flesh and the vivification of the spirit. This is clearly expressed by the prophets, although in a simple and homely manner, according to the capacity of a carnal people, when they say, "Depart from evil, and do good." (b) Again: "Wash you, make you clean; put away the evil of your doings from before mine eyes; cease to do evil; learn to do well; seek judgment; relieve the oppressed," &c. (c) For when they call men from the paths of wickedness, they require the total destruction of the flesh, which is full of wickedness and perverseness. It is a thing truly difficult and arduous to put off ourselves, and to depart from the native bias of our minds. Nor must the flesh be considered as entirely dead, unless all that we have of ourselves be destroyed. But since the universal disposition of the flesh

---

(a) 2 Cor. vii. 10.   (b) Psalm xxxiv. 14.   (c) Isaiah i. 16, 17.

is settled "enmity against God," (d) the first step to an obedience of the law is this renunciation of our own nature. They afterwards designate the renovation by its fruits — righteousness, judgment, and mercy. For a punctual performance of these external duties would not be sufficient, unless the mind and heart had previously acquired a disposition of righteousness, judgment, and mercy. This takes place when the Spirit of God has tinctured our souls with his holiness, and given them such new thoughts and affections, that they may be justly considered as new, [or altogether different from what they were before.] And certainly, as we have a natural aversion to God, we shall never aim at that which is right, without a previous renunciation of ourselves. Therefore we are so frequently commanded to put off the old man, to renounce the world and the flesh, to forsake our lusts, and to be renewed in the spirit of our mind. Besides, the very word *mortification* reminds us how difficult it is to forget our former nature; for it implies that we cannot be formed to the fear of God, and learn the rudiments of piety, without being violently slain and annihilated by the sword of the Spirit. As though God had pronounced that, in order to our being numbered among his children, there is a necessity for the destruction of our common nature.

IX. Both these branches of repentance are effects of our participation of Christ. For if we truly partake of his death, our old man is crucified by its power, and the body of sin expires, so that the corruption of our former nature loses all its vigour. (e) If we are partakers of his resurrection, we are raised by it to a newness of life, which corresponds with the righteousness of God. In one word I apprehend repentance to be regeneration, the end of which is the restoration of the Divine image within us; which was defaced, and almost obliterated, by the transgression of Adam. Thus the apostle teaches us, when he says, "But we all, with open face beholding as in a glass the glory of the Lord, are changed into the same image from glory to glory, even as by the Spirit of the Lord." (f) Again: "Be ye renewed in the spirit of your mind; and put on the new man, which after God is created in righteousness and true holiness." (g) Again, in another place: "And ye have put on the new man, which is renewed in knowledge after the image of him that created him." (h) Wherefore, in this regeneration, we are restored by the grace of Christ to the righteousness of God, from which we fell in Adam; in which manner the Lord is pleased completely to restore all those whom

(d) Rom. viii. 7. (e) Rom. vi 5, 6. (f) 2 Cor. iii. 18.
(g) Eph iv. 23, 24. (h) Col. iii. 10.

he adopts to the inheritance of life. And this restoration is not accomplished in a single moment, or day, or year; but by continual, and sometimes even tardy advances, the Lord destroys the carnal corruptions of his chosen, purifies them from all pollution, and consecrates them as temples to himself; renewing all their senses to real purity, that they may employ their whole life in the exercise of repentance, and know that this warfare will be terminated only by death. And so much the greater is the wickedness of that impure and quarrelsome apostate Staphylus, who idly pretends that I confound the state of the present life with the glory of heaven, when I explain the image of God, according to Paul, to be righteousness and true holiness. As if, indeed, when any thing is to be defined, we are not to inquire after the completeness and perfection of it. It is not denied that there is room for further advances; but I assert, that as far as any man approaches to a resemblance of God, so far the image of God is displayed in him. That believers may attain to this, God assigns them the race of repentance to run during their whole life.

X. Thus, therefore, the children of God are liberated by regeneration from the servitude of sin; not that they have already obtained the full possession of liberty, and experience no more trouble from the flesh, but there remains in them a perpetual cause of contention to exercise them; and not only to exercise them, but also to make them better acquainted with their own infirmity. And on this subject all sound writers are agreed — that there still remains in a regenerate man a fountain of evil, continually producing irregular desires, which allure and stimulate him to the commission of sin. They acknowledge, also, that saints are still so afflicted with the disease of concupiscence, that they cannot prevent their being frequently stimulated and incited either to lust, or to avarice, or to ambition, or to other vices. There is no need of a laborious investigation, to learn what were the sentiments of the fathers on this subject: it will be sufficient to consult Augustine alone, who with great diligence and fidelity has collected the opinions of them all. From him, then, the reader may receive all the certainty he can desire concerning the sense of antiquity. Between him and us, this difference may be discovered — that while he concedes that believers, as long as they inhabit a mortal body, are so bound by concupiscence that they cannot but feel irregular desires, yet he ventures not to call this disease by the name of *sin*, but, content with designating it by the appellation of infirmity, teaches that it only becomes sin in cases where either action or consent is added to the conception or apprehension of the mind, that is, where the will yields to the first impulse of appetite. But we, on the contrary, deem it to be sin, whenever a man feels any evil desires contrary to the Divine law; and we also assert the depravity itself to be sin, which produces these desires in our minds. We maintain, therefore, that sin always exists in the saints, till they are divested of the mortal body; because their flesh is the residence of that depravity of concupiscence, which is repugnant to all rectitude. Nevertheless, he has not always refrained from using the word *sin* in this sense; as when he says, "Paul gives the appellation of sin to this, from which all sins proceed, that is, to carnal concupiscence. This, as it respects the saints, loses its kingdom on earth, and has no existence in heaven." In these words he acknowledges that believers are guilty of sin, inasmuch as they are the subjects of carnal concupiscence.

XI. But when God is said "to cleanse his church" (*i*) from all sin, to promise the grace of deliverance in baptism, and to fulfil it in his elect,—we refer these phrases rather to the guilt of sin, than to the existence of sin. In the regeneration of his children, God does indeed destroy the kingdom of sin in them, (for the Spirit supplies them with strength, which renders them victorious in the conflict;) but though it ceases to reign, it continues to dwell in them. Wherefore we say, that "the old man is crucified,"(*k*) that the law of sin is abolished in the children of God, yet so that some relics remain; not to predominate over them, but to humble them with a consciousness of their infirmity. We grant, indeed, that they are not imputed, any more than if they did not exist; but we likewise contend that it is owing to the mercy of God that the saints are delivered from this guilt, who would otherwise be justly accounted sinners and guilty before him. Nor will it be difficult for us to confirm this opinion, since there are clear testimonies of Scripture to support it. What can we desire more explicit than the declaration of Paul to the Romans? (*l*) In the first place, that he there speaks in the character of a regenerate man, we have already shown; and Augustine has evinced the same by the strongest arguments. I say nothing of his using the words *evil* and *sin*. However those who wish to oppose us may cavil at those words, yet who can deny that a resistance to the Divine law is evil? who can deny that an opposition to righteousness is sin? finally, who will not admit that there is guilt wherever there is spiritual misery? But all these things are affirmed by Paul respecting this disease. Besides, we have a certain demonstration from the law, by which this whole question may be briefly decided. For we are commanded to love God with all our heart, with all our mind, and with all our

(*i*) Eph. v. 26.   (*k*) Rom. vi. 6.   (*l*) Rom. vii.

strength. Since all the powers of our soul ought to be thus occupied by the love of God, it is evident that the precept is not fulfilled by those who receive into their hearts the least desire, or admit into their minds any thought, which may draw them aside from the love of God into vanity. What then? Are not these properties of the soul, — to be affected with sudden emotions, to apprehend in the sensory, and to form conceptions in the mind? When these, therefore, open a way for the admission of vain and corrupt thoughts, do they not show that they are so far destitute of the love of God? Whoever, therefore, refuses to acknowledge that all the inordinate desires of the flesh are sins, and that that malady of concupiscence, which they call an incentive to sin, is the source of sin, must necessarily deny the transgression of the law to be sin.

XII. If it be thought absurd, that all the natural appetites of man should be thus universally condemned, since they were implanted by God, the author of nature, — we reply, that we by no means condemn those desires, which God implanted so deeply in the nature of man at his first creation that they cannot be eradicated from it without destroying humanity itself, but only those insolent and lawless appetites which resist the commands of God. But now, since, through the depravity of nature, all its powers are so vitiated and corrupted, that disorder and intemperance are visible in all our actions; because the appetites are inseparable from such excesses, therefore we maintain that they are corrupt. Or, if it be wished to have the substance of our opinion in fewer words, we say, that all the desires of men are evil; and we consider them to be sinful, not as they are natural, but because they are inordinate; and we affirm they are inordinate, because nothing pure or immaculate can proceed from a corrupted and polluted nature. Nor does Augustine deviate from this doctrine so much as he appears to do. When he is too much afraid of the odium with which the Pelagians endeavoured to overwhelm him, he sometimes refrains from using the word *sin:* yet when he says, " that the law of sin remains in the saints, and that only the guilt is abolished," he sufficiently indicates that he is not averse to our opinion.

XIII. We will adduce some other passages, from which his sentiments will more fully appear. In his second book against Julian: " This law of sin is both abolished in the spiritual regeneration, and continues in the mortal flesh; abolished, since the guilt is removed in the sacrament, by which believers are regenerated; but continues, because it produces those desires against which also believers contend." Again: " Therefore the law of sin, which was in the members even of so great an apostle, is abolished in baptism, but not finally destroyed." Again: " The law of sin, the remaining guilt of which is removed in baptism. Ambrose has called *iniquity;* because it is iniquitous for the flesh to lust against the spirit." Again: " Sin is dead in that guilt in which it held us; and, although dead, it will rebel till it is cured by the perfection of burial." In the fifth book, he is still more explicit: " As blindness of heart is both a sin, which consists in a man's not believing in God; and a punishment for sin, by which a proud heart is deservedly punished; and also a cause of sin, when any is committed through the error of a blind heart; so the concupiscence of the flesh, against which the good spirit lusteth, is both a sin, because it is a disobedience against the government of the mind; and a punishment for sin, because it is inflicted for the demerits of the disobedient; and also a cause of sin, consenting by defection, or produced from contagion." Here he styles it *sin*, without any ambiguity; because, having overthrown error and confirmed the truth, he is not so much afraid of calumnies; as also in the forty-first homily on John, where he undoubtedly speaks the real sentiments of his mind: " If in the flesh you serve the law of sin, do what the apostle himself says — 'Let not sin reign in your mortal body, that ye should obey it in the lusts thereof.' (*m*) He says not, let it not exist; but, let it not reign. As long as you live, sin must necessarily exist in your members; let it at least be divested of its kingdom, so that its commands may not be fulfilled." Those who contend that concupiscence is not sin, commonly object this passage of James — " When lust hath conceived, it bringeth forth sin." (*n*) But this objection is easily repelled; for, unless we understand him there to speak of evil works exclusively, or of actual sins, even an evil volition cannot be accounted sin. But from his calling flagitious and criminal actions the offspring of lust, and attributing to them the name of sin, it does not necessarily follow that concupiscence is not an evil thing, and deserving of condemnation in the sight of God.

XIV. Some Anabaptists, in the present age, imagine I know not what frantic intemperance, instead of spiritual regeneration — that the children of God, being restored to a state of innocence, are no longer obliged to be solicitous to restrain the licentiousness of the flesh, but that they ought to follow the leadings of the Spirit, under whose direction it is impossible ever to err. It would be incredible that the mind of man should fall into such madness, did they not publicly and haughtily disseminate this opinion. It is indeed truly prodigious; but it is just and reasonable, that those who have persuaded themselves to pervert the truth of God into a falsehood, should suffer such punishment for their sacrilegious presumption. Must all distinction, then, of honour and turpitude, justice and injustice, good

(*m*) Rom. vi. 12.   (*n*) James i. 15.

and evil, virtue and vice, be annihilated? This difference, they say, proceeds from the malediction of the old Adam, from which we are delivered by Christ. Then there will be no difference now between chastity and fornication, sincerity and knavery, truth and falsehood, equity and rapine. Dismiss (they say) all vain fear; the Spirit will command you nothing that is evil, provided you securely and intrepidly resign yourself to his direction. Who is not astonished at these monstrous notions? Yet this is a popular philosophy among those, who, blinded by the violence of their appetites, have discarded common sense. But what kind of a Christ, and what kind of a Spirit, have they fabricated for us? For we acknowledge one Christ and his Spirit alone; whom the prophets have celebrated, whom the gospel proclaims as revealed, but of whom it gives us no such account as this. That Spirit is not the patron of murder, fornication, drunkenness, pride, contention, avarice, or fraud; but the author of love, chastity, sobriety, modesty, peace, moderation, and truth. He is not a Spirit of fanaticism, rushing precipitately, without any consideration, through right and wrong; but is full of wisdom and understanding, rightly to discern between justice and injustice. He never instigates to dissolute and unrestrained licentiousness; but, discriminating between what is lawful and what is unlawful, inculcates temperance and moderation. But why should we spend any more labour in refuting this monstrous frenzy? To Christians the Spirit of the Lord is not a turbulent phantom, which they have either spawned themselves in a dream, or received from the invention of others; but they religiously seek the knowledge of him in the Scriptures, where these two things are delivered concerning him — first, that he is given to us in order to our sanctification, to purify us from all our pollutions, and lead us to obey the Divine righteousness; which obedience cannot exist without the subjugation of the appetites, to which these men would allow an unlimited license: in the next place, that we are so purified by his sanctification, that we are nevertheless still encompassed with numerous vices and great infirmity, as long as we are burdened with the body. Wherefore, being at a great distance from perfection, it behoves us to make continual advances; and being entangled in vices, we have need to strive against them every day. Hence, also, it follows that we ought to shake off all slothful security, and exert the most vigilant attention, lest, without caution, we should be surprised and overcome by the snares of our flesh; unless we are well assured that we have made a greater progress than the apostle; who, nevertheless, was buffeted by the "messenger of Satan," (o)

(o) 2 Cor. xii. 7, 9.

that his strength might be "made perfect in weakness;" (*p*) and who faithfully represented the conflict between the flesh and the Spirit, which he experienced in his own person.

XV. When the apostle, in a description of repentance, enumerates seven things, which are either causes producing it, or effects proceeding from it, or members and parts of it, he does it for a very good reason. These things are, carefulness, excuse, indignation, fear, vehement desire, zeal, revenge. (*q*) Nor ought it to be thought strange that I venture not to determine whether they should be considered as causes or effects; for arguments may be adduced in support of both. They may also be styled affections connected with repentance; but as we may discover the meaning of Paul without discussing these questions, we shall be content with a simple exposition of them. He says, then, that godly sorrow produces *solicitude*. For a person who is affected with a serious sense of displeasure because he has sinned against his God, is at the same time stimulated to diligence and attention, that he may completely extricate himself from the snares of the devil, and be more cautious of his insidious attacks, that he may not in future disobey the government of the Spirit, or be overcome with a careless security. The next thing is *self-excuse*, which in this place signifies not a defence by which a sinner tries to escape the judgment of God, either by denying his transgressions or extenuating his guilt, but a kind of excuse, consisting rather in deprecation of punishment than in confidence of his cause. Just as children, who are not absolutely lost to all sense of duty, while they acknowledge and confess their faults, at the same time deprecate punishment, and, in order to succeed, testify by every possible method that they have not cast off that reverence which is due to their parents; in a word, they excuse themselves in such a manner, not to prove themselves righteous and innocent, but only to obtain pardon. This is followed by *indignation*, in which the sinner laments within himself, expostulates with himself, and is angry with himself, while he recollects his perverseness and ingratitude to God. The word *fear* denotes that trepidation with which our minds are penetrated, whenever we reflect upon our demerits, and on the terrible severity of the Divine wrath against sinners. For we cannot but be agitated with an amazing inquietude, which teaches us humility, and renders us more cautious for the future. Now, if the solicitude before mentioned be the offspring of fear, we see the connection and coherence between them. He appears to me to have used the word *desire* to denote diligence in duty and alacrity of obedience, to which the

(*p*) Rom. vii.   (*q*) 2 Cor. vii. 11.

knowledge of our faults ought to be a most powerful stimulus. Similar to this is the meaning of *zeal,* which he immediately subjoins; for it signifies the ardour with which we are inflamed, when we are roused with such thoughts as these: "What have I done? Whither had I precipitated myself, if I had not been succoured by the mercy of God?" The last thing is *revenge,* or punishment; for the greater our severity is towards ourselves, and the stricter inquisition we make concerning our sins, so much the stronger hope ought we to entertain that God will be propitious and merciful. And, indeed, it is impossible but that a soul, impressed with a dread of the Divine judgment, must inflict some punishment on itself. Truly pious persons experience what punishments are contained in shame, confusion, lamentation, displeasure with themselves, and the other affections which arise from a serious acknowledgment of their transgressions. But let us remember that some limit must be observed, that we may not be overwhelmed in sorrow; for to nothing are terrified consciences more liable than to fall into despair. And with this artifice, also, whomsoever Satan perceives to be dejected by a fear of God, he plunges them further and further into the deep gulf of sorrow, that they may never arise again. That fear, indeed, cannot be excessive, which terminates in humility, and departs not from the hope of pardon. Nevertheless, the sinner should always be on his guard, according to the direction of the apostle, (r) lest while he excites his heart to be displeased with himself, he *be wearied* with excessive dread, and *faint in his mind;* for this would drive us away from God, who calls us to himself by repentance. On this subject, Bernard also gives a very useful admonition: "Sorrow for sin is necessary, if it be not perpetual. I advise you sometimes to quit the anxious and painful recollection of your own ways, and to arise to an agreeable and serene remembrance of the Divine blessings. Let us mingle honey with wormwood, that its salutary bitterness may restore our health, when it shall be drunk tempered with a mixture of sweetness; and if you reflect on your own meanness, reflect also on the goodness of the Lord."

XVI. Now, it may also be understood what are the fruits of repentance. They are, the duties of piety towards God, and of charity towards men, with sanctity and purity in our whole life. In a word, the more diligently any one examines his life by the rule of the Divine law, so much the more certain evidences he discovers of his repentance. The Spirit, therefore, in frequently exhorting us to repentance, calls our attention, sometimes to all the precepts of the law, sometimes to the

(r) Heb. xii. 3.

duties of the second table; though in other places, after having condemned impurity in the very fountain of the heart, he proceeds to those external testimonies which evidence a sincere repentance; a view of which I will soon exhibit to the reader, in a description of the Christian life. I shall not collect testimonies from the prophets, in which they partly ridicule the follies of those who attempt to appease God by ceremonies, and demonstrate them to be mere mockeries; and partly inculcate, that external integrity of life is not the principal branch of repentance, because God looks at the heart. He that is but ordinarily acquainted with the Scripture, will discover of himself, without being informed by any one, that in our concerns with God, we advance not a single step unless we begin with the internal affection of the heart. And this passage of Joel will afford us no small assistance in the interpretation of others: "Rend your heart, and not your garments." (s) Both these ideas are briefly expressed in these words of James — "Cleanse your hands, ye sinners; and purify your hearts, ye double minded;" (t) where there is indeed an addition made to the first clause; but the fountain, or original, is next discovered, showing the necessity of cleansing the secret pollution, that an altar may be erected to God even in the heart. There are likewise some external exercises which we use, in private, as remedies either to humble ourselves, or to subdue our carnality; and in public, to testify our repentance. They proceed from the *revenge* mentioned by Paul; (u) for it is natural to an afflicted mind to continue in a squalid condition, groaning and weeping, to avoid every kind of splendour and pomp, and to forsake all pleasures. He who experiences the great evil of the rebellion of the flesh, seeks every remedy to restrain it. He who properly considers what a grievous thing it is to have offended the justice of God, can enjoy no repose till he has glorified God by his humility. Such exercises are frequently mentioned by the old writers, when they speak of the fruits of repentance. And though they by no means make repentance wholly to consist in them, yet the reader will pardon me if I deliver my opinion, that they appear to me to insist upon them more than they ought. And I hope every one, on a sober examination, will agree with me, that they have gone beyond all due bounds in two respects. For when they so strongly urged and so extravagantly recommended that corporeal discipline, the consequence was indeed that the common people adopted it with great ardour; but they also obscured that which ought to be esteemed of infinitely greater importance. Secondly, in the infliction of castigations, they

(s) Joel ii. 13.   (t) James iv. 8.   (u) 2 Cor. vii. 11.

used rather more rigour than was consistent with ecclesiastical gentleness. But we shall have to treat of this in another place.

XVII. But as some persons, when they find weeping, fasting, and ashes mentioned, not only in many other passages of Scripture, but particularly in Joel, (v) consider fasting and weeping as the principal part of repentance, their mistake requires to be rectified. What is there said of the conversion of the whole heart to the Lord, and of rending not the garments, but the heart, properly belongs to repentance; but weeping and fasting are not added as perpetual or necessary effects of it, but as circumstances belonging to a particular case. Having prophesied that a most grievous destruction was impending over the Jews, he persuades them to prevent the Divine wrath, not only by repentance, but also by exhibiting external demonstrations of sorrow. For as it was customary, in ancient times, for an accused person to present himself in a suppliant posture, with a long beard, dishevelled hair, and mourning apparel, in order to conciliate the compassion of the judge, so it became those who stood as criminals before the tribunal of God, to deprecate his severity in a condition calculated to excite commiseration. Though sackcloth and ashes were perhaps more suitable to those times, yet it is evident that the practice of weeping and fasting would be very seasonable among us, whenever the Lord appears to threaten us with any affliction or calamity. For when he causes danger to appear, he, as it were, denounces that he is prepared and armed for the exercise of vengeance. The prophet, therefore, was right in exhorting his countrymen to weeping and fasting; that is, to the sadness of persons under accusation, into whose offences he had just before said that an examination was instituted. Neither would the pastors of the church act improperly in the present age, if, when they perceived calamity impending over the heads of their people, they called them to immediate weeping and fasting; provided they always insisted with the greatest fervour and diligence on the principal point, which is, that they must rend their hearts, and not their garments. It is certain, that fasting is not always the concomitant of repentance, but is appointed for times of peculiar calamity; wherefore Christ connects it with mourning, when he frees the apostles from any obligation to it, till they should be affected with grief at the loss of his presence. (w) I speak of solemn fasting. For the life of the pious ought at all times to be regulated by frugality and sobriety, that through its whole progress it may appear to be a kind of perpetual fast. But as the whole of this subject must be discussed again, when we come to treat of Ecclesiastical Discipline, I touch the more slightly upon it at present.

(v) Joel ii. 12.   (w) Matt. ix. 15.

XVIII. I will again remark, however, that when the word *repentance* is transferred to this external profession, it is improperly changed from the genuine signification which I have stated. For this external profession is not so much a conversion to God, as a confession of sin, with a deprecation of punishment and guilt. Thus to "repent in sackcloth and ashes," (*x*) is only a declaration of our displeasure against ourselves, when God is angry with us on account of our grievous offences. And this is a public species of confession, by which condemning ourselves before angels and men, we prevent the judgment of God. For Paul rebukes the sluggishness of those who indulge their sins, saying, "If we would judge ourselves, we should not be judged." (*y*) It is not necessary, in all cases, publicly to make men witnesses of our repentance; but a private confession to God is a branch of true penitence which cannot be omitted. For nothing is more unreasonable than that God should pardon sins, in which we encourage ourselves, and which, lest he should bring them to light, we conceal under the garb of hypocrisy. And it is not only necessary to confess the sins which we commit from day to day; more grievous falls ought to lead us further, and to recall to our remembrance those which appear to have been long buried in oblivion. We learn this from the example of David; (*z*) for, being ashamed of a recent and flagitious crime, he examines himself back to the time of his conception, and acknowledges that even then he was corrupted and contaminated with carnal impurity; and this not to extenuate his guilt, as many conceal themselves in a multitude, and endeavour to escape with impunity by implicating others with themselves. Very different was the conduct of David, who ingenuously aggravated his guilt, by confessing that he was corrupted from his earliest infancy, and had never ceased to accumulate crimes upon crimes. In another place, also, he enters on such an examination of his past life, that he implores the Divine mercy to pardon the sins of his youth. (*a*) And certainly we shall never give proof that we have shaken off our lethargy, till, groaning under the burden, and bewailing our misery, we pray to God for relief. It is further to be remarked, that the repentance which we are commanded constantly to practise, differs from that which arouses, as it were, from death those who have either fallen into some great enormity, or abandoned themselves to a course of sin with unrestrained license, or by any rebellion shaken off the Divine yoke. For when the Scripture exhorts to repentance, it frequently signifies a kind of transition and resurrection from death to life; and when it states that the people repented, it

(*x*) Matt. xi. 21.   (*y*) 1 Cor. xi. 31.   (*z*) Psalm li. 5.   (*a*) Psalm xxv. 7.

means that they departed from idolatry and other gross enormities; in which sense Paul declares his grief for sinners, who "have not repented of their uncleanness, and fornication, and lasciviousness." (b) This difference should be carefully observed, lest, when we hear that few are called to repentance, we fall into a supine security, as though we had no more to do with the mortification of the flesh, from which the depraved appetites that perpetually disturb us, and the vices that often arise in us, will never permit us to relax. The special repentance, therefore, which is only required of some whom the devil has seduced from the fear of God, and entangled in his fatal snares, supersedes not that ordinary repentance, which the corruption of nature obliges us to practise during the whole course of our lives.

XIX. Now, if it be true, as it certainly is, that the whole substance of the gospel is comprised in these two points, repentance and remission of sins, — do not we perceive that the Lord freely justifies his children, that he may also restore them to true righteousness by the sanctification of his Spirit? John, the "messenger sent before the face" of Christ to "prepare his way before him," (c) preached, "Repent ye, for the kingdom of heaven is at hand." (d) By calling men to repentance, he taught them to acknowledge themselves to be sinners, and every thing belonging to them to be condemned before God, that they might earnestly desire and pray for a mortification of the flesh, and new regeneration in the Spirit. By announcing the kingdom of God, he called them to exercise faith; for by "the kingdom of God," the approach of which he proclaimed, he intended remission of sins, salvation, life, and in general all the benefits that we obtain in Christ. Wherefore, in the other evangelists, it is said, that "John came, preaching the baptism of repentance for the remission of sins." (e) What was intended by this, but that, oppressed and wearied with the burden of sins, men should turn themselves to the Lord, and entertain a hope of remission and salvation? Thus, also, Christ commenced his public ministrations. "The kingdom of God is at hand: repent ye, and believe the gospel." (f) First, he declares that the treasures of mercy are opened in himself; then he requires repentance; and lastly, a reliance on the Divine promises. Therefore, when he would give a brief summary of the whole gospel, he said, that "it behoved him to suffer, and to rise from the dead; and that repentance and remission of sins should be preached in his name." (g) The apostles also, after his resurrection, preached that he was exalted

(b) 2 Cor. xii. 21.   (d) Matt. iii. 2.   (f) Mark i. 15.
(c) Matt. xi. 10.   (e) Luke iii. 3. Mark i. 4.   (g) Luke xxiv. 46, 47.

by God, "to give repentance to Israel and remission of sins." (*h*) Repentance is preached in the name of Christ, when men are informed, by the doctrine of the gospel, that all their thoughts, their affections, and their pursuits, are corrupt and vicious; and that therefore it is necessary for them to be born again, if they wish to enter the kingdom of God. Remission of sins is preached, when men are taught that Christ is made unto them "wisdom, and righteousness, and sanctification, and redemption;" (*i*) in whose name they are gratuitously accounted righteous and innocent in the sight of God. Both these blessings of grace, as we have already shown, are apprehended by faith; yet since the goodness of God in the remission of sins is the peculiar object of faith, it was necessary that it should be carefully distinguished from repentance.

XX. Now, as a hatred of sin, which is the commencement of repentance, is our first introduction to the knowledge of Christ, who reveals himself to none but miserable and distressed sinners, who mourn, and labour, and are heavy laden; who hunger and thirst, and are pining away with grief and misery; (*k*) so it is necessary for us, if we desire to abide in Christ, to strive for this repentance, to devote our whole lives to it, and to pursue it to the last. For he "came to call sinners," but it was to call them "to repentance." (*l*) He was "sent to bless" the unworthy; but it was "in turning away every one from his iniquities." (*m*) The Scripture is full of such expressions. Wherefore, when God offers remission of sins, he generally requires repentance on the part of the sinner; implying that his mercy ought to furnish a motive to excite us to repentance. "Keep ye judgment, and do justice; for my salvation is near." (*n*) Again: "The Redeemer shall come to Zion, and unto them that turn from transgression in Jacob." (*o*) Again: "Seek ye the Lord while he may be found, call ye upon him while he is near: let the wicked forsake his way, and the unrighteous man his thoughts; and let him return unto the Lord, and he will have mercy upon him." (*p*) Again: "Repent, and be converted, that your sins may be blotted out." (*q*) Here it must be remarked, however, that this condition is not annexed in such a manner, as though our repentance were the fundamental and meritorious cause of pardon; but rather, because the Lord has determined to have mercy upon men, in order that they may repent, he informs them what course they must take if they wish to obtain his favour. Therefore, as long as we inhabit the prison of our body, we shall have to maintain an incessant conflict with the vices of

(*h*) Acts v. 31.   (*i*) 1 Cor. i. 30.   (*k*) Isaiah lxi. 1.   Matt. xi. 5.   Luke iv. 18.
    (*l*) Matt. ix. 13.   (*m*) Acts iii. 26.   (*n*) Isaiah lvi. 1.
    (*o*) Isaiah lix. 20.   (*p*) Isaiah lv. 6, 7.   (*q*) Acts iii. 19.

our corrupt nature, and even with our natural soul. Plato sometimes says, that the life of a philosopher is a meditation of death. We may assert with more truth, that the life of a Christian is perpetually employed in the mortification of the flesh, till it is utterly destroyed, and the Spirit of God obtains the sole empire within us. Wherefore I think that he has made a very considerable proficiency, who has learned to be exceedingly displeased with himself: not that he should remain in this distress, and advance no further, but rather hasten and aspire towards God; that being ingrafted into the death and life of Christ, he may make repentance the object of his constant meditation and pursuit. And this cannot but be the conduct of those who feel a genuine hatred of sin; for no man ever hated sin, without having been previously captivated with the love of righteousness. This doctrine, as it is the most simple of all, so also it appears to me to be most consistent with the truth of the Scripture.

XXI. That repentance is a peculiar gift of God, must, I think, be so evident from the doctrine just stated, as to preclude the necessity of a long discourse to prove it. Therefore the Church praises and admires the goodness of God, that he "hath granted to the Gentiles repentance unto life;" (r) and Paul, when he enjoins Timothy to be patient and gentle towards unbelievers, says, "If God, peradventure, will give them repentance, that they may recover themselves out of the snare of the devil." (s) God affirms, indeed, that he wills the conversion of all men, and directs his exhortations promiscuously to all; but the efficacy of these exhortations depends on the Spirit of regeneration. For it were more easy to make ourselves men, than by our own power to endue ourselves with a more excellent nature. Therefore, in the whole course of regeneration, we are justly styled God's "workmanship, created unto good works, which God hath before ordained that we should walk in them." (t) Whomsoever God chooses to rescue from destruction, them he vivifies by the Spirit of regeneration: not that repentance is properly the cause of salvation, but because, as we have already seen, it is inseparable from faith and the mercy of God; since, according to the testimony of Isaiah, "the Redeemer shall come to Zion, and unto them that turn from transgression in Jacob." (u) It remains an unshaken truth, that wherever the fear of God prevails in the heart, the Spirit has operated to the salvation of that individual. Therefore, in Isaiah, where believers are bewailing and deploring their being deserted by God, they mention this as a sign of reprobation, that their hearts are hardened by him. (w) The apostle also,

(r) Acts xi. 18.   (s) 2 Tim. ii. 25, 26.   (t) Eph. ii. 10.
(u) Isaiah lix. 20.   (w) Isaiah lxiii. 17.

intending to exclude apostates from all hope of salvation, asserts, as a reason, that "it is impossible to renew them again unto repentance;" (*x*) because God, in the renewal of those whom he will not suffer to perish, discovers an evidence of his paternal favour, and attracts them to himself with the radiance of his serene and joyful countenance; whilst, on the contrary, he displays his wrath in hardening the reprobate, whose impiety is never to be forgiven. (*y*) This kind of vengeance the apostle denounces against wilful apostates, who, when they depart from the faith of the gospel, deride God, contumeliously reject his grace, profane and trample on the blood of Christ, and do all in their power to crucify him again. For he does not, as is pretended by some preposterously severe persons, preclude all voluntary sinners from a hope of pardon. His design is to show that apostasy is unworthy of every excuse, and therefore it is not strange that God punishes such a sacrilegious contempt of himself with inexorable rigour. "For it is impossible (he tells us) for those who were once enlightened, and have tasted of the heavenly gift, and were made partakers of the Holy Ghost, and have tasted the good word of God, and the powers of the world to come, if they shall fall away, to renew them again unto repentance; seeing they crucify to themselves the Son of God afresh, and put him to an open shame." (*z*) Again: "If we sin wilfully after that we have received the knowledge of the truth, there remaineth no more sacrifice for sins, but a certain fearful looking-for of judgment." (*a*) These are the passages, from a misinterpretation of which the Novatians formerly derived a pretence for their extravagant opinions; and the apparent harshness of which has offended some good men, and induced them to believe that this Epistle is supposititious, though every part of it contains unequivocal evidences of the apostolic spirit. But as we are contending only with those who receive it, it is easy to show that these passages afford not the least countenance to their error. In the first place, the apostle must necessarily be in unison with his Master, who affirms that "all sin and blasphemy shall be forgiven unto men, but the blasphemy against the Holy Ghost, which shall not be forgiven, neither in this world, neither in the world to come." (*b*) The apostle, I say, must certainly have been content with this exception, unless we wish to make him an enemy to the grace of Christ. Whence it follows, that pardon is denied to no particular sins, except one, which proceeds from desperate fury, and cannot be attributed to infirmity, but clearly proves a man to be possessed by the devil.

(*x*) Heb. vi. 4. (*y*) Heb. x. 29. (*z*) Heb. vi. 4—6.
(*a*) Heb. x. 26, 27. (*b*) Matt. xii. 31, 32. Mark iii. 28, 29. Luke xii. 10.

XXII. But, for the further elucidation of this subject, it is necessary to inquire into the nature of that dreadful crime which will obtain no forgiveness. Augustine somewhere defines it to be an obstinate perverseness, attended with a despair of pardon, and continued till death; but this is not consistent with the language of Christ, that "it shall not be forgiven in this world." For either this is a vain assertion, or the sin may be committed in this life. But if the definition of Augustine be right, it is never committed unless it continue till death. Others say, that a man sins against the Holy Ghost, who envies the grace bestowed on his brother. I know no foundation for this notion. But we will adduce the true definition; which when it shall have been proved by strong testimonies, will of itself easily overturn all others. I say, then, that the sin against the Holy Ghost is committed by those who, though they are so overpowered with the splendour of Divine truth that they cannot pretend ignorance, nevertheless resist it with determined malice, merely for the sake of resisting it. For Christ, in explanation of what he had asserted, immediately subjoins, "Whosoever speaketh a word against the Son of man, it shall be forgiven him; but whosoever speaketh against the Holy Ghost, it shall not be forgiven him." (c) And Matthew, instead of "blasphemy against the Spirit," says, "blasphemy of the Spirit."* How can any one cast a reproach on the Son, that is not also directed against the Spirit? Those who unadvisedly offend against the truth of God, which they know not, and who ignorantly revile Christ, but at the same time have such a disposition that they would not extinguish the Divine truth if revealed to them, or utter one injurious word against him whom they knew to be the Lord's Christ, — they sin against the Father and the Son. Thus there are many, in the present day, who most inveterately execrate the doctrines of the gospel, which if they knew to be the evangelical doctrine, they would be ready to venerate with their whole heart. But those who are convinced in their conscience, that it is the word of God which they reject and oppose, and yet continue their opposition, — they are said to blaspheme against the Spirit, because they strive against the illumination which is the work of the Holy Spirit. Such were some among the Jews, who, when they were not able to resist the Spirit (d) that spake by Stephen, yet obstinately strove to resist. Many of them were undoubtedly urged to this conduct by a zeal for the law; but it appears that there were others, who were infuriated by a malignant impiety against

---

* τοῦ Πνεύματος βλασφημία, Matt. xii. 31.

(c) Matt. xii. 32.   (d) Acts vi. 10.

God himself, that is, against the doctrine which they knew to be from God. Such also were the Pharisees, whom the Lord rebuked; who, in order to counteract the influence of the Holy Spirit, slanderously ascribed it to the power of Beelzebub. (*e*) This, then, is "blasphemy of the Spirit," where the presumption of man deliberately strives to annihilate the glory of God. This is implied in the observation of Paul, that he "obtained mercy, because" he had "ignorantly in unbelief" committed those crimes, the demerits of which would otherwise have excluded him from the grace of the Lord. (*f*) If the union of ignorance and unbelief was the reason of his obtaining pardon, it follows that there is no room for pardon where unbelief has been attended with knowledge.

XXIII. But, on a careful observation, you will perceive that the apostle speaks not of one or more particular falls, but of the universal defection, by which the reprobate exclude themselves from salvation. We need not wonder that those whom John, in his canonical Epistle, affirms not to have been of the number of the elect from whom they departed, experience God to be implacable towards them. (*g*) For he directs his discourse against those who imagined that they might return to the Christian religion, although they had once apostatized from it; to whom he contradicts this false and pernicious notion, declaring, what is absolutely true, that it is impossible for persons to return to the communion of Christ, who have knowingly and wilfully rejected it. And it is rejected, not by those who simply transgress the word of the Lord by a dissolute and licentious life, but by those who professedly renounce all his doctrines. Therefore the fallacy lies in the terms *falling away* and *sinning*; for the Novatians explain *falling away* to take place, when any one, after having been instructed by the law of the Lord that theft and fornication ought not to be committed, yet abstains not from either of these sins. But, on the contrary, I affirm that there is a tacit antithesis understood, which ought to contain a repetition of all the opposites of the things which had been previously mentioned; so that this passage expresses not any particular vice, but a universal defection from God, and if I may use the expression, an apostasy of the whole man. When he speaks, therefore, of some who fell away, "after they were once enlightened, and had tasted of the heavenly gift, and were made partakers of the Holy Ghost, and the powers of the world to come," (*h*) it must be understood of persons who, with deliberate impiety, have smothered the light of the Spirit, rejected the taste of the heavenly gift, alienated themselves from the sanctification of the Spirit, and trampled on the word of God

(*e*) Matt. ix. 34; xii. 24
(*f*) 1 Tim. i. 13.
(*g*) 1 John ii. 19.
(*h*) Heb. vi. 4—6.

and the powers of the world to come. And the more fully to express that decided determination of impiety, he afterwards, in another place, adds the word *wilfully*. For when he says, that "if we sin wilfully after that we have received the knowledge of the truth, there remaineth no more sacrifice," (*i*) he denies not that Christ is a perpetual sacrifice to expiate the iniquities of the saints, which almost the whole Epistle expressly proclaims in describing the priesthood of Christ, but intends that there remains no other where that is rejected. But it is rejected, when the truth of the gospel is avowedly renounced.

XXIV. The objection of some, who conceive it to be severe and inconsistent with the Divine clemency, that pardon should be refused to any who flee to the Lord imploring his mercy, is easily answered. For he affirms not that pardon is denied to them if they turn themselves to the Lord; but he absolutely denies the possibility of their attaining to repentance, because they are stricken with eternal blindness by the righteous judgment of God, on account of their ingratitude. Nor is it any objection that the same apostle afterwards accommodates to this subject the example of Esau, who vainly endeavoured with weeping and lamentation to recover his lost rights of primogeniture. Nor that the prophet utters this denunciation: "though they shall cry unto me, I will not hearken unto them." (*k*) For such forms of expression signify neither true conversion nor invocation of God, but the anxiety felt by the impious in extreme calamity, which constrains them to consider, what before they carelessly disregarded, that nothing can do them any good but the assistance of the Lord. And this they do not so much implore, as bewail its being withheld from them. Therefore the prophet intends by *crying*, and the apostle by *weeping*, only that dreadful torment which excruciates the impious with the agonies of despair. This requires to be carefully observed, because otherwise this procedure of God would contradict his proclamation by the mouth of the prophet, that as soon as the sinner shall have turned, he will be propitious to him. (*l*) And, as I have already remarked, it is certain that the human mind is not changed for the better, except by the previous influence of his grace. Nor will his promise respecting those who call upon him, ever deceive; but it is improper to apply the terms *conversion* and *prayer* to that blind torment by which the reprobate are distracted, when they see that it is necessary for them to seek God in order to find a remedy for their miseries, while at the same time they continue to flee from his approach.

(*i*) Heb. x. 26.   (*k*) Jer. xi. 11.   (*l*) Ezek. xviii. 21.

XXV. But it is inquired, since the apostle denies that God is appeased by a hypocritical repentance, how Ahab obtained pardon, and averted the punishment with which he had been threatened, though he appears, from the subsequent tenor of his life, to have been only terrified by a sudden consternation. He clothed himself with sackcloth, sprinkled ashes upon his head, lay on the ground, and, as it is declared concerning him, "humbled himself before God;" (*m*) but it was nothing to rend his garments, while his heart remained perverse and inflated with wickedness. Yet we see how God is inclined to clemency. I reply, that sometimes hypocrites are thus spared for a season, yet that the wrath of God always abides upon them, and that this is done not so much for their sakes, as for a public example. For what benefit did Ahab receive from the mitigation of the threatened punishment, but a respite from it during his continuance in this world? The malediction of God, therefore, although concealed, fixed itself in his family, and he himself went forward to eternal perdition. The same may be observed in the case of Esau; for though he suffered a repulse, yet a temporal benediction was granted to his tears. (*n*) But since the spiritual inheritance, according to the oracle of God, could remain only with one of the brothers, when Jacob was chosen and Esau rejected, that preterition shut out the Divine mercy; yet this consolation was left to him as to a man on a level with the brutes, that he should be enriched with "the fatness of the earth and the dew of heaven." This is what I have just observed ought to be considered as an example to others, that we may learn to devote our minds and our exertions with more alacrity to sincere repentance; because it is not to be doubted that those who are truly and cordially converted will find God readily disposed to forgiveness, whose clemency extends itself even to the unworthy, as long as they manifest any appearance of contrition. At the same time, also, we are taught what dreadful vengeance awaits all the obstinate, who, with impudent countenances and hardened hearts, despise, disregard, and ridicule the Divine threatenings. Thus he frequently extended his hand to the children of Israel, to alleviate their distresses, notwithstanding their supplications were hypocritical, and their hearts full of duplicity and perfidy; as he complains in one of the Psalms, (*o*) that they immediately after returned to their former courses. He designed by his merciful kindness, either to bring them to a serious conversion, or to render them inexcusable. Yet, by the temporary remission of punishments, he imposes on himself no perpetual law, but sometimes arises against hypocrites with the greater seve-

(*m*) 1 Kings xxi. 27, &c.   (*n*) Gen. xxvii. 38, 39.   (*o*) Psalm lxxviii. 36, 37.

rity, and enhances their punishments, to manifest his extreme displeasure against hypocrisy. But he exhibits, as I have observed, some examples of his readiness to pardon, in order to animate the pious to a correction of their lives, and the more severely to condemn the pride of those who obstinately kick against the goads.

CHAPTER IV.

THE SOPHISTRY AND JARGON OF THE SCHOOLS CONCERNING REPENTANCE, VERY REMOTE FROM THE PURITY OF THE GOSPEL. ON CONFESSION AND SATISFACTION.

I COME now to the discussion of those things which have been advanced by the sophists of the schools concerning Repentance, which I shall run over as briefly as possible; for it is not my design to pursue the subject at large, lest this book, which I am endeavouring to make a compendium of doctrine, should be drawn out to an immoderate extent. They have involved a subject, otherwise not very intricate, in so many perplexities, that those who have entered but a little way into their labyrinths will not find it easy to extricate themselves. In the first place, the definition they have given of repentance, clearly shows that they never understood what it was; for they catch at some passages in the writings of the fathers, which by no means express the nature of repentance; as, "that to repent is to weep for sins previously committed, and not to commit sins to be wept for." Again: "that it is to lament evils that are past, and not to commit new ones to be lamented." Again: "that it is a kind of mournful vengeance, punishing in ourselves what we bewail having committed." Again: "that it is a sorrow of heart and bitterness of soul on account of the evils which a man has committed, or to which he has consented." But though we concede that these expressions were properly used by the fathers, which, however, a contentious man would find no difficulty in denying, yet they were used not with a view to describe repentance, but only to exhort their readers to avoid relapsing into those crimes from which they had been delivered. But if we are disposed to convert all observations of this kind into definitions, others may be added with equal propriety. As this of Chrysostom, "Repentance is a medicine which destroys sin, a gift bestowed from heaven, an admirable virtue, a grace exceeding the power of laws." Moreover, the doctrine which they afterwards advance is still worse than these definitions;

for they are so obstinately riveted to external exercises, that one can collect nothing else from immense volumes, but that repentance is an austere discipline, which serves partly to subdue the flesh, partly to chastise and punish vices; but concerning the internal renovation of the mind, which is attended with a real reformation of the life, they observe a wonderful silence. Of *contrition* and *attrition*, indeed, they treat largely; they torment souls with a multitude of scruples, and drive them to extreme trouble and anxiety; but when they appear to have thoroughly wounded the heart, they heal all the bitterness by a slight sprinkling of ceremonies. Having thus quaintly defined repentance, they divide it into contrition of heart, confession of mouth, and satisfaction of work — a division which is no more agreeable to the rules of logic than their definition, though they would be thought to have spent their whole lives in composing syllogisms. But should any one reason from the definition, (which is a kind of argumentation common among logicians,) that a man may weep for sins previously committed, and commit no more to be wept for; may lament evils that are past, and commit no more to be lamented; may punish what he mourns that he has committed, &c., although he makes no confession with his mouth; how will they defend their division? For if he who confesses not, be nevertheless truly penitent, repentance may exist where there is no confession. But if they reply that this division refers to repentance as a sacrament, or is to be understood of the complete perfection of repentance, which they comprehend not in their definition, they have no reason to accuse me; let them impute the blame to themselves, for not giving definitions with more correctness and perspicuity. For myself, indeed, according to my dull capacity, in all controversies I refer every thing to the definition, which is the hinge and foundation of the whole argument. But, admitting this to be their magisterial license, we proceed to an attentive examination of the parts themselves in order. When I neglect, and pass over as frivolous, things which, with supercilious gravity, they represent as mysteries, I never do it without design; not that I should find it very laborious to canvass the arguments in which they conceive themselves to have discovered most shrewdness and subtilty; but I could not conscientiously fatigue my readers with such impertinences to no good purpose. From the questions which they raise and agitate, and with which they miserably embarrass themselves, it is easy to see, that they talk of subjects of which they are utterly ignorant; such as this: Whether repentance for one sin be pleasing to God during an obstinate continuance in others. Again: Whether punishments inflicted by God be available for satisfaction. Again: Whether repentance may be frequently repeated for mortal sins. On this point they shamefully and impiously determine, that repentance is daily practised only for venial sins. They also torment themselves much with a gross error, in an expression of Jerome, "That repentance is a second plank after a shipwreck;" thus giving proof, that they have never been awakened from their brutish stupidity, so as to have even the most distant view of the thousandth part of their sins.

II. I wish the reader to consider, that this is not a contention about an insignificant trifle, but a question respecting the most serious of all subjects — remission of sins. For by requiring, in repentance, compunction of heart, confession of mouth, and satisfaction of work, they maintain, that these three things are necessary to procure the remission of sins. But if it be important for us to know any thing in the whole science of religion, it is certainly of the greatest importance to apprehend, and fully to understand, by what means, by what law, on what condition, and with what facility or difficulty, remission of sins may be obtained. Unless this knowledge be clear and certain, the conscience can have no rest, no peace with God, no confidence or security; but is the subject of perpetual trepidations and fluctuations, is disturbed, tormented, and harassed, and dreads, hates, and avoids the presence of God. But if remission of sins depend on those conditions to which they confine it, we are in a most miserable and deplorable situation. They make contrition the first step towards obtaining pardon, and require such as is due from us, that is, such as is just and perfect; but they have not determined, when a man may be assured that he has arrived at this degree of perfect contrition. I grant, indeed, that every man ought to be sedulously and earnestly urged, that by bitterly mourning for his sins, he may continually augment his displeasure and hatred against them. For this "sorrow worketh repentance to salvation, not to be repented of." (p) But when such an anguish of sorrow is required as may correspond to the magnitude of the guilt, and may be weighed in the balance with confidence of pardon, then the wretched conscience is wonderfully tormented and agitated, when it sees a due contrition for sins imposed on it, and understands not the extent of the debt so as to be able to decide with itself that it has discharged what was due from it. If they say that we must do what we can, we still return to the same point; for when will any man presume to flatter himself that he has exerted all his power in bewailing his sins? Consciences, therefore, that have been long striving with themselves, and exercised in tedious conflicts, but without finding

(p) 2 Cor. vii. 10.

at length any place of rest, endeavour to procure some small alleviation, extorting from themselves some sorrow, and forcing out some tears to complete their contrition.

III. If they charge me with calumny, let them come forth and produce a single individual, who has not, by this doctrine of contrition, either been driven into despair, or endeavoured to avert the Divine judgment by a pretended sorrow instead of real compunction. We have said ourselves, that forgiveness of sins is never enjoyed without repentance, because none but those who are afflicted and wounded with a consciousness of sins, can sincerely implore the mercy of God; but we have likewise added, that repentance is not the cause of remission of sins. But those torments of soul, which they say are duties to be performed, we have put aside. We have taught the sinner not to look on his compunction or on his tears, but to fix both his eyes solely on the mercy of God. We have only declared, that Christ called the labouring and heavy-laden, when he was sent "to preach the gospel to the poor, to heal the broken-hearted, to preach deliverance to the captives, and the opening of the prison to them that are bound, and to comfort all that mourn." (q) This would exclude the Pharisees, who, satisfied with their own righteousness, acknowledge not their poverty; and despisers, who, careless of the wrath of God, seek no remedy for their disease; for such neither labour, nor are heavy-laden; they are not broken-hearted, or in bondage, or in captivity. But there is a considerable difference, whether a man be taught to merit remission of sins by a true and perfect contrition, (which no sinner can ever perform,) or be instructed to hunger and thirst for the Divine mercy, that by the knowledge of his misery, by his disquietude, fatigue, and captivity, he may be shown where he ought to seek for consolation, rest, and liberty, and may learn to glorify God by his humility.

IV. Concerning confession, there has always been a great controversy between the canonists and the scholastic divines; the latter contending, that confession is commanded by the word of God; the other, on the contrary, maintaining that it is enjoined only by the ecclesiastical constitutions. But this controversy has discovered the singular impudence of the theologians, who have corrupted and violently distorted all the passages of Scripture which they have cited in favour of their argument. And when they perceived that they could not even thus obtain what they desired, those who would appear more shrewd than others, resorted to this subterfuge, that confession, as to the substance of it, came from the Divine law, but afterwards derived its form from a positive law. In a similar man-

(q) Matt. xi. 28. Luke iv. 18. Isaiah lxi. 1, &c

ner the most foolish lawyers pretend, that citations originated from the Divine law, because it is said, "Adam, where art thou?" (r) and exceptions also, because Adam answered, as if by way of exception, "The woman whom thou gavest to be with me," &c.; but that both received their form from the civil code. But let us examine by what arguments they prove this confession, either formal or informal, to have been commanded by God. The Lord, say they, sent leprous persons to the priests. What then? Did he send them to confession? Who ever heard that the Levitical priests were appointed to hear confessions? Therefore they resort to allegories: it was enacted by the Mosaic law, that the priests should distinguish between leprosy and leprosy; sin is a spiritual leprosy, concerning which it is the office of the priests to decide. Before I reply to this, I would inquire, by the way, if this passage constitutes them judges of the spiritual leprosy, why do they arrogate to themselves the cognizance of the natural and corporeal leprosy? Is not this trifling with the Scriptures? The law commits to the Levitical priests the cognizance of the leprosy; let us usurp this to ourselves. Sin is a spiritual leprosy; let us also take cognizance of sin. Now, I reply, "The priesthood being changed, there is made, of necessity, a change also of the law."(s) All the priestly functions have been transferred to Christ; in him they are fulfilled and finished; therefore every privilege and honour of the sacerdotal office has been transferred to him alone. If they are so extremely fond of pursuing allegories, let them propose Christ to themselves as the only priest, and accumulate on his tribunal the unlimited jurisdiction over all things; this we shall easily admit. Besides, this allegory of theirs is very absurd, since it places among the ceremonies a law that was merely political. Why, then, does Christ send leprous persons to the priests? To preclude the priests from calumniating him with a violation of the law, which commanded him that was cured of the leprosy to show himself to the priest, and to be purged by the oblation of a sacrifice. "Go (said he) show thyself to the priest, and offer the gift that Moses commanded, for a testimony unto them." (t) And truly this miracle was to be a testimony to them; for they had pronounced him leprous, now they pronounce him healed. Are they not, whether willingly or reluctantly, constrained to become witnesses of the miracles of Christ? Christ gives them his miracle for their examination; they cannot deny it; but because they still cavil, this work is a testimony to them. Thus it is said, "This gospel shall be preached in all the world, for a witness unto

(r) Gen. iii. 9, 12.   (s) Heb. vii. 12.
(t) Matt. viii. 4.   Luke v. 14; xvii. 14.   Lev. xiv. 2, &c.

all nations." (u) Again: "Ye shall be brought before governors and kings, for a testimony against them." (w) That is, that they may be more powerfully convicted at the judgment of God. But if they would rather coincide with Chrysostom, he also teaches, that Christ did this on account of the Jews, that he might not be deemed a transgressor of the law. Though on a point so clear I am ashamed to adduce the suffrage of any man; when Christ declares that he leaves the legal rights entirely to the priests, as the professed enemies of the gospel, who were always ready to cavil, if their mouths were not stopped. Wherefore the Popish priests, in order to retain this possession, should publicly espouse the party of those whom it is necessary to restrain by force from uttering their curses against Christ. For with this his true ministers have no concern.

V. Their second argument they derive from the same source, that is, from allegory; as though allegories were sufficient for the confirmation of any dogma. Let them be admitted as sufficient, if I do not prove that those very allegories may be urged by me with more plausibility than they possibly can by them. They plead, therefore, that the Lord commanded his disciples to loose Lazarus from his bandages, when he was raised from the grave. (x) Here, in the first place, they are guilty of falsehood; for it is nowhere recorded, that the Lord said this to his disciples; and it is much more probable that he said it to the Jews who were standing near him, that the miracle might be rendered more evident, beyond all suspicion of fraud, and that his power might appear the greater, from his raising the dead to life without the least touch, solely by the call of his voice. For I apprehend, that the Lord, in order to remove from the minds of the Jews every unfavourable suspicion, chose that they should roll back the stone, should perceive the fetid odour, should see the certain tokens of death, should behold him rising by the sole energy of a word, and be the first to touch him on his restoration to life. And this is the opinion of Chrysostom. But admitting this to have been addressed to the disciples, what will they gain by it? That the Lord gave his apostles the power of loosing; but with how much more aptitude and skill might these words be handled in an allegorical sense, if we should say, that God intended by this emblem to instruct believers, that they ought to loose those whom he has raised to life; that is, that they should not recall to remembrance the sins which he had forgotten; that they should not condemn as sinners those whom he had absolved; that they should not continue to upbraid with offences

(u) Matt. xxiv. 14.   (w) Matt. x. 18.   (x) John xi. 44.

which he had forgiven; that where he is merciful and ready to spare, they should not be severe and rigorous to punish! Nothing, surely, ought to be a stronger motive to the exercise of forgiveness by us, than the example of that judge, who threatens to be implacable towards them who are too rigorous and cruel. Let them go now and boast of their allegories.

VI. They come to a closer contest, when they oppose us with what they apprehend to be plain passages. Those who came to the baptism of John confessed their sins; (*y*) and James directs us to confess our sins one to another. (*z*) It is no wonder, if those who desired to be baptized confessed their sins, for it is said, that John "preached the baptism of repentance," and "baptized with water unto repentance." Whom, then, should he baptize, but such as confessed themselves sinners? Baptism is an emblem of remission of sins; and who should be admitted to this emblem but sinners, and those who acknowledged themselves to be such? They confessed their sins, therefore, in order to be baptized. Nor is it without reason that James directs us to confess one to another. But if they would observe what immediately follows, they would perceive, that this also affords them very little support. "Confess (says he) your faults one to another, and pray for one another." He connects mutual confession and mutual prayer. If our confessions must be made only to priests, then our prayers ought to be offered up for them alone. But would it not follow from the language of James, that priests alone might make confessions? For when he enjoins mutual confession, he addresses such only as have a right to hear the confessions of others. Αλληλοι implies mutually, by turns, successively, or reciprocally. But none can reciprocally confess, but those who are qualified to hear confessions. And since they dignify the priests exclusively with this prerogative, we also relinquish to them alone the task of making confession. Then let us dismiss such impertinences, and attend to the real meaning of the apostle, which is simple and clear; it is, that we should reciprocally communicate our infirmities to each other, to receive from one another mutual advice, mutual compassion, and mutual consolation; and, also, that being mutually conscious of the infirmities of our brethren, we should pray to the Lord on their behalf. Why, then, do they quote James in opposition to us, when we so strongly urge a confession of the Divine mercy? But no man can confess the mercy of God, if he has not previously confessed his own misery. Indeed, we rather pronounce an anathema against him who has not confessed himself a sinner before God, before his

(*y*) Matt. iii. 6. (*z*) James v. 16.

angels, before the Church, and, in a word, before all mankind. "For the Scripture hath concluded all under sin — that every mouth may be stopped, and all the world may become guilty before God;" (*a*) and that he alone may be justified and exalted.

VII. But I wonder with what face they can presume to contend, that the confession of which they speak is of Divine appointment. The practice we admit to be very ancient, but we can easily prove, that Christians were formerly quite at liberty as to the use of it. That there was no fixed law or constitution respecting it till the time of Innocent III., is certain from the testimony of their own histories. Surely, if there had been a more ancient law, they would rather have cited it, than, by being content with a decree of the Council of Lateran, have rendered themselves ridiculous even in the eyes of children. They hesitate not in other cases to fabricate fictitious decrees, which they ascribe to the most ancient councils, that they may dazzle the eyes of the simple by a veneration for antiquity. In this instance they never thought of obtruding such a forgery. Therefore, according to their own testimony, three hundred years have not yet elapsed, since Innocent III. introduced the snare, and imposed the necessity of confession. But, to say nothing respecting the time, the barbarism of the diction is, of itself, sufficient to deprive that law of all credit. For the good fathers enjoin, that every person, of both sexes, shall, once in every year, make a particular confession of all sins to the proper priest; but some wits facetiously object, that this precept binds none but hermaphrodites, and relates to no one who is either a male or a female. Moreover, their disciples have betrayed still greater folly, in their inability to explain what is meant by the proper priest. Whatever may be clamorously pretended by all the Pope's mercenary disputants, we are certain, that Christ was not the author of this law, which compels men to enumerate their sins, and that twelve centuries passed away after the resurrection of Christ, before any such law was promulgated; so that this tyranny was not introduced till after the extinction of piety and learning, when masques, occupying the place of pastors, had assumed an unlimited license of doing whatever they pleased. There are also plain testimonies, in histories and other ancient writings, which inform us, that this was a political discipline instituted by bishops, not a law given by Christ or his apostles. Of a great number, I shall produce only one, which will be a clear proof of this assertion. Sozomen, in his Ecclesiastical History, relates, that this ordinance of the bishops

(*a*) Gal. iii. 22. Rom. iii. 9, 19.

was diligently observed in all the Western Churches, and especially at Rome. He fully implies that it was not the universal custom of all the churches, and says, that one of the Presbyters was peculiarly appointed to this office. In this, he abundantly confutes the false pretensions of these men, that the keys were given promiscuously, for this use, to the whole sacerdotal order, since it was not the common function of all priests, but the peculiar department of one who was chosen to it by the bishop. This is the same, who, in the present day, in every cathedral church is called the Penitentiary, who takes cognizance of crimes of peculiar enormity, and such as are censured for the sake of example. The historian immediately adds, that this was the custom also at Constantinople, till a certain matron, pretending to go to confession, was discovered to have concealed, under this specious pretext, a criminal connection with the deacon of that church. On account of this crime, Nectarius, the bishop of the church, (a man eminent for sanctity and erudition,) abolished the ceremony of confession. Here let them erect their asinine ears. If auricular confession had been a law of God, how could Nectarius have presumed to reverse and disannul it? Will they accuse Nectarius of heresy and schism, who is acknowledged by all the fathers to have been a holy man of God? But the same sentence would condemn the Constantinopolitan church, in which Sozomen affirms the custom of confession not only to have been discontinued for a season, but to have been altogether disused down to his time. And they would accuse of apostasy, not only the church of Constantinople, but all the Oriental churches, who neglected a law which they maintain to be inviolable and obligatory on all Christians.

VIII. But this abrogation is plainly attested by Chrysostom, who was himself also a bishop of the church of Constantinople, in so many places, that it is surprising how they dare to open their mouths in contradiction of it. "Confess your sins, (says he,) that you may obliterate them. If you are ashamed to tell any one what sins you have committed, confess them daily in your soul. I say not, that you should confess them to your fellow-servant, who may reproach you; confess them to God, who cures them. Confess your sins on your bed, that there your conscience may daily recognize its crimes." Again: "But, now, it is not necessary to confess in the presence of witnesses; let an inquisition into your transgressions be the work of your own thoughts; let there be no witness of this judgment; let God alone see you confessing." Again: "I conduct you not into the public view of your fellow-servants; I do not oblige you to reveal your sins to men; lay open your conscience in the presence of God. Show your wounds to the Lord, who is the best physician, and implore a remedy from him; show them to him, who upbraideth not, but most mercifully heals." Again: "You certainly should not tell it to a man, lest he reproach you; nor is confession to be made to a fellow-servant, who may publish it; but show your wounds to the Lord, who exercises his care over you, and is a most merciful physician." He afterwards introduces God, speaking thus: "I constrain you not to come forth into the midst of a theatre, and assemble a multitude of witnesses; declare your sin privately to me alone, that I may heal your wound." Shall we say, that Chrysostom proceeded to such a degree of temerity, when he wrote those and similar passages, as to liberate the consciences of men from obligations imposed on them by the Divine law? Certainly not. But he dares not to require as necessary what he knows is never prescribed in the word of God.

IX. But to place the whole subject in a more plain and familiar light, we will first faithfully state what kind of confession is taught in the word of God; and then we will subjoin an account of those inventions of the Papists, not indeed of all, (for who could exhaust that immense ocean?) but only of those which comprise the substance of their doctrine respecting secret confession. Here it grieves me to mention, how frequently the old translator has translated *confess* instead of *praise;* which is well known even to the most unlearned; only it is necessary to expose their audacity, in transferring to their own tyrannical edict what was written with reference to the praises of God. To prove the virtue of confession to exhilarate the mind, they produce this passage from the Psalmist: "With the voice of exultation and confession." (*b*) But if such a metamorphosis of the passage be admitted, we shall be able to infer any thing from any thing. But since they are thus lost to all sense of shame, let the pious reader remember, that they have been consigned over to a reprobate mind by the righteous vengeance of God, to render their presumption the more detestable. If we are satisfied with the simple doctrine of the Scripture, we shall be in no danger of being deluded by such fallacies; for there one method of confession is prescribed; which is, that since it is the Lord who forgives, forgets, and obliterates sins, we should confess our sins to him, that we may obtain pardon. He is a physician; to him, then, let us discover our wounds. He is injured and offended; let us pray to him for peace. He is the searcher of hearts, and privy to all thoughts; let us hasten to pour out our hearts before him. Finally, it is he who calls sinners; let us not delay to approach him. David says, "I acknowledge my sin unto thee, and mine iniquity have I not hid. I said, I will confess my

(*b*) Psalm xlii. 4.

transgressions unto the Lord; and thou forgavest the iniquity of my sin."(c) Similar to this is another confession of David: "Have mercy upon me, O God, according unto the multitude of thy tender mercies."(d) Such, also, is the confession of Daniel: "We have sinned, and have committed iniquity, and have done wickedly, and have rebelled, even by departing from thy precepts."(e) And such are the other confessions, which frequently occur in the Scriptures, the recital of which would almost fill a volume. John says, "If we confess our sins, God is faithful and just to forgive us our sins."(f) To whom must we confess? To him, certainly; and this we do, if we prostrate ourselves before him with a distressed and humbled heart; if we sincerely accuse and condemn ourselves in his presence, and pray to be pardoned by his goodness and mercy.

X. Whoever from the heart makes this confession before God, will also, without doubt, have a tongue prepared for confession, as often as it shall be necessary to proclaim the Divine mercy among men; and not only to whisper the secret of his mind once into the ear of an individual, but frequently and publicly, and in the hearing of the whole world, ingenuously to declare, both his own ignominy, and the magnificence and glory of God. In this manner, when David was reproved by Nathan, he felt compunction of conscience, and confessed his sin both to God and to men: "I have sinned (said he) against the Lord;"(g) that is, I now make no excuse, nor use the least subterfuge to prevent all men from condemning me as a sinner, and what I wished to conceal from the Lord, from being revealed also to men. The secret confession, therefore, which is made to God, is followed by a voluntary confession before men, whenever it contributes either to the Divine glory or to our humiliation. For this reason, the Lord anciently enjoined upon the Israelites, that all the people should confess their iniquities publicly in the temple, by the mouth of the priest.(h) For he foresaw this assistance to be necessary for them, to bring every person to a proper view of himself. And it is reasonable, that, by the confession of our misery, we should glorify the goodness and mercy of God, both among ourselves and before the whole world.

XI. This kind of confession ought to be both ordinary, in the Church; and extraordinary, to be practised in a particular manner whenever the people at large are chargeable with the guilt of any common crime. We have an example of the latter in that solemn confession which was made by all the people under the auspices of Ezra and Nehemiah. For as

(c) Psalm xxxii. 5. (e) Dan. ix. 5. (g) 2 Sam. xii. 13.
(d) Psalm li. 1. (f) 1 John i. 9. (h) Lev. xvi. 21

their long exile, the destruction of their city and temple, and the subversion of their religion, were punishments of the common defection of all, they could not properly acknowledge the blessing of deliverance, unless they had first confessed their guilt. Nor is it of any importance if, in a congregation, there be sometimes a few innocent persons; for as they are members of a languid and diseased body, they ought not to boast of health. Nor is it possible, indeed, but they must contract some of the pollution, and sustain part of the guilt. Therefore, whenever we are afflicted with pestilence, or war, or sterility, or any other calamity, if it be our duty to resort to mourning, to fasting, and other expressions of guilt, — confession itself, on which all these other things depend, ought by no means to be neglected. The ordinary confession is not only recommended from the mouth of the Lord, but no judicious man, who has considered its usefulness, will venture to condemn it. For since, in every religious assembly, we introduce ourselves into the presence of God and angels, how shall we commence our services, except by an acknowledgment of our unworthiness? But this, you will say, is done in every prayer; for whenever we pray for pardon, we make a confession of our sins. This I acknowledge. But, if you consider our extreme carelessness, or drowsiness, or stupidity, you will admit to me, that it would be a salutary regulation, if the generality of Christians were accustomed to humble themselves by some solemn act of confession. For though the ceremony, which the Lord enjoined on the Israelites, was a part of the tutelage of the law, yet the thing itself, in some measure, belongs also to us. And, indeed, we see that in all well-regulated churches this custom is advantageously observed; that on every Lord's day the minister makes a formal confession, in which he represents all as guilty of sin, and supplicates pardon from the Lord on behalf of all. Finally, by this key the gate of prayer is opened, both to individuals in private, and in public to all the congregation.

XII. Moreover, the Scripture sanctions two kinds of private confession; one to be made for our own sake, which is referred to in the direction of James, that we should " confess our faults one to another;" (*i*) for he means, that, revealing our infirmities to one another, we should assist each other with mutual advice and consolation; another, which is to be made for the sake of our neighbour, to pacify and reconcile him to us, if we have done him any injury. In the former species of confession, though James, by not expressly appointing any one into whose bosom we should disburden ourselves, leaves us quite at liberty to confess to any member of the church who shall appear most

(*i*) James v. 16.

suitable; yet, since the pastors must generally be considered more proper than others, we ought chiefly to make choice of them. I say that they are more suitable than others, since, in their very vocation to the ministry, they are designated by the Lord, to instruct us to subdue and correct our sins, and to console us with a confidence of pardon. For though the office of mutual admonition and reproof is committed to all, yet it is especially confided to ministers. And so, while we all ought mutually to console and confirm each other in a confidence of the Divine mercy, yet we see, that ministers are constituted witnesses and sureties of it, that they may afford our consciences a stronger assurance of the remission of sins; insomuch that they themselves are said to remit sins and to loose souls. (*k*) When you find this attributed to them, consider that it is for your benefit. Therefore, let every believer remember that it is his duty, if he feels such secret anguish or affliction from a sense of his sins, that he cannot extricate himself without some exterior aid, not to neglect the remedy offered him by the Lord; which is, that in order to alleviate his distress, he should use private confession with his pastor, and, to obtain consolation, should privately implore his assistance, whose office it is, both publicly and privately, to comfort the people of God with the doctrine of the gospel. But we should always observe such a degree of moderation, as to lay no yoke on the conscience, where God has given no positive command. Hence it follows, that such confession ought to be free, so as not to be required of all, but only to be recommended to those who conceive themselves to need it. It follows also, that they who practise it on account of their need of it, should neither be compelled by any precept, nor be induced by any artifice, to enumerate all their sins; but only so far as they shall think beneficial to themselves, that they may receive solid consolation. Faithful pastors ought not only to leave the churches in possession of this liberty, but also to defend and vindicate it with all their power, if they wish to preserve their ministry from tyranny, and the people from superstition.

XIII. Concerning the other species of confession, Christ says, in the Gospel of Matthew, "If thou bring thy gift to the altar, and there rememberest that thy brother hath ought against thee, leave there thy gift before the altar, and go thy way; first be reconciled to thy brother, and then come and offer thy gift." (*l*) Thus is that charity, which has been broken by our offence, to be repaired by acknowledging the fault we have committed, and imploring forgiveness. In this kind is comprehended the confession of those who have sinned to

---

(*k*) Matt. xvi. 19; xviii. 18. John xx. 23.   (*l*) Matt. v. 23, 24.

the offence of the whole Church. For, if Christ esteems the private offence of one man of such importance, as to prohibit from the sacred ordinances all those who have sinned against their brethren till they have been restored to favour by an adequate satisfaction,—how much stronger is the reason, that he who, by any evil example, has injured the whole Church, should reconcile it to himself by an acknowledgment of his guilt! Thus was the Corinthian readmitted to the communion, after having submitted to reproof. (*m*) This mode of confession is stated by Cyprian to have been practised in the ancient Church. "They repent (says he) in due time; and afterwards they come to confession; and by the imposition of the hands of the bishop and clergy, they receive a right to communion." The Scripture knows nothing of any other method or form of confession; and it is not our province to impose new chains on men's consciences, which Christ most strictly forbids to reduce under the yoke of bondage. But that the sheep should present themselves to their pastor, whenever they desire to partake of the sacred supper, I am so far from opposing, that I earnestly wish it were universally observed. For those who experience distress of conscience may receive singular benefit from such an interview; and those who require to be admonished, will thus afford an opportunity for admonitions; provided that care be always taken to guard against tyranny and superstition.

XIV. The power of the keys is exercised in these three kinds of confession: either when the whole church implores pardon by a solemn acknowledgment of its transgressions; or when an individual, who, by any remarkable crime, has occasioned a common offence, declares his repentance; or when he who needs the assistance of the minister on account of the disquietude of his conscience, discloses his infirmity to him. The removal of an offence proceeds on a different principle; because, though it is also designed to produce peace of conscience, yet the principal end is, that animosity may be destroyed, and the minds of men united in the bonds of peace. But this advantage, which I have mentioned, is by no means to be despised, that we may confess our sins with the greater readiness. For, when the whole church stands, as it were, before the tribunal of God, when they confess themselves guilty, and have no refuge but in the Divine mercy,—it is no mean or trivial consolation to have Christ's ambassador present, furnished with the mandate of reconciliation, by whom they may have their absolution pronounced. Here the usefulness of the keys is deservedly celebrated, when this embassy is rightly performed,

(*m*) 2 Cor. ii. 6.

with becoming order and reverence. So, when he who had, in some measure, alienated himself from the Church, is pardoned and restored to the unity of the brethren, how great a blessing does he experience in knowing himself to be forgiven by them, to whom Christ has said, " Whose soever sins ye shall remit on earth, they shall be remitted in heaven!" (n) Nor is private absolution less efficacious or beneficial, when it is requested by those who need a particular remedy for the relief of their infirmities. For it frequently happens, that he who hears the general promises, which are addressed to the whole congregation of believers, nevertheless remains in some suspense, and his mind is still disquieted with doubts of the forgiveness of his sins. The same person, if he discloses to his pastor the secret distress of his mind, and hears this language of the gospel particularly directed to him, " Be of good cheer; thy sins be forgiven thee," (o) will encourage his mind to an assurance, and will be liberated from that trepidation with which he was before disturbed. But when we are treating of the keys, we must always be cautious not to dream of any power distinct from the preaching of the gospel. This subject will again be discussed more fully in another place, where we shall have to treat of the government of the Church; and there we shall see, that all the power of binding and loosing, which Christ has conferred on the Church, is inseparable from the word. But this is chiefly applicable to the ministry of the keys, the whole force and meaning of which consist in this, that the grace of the gospel should be confirmed and sealed, as it were, to the minds of the faithful, in public as well as private, by those whom the Lord has ordained to this office; which cannot be done but by preaching alone.

XV. But what is the doctrine of the Romish divines? They maintain, that all persons, of both sexes, as soon as they shall have arrived at years of discretion, should, once at least in every year, confess all their sins to their own priest; that there is no remission of sin, unless they have firmly resolved to confess it; that unless they fulfil this resolution, when opportunity offers, there is no admittance for them into Paradise; and, moreover, that the priest has the power of the keys, with which he may loose the sinner or bind him; because Christ has not said in vain, " Whatsoever ye shall bind on earth shall be bound in heaven." (p) But concerning this power, they have obstinate contentions among themselves. Some say, that there is essentially but one key, namely, the power of binding and loosing; that knowledge is required, indeed, for the good use of it, but that it is only like an accessary, not an essential con-

(n) Matt. xviii. 18. John xx. 23.   (o) Matt. ix. 2.   (p) Matt. xviii. 18.

comitant. Others, perceiving this to be too unlimited a license, have mentioned two keys, discretion and power. Others, again, observing that the wickedness of the priests was restrained by such moderation, have invented other keys, an authority of discerning which they might use in pronouncing decisions; and a power, which they might exert in executing their sentences; with knowledge, to assist as a counsellor. But they venture not to explain this binding and loosing simply to mean, forgiving and obliterating sins; because they hear the Lord proclaiming by the prophet, "I am the Lord, and beside me there is no Saviour. I, even I, am he which blotteth out thy transgressions." (*q*) But they say, that it belongs to the priest to pronounce who are bound or loosed, and to declare whose sins are remitted or retained; and that he declares it, either by confession, when he absolves and retains sins; or by his sentence, when he excommunicates, and when he receives to the communion of the sacraments. Lastly, when they perceive that they are not yet extricated from this difficulty, but that it may always be objected, that their priests frequently bind and loose improper persons, who are not therefore bound or loosed in heaven,—as their last resource, they reply, that the commission of the keys must be understood with some limitation, Christ having promised, that the sentence of the priest, which has been justly delivered, according to the merits of the persons bound or loosed, shall be confirmed at his tribunal. They add also, that these keys were given by Christ to all priests, who receive them from the bishops on their promotion to the sacerdotal office; but that the free use of them belongs only to those who exercise ecclesiastical functions; that the keys themselves remain, indeed, with the excommunicated or suspended ones, but that they are rusty and disused. And those who advance these things may justly be considered modest and sober, in comparison with others, who, on a new anvil, have fabricated new keys, with which they tell us the treasure of the Church is locked up; which we shall examine in the proper place.

XVI. I shall briefly reply to each of these things; though without noticing, at present, the justice or injustice with which they bind the souls of the faithful by their laws; as that will be considered in due order. But when they impose a law respecting the enumeration of all sins; when they deny that sin is forgiven, but on condition that a firm resolution has been formed to confess it; when they say that there remains no entrance into Paradise, if the opportunity of confession has been neglected,—this is altogether intolerable. Must all sins

(*q*) Isaiah xliii. 11, 25.

be enumerated? David, who (I suppose) had often meditated the confession of his sins, nevertheless exclaimed, "Who can understand his errors? cleanse thou me from secret faults." (r) And in another place: "Mine iniquities are gone over mine head; as a heavy burden they are too heavy for me." (s) He had just apprehensions of the vast abyss of our sins, of the numerous species of our crimes, of the many heads this monster bore, and the long tail it drew after it. Therefore he attempted not to detail his transgressions, but from the abyss of his distresses cried to the Lord, "I am afflicted and ready to die; my spirit is overwhelmed within me; I dwell in darkness, as those that have been long dead;" (t) "the sorrows of death compassed me, and the pains of hell gat hold upon me;" (v) "I sink in deep mire; deliver me out of the mire, and let me not sink." (w) Who can now think of recounting his sins, when he sees that David was unable to enter on an enumeration of his?

XVII. The souls of those who have been affected with any discoveries of God, have been most cruelly tormented by this fatal delusion. First, they called themselves to an account; they divided sins into boughs, branches, twigs, and leaves, according to the distinctions of these confessors: then they examined the qualities, quantities, and circumstances; and the business made some little progress. But, when they had advanced further, they were surrounded on all sides by the sea and the sky, no port, no haven in prospect; the more they had passed over, the greater mass was always accumulating on their view; they beheld, as it were, lofty mountains rising before them, and no time or labour seemed to encourage the least hope of escaping. Thus they remained in extreme distress, and after all, found it terminate in nothing but despair. Then the remedy applied by those cruel murderers, to alleviate the wounds which they had made, was, that every one should do to the uttermost of his ability. But new cares again disturbed, and new agonies again excruciated, these miserable souls: I have not devoted sufficient time; I have not applied with proper diligence; I have omitted many things through negligence, and the forgetfulness which arises from negligence is inexcusable. To assuage such pains, other remedies were now added: Repent of your negligence; if it be not too great, it will be forgiven. But all these things cannot heal the wound; nor do they act as alleviations of the malady, but rather as poisons concealed in honey, that they may not by their harshness offend at the first taste, but may penetrate into the inmost parts before they are perceived. This terrible injunction, therefore, is always pursuing them and resounding in their ears: "Confess

---

(r) Psalm xix. 12.   (s) Psalm lxxxviii. 15.   (t) Psalm cxliii. 3, 4.
(v) Psalm cxvi. 3   (w) Psalm lxix. 2, 14.

all your sins;" nor can that terror be appeased but by some certain consolation. Here let the reader consider the possibility of taking an account of the actions of a whole year, and selecting the sins of every day; since experience convinces every man that, when at evening he comes to examine the delinquencies of only one day, his memory is confounded by their great multitude and variety. I speak not of stupid hypocrites, who, if they have noticed three or four gross sins, imagine they have discharged their duty; but of the true worshippers of God, who, when they find themselves overwhelmed with the examination they have made, conclude, in the language of John, "If our heart condemn us, God is greater than our heart." (x) They tremble, therefore, before that Judge, whose knowledge far exceeds our apprehension.

XVIII. The acquiescence of a great part of the world in such soothing arts, employed to temper this mortal poison, was not indulged from a belief that God was satisfied, or because they were altogether satisfied themselves; but that, like mariners, having cast anchor in the midst of the sea, they might enjoy a short respite from the toils of navigation, or like a fatigued and fainting traveller, might lie down in the road. I shall not take much trouble to establish this point; for every man may be his own witness of it. I will briefly state the nature of this law. First, it is absolutely impracticable; therefore it can only destroy, condemn, confound, and precipitate into ruin and despair. In the next place, it diverts sinners from a true sense of their sins, and makes them hypocrites, ignorant both of God and themselves. For while they are wholly employed in enumerating their sins, they forget, in the mean time, that latent source of vices, their secret iniquities and inward pollutions, a knowledge of which is above all things necessary to a consideration of their misery. But the most certain rule of confession is to acknowledge and confess the abyss of our guilt to be vast beyond all our comprehension. The publican's confession appears to have been composed according to this rule — "God be merciful to me a sinner." (y) As though he had said, "All that I am is utterly sinful; I cannot reach the magnitude of my sins, either with my tongue or with my mind; let the abyss of thy mercy swallow up this abyss of sin." But you will say, Are not particular sins, then, to be confessed? Is no confession accepted by God unless it be comprised in these precise words, "I am a sinner?" I reply, that we should rather endeavour, as far as we possibly can, to pour out our whole heart before the Lord; and not only confess ourselves sinners in a single expression, but truly and

(x) 1 John iii. 20.   (y) Luke xviii. 13.

cordially acknowledge ourselves such; and consider in all our reflections, how great and various is the pollution of sin; not only that we are unclean, but the nature and extent of our impurity; not only that we are debtors, but the magnitude and number of the debts with which we are burdened; not only that we are wounded, but what a multitude of mortal wounds we have received. Yet when the sinner has wholly unbosomed himself before God in this acknowledgment, let him seriously and sincerely reflect, that more sins still remain, and that the secret recesses of his guilt are too deep to be entirely disclosed. And therefore let him exclaim with David, " Who can understand his errors? Cleanse thou me from secret faults." (*w*) Now, when they affirm, that sins are not forgiven without a strong resolution having been formed to confess them, and that the gate of Paradise is shut against him who has neglected an opportunity afforded him of confessing, — far be it from us to make them such a concession. For there is no other remission of sins now than there always has been. Among all those who are said to have obtained remission of sins from Christ, none are said to have made a confession in the ear of any priest. Nor, indeed, was it possible for them thus to confess, when there were no confessionary priests, and confession itself was altogether unknown. And this confession was unheard of for many ages after, during which sins were forgiven without this condition. But, not to debate any longer as respecting a doubtful point, " the word of God which abideth for ever," (*x*) is perfectly clear: " If the wicked will turn from all his sins, all his transgressions that he hath committed, they shall not be mentioned unto him." (*y*) He who presumes to make any addition to this declaration, does not bind sins, but limits the mercy of God. When they contend that judgment cannot be given without a trial of the cause, we are prepared with an answer — that they are guilty of arrogant presumption in creating themselves judges. And it is surprising that they so securely fabricate principles for themselves, which no man of sound understanding will admit. They boast that the office of binding and loosing is committed to them, as though it were a kind of jurisdiction annexed to examination. That the apostles were strangers to this authority, their whole doctrine proclaims; and to know certainly whether the sinner be loosed, belongs not to the priest, but to Him of whom absolution is implored; since the priest who hears the confession, can never know whether the enumeration of sins be true and perfect. Thus there would be no absolution, but what must be restricted to the words of the person to be

(*w*) Psalm xix. 12.   (*x*) 1 Peter i. 23.   (*y*) Ezek. xviii. 21, 22.

judged. Besides, the loosing of sins depends entirely on faith and repentance; which both elude the knowledge of man, when sentence is to be given respecting another. It follows, therefore, that the certainty of binding and loosing is not subject to the decision of an earthly judge; because a minister, in the legitimate execution of his office, can pronounce only a conditional absolution; but that the declaration, "*Whose soever sins ye remit, they are remitted*," is spoken for the sake of sinners, to preclude every doubt that the pardon, which is promised according to the command and word of God, will be ratified in heaven.

XIX. It is not to be wondered at, therefore, if we condemn and desire the total removal of this auricular confession — a thing so pestilent, and in so many respects injurious to the Church. Even if it were a thing abstractedly indifferent, yet, since it is of no use or benefit, but has occasioned so much impiety, sacrilege, and error, — who can refuse to admit, that it ought to be immediately abolished? They mention, indeed, some uses, which they boast of as very beneficial; but these are mere fictions, or productive of no advantage whatever. One circumstance they state as a peculiar recommendation, that the shame of the person who confesses is a grievous punishment, by which the sinner is rendered more cautious in future, and prevents the vengeance of God by punishing himself. As though we humble not a man with a sufficient degree of shame, when we summon him to the supreme tribunal of heaven — to the cognizance of God! It is a wonderful advantage, indeed, if we cease to sin through a shame of one man, but are never ashamed of having God for a witness of our evil conscience! Though this very notion is utterly false; for it is universally observable, that nothing produces a greater confidence or licentiousness in sinning, than the idea entertained by some men, after they have made their confession to a priest, that they may " wipe their mouth and say, I have done no wickedness."(z) And they not only become more presumptuous in their sins throughout the year, but, having no concern about confession for the rest of the year, they never aspire after God, they never retire into themselves, but accumulate sins upon sins, till they disembogue them, as they imagine, all at once. But when they have done this, they conceive themselves to be exonerated of their burden, and to have transferred from God the judgment they have conferred on the priest; and that they have deprived God of remembrance, by the information they have communicated to the priest. Besides, who rejoices to see the day of confession approaching? Who goes to confess with alacrity of heart; and does not rather come with unwillingness and re-

(z) Prov. xxx. 20.

luctance, as though he were forcibly dragged to a prison; except perhaps the priests, who pleasantly entertain themselves with mutual narrations of their exploits, as with humorous anecdotes? I will not soil much paper by relating the monstrous abominations with which auricular confession abounds. I only remark, if that holy man was not guilty of indiscretion, who, on account of one rumour of fornication, banished confession from his church, or rather from the memory of his people,—we are thus reminded of what ought to be done in the present day, when rapes, adulteries, incests, and seductions exceed all enumeration.

XX. As the advocates of confession plead the power of the keys, and rest upon it all the merits of their cause, we must examine the weight that is due to this argument. Are the keys, then, (say they,) given without any reason? Is it without any cause that it is said, "Whatsoever ye shall loose on earth, shall be loosed in heaven?" (*a*) Do we, then, frustrate the declaration of Christ? I reply, that there was an important reason why the keys should be given; as I have already stated, and shall again more explicitly show, when I come to treat of excommunication. But what if I refute the whole of their pretensions with one argument, that their priests are not vicars, or successors of the apostles? But this, also, will be discussed in another place. Now, they set up, as their principal defence, an engine by which their whole structure may be completely demolished. For Christ never conferred on his apostles the power of binding and loosing, till after he had given them the Holy Ghost. I deny, therefore, that the power of the keys belongs to any, who have not previously received the Holy Ghost. I deny that any one can use the keys, unless the Spirit guide and instruct him, and direct him how he ought to act. They impertinently pretend, that they have the Holy Ghost; but in reality they deny it; unless perhaps they imagine, as they certainly do, that the Holy Ghost is a useless and worthless thing; but they will not be believed. By this weapon they are completely vanquished. Of whatever door they pretend to have the key, they should always be asked, whether they have the Holy Ghost, who is the arbiter and governor of the keys. If they reply in the affirmative, they must be questioned again, whether it be possible for the Holy Ghost to err. This they will not dare expressly to avow, though they obliquely insinuate it in their doctrine. We may justly infer, therefore, that no priests have the power of the keys, who, without discrimination, frequently loose what the Lord had designed to be bound, and bind what he had commanded to be loosed.

XXI. When they find themselves convinced, by evident

(*a*) Matt. xviii. 18.

experience, that they promiscuously loose and bind the worthy and the unworthy, they arrogate to themselves the power without knowledge. And though they dare not deny that knowledge is requisite to a good use of it, yet they tell us, that the power itself is committed to improper dispensers of it. But this is the power — " Whatsoever thou bindest or loosest on earth, shall be bound or loosed in heaven." Either the promise of Christ must be false, or the binding and loosing is rightly performed by those who are endued with this power. Nor is there any room for them to quibble, that the declaration of Christ is limited according to the merits of the person that is bound or loosed. We also acknowledge, that none can be bound or loosed, but such as are worthy to be bound or loosed. But the preachers of the gospel, and the Church, have the word as the standard of this worthiness. In this word, the ministers of the gospel may promise to all remission of sins in Christ through faith; they may denounce damnation against all and upon all who receive not Christ. In this word, the Church pronounces, that fornicators, adulterers, thieves, murderers, misers, and extortioners, have no part in the kingdom of God; and binds such with the firmest bonds. In the same word, the Church looses and comforts those who repent. (*b*) But what kind of power will it be, not to know what ought to be bound or loosed? and not to be able to bind or loose without this knowledge? Why, then, do they say, that they absolve by the authority committed to them, when their absolution is uncertain? Why should we concern ourselves about this imaginary power, if it be quite useless? But I have already ascertained, either that it has no existence, or that it is too uncertain to be considered of any value. For, as they confess that there are many of the priests who make no right use of the keys, and that the power has no efficacy without a legitimate use of it, who will assure me, that he by whom I am loosed is a good dispenser of the keys? But if he be a bad one, what else does he possess but this frivolous dispensation of them: " What ought to be bound or loosed in you, I know not, since I am destitute of the proper use of the keys; but if you deserve it, I absolve you?" But as much as this might be done, I will not say by a layman, (since they could not hear that with any patience,) but by a Turk or a devil. For it is equivalent to saying, "I have not the word of God, which is the certain rule of loosing; but I am invested with authority to absolve you, on condition that your merits deserve it." We see, then, what they intended, when they defined the keys to be an authority of discerning, and a power of executing, attended with knowledge as a counsellor, to promote the good

(*b*) 1 Cor. vi. 9—11.

use. The truth is, that they wished to reign according to their own licentious inclinations, independently of God and his word.

XXII. If it be objected, that the legitimate ministers of Christ will be equally perplexed in their office, since the absolution, which depends on faith, will ever be doubtful, and that therefore sinners will have but a slight consolation, or none at all, since the minister himself, who is not a competent judge of their faith, is not certain of their absolution, — we are prepared with an answer. They say, that no sins are remitted by the priest, but those which fall under his cognizance; thus, according to them, remission depends on the judgment of the priest; and unless he sagaciously discerns who are worthy of pardon, the whole transaction is frivolous and useless. In short, the power of which they speak is a jurisdiction annexed to examination, to which pardon and absolution are restricted. In this statement, we find no firm footing, but rather a bottomless abyss; for where the confession is deficient, the hope of pardon is also imperfect; in the next place, the priest himself must necessarily remain in suspense, while he is ignorant whether the sinner faithfully enumerates all his crimes; lastly, such is the ignorance and inexperience of priests, that the majority of them are no more qualified for the exercise of this office, than a shoemaker for cultivating the ground; and almost all the rest ought justly to be suspicious of themselves. Hence, then, the perplexity and doubtfulness of the Papal absolution, because they maintain it to be founded on the person of the priest; and not only so, but on his knowledge, so that he can only judge of what he hears, examines, and ascertains. Now, should any one inquire of these good doctors, whether a sinner be reconciled to God on the remission of part of his sins, I know not what answer they can give, without being constrained to acknowledge the inefficacy of whatever the priest may pronounce concerning the remission of sins which he has heard enumerated, as long as the guilt of others still remains. What a pernicious anxiety must oppress the conscience of the person that confesses, appears from this consideration, that while he relies on the discretion of the priest, (as they express themselves,) he decides nothing by the word of God. The doctrine maintained by us, is perfectly free from all these absurdities. For absolution is conditional, in such a way, that the sinner may be confident that God is propitious to him, provided he sincerely seeks an atonement in the sacrifice of Christ, and relies upon the grace offered to him. Thus it is impossible for him to err, who, according to his duty as a preacher, promulgates what he has been taught by the Divine word; and the sinner may receive a certain and clear absolution, simply on condition of embracing the grace of Christ, according to that general rule of our Lord himself, which has been impiously despised among the Papists — "According to your faith be it unto you." (c)

XXIII. Their absurd confusion of the clear representations of the Scripture concerning the power of the keys, I have promised to expose in another place; and a more suitable opportunity will present itself, in discussing the government of the Church. But let the reader remember, that they preposterously pervert to auricular and secret confession, passages which are spoken by Christ, partly of the preaching of the gospel, and partly of excommunication. Wherefore, when they object that the power of loosing was committed to the apostles, which is now exercised by the priests in remitting the sins confessed to them, it is evidently an assumption of a false and frivolous principle; for the absolution consequent on faith, is nothing but a declaration of pardon taken from the gracious promise of the gospel; but the other absolution, which depends on ecclesiastical discipline, relates not to secret sins, but is rather for the sake of example, that the public offence of the Church may be removed. They rake together testimonies from every quarter, to prove, that it is not sufficient to make a confession of sins to God, or to laymen, unless they are likewise submitted to the cognizance of a priest; but they ought to be ashamed of such a disgusting employment. For, if the ancient fathers sometimes persuade sinners to disburden themselves to their own pastor, it cannot be understood of a particular enumeration of sins, which was not then practised. Moreover, Lombard and others of the same class have been so unfair, that they appear to have designedly consulted spurious books, in order to use them as a pretext to deceive the unwary. They do, indeed, properly acknowledge, that since loosing always accompanies repentance, there really remains no bond where any one has experienced repentance, although he may not yet have made a confession; and, therefore, that then the priest does not so much remit sins, as pronounce and declare them to be remitted. Though in the word *declare* they insinuate a gross error, substituting a ceremony in the place of instruction; but by adding, that he who had already obtained pardon before God, is absolved in the view of the Church, they unseasonably apply to the particular use of every individual, what we have already asserted to have been appointed as a part of the common discipline of the Church, when the offence of some great and notorious crime requires to be removed. But they presently corrupt and destroy all the moderation they had observed, by adding another mode of remission, that is, with an injunction

(c) Matt. ix. 29.

of punishment and satisfaction; by which they arrogantly ascribe to their priests the power of dividing into two parts what God has every where promised as complete. For, as he simply requires repentance and faith, this partition or exception is an evident sacrilege. For it is just as if the priest, sustaining the character of a tribune, should interpose his *veto*, and not suffer God of his mere goodness to receive any one into favour, unless he had lain prostrate before the tribunitial seat, and there been punished.

XXIV. The whole argument comes to this — that if they will represent God as the author of this fictitious confession, it is a full proof of their error; for I have pointed out their fallacies in the few passages which they quote. But since it is evident that this is a law of human imposition, I assert that it is also tyrannical and injurious to God, who binds the consciences of men by his word, and whose will it is that they should be free from the authority of men. Now, when they prescribe as a necessary prerequisite to pardon that which God has chosen should be free, I maintain that it is an intolerable sacrilege; for nothing is more peculiarly the prerogative of God than the remission of sins, in which our salvation consists. I have moreover proved, that this tyranny was not introduced till the world was oppressed with the rudest barbarism. I have likewise shown that it is a pestilent law, because, if wretched souls are affected with the fear of God, it precipitates them into despair; or if they are in a state of careless security, it soothes them with vain flatteries, and renders them still more insensible. Lastly, I have stated, that all the mitigations which they add, have no other tendency than to perplex, obscure, and corrupt the pure doctrine, and to conceal their impieties under false and illusive colours.

XXV. The third place in repentance they assign to *satisfaction*; all their jargon concerning which may be overturned in one word. They say, that it is not sufficient for a penitent to abstain from his former sins, and to change his morals for the better, unless he make satisfaction to God for the crimes which he has committed; and that there are many helps by which we may redeem sins, such as tears, fastings, oblations, and works of charity; that by these the Lord is to be propitiated, by these our debts are to be paid to the Divine justice, by these we must compensate for the guilt of our sins, by these we must merit pardon; for that though, in the plenitude of his mercy, he has remitted our sins, yet, in the discipline of justice, he retains the punishment, and that this is the punishment which must be redeemed by *satisfactions*. All that they say, however, comes to this conclusion — that we obtain the pardon of our transgressions from the mercy of God, but that it is by the intervention of the merit of works, by which the evil of our sins must be compensated, that the Divine justice may receive the satisfaction which is due to it. To such falsehoods I oppose the gratuitous remission of sins, than which there is nothing more clearly revealed in the Scripture. In the first place, what is remission, but a gift of mere liberality? For the creditor is not said to forgive, who testifies by a receipt that the debt has been paid, but he who, without any payment, merely through his beneficence, voluntarily cancels the obligation. In the next place, why is this said to be free, but to preclude every idea of satisfaction? With what confidence, then, can they still set up their *satisfactions*, which are overthrown by such a mighty thunderbolt? But when the Lord proclaims by Isaiah, "I, even I, am he that blotteth out thy transgressions for mine own sake, and will not remember thy sins," (*d*) does he not evidently declare, that he derives the cause and foundation of forgiveness merely from his own goodness? Besides, while the whole Scripture bears testimony to Christ, that "remission of sins" is to be "received through his name," (*e*) does it not exclude all other names? How, then, do they teach, that it is received through the name of *satisfactions?* Nor can they deny that they ascribe this to satisfactions, although they call their intervention *subsidiary*. For when the Scripture states it to be "through the name of Christ," it signifies, that we bring nothing, that we plead nothing, of our own, but rely solely on the mediation of Christ; as Paul, after affirming, "that God was in Christ reconciling the world unto himself, not imputing their trespasses unto them," immediately adds the method and nature of it, "for he hath made him, who knew no sin, to be sin for us." (*f*)

XXVI. But such is their perverseness, they reply that both remission of sins and reconciliation are obtained at once, when in baptism we are received into the favour of God, through Christ; that if we fall after baptism, we are to be raised up again by *satisfactions;* and that the blood of Christ avails us nothing, any further than it is dispensed by the keys of the Church. I am not speaking of a doubtful point, for they have betrayed their impurity in the most explicit terms; and this is the case not only of two or three, but of all the schoolmen. For their master, Lombard, after having confessed that, according to the doctrine of Peter, Christ suffered the punishment of sins on the cross, (*g*) immediately corrects that sentiment by the addition of the following exception: that all the temporal punishments of sins are remitted in baptism; but

(*d*) Isaiah xliii. 25.   (*f*) 2 Cor. v. 19, 21.
(*e*) Acts x. 43.   (*g*) 1 Peter ii. 24.

that after baptism they are diminished by means of repentance, so that our repentance coöperates with the cross of Christ. But John speaks a very different language: "If any man sin, we have an Advocate with the Father, Jesus Christ the righteous; and he is the propitiation for our sins: I write unto you, little children, because your sins are forgiven you for his name's sake." (*h*) He certainly addresses believers, and when he exhibits Christ to them as the propitiation for sins, proves that there is no other satisfaction by which our offended God may be propitiated or appeased. He says not, God was once reconciled to you by Christ, now seek some other means; but represents him as a perpetual advocate, who by his intercession restores us to the Father's favour for ever, and as a perpetual propitiation by which our sins are expiated. For this is perpetually true, that was declared by the other John, "Behold the Lamb of God, which taketh away the sins of the world." (*i*) He takes them away himself, I say, and no other; that is, since he alone is the Lamb of God, he alone is the oblation, the expiation, the satisfaction for sins. For the right and power to forgive being the peculiar prerogative of the Father, as distinguished from the Son, as we have already seen, Christ is here represented in another capacity, since by transferring to himself the punishment we deserved, he has obliterated our guilt before the throne of God. Whence it follows, that we shall not be partakers of the atonement of Christ in any other way, unless he remain in the exclusive possession of that honour, which they unjustly assume to themselves who endeavour to appease God by *satisfactions* of their own.

XXVII. And here two things demand our consideration — that the honour, which belongs to Christ, should be preserved to him entire and undiminished; and that consciences assured of the pardon of their sins, should have peace with God. Isaiah says, "The Lord hath laid on him the iniquity of us all," and "With his stripes we are healed." (*k*) Peter, repeating the same truth in different words, says, that Christ "bare our sins in his own body on the tree." (*l*) Paul informs us, that "sin was condemned in the flesh," (*m*) when "Christ was made sin for us;" (*n*) that is, that the power and curse of sin were destroyed in his flesh, when he was given as a victim, to sustain the whole load of our sins, with their curse and execrations, with the dreadful judgment of God, and the condemnation of death. We cannot here listen to those foolish fictions; that after the initial purgation or baptism, none of us can have any further experience of the efficacy of the sufferings of

(*h*) 1 John ii. 1, 2, 12.
(*i*) John i. 29.
(*k*) Isaiah liii. 5, 6.
(*l*) 1 Peter ii. 24.
(*m*) Rom. viii. 3.
(*n*) 2 Cor. v. 21. Gal. iii. 13.

Christ, than in proportion to a satisfactory repentance. But whenever we have fallen, the Scripture recalls us to the satisfaction of Christ alone. Now, review their pestilent follies; " that the grace of God operates alone in the first remission of sins; but that if we afterwards fall, our works coöperate with it in the impetration of a second pardon." If these things be admitted, does Christ remain exclusively possessed of what we have before attributed to him? How immensely wide is the difference between these positions — that our iniquities are laid on Christ to be expiated by him, and that they are expiated by our own works! that Christ is the propitiation for our sins, and that God must be propitiated by works! But with respect to pacifying the conscience, what peace will it afford any one, to hear that sins are redeemed by satisfactions? When will he be assured of the accomplishment of satisfaction? Therefore he will always doubt whether God be propitious to him, he will always be in a state of fluctuation and terror. For those who content themselves with trivial satisfactions, have too contemptuous sentiments of the judgment of God, and reflect very little on the vast evil of sin, as we shall elsewhere observe. But though we should allow them to expiate some sins by a proper satisfaction, yet what will they do when they are overwhelmed with so many sins, that to make adequate satisfactions for them, even a hundred lives entirely devoted to it could not possibly be sufficient? Besides, all the passages in which remission of sins is declared, are not addressed to catechumens, [or persons not yet baptized,] but to the regenerated sons of God, and those who have been long nurtured in the bosom of the Church. That embassy which Paul so splendidly extols, " We pray you in Christ's stead, be ye reconciled to God," (o) is directed not to strangers, but to those who had already been regenerated. But, dismissing all satisfactions, he sends them to the cross of Christ. Thus, when he writes to the Colossians, that " Christ had made peace by the blood of his cross, and reconciled all things both in earth and in heaven," (p) he restricts not this to the moment of our reception into the Church, but extends it through our whole course; as is evident from the context, where he says that believers " have redemption through his blood, even the forgiveness of sins." But it is unnecessary to accumulate more passages, which are frequently occurring.

XXVIII. Here they take refuge in a foolish distinction, that some sins are *venial*, and some *mortal;* that a great satisfaction is due for mortal sins; but that those which are venial are purged away by easier remedies, by the Lord's prayer, the

(o) 2 Cor. v. 20.   (p) Col. i. 20.

aspersion of holy water, and the absolution of the mass. Thus they sport and trifle with God. But though they are incessantly talking of venial and mortal sins, yet they have never been able to discriminate one from the other, except by making impiety and impurity of heart a venial sin. But we maintain, according to the doctrine of the Scripture, the only standard of righteousness and sin, that "the wages of sin is death," and "the soul that sinneth, it shall die;" (*q*) but that the sins of believers are venial, not because they are not deserving of death, but because, through the mercy of God, "there is no condemnation to them which are in Christ Jesus;" (*r*) because they are not imputed to them, but obliterated by a pardon. I know their unjust calumnies against this doctrine of ours; they assert it to be the Stoical paradox concerning the equality of sins; but they will easily be refuted out of their own lips. For I ask, whether among those very sins which they confess to be mortal, they do not acknowledge one to be greater or less than another? It does not, therefore, immediately follow, that sins are equal because they are alike mortal. Since the Scripture declares that the wages of sin is death, that obedience to the law is the way of life, and the transgression of it death, they cannot evade this decision. What end, then, will they find to satisfactions in so great an accumulation of sins? If it be the business of one day to satisfy for one sin, while they are employed in that, they involve themselves in more; for the most righteous man cannot pass a single day without falling several times. While they shall be preparing themselves to make satisfaction for these, they will accumulate a numerous, or rather an innumerable multitude. Now, all confidence in satisfaction is cut off: on what do they depend? How do they still presume to think of making satisfaction?

XXIX. They endeavour to extricate themselves from this difficulty, but without success. They invent a distinction between the guilt and the punishment; and acknowledge that the guilt is forgiven by the Divine mercy, but maintain, that after the remission of the guilt, there still remains the punishment, which the Divine justice requires to be suffered; and, therefore, that satisfactions properly relate to the remission of the punishment. What desultory levity is this! Now, they confess that remission of guilt is proposed as gratuitous, which they are continually teaching men to merit by prayers and tears, and other preparations of various kinds. But every thing delivered in the Scripture concerning remission of sins is diametrically opposite to this distinction. And though I think I have fully established this point already, I will subjoin some

(*q*) Rom. vi. 23. Ezek. xviii. 20.   (*r*) Rom. viii. 1.

additional testimonies, by which our opponents will be so much embarrassed, as, notwithstanding all their serpentine lubricity, to be totally unable ever to extricate themselves. "This is the new covenant," which God has made with us in Christ, "that he will not remember our iniquities." (*s*) The import of these expressions we learn from another prophet, by whom the Lord says, "When the righteous turneth away from his righteousness, all his righteousness that he hath done shall not be mentioned. When the wicked man turneth away from his wickedness, he shall surely live, he shall not die." (*t*) "Not to mention righteousness," signifies, not to notice it so as to reward it; and "not to remember sins," is, not to inflict punishment for them. This is expressed in other passages by the following phrases: to "cast behind the back," to "blot out as a cloud," to "cast into the depths of the sea," "not to impute," to "cover." (*u*) These forms of expression would clearly convey to us the sense of the Holy Spirit, if we attended to them with docility. If God punishes sins, he certainly imputes them; if he avenges them, he remembers them; if he cites them to judgment, he does not cover them; if he examines them, he has not cast them behind his back; if he inspects them, he has not blotted them out as a cloud; if he scrutinizes them, he has not cast them into the depths of the sea. And in this manner the subject is clearly explained by Augustine. "If God has covered sins, he would not look at them; if he would not look at them, he would not take cognizance of them; if he would not take cognizance of them, he would not punish them; he would not know them, he would rather forgive them. Why, then, has he said that sins are covered? That they might not be seen. For what is meant by God's seeing sin, but his punishing it?" Let us also hear from another passage of the prophet, on what conditions God remits sins. "Though your sins be as scarlet, (says he,) they shall be as white as snow; though they be red like crimson, they shall be as wool." (*w*) And in Jeremiah we find this declaration: "In that time the iniquities of Israel shall be sought for, and there shall be none; and the sins of Judah, and they shall not be found; for I will pardon them whom I reserve." (*x*) Would you briefly know what is the meaning of these words? Consider, on the contrary, the import of the following expressions: "the Lord seweth up iniquity in a bag;" "iniquity is bound up;" "sin is hid;" to "write sins with a pen of iron, and engrave them with the point of a diamond." (*y*) If they signify

---

(*s*) Jer. xxxi. 31—34.   (*t*) Ezek. xviii. 21—28.
(*u*) Isaiah xxxviii. 17; xliv. 22. Micah vii. 19. Psalm xxxii. 1, 2.
(*w*) Isaiah i. 18.   (*x*) Jeremiah l. 20.
(*y*) Job xiv. 17. Hos. xiii. 12. Jeremiah xvii. 1.

that God will execute vengeance, as they undoubtedly do, neither can it be doubted but that, by the contrary declaration, the Lord proclaims his remission of all vindictive punishment. Here I must conjure my readers not to listen to my expositions, but only to pay some deference to the word of God.

XXX. What would Christ have done for us, if punishment for sins were still inflicted on us? For when we say, that he "bare all our sins in his own body on the tree," (z) we intend only, that he sustained the vindictive punishment which was due to our sins. This sentiment is more significantly expressed by Isaiah, when he says that the "chastisement (or correction) of our peace was upon him." (a) Now, what is the correction of our peace, but the punishment due to sins, and which we must have suffered before we could be reconciled to God, if he had not become our substitute? Thus we see clearly, that Christ bore the punishment of sins, that he might deliver his people from it. And whenever Paul mentions the redemption accomplished by him, he generally calls it ἀπολύτρωσις, (b) which signifies not simply redemption, as it is commonly understood, but the price and satisfaction of redemption. Thus he says that Christ " gave himself a ransom " (ἀντίλυτρον) for us. (c) " What propitiation is there with the Lord (says Augustine) but sacrifice? And what sacrifice is there, but that which has been offered for us in the death of Christ?" But the institutions of the law of Moses, respecting expiations for sins, furnish us with a most powerful argument. For there the Lord prescribes not this or the other method of satisfying, but requires the whole compensation in sacrifices; though he specifies all the rites of expiation with the most particular care, and in the most exact order. How is it that he commands the expiation of sins without any works at all, requiring no other atonement than by sacrifices, but because he intends in this way to declare, that there is only one kind of satisfaction by which his justice is appeased? For the sacrifices then immolated by the Israelites were not considered as the works of men, but were estimated according to their antitype, that is, the one sacrifice of Christ alone. The nature of the compensation which the Lord receives from us is concisely and beautifully expressed by Hosea: " Take away (saith he) all iniquity, O Lord; " here is remission of sins; "so will we render the calves of our lips; " (d) here is satisfaction, [which is no other than thanksgiving.] I am aware of another still more subtle evasion to which they resort, by distinguishing between eternal punishments and those which are temporal. But when

(z) 1 Peter ii. 24. (a) Isaiah liii. 6. (b) Rom. iii. 24, &c.
(c) 1 Tim. ii. 6. (d) Hosea xiv. 2.

they assert that temporal punishment is any suffering inflicted by God on the body or the soul, eternal death only excepted, this limitation affords them but little assistance. For the passages which we have cited above, expressly signify, that God receives us into favour on this condition, that in forgiving our guilt, he remits all the punishment that we had deserved. And whenever David or the other prophets implore the pardon of their sins, they at the same time deprecate the punishment; and to this they are impelled by an apprehension of the Divine judgment. Again: when they promise mercy from the Lord, they almost always professedly speak of punishments, and of the remission of them. Certainly when the Lord announces by Ezekiel, that he will put an end to the Babylonian captivity, and that for his own sake, not for the sake of the Jews, he sufficiently shows this deliverance to be gratuitous. Finally, if Christ delivers us from guilt, the punishments consequent upon it must necessarily cease.

XXXI. But as our adversaries also, on their part, arm themselves with testimonies from the Scripture, let us examine what arguments they offer. They reason in this way: David, after having been reproved by Nathan the prophet for adultery and murder, receives the pardon of his sin; and yet is afterwards punished by the death of the son that was the fruit of his adultery. (*e*) We are taught to compensate by satisfactions for such punishments as would be inflicted even after the remission of the guilt. For Daniel exhorted Nebuchadnezzar to atone for his sins by acts of mercy. (*f*) And Solomon says, "By mercy and truth, iniquity is purged." (*g*) And that "charity shall cover a multitude of sins," (*h*) is a sentiment confirmed by the united testimony of Solomon and Peter. The Lord also says in Luke, concerning the woman that had been a sinner, "Her sins are forgiven; for she loved much." (*i*) How perversely and preposterously they always estimate the Divine proceedings! But if they had observed, what should by no means have been overlooked, that there are two kinds of Divine judgment, they would have seen, in this correction of David, a species of punishment very different from that which may be considered as vindictive. But since it highly concerns us all to understand the design of those chastisements with which God corrects our sins, and how greatly they differ from the examples of his indignation pursuing the impious and reprobate, I conceive it will not be unseasonable to give a summary account of them. For the sake of perspicuity, let us call one *vengeance*, or *vindictive judgment*, and the other

(*e*) 2 Sam. xii. 13, 14.   (*f*) Dan. iv. 27.   (*g*) Prov. xvi. 6.
(*h*) Prov. x. 12.   1 Peter iv. 8.   (*i*) Luke vii. 47.

chastisement, or *disciplinary judgment*. In vindictive judgment, God is to be contemplated as taking vengeance on his enemies, so as to exert his wrath against them, to confound, dissipate, and reduce them to nothing. We consider it, therefore, strictly speaking, to be the vengeance of God, when the punishment he inflicts is attended with his indignation. In disciplinary judgment, he is not so severe as to be angry; nor does he punish in order to destroy or precipitate into perdition. Wherefore, it is not properly punishment or vengeance, but correction and admonition. The former is the part of a judge, the latter of a father. For a judge, when he punishes an offender, attends to the crime itself, and inflicts punishment according to the nature and aggravations of it. When a father corrects his child with severity, he does it not to take vengeance or satisfaction, but rather to teach him, and render him more cautious for the future. Chrysostom somewhere uses a comparison a little different, which, nevertheless, comes to the same point. "A son (says he) is beaten; a servant also is beaten; but the latter is punished as a slave, because he has transgressed; the former is chastised as free and a son, that needs to be disciplined." Correction serves to the latter for a probation and reformation, to the former for a scourge and a punishment.

XXXII. To obtain a clear view of the whole subject in a small compass, it is necessary to state two distinctions respecting it. The first is, that wherever there is vindictive punishment, there also is a manifestation of the curse and wrath of God, which he always withholds from believers. Chastisement, on the contrary, is, as the Scripture teaches us, both a blessing of God, and a testimony of his love. This difference is sufficiently marked in every part of the Divine word. For all the afflictions which the impious endure in the present life, are represented to us as constituting a kind of antechamber of hell, whence they already have a distant prospect of their eternal damnation; and they are so far from being reformed, or receiving any benefit from this, that they are rather prepared by such preludes for that most tremendous vengeance which finally awaits them. On the contrary, the Lord repeatedly chastises his servants, yet does not deliver them over to death; (*k*) wherefore they confess that the strokes of his rod were highly beneficial and instructive to them. As we every where find that the saints bore these corrections with resignation of soul, so they always earnestly deprecated punishments of the former kind. Jeremiah says, " O Lord, correct me, but with judgment; not in thine anger, lest thou bring me to nothing. Pour out

---

(*k*) Job v. 17. Prov. iii. 11. Heb. xii. 5—11. Psalm cxviii. 18; cxix. 71.

thy fury upon the heathen that know thee not, and upon the families that call not upon thy name." (*l*) And David: "O Lord, rebuke me not in thine anger, neither chasten me in thy hot displeasure." (*m*) Nor is it any objection to this, that the Lord is frequently said to be angry with his saints, when he chastises them for their sins. As in Isaiah: "O Lord, I will praise thee; though thou wast angry with me, thine anger is turned away, and thou comfortedst me." (*n*) Habakkuk also: "In wrath remember mercy." (*o*) And Micah: "I will bear the indignation of the Lord, because I have sinned against him." (*p*) Which reminds us, not only that those who are justly punished, receive no advantage from murmuring, but that the faithful derive a mitigation of their sorrow from a consideration of the intention of God. For on the same account he is said to profane his own inheritance, which, however, we know, he never will profane. (*q*) That relates not to the design or disposition of God in punishing, but to the vehement sense of sorrow experienced by those who suffer any of his severity. He not only distresses his believing people with no small degree of rigour, but sometimes wounds them in such a manner, that they seem to themselves to be on the brink of infernal destruction. Thus he declares, that they have deserved his wrath; and this in order that they may be displeased with themselves in their distresses, may be influenced by a greater concern to appease God, and may hasten with solicitude to implore his pardon; but in this very procedure he exhibits a brighter testimony of his clemency than of his wrath. The covenant still remains which was made with us in our true Solomon, and the validity of which he, who cannot deceive, has declared shall never be diminished: "If his children forsake my law, and walk not in my commandments; if they break my statutes, and keep not my commandments; then will I visit their transgressions with the rod, and their iniquities with stripes. Nevertheless, my loving-kindness will I not utterly take from him." (*r*) To assure us of this loving-kindness, he says, that the rod with which he will chastise the posterity of Solomon, and the stripes he will inflict on them, will be "the rod of men, and the stripes of the children of men." (*s*) While by these phrases he signifies moderation and lenity, he also implies that those who feel his hand exerted against them cannot but be confounded with an extreme and deadly horror. How much he observes this lenity in chastising his Israel, he shows by the prophet: "I have refined thee, (says he,) but not with silver; (*t*) for thou wouldst have been

(*l*) Jer. x. 24, 25.
(*m*) Ps. vi. 1; xxxviii. 1.
(*n*) Isaiah xii. 1.
(*o*) Hab. iii. 2.
(*p*) Micah vii. 9.
(*q*) Is. xliii. 28; xlvii. 6.
(*r*) Ps. lxxxix. 30—33.
(*s*) 2 Sam. vii. 14.
(*t*) Is. xlviii. 10.

wholly consumed." Though he teaches him that chastisements serve to purify him, yet he adds that he so far moderates them, that they may not exceed what he is able to bear. And this is highly necessary; for the more a man reveres God and devotes himself to the cultivation of piety, he is so much the more tender to bear his wrath. For though the reprobate groan under his scourges, yet because they consider not the cause, but rather turn their backs both on their sins and on the Divine judgments, from this carelessness they contract an insensibility; or because they murmur and resist, and rebel against their judge, that furious impetuosity stupefies them with madness and rage. But believers, admonished by the Divine corrections, immediately descend to the consideration of their sins, and, stricken with fear and dread, resort to a suppliant deprecation of punishment. If God did not mitigate these sorrows, with which wretched souls torment themselves, they would be continually fainting, even under slight tokens of his wrath.

XXXIII. The second distinction is, that when the reprobate are lashed by the scourges of God in this world, they already begin to suffer his vindictive punishments; and though they will not escape with impunity for having disregarded such indications of the Divine wrath, yet they are not punished in order to their repentance, but only that, from their great misery, they may prove God to be a judge who will inflict vengeance according to their crimes. On the contrary, the children of God are chastised, not to make satisfaction to him for their sins, but that they may thereby be benefited and brought to repentance. Wherefore we see, that such chastisements relate to the future rather than the past. To express this, I would prefer Chrysostom's language to my own. "For this reason (says he) God punishes us, not to take vengeance for our sins, but to correct us for the future." Thus also Augustine: "That which you suffer, and which causes you to mourn, is a medicine to you, not a punishment; a chastisement, and not damnation. Reject not the scourge, if you desire not to be rejected from the inheritance. All this misery of mankind, under which the world groans, know, brethren, that it is a medicinal sorrow, not a penal sentence." These passages I have therefore thought proper to quote, that no one might consider the phraseology which I have adopted to be novel or unusual. And to the same purpose are the indignant complaints in which the Lord frequently expostulates on account of the ingratitude of the people, and their obstinate contempt of all their punishments. In Isaiah: "Why should ye be stricken any more? From the sole of the foot even unto the head there is no soundness." (*u*) But as the prophets

(*u*) Isaiah i. 5, 6.

abound in such passages, it will be sufficient briefly to have suggested, that God punishes his Church with no other design than to subdue it to repentance. Therefore, when he rejected Saul from the kingdom, he punished him in a vindictive manner; (*x*) when he deprived David of his infant son, he corrected him in order to his reformation. (*y*) In this sense we must understand the observation of Paul: "When we are judged, we are chastened of the Lord, that we should not be condemned with the world." (*z*) That is, when we, the children of God, are afflicted by the hand of our heavenly Father, this is not a punishment to confound us, but only a chastisement to instruct us. In which Augustine evidently coincides with us; for he teaches that the punishments with which men are equally chastised by God, are to be considered in different points of view; because to the saints, after the remission of their sins, they are conflicts and exercises, but to the reprobate, whose sins are not forgiven, they are the penalties due to their iniquity. He also mentions the punishments inflicted on David and other pious persons, and says, that those chastisements tended to promote their humility, and thereby to exercise and prove their piety. And the declaration of Isaiah, that Jerusalem's "iniquity is pardoned, for she hath received of the Lord's hand double for all her sins," (*a*) proves not the pardon of transgressions to depend on the suffering of the punishment, but is just as though he had said, "Punishments enough have now been inflicted on you; and as the severity and multitude of them have harassed you with a long continuance of grief and sorrow, it is time for you to receive the message of complete mercy, that your hearts may be expanded with joy, and experience me to be your Father." For God there assumes the character of a Father, who repents even of his righteous severity, when he has been constrained to chastise his son with any degree of rigour.

XXXIV. It is necessary that the faithful should be provided with these reflections in the anguish of afflictions. "The time is come that judgment must begin at the house of God, upon which his name is called." (*b*) What would the children of God do, if they believed the severity which they feel to be the vengeance of God upon them? For he who, under the strokes of the Divine hand, considers God as an avenging Judge, cannot but conceive of Him as incensed against him, and hostile to him, and will therefore detest his scourge itself as a curse and condemnation; in a word, he who thinks that God is still determined to punish him, can never be persuaded to believe him-

---

(*x*) 1 Sam. xv. 23.   (*y*) 2 Sam. xii. 18.   (*z*) 1 Cor. xi. 32.
(*a*) Isaiah xl. 2.   (*b*) 1 Peter iv. 17. Jer. xxv. 29, marg. read.

self an object of the Divine love. The only one who receives any benefit from the Divine chastisements, is he who considers God as angry with his crimes, but propitious and benevolent towards his person. For otherwise the case must necessarily be similar to what the Psalmist complains of having experienced: "Thy fierce wrath goeth over me; thy terrors have cut me off."(c) And what Moses also speaks of: "For we are consumed by thine anger, and by thy wrath are we troubled. Thou hast set our iniquities before thee, our secret sins in the light of thy countenance. For all our days are passed away in thy wrath: we spend our years as a tale that is told."(d) On the contrary, David, speaking of his paternal chastisements, in order to show that believers are rather assisted than oppressed by them, sings: "Blessed is the man whom thou chastenest, O Lord, and teachest him out of thy law; that thou mayest give him rest from the days of adversity, until the pit be digged for the wicked."(e) It is certainly a severe temptation, when the Lord spares unbelievers, and conceals their crimes, while he appears more rigorous towards his own children. For their consolation, therefore, he adds the admonition of the law, whence they may learn, that it is for the promotion of their salvation when they are recalled into the way, but that the impious are precipitated into their errors, which end in the pit. Nor is it of any importance whether the punishment be eternal or temporal. For wars, famines, plagues, and diseases are curses from God, as well as the judgment of eternal death itself, when they are inflicted as the instruments of the Lord's wrath and vengeance against the reprobate.

XXXV. Every one, I presume, now perceives the design of the Lord's correction of David, that it was to be a proof of God's extreme displeasure against murder and adultery, with which he declared himself to be so greatly offended in his beloved and faithful servant, and to teach David never again to be guilty of such crimes; but not as a punishment, by which he was to render God a satisfaction for his offence. And we ought to form the same judgment concerning the other correction, in which the Lord afflicted the people with a violent pestilence, on account of the disobedience of David in numbering them. For he freely forgave David the guilt of his sin; but because it was necessary, as a public example to all ages, and also to the humiliation of David, that such an offence should not remain unpunished, he chastised him with extreme severity. This end we should keep in view also in the universal curse of mankind. For since we all, even after having obtained pardon, still suffer the miseries which were inflicted on our first parent

---

(c) Psalm lxxxviii. 16.   (d) Psalm xc. 7—9.   (e) Psalm xciv. 12, 13.

as the punishment of sin, we consider such afflictions as admonitions how grievously God is displeased with the transgression of his law; that being thus dejected and humbled with a consciousness of our miserable condition, we may aspire with greater ardour after true blessedness. Now, he is very unwise, who imagines that the calamities of the present life are inflicted upon us as satisfactions for the guilt of sin. This appears to me to have been the meaning of Chrysostom, when he said, "If God therefore inflicts punishments on us, that while we are persisting in sins he may call us to repentance,—after a discovery of repentance, the punishment will be unnecessary." Wherefore he treats one person with greater severity, and another with more tender indulgence, as he knows to be suitable to every man's particular disposition. Therefore, when he means to suggest that he is not excessively severe in the infliction of punishment, he reproaches an obdurate and obstinate people, that though they have been corrected, they have not forsaken their sins. (*f*) In this sense he complains, that "Ephraim is a cake not turned," (*g*) that is, scorched on one side, unbaked on the other; because his corrections did not penetrate the hearts of the people, so as to expel their vices and render them proper objects of pardon. By expressing himself in this manner, he certainly gives us to understand, that as soon as they shall have repented, he will be immediately appeased, and that the rigour which he exercises in chastising offences is extorted from him by our obstinacy, but would be prevented by a voluntary reformation. Yet since our obduracy and ignorance are such as universally to need castigation, our most wise Father is pleased to exercise all his children, without exception, with the strokes of his rod, as long as they live. It is astonishing why they fix their eyes thus on the example of David alone, and are unaffected by so many instances in which they might behold a gratuitous remission of sins. The publican is said to have gone down from the temple justified; (*h*) no punishment follows. Peter obtained the pardon of his sins. "We read," says Ambrose, "of his tears, but not of his satisfaction." (*i*) And a paralytic hears the following address: "Be of good cheer; thy sins be forgiven thee;" (*k*) no punishment is inflicted. All the absolutions which are mentioned in the Scripture, are described as gratuitous. A general rule ought rather to be deduced from these numerous examples, than from that single case which is attended with peculiar circumstances.

XXXVI. When Daniel exhorted Nebuchadnezzar to "break

(*f*) Jer. v. 3.   (*g*) Hosea vii. 8.   (*h*) Luke xviii. 14.
(*i*) Luke xxii. 62.   (*k*) Matt. ix. 2.

off his sins by righteousness, and his iniquities by showing mercy to the poor," (*l*) he meant not to intimate that righteousness and mercy propitiate God and atone for sins; for God forbid that there should ever be any other redemption than the blood of Christ. But he used the term *break off* with reference to men, rather than to God; as though he had said, "Thou hast exercised, O king, an unrighteous and violent despotism; thou hast oppressed the weak; thou hast plundered the poor; thou hast treated thy people with harshness and iniquity; instead of unjust exactions, instead of violence and oppression, now substitute mercy and righteousness." In a similar sense Solomon says, that "love covereth all sins;" not with reference to God, but among men. For the whole verse is as follows: "Hatred stirreth up strifes; but love covereth all sins." (*m*) In which verse, he, according to his usual custom, contrasts the evils arising from hatred with the fruits of love; signifying, that they who hate each other, reciprocally harass, criminate, reproach, revile, and convert every thing into a fault; but that they who love one another, mutually conceal, connive at, and reciprocally forgive, many things among themselves; not that they approve each other's faults, but bear with them, and heal them by admonition, rather than aggravate them by invectives. Nor can we doubt that Peter intended the same in his citation of this passage, (*n*) unless we mean to accuse him of corrupting, and craftily perverting the Scriptures. When Solomon says, that "by mercy and truth iniquity is purged," (*o*) he intends not a compensation in the Divine view, so that God, being appeased with such a satisfaction, remits the punishment which he would otherwise have inflicted; but, in the familiar manner of Scripture, he signifies, that they shall find him propitious to them who have forsaken their former vices and iniquities, and are converted to him in piety and truth; as though he had said, that the wrath of God subsides, and his judgment ceases, when we cease from our sins. He describes not the cause of pardon, but the mode of true conversion. Just as the prophets frequently declare that it is in vain for hypocrites to offer to God ostentatious ceremonies instead of repentance, since he is only pleased with integrity and the duties of charity; and as the author of the Epistle to the Hebrews, when he recommends us "to do good and to communicate," informs us that "with such sacrifices God is well pleased." (*p*) And when Christ ridicules the Pharisees for having attended only to the cleansing of dishes, and neglected all purity of heart, and commands them to give alms that all

(*l*) Dan. iv. 27.   (*m*) Prov. x. 12.   (*n*) 1 Peter iv. 8.
(*o*) Prov. xvi. 6.   (*p*) Heb. xiii. 16.

might be clean, (*q*) he is not exhorting them to make a satisfaction, but only teaching them what kind of purity obtains the Divine approbation. But of this expression we have treated in another work.*

XXXVII. With respect to the passage of Luke, (*r*) no one, who has read with a sound judgment the parable the Lord there proposes, will enter into any controversy with us concerning it. The Pharisee thought within himself, that the Lord did not know the woman, whom he had so easily admitted to his presence. For he imagined that Christ would not have admitted her, if he had known what kind of a sinner she was. And thence he inferred that Christ, who was capable of being so deceived, was not a prophet. To show that she was not a sinner, her sins having already been forgiven, the Lord proposed this parable: "There was a certain creditor, which had two debtors; the one owed five hundred pence, and the other fifty. He frankly forgave them both. Which of them will love him most?" The Pharisee answered, "He to whom he forgave most." The Lord rejoins, Hence know that "this woman's sins, which are many, are forgiven; for she loved much." In these words, you see, he makes her love, not the cause of the remission of her sins, but the proof of it. For they are taken from a comparison of that debtor to whom five hundred pence had been forgiven, of whom it is said, not that his debt was forgiven, because he had loved much, but that he loved much because his debt had been forgiven. And this similitude may be applied to the case of the woman in the following manner: "You suppose this woman to be a sinner; but you ought to know that she is not such, since her sins are forgiven her. And her love ought to convince you of the remission of her sins, by the grateful return she makes for this blessing." It is an *argumentum a posteriori*, by which any thing is proved from its consequences. By what means she obtained remission of sins, the Lord plainly declares: "Thy faith," says he, "hath saved thee." By faith therefore we obtain remission, by love we give thanks and declare the goodness of the Lord.

XXXVIII. To those things which frequently occur in the works of the fathers concerning *satisfaction*, I pay little regard. I see, indeed, that some of them, or, to speak plainly, almost all whose writings are extant, have either erred on this point, or expressed themselves too harshly. But I shall not admit that they were so ignorant and inexperienced, as to write those things in the sense in which they are understood by the modern advocates for satisfaction. Chrysostom somewhere

(*q*) Luke xi. 39—41.   * In Harm. Evang.   (*r*) Luke vii. 39.

expresses himself thus: "Where mercy is requested, examination ceases; where mercy is implored, judgment is not severe; where mercy is sought, there is no room for punishment; where there is mercy, there is no inquiry; where mercy is, an answer is freely given." These expressions, however they may be distorted, can never be reconciled with the dogmas of the schools. In the treatise On Ecclesiastical Doctrines, which is ascribed to Augustine, we read the following passage: "The satisfaction of repentance is to cut off the causes of sins, and not to indulge an entrance to their suggestions." Whence it appears, that even in those times the doctrine of satisfaction, as a compensation for sins committed, was universally rejected, since he refers all satisfaction to a cautious abstinence from sins in future. I will not quote what is further asserted by Chrysostom, that the Lord requires of us nothing more than to confess our sins before him with tears; for passages of this kind frequently occur in his writings, and in those of other fathers. Augustine somewhere calls works of mercy "remedies for obtaining remission of sins;" but lest any one should stumble at that expression, he explains himself more fully in another place. "The flesh of Christ," says he, "is the true and sole sacrifice for sins, not only for those which are all obliterated in baptism, but also for those which afterwards creep in through infirmity; on account of which the whole Church at present exclaims, Forgive us our debts; (s) and they are forgiven through that single sacrifice."

XXXIX. But they most commonly used the word "satisfaction" to signify, not a compensation rendered to God, but a public testification, by which those who had been punished with excommunication, when they wished to be readmitted to communion, gave the Church an assurance of their repentance. For there were enjoined on those penitents certain fastings, and other observances, by which they might prove themselves truly and cordially weary of their former life, or rather obliterate the memory of their past actions; and thus they were said to make satisfaction, not to God, but to the Church. This is also expressed by Augustine in these very words, in his Enchiridion ad Laurentium. From that ancient custom have originated the confessions and satisfactions which are used in the present age; a viperous brood which retain not even the shadow of that original form. I know that the fathers sometimes express themselves rather harshly; nor do I deny, what I have just asserted, that perhaps they have erred. But their writings, which were only besprinkled with a few spots, after they have been handled by such foul hands, became thoroughly soiled. And if we

(s) Matt. vi. 12.

must contend with the authority of fathers, what fathers do they obtrude upon us? Most of those passages, of which Lombard, their champion, has compiled his heterogeneous collection, are extracted from the insipid reveries of some monks, which are circulated under the names of Ambrose, Jerome, Augustine, and Chrysostom. Thus, on the present argument, he borrows almost every thing from a Treatise on Repentance, which is a ridiculous selection from various authors, good and bad; it bears the name of Augustine indeed, but no man even of moderate learning can deign to admit it as really his. For not entering into a more particular examination of their absurdities, I request the pardon of the reader, whom I wish to spare that trouble. It would be both easy and plausible for me to expose to the greatest contempt, what they have heretofore celebrated as mysteries; but I forbear, as my object is to write what may tend to edification.

CHAPTER V.

INDULGENCES AND PURGATORY. THE SUPPLEMENTS TO THEIR DOCTRINE OF SATISFACTIONS.

This doctrine of *satisfaction* has given rise to *indulgences*. For by indulgences they pretend, that the deficiency of our abilities to make satisfaction is supplied, and even proceed to the extravagance of defining them to be the dispensation of the merits of Christ and of the martyrs, which the Pope distributes in his bulls. Now, though such persons are fitter subjects for a mad-house than for arguments, so that it would be of little use to engage in refuting errors so frivolous, which have been shaken by many attacks, and begin of themselves to grow obsolete, and totter towards a fall, yet, as a brief refutation will be useful to some minds hitherto uninformed on the subject, I shall not altogether omit it. And indeed the establishment and long continuance of indulgences, with the unlimited influence retained by them amidst such outrageous and furious licentiousness, may serve to convince us in what a deep night of errors men were immersed for several ages. They saw, that they were themselves objects of the public and undissembled ridicule of the Pope and the dispensers of his bulls; that lucrative bargains were made concerning the salvation of their souls; that the price of salvation was fixed at a trifling sum of money, and nothing presented gratuitously; that under this pretext, contributions were extorted from them, which were vilely consumed on brothels, pimps, and revellings; that the greatest advocates of indulgences were the greatest despisers of them; that this monster was daily making longer strides in licentious power and luxury, and that there was no end, that more trash was continually produced, and more money continually extorted. Yet they received indulgences with the greatest veneration, adored them and purchased them; and those who had more discernment than others, yet considered them as pious frauds, by which they might be deceived with some advantage. At length, since the world has permitted itself to recover a little the exercise of reason, indulgences become more and more discredited, till they altogether disappear.

II. But since many, who see the pollution, imposture, robbery, and rapacity, with which the dispensers of indulgences have hitherto amused themselves and cajoled us, do not perceive the fountain of all this impiety, — it will be necessary to show, not only the nature of indulgences as commonly used, but what they are in themselves when abstracted from every adventitious blemish. The merits of Christ and of the holy apostles and martyrs, they style "the treasury of the Church." The principal custody of this repository they pretend to have been delivered, as I have already hinted, to the bishop of Rome, who has the dispensation of such great benefits, so that he can both bestow them himself, and delegate the power of bestowing them to others. Hence from the Pope are received sometimes plenary indulgences, sometimes indulgences for a certain number of years; from Cardinals, for a hundred days; from Bishops, for forty days. But to describe them correctly, they are a profanation of the blood of Christ and a delusion of Satan, by which they seduce Christians from the grace of God and the life which is in Christ, and turn them aside from the right way of salvation. For how could the blood of Christ be more basely profaned, than when it is denied to be sufficient for the remission of sins, for reconciliation and satisfaction, unless its deficiency be supplied from some other quarter? "To him," says Peter, "give all the prophets witness, that through his name, whosoever believeth on him shall receive remission of sins." (*t*) Indulgences dispense remission of sins through Peter, and Paul, and the martyrs. "The blood of Jesus Christ," says John, "cleanseth us from all sin." (*u*) Indulgences make the blood of the martyrs the ablution of sins. Paul says, that Christ, "who knew no sin, was made sin for us;" that is, a satisfaction for sin, "that we might be made the righteousness of God in him." (*w*) Indulgences place sa-

---

(*t*) Acts x. 43. (*u*) 1 John i. 7. (*w*) 2 Cor. v. 21.

tisfaction for sins in the blood of the martyrs. Paul declared to the Corinthians, that Christ alone was crucified and died for them. (*x*) Indulgences pronounce that Paul and others died for us. In another place he says, that Christ "hath purchased the Church with his own blood." (*y*) Indulgences assign another price of this purchase, in the blood of the martyrs. The apostle says, that "by one offering Christ hath perfected for ever them that are sanctified." (*z*) Indulgences, on the contrary, proclaim that sanctification, which were otherwise insufficient, receives its perfection from the martyrs. John declares that all saints "have washed their robes in the blood of the Lamb." (*a*) Indulgences teach us to wash our robes in the blood of the saints.

III. Leo, bishop of Rome, excellently opposes these sacrilegious pretensions in his epistle to the Bishops of Palestine. "Although the death of many saints," he says, "has been precious in the sight of the Lord, yet the murder of no innocent person has been the propitiation of the world. The righteous have received, not bestowed, crowns; and from the fortitude of the faithful have arisen examples of patience, not gifts of righteousness. For their deaths have been all singular, nor has any one by his death discharged the debt of another; for it is the Lord Christ alone, in whom all are crucified, dead, buried, and raised from the dead." This passage being worthy of remembrance, he repeats it in another place. Surely nothing clearer can be desired, in confutation of this impious doctrine of indulgences. And Augustine expresses himself with equal propriety to the same purpose. He says, "Although we die, brethren for brethren, yet the blood of no martyr is ever shed for the remission of sins. Christ has done this for us; and in doing it has not given an example in which we should imitate him, but conferred a favour for which we should thank him." Again, in another place : "As the Son of God alone became the Son of man, to make us with himself sons of God, so he alone, without any demerits, sustained the punishment for us, that we, without any merits, might through him obtain undeserved grace." Indeed, whilst their whole doctrine is a compound of horrible sacrilege and blasphemies, yet this is a blasphemy more monstrous than the rest. Let them acknowledge whether these be not their opinions, that the martyrs have by their death performed for God, and merited from him, more than was necessary for themselves; that they had so great a redundance of merits, as to superabound to others; that therefore, lest so great a blessing should be superfluous, their blood is commingled with the blood of Christ, and

(*x*) 1 Cor. i. 13.   (*y*) Acts xx. 28.   (*z*) Heb. x. 14.   (*a*) Rev. vii. 14.

that of both these is formed the treasury of the Church for the remission and expiation of sins; and that in this sense we ought to understand the declaration of Paul, "I fill up that which is behind of the afflictions of Christ in my flesh, for his body's sake, which is the Church." (*b*) What is this but leaving Christ a mere name, and in other respects making him an inferior saint of the common order, scarcely distinguishable among the multitude? He alone ought to have been preached, he alone exhibited, he alone mentioned, he alone regarded, in all discourses on the procurement of remission of sins, expiation, and sanctification. But let us hear their grand argument: That the blood of the martyrs may not be shed in vain, let it be applied to the common benefit of the Church. Indeed? Was it no advantage to glorify God by their death? to subscribe to his truth with their blood? to testify by their contempt of the present life, that they sought a better one? by their constancy, to confirm the faith of the Church, and vanquish the obstinacy of their enemies? But this is the fact: they acknowledge no benefit, if Christ alone be the propitiator, if he alone died for our sins, if he alone was offered for our redemption. Peter and Paul, they say, might nevertheless have obtained the crown of victory, if they had expired in their beds. But since they contended even to blood, it would be incompatible with the justice of God to leave this *barren* or *unfruitful*. As if God knew not how to augment the glory of his servants according to the extent of his gifts. But the Church in general receives an advantage sufficiently great, when by their triumphs it is inflamed with the same zeal for similar exertions and conflicts.

IV. But how maliciously they pervert that passage of Paul, where he says, "that he fills up in his own flesh that which is behind of the afflictions of Christ!" (*c*) For he refers that deficiency and supplement, not to the work of redemption, satisfaction, or expiation, but to those afflictions, with which the members of Christ, even all the faithful, must necessarily be exercised as long as they live in the present state. He says, therefore, that this remains of the afflictions of Christ, that having once suffered in himself, he daily suffers in his members. Christ honors us so far as to consider our afflictions as his. When Paul adds that he suffered "for the Church," he means not for the redemption, reconciliation, or atonement of the Church, but for its edification and profit. As in another place he says, "I endure all things for the elect's sakes, that they may also obtain the salvation which is in Christ Jesus." (*d*) He writes to the Corinthians, that whatever tribulations he

(*b*) Col. i. 24.   (*c*) Col. i. 24.   (*d*) 2 Tim. ii. 10.

endured, he was "afflicted for their consolation and salvation." (e) And he immediately proceeds to explain himself, by adding, that he was made a minister of the Church, not for its redemption, but according to the dispensation which had been committed to him, to preach the gospel of Christ. (f) But if they require also another expositor, let them attend to Augustine: "The sufferings of Christ," says he, "are in Christ alone, as in the head; in Christ and the Church, as in the whole body. Whence Paul, one of the members, says, I fill up in my flesh that which is behind of the afflictions of Christ. If you, therefore, whoever you are that read this, are one of the members of Christ, all that you suffer from such as are not members of Christ, was behind in the afflictions of Christ." But the tendency of the sufferings of the apostles, sustained on account of the Church, is stated by him in another place: "Christ is my door to you; because you are the sheep of Christ, purchased with his blood: acknowledge your price, which is not given by me, but preached by me." Then he adds, "As he has laid down his life, so we ought also to lay down our lives for the brethren, for the establishment of peace and the confirmation of faith." This is the language of Augustine. But let it not be imagined, that Paul thought there was any deficiency in the sufferings of Christ, with respect to all the plenitude of righteousness, salvation, and life; or that any addition to them was intended by him, who so clearly and magnificently proclaims, that the "abundance of grace by Christ" was poured forth with such liberality, that it "much more abounded" beyond all the aboundings of sin. (g) It is not by the merit of their own life or death, but by this grace alone, that all the saints have been saved, as Peter expressly testifies; (h) so that he would be guilty of an injurious contempt of God and of his Christ, who should place the worthiness of any saint in any thing else but the mere mercy of God. But why do I dwell any longer on this subject, as though it were still involved in obscurity? whereas the statement of such monstrous notions is of itself a complete refutation of them.

V. Now, to pass from such abominations, who taught the Pope to enclose in lead and parchment the grace of Jesus Christ, which the Lord designed to be dispensed by the word of the gospel? Either the gospel of God must be false, or their indulgences fallacious. For that Christ is offered to us in the gospel, with all his plenitude of heavenly blessings, with all his merits, with all his righteousness, wisdom, and grace, without any exception, is testified by Paul, when he says, "God hath committed unto us the word of reconciliation.

(e) 2 Cor. i. 6.   (f) Col. i. 25.   (g) Rom. v. 17—20.   (h) Acts xv. 11.

Now, then, we are ambassadors for Christ, as though God did beseech you by us; we pray you in Christ's stead, be ye reconciled to God. For he hath made him, who knew no sin, to be sin for us; that we might be made the righteousness of God in him." (*i*) And believers know the meaning of that "fellowship of Christ," (*k*) which, according to the testimony of the same apostle, is offered to our enjoyment in the gospel. Indulgences, on the contrary, produce a certain allowance of grace from the Pope's repository, fix it to lead and parchment, and even to a particular place, and separate it from the word of God. Now, if any one inquire the origin of this abuse, it seems to have arisen from an ancient custom, that when more severe satisfactions were imposed on penitents than could possibly be borne by all, they who felt themselves oppressed beyond measure, petitioned the Church for some relaxation of rigour. The remission granted to such persons was called indulgence. But when they transferred satisfactions to God, and said that they were compensations, by which men might redeem themselves from the judgment of God, they also converted these indulgences into expiatory remedies, to deliver us from deserved punishments. But the blasphemies which we have mentioned have been fabricated with such consummate impudence, that they have not even the least appearance of plausibility.

VI. Nor let them now trouble us any more about their purgatory, since it is utterly demolished by this argument. For I cannot coincide with some, who think it best to be silent on this point, and to omit the mention of purgatory, from which, they say, many sharp contentions arise, but very little edification results. Indeed, I should myself be of opinion that such trifles are unworthy of notice, if they did not consider them as matters of importance. But since purgatory has been erected with a multitude of blasphemies, and is daily propped by new ones, and since it excites many and grievous offences, it really must not pass without notice. It might be possible for a time to conceal that it was a fiction of curious and presumptuous temerity, unsupported by the word of God; that it was accredited by I know not what revelation invented by the subtlety of Satan; that for its confirmation some passages of Scripture were absurdly perverted. The Lord, however, suffers not human presumption thus violently to break into the hidden recesses of his judgment; (*l*) and has severely prohibited the neglect of his word and the inquiry after truth among the dead; and does not permit his word to be thus irreverently dishonoured. Nevertheless, admitting that all these things

(*i*) 2 Cor. v. 18, &c.   (*k*) 1 Cor. i. 9.   (*l*) Deut. xviii. 10—12.

might for a short time have been tolerated as matters of small importance, yet when expiation of sins is sought any where but in the blood of Christ, when satisfaction is transferred to any other, silence becomes dangerous in the extreme. Therefore we should exclaim with all our might, that purgatory is a pernicious fiction of Satan, that it makes void the cross of Christ, that it intolerably insults the Divine mercy, and weakens and overturns our faith. For what is their purgatory, but a satisfaction for sins paid after death by the souls of the deceased? Thus the notion of satisfaction being overthrown, purgatory itself is immediately subverted from its very foundations. But if it has been fully evinced, that the blood of Christ is the only satisfaction, expiation, and purgation for the sins of the faithful, what is the necessary inference, but that purgatory is nothing but a horrible blasphemy against Christ? I pass by the sacrilegious pretences with which it is daily defended, the offences which it produces in religion, and the other innumerable evils which we perceive to have proceeded from such a source of impiety.

VII. It is worth while, however, to wrest out of their hands those passages of Scripture, which they have falsely and corruptly pressed into their service. The assertion of the Lord, that the sin against the Holy Ghost "shall not be forgiven, neither in this world, neither in the world to come," (*m*) implies, they say, that there is a forgiveness of some sins in the world to come. But who does not see, that the Lord there speaks of the guilt of sin? And if this be the case, what has it to do with their purgatory, for there they suppose punishment to be inflicted for sins, the guilt of which they do not deny to have been forgiven in the present life? But to prevent all further cavils, they shall have a plainer answer. When the Lord intended to cut off from such flagitious iniquity all hope of pardon, he thought it not sufficient to say that it should never be forgiven; but for the sake of further amplification he adopted a distinction, comprehending both the judgment which the conscience of every individual feels in this life, and that final judgment which will be publicly held at the resurrection; as though he had said, "Beware of malicious rebellion, as of immediate perdition; for he who shall have purposely endeavoured to extinguish the offered light of the Spirit, shall never obtain pardon, neither in this life, which is allotted to sinners for their conversion, nor in the last day, when the lambs shall be separated from the goats by the angels of God, and the kingdom of heaven shall be purged from every offence." They next adduce this parable from Matthew: "Agree with thine

(*m*) Matt. xii. 32.

adversary; lest at any time the adversary deliver thee to the judge, and the judge deliver thee to the officer, and thou be cast into prison. Thou shalt by no means come out thence, till thou hast paid the uttermost farthing." (*n*) If in this place the judge signify God, the adversary the devil, the officer an angel, the prison purgatory, I will readily submit to them. But if it be evident to every one, that Christ there intended to show to how many dangers and calamities persons exposed themselves, who prefer obstinately exerting the rigour of the law, to acting upon the principles of equity and kindness, in order the more earnestly to exhort his disciples to an equitable concord, pray where will purgatory be found?

VIII. They derive an argument from the language of Paul, where he has affirmed, "that at the name of Jesus every knee should bow, of things in heaven, and things in earth, and things under the earth." (*o*) For they assume it as granted, that "things (or persons) under the earth" cannot be understood of those who are consigned to eternal damnation. It follows, therefore, that they must be the souls suffering in purgatory. Their reasoning would not be very bad, if, by genuflection, the apostle designed truly pious worship; but since he simply teaches, that dominion is committed to Christ, by which all creatures must be subjugated, why may we not understand this phrase of the devils, who will indeed stand at the tribunal of the Lord, and acknowledge him as their Judge with fear and trembling? As Paul himself elsewhere explains the same prophecy: "We shall all stand," says he, "before the judgment seat of Christ. For it is written, As I live, saith the Lord, every knee shall bow to me," &c. (*p*) But they reply, we cannot give the same kind of interpretation to this passage in the Revelation: "Every creature which is in heaven, and on the earth, and under the earth, and such as are in the sea, and all that are in them, heard I saying, Blessing, and honour, and glory, and power, be unto him that sitteth upon the throne, and unto the Lamb for ever and ever." (*q*) This I readily concede; but what creatures do they suppose to be here enumerated? for it is very certain, that the expressions comprehend creatures both irrational and inanimate. It is a mere declaration that all the parts of the world, from the summit of the heavens to the centre of the earth, celebrate, in their respective ways, the glory of the Creator. What they produce from the history of the Maccabees, I shall not honour with an answer, that I may not be supposed to place that work in the catalogue of sacred books. But Augustine, they say, received it as canonical. I inquire, first, With what degree of credit did he

(*n*) Matt. v. 25.
(*o*) Phil. ii. 10.
(*p*) Rom. xiv. 10, 11.
(*q*) Rev. v. 13.

receive it? He says, "The history of the Maccabees is not esteemed by the Jews as the law, and the prophets, and the Psalms, to which the Lord gives a testimony, as being witnesses concerning him, saying, 'All things must be fulfilled, which were written in the law of Moses, and in the prophets, and in the Psalms, concerning me.' (r) But it has been received by the Church, and not altogether unprofitably, if it be read or heard with sobriety," &c. Jerome, without any scruple, inculcates, that its authority is of no force in the support of doctrines. And from that old treatise on the Exposition of the Creed, which is ascribed to Cyprian, it clearly appears that it was not admitted in the ancient Church. But why am I now contending to no purpose? as though the author himself did not sufficiently show what deference is due to him, when, at the conclusion, he begs pardon if he should have spoken any thing improperly. Certainly he who confesses that his writings need pardon, proclaims them not to be the oracles of the Holy Spirit. Besides, the piety of Judas Maccabeus is commended on no other ground, but because he had a firm hope of the final resurrection, when he sent to Jerusalem an oblation for the dead. Nor does the historian represent this oblation as intended to be a price of redemption, but that those in whose names it was offered might be partakers of eternal life with the rest of the faithful who had died in defence of their country and religion. This action was accompanied, indeed, by superstition and preposterous zeal; but they are more than infatuated who apply to us a sacrifice offered under the law; since we know, that all such ancient usages ceased at the advent of Christ.

IX. But they find in Paul an invincible argument, which cannot be so easily answered. "If any man," says he, "build upon this foundation gold, silver, precious stones, wood, hay, stubble, every man's work shall be made manifest; for the day shall declare it, because it shall be revealed by fire; and the fire shall try every man's work, of what sort it is. If any man's work shall be burned, he shall suffer loss; but he himself shall be saved; yet so as by fire." (s) What can this be, they ask, but purgatorial fire, by which the pollution of sins is cleansed, that we may enter pure into the kingdom of God? But most of the fathers were of a different opinion, understanding the word "fire" to mean tribulation, or the cross, by which the Lord tries his children, to purify them from all carnal pollution; and this is much more probable than the notion of purgatory. I cannot, however, coincide with them; for I think I have discovered a far more certain and lucid interpreta-

(r) Luke xxiv. 44.   (s) 1 Cor. iii. 12.

tion of this passage. But before I state it, I could wish them to answer this question — whether they suppose it was necessary for the apostles and all the saints to pass through this purgatorial fire. I know they will answer in the negative; for it were too absurd, that purification should be necessary to those whose redundant merits they vainly imagine to superabound to all the members of the Church. But the apostle affirms this; for he says, not that the work of some, but that the work of all, shall be proved. Nor is this my own argument, but Augustine's, who thus opposes the interpretation now adopted by our adversaries. And, what would be still more absurd, he says, not that they shall pass through the fire on account of any works, but that if they have edified the Church with perfect fidelity, they shall receive a reward, when their work shall have been tried by fire. In the first place, we see that the apostle uses a metaphor, when he calls doctrines of human invention " wood, hay, stubble." The reason of the metaphor also is evident; that as wood, immediately on being placed in contact with fire, consumes and wastes away, so neither will those doctrines be able to abide the test of examination. Now, it is well known that such an examination proceeds from the Spirit of God. Therefore, to pursue the thread of the metaphor, and to adapt the parts by a proper relation to each other, he gives the Holy Spirit's examination the appellation of *fire*. For as gold and silver afford a more certain proof of their goodness and purity in proportion to their proximity to the fire, so Divine truth receives the stronger confirmation of its authority, in proportion to the strictness of spiritual examination by which it is investigated. As wood, hay, and stubble, brought into contact with fire, are speedily consumed, so the inventions of men, unsupported by the word of God, cannot bear the examination of the Holy Spirit, but must immediately fall to the ground. Finally, if false doctrines are compared to wood, hay, and stubble, because, like wood, hay, and stubble, they are consumed by fire and entirely destroyed, and if they are overcome only by the Spirit of the Lord, it follows that the Spirit is that fire by which they will be proved. This trial Paul calls *the day*, or *the day of the Lord*, according to the common phraseology of Scripture. For that is called the day of the Lord, whenever he manifests his presence to men. Now, we enjoy most of the light of his countenance when we are favoured with the radiance of his truth. It has been evinced that Paul means no other fire than the examination of the Holy Spirit. But how are they saved by the fire, who suffer the loss of their work? This it will not be difficult to comprehend, if we consider of what class of men he is speaking. For he characterizes them as builders of the

Church, who retain their legitimate foundation, but raise the superstructure of unequal materials; they are such as do not deviate from the principal and essential articles of the faith, but err in inferior and less important ones, mixing their own inventions with the word of God. Such, I say, must suffer the loss of their work, by their inventions being destroyed; but they are themselves saved, yet so as by fire; that is, not because their ignorance and error can be approved by the Lord, but because they are purified from them by the grace and power of the Holy Spirit. Wherefore, whoever have corrupted the pure gold of the Divine word with this filth of purgatory, must necessarily suffer the loss of their work.

X. Our opponents will reply, that it has been a very ancient opinion in the Church. Paul removes this objection when he comprehends even his own age in this sentence, where he denounces, that all must suffer the loss of their work, who, in the structure of the Church, should place any thing not corresponding to the foundation. When our adversaries, therefore, object to me, that to offer prayers for the dead has been the practice of more than thirteen hundred years, I inquire of them, on the contrary, by what word of God, by what revelation, by what example, it is sanctioned. For they are not only destitute of any testimonies of Scripture in favour of it, but none of the examples of the saints there recorded exhibit any thing like it. Respecting mourning and funeral offices, it contains many and sometimes long accounts; but of prayers for persons deceased, you cannot discover the smallest hint. But the greater the importance of the subject, so much the rather ought it to have been particularly mentioned. Even the fathers themselves, who offered up prayers for the dead, saw that they had neither a Divine command, nor a legitimate example, to justify the practice. Why, then, did they presume to adopt it? In this, I say, they discovered themselves to be but men; and therefore I contend, that what they did ought not to be enforced for the imitation of others. For since believers ought not to undertake any thing without an assurance of conscience, according to the direction of Paul, (*t*) this assurance is chiefly requisite in prayer. Yet it will be urged, It is probable that they were impelled to it by some reason. I reply, Perhaps they sought some consolation to alleviate their sorrow, and it might appear inhuman not to give some testimony of their love towards the dead in the presence of God. The propensity of the human mind to this affection, all men know by experience. The custom, also, when received, was like a flame, kindling ardour in the minds of multitudes. We

(*t*) Rom. xiv. 23.

know that funeral rites have been performed to the dead among all nations, and in every age, and that lustrations have been annually made for their departed spirits. For though Satan has deluded foolish mortals with these fallacies, yet he has borrowed the occasion of the deception from a true principle — that death is not an annihilation, but a transition from this life into another. Nor can it be doubted, but that even superstition itself convicts the heathen before the tribunal of God, for neglecting all the concerns of a future life, which they professed to believe. Now, Christians, because they would not be inferior to the heathen, were ashamed to perform no services for the dead, as though they had wholly ceased to exist. Hence that inconsiderate officiousness; because if they were negligent in attending to funerals, feasts, and oblations, they were afraid they should expose themselves to great disgrace. What first proceeded from a perverse emulation, has been so repeatedly augmented by novel additions, that the principal sanctity of Popery consists in relieving the distresses of the dead. But the Scripture administers another consolation, far better and more substantial, when it declares that "Blessed are the dead which die in the Lord;" and adds as a reason, "that they may rest from their labours."(*u*) But we ought not to indulge our own affection so far as to introduce a corrupt method of praying into the Church. Certainly, he that has but a moderate share of penetration, will easily discover all that we find on this subject in the fathers to have been in compliance with general practice and vulgar ignorance. I confess, they were also involved in the error themselves, from an inconsiderate credulity which frequently deprives the human mind of its judgment. But in the mean time, the mere reading of them demonstrates with what hesitation they recommend prayers for the dead. Augustine, in his Book of Confessions, relates that Monica, his mother, had vehemently entreated to be remembered in the celebration of the mysteries at the altar. This was the wish of an old woman, which her son did not examine by the standard of Scripture; but from his natural affection for her, wished it to gain the approbation of others. But the treatise composed by him, on Care for the Dead, contains so many hesitations, that it ought by its coolness to extinguish the heat of imprudent zeal. If any one desires to be an intercessor for the dead, this treatise, with its frigid probabilites, will certainly remove all the solicitude he may have previously experienced. For this is its only support, that since it has been customary to pray for the dead, it is a duty not to be despised. But though I concede, that the ancient writers of the Church esteemed it a pious act

(*u*) Rev. xiv. 13.

to pray for the dead, yet we must always remember a rule which can never deceive — that it is not right for us in our prayers to introduce any thing of our own, but that our desires must be submitted to the word of God; because he chooses to prescribe what he designs we should ask. Now, since there is not a syllable, in all the law or the gospel, which allows us to pray for the dead, it is a profane abuse of the name of God, to attempt more than he enjoins. But that our adversaries may not glory, as though the ancient Church were associated with them in their error, I assert that there is a considerable difference between them. The ancients preserved the memory of the dead, that they might not seem to have cast off all concern for them; but they at the same time confessed their uncertainty concerning their state. Respecting purgatory they asserted nothing, but considered it as quite uncertain. The moderns expect their reveries concerning purgatory to be admitted as unquestionable articles of faith. The fathers, in the communion of the sacred supper, merely recommended their deceased friends to the mercy of God. The Papists are incessantly urging a concern for the dead; and by their importunate declamations cause it to be preferred to all the duties of charity. Besides, it would not be difficult for us to produce some testimonies from the fathers which manifestly overthrow all those prayers for the dead which were then used. Such is this of Augustine; when he teaches that all men expect the resurrection of the body and eternal glory, and that every individual enters on the fruition of that rest which follows after death, if he is worthy of it when he dies. Therefore he declares that all the pious, as well as the prophets, apostles, and martyrs, enjoy a blessed repose immediately after death. If such be their condition, what advantage will our prayers confer on them? I pass over those grosser superstitions with which they have fascinated the minds of the simple; which nevertheless are innumerable, and for the most part so monstrous, that they cannot be varnished over by any honest pretext. I omit, also, that most disgraceful traffic which they licentiously carried on while the world was in such a state of stupidity. For I should never arrive at a conclusion, and I have already furnished the pious reader with sufficient to establish his conscience.

CHAPTER VI.

THE LIFE OF A CHRISTIAN. SCRIPTURAL ARGUMENTS AND EXHORTATIONS TO IT.

We have said that the end of regeneration is, that the life of believers may exhibit a symmetry and agreement between the righteousness of God and their obedience; and that thus they may confirm the adoption by which they are accepted as his children. But though the law of God contains in it that newness of life by which his image is restored in us, yet since our tardiness needs much stimulation and assistance, it will be useful to collect from various places of Scripture a rule for the reformation of the life, that they who cordially repent may not be bewildered in their pursuits. Now, when I undertake the regulation of a Christian's life, I know that I am entering on an argument various and copious, and the magnitude of which might fill a large volume, if I designed a complete discussion of every part of it. For we see to what great prolixity the fathers have extended the exhortations composed by them only on single virtues; and that without any excessive loquacity; for, whatever virtue it is intended to recommend in an oration, the copiousness of the matter naturally produces such a diffusiveness of style, that unless you have spoken largely, you seem not to have done justice to the subject. But my design is not to extend the plan of life, which I am now about to deliver, so far as particularly to discourse on each distinct virtue, and expatiate into exhortations. These things may be sought in the writings of others, especially in the homilies of the fathers. It will be sufficient for me if I point out a method by which a pious man may be conducted to the right end in the regulation of his life, and briefly assign a universal rule, by which he may properly estimate his duties. There will, perhaps, at some future period be a suitable opportunity for declamations; or I shall leave to others an office for which I am not calculated. I am naturally fond of brevity; and, perhaps, were I desirous of speaking in a more copious manner, I should not succeed. And if a more prolix method of teaching were most acceptable, yet I should scarcely be inclined to make the trial. The plan of the present work, however, requires me to treat a simple doctrine with all possible brevity. As the philosophers have certain principles of rectitude and honour, whence they deduce particular duties and the whole circle of virtues, so the Scripture is not without its order in this respect, but maintains an economy superlatively beautiful, and far more certain, than all the systems of the philosophers. There is only this difference — that, the philosophers being ambitious men, they have sedulously affected an exquisite perspicuity of method, in order to make an ostentatious display of their ingenious dexterity. But the Spirit, whose teaching is void of affectation, has not so exactly or perpetually observed a methodical plan; which, nevertheless, by using it in some places, he sufficiently indicates ought not to be neglected by us.

II. This Scripture plan, of which we are now treating, consists chiefly in these two things — the first, that a love of righteousness, to which we have otherwise no natural propensity, be instilled and introduced into our hearts; the second, that a rule be prescribed to us, to prevent our taking any devious steps in the race of righteousness. Now, in the recommendation of righteousness, it uses a great number of very excellent arguments, many of which we have before noticed on different occasions, and some we shall briefly touch on in this place. With what better foundation can it begin, than when it admonishes us that we ought to be holy, because *our God is holy?* (*w*) For when we were dispersed like scattered sheep, and lost in the labyrinth of the world, he gathered us together again, that he might associate us to himself. When we hear any mention of our union with God, we should remember, that holiness must be the bond of it; not that we attain communion with him by the merit of holiness, (since it is rather necessary for us, in the first place, to adhere to him, in order that, being endued with his holiness, we may follow whither he calls:) but because it is a peculiar property of his glory not to have any intercourse with iniquity and uncleanness. Wherefore also it teaches, that this is the end of our vocation, which it is requisite for us always to keep in view, if we desire to correspond to the design of God in calling us. For to what purpose was it that we were delivered from the iniquity and pollution of the world, in which we had been immerged, if we permit ourselves to wallow in them as long as we live? Besides, it also admonishes us that, to be numbered among the people of God, we must inhabit the holy city Jerusalem; (*x*) which, he having consecrated it to himself, cannot without impiety be profaned by impure inhabitants. Whence these expressions: "He shall abide in the tabernacle of the Lord, that walketh uprightly and worketh righteousness," &c., (*y*) because it is very unbecoming the sanctuary which he inhabits, to be rendered as filthy as a stable.

(*w*) Lev. xix. 2. 1 Peter i. 16.   (*x*) Isaiah xxxv. 10
(*y*) Psalm xv. 1, 2; xxiv. 3, 4.

III. And as a further incitement to us, it shows, that as God the Father has reconciled us to himself in Christ, so he has exhibited to us in him a pattern, to which it is his will that we should be conformed. (*z*) Now, let those who are of opinion that the philosophers have the only just and orderly systems of moral philosophy, show me, in any of their works, a more excellent economy than that which I have stated. When they intend to exhort us to the sublimest virtue, they advance no argument but that we ought to live agreeably to nature ; but the Scripture deduces its exhortation from the true source, when it not only enjoins us to refer our life to God the author of it, to whom it belongs, but, after having taught us, that we are degenerated from the original state in which we were created, adds, that Christ, by whom we have been reconciled to God, is proposed to us as an example, whose character we should exhibit in our lives. What can be required more efficacious than this one consideration ? indeed, what can be required besides? For if the Lord has adopted us as his sons on this condition, — that we exhibit in our life an imitation of Christ the bond of our adoption, — unless we addict and devote ourselves to righteousness, we not only most perfidiously revolt from our Creator, but also abjure him as our Saviour. The Scripture derives matter of exhortation from all the blessings of God which it recounts to us, and from all the parts of our salvation. It argues, that since God has discovered himself as a Father to us, we must be convicted of the basest ingratitude, unless we, on our part, manifest ourselves to be his children ; that since Christ has purified us in the laver of his blood, and has communicated this purification by baptism, it does not become us to be defiled with fresh pollution ; that since he has united us to his body, we should, as his members, solicitously beware lest we asperse ourselves with any blemish or disgrace ; that since he who is our Head has ascended to heaven, we ought to divest ourselves of all terrestrial affection, and aspire thither with all our soul ; that since the Holy Spirit has dedicated us as temples to God, we should use our utmost exertions, that the glory of God may be displayed by us ; and ought not to allow ourselves to be profaned with the pollution of sin ; that since both our soul and our body are destined to heavenly incorruption and a never-fading crown, we ought to exert our most strenuous efforts to preserve them pure and uncorrupt till the day of the Lord. These, I say, are the best foundations for the proper regulation of the life, such as we cannot find in the philosophers ; who, in the recommendation of virtue, never rise above the natural dignity of man.

(*z*) Rom. vi. 4, &c. ; viii. 29.

IV. This is a proper place to address those who have nothing but the name and the symbol of Christ, and yet would be denominated Christians. But with what face do they glory in his sacred name? For none have any intercourse with Christ but those who have received the true knowledge of him from the word of the gospel. Now, the apostle denies that any have rightly learned Christ, who have not been taught that they must put off the old man, which is corrupt according to the deceitful lusts, and put on Christ. (*a*) Their knowledge of Christ, then, is proved to be a false and injurious pretence, with whatever eloquence and volubility they may talk concerning the gospel. For it is a doctrine not of the tongue, but of the life; and is not apprehended merely with the understanding and memory, like other sciences, but is then only received, when it possesses the whole soul, and finds a seat and residence in the inmost affection of the heart. Let them, therefore, either cease to insult God by boasting themselves to be what they are not, or show themselves disciples not unworthy of Christ, their Master. We have allotted the first place to the doctrine which contains our religion, because it is the origin of our salvation; but that it may not be unprofitable to us, it must be transfused into our breast, pervade our manners, and thus transform us into itself. If the philosophers are justly incensed against, and banish with disgrace from their society, those who, while they profess an art which ought to be a rule of life, convert it into a sophistical loquacity, — with how much better reason may we detest those sophists who are contented to have the gospel on their lips, whilst its efficacy ought to penetrate the inmost affections of the heart, to dwell in the soul, and to affect the whole man with a hundred times more energy than the frigid exhortations of the philosophers!

V. Yet I would not insist upon it as absolutely necessary, that the manners of a Christian should breathe nothing but the perfect gospel; which, nevertheless, ought both to be wished and to be aimed at. But I do not so rigorously require evangelical perfection as not to acknowledge as a Christian, one who has not yet attained to it; for then all would be excluded from the Church; since no man can be found who is not still at a great distance from it; and many have hitherto made but a very small progress, whom it would, nevertheless, be unjust to reject. What then? let us set before our eyes that mark, to which alone our pursuit must be directed. Let that be prescribed as the goal towards which we must earnestly tend. For it is not lawful for you to make such a compromise with God, as to undertake a part of the duties prescribed

(*a*) Eph. iv. 20, &c.

to you in his word, and to omit part of them, at your own pleasure. For, in the first place, he every where recommends integrity as a principal branch of his worship; by which he intends a sincere simplicity of heart, free from all guile and falsehood; the opposite of which is a double heart; as though it had been said, that the beginning of a life of uprightness is spiritual, when the internal affection of the mind is unfeignedly devoted to God in the cultivation of holiness and righteousness. But since no man in this terrestrial and corporeal prison has strength sufficient to press forward in his course with a due degree of alacrity, and the majority are oppressed with such great debility, that they stagger and halt, and even creep on the ground, and so make very inconsiderable advances, — let us every one proceed according to our small ability, and prosecute the journey we have begun. No man will be so unhappy, but that he may every day make some progress, however small. Therefore, let us not cease to strive, that we may be incessantly advancing in the way of the Lord; nor let us despair on account of the smallness of our success; for however our success may not correspond to our wishes, yet our labour is not lost, when this day surpasses the preceding one; provided that, with sincere simplicity, we keep our end in view, and press forward to the goal, not practising self-adulation, nor indulging our own evil propensities, but perpetually exerting our endeavours after increasing degrees of amelioration, till we shall have arrived at a perfection of goodness, which, indeed, we seek and pursue as long as we live, and shall then attain, when, divested of all corporeal infirmity, we shall be admitted by God into complete communion with him.

CHAPTER VII.

SUMMARY OF THE CHRISTIAN LIFE. SELF-DENIAL.

ALTHOUGH the Divine law contains a most excellent and well-arranged plan for the regulation of life, yet it has pleased the heavenly Teacher to conform men by a more accurate doctrine to the rule which he had prescribed in the law. And the principle of that doctrine is this — that it is the duty of believers to "present their bodies a living sacrifice, holy, acceptable unto God;" (b) and that in this consists the legitimate worship of

(b) Rom. xii. 1.

him. Hence is deduced an argument for exhorting them, "Be not conformed to this world; but be ye transformed by the renewing of your mind, that ye may prove what is that will of God." This is a very important consideration, that we are consecrated and dedicated to God; that we may not hereafter think, speak, meditate, or do any thing but with a view to his glory. For that which is sacred cannot, without great injustice towards him, be applied to unholy uses. If we are not our own, but the Lord's, it is manifest both what error we must avoid, and to what end all the actions of our lives are to be directed. We are not our own; therefore neither our reason nor our will should predominate in our deliberations and actions. We are not our own; therefore let us not propose it as our end, to seek what may be expedient for us according to the flesh. We are not our own; therefore let us, as far as possible, forget ourselves and all things that are ours. On the contrary, we are God's; to him, therefore, let us live and die. We are God's; therefore let his wisdom and will preside in all our actions. We are God's; towards him, therefore, as our only legitimate end, let every part of our lives be directed. O, how great a proficiency has that man made, who, having been taught that he is not his own, has taken the sovereignty and government of himself from his own reason, to surrender it to God! For as compliance with their own inclinations leads men most effectually to ruin, so to place no dependence on our own knowledge or will, but merely to follow the guidance of the Lord, is the only way of safety. Let this, then, be the first step, to depart from ourselves, that we may apply all the vigour of our faculties to the service of the Lord. By service I mean, not that only which consists in verbal obedience, but that by which the human mind, divested of its natural carnality, resigns itself wholly to the direction of the Divine Spirit. Of this transformation, which Paul styles a renovation of the mind, (c) though it is the first entrance into life, all the philosophers were ignorant. For they set up Reason as the sole directress of man; they think that she is exclusively to be attended to; in short, to her alone they assign the government of the conduct. But the Christian philosophy commands her to give place and submit to the Holy Spirit; so that now the man himself lives not, but carries about Christ living and reigning within him. (d)

II. Hence also that other consequence, that we should seek not our own things, but those which are agreeable to the will of the Lord, and conducive to the promotion of his glory. This also argues a great proficiency, that almost forgetting our-

(c) Eph. iv. 23.   (d) Gal. ii. 20.

selves, and certainly neglecting all selfish regards, we endeavour faithfully to devote our attention to God and his commandments. For when the Scripture enjoins us to discard all private and selfish considerations, it not only erases from our minds the cupidity of wealth, the lust of power, and the favour of men, but also eradicates ambition and all appetite after human glory, with other more secret plagues. Indeed, a Christian man ought to be so disposed and prepared, as to reflect that he has to do with God every moment of his life. Thus, as he will measure all his actions by his will and determination, so he will refer the whole bias of his mind religiously to him. For he who has learned to regard God in every undertaking, is also raised above every vain imagination. This is that denial of ourselves, which Christ, from the commencement of their course, so diligently enjoins on his disciples; which, when it has once obtained the government of the heart, leaves room neither for pride, haughtiness, or ostentation, nor for avarice, libidinousness, luxury, effeminacy, or any other evils which are the offspring of self-love. On the contrary, wherever it does not reign, there either the grossest vices are indulged without the least shame; or, if there exist any appearance of virtue, it is vitiated by a depraved passion for glory. Show me, if you can, a single individual, who, unless he has renounced himself according to the command of the Lord, is voluntarily disposed to practise virtue among men. For all who have not been influenced by this disposition, have followed virtue merely from the love of praise. And even those of the philosophers who have ever contended that virtue is desirable for its own sake, have been inflated with so much arrogance, that it is evident they desired virtue for no other reason than to furnish them occasion for the exercise of pride. But God is so far from being delighted, either with those who are ambitious of popular praise, or with hearts so full of pride and presumption, that he pronounces "they have their reward" in this world, and represents harlots and publicans as nearer to the kingdom of heaven than such persons. But we have not yet clearly stated the number and magnitude of the obstacles by which a man is impeded in the pursuit of that which is right, as long as he has refrained from all self-denial. For it is an ancient and true observation, that there is a world of vices concealed in the soul of man. Nor can you find any other remedy than to deny yourself and discard all selfish considerations, and to devote your whole attention to the pursuit of those things which the Lord requires of you, and which ought to be pursued for this sole reason, because they are pleasing to him.

III. The same apostle, in another place, gives a more distinct, though a brief, representation of all the parts of a well-regulated life. "The grace of God that bringeth salvation hath appeared to all men, teaching us, that, denying ungodliness and worldly lusts, we should live soberly, righteously, and godly, in this present world; looking for that blessed hope, and the glorious appearing of the great God and our Saviour Jesus Christ, who gave himself for us, that he might redeem us from all iniquity, and purify unto himself a peculiar people, zealous of good works."(e) For after having proposed the grace of God to animate us, in order to prepare the way for us truly to worship God, he removes two obstacles, which are our chief impediments; first, ungodliness, to which we have naturally too strong a propensity, and secondly, worldly lusts, which extend themselves further. The term " ungodliness " not only denotes superstitions, but comprehends also every thing that is repugnant to the serious fear of God. And " worldly lusts " mean the carnal affections. Therefore he enjoins us, with reference to both tables of the law, to forsake our former propensities, and to renounce all the dictates of our own reason and will. He reduces all the actions of life to three classes — sobriety, righteousness, and godliness. "Sobriety" undoubtedly denotes chastity and temperance, as well as a pure and frugal use of temporal blessings, and patience under poverty. "Righteousness" includes all the duties of equity, that every man may receive what is his due. "Godliness" separates us from the pollutions of the world, and by true holiness unites us to God. When these virtues are indissolubly connected, they produce absolute perfection. But since nothing is more difficult than to forsake all carnal considerations, to subdue and renounce our appetites, to devote ourselves to God and our brethren, and to live the life of angels amidst the corruptions of the world, — in order to extricate our minds from every snare, Paul recalls our attention to the hope of a blessed immortality; apprizing us that our efforts are not in vain; because, as Christ once appeared as a Redeemer, so, at his final advent, he will manifest the benefits of the salvation he has obtained. Thus he dispels the fascinations which blind us, and prevent our aspiring with becoming ardour to the glories of heaven, and at the same time teaches us that we must live as strangers and pilgrims in the world, that we may not lose the heavenly inheritance.

IV. In these words we perceive, that self-denial relates partly to men, but partly, and indeed principally, to God. For when the Scripture enjoins us to conduct ourselves in such a manner towards men, as in honour to prefer one another, and faithfully to devote our whole attention to the promotion of their ad-

(e) Titus ii. 11—14.

vantage, (*f*) it gives such commands as our heart can by no means receive, without having been previously divested of its natural bias. For we are all so blinded and fascinated with self-love, that every one imagines he has a just right to exalt himself, and to undervalue all others who stand in competition with him. If God has conferred on us any valuable qualification, relying thereon, our hearts are immediately lifted up; and we not only swell, but almost burst with pride. The vices in which we abound, we sedulously conceal from others, and flatter ourselves with the pretence that they are diminutive and trivial, and even sometimes embrace them as virtues. If the same talents which we admire in ourselves, or even superior ones, appear in others, in order that we may not be obliged to acknowledge their superiority, we depreciate and diminish them with the utmost malignity: if they have any vices, not content to notice them with severe and sharp animadversions, we odiously amplify them. Hence that insolence, that every one of us, as if exempted from the common lot, is desirous of pre-eminence above the rest of mankind; and severely and haughtily contemns every man, or at least despises him as an inferior. The poor yield to the rich, plebeians to nobles, servants to masters, the illiterate to the learned; but there is no man who does not cherish within him some idea of his own excellence. Thus all men, in flattering themselves, carry, as it were, a kingdom in their own breast; for arrogating to themselves the height of self-gratulation, they pass censure on the understandings and conduct of others; but if any contention arises, it produces an eruption of the poison. For many discover some gentleness, as long as they find every thing pleasant and amiable; but how many are there who preserve the same constant course of good humour when they are disturbed and irritated? Nor is there any other remedy, than the eradication from the inmost recesses of the heart of this most noxious pest of ambition and self-love; as it is indeed eradicated by the doctrine of the Scripture. For if we attend to its instructions, we must remember, that the talents with which God has favoured us, are not excellences originating from ourselves, but free gifts of God; of which if any are proud, they betray their ingratitude. "Who maketh thee to differ?" saith Paul. "Now, if thou didst receive all things, why dost thou glory, as if thou hadst not received them?" (*g*) In the next place, by assiduous observation and acknowledgment of our faults, we must recall our minds to humility. Thus there will remain in us nothing to inflate us, but great reason for dejection. On the other hand, we are enjoined, whatever gifts of God we perceive in

(*f*) Rom. xii. 10. Phil. ii. 4.   (*g*) 1 Cor. iv. 7.

others, to revere and esteem them, so as to honour those in whom they reside. For it would betray great wickedness in us to rob them of that honour which God has given them. Their faults we are taught to overlook, not indeed to encourage them by adulation, but never on account of them to insult those whom we ought to cherish with benevolence and honour. The result of attention to these directions will be, that with whomsoever we are concerned, we shall conduct ourselves not only with moderation and good humour, but with civility and friendship. For we shall never arrive at true meekness by any other way, than by having our hearts imbued with self-abasement and a respect for others.

V. How extremely difficult it is for you to discharge your duty in seeking the advantage of your neighbour! Unless you quit all selfish considerations, and, as it were, lay aside yourself, you will effect nothing in this duty. For how can you perform those which Paul inculcates as works of charity, unless you renounce yourself, and devote yourself wholly to serve others? "Charity," says he, "suffereth long, and is kind; charity envieth not; charity vaunteth not itself, is not puffed up, doth not behave itself unseemly, seeketh not her own, is not easily provoked," &c. (*h*) If this be all that is required, that we seek not our own, yet we must do no small violence to nature, which so strongly inclines us to the exclusive love of ourselves, that it does not so easily permit us to neglect ourselves and our own concerns in order to be vigilant for the advantage of others, and even voluntarily to recede from our right, to resign it to another. But the Scripture leads us to this, admonishes us, that whatever favours we obtain from the Lord, we are intrusted with them on this condition, that they should be applied to the common benefit of the Church; and that, therefore, the legitimate use of all his favours, is a liberal and kind communication of them to others. There cannot be imagined a more certain rule, or a more powerful exhortation to the observance of it, than when we are taught, that all the blessings we enjoy are Divine deposits, committed to our trust on this condition, that they should be dispensed for the benefit of our neighbours. But the Scripture goes still further, when it compares them to the powers with which the members of the human body are endued. For no member has its power for itself, nor applies it to its private use; but transfuses it among its fellow-members, receiving no advantage from it but what proceeds from the common convenience of the whole body. So, whatever ability a pious man possesses, he ought to possess it for his brethren, consulting his own private interest in no

---

(*h*) 1 Cor. xiii. 4—8.

way inconsistent with a cordial attention to the common edification of the Church. Let this, then, be our rule for benignity and beneficence, — that whatever God has conferred on us, which enables us to assist our neighbour, we are the stewards of it, and must one day render an account of our stewardship; and that the only right dispensation of what has been committed to us, is that which is regulated by the law of love. Thus we shall not only always connect the study to promote the advantage of others with a concern for our own private interests, but shall prefer the good of others to our own. To teach us that the dispensation of the gifts we receive from heaven ought to be regulated by this law, God anciently enjoined the same even in regard to the smallest bounties of his liberality. For he commanded the people to offer to him the first-fruits of the corn, as a solemn avowal that it was unlawful for them to enjoy any blessings not previously consecrated to him. And if the gifts of God are not sanctified to us till after we have with our own hands dedicated them to their Author, that must evidently be a sinful abuse which is unconnected with such a dedication. But in vain would you attempt to enrich the Lord by a communication of your possessions. Therefore, since your "goodness extendeth not to him," (*i*) as the Psalmist says, you must exercise it "towards the saints that are in the earth;" and alms are compared to sacred oblations, to show that these exercises of charity under the gospel, correspond to those offerings under the law.

VI. Moreover, that we may not be weary of doing good, which otherwise would of necessity soon be the case, we must add also the other character mentioned by the apostle, that " charity suffereth long, and is not easily provoked." The Lord commands us to do " good unto all men," (*k*) universally, a great part of whom, estimated according to their own merits, are very undeserving ; but here the Scripture assists us with an excellent rule, when it inculcates, that we must not regard the intrinsic merit of men, but must consider the image of God in them, to which we owe all possible honour and love ; but that this image is most carefully to be observed in them " who are of the household of faith," (*l*) inasmuch as it is renewed and restored by the Spirit of Christ. Whoever, therefore, is presented to you that needs your kind offices, you have no reason to refuse him your assistance. Say that he is a stranger ; yet the Lord has impressed on him a character which ought to be familiar to you ; for which reason he forbids you to despise your own flesh. (*m*) Say that he is contemptible and worthless ; but the Lord shows him to be one whom he has deigned

---

(*i*) Psalm xvi. 2, 3   (*k*) Heb. xiii. 16.   (*l*) Gal. vi. 10.   (*m*) Isaiah lviii. 7

to grace with his own image. Say that you are obliged to him for no services; but God has made him, as it were, his substitute, to whom you acknowledge yourself to be under obligations for numerous and important benefits. Say that he is unworthy of your making the smallest exertion on his account; but the image of God, by which he is recommended to you, deserves your surrender of yourself and all that you possess. If he not only has deserved no favour, but, on the contrary, has provoked you with injuries and insults, — even this is no just reason why you should cease to embrace him with your affection, and to perform to him the offices of love. He has deserved, you will say, very different treatment from me. But what has the Lord deserved? who, when he commands you to forgive men all their offences against you, certainly intends that they should be charged to himself. This is the only way of attaining that which is not only difficult, but utterly repugnant to the nature of man — to love them who hate us, (n) to requite injuries with kindnesses, and to return blessings for curses. (o) We should remember, that we must not reflect on the wickedness of men, but contemplate the Divine image in them; which, concealing and obliterating their faults, by its beauty and dignity allures us to embrace them in the arms of our love.

VII. This mortification, therefore, will not take place in us unless we fulfil all the duties of charity. These are fulfilled, not by him who merely performs all the external offices of charity, even without the omission of one, but by him who does this from a sincere principle of love. For it may happen, that a man may fully discharge his duty to all men, with respect to external actions, and, at the same time, be very far from discharging it in the right way. For you may see some men who would be thought extremely liberal, and yet never bestow any thing without upbraiding, either by pride of countenance, or by insolence of language. And we are sunk to such a depth of calamity in this unhappy age, that scarcely any alms are given, at least by the majority of mankind, but in a haughty and contemptuous manner — a corruption which ought not to have been tolerated even among heathen; for of Christians there is something further required, than to display a cheerfulness of countenance, and to render their benefactions amiable by civility of language. In the first place, they ought to imagine themselves in the situation of the person who needs their assistance, and to commiserate his case, just as though they themselves felt and suffered the same; so that they may be impelled, by a sense of mercy and humanity, to afford assistance to him as readily as if it were to themselves. He who comes to the assistance of

(n) Matt. v. 44.   (o) Luke xvii. 3, 4.

his brethren under the influence of such a disposition, not only will not contaminate his services with arrogance or reproach, but will neither despise his brother who is the object of his beneficence, as needing assistance, nor domineer over him as under an obligation to him; no more, for instance, than we insult a diseased member, for whose restoration the rest of the body labours, or suppose it to be under particular obligations to the other members, because it has needed more assistance than it returned. For the communication of services between the members of the body, is esteemed to be in no sense gratuitous, but rather a discharge of that which, being due by the law of nature, it would be monstrous to refuse. And for this reason, he will not suppose himself to have discharged all his duty, who has performed one kind of service; as it generally happens, that a rich man, after having bestowed some part of his property, leaves other burdens to be borne by other persons, and considers himself as exempted from all concern about them. On the contrary, every man will reflect with himself, that however great he may be, he is a debtor to his neighbour, and that no bounds should be fixed to the exercise of beneficence towards them, except when his ability fails, which, as far as it extends, ought to be limited by the rule of charity.

VIII. Let us describe again, more at large, the principal branch of self-denial, which we have said relates to God; and indeed many observations have already been made concerning it, which it would be needless to repeat: it will be sufficient to show how it habituates us to equanimity and patience. First, therefore, in seeking the convenience or tranquillity of the present life, the Scripture calls us to this point; that resigning ourselves and all that we have to the will of God, we should surrender to him the affections of our heart, to be conquered and reduced to subjection. To desire wealth and honours, to be ambitious of power, to accumulate riches, to amass all those vanities which appear conducive to magnificence and pomp, our passion is furious, and our cupidity unbounded. On the contrary, to poverty, obscurity, and meanness, we feel a wonderful fear and abhorrence, which stimulate us to avoid them by all possible means. Hence we may see, how restless the minds of all those persons are, who regulate their lives according to their own reason; how many arts they try, and with what exertions they fatigue themselves, in order, on the one hand, to obtain the objects of ambition or avarice, on the other, to avoid poverty and meanness. Pious men, therefore, that they may not be involved in such snares, must pursue the following course: First, let them neither desire, nor hope, nor entertain a thought of prosperity, from any other cause than the Divine blessing; and on that let them securely and confidently depend. For however the flesh may appear to itself to be abundantly sufficient, when it either attempts by its own industry, or strenuous exertions, to attain honours and wealth, or is assisted by the favour of man, — yet it is certain, that all these things are nothing, and that we shall obtain no advantage, either by ingenuity or by labour, but as far as the Lord shall prosper both. On the contrary, his benediction alone finds a way, even through all impediments, so as to bring all our affairs to a joyful and prosperous conclusion. And though we may, for the most part, be able without it to obtain for ourselves some degree of opulence and glory, as we daily behold impious men accumulating great honours and enormous wealth, yet, since those who are under the curse of God enjoy not even the smallest particle of happiness, we shall acquire nothing without the Divine blessing, which will not eventually prove a calamity to us. And that is by no means to be desired, the acquisition of which renders men more miserable.

IX. Therefore, if we believe that all the cause of desirable prosperity consists in the Divine benediction alone, without which miseries and calamities of every kind await us, it follows also, that we should not passionately strive for wealth and honours, either relying on our own diligence or acuteness of understanding, or depending on the favour of men, or confiding in a vain imagination of chance ; but that we should always regard the Lord, to be conducted by his direction to whatsoever lot he has provided for us. The consequence of this will be, in the first place, that we shall not rush forward to seize on wealth or honours by unlawful actions, by deceitful and criminal arts, by rapacity and injury of our neighbours ; but shall confine ourselves to the pursuit of those interests, which will not seduce us from the path of innocence. For who can expect the assistance of the Divine benediction, amidst fraud, rapine, and other iniquitous acts ? For as that follows him only whose thoughts are pure, and whose actions are upright, so it calls away all those by whom it is sought, from irregular thoughts and corrupt practices. In the next place, we shall find a restraint laid upon us, to keep us from being inflamed with an inordinate desire of growing rich, and from ambitiously aspiring after honours. For with what face can any man confide in the assistance of God, towards obtaining things which he desires in opposition to the Divine word ? Far be it from God to follow with the aid of his blessing, what he curses with his mouth. Lastly, if our success be not equal to our wishes and hopes, yet we shall be restrained from impatience, and from execrating our condition, whatever it may be ; because we shall know, that this would be murmuring against God, at whose pleasure are dispensed riches and poverty, honour and contempt. In short, he who shall repose himself, in the manner we have mentioned, on the Divine blessing, will neither hunt after the objects violently coveted by men in general, by evil methods, from which he will expect no advantage; nor will he impute any prosperous event to himself, and to his own diligence, industry, or good fortune; but will acknowledge God to be the author of it. If, while the affairs of others are flourishing, he makes but a small progress, or even moves in a retrograde direction, yet he will bear his poverty with more equanimity and moderation, than any profane man would feel with a mediocrity of success, which would merely be inferior to his wishes; possessing, indeed, a consolation in which he may enjoy more tranquil satisfaction, than in the zenith of opulence or power; because he considers, that his affairs are ordered by the Lord in such a manner as is conducive to his salvation. This, we see, was the disposition of David, who, while he follows God, surrenders himself to his government, and declares, that he is "as a child that is weaned of his mother; neither do I exercise myself," says he, "in great matters, or in things too high for me." (*p*)

X. Nor is this the only instance in which pious persons should feel such tranquillity and patience; the same state of mind ought to be extended to all the events to which the present life is exposed. Therefore no man has rightly renounced himself, but he who has wholly resigned himself to the Lord, so as to leave all the parts of his life to be governed by his will. He whose mind is thus composed, whatever may befall him, will neither think himself miserable, nor invidiously complain against God on account of his lot. The great necessity of this disposition will appear, if we consider the numerous accidents to which we are subject. Diseases of various kinds frequently attack us: at one time, the pestilence is raging; at another, we are cruelly harassed with the calamities of war; at another time, frost or hail, devouring the hopes of the year, produces sterility, which brings us to penury; a wife, parents, children, or other relatives, are snatched away by death; our dwelling is consumed by a fire; these are the events, on the occurrence of which, men curse this life, or their natal day, execrate heaven and earth, reproach God, and, as they are eloquent to blaspheme, accuse him of injustice and cruelty. But it behoves a believer, even in these events, to contemplate the clemency and truly paternal goodness of God. Wherefore, if he sees his relatives removed, and his house rendered a solitary place, he must not cease to bless the Lord, but rather have recourse to this reflection: Yet the grace of the Lord, which inhabits my

(*p*) Psalm cxxxi. 1, 2.

house, will not leave it desolate. Or if he sees his crops bitten or destroyed by frost, or beaten down by hail, and famine threatening him, yet he will not sink into despondency or displeasure against God, but will abide in this confidence — We are under the guardian care of God, we are "the sheep of his pasture;" (q) he therefore will supply us with food even in seasons of the greatest barrenness. If he shall be afflicted with disease, even then he will not be so far discouraged by the bitterness of his pain, as to break out into impatience, and to complain against God; but will rather strengthen his patience by a consideration of the justice and lenity of the Divine correction. Finally, whatever may happen, knowing it to be ordained by the Lord, he will receive it with a placid and grateful heart, that he may not be guilty of contumaciously resisting his authority, to whose power he has once resigned himself and all that belongs to him. Far, therefore, from the heart of a Christian man be that foolish and most wretched consolation of the heathen, who, to fortify their minds against adversity, imputed it to Fortune; with whom they esteemed it foolish to be displeased, because she was thoughtless and rash, and blindly wounded without discrimination the worthy and the unworthy. On the contrary, the rule of piety is, that God alone is the arbiter and governor of all events, both prosperous and adverse, and that he does not proceed with inconsiderate impetuosity, but dispenses to us blessings and calamities with the most systematic justice.

CHAPTER VIII.

BEARING THE CROSS, WHICH IS A BRANCH OF SELF-DENIAL.

But it becomes a pious mind to rise still higher, even to that to which Christ calls his disciples; that every one should "take up his cross." (r) For all whom the Lord has chosen and honoured with admission into the society of his saints, ought to prepare themselves for a life, hard, laborious, unquiet, and replete with numerous and various calamities. It is the will of their heavenly Father to exercise them in this manner, that he may have a certain proof of those that belong to him. Having begun with Christ his first begotten Son, he pursues this method towards all his children. For though Christ was above all others the beloved Son, in whom the Father was

(q) Psalm lxxix. 13.   (r) Matt. xvi. 24.

always well pleased, (*s*) yet we see how little indulgence and tenderness he experienced; so that it may be truly said, not only that he was perpetually burdened with a cross during his residence on earth, but that his whole life was nothing but a kind of perpetual cross. The apostle assigns the reason, that it was necessary for him to "learn obedience by the things which he suffered." (*t*) Why, then, should we exempt ourselves from that condition, to which it behoved Christ our head to be subject; especially since his submission was on our account, that he might exhibit to us an example of patience in his own person? Wherefore the apostle teaches, that it is the destination of all the children of God "to be conformed to him." (*u*) It is also a source of signal consolation to us, in unpleasant and severe circumstances, which are esteemed adversities and calamities, that we partake of the sufferings of Christ; that as he from a labyrinth of all evils entered into the glory of heaven, so we are conducted forward through various tribulations to the same glory; (*w*) for Paul teaches us, that when we "know the fellowship of his sufferings," we also apprehend "the power of his resurrection;" that while we are conformed to his death, we are thus prepared to partake of his glorious resurrection. (*x*) How much is this adapted to alleviate all the bitterness of the cross, that the more we are afflicted by adversities, our fellowship with Christ is so much the more certainly confirmed! By this communion the sufferings themselves not only become blessings to us, but afford considerable assistance towards promoting our salvation.

II. Besides, our Lord was under no necessity of bearing the cross, except to testify and prove his obedience to his Father; but there are many reasons which render it necessary for us to live under a continual cross. First, as we are naturally too prone to attribute every thing to our flesh, unless we have, as it were, ocular demonstration of our imbecility, we easily form an extravagant estimate of our strength, presuming that whatever may happen, it will remain undaunted and invincible amidst all difficulties. This inflates us with a foolish, vain, carnal confidence; relying on which, we become contumacious and proud, in opposition to God himself, just as though our own powers were sufficient for us without his grace. This arrogance he cannot better repress, than by proving to us from experience, not only our great imbecility, but also our extreme frailty. Therefore he afflicts us with ignominy, or poverty, or loss of relatives, or disease, or other calamities; to the bearing of which being in ourselves unequal, we ere long

(*s*) Matt. iii. 17; xvii. 5.   (*t*) Heb. v. 8.   (*u*) Rom. viii. 29.
(*w*) Acts xiv. 22.   (*x*) Phil. iii. 10.

sink under them. Thus being humbled, we learn to invoke his strength, which alone causes us to stand erect under a load of afflictions. Moreover, the greatest saints, though sensible that they stand by the grace of God, not by their own strength, are nevertheless more secure than they ought to be of their fortitude and constancy, unless he leads them by the discipline of the cross into a deeper knowledge of themselves. This presumption insinuated itself even into David: "In my prosperity I said, I shall never be moved; Lord, by thy favour thou hast made my mountain to stand strong. Thou didst hide thy face, and I was troubled." (y) For he confesses that his senses were so stupefied and benumbed by prosperity, that disregarding the grace of God, on which he ought to have depended, he relied on himself, so as to promise himself a permanent standing. If this happened to so great a prophet, who of us should not be fearful and cautious? Though in prosperity, therefore, they have flattered themselves with the notion of superior constancy and patience, yet when humbled by adversity, they learn that this was mere hypocrisy. Admonished by such evidences of their maladies, believers advance in humility, and, divested of corrupt confidence in the flesh, betake themselves to the grace of God; and when they have applied to it, they experience the presence of the Divine strength, in which they find abundant protection.

III. This is what Paul teaches, that "tribulation worketh patience, and patience experience." (z) For the promise of God to believers, that he will assist them in tribulations, they experience to be true, when they patiently stand supported by his power, which they certainly could not do by their own strength. Patience, therefore, affords a proof to the saints, that God will really give the assistance he has promised in every time of need. This also confirms their hope; for it would be too much ingratitude not to rely on the truth of God for the future, which they have hitherto experienced to be constant and certain. We see now what a series of benefits we derive from the cross. For, subverting the opinion which we have falsely preconceived of our own strength, and detecting our hypocrisy, with which we are enamoured, it expels pernicious and carnal confidence; when we are thus humbled, it teaches us to rely upon God alone, which keeps us from sinking under afflictions. And victory is followed by hope; inasmuch as the Lord, by the performance of his promises, establishes his truth for the future. Though these were the only reasons that could be given, they are sufficient to show the necessity of the discipline of the cross. For it is no small advantage to be

(y) Psalm xxx. 6, 7.   (z) Rom. v. 3, 4.

divested of a blind self-love, that we may be fully conscious of our imbecility; to be affected with a sense of our imbecility, that we may learn to be diffident of ourselves; to be diffident of ourselves, that we may transfer our confidence to God; to depend with unreserved confidence on God, that, relying on his assistance, we may persevere unconquered to the end; to stand in his grace, that we may know his veracity in his promises; to experience the certainty of his promises, that our hope may thereby be strengthened.

IV. The Lord has also another end in afflicting his children; to try their patience, and teach them obedience. Not, indeed, that they can perform any other obedience to him than that which he has given them; but he is pleased in this manner, by clear evidences, to exhibit and testify the graces which he has conferred on his saints, that they may not be concealed in inactivity within them. Therefore, in giving an open manifestation of the strength and constancy in suffering, with which he has furnished his servants, he is said to try their patience. Hence these expressions, that "God did tempt Abraham," and prove his piety, from the circumstance of his not refusing to sacrifice his own and only son. (*a*) Wherefore Peter states, that our faith is tried by tribulations, just as gold is tried by fire in a furnace. (*b*) Now, who can say that it is not necessary for this most excellent gift of patience, which a believer has received from his God, to be brought forward into use, that it may be ascertained and manifested? For otherwise men will never esteem it as it deserves. But if God himself acts justly, when, to prevent the virtues which he has conferred on believers from being concealed in obscurity and remaining useless and perishing, he furnishes an occasion for exciting them, — there is the best of reasons for the afflictions of the saints, without which they would have no patience. By the cross they are also, I say, instructed to obedience; because they are thus taught to live, not according to their own inclination, but according to the will of God. If every thing succeeded with them according to their wishes, they would not know what it is to follow God. But Seneca mentions that this was an ancient proverb, when they would exhort any one to bear adversity with patience, "Follow God." This implied that man submitted to the yoke of God, only when he resigned himself to his corrections. Now, if it is most reasonable that we should prove ourselves in all things obedient to our heavenly Father, we certainly ought not to deny him the use of every method to accustom us to practise this obedience.

V. Yet we do not perceive how necessary this obedience is

(*a*) Gen. xxii. 1, 12.   (*b*) 1 Peter i. 7.

to us, unless we at the same time reflect on the great wantonness of our flesh to shake off the Divine yoke, as soon as we have been treated with a little tenderness and indulgence. The case is exactly the same as with refractory horses, which, after having been pampered for some days in idleness, grow fierce and untamable, and regard not the rider, to whose management they previously submitted. And we are perpetual examples of what God complains of in the people of Israel: when we are "waxen fat," and are "covered with fatness," (c) we kick against him who has cherished and supported us. The beneficence of God ought to have allured us to the consideration and love of his goodness; but since such is our ingratitude, that we are rather constantly corrupted by his indulgence, it is highly necessary for us to be restrained by some discipline from breaking out into such petulance. Therefore, that we may not be made haughty by an excessive abundance of wealth, that we may not become proud on being distinguished with honours, that we may not be rendered insolent by being inflated with other advantages, mental, corporeal, or external, the Lord himself, as he foresees will be expedient, by the remedy of the cross, opposes, restrains, and subdues the haughtiness of our flesh; and that by various methods, adapted to promote the benefit of each individual. For we are not all equally afflicted with the same diseases, or all in need of an equally severe method of cure. Hence we see different persons exercised with different kinds of crosses. But whilst the heavenly Physician, consulting the health of all his patients, practises a milder treatment towards some, and cures others with rougher remedies, yet he leaves no one completely exempted, because he knows we are all diseased, without the exception of a single individual.

VI. Moreover it is necessary that our most merciful Father should not only prevent our infirmity for the future, but also frequently correct our past offences, to preserve us in a course of legitimate obedience to himself. Wherefore in every affliction we ought immediately to recollect the course of our past life. In reviewing it, we shall certainly find that we have committed what was deserving of such chastisement. Nevertheless the exhortation to patience must not be principally founded on a consciousness of sin. For the Scripture furnishes a far better consideration, when it informs us, that in adversity "we are chastened of the Lord, that we should not be condemned with the world." (d) Therefore, even in the bitterness of tribulations, it becomes us to acknowledge the clemency and benignity of our Father towards us; since even then he ceases

(c) Deut. xxxii. 15.   (d) 1 Cor. xi. 32.

not to promote our salvation. For he afflicts, not to ruin or destroy us, but rather to deliver us from the condemnation of the world. This idea will lead us to what the Scripture inculcates in another place: "My son, despise not the chastening of the Lord, neither be weary of his correction; for whom the Lord loveth he correcteth, even as a father the son in whom he delighteth." (e) When we recognize the rod of a father, is it not our duty rather to show ourselves obedient and docile children, than contumaciously to imitate desperate men, who have been hardened in their transgressions? God loses us, unless he recalls us after our defections from him; so that the apostle correctly remarks, "If ye be without chastisement, then are ye bastards, and not sons." (f) We are extremely perverse, therefore, if we cannot bear with him, while he declares his benevolence towards us, and his great concern for our salvation. The Scripture points out this difference between believers and unbelievers; the latter, as the slaves of an inveterate and incurable iniquity, are only rendered more wicked and obstinate by correction; the former, like ingenuous children, are led to a salutary repentance. You have to choose now in which number you would prefer to stand. But having treated of this subject elsewhere, I shall conclude, contenting myself with having thus briefly touched on it here.

VII. But it is a source of peculiar consolation when we suffer persecution "for righteousness' sake." (g) For we ought then to reflect how greatly we are honoured by God, when he thus distinguishes us with the peculiar characteristic of his service. I call it persecution for righteousness' sake, not only when we suffer in defence of the gospel, but also when we are molested in the vindication of any just cause. Whether, therefore, in asserting the truth of God, in opposition to the falsehoods of Satan, or in undertaking the protection of good and innocent men against the injuries of the wicked, it be necessary for us to incur the resentment and hatred of the world, by which our lives, our fortunes, or our reputation, may be endangered, — let it not be grievous or irksome to us thus far to employ ourselves in the service of God; nor let us imagine ourselves to be miserable in those respects in which he has with his own mouth pronounced us blessed. It is true, that poverty, considered in itself, is misery; and the same may be said of exile, contempt, imprisonment, ignominy; finally, death is of all calamities the last and worst. But with the favour of our God, they are all conducive to our happiness. Let us therefore be content with the testimony of Christ, rather than with the false opinion of the flesh. Thus we shall rejoice,

(e) Prov. iii. 11, 12.   (f) Heb. xii. 8.   (g) Matt. v. 10.

like the apostles, whenever he shall "count us worthy to suffer shame for his name." (*h*) For if, being innocent and conscious of our own integrity, we are stripped of our property by the villany of the wicked, we are reduced to poverty indeed among men, but we thereby obtain an increase of true riches with God in heaven; if we are banished from our country, we are more intimately received into the family of God; if we meet with vexation and contempt, we are so much the more firmly rooted in Christ; if we are stigmatized with reproach and ignominy, we are so much the more exalted in the kingdom of God; if we are massacred, it opens an entrance for us into a life of blessedness. We ought to be ashamed of setting a lower estimation on things on which the Lord has attached such a great value, than on the shadowy and evanescent pleasures of the present life.

VIII. Since the Scripture, therefore, by these and similar instructions, affords abundant consolation under all the ignominy and calamity which we sustain in the defence of righteousness, we are chargeable with extreme ingratitude if we do not receive them from the hand of the Lord with cheerful resignation; especially since this is the species of affliction, or the cross, most peculiar to believers, by which Christ will be glorified in us, according to the declaration of Peter. (*i*) And contumelious treatment being to ingenuous minds more intolerable than a hundred deaths, Paul expressly apprizes us, that not only persecutions, but *reproaches* await us, "because we trust in the living God." (*k*) As in another place he directs us by his example to go through "evil report and good report." (*l*) Nor are we required to exercise such a cheerfulness as to banish all sense of bitterness and sorrow; the saints could discover no patience under the cross, unless they were tormented with sorrow and harassed with grief. If there were no hardship in poverty, no agony in diseases, no distress in ignominy, no horror in death, — what fortitude or moderation would be displayed in regarding them with absolute indifference? But since each of these, by its own essential bitterness, naturally preys on all our hearts, herein the fortitude of a believer is manifested, if, when he experiences such bitterness, how grievously soever he may be distressed by it, yet by valiantly resisting, he at length overcomes it; his patience displays itself, if, when he is sharply provoked, he is nevertheless restrained by the fear of God from any eruptions of intemperance: his cheerfulness is conspicuous, if, when he is wounded by sadness and sorrow, he is satisfied with the spiritual consolation of God.

IX. This conflict, which believers sustain against the na-

(*h*) Acts v. 41.   (*i*) 1 Peter iv. 14.   (*k*) 1 Tim. iv. 10.   (*l*) 2 Cor. vi. 8

tural emotions of sorrow, while they cultivate patience and moderation, Paul has beautifully described in the following words: "We are troubled on every side, yet not distressed; we are perplexed, but not in despair; persecuted, but not forsaken; cast down, but not destroyed." (*m*) You see that patiently to bear the cross does not consist in an absolute stupefaction and privation of all sense of sorrow, according to the foolish description given by the ancient Stoics of a magnanimous man, as one who, divested of the feelings of human nature, is alike unaffected by adverse and prosperous events, by sorrowful and joyful ones. And what advantage have they derived from this sublime wisdom? They have depicted an image of patience, such as never has been found, such as never can exist among men; but in their ardour for a patience too perfect and precise, they have banished its influence from human life. At present also among Christians there are modern Stoics, who esteem it sinful not only to groan and weep, but even to discover sadness and solicitude. These paradoxes generally proceed from idle men, who, employing themselves more in speculation than in action, can produce nothing but such paradoxical notions. But we have nothing to do with that iron-hearted philosophy, which our Master and Lord has condemned not only in words, but even by his own example. For he mourned and wept both for his own calamities and for those of others. Nor did he teach his disciples a different conduct. "The world," says he, "shall rejoice, but ye shall weep and lament." (*n*) And that no man might pervert it into a crime, he has formally pronounced a blessing on them that mourn; (*o*) and no wonder. For if all tears be reprobated, what judgment shall we form concerning the Lord himself, from whose body distilled tears of blood? (*p*) If every terror be stigmatized with the charge of unbelief, what character shall we attribute to that horror and consternation with which we read that he was so violently depressed? If all sorrow be displeasing, how can we be pleased with his confessing that his "soul" was "sorrowful even unto death?"

X. I have thought proper to mention these things, in order to preserve pious minds from despair; that they may not hastily renounce the study of patience, because they cannot divest themselves of the natural affection of sorrow. This must necessarily be the case with those who degrade patience into insensibility, and a man of fortitude and constancy into a senseless block. For the Scripture applauds the saints for their patience, when they are afflicted with severe calamities, but not broken and overcome by them; when they are bitterly dis-

(*m*) 2 Cor. iv. 8, 9.   (*n*) John xvi. 20.   (*o*) Matt. v. 4.   (*p*) Luke xxii. 44

tressed, but are filled at the same time with spiritual joy; when they are oppressed with anxiety, but are revived and exhilarated with Divine consolation. At the same time there is that opposition in their hearts, that the feelings of nature avoid and dread those things which they experience to be inimical to it; but the affection of piety struggles even through these difficulties to obey the Divine will. This opposition the Lord expressed, when he thus addressed Peter: "When thou wast young, thou girdedst thyself, and walkedst whither thou wouldest; but when thou shalt be old, another shall gird thee, and carry thee whither thou wouldest not." (*q*) It is not probable that Peter, when he was called to glorify God by his death, was drawn to it with reluctance and resistance; in this case his martyrdom would be entitled to little applause. But however he might submit with the greatest alacrity of heart to the Divine appointment, yet, not having divested himself of human nature, he was distracted by two contrary inclinations. For when he contemplated the bloody death he was about to undergo, stricken with a dread of it, he would gladly have escaped. On the contrary, when he considered that he was called to it by the Divine will, suppressing all fear, he unreluctantly and even cheerfully submitted to it. It must be our study, therefore, if we would be the disciples of Christ, that our minds may be imbued with so great a reverence for God, and such an unreserved obedience to him, as may overcome all contrary affections, and make them submit to his appointments. Thus, whatever kind of affliction we endure, even in the greatest distresses of the mind, we shall constantly retain our patience. For adversity itself will have its stings, with which we shall be wounded. Thus, when afflicted with disease, we shall groan and be disquieted, and pray for the restoration of health; thus, when oppressed with poverty, we shall feel the stings of solicitude and sorrow; thus we shall be affected with the grief of ignominy, contempt, and injury; thus we shall shed the tears due to nature at the funerals of our friends; but we shall always recur to this conclusion, This affliction is appointed by the Lord, therefore let us submit to his will. Even in the agonies of grief, amid groans and tears, there is a necessity for the intervention of this reflection, in order to incline the heart cheerfully to bear those things by which it is so affected.

XI. But as we have deduced the principal reason for bearing the cross from a consideration of the Divine will, we must briefly point out the difference between philosophical and Christian patience. For very few of the philosophers have risen to such an eminence of reason, as to perceive that we are

(*q*) John xxi. 18.

exercised with afflictions by the Divine hand, and to conclude that God ought to be obeyed in these occurrences; and even those who have gone to this length, adduce no other reason, than because it is necessary. What is this but saying, that we must submit to God, because it were in vain to contend against him? For if we obey God only from necessity, if it were possible to escape from him, our obedience would cease. But the Scripture enjoins us to consider the Divine will in a very different point of view; first, as consistent with justice and equity; secondly, as directed to the accomplishment of our salvation. Christian exhortations to patience, then, are such as these: Whether we are afflicted with poverty, or exile, or imprisonment, or reproach, or disease, or loss of relatives, or any other similar calamity, we must reflect that none of these things happen without the appointment and providence of God; and, moreover, that he does nothing but with the most systematic justice. Do not our innumerable and daily transgressions deserve more severe and grievous chastisements than those which his clemency inflicts on us? Is it not highly reasonable that our flesh should be subdued, and as it were accustomed to the yoke, lest it should break out, according to its propensities, into lawless excesses? Are not the righteousness and truth of God worthy of our labours on their account? But if the equity of God evidently appears in our afflictions, we cannot without iniquity either murmur or resist. We no longer hear that frigid maxim of the philosophers, We must submit to necessity; but a lesson lively and full of efficacy, We must obey, because it is unlawful to resist; we must patiently suffer, because impatience is a rebellious opposition to the justice of God. Because nothing is really amiable to us but what we know to be conducive to our benefit and salvation, our most merciful Father affords us consolation also in this respect, by declaring, that even in afflicting us with the cross, he promotes our salvation. But if it be evident that tribulations are salutary for us, why should we not endure them with grateful and placid hearts? In patiently bearing them, therefore, we do not submit to necessity, but acquiesce in our own benefit. The effect of these considerations is, that in proportion as our minds are oppressed under the cross with the natural sense of affliction, so greatly are they dilated with spiritual joy. This is attended also by thanksgiving, which cannot be without joy. But if praise and thanksgiving to the Lord can only proceed from a cheerful and joyful heart, — and there is nothing which ought to repress these emotions within us, — this shows how necessary it is that the bitterness of the cross should be tempered with spiritual joy.

CHAPTER IX.

MEDITATION ON THE FUTURE LIFE.

WITH whatever kind of tribulation we may be afflicted, we should always keep this end in view — to habituate ourselves to a contempt of the present life, that we may thereby be excited to meditation on that which is to come. For the Lord, well knowing our strong natural inclination to a brutish love of the world, adopts a most excellent method to reclaim us and rouse us from our insensibility, that we may not be too tenaciously attached to that foolish affection. There is not one of us who is not desirous of appearing, through the whole course of his life, to aspire and strive after celestial immortality. For we are ashamed of excelling in no respect the brutal herds, whose condition would not be at all inferior to ours, unless there remained to us a hope of eternity after death. But if you examine the designs, pursuits, and actions of every individual, you will find nothing in them but what is terrestrial. Hence that stupidity, that the mental eyes, dazzled with the vain splendour of riches, power, and honours, cannot see to any considerable distance. The heart also, occupied and oppressed with avarice, ambition, and other inordinate desires, cannot rise to any eminence. In a word, the whole soul, fascinated by carnal allurements, seeks its felicity on earth. To oppose this evil, the Lord, by continual lessons of miseries, teaches his children the vanity of the present life. That they may not promise themselves profound and secure peace in it, therefore he permits them to be frequently disquieted and infested with wars or tumults, with robberies or other injuries. That they may not aspire with too much avidity after transient and uncertain riches, or depend on those which they possess, — sometimes by exile, sometimes by the sterility of the land, sometimes by a conflagration, sometimes by other means, he reduces them to indigence, or at least confines them within the limits of mediocrity. That they may not be too complacently delighted with conjugal blessings, he either causes them to be distressed with the wickedness of their wives, or humbles them with a wicked offspring, or afflicts them with want or loss of children. But if in all these things he is more indulgent to them, yet that they may not be inflated with vain glory, or improper confidence, he shows them by diseases and dangers the unstable and transitory nature of all mortal blessings. We therefore truly derive advantage from the discipline of the cross, only when we learn that this life, considered in itself, is unquiet, turbulent, miserable in numberless instances, and in no respect altogether happy; and that all its reputed blessings are uncertain, transient, vain, and adulterated with a mixture of many evils; and in consequence of this at once conclude, that nothing can be sought or expected on earth but conflict, and that when we think of a crown we must raise our eyes towards heaven. For it must be admitted, that the mind is never seriously excited to desire and meditate on the future life, without having previously imbibed a contempt of the present.

II. There is no medium between these two extremes; either the earth must become vile in our estimation, or it must retain our immoderate love. Wherefore, if we have any concern about eternity, we must use our most diligent efforts to extricate ourselves from these fetters. Now, since the present life has numerous blandishments to attract us, and much pleasure, beauty, and sweetness to delight us, — it is very necessary to our highest interests, that we should be frequently called off, that we may not be fascinated with such allurements. For what would be the consequence, if we were perpetually happy in the enjoyment of the blessings of this life; since we cannot, even by the incessant stimulus of calamity after calamity, be sufficiently aroused to a consideration of its misery? That human life is like a vapour or a shadow, is not only known to the learned, but even the vulgar have no proverb more common; and perceiving it to be a thing the knowledge of which would be eminently useful, they have represented it in many remarkable sentences. But there is scarcely any thing which we more carelessly consider, or sooner forget; for we undertake every thing as though we were erecting for ourselves an immortality on earth. If a funeral pass by, or we walk among the tombs, because the image of death is then presented to our eyes, we philosophize, I confess, in an admirable manner concerning the vanity of the present life; although even that is not always the case, for frequently we are quite unaffected with all these things. But when this effect is produced, our philosophy is momentary, vanishing as soon as we withdraw, and leaving not even the smallest vestige behind it; in short, it passes away, and is forgotten just like the plaudits of a theatre at any entertaining exhibition. And forgetting not only death, but mortality itself, as though no rumour concerning it had ever reached us, we relapse into a supine security of immortality on earth. If any one, in the mean time, reminds us of the unwelcome proverb, that man is a creature of a day, we acknowledge the truth of it indeed, but with such inattention that the idea of perpetually living here still remains fixed in our minds. Who, then, can deny, that it is highly useful to us all, I do not say to be admonished by words, but by every possible evidence to be convinced, of the miserable condition of the present life; since even after we are convinced of it, we scarcely cease to be besotted with a perverse and foolish admiration of it, as though it contained the greatest attainable blessings? But if it be necessary for God to instruct us, it is, on the other hand, our duty to listen to him when he calls, and rebukes our sluggishness; in order that, despising the world, we may apply ourselves with our whole heart to meditate on the life which is to come.

III. But believers should accustom themselves to such a contempt of the present life, as may not generate either hatred of life, or ingratitude towards God. For this life, though it is replete with innumerable miseries, is yet deservedly reckoned among the Divine blessings which must not be despised. Wherefore, if we discover nothing of the Divine beneficence in it, we are already guilty of no small ingratitude towards God himself. But to believers especially it should be a testimony of the Divine benevolence, since the whole of it is destined to the advancement of their salvation. For before he openly discovers to us the inheritance of eternal glory, he intends to reveal himself as our Father in inferior instances; and those are the benefits which he daily confers on us. Since this life, then, is subservient to a knowledge of the Divine goodness, shall we fastidiously scorn it, as though it contained no particle of goodness in it? We must therefore have this sense and affection, to class it among the bounties of the Divine benignity which are not to be rejected. For if Scripture testimonies were wanting, which are very numerous and clear, even nature itself exhorts us to give thanks to the Lord for having introduced us to the light of life, for granting us the use of it, and giving us all the helps necessary to its preservation. And it is a far superior reason for gratitude, if we consider that here we are in some measure prepared for the glory of the heavenly kingdom. For the Lord has ordained, that they who are to be hereafter crowned in heaven, must first engage in conflicts on earth, that they may not triumph without having surmounted the difficulties of warfare and obtained the victory. Another reason is, that here we begin in various blessings to taste the sweetness of the Divine benignity, that our hope and desire may be excited after the full revelation of it. When we have come to this conclusion, that our life in this world is a gift of the Divine clemency, which, as we owe to him, we ought to remember with gratitude, it will then be time for us to descend to a consideration of its most miserable condition, that we may be delivered from excessive love of it, to which, as has been observed, we are naturally inclined.

IV. Now, whatever is abstracted from the corrupt love of this life should be added to the desire of a better. I grant, indeed, the correctness of their opinion, who considered it as the greatest blessing not to be born, and as the next, to die immediately. For, being heathens, destitute of the knowledge of God and of true religion, what could they see in it but unhappiness and misery? Nor was there any thing irrational in the conduct of those who mourned and wept at the births of their relations, and solemnly rejoiced at their funerals. But they practised this without any advantage; for, destitute of the true doctrine of faith, they did not perceive how that can conduce to the benefit of the pious, which in itself is neither blessed nor desirable; and so their views terminated in despair. It should be the object of believers, therefore, in judging of this mortal life, that understanding it to be of itself nothing but misery, they may apply themselves wholly, with increasing cheerfulness and readiness, to meditate on the future and eternal life. When we come to this comparison, then indeed the former may be not only securely neglected, but, in competition with the latter, altogether despised and abhorred. For if heaven is our country, what is the earth but a place of exile? If the departure out of the world is an entrance into life, what is the world but a sepulchre? What is a continuance in it but an absorption in death? If deliverance from the body is an introduction into complete liberty, what is the body but a prison? If to enjoy the presence of God is the summit of felicity, is it not misery to be destitute of it? But till we escape out of the world, "we are absent from the Lord." (r) Therefore, if the terrestrial life be compared with the celestial, it should undoubtedly be despised and accounted of no value. It certainly is never to be hated, except in as much as it keeps us obnoxious to sin; although even that hatred is not properly to be applied to life itself. It becomes us, however, to be so affected with weariness or hatred of it, as to desire its end, but to be also prepared to remain in it during the Divine pleasure; that is to say, our weariness should be remote from all murmuring and impatience. For it is a post at which the Lord has placed us, to be retained by us till he call us away. Paul, indeed, bewails his lot, that he is kept in bondage by the fetters of the body longer than he would wish, and sighs with an ardent desire of deliverance; (s) nevertheless, obedient to the Divine authority, he professes himself prepared for both; for he acknowledges himself under an obligation to God to glorify

(r) 2 Cor. v. 6.   (s) Rom. vii. 24.

his name either by life or by death; (*t*) but that it belongs to the Lord to determine what will conduce most to his glory. Therefore, if it becomes us "to live and to die to the Lord," (*u*) let us leave the limits of our life and death to his decision; yet in such a manner, as ardently to desire and continually to meditate on the latter, but to despise the former in comparison with future immortality, and on account of the servitude of sin, to wish to forsake it whenever it shall please the Lord.

V. But it is monstrous, that instead of this desire of death, multitudes who boast themselves to be Christians, are filled with such a dread of it, that they tremble whenever it is mentioned, as if it were the greatest calamity that could befall them. It is no wonder, indeed, if our natural feelings should be alarmed at hearing of our dissolution. But it is intolerable that there should not be in a Christian breast sufficient light of piety to overcome and suppress all that fear with superior consolation. For if we consider, that this unstable, depraved, corruptible, frail, withering, and rotten tabernacle of our body is dissolved, in order that it may hereafter be restored to a durable, perfect, incorruptible, and heavenly glory,—will not faith constrain us ardently to desire what nature dreads? If we consider, that by death we are recalled from exile to inhabit our own country, and that a heavenly one, shall we derive thence no consolation? But it will be said, There is nothing that does not desire to be permanent. I admit it; and contend that we ought therefore to direct our views to a future immortality, where we may obtain a fixed condition, which is nowhere to be found on earth. For Paul excellently teaches believers to go with alacrity to death, " not for that they would be unclothed, but clothed upon." (*x*) Shall brute animals, and even inanimate creatures, down to stocks and stones, conscious of their present vanity, be looking forward to the resurrection at the last day, that they may be delivered from vanity, together with the children of God; and shall we, endued with the light of understanding, and, what is superior to the natural understanding, illuminated with the Spirit of God, when the question respects our own existence, not raise our minds above the corruption of this world? But it is not necessary to my present design, nor suitable in this place, to argue against such extreme perverseness. And I have already declared in the beginning, that I would not undertake a diffuse discussion of commonplace topics. I would persuade such timid minds to read Cyprian's treatise on Mortality, did they not deserve rather to be referred to the philosophers, that they may begin to blush, when they see the contempt of death

(*t*) Phil. i. 20.   (*u*) Rom. xiv. 7, 8.   (*x*) 2 Cor. v. 4.

discovered by them. But this we may positive.y conclude, that no man has made any good proficiency in the school of Christ, but he who joyfully expects both the day of death and that of the final resurrection. For Paul describes all believers by this character, (*y*) and the Scripture often recalls our attention to it, when it intends to furnish us with a reason for true joy. "Look up," saith the Lord, "and lift up your heads; for your redemption draweth nigh." (*z*) Is it reasonable, that what he designed so powerfully to excite us to exultation and alacrity, should produce nothing but sorrow and consternation? If this be the case, why do we still glory in him as our Master? Let us therefore acquire a sounder judgment; and notwithstanding the opposition of the blind and stupid cupidity of our flesh, let us not hesitate ardently to desire the advent of the Lord, as of all events the most auspicious. For he shall come to us as a Redeemer, to deliver us from this bottomless gulf of all evils and miseries, and introduce us into that blessed inheritance of his life and glory.

VI. It is certainly true, that the whole family of believers, as long as they dwell on the earth, must be "accounted as sheep for the slaughter," (*a*) that they may be conformed to Christ their Head. Their state, therefore, would be extremely deplorable, if they did not elevate their thoughts towards heaven, rise above all sublunary things, and look beyond present appearances. (*b*) On the contrary, when they have once raised their heads above this world, although they see the impious flourishing in riches and honours, and enjoying the most profound tranquillity; though they see them boasting of their splendour and luxury, and behold them abounding in every delight; though they may also be harassed by their wickedness, insulted by their pride, defrauded by their avarice, and may receive from them any other lawless provocations, — yet they will find no difficulty in supporting themselves even under such calamities as these. For they will keep in view that day when the Lord will receive his faithful servants into his peaceful kingdom; will wipe every tear from their eyes, (*c*) invest them with robes of joy, adorn them with crowns of glory, entertain them with his ineffable delights, exalt them to fellowship with his majesty, and, in a word, honour them with a participation of his happiness. But the impious, who have been great in this world, he will precipitate down to the lowest ignominy; he will change their delights into torments, and their laughter and mirth into weeping and gnashing of teeth; he will disturb their tranquillity with dreadful agonies of con-

(*y*) Titus ii. 13. (*z*) Luke xxi. 28.
(*a*) Rom. viii. 36. (*b*) 1 Cor. xv. 19. (*c*) Isaiah xxv. 8. Rev. vii. 17.

science, and will punish their delicacy with inextinguishable fire, and even put them in subjection to the pious, whose patience they have abused. For, according to Paul, "it is a righteous thing with God to recompense tribulation to them that trouble" the saints, "and to" them "who are troubled, rest, when the Lord Jesus shall be revealed from heaven." (d) This is our only consolation; and deprived of this, we must of necessity either sink into despondency of mind, or solace ourselves to our own destruction with the vain pleasures of the world. For even the Psalmist confesses that he staggered, (e) when he was too much engaged in contemplating the present prosperity of the impious; and that he could no otherwise establish himself, till he entered the sanctuary of God, and directed his views to the last end of the godly and of the wicked. To conclude in one word, the cross of Christ triumphs, in the hearts of believers, over the devil and the flesh, over sin and impious men, only when their eyes are directed to the power of the resurrection.

CHAPTER X.

THE RIGHT USE OF THE PRESENT LIFE AND ITS SUPPORTS.

BY such principles, the Scripture also fully instructs us in the right use of terrestrial blessings — a thing that ought not to be neglected in a plan for the regulation of life. For if we must live, we must also use the necessary supports of life; nor can we avoid even those things which appear to subserve our pleasures rather than our necessities. It behooves us, therefore, to observe moderation, that we may use them with a pure conscience, whether for necessity or for pleasure. This the Lord prescribes in his word, when he teaches us, that to his servants the present life is like a pilgrimage, in which they are travelling towards the celestial kingdom. If we are only to pass through the earth, we ought undoubtedly to make such a use of its blessings as will rather assist than retard us in our journey. It is not without reason, therefore, that Paul advises us to use this world as though we used it not, and to buy with the same disposition with which we sell. (f) But as this is a difficult subject, and there is danger of falling into one of two opposite errors, let us endeavour to proceed on safe ground, that we may avoid both extremes. For there have

(d) 2 Thess. i. 6, 7.   (e) Psalm lxxiii. 2, &c.   (f) 1 Cor. vii. 30, 31.

been some, in other respects good and holy men, who, seeing that intemperance and luxury, unless restrained with more than ordinary severity, would perpetually indulge the most extravagant excesses, and desiring to correct such a pernicious evil, have adopted the only method which occurred to them, by permitting men to use corporeal blessings no further than their necessity should absolutely require. This advice was well intended, but they were far too austere. For they committed the very dangerous error of imposing on the conscience stricter rules than those which are prescribed to it by the word of the Lord. By restriction within the demands of necessity, they meant an abstinence from every thing from which it is possible to abstain; so that, according to them, it would scarcely be lawful to eat or drink any thing but bread and water. Others have discovered still greater austerity, like Crates the Theban, who is said to have thrown his wealth into the sea, from an apprehension that, unless it were destroyed, he should himself be destroyed by it. On the contrary, many in the present day, who seek a pretext to excuse intemperance in the use of external things, and at the same time desire to indulge the licentiousness of the flesh, assume as granted, what I by no means concede to them, that this liberty is not to be restricted by any limitation; but that it ought to be left to the conscience of every individual to use as much as he thinks lawful for himself. I grant, indeed, that it is neither right nor possible to bind the conscience with the fixed and precise rules of law in this case; but since the Scripture delivers general rules for the lawful use of earthly things, our practice ought certainly to be regulated by them.

II. It must be laid down as a principle, that the use of the gifts of God is not erroneous, when it is directed to the same end for which the Creator himself has created and appointed them for us; since he has created them for our benefit, not for our injury. Wherefore, no one will observe a more proper rule, than he who shall diligently regard this end. Now, if we consider for what end he has created the various kinds of aliment, we shall find that he intended to provide not only for our necessity, but likewise for our pleasure and delight. So in clothing, he has had in view not mere necessity, but propriety and decency. In herbs, trees, and fruits, beside their various uses, his design has been to gratify us by graceful forms and pleasant odours. For if this were not true, the Psalmist would not recount among the Divine blessings, " wine that maketh glad the heart of man, and oil to make his face to shine ;" (*g*) nor would the Scriptures universally declare, in commendation of his goodness, that he has given all these things to men. And

(*g*) Psalm civ. 15.

even the natural properties of things sufficiently indicate for what end, and to what extent, it is lawful to use them. But shall the Lord have endued flowers with such beauty, to present itself to our eyes, with such sweetness of smell, to impress our sense of smelling; and shall it be unlawful for our eyes to be affected with the beautiful sight, or our olfactory nerves with the agreeable odour? What! has he not made such a distinction of colours as to render some more agreeable than others? Has he not given to gold and silver, to ivory and marble, a beauty which makes them more precious than other metals or stones? In a word, has he not made many things worthy of our estimation, independently of any necessary use?

III. Let us discard, therefore, that inhuman philosophy which, allowing no use of the creatures but what is absolutely necessary, not only malignantly deprives us of the lawful enjoyment of the Divine beneficence, but which cannot be embraced till it has despoiled man of all his senses, and reduced him to a senseless block. But, on the other hand, we must, with equal diligence, oppose the licentiousness of the flesh; which, unless it be rigidly restrained, transgresses every bound. And, as I have observed, it has its advocates, who, under the pretext of liberty, allow it every thing. In the first place, it will be one check to it, if it be concluded, that all things are made for us, in order that we may know and acknowledge their Author, and celebrate his goodness towards us by giving him thanks. What will become of thanksgiving, if you overcharge yourself with dainties or wine, so as to be stupefied or rendered unfit for the duties of piety and the business of your station? Where is any acknowledgment of God, if your body, in consequence of excessive abundance, being inflamed with the vilest passions, infects the mind with its impurity, so that you cannot discern what is right or virtuous? Where is gratitude towards God for clothing, if, on account of our sumptuous apparel, we admire ourselves and despise others? if with the elegance and beauty of it, we prepare ourselves for unchastity? Where is our acknowledgment of God, if our minds be fixed on the splendour of our garments? For many so entirely devote all their senses to the pursuit of pleasure, that the mind is, as it were, buried in it; many are so delighted with marble, gold, and pictures, that they become like statues, are, as it were, metamorphosed into metal, and resemble painted images. The flavour of meats, or the sweetness of odours, so stupefies some, that they have no relish for any thing spiritual. The same may be observed in other cases. Wherefore it is evident, that this principle lays some restraint on the license of abusing the Divine bounties, and confirms the rule given us by Paul, that we " make not provision for the flesh, to fulfil the lusts thereof;" (*i*) which, if they are allowed too much latitude, will transgress all the bounds of temperance and moderation.

IV. But there is no way more certain or concise, than what we derive from a contempt of the present life, and meditation on a heavenly immortality. For thence follow two rules. The first is, "that they that have wives be as though they had none; and they that buy, as though they possessed not; and they that use this world, as not abusing it;" (*k*) according to the direction of Paul: the second, that we should learn to bear penury with tranquillity and patience, as well as to enjoy abundance with moderation. He who commands us to use this world as though we used it not, prohibits not only all intemperance in eating and drinking, and excessive delicacy, ambition, pride, haughtiness, and fastidiousness in our furniture, our habitations, and our apparel, but every care and affection, which would either seduce or disturb us from thoughts of the heavenly life, and attention to the improvement of our souls. Now, it was anciently and truly observed by Cato, That there is a great concern about adorning the body, and a great carelessness about virtue; and it is an old proverb, That they who are much engaged in the care of the body, are generally negligent of the soul. Therefore, though the liberty of believers in external things cannot be reduced to certain rules, yet it is evidently subject to this law, That they should indulge themselves as little as possible; that, on the contrary, they should perpetually and resolutely exert themselves to retrench all superfluities and to restrain luxury; and that they should diligently beware lest they pervert into impediments things which were given for their assistance.

V. The other rule will be, That persons whose property is small should learn to be patient under their privations, that they may not be tormented with an immoderate desire of riches. They who observe this moderation, have attained no small proficiency in the school of the Lord, as he who has made no proficiency in this point can scarcely give any proof of his being a disciple of Christ. For besides that an inordinate desire of earthly things is accompanied by most other vices, he who is impatient under penury, in abundance generally betrays the opposite passion. By this I mean, that he who is ashamed of a mean garment, will be proud of a splendid one; he who, not content with a slender meal, is disquieted with the desire of a more sumptuous one, would also intemperately abuse those dainties, should they fall to his lot; he who bears a private and mean condition with discontent and disquietude, would not abstain from pride and arrogance, should he

(*i*) Rom. xiii. 14.   (*k*) 1 Cor. vii. 29, 30, 31.

rise to eminence and honours. Let all, therefore, who are sincere in the practice of piety, earnestly endeavour to learn, after the apostolic example, "both to be full and to be hungry, both to abound and to suffer need." (*l*) The Scripture has also a third rule, by which it regulates the use of earthly things: of which something was said, when we treated of the precepts of charity. For it states, that while all these things are given to us by the Divine goodness, and appointed for our benefit, they are, as it were, deposits intrusted to our care, of which we must one day give an account. We ought, therefore, to manage them in such a manner that this alarm may be incessantly sounding in our ears, "Give an account of thy stewardship." (*m*) Let it also be remembered by whom this account is demanded; that it is by him who has so highly recommended abstinence, sobriety, frugality, and modesty; who abhors profusion, pride, ostentation, and vanity; who approves of no other management of his blessings, than such as is connected with charity; who has with his own mouth already condemned all those pleasures which seduce the heart from chastity and purity, or tend to impair the understanding.

VI. Lastly, it is to be remarked, that the Lord commands every one of us, in all the actions of life, to regard his vocation. For he knows with what great inquietude the human mind is inflamed, with what desultory levity it is hurried hither and thither, and how insatiable is its ambition to grasp different things at once. Therefore, to prevent universal confusion being produced by our folly and temerity, he has appointed to all their particular duties in different spheres of life. And that no one might rashly transgress the limits prescribed, he has styled such spheres of life *vocations*, or *callings*. Every individual's line of life, therefore, is, as it were, a post assigned him by the Lord, that he may not wander about in uncertainty all his days. And so necessary is this distinction, that in his sight all our actions are estimated according to it, and often very differently from the sentence of human reason and philosophy. There is no exploit esteemed more honourable, even among philosophers, than to deliver our country from tyranny; but the voice of the celestial Judge openly condemns the private man who lays violent hands on a tyrant. It is not my design, however, to stay to enumerate examples. It is sufficient if we know that the principle and foundation of right conduct in every case is the vocation of the Lord, and that he who disregards it will never keep the right way in the duties of his station. He may sometimes, perhaps, achieve something apparently laudable; but however it may appear in the eyes of men,

(*l*) Phil. iv. 12. (*m*) Luke xvi. 2.

it will be rejected at the throne of God; besides which, there will be no consistency between the various parts of his life. Our life, therefore, will then be best regulated, when it is directed to this mark; since no one will be impelled by his own temerity to attempt more than is compatible with his calling, because he will know that it is unlawful to transgress the bounds assigned him. He that is in obscurity will lead a private life without discontent, so as not to desert the station in which God has placed him. It will also be no small alleviation of his cares, labours, troubles, and other burdens, when a man knows that in all these things he has God for his guide. The magistrate will execute his office with greater pleasure, the father of a family will confine himself to his duty with more satisfaction, and all, in their respective spheres of life, will bear and surmount the inconveniences, cares, disappointments, and anxieties which befall them, when they shall be persuaded that every individual has his burden laid upon him by God. Hence also will arise peculiar consolation, since there will be no employment so mean and sordid (provided we follow our vocation) as not to appear truly respectable, and be deemed highly important in the sight of God.

CHAPTER XI.

JUSTIFICATION BY FAITH. THE NAME AND THING DEFINED.

I think I have already explained, with sufficient care, how that men, being subject to the curse of the law, have no means left of attaining salvation but through faith alone; and also what faith itself is, what Divine blessings it confers on man, and what effects it produces in him. The substance of what I have advanced is, that Christ, being given to us by the goodness of God, is apprehended and possessed by us by faith, by a participation of whom we receive especially two benefits. In the first place, being by his innocence reconciled to God, we have in heaven a propitious father instead of a judge; in the next place, being sanctified by his Spirit, we devote ourselves to innocence and purity of life. Of regeneration, which is the second benefit, I have said what I thought was sufficient. The method of justification has been but slightly touched, because it was necessary, first to understand that the faith, by which alone we attain gratuitous justification through the Divine mercy, is not unattended with good works, and what is the nature of the good works of the saints, in which part of this question consists. The subject of justification, therefore, must now be fully discussed, and discussed with the recollection that it is the principal hinge by which religion is supported, in order that we may apply to it with the greater attention and care. For unless we first of all apprehend in what situation we stand with respect to God, and what his judgment is concerning us, we have no foundation either for a certainty of salvation, or for the exercise of piety towards God. But the necessity of knowing this subject will be more evident from the knowledge itself.

II. But that we may not stumble at the threshold, (which would be the case were we to enter on a disputation concerning a subject not understood by us,) let us first explain the meaning of these expressions *To be justified in the sight of God, To be justified by faith or by works.* He is said to be *justified in the sight of God* who in the Divine judgment is reputed righteous, and accepted on account of his righteousness; for as iniquity is abominable to God, so no sinner can find favour in his sight, as a sinner, or so long as he is considered as such. Wherever sin is, therefore, it is accompanied with the wrath and vengeance of God. He is justified who is considered not as a sinner, but as a righteous person, and on that account stands in safety before the tribunal of God, where all sinners are confounded and ruined. As, if an innocent man be brought under an accusation before the tribunal of a just judge, when judgment is passed according to his innocence, he is said to be justified or acquitted before the judge, so he is justified before God, who, not being numbered among sinners, has God for a witness and asserter of his righteousness. Thus he must be said, therefore, to be *justified by works*, whose life discovers such purity and holiness, as to deserve the character of righteousness before the throne of God; or who, by the integrity of his works, can answer and satisfy the divine judgment. On the other hand, he will be *justified by faith*, who, being excluded from the righteousness of works, apprehends by faith the righteousness of Christ, invested in which, he appears, in the sight of God, not as a sinner, but as a righteous man. Thus we simply explain justification to be an acceptance, by which God receives us into his favour, and esteems us as righteous persons; and we say that it consists in the remission of sins and the imputation of the righteousness of Christ.

III. For the confirmation of this point there are many plain testimonies of Scripture. In the first place, that this is the proper and most usual signification of the word, cannot be denied. But since it would be too tedious to collect all the passages and compare them together, let it suffice to have suggested it to the reader; for he will easily observe it of himself. I will only produce a few places, where this justification, which we speak of, is expressly handled. First, where Luke relates that "the people that heard Christ justified God;" and where Christ pronounces that "wisdom is justified of all her children." (*n*) *To justify God*, in the former passage, does not signify to confer righteousness, which always remains perfect in him, although the whole world endeavour to rob him of it; nor, in the latter passage, does *the justifying of wisdom* denote making the doctrine of salvation righteous, which is so of itself; but both passages imply an ascription to God and to his doctrine of the praise which they deserve. Again, when Christ reprehends the Pharisees for "justifying themselves," (*o*) he does not mean that they attained righteousness by doing what was right, but that they ostentatiously endeavoured to gain the character of righteousness, of which they were destitute. This is better understood by persons who are skilled in the Hebrew language; which gives the appellation of *sinners*, not only to those who are conscious to themselves of sin, but to persons who fall under a sentence of condemnation. For Bathsheba, when she says, "I and my son Solomon shall be counted offenders," or sinners, (*p*) confesses no crime, but complains, that she and her son will be exposed to the disgrace of being numbered among condemned criminals. And it appears from the context, that this word, even in the translation, cannot be understood in any other than a relative sense, and that it does not denote the real character. But with respect to the present subject, where Paul says, "The Scripture foresaw that God would justify the heathen through faith," (*q*) what can we understand, but that God imputes righteousness through faith? Again, when he says that God "justifieth the ungodly which believeth in Jesus," (*r*) what can be the meaning, but that he delivers him by the blessing of faith from the condemnation deserved by his ungodliness? He speaks still more plainly in the conclusion, when he thus exclaims: "Who shall lay any thing to the charge of God's elect? It is God that justifieth. Who is he that condemneth? It is Christ that died, yea rather, that is risen again, who also maketh intercession for us." (*s*) For it is just as if he had said, Who shall accuse them whom God absolves? Who shall condemn those for whom Christ intercedes? Justification, therefore, is no other than an acquittal from guilt of him who was accused, as though his innocence had been proved. Since God, therefore, justifies us through the mediation of Christ, he acquits us, not by an admission of our personal innocence, but

(*n*) Luke vii. 29, 35.   (*p*) 1 Kings i. 21.   (*r*) Rom. iii. 26; iv. 5.
(*o*) Luke xvi. 15.   (*q*) Gal. iii. 8.   (*s*) Rom. viii. 33, 34.

by an imputation of righteousness; so that we, who are unrighteous in ourselves, are considered as righteous in Christ. This is the doctrine preached by Paul in the thirteenth chapter of the Acts: "Through this man is preached unto you the forgiveness of sins; and by him all that believe are justified from all things, from which ye could not be justified by the law of Moses." (t) We see that after remission of sins, this justification is mentioned, as if by way of explanation: we see clearly that it means an acquittal; that it is separated from the works of the law; that it is a mere favour of Christ; that it is apprehended by faith: we see, finally, the interposition of a satisfaction, when he says that we are justified from sins by Christ. Thus, when it is said, that the publican "went down to his house justified," (u) we cannot say that he obtained righteousness by any merit of works. The meaning therefore is, that after he had obtained the pardon of his sins, he was considered as righteous in the sight of God. He was righteous, therefore, not through any approbation of his works, but through God's gracious absolution. Wherefore Ambrose beautifully styles confession of sins, a legitimate justification.

IV. But leaving all contention about the term, if we attend to the thing itself, as it is described to us, every doubt will be removed. For Paul certainly describes justification as an acceptance, when he says to the Ephesians, "God hath predestinated us to the adoption of children by Jesus Christ to himself, according to the good pleasure of his will, to the praise of the glory of his grace, wherein he hath made us accepted." (w) The meaning of this passage is the same as when in another place we are said to be "justified freely by his grace." (x) But in the fourth chapter to the Romans, he first mentions an imputation of righteousness, and immediately represents it as consisting in remission of sins. "David," says he, "describeth the blessedness of the man unto whom God imputeth righteousness without works, saying, Blessed are they whose iniquities are forgiven," &c. (y) He there, indeed, argues not concerning a branch, but the whole of justification. He also adduces the definition of it given by David, when he pronounces them to be blessed who receive the free forgiveness of their sins; whence it appears, that this righteousness of which he speaks is simply opposed to guilt. But the most decisive passage of all on this point, is where he teaches us that the grand object of the ministry of the gospel is, that we may "be reconciled to God," because he is pleased to receive us into his favour through Christ, "not imputing" our "trespasses unto"

(t) Acts xiii. 38, 39.   (u) Luke xviii. 14.   (w) Eph. i. 5, 6.
(x) Rom. iii. 24.   (y) Rom. iv. 6—8.

us. (z) Let the reader carefully examine the whole context; for when, by way of explanation, he just after adds, in order to describe the method of reconciliation, that Christ, "who knew no sin," was "made sin for us," (a) he undoubtedly means by the term "reconciliation," no other than justification. Nor would there be any truth in what he affirms in another place, that we are "made righteous by the obedience of Christ," (b) unless we are reputed righteous before God, in him, and out of ourselves.

V. But since Osiander has introduced I know not what monstrous notion of essential righteousness, by which, though he had no intention to destroy justification by grace, yet he has involved it in such obscurity as darkens pious minds, and deprives them of a serious sense of the grace of Christ, — it will be worth while, before I pass to any thing else, to refute this idle notion. In the first place, this speculation is the mere fruit of insatiable curiosity. He accumulates, indeed, many testimonies of Scripture, to prove that Christ is one with us, and we one with him, of which there is no proof necessary; but for want of observing the bond of this union, he bewilders himself. For us, however, who hold that we are united to Christ by the secret energy of his Spirit, it will be easy to obviate all his sophisms. He had conceived a notion similar to what was held by the Manichæans, so that he wished to transfuse the Divine essence into men. Hence another discovery of his, that Adam was formed in the image of God, because, even antecedently to the fall, Christ had been appointed the exemplar of the human nature. But for the sake of brevity, I shall only insist on the subject now before us. He says that we are one with Christ. This we admit; but we at the same time deny that Christ's essence is blended with ours. In the next place, we assert that this principle — that Christ is our righteousness because he is the eternal God, the fountain of righteousness, and the essential righteousness of God — is grossly perverted to support his fallacies. The reader will excuse me, if I now just hint at these things, which the order of the treatise requires to be deferred to another place. But though he alleges, in vindication of himself, that by the term *essential righteousness* he only intends to oppose the opinion that we are reputed righteous for the sake of Christ, yet he manifestly shows, that, not content with that righteousness which has been procured for us by the obedience and sacrificial death of Christ, he imagines that we are substantially righteous in God, by the infusion of his essence as well as his character. For this is the reason why he so vehemently contends, that

(z) 2 Cor. v. 18, 19.   (a) 2 Cor. v. 21.   (b) Rom. v. 19.

not only Christ, but the Father and the Holy Spirit also dwell in us; which, though I allow it to be a truth, yet I maintain that he has grossly perverted. For he ought to have fully considered the nature of this inhabitation; namely, that the Father and the Spirit are in Christ; and that as "all the fulness of the Godhead dwelleth in him," (z) so in him we possess the whole Deity. Whatever, therefore, he advances concerning the Father and the Spirit separately, has no other tendency but to seduce the simple from Christ. In the next place, he introduces a mixture of substances, by which God, transfusing himself into us, makes us, as it were, a part of himself. For he considers it as of no importance, that the power of the Holy Spirit unites us to Christ, so that he becomes our head and we become his members, unless his essence be blended with ours. But when speaking of the Father and the Spirit, he more openly betrays his opinion; which is, that we are not justified by the sole grace of the Mediator, and that righteousness is not simply or really offered to us in his person; but that we are made partakers of the Divine righteousness when God is essentially united with us.

VI. If he had only said, that Christ in justifying us becomes ours by an essential union, and that he is our head not only as man, but that the essence of his Divine nature also is infused into us, — he might have entertained himself with his fancies with less mischief, nor perhaps would so great a contention have been excited about this reverie. But as this principle is like a cuttlefish, which, by the emission of black and turbid blood, conceals its many tails, there is a necessity for a vigorous opposition to it, unless we mean to submit to be openly robbed of that righteousness which alone affords us any confidence concerning our salvation. For throughout this discussion, the terms *righteousness* and *justify* are extended by him to two things. First, he understands that "to be justified" denotes not only to be reconciled to God by a free pardon, but also to be made righteous; and that righteousness is not a gratuitous imputation, but a sanctity and integrity inspired by the Divine essence which resides in us. Secondly, he resolutely denies that Christ is our righteousness, as having, in the character of a priest, expiated our sins and appeased the Father on our behalf, but as being the eternal God and everlasting life. To prove the first assertion, that God justifies not only by pardoning, but also by regenerating, he inquires whether God leaves those whom he justifies in their natural state, without any reformation of their manners. The answer is very easy; as Christ cannot be divided, so these two blessings, which we receive together

(z) Col. ii. 9.

in him, are also inseparable. Whomsoever, therefore, God receives into his favour, he likewise gives them the Spirit of adoption, by whose power he renews them in his own image. But if the brightness of the sun be inseparable from his heat, shall we therefore say that the earth is warmed by his light, and illuminated by his heat? Nothing can be more apposite to the present subject than this similitude. The beams of the sun quicken and fertilize the earth, his rays brighten and illuminate it. Here is a mutual and indivisible connection. Yet reason itself prohibits us to transfer to one what is peculiar to the other. In this confusion of two blessings which Osiander obtrudes on us, there is a similar absurdity. For as God actually renews to the practice of righteousness those whom he gratuitously accepts as righteous, Osiander confounds that gift of regeneration with this gracious acceptance, and contends that they are one and the same. But the Scripture, though it connects them together, yet enumerates them distinctly, that the manifold grace of God may be the more evident to us. For that passage of Paul is not superfluous, that "Christ is made unto us righteousness and sanctification." (*a*) And whenever he argues, from the salvation procured for us, from the paternal love of God, and from the grace of Christ, that we are called to holiness and purity, he plainly indicates that it is one thing to be justified, and another thing to be made new creatures. When Osiander appeals to the Scripture, he corrupts as many passages as he cites. The assertion of Paul, that "to him that worketh not, but believeth on him that justifieth the ungodly, his faith is counted for righteousness," (*b*) is explained by Osiander to denote making a man righteous. With the same temerity he corrupts the whole of that fourth chapter to the Romans, and hesitates not to impose the same false gloss on the passage just cited, "Who shall lay any thing to the charge of God's elect? It is God that justifieth;" where it is evident that the apostle is treating simply of accusation and absolution, and that his meaning wholly rests on the antithesis. His folly, therefore, betrays itself both in his arguments and in his citations of Scripture proofs. With no more propriety does he treat of the word righteousness, when he says, "that faith was reckoned to Abraham for righteousness," because that after having embraced Christ, (who is the righteousness of God, and God himself,) he was eminent for the greatest virtues. Whence it appears, that of two good parts, he erroneously makes one corrupt whole; for the righteousness there mentioned does not belong to the whole course of Abraham's life; but rather the Spirit testifies that,

---

(*a*) 1 Cor. i. 30.   (*b*) Rom. iv. 5.

notwithstanding the singular eminence of Abraham's virtues, and his laudable and persevering advancement in them, yet he did not please God any otherwise than in receiving by faith the grace offered in the promise. Whence it follows, that in justification there is no regard paid to works, as Paul conclusively argues in that passage.

VII. His objection, that the power of justifying belongs not to faith of itself, but only as it receives Christ, I readily admit. For if faith were to justify of itself, or by an intrinsic efficacy, as it is expressed, being always weak and imperfect, it never could effect this but in part; and thus it would be a defective justification, which would only confer on us a partial salvation. Now, we entertain no such notion as the objection supposes; on the contrary, we affirm that, strictly speaking, "it is God that justifies;" and then we transfer this to Christ, because he is given to us for righteousness. Faith we compare to a vessel: for unless we come empty with the mouth of our soul open to implore the grace of Christ, we cannot receive Christ. Whence it may be inferred, that we do not detract from Christ the power of justifying, when we teach that faith receives him before it receives his righteousness. Nevertheless, I cannot admit the intricate comparisons of this sophist, when he says that faith is Christ; as though an earthen vessel were a treasure, because gold is concealed in it. For faith, although intrinsically it is of no dignity or value, justifies us by an application of Christ, just as a vessel full of money constitutes a man rich. Therefore I maintain that faith, which is only the instrument by which righteousness is received, cannot without absurdity be confounded with Christ, who is the material cause, and at once the author and dispenser of so great a benefit. We have now removed the difficulty as to the sense in which the word *faith* ought to be understood, when it is applied to justification.

VIII. Respecting the reception of Christ, he goes still greater lengths; asserting that the internal word is received by the ministry of the external word, by which he would divert us from the priesthood of Christ and the person of the Mediator, to his eternal divinity. We do not divide Christ, but we maintain that the same person, who, by reconciling us to the Father in his own flesh, has given us righteousness, is the eternal Word of God; and we confess that he could not otherwise have discharged the office of Mediator, and procured righteousness for us, if he were not the eternal God. But the opinion of Osiander is, that since Christ is both God and man, he is made righteousness to us, in respect of his Divine, not his human nature. Now, if this properly belong to the Divinity, it will not be peculiar to Christ, but common also to the Father and the Spirit; since the righteousness of one is the same as that of the others. Besides, what has been naturally eternal, cannot with propriety be said to be "made unto us." But though we grant that God is made righteousness unto us, how will it agree with the clause which is inserted, that "of God," he "is made unto us righteousness?" This is certainly peculiar to the character of the Mediator, who, though he contains in himself the Divine nature, yet is designated by this appropriate title, by which he is distinguished from the Father and the Spirit. But he ridiculously triumphs in that single expression of Jeremiah, where he promises that "the Lord," *Jehovah*, will be "our righteousness." (c) He can deduce nothing from this, but that Christ, who is our righteousness, is God manifested in the flesh. We have elsewhere recited from Paul's sermon, that "God hath purchased the Church with his own blood." (d) If any should infer from this, that the blood by which our sins were expiated, was Divine, and part of the Divine nature, who could bear so monstrous an error? But Osiander thinks he has gained every thing by this very puerile cavil; he swells, exults, and fills many pages with his swelling words, though the passage is simply and readily explained, by saying that Jehovah, when he should become the seed of David, would be the righteousness of the pious; and in the same sense Isaiah informs us, "by his knowledge shall my righteous servant justify many." (e) Let us remark, that the speaker here is the Father; that he attributes to his Son the office of justifying; that he adds as a reason, that he is righteous; and that he places the mode or means of effecting this, in the doctrine by which Christ is made known. For it is more suitable to understand the word דעתו in a passive sense. Hence I conclude, first, that Christ was made righteousness when he assumed the form of a servant; secondly, that he justifies us by his own obedience to the Father; and, therefore, that he does this for us, not according to his Divine nature, but by reason of the dispensation committed to him. For though God alone is the fountain of righteousness, and we are righteous only by a participation of him, yet, because we have been alienated from his righteousness through the unhappy breach occasioned by the fall, we are under the necessity of descending to this inferior remedy, to be justified by Christ, by the efficacy of his death and resurrection.

IX. If Osiander object, that the excellence of this work surpasses the nature of man, and therefore can be ascribed only to the Divine nature,— the former part of the objection I admit, but in the latter I maintain that he is grossly mistaken. For although Christ could neither purify our souls with his blood,

---

(c) Jer. xxiii. 6; xxxiii. 16.   (d) Acts xx. 28.   (e) Isaiah liii. 11.

nor appease the Father by his sacrifice, nor absolve us from guilt, nor, in short, perform the functions of a priest, if he were not truly God, because human power would have been unequal to so great a burden, yet it is certain that he performed all these things in his human nature. For if it be inquired, How are we justified? Paul replies, "By the obedience" of Christ. (*f*) But has he obeyed in any other way than by assuming the form of a servant? Hence we infer, that righteousness is presented to us in his flesh. In the other passage also, which I much wonder that Osiander is not ashamed to quote so frequently, Paul places the source of righteousness wholly in the humanity of Christ. "He hath made him to be sin for us, who knew no sin, that we might be made the righteousness of God in him." (*g*) Osiander lays great stress on "the righteousness of God," and triumphs as though he had evinced it to be his notion of essential righteousness; whereas the words convey a very different idea,—that we are righteous through the expiation effected by Christ. That "the righteousness of God" means that which God approves, ought to have been known to the youngest novices; just as in John "the praise of God" is opposed to "the praise of men." (*h*) I know that "the righteousness of God" sometimes denotes that of which he is the author, and which he bestows upon us; but, without any observation of mine, the judicious reader will perceive that the meaning of this passage is only, that we stand before the tribunal of God supported by the atoning death of Christ. Nor is the term of such great importance, provided that Osiander coincides with us in this, that we are justified in Christ, inasmuch as he was made an expiatory sacrifice for us; which is altogether incompatible with his Divine nature. For this reason, when Christ designs to seal the righteousness and salvation which he has presented to us, he exhibits a certain pledge of it in his flesh. He calls himself, indeed, "living bread;" but adds, by way of explanation, "my flesh is meat indeed, and my blood is drink indeed." This method of instruction is discovered in the sacraments; which, although they direct our faith to the whole of the person of Christ, not to a part of him only, yet at the same time teach that the matter of justification and salvation resides in his human nature; not that he either justifies or vivifies, of himself as a mere man, but because it has pleased God to manifest in the Mediator that which was incomprehensible and hidden in himself. Wherefore I am accustomed to say, that Christ is, as it were, a fountain opened to us, whence we may draw what were otherwise concealed and useless in that secret

(*f*) Rom. v. 19.   (*g*) 2 Cor. v. 21.   (*h*) John xii. 43.

and deep fountain which flows to us in the person of the Mediator. In this manner, and in this sense, provided he will submit to the clear and forcible arguments which I have adduced, I do not deny that Christ justifies us, as he is God and man, and that this work is common also to the Father and the Spirit; and, finally, that the righteousness of which Christ makes us partakers, is the eternal righteousness of the eternal God.

X. Moreover, that his cavils may not deceive the inexperienced, I confess that we are destitute of this incomparable blessing, till Christ becomes ours. I attribute, therefore, the highest importance to the connection between the head and members; to the inhabitation of Christ in our hearts; in a word, to the mystical union by which we enjoy him, so that being made ours, he makes us partakers of the blessings with which he is furnished. We do not, then, contemplate him at a distance out of ourselves, that his righteousness may be imputed to us; but because we have put him on, and are ingrafted into his body, and because he has deigned to unite us to himself, therefore we glory in a participation of his righteousness. Thus we refute the cavil of Osiander, that faith is considered by us as righteousness; as though we despoiled Christ of his right, when we affirm, that by faith we come to him empty, that he alone may fill us with his grace. But Osiander, despising this spiritual connection, insists on a gross mixture of Christ with believers; and therefore invidiously gives the appellation of Zuinglians to all who do not subscribe to his fanatical error concerning essential righteousness; because they are not of opinion that Christ is substantially eaten in the sacred supper. As for myself, indeed, I consider it the highest honour to be thus reproached by a man so proud and so absorbed in his own delusions; although he attacks not me alone, but other writers well known in the world, whom he ought to have treated with modest respect. But this does not at all affect me, who am supporting no private interest; wherefore I the more unreservedly advocate this cause, conscious that I am free from every sinister motive. His great importunity in insisting on essential righteousness, and an essential inhabitation of Christ in us, goes to this length — first, that God transfuses himself into us by a gross mixture of himself with us, as he pretends that there is a carnal eating in the sacred supper; secondly, that God inspires his righteousness into us, by which we are really righteous with him, since, according to this man, such righteousness is as really God himself, as the goodness, or holiness, or perfection of God. I shall not take much trouble to refute the testimonies adduced by him, which he violently perverts from the celestial to the present state. By Christ, says

Peter, "are given unto us exceeding great and precious promises; that by these ye might be partakers of the Divine nature." (*i*) As though we were now such as the gospel promises we shall be at the second advent of Christ; nay, John apprizes us, that *then* " we shall be like God; for we shall see him as he is." (*k*) I have thought proper to give the reader only a small specimen, and endeavoured to pass over these impertinences, not that it is difficult to refute them, but because I am unwilling to be tedious in labouring to no purpose.

XI. There is yet more latent poison in the second particular, in which he maintains, that we are righteous together with God. I think I have already sufficiently demonstrated, that although this dogma were not so pestiferous, yet because it is weak and unsatisfactory, and evaporates through its own inanity, it ought justly to be rejected by all judicious and pious readers. But this is an impiety not to be tolerated — under the pretext of a twofold righteousness to weaken the assurance of salvation, and to elevate us above the clouds, that we may not embrace by faith the grace of expiation, and call upon God with tranquillity of mind. Osiander ridicules those who say that justification is a forensic term, because it is necessary for us to be actually righteous: nor is there any thing that he more dislikes than the doctrine that we are justified by gratuitous imputation. Now, if God do not justify by absolving and pardoning us, what is the meaning of this declaration of Paul? "God was in Christ, reconciling the world unto himself, not imputing their trespasses unto them. For he hath made him to be sin for us, who knew no sin; that we might be made the righteousness of God in him." (*l*) First I find, that they are accounted righteous who are reconciled to God: the manner is specified, that God justifies by pardoning; just as, in another passage, justification is opposed to accusation; which antithesis clearly demonstrates, that the form of expression is borrowed from the practice of courts. Nor is there any one, but tolerably versed in the Hebrew language, provided at the same time that he be in his sound senses, who can be ignorant that this is the original of the phrase, and that this is its import and meaning. Now, let Osiander answer me whether, where Paul says that "David describeth righteousness without works, saying, Blessed are they whose iniquities are forgiven," (*m*) whether, I say, this be a complete definition or a partial one. Certainly Paul does not adduce the testimony of the Psalmist, as teaching that pardon of sins is a part of righteousness, or concurs to the justification of a man; but he includes the whole of righteousness in a free remission, pronouncing, "Blessed are they whose

(*i*) 2 Peter i. 4.   (*k*) 1 John iii. 2.   (*l*) 2 Cor. v. 19, 21.   (*m*) Rom. iv. 6—8.

iniquities are forgiven, and whose sins are covered. Blessed is the man to whom the Lord will not impute sin." He thence estimates and judges of the felicity of such a man, because in this way he becomes righteous, not actually, but by imputation. Osiander objects, that it would be dishonourable to God, and contrary to his nature, if he justified those who still remain actually impious. But it should be remembered that, as I have already observed, the grace of justification is inseparable from regeneration, although they are distinct things. But since it is sufficiently known from experience, that some relics of sin always remain in the righteous, the manner of their justification must of necessity be very different from that of their renovation to newness of life. For the latter God commences in his elect, and as long as they live carries it on gradually, and sometimes slowly, so that they are always obnoxious at his tribunal to the sentence of death. He justifies them, however, not in a partial manner, but so completely, that they may boldly appear in heaven, as being invested with the purity of Christ. For no portion of righteousness could satisfy our consciences, till we have ascertained that God is pleased with us, as being unexceptionably righteous before him. Whence it follows, that the doctrine of justification is perverted and totally overturned, when doubts are injected into the mind, when the confidence of salvation is shaken, when bold and fearless worship is interrupted, and when quiet and tranquillity with spiritual joy are not established. Whence Paul argues from the incompatibility of things contrary to each other, that the inheritance is not of the law, because then faith would be rendered vain; (n) which, if it be fixed upon works, must inevitably fall; since not even the most holy of all saints will find them afford any ground of confidence. This difference between justification and regeneration (which Osiander confounds together, and denominates a twofold righteousness) is beautifully expressed by Paul; for, speaking of his real righteousness, or of the integrity which he possessed, to which Osiander gives the appellation of essential righteousness, he sorrowfully exclaims, " O wretched man that I am! who shall deliver me from the body of this death?" (o) But resorting to the righteousness which is founded in the Divine mercy alone, he nobly triumphs over life, and death, and reproaches, and famine, and the sword, and all adverse things and persons. " Who shall lay any thing to the charge of God's elect? It is God that justifieth. For I am persuaded, that nothing shall be able to separate us from the love of God, which is in Christ Jesus our Lord." (p) He plainly declares himself to be pos-

(n) Gal. iii 18.   (o) Rom. vii. 24.   (p) Rom. viii. 33, 38, 39.

sessed of that righteousness, which alone is fully sufficient for salvation in the sight of God; so that the miserable servitude, in a consciousness of which he was just before bewailing his condition, neither diminishes, nor in the smallest degree interrupts, the confidence with which he triumphs. This diversity is sufficiently known, and is even familiar to all the saints, who groan under the burden of their iniquities, and yet with victorious confidence rise superior to every fear. But the objection of Osiander, that it is incongruous to the nature of God, recoils upon himself; for, although he invests the saints with a twofold righteousness, as with a garment covered with skins, he is, notwithstanding, constrained to acknowledge that no man can please God without the remission of his sins. If this be true, he should at least grant that they who are not actually righteous, are accounted righteous in proportion, as it is expressed, to the degree of imputation. But how far shall a sinner extend this gracious acceptance, which is substituted in the place of righteousness? Shall he estimate it by the weight? Truly he will be in great uncertainty to which side to incline the balance; because he will not be able to assume to himself as much righteousness as may be necessary to his confidence. It is well that he, who would wish to prescribe laws to God, is not the arbiter of this cause. But this address of David to God will remain: "That thou mightest be justified when thou speakest, and be clear when thou judgest." (*q*) And what extreme arrogance it is to condemn the supreme Judge when he freely absolves, and not to be satisfied with this answer, "I will show mercy on whom I will show mercy!" (*r*) And yet the intercession of Moses, which God checked with this reply, was not that he would spare none, but that, though they were guilty, he would remove their guilt and absolve them all at once. We affirm, therefore, that those who were undone are justified before God by the obliteration of their sins; because, sin being the object of his hatred, he can love none but those whom he justifies. But this is a wonderful method of justification, that sinners, being invested with the righteousness of Christ, dread not the judgment which they have deserved; and that, while they justly condemn themselves, they are accounted righteous out of themselves.

XII. But the readers must be cautioned to pay a strict attention to the mystery which Osiander boasts that he will not conceal from them. For, after having contended with great prolixity, that we do not obtain favour with God solely through the imputation of the righteousness of Christ, because 't would be impossible for him to esteem those as righteous

(*q*) Psalm li. 4.   (*r*) Exod. xxxiii. 19.

who are not so, (I use his own words,) he at length concludes, that Christ is given to us for righteousness, not in respect of his human, but of his Divine nature; and that, though this righteousness can only be found in the person of the Mediator, yet it is the righteousness, not of man, but of God. He does not combine two righteousnesses, but evidently deprives the humanity of Christ of all concern in the matter of justification. It is worth while, however, to hear what arguments he adduces. It is said in the passage referred to, that "Christ is made unto us wisdom,"(s) which is applicable only to the eternal Word. Neither, therefore, is Christ, considered as man our righteousness. I reply, that the only begotten Son of God was indeed his eternal wisdom; but this title is here ascribed to him by Paul in a different sense, because "in him are hid all the treasures of wisdom and knowledge." (t) What, therefore, he had with the Father, he has manifested to us; and so what Paul says, refers not to the essence of the Son of God, but to our benefit, and is rightly applied to the humanity of Christ; because, although he was a light shining in darkness before his assumption of the flesh, yet he was a hidden light till he appeared in the nature of man "as the Sun of righteousness;" (u) wherefore he calls himself "the light of the world." (w) Osiander betrays his folly likewise in objecting, that justification exceeds the power of angels and men; since it depends not upon the dignity of any creature, but upon the appointment of God. If angels were desirous to offer a satisfaction to God, it would be unavailing; because they have not been appointed to it. This was peculiar to the man Christ, who was "made under the law, to redeem us from the curse of the law." (x) He likewise very unjustly accuses those who deny that Christ is our righteousness according to his Divine nature, of retaining only one part of Christ, and (what is worse) making two Gods; because, though they acknowledge that God dwells in us, yet they flatly deny that we are righteous through the righteousness of God. For if we call Christ the author of life in consequence of his having suffered death, "that he might destroy him that had the power of death," (y) it is not to be inferred that we deny this honour to his complete person, as God manifested in the flesh: we only state with precision the means by which the righteousness of God is conveyed to us, so that we may enjoy it. In this, Osiander has fallen into a very pernicious error. We do not deny, that what is openly exhibited to us in Christ flows from the secret grace and power of God; nor do we refuse to admit, that the

---

(s) 1 Cor. i. 30. (u) Mal. iv. 2. (x) Gal. iii. 13; iv. 4.
(t) Col. ii. 3. (w) John viii. 12. (y) Heb. ii. 14.

righteousness conferred on us by Christ is the righteousness of God as proceeding from him: but we constantly maintain that we have righteousness and life in the death and resurrection of Christ. I pass over that shameful accumulation of passages, with which, without any discrimination, and even without common sense, he has burdened the reader, in order to evince, that wherever mention is made of righteousness, it ought to be understood of this essential righteousness; as where David implores the righteousness of God to assist him; which as he does above a hundred times, Osiander hesitates not to pervert such a great number of passages. Nor is there any thing more solid in his other objection, that the term "righteousness" is properly and rightly applied to that by which we are excited to rectitude of conduct, and that God alone "worketh in us both to will and to do." (z) Now, we do not deny, that God renews us by his Spirit to holiness and righteousness of life; but it should first be inquired, whether he does this immediately by himself, or through the medium of his Son, with whom he has deposited all the plenitude of his Spirit, that with his abundance he might relieve the necessities of his members. Besides, though righteousness flows to us from the secret fountain of the Divinity, yet it does not follow that Christ, who in the flesh sanctified himself for our sakes, (a) is our righteousness with respect to his Divine nature. Equally frivolous is his assertion, that Christ himself was righteous with the righteousness of God; because, if he had not been influenced by the will of the Father, not even he could have performed the part assigned him. For though it has been elsewhere observed, that all the merit of Christ himself flows from the mere favour of God, yet this affords no countenance to the fanciful notion with which Osiander fascinates his own eyes and those of the injudicious. For who would admit the inference, that because God is the original source of our righteousness, we are therefore essentially righteous, and have the essence of the Divine righteousness residing in us? In redeeming the Church (Isaiah says) God "put on righteousness as a breastplate;" (b) but was it to spoil Christ of the armour which he had given him, and to prevent his being a perfect Redeemer? The prophet only meant that God borrowed nothing extrinsic to himself, and had no assistance in the work of our redemption. Paul has briefly intimated the same in other words, saying that he has given us salvation in order "to declare his righteousness." (c) Nor does this at all contradict what he states in another place, "that by the

(z) Phil. ii. 13.
(a) John xvii. 19.
(b) Isaiah lix. 17.
(c) Rom. iii. 24, 25.

obedience of one we are made righteous." (d) To conclude: whoever fabricates a twofold righteousness, that wretched souls may not rely wholly and exclusively on the Divine mercy, makes Christ an object of contempt, and crowns him with platted thorns.

XIII. But as many persons imagine righteousness to be composed of faith and works, let us also prove, before we proceed, that the righteousness of faith is so exceedingly different from that of works, that if one be established, the other must necessarily be subverted. The apostle says, "I count all things but dung, that I may win Christ, and be found in him, not having mine own righteousness, which is of the law, but that which is through the faith of Christ, the righteousness which is of God by faith." (e) Here we see a comparison of two opposites, and an implication that his own righteousness must be forsaken by him who wishes to obtain the righteousness of Christ. Wherefore, in another place, he states this to have been the cause of the ruin of the Jews, that, "going about to establish their own righteousness, they have not submitted themselves unto the righteousness of God." (f) If, by establishing our own righteousness, we reject the righteousness of God, then, in order to obtain the latter, the former must doubtless be entirely renounced. He conveys the same sentiment when he asserts, that "boasting is excluded. By what law? of works? Nay; but by the law of faith." (g) Whence it follows, that as long as there remains the least particle of righteousness in our works, we retain some cause for boasting. But if faith excludes all boasting, the righteousness of works can by no means be associated with the righteousness of faith. To this purpose he speaks so clearly in the fourth chapter to the Romans, as to leave no room for cavil or evasion. "If Abraham (says he) were justified by works, he hath whereof to glory." He adds, "but" he hath "not" whereof to glory "before God." (h) It follows, therefore, that he was not justified by works. Then he advances another argument from two opposites. "To him that worketh is the reward not reckoned of grace, but of debt." (i) But righteousness is attributed to faith through grace. Therefore it is not from the merit of works. Adieu, therefore, to the fanciful notion of those who imagine a righteousness compounded of faith and works.

XIV. The sophists, who amuse and delight themselves with perversion of the Scripture and vain cavils, think they have found a most excellent subterfuge, when they explain *works*, in these passages, to mean those which men yet unregenerate

(d) Rom. v. 19.   (f) Rom. x. 3.   (h) Rom. iv. 2.
(e) Phil. iii. 8, 9.   (g) Rom iii. 27.   (i) Rom. iv. 4.

perform without the grace of Christ, merely through the unassisted efforts of their own free-will; and deny that they relate to spiritual works. Thus, according to them, a man is justified both by faith and by works, only the works are not properly his own, but the gifts of Christ and the fruits of regeneration. For they say that Paul spoke in this manner, only that the Jews, who relied on their own strength, might be convinced of their folly in arrogating righteousness to themselves, whereas it is conferred on us solely by the Spirit of Christ, not by any exertion properly our own. But they do not observe, that in the contrast of legal and evangelical righteousness, which Paul introduces in another place, all works are excluded, by what title soever they may be distinguished. For he teaches that this is the righteousness of the law, that he who has fulfilled the command of the law shall obtain salvation; (*k*) but that the righteousness of faith consists in believing that Christ has died and is risen again. (*l*) Besides, we shall see, as we proceed, in its proper place, that sanctification and righteousness are separate blessings of Christ. Whence it follows, that even spiritual works are not taken into the account, when the power of justifying is attributed to faith. And the assertion of Paul, in the place just cited, that Abraham has not whereof to glory before God, since he was not justified by works, ought not to be restricted to any literal appearance or external display of virtue, or to any efforts of free-will; but though the life of the patriarch was spiritual, and almost angelic, yet his works did not possess sufficient merit to justify him before God.

XV. The errors of the schoolmen, who mingle their preparations, are rather more gross; but they instil into the simple and incautious a doctrine equally corrupt, while under the pretext of the Spirit and of grace, they conceal the mercy of God, which alone can calm the terrors of the conscience. We confess, indeed, with Paul, that "the doers of the law are justified before God;" (*m*) but since we are all far from being observers of the law, we conclude, that those works which should be principally available to justification, afford us no assistance, because we are destitute of them. With respect to the common Papists, or schoolmen, they are in this matter doubly deceived; both in denominating faith a certainty of conscience in expecting from God a reward of merit, and in explaining the grace of God to be, not an imputation of gratuitous righteousness, but the Spirit assisting to the pursuit of holiness. They read in the apostle, "He that cometh to God must believe that he is, and that he is a rewarder of them that diligently seek him." (*n*) But they do not consider the man-

---

(*k*) Rom. x. 5, &c.   (*l*) Gal. iii. 11.   (*m*) Rom. ii. 13.   (*n*) Heb. xi. 6.

ner of seeking him. And that they mistake the sense of the word "grace," is evident from their writings. For Lombard represents justification by Christ as given us in two ways. He says, "The death of Christ justifies us, first, because it excites charity in our hearts, by which we are made actually righteous; secondly, because it destroys sin, by which the devil held us in captivity, so that now it cannot condemn us." We see how he considers the grace of God in justification to consist in our being directed to good works by the grace of the Holy Spirit. He wished, indeed, to follow the opinion of Augustine; but he follows him at a great distance, and even deviates considerably from a close imitation of him; for whatever he finds clearly stated by him, he obscures, and whatever he finds pure in him, he corrupts. The schools have always been running into worse and worse errors, till at length they have precipitated themselves into a kind of Pelagianism. Nor, indeed, is the opinion of Augustine, or at least his manner of expression, to be altogether admitted. For though he excellently despoils man of all the praise of righteousness, and ascribes the whole to the grace of God, yet he refers grace to sanctification, in which we are regenerated by the Spirit to newness of life.

XVI. The Scripture, when speaking of the righteousness of faith, leads us to something very different. It teaches us, that being diverted from the contemplation of our own works, we should regard nothing but the mercy of God and the perfection of Christ. For it states this to be the order of justification; that from the beginning God deigns to embrace sinful man with his pure and gratuitous goodness, contemplating nothing in him to excite mercy, but his misery; (for God beholds him utterly destitute of all good works;) deriving from himself the motive for blessing him, that he may affect the sinner himself with a sense of his supreme goodness, who, losing all confidence in his own works, rests the whole of his salvation on the Divine mercy. This is the sentiment of faith, by which the sinner comes to the enjoyment of his salvation, when he knows from the doctrine of the gospel that he is reconciled to God; that having obtained remission of sins, he is justified by the intervention of the righteousness of Christ; and though regenerated by the Spirit of God, he thinks on everlasting righteousness reserved for him, not in the good works to which he devotes himself, but solely in the righteousness of Christ. When all these things shall have been particularly examined, they will afford a perspicuous explication of our opinion. They will, however, be better digested in a different order from that in which they have been proposed. But it is of little importance, provided they are so connected with each other, that we may have the whole subject rightly stated and well confirmed.

XVII. Here it is proper to recall to remembrance the relation we have before stated between faith and the gospel; since the reason why faith is said to justify, is, that it receives and embraces the righteousness offered in the gospel. But its being offered by the gospel absolutely excludes all consideration of works. This Paul very clearly demonstrates on various occasions; and particularly in two passages. In his Epistle to the Romans, contrasting the law and the gospel, he says, "Moses describeth the righteousness which is of the law, that the man which doeth those things shall live by them. But the righteousness which is of faith speaketh on this wise: That if thou shalt confess with thy mouth the Lord Jesus, and shalt believe in thine heart that God hath raised him from the dead, thou shalt be saved." (*o*) Do you perceive how he thus discriminates between the law and the gospel, that the former attributes righteousness to works, but the latter bestows it freely, without the assistance of works? It is a remarkable passage, and may serve to extricate us from a multitude of difficulties, if we understand that the righteousness which is given us by the gospel is free from all legal conditions. This is the reason why he more than once strongly opposes the *promise* to the *law*. "If the inheritance be of the law, it is no more of promise;" (*p*) and more in the same chapter to the same purpose. It is certain that the law also has its promises. Wherefore, unless we will confess the comparison to be improper, there must be something distinct and different in the promises of the gospel. Now, what can that be, but that they are gratuitous and solely dependent on the Divine mercy, whilst the promises of the law depend on the condition of works? Nor let any one object, that it is only the righteousness which men would obtrude on God from their own natural powers and free-will that is rejected; since Paul teaches it as a universal truth, that the precepts of the law are unprofitable, because, not only among the vulgar, but even among the very best of men, there is not one who can fulfil them. (*q*) Love is certainly the principal branch of the law: when the Spirit of God forms us to it, why does it not constitute any part of our righteousness, but because even in the saints it is imperfect, and therefore of itself deserves no reward?

XVIII. The other passage is as follows: "That no man is justified by the law in the sight of God, it is evident; for, The just shall live by faith. And the law is not of faith; but, The man that doeth them shall live in them." (*r*) How could this argument be supported, unless it were certain that works do not come into the account of faith, but are to be entirely sepa-

(*o*) Rom. x. 5, 6, 9.   (*q*) Rom. iii. 10, &c.
(*p*) Gal. iii. 18.   (*r*) Gal. iii. 11, 12.

rated from it? The law, he says, differs from faith. Why? Because works are required to the righteousness of the law. It follows, therefore, that works are not required to the righteousness of faith. From this statement it appears, that they who are justified by faith, are justified without the merit of works, and beyond the merit of works; for faith receives that righteousness which the gospel bestows; and the gospel differs from the law in this respect, that it does not confine righteousness to works, but rests it entirely on the mercy of God. He argues in a similar manner to the Romans, that " Abraham had not whereof to glory; for he believed God, and it was counted unto him for righteousness;" (s) and by way of confirmation he subjoins, that then there is room for the righteousness of faith when there are no works which merit any reward. He tells us, that where there are works, they receive a reward " of debt," but that what is given to faith is " of grace;" for this is the clear import of the language which he there uses. When he adds, a little after, " Therefore it is of faith " that we obtain the inheritance, in order " that it might be by grace," (t) he infers that the inheritance is gratuitous, because it is received by faith: and why is this, but because faith, without any assistance of works, depends wholly on the Divine mercy? And in the same sense undoubtedly he elsewhere teaches us, that " the righteousness of God without the law is manifested, being witnessed by the law and the prophets;" (u) because, by excluding the law, he denies that righteousness is assisted by works, or that we obtain it by working, but asserts that we come empty in order to receive it.

XIX. The reader will now discover, with what justice the sophists of the present day cavil at our doctrine, when we say *that a man is justified by faith only.* That a man is justified *by faith,* they do not deny, because the Scripture so often declares it; but since it is nowhere expressly said to be by faith *only,* they cannot bear this addition to be made. But what reply will they give to these words of Paul, where he contends that " righteousness is not of faith unless it be gratuitous?" (w) How can any thing gratuitous consist with works? And by what cavils will they elude what he asserts in another place, that in the gospel " is the righteousness of God revealed?" (x) If righteousness is revealed in the gospel, it is certainly not a mutilated and partial, but a complete and perfect one. The law, therefore, has no concern in it. And respecting this exclusive particle, *only,* they rest on an evasion which is not only false, but glaringly ridiculous. For does not

(s) Rom. iv. 2, 3.   (t) Rom. iv. 16.   (u) Rom. iii. 21.
(w) Rom. iv. 2.   (x) Rom. i. 17.

he most completely attribute every thing to faith alone, who denies every thing to works? What is the meaning of these expressions of Paul? "Righteousness is manifested without the law," "justified freely by his grace," "justified without the deeds of the law." (*y*) Here they have an ingenious subterfuge, which, though it is not of their own invention, but borrowed from Origen and some of the ancients, is nevertheless very absurd. They pretend that the works excluded are the ceremonial works of the law, not the moral works. They have made such a proficiency by their perpetual disputations, that they have forgotten the first elements of logic. Do they suppose the apostle to have been insane, when he adduced these passages in proof of his doctrine? "The man that doeth them shall live in them;" and "Cursed is every one that continueth not in all things which are written in the book of the law to do them." (*z*) If they be in their sober senses, they will not assert that life was promised to the observers of ceremonies, and the curse denounced merely on the transgressors of them. If these places are to be understood of the moral law, it is beyond a doubt, that moral works likewise are excluded from the power to justify. To the same purpose are these arguments which he uses: "For by the law is the knowledge of sin;" consequently not righteousness. "Because the law worketh wrath," (*a*) therefore not righteousness. Since the law cannot assure our consciences, neither can it confer righteousness. Since faith is counted for righteousness, consequently righteousness is not a reward of works, but is gratuitously bestowed. Since we are justified by faith, boasting is precluded. "If there had been a law given which could have given life, verily righteousness should have been by the law. But the Scripture hath concluded all under sin, that the promise by faith of Jesus Christ might be given to them that believe." (*b*) Let them idly pretend, if they dare, that these are applicable to ceremonies, not to morals; but even children would explode such consummate impudence. We may therefore be assured, that when the power of justifying is denied to the law, the whole law is included.

XX. If any one should wonder why the apostle does not content himself with simply mentioning *works*, but says *works of the law*, the reason is obvious. For though works are so greatly esteemed, they derive their value from the Divine approbation rather than from any intrinsic excellence. For who can dare to boast to God of any righteousness of works, but what he has approved? Who can dare to claim any reward as due to them, but what he has promised? It is owing, therefore,

(*y*) Rom. iii. 21, 24, 28.
(*z*) Gal. iii. 10, 12.
(*a*) Rom. iii. 20; iv. 15.
(*b*) Gal. iii. 21, 22.

to the Divine favour, that they are accounted worthy both of the title and of the reward of righteousness; and so they are valuable, only when they are intended as acts of obedience to God. Wherefore the apostle, in another place, in order to prove that Abraham could not be justified by works, alleges, that "the law was four hundred and thirty years after the covenant was confirmed." (*c*) Ignorant persons would ridicule such an argument, because there might have been righteous works before the promulgation of the law; but knowing that works have no such intrinsic worth, independently of the testimony and esteem of God, he has taken it for granted that, antecedently to the law, they had no power to justify. We know why he expressly mentions "the works of the law," when he means to deny justification by works; it is because they alone can furnish any occasion of controversy. However, he likewise excludes all works, without any limitation, as when he says, "David describeth the blessedness of the man, unto whom God imputeth righteousness without works." (*d*) They cannot, therefore, by any subtleties prevent us from retaining this general exclusive particle. It is in vain, also, that they catch at another frivolous subtlety, alleging that we are justified only by that "faith which worketh by love;" (*e*) with a view to represent righteousness as depending on love. We acknowledge, indeed, with Paul, that no other faith justifies, except that "which worketh by love;" but it does not derive its power to justify from the efficacy of that love. It justifies in no other way than as it introduces us into a participation of the righteousness of Christ. Otherwise there would be no force in the argument so strenuously urged by the apostle. "To him that worketh," says he, "is the reward not reckoned of grace, but of debt. But to him that worketh not, but believeth on him that justifieth the ungodly, his faith is counted for righteousness." (*f*) Was it possible for him to speak more plainly than by thus asserting, that there is no righteousness of faith, except where there are no works entitled to any reward; and that faith is imputed for righteousness, only when righteousness is conferred through unmerited grace?

XXI. Now, let us examine the truth of what has been asserted in the definition, that the righteousness of faith is a reconciliation with God, which consists solely in remission of sins. (*g*) We must always return to this axiom — That the Divine wrath remains on all men, as long as they continue to be sinners. This Isaiah has beautifully expressed in the following words: "The Lord's hand is not shortened, that it cannot save; neither is his ear heavy, that it cannot hear; but your

(*c*) Gal. iii. 17.   (*d*) Rom. iv. 6.   (*e*) Gal. v. 6.
(*f*) Rom. iv. 4, 5.   (*g*) Sect. II.

iniquities have separated between you and your God, and your sins have hid his face from you, that he will not hear." (*h*) We are informed, that sin makes a division between man and God, and turns the Divine countenance away from the sinner. Nor can it be otherwise; because it is incompatible with his righteousness to have any communion with sin. Hence the apostle teaches, that man is an enemy to God, till he be reconciled to him through Christ. (*i*) Whom, therefore, the Lord receives into fellowship, him he is said to justify; because he cannot receive any one into favour or into fellowship with himself, without making him from a sinner to be a righteous person. This, we add, is accomplished by the remission of sins. For if they, whom the Lord has reconciled to himself, be judged according to their works, they will still be found actually sinners; who, notwithstanding, must be absolved and free from sin. It appears, then, that those whom God receives, are made righteous no otherwise than as they are purified by being cleansed from all their defilements by the remission of their sins; so that such a righteousness may, in one word, be denominated a remission of sins.

XXII. Both these points are fully established by the language of Paul, which I have already recited. "God was in Christ, reconciling the world unto himself, not imputing their trespasses unto them; and hath committed unto us the word of reconciliation." (*k*) Then he adds the substance of his ministry: "He hath made him to be sin for us, who knew no sin; that we might be made the righteousness of God in him." (*l*) The terms "righteousness" and "reconciliation" are here used by him indiscriminately, to teach us that they are mutually comprehended in each other. And he states the manner of obtaining this righteousness to consist in our transgressions not being imputed to us. Wherefore we can no longer doubt how God justifies, when we hear that he reconciles us to himself by not imputing our sins to us. Thus, in the Epistle to the Romans, the apostle proves, that "God imputeth righteousness without works," from the testimony of David, who declares, "Blessed are they whose iniquities are forgiven, and whose sins are covered. Blessed is the man to whom the Lord will not impute sin." (*m*) By "blessedness," in this passage, he undoubtedly means righteousness; for since he asserts it to consist in remission of sins, there is no reason for our adopting any other definition of it. Wherefore Zachariah, the father of John the Baptist, places "the knowledge of salvation" in "the remission of sins." (*n*) And Paul, observing the same rule in the sermon which he preached to

(*h*) Isaiah lix. 1, 2. (*k*) 2 Cor. v. 19. (*m*) Rom. iv. 6—8.
(*i*) Rom. v. 8—10. (*l*) 2 Cor. v. 21. (*n*) Luke i. 77.

the people of Antioch on the subject of salvation, is stated by Luke to have concluded in the following manner: " Through this man is preached unto you the forgiveness of sins; and by him all that believe are justified from all things, from which ye could not be justified by the law of Moses."(*o*) The apostle thus connects " forgiveness of sins " with "justification," to show that they are identically the same; whence he justly argues, that this righteousness which we obtain through the favour of God is gratuitously bestowed upon us. Nor should it be thought a strange expression, that believers are justified before God, not by their works, but by his gracious acceptance of them; since it occurs so frequently in the Scripture, and sometimes also in the fathers. Augustine says, " The righteousness of the saints, in this world, consists rather in the remission of their sins than in the perfection of their virtues." With which corresponds the remarkable observation of Bernard: " Not to sin at all, is the righteousness of God; but the righteousness of man is the Divine grace and mercy." He had before asserted, " that Christ is righteousness to us in absolution, and therefore that they alone are righteous who have obtained pardon through his mercy."

XXIII. Hence, also, it is evident, that we obtain justification before God, solely by the intervention of the righteousness of Christ. Which is equivalent to saying, that a man is righteous, not in himself, but because the righteousness of Christ is communicated to him by imputation; and this is a point which deserves an attentive consideration. For it supersedes that idle notion, that a man is justified by faith, because faith receives the Spirit of God by whom he is made righteous; which is too repugnant to the foregoing doctrine, ever to be reconcilable to it. For he must certainly be destitute of all righteousness of his own, who is taught to seek a righteousness out of himself. This is most clearly asserted by the apostle, when he says, " He hath made him to be sin for us, who knew no sin; that we might be made the righteousness of God in him."(*p*) We see that our righteousness is not in ourselves, but in Christ; and that all our title to it rests solely on our being partakers of Christ; for in possessing him, we possess all his riches with him. Nor does any objection arise from what he states in another place, that " God, sending his own Son in the likeness of sinful flesh, and for sin, condemned sin in the flesh; that the righteousness of the law might be fulfilled in us; " (*q*) where he intends no other fulfilment than what we obtain by imputation. For the Lord Christ so communicates his righteousness to us, that, with reference to the Divine judgment, he transfuses its virtue into us in a most wonderful manner. That the apostle intended

(*o*) Acts xiii. 38, 39.   (*p*) 2 Cor. v. 21.   (*q*) Rom. viii. 3, 4.

no other, abundantly appears from another declaration, which he had made just before: "As by one man's disobedience many were made sinners, so by the obedience of one shall many be made righteous." (r) What is placing our righteousness in the obedience of Christ, but asserting, that we are accounted righteous only because his obedience is accepted for us as if it were our own? Wherefore Ambrose appears to me to have very beautifully exemplified this righteousness in the benediction of Jacob; that as he, who had on his own account no claim to the privileges of primogeniture, being concealed in his brother's habit, and invested with his garment, which diffused a most excellent odour, insinuated himself into the favour of his father, that he might receive the benediction to his own advantage, under the character of another; so we shelter ourselves under the precious purity of Christ our elder brother, that we may obtain the testimony of righteousness in the sight of God. The words of Ambrose are, "That Isaac smelled the odour of the garments, perhaps indicates, that we are justified not by works, but by faith; since the infirmity of the flesh is an impediment to works, but the brightness of faith, which merits the pardon of sin, conceals the error of our actions." And such is indeed the real fact; for that we may appear before the face of God to salvation, it is necessary for us to be perfumed with his fragrance, and to have all our deformities concealed and absorbed in his perfection.

CHAPTER XII.

A CONSIDERATION OF THE DIVINE TRIBUNAL, NECESSARY TO A SERIOUS CONVICTION OF GRATUITOUS JUSTIFICATION.

Though it appears, from the plainest testimonies, that all these things are strictly true, yet we shall not clearly discover how necessary they are, till we shall have taken a view of what ought to be the foundation of all this argument. In the first place, therefore, we should reflect that we are not treating of the righteousness of a human court, but of that of the heavenly tribunal; in order that we may not apply any diminutive standard of our own, to estimate the integrity of conduct required to satisfy the Divine justice. But it is wonderful, with what temerity and presumption this is commonly decided; and it is even observable, that no men give us more confident or pompous declamations concerning the righteousness of works, than

(r) Rom. v. 19.

those who are notoriously guilty of open sins or addicted to secret vices. This arises from their never thinking of the righteousness of God, the smallest sense of which would prevent them from treating it with such contempt. And certainly it is exceedingly undervalued, if it be not acknowledged to be so perfect that nothing can be acceptable to it but what is absolutely complete and immaculate, such as it never was, nor ever will be, possible to find in fallen man. It is easy for any one in the cloisters of the schools, to indulge himself in idle speculations on the merit of works to justify men; but when he comes into the presence of God, he must bid farewell to these amusements, for there the business is transacted with seriousness, and no ludicrous logomachy practised. To this point, then, must our attention be directed, if we wish to make any useful inquiry concerning true righteousness; how we can answer the celestial Judge, when he shall call us to an account. Let us place that Judge before our eyes, not according to the spontaneous imaginations of our minds, but according to the descriptions given of him in the Scripture; which represents him as one whose refulgence eclipses the stars, whose power melts the mountains, whose anger shakes the earth, whose wisdom takes the subtle in their own craftiness, whose purity makes all things appear polluted, whose righteousness even the angels are unable to bear, who acquits not the guilty, whose vengeance, when it is once kindled, penetrates even to the abyss of hell.* Let him seat himself, I say, on the tribunal, to examine the actions of men: who will present himself fearless before his throne? "Who shall dwell with the devouring fire?" saith the prophet. "Who shall dwell with everlasting burnings? He that walketh righteously and speaketh uprightly," &c. (s) Now let him come forward, whoever he is. But this answer causes not one to appear. For, on the contrary, we hear this fearful speech, "If thou, Lord, shouldst mark iniquities, O Lord, who shall stand?" (t) In truth, all must speedily perish, as it is written in another place, "Shall mortal man be more just than God? Shall a man be more pure than his Maker? Behold, he put no trust in his servants; and his angels he charged with folly; how much less in them that dwell in houses of clay, whose foundation is in the dust, which are crushed before the moth? They are destroyed from morning to evening." (u) Again: "Behold, he putteth no trust in his saints; yea, the heavens are not clean in his sight; how much more abominable and filthy is man, which drinketh iniquity like water?" (w) I confess that in the Book of Job mention is made of a right-

---

* See particularly the Book of Job. (s) Isaiah xxxiii. 14, 15.
(t) Psalm cxxx. 3.   (u) Job iv. 17—20.   (w) Job xv. 15, 16.

eousness which is superior to the observance of the law. And it will be of use to remember this distinction; because, though any one could satisfy the law, he could not even then stand the scrutiny of that righteousness which exceeds all comprehension. Therefore, though Job is conscious of his own integrity, yet he is mute with astonishment, when he sees that God could not be pleased even with the sanctity of angels, if he were to enter into a strict examination of their works. I shall, therefore, now pass over that righteousness to which I have alluded, because it is incomprehensible, and content myself with asserting, that we must be worse than stupid, if, on an examination of our lives by the rule of the written law, we are not tormented with awful dread in consequence of so many maledictions, which God has designed to arouse us, and among the rest this general one: " Cursed be he that confirmeth not all the words of this law to do them." (x) In short, this whole controversy will be uninteresting and useless, unless every one present himself as a criminal before the celestial Judge, and voluntarily prostrate and humble himself in deep solicitude concerning his absolution.

II. To this point our eyes ought to have been raised, that we might learn rather to tremble through fear, than to indulge in vain exultation. It is easy, indeed, while the comparison is made only between men, for every man to imagine himself to be possessed of something which others ought not to contemn; but when we ascend to the contemplation of God, that confidence is immediately lost. And the case of our soul with respect to God is similar to that of our body with respect to the visible heavens; for the eye, as long as it is employed in beholding adjacent objects, receives proofs of its own perspicacity; but if it be directed towards the sun, dazzled and confounded with his overpowering brightness, it feels no less debility in beholding him, than strength in the view of inferior objects. Let us not, then, deceive ourselves with a vain confidence, although we consider ourselves equal or superior to other men. That is nothing to God, to whose decision this cause must be submitted. But if our insolence cannot be restrained by these admonitions, he will reply to us in the language which he addressed to the Pharisees: " Ye are they which justify yourselves before men; but that which is highly esteemed among men, is abomination in the sight of God." (y) Go now, and among men proudly glory in your righteousness, while the God of heaven abominates it. But what is the language of the servants of God, who are truly taught by his Spirit? One says, " Enter not into judgment with thy servant; for in thy sight shall no man living be justified." (z) And another,

(x) Deut. xxvii. 26. (y) Luke xvi. 15. (z) Psalm cxliii. 2.

though in a sense somewhat different, "How should man be just with God? If he will contend with him, he cannot answer him one of a thousand." (*a*) Here we are plainly informed respecting the righteousness of God, that it is such as no human works can satisfy; and such as renders it impossible for us, if accused of a thousand crimes, to exculpate ourselves from one of them. The same idea of this righteousness had very properly been entertained by Paul, that "chosen vessel" (*b*) of God, when he professed, "I am conscious to myself of nothing; yet am I not hereby justified." (*c*)

III. Nor is it only in the sacred Scriptures that such examples are found. All pious writers discover similar sentiments. Thus Augustine says, "The only hope of all the pious, who groan under this burden of corruptible flesh, and amidst the infirmities of this life, is, that we have a Mediator, Jesus Christ the righteous; and he is the propitiation for our sins." What is the meaning of this observation? If this is their only hope, where is any confidence in works? For when he asserts this to be the only one, he precludes every other. Bernard also says, "And in fact where can be found safe and solid rest and security for the weak, but in the wounds of the Saviour? There I dwell with the greater security, in proportion to his power to save. The world rages, the body oppresses, the devil lies in wait to destroy. I do not fall, because my foundation is on a firm rock. I have committed heinous sin. My conscience is disturbed, but shall not fall into despair, because I shall recall to remembrance the wounds of the Lord." From these considerations he afterwards concludes, "My merit, therefore, is the compassion of the Lord: I am clearly not destitute of merit, as long as he is not destitute of compassions. But if the mercies of the Lord be a multitude of mercies, my merits are likewise equally numerous. Shall I sing of my own righteousness? O Lord, I will remember thy righteousness alone. For it is mine also, since he is made of God righteousness unto me." Again, in another place: "This is the whole merit of man — to fix all his hope on him who saves the whole man." Likewise in another place, retaining peace to himself, and ascribing the glory to God, he says, "To thee let the glory remain undiminished. It is happy for me, if I have peace. The glory I entirely renounce; lest, if I usurp what is not mine, I lose also that which is offered me." In another place he is still more explicit: "Why should the Church be solicitous about merits, while it has a stronger and more secure reason for glorying in the designs of God? You need not inquire on account of what merits we hope for blessings, especially when you read in the prophet, 'Thus saith the

(*a*) Job ix. 2, 3.   (*b*) Acts ix. 15.   (*c*) 1 Cor. iv. 4.

Lord God; I do not this for your sakes, but for mine holy name's sake.' (*d*) It suffices with respect to merit, to know that merits are not sufficient; but as it suffices for merit not to presume on merits, so to be destitute of merits is sufficient cause of condemnation." We must excuse his custom of freely using the word *merits* for good works. But his ultimate design was to terrify hypocrites, who indulge themselves in a licentious course of sin against the grace of God; as he presently declares: "Happy is the Church which wants neither merits without presumption, nor presumption without merits. It has some ground of presumption, but not merits. It has merits, but in order to deserve, not to presume. Is not the absence of presumption itself a merit? Therefore the Church presumes the more securely, because it does not presume, having ample cause for glorying in the multitude of the Divine mercies."

IV. This is the real truth. The troubled conscience finds this to be the only asylum of safety, where it can enjoy any tranquillity, when it has to do with the Divine justice. For if the stars, which appeared most brilliant during the night, lose their splendour on the rising of the sun, what can we suppose will be the case with the most excellent innocence of man, when compared with the purity of God? For that will be an examination inconceivably severe, which shall penetrate into all the most secret thoughts of the heart, and, as Paul says, "bring to light the hidden things of darkness, and make manifest the counsels of the hearts;" (*e*) which shall constrain the reluctant conscience to confess all those things which have now passed away even from our own remembrance. We shall be urged by an accusing devil, who has been privy to all the crimes which he has impelled us to perpetrate. There the external appearance of good works, which now is the sole object of esteem, will be of no avail; sincerity of heart is all that will be required. Wherefore hypocrisy, not only that by which a man, conscious of his guilt before God, affects ostentation before men, but that also by which every man imposes on himself before God, for we are all prone to self-complacency and adulation; hypocrisy in all its forms will then be overwhelmed with confusion, however it may now be intoxicated with presumption and pride. Persons who never look forward to such a spectacle, may, indeed, delightfully and complacently compose for themselves a temporary righteousness, of which they will immediately be stripped at the Divine judgment; just as immense riches, accumulated by us in a dream, vanish as soon as we awake. But they who inquire seriously, and as in the presence of God, respecting the true standard of righteousness, will certainly find that all the actions of men, if estimated

(*d*) Ezek. xxxvi. 22.   (*e*) 1 Cor. iv. 5.

according to their intrinsic worth, are utterly defiled and polluted; that what is commonly considered as righteousness, is, in the Divine view, nothing but iniquity; that what is accounted integrity, is mere pollution; and that what is reputed glory, is real ignominy.

V. From this contemplation of the Divine perfection, let us not be unwilling to descend to take a view of ourselves, without adulation or blind self-love. For it is not to be wondered at, if we are so extremely blind in this respect, since not one of us is sufficiently cautious of that pestilent self-indulgence, which the Scripture declares to be naturally inherent in us all. "Every way of man," says Solomon, "is right in his own eyes." (*f*) Again: "All the ways of a man are clean in his own eyes." (*g*) But what follows from this? Is he absolved from guilt by this delusion? Not at all; but, as is immediately added, "the Lord weigheth the spirits;" that is, while men are congratulating themselves on account of the external mask of righteousness which they wear, the Lord is at the same time weighing in his own balance the latent impurity of their hearts. Since we are so far from deriving any advantage, therefore, from such blandishments, let us not voluntarily delude ourselves to our own perdition. That we may examine ourselves properly, it is necessary for us to summon our conscience to the tribunal of God. For we have the greatest need of his light in order to detect the recesses of our depravity, which otherwise are too deeply concealed. For then only shall we clearly perceive the force of this language: "How can man be justified with God— man, who is" corruption and "a worm, abominable and filthy, and who drinketh iniquity like water?" (*h*) "Who can bring a clean thing out of an unclean? Not one." (*i*) Then also we shall experience what Job said concerning himself: "If I justify myself, mine own mouth shall condemn me; if I say I am perfect, it shall also prove me perverse." (*k*) For the complaint, which the prophet formerly made respecting Israel, "All we like sheep have gone astray; we have turned every one to his own way;" (*l*) is applicable not only to one period of time, but to all ages. For he there comprehends all to whom the grace of redemption was to extend; and the rigour of this examination ought to proceed till it shall have filled us with complete consternation, and thus prepared us to receive the grace of Christ. For he is deceived who supposes himself capable of this enjoyment, without having first been truly humbled. It is a well-known observation, that "God resisteth the proud, and giveth grace to the humble." (*m*)

VI. But what means have we of humbling ourselves, except by submitting, all poor and destitute, to the Divine mercy?

(*f*) Prov. xxi. 2.   (*g*) Prov. xvi. 2.   (*h*) Job xv. 16; xxv. 4, 6.
(*i*) Job xiv. 4.   (*k*) Job ix. 20.   (*l*) Isaiah liii. 6.   (*m*) 1 Peter v. 5.

For I do not call it humility, if we suppose that we have any thing left. And hitherto they have taught a pernicious hypocrisy, who have connected these two maxims — that we should entertain humble thoughts of ourselves before God, and that we should attach some dignity to our own righteousness. For if we address to God a confession which is contrary to our real sentiments, we are guilty of telling him an impudent falsehood; but we cannot think of ourselves as we ought to think, without utterly despising every thing that may be supposed an excellence in us. When we hear, therefore, from the Psalmist, that "God will save the afflicted people, but will bring down high looks," (*n*) let us consider, first, that there is no way of salvation till we have laid aside all pride, and attained sincere humility; secondly, that this humility is not a species of modesty, consisting in conceding to God a small portion of what we might justly claim, as they are called humble among men, who neither haughtily exalt themselves nor behave with insolence to others, while they nevertheless entertain some consciousness of excellence: this humility is the unfeigned submission of a mind overwhelmed with a weighty sense of its own misery and poverty; for such is the uniform description of it in the word of God. When the Lord speaks thus in Zephaniah, "I will take away out of the midst of thee them that rejoice in thy pride; I will also leave in the midst of thee an afflicted and poor people, and they shall trust in the name of the Lord;" (*o*) does he not clearly show who are truly humble? even such as are afflicted with a knowledge of their own poverty. On the contrary, he describes the proud as persons "rejoicing," because this is the usual consequence of prosperity. But to the humble, whom he intends to save, he leaves nothing but that "they trust in the name of the Lord." Thus also in Isaiah, "To this man will I look, even to him that is poor and of a contrite spirit, and trembleth at my word." (*p*) Again: "Thus saith the high and lofty One that inhabiteth eternity, whose name is Holy; I dwell in the high and holy place, with him also that is of a contrite and humble spirit, to revive the spirit of the humble, and to revive the heart of the contrite ones." (*q*) By the contrition so frequently mentioned, we must understand a wounded heart, which prevents a man from rising when humbled in the dust. With such contrition must our heart be wounded, if we desire, according to the declaration of the Lord, to be exalted with the humble. If this be not the case, we shall be abased by the powerful hand of God to our shame and disgrace. (*r*)

VII. And, not content with mere precepts, our excellent

(*n*) Psalm xviii. 27. (*p*) Isaiah lxvi. 2. (*r*) Matt. xxiii. 12. Luke xiv.
(*o*) Zeph. iii. 11, 12. (*q*) Isaiah lvii. 15. 11; xviii. 14.

Master, in a parable, as in a picture, has presented us with an example of genuine humility. For he introduces a publican, who, "standing afar off, would not lift up so much as his eyes unto heaven, but smote upon his breast, saying, God be merciful to me a sinner." (s) We must not conclude these circumstances — his not presuming to look upwards, standing afar off, smiting upon his breast, and confessing himself a sinner — to be marks of feigned modesty; we may be certain that they were sincere evidences of the disposition of his heart. To him our Lord opposes a Pharisee, who said, "God, I thank thee that I am not as other men are, extortioners, unjust, adulterers, or even as this publican. I fast twice in the week, I give tithes of all that I possess." He openly confesses the righteousness which he has, to be the gift of God; but because he confides in his being righteous, he departs from the presence of God unacceptable and hateful to him. The publican, acknowledging his iniquity is justified. Hence we may see how very pleasing our humiliation is in the sight of God; so that the heart is not open for the reception of his mercy unless it be divested of all idea of its own dignity. When this notion has occupied the mind, it precludes the admission of Divine mercy. That no one might have any doubt of this, Christ was sent by his Father into the world with a commission, "to preach good tidings unto the meek; to bind up the broken-hearted; to proclaim liberty to the captives, and the opening of the prison to them that are bound; to comfort all that mourn; to give unto them beauty for ashes, the oil of joy for mourning, the garment of praise for the spirit of heaviness." (t) In pursuance of this commission, he invites to a participation of his benefits none but those who "labour and are heavy laden." (u) And in another place he says, " I am not come to call the righteous, but sinners to repentance." (v)

VIII. Therefore, if we would obey the call of Christ, let us dismiss all arrogance and carelessness from our minds. The former arises from a foolish persuasion of our own righteousness, when a man supposes himself to be possessed of any thing, the merit of which can recommend him to God; the latter may exist without any consideration of works. For multitudes of sinners, inebriated with criminal pleasures, and forgetful of the Divine judgment, are in a state, as it were, of lethargic insensibility, so that they never aspire after the mercy which is offered to them. But it is equally necessary for us to shake off such stupidity, and to reject all confidence in ourselves, in order that, being freed from every incumbrance, we may hasten to Christ, all destitute and hungry, to be filled with his blessings. For we shall never have sufficient confidence in him, unless

(s) Luke xviii. 13.   (t) Isaiah lxi. 1—3.   (u) Matt. xi. 28.   (v) Matt. ix. 13.

we entirely lose all confidence in ourselves; we shall never find sufficient encouragement in him, unless we are previously dejected in ourselves; we shall never enjoy sufficient consolation in him, unless we are utterly disconsolate in ourselves. We are prepared, therefore, to seek and obtain the grace of God, discarding at the same time all confidence in ourselves, and relying solely on the assurance of his mercy, "when," as Augustine says, "forgetting our own merits, we embrace the free gifts of Christ; because, if he sought merits in us, we should not come to his free gifts." With him Bernard fully agrees, when he compares proud men, that arrogate ever so little to their own merits, to unfaithful servants, because they unjustly claim the praise of the grace which passes through them; just as though a wall should say that it produces the sunbeams which it receives through a window. But not to dwell any longer on this, we may lay it down as a brief, but general and certain maxim, that he is prepared for a participation of the benefits of Divine mercy, who has wholly divested himself, I will not say of his righteousness, which is a mere nullity, but of the vain and airy phantom of righteousness; for as far as any man is satisfied with himself, so far he raises an impediment to the exercise of the grace of God.

CHAPTER XIII.

TWO THINGS NECESSARY TO BE OBSERVED IN GRATUITOUS JUSTIFICATION.

HERE are two things to which we must always be particularly attentive; to maintain the glory of the Lord unimpaired and undiminished, and to preserve in our own consciences a placid composure and serene tranquillity with regard to the Divine judgment. We see how frequently and solicitously the Scripture exhorts us to render ascriptions of praise to God alone, when it treats of justification. And, indeed, the apostle assures us that the design of the Lord in conferring righteousness upon us in Christ, is to manifest his own righteousness. The nature of that manifestation he immediately subjoins: it is, "that he might be just, and the justifier of him which believeth in Jesus." (*w*) The righteousness of God, we see, is not sufficiently illustrious, unless he alone be esteemed righteous, and communicate the grace of justification to the unworthy. For this reason it is his will "that every mouth be stopped, and all

(*w*) Rom. iii. 26.

the world become guilty before him;" (*x*) because, as long as
man has any thing to allege in his own defence, it detracts
something from the glory of God. Thus in Ezekiel he
teaches us how greatly we glorify his name by an acknowledgment of our iniquity: "Ye shall remember your ways,
(saith he,) and all your doings, wherein ye have been defiled;
and ye shall loathe yourselves in your own sight for all your
evils that ye have committed. And ye shall know that I am
the Lord, when I have wrought with you for my name's sake,
not according to your wicked ways, nor according to your corrupt doings." (*y*) If these things are contained in the true
knowledge of God, that, humbled with a consciousness of our
iniquity, we should consider him as indulging us with blessings of which we are unworthy, why do we attempt, to our
own serious injury, to pilfer the smallest particle of the praise
due to his gratuitous goodness? Thus also when Jeremiah
proclaims, "Let not the wise man glory in his wisdom, neither
let the mighty man glory in his might, let not the rich man
glory in his riches; but let him that glorieth glory in the
Lord;" (*z*) does he not suggest that the glory of God sustains
some diminution, if any man glory in himself? To this use
these words are clearly applied by Paul, when he states, that
all the branches of our salvation are deposited with Christ,
that we may not glory except in the Lord. (*a*) For he intimates, that they who suppose themselves to have even the
least ground for glorying in themselves, are guilty of rebelling
against God, and obscuring his glory.

II. The truth, then, is, that we never truly glory in him, till
we have entirely renounced all glory of our own. On the
converse, this may be admitted as an axiom universally true, that
they who glory in themselves, glory in opposition to God. For
Paul is of opinion that the world is not "subject to the judgment of God," till men are deprived of all foundation for glorying. (*b*) Therefore Isaiah, when he announces, that "in the
Lord shall all the seed of Israel be justified," adds also, "and
shall glory;" as though he had said, that the end of God in
justifying the elect was, that they might glory in himself, and
in no other. But how we should glory in the Lord, he had
stated in the preceding verse: "Surely, shall one say, in the
Lord have I righteousness and strength." Let us observe, that
what is required is not a simple confession, but a confession
confirmed by an oath; that we may not suppose any fictitious
pretence of humility to be sufficient. (*c*) Here let no one plead
that he does not glory at all, when without arrogance he recognizes his own righteousness; for such an opinion cannot exist

(*x*) Rom. iii. 19.
(*y*) Ezek. xx. 43, 44.
(*z*) Jer. ix. 23, 24.
(*a*) 1 Cor. i. 29—31.
(*b*) Rom. iii. 19.
(*c*) Isaiah xlv. 23—25.

without generating confidence, nor confidence without being attended with glorying. Let us remember, therefore, in the whole controversy concerning righteousness, that this end must be kept in view, that all the praise of it may remain perfect and undiminished with the Lord; because, according to the apostle's testimony, he has bestowed his grace on us in order "to declare his righteousness; that he might be just, and the justifier of him which believeth in Jesus." (*d*) Wherefore, in another place, after having declared that the Lord has conferred salvation on us in order to display "the praise of the glory of his grace," (*e*) repeating, as it were, the same sentiment, he adds, "By grace are ye saved through faith; and that not of yourselves; it is the gift of God; not of works, lest any man should boast." (*f*) And when Peter admonishes us that we are called to the hope of salvation, "that we should show forth the praises (or virtues) of him who hath called us out of darkness into his marvellous light," (*g*) he evidently means that the praises of God alone should resound in the ears of believers, so as to impose total silence on all the presumption of the flesh. The conclusion of the whole is, that man cannot without sacrilege arrogate to himself the least particle of righteousness, because it is so much detracted and diminished from the glory of the righteousness of God.

III. Now, if we inquire by what means the conscience can obtain peace before God, we shall find no other than our reception of gratuitous righteousness from his free gift. Let us always remember the inquiry of Solomon — "Who can say, I have made my heart clean, I am pure from my sin?" (*h*) It is certain that there is no man who is not covered with infinite pollution. Let a man of the most perfect character, then, retire into his own conscience, and enter into a scrutiny of his actions, and what will be the result? Will he feel a high degree of satisfaction, as though there were the most entire agreement between God and him? or will he not rather be lacerated with terrible agonies, on perceiving in himself such ample cause for condemnation, if he be judged according to his works? If the conscience reflect on God, it must either enjoy a solid peace with his judgment, or be surrounded with the terrors of hell. We gain nothing, therefore, in our discussions of this point, unless we establish a righteousness, the stability of which will support our souls under the scrutiny of the Divine judgment. When our souls shall possess what will enable them to appear with boldness in the presence of God, and to await and receive his judgment without any fear, then, and not before, we may be assured that we have found a righteousness which truly

(*d*) Rom. iii. 26.   (*e*) Ephes. i. 6.   (*f*) Ephes. ii. 8.
(*g*) 1 Peter ii. 9.   (*h*) Prov. xx. 9.

deserves the name. It is not without reason, therefore, that this subject is so largely insisted on by the apostle, whose words I prefer to my own: "For if they which are of the law be heirs, faith is made void, and the promise is made of none effect." (*i*) He first infers, that faith is annulled and superseded, if the promise of righteousness respect the merit of our works, or depend on our observance of the law. For no man could ever securely rely on it, since he never would be able to determine with certainty for himself that he had fulfilled the law, as in fact no man ever does completely satisfy it by any works of his own. Not to seek far for testimonies of this fact, every individual may be his own witness of it, who will enter unprejudiced into an examination of himself. And hence it appears in what deep and dark recesses hypocrisy buries the minds of men, while they indulge themselves in such great security, and hesitate not to oppose their self-adulation to the judgment of God, as though they would stop the proceedings of his tribunal. But believers, who sincerely examine themselves, are troubled and distressed with a solicitude of a very different nature. The minds of men universally, therefore, ought to feel first hesitation, and then despair, while considering, every one for himself, the magnitude of the debt with which they are still oppressed, and their immense distance from the conditions prescribed to them. Behold their confidence already broken and extinguished; for to confide is not to fluctuate, to vary, to be hurried hither and thither, to hesitate, to be kept in suspense, to stagger, and finally to despair; but it is, to strengthen the mind with content, certainty, and solid security, and to have somewhat upon which to stand and to rest.

IV. He adds likewise another consideration, that the promise would be void and of none effect. For if the fulfilment of it depend on our merit, when shall we have made such a progress as to deserve the favour of God? Besides, this second argument is a consequence of the former, since the promise will be fulfilled to those alone who shall exercise faith in it. Therefore, if faith be wanting, the promise will retain no force. "Therefore the inheritance is of faith, that it might be by grace; to the end the promise might be sure to all the seed." (*k*) For it is abundantly confirmed, when it depends solely on the Divine mercy; because mercy and truth are connected by an indissoluble bond, and whatever God mercifully promises, he also faithfully performs. Thus David, before he implores salvation for himself according to the word of God, first represents it as originating in his mercy: "According to thy word unto thy servant, let thy tender mercies come unto me, that I may live." (*l*) And for this there is sufficient reason, since

(*i*) Rom. iv. 14. (*k*) Rom. iv. 16. (*l*) Psalm cxix. 76, 77.

God has no other inducement to promise than what arises from his mere mercy. Here, then, we must place, and, as it were, deeply fix, all our hopes, without regarding our own works, or seeking any assistance from them. Nor must it be supposed that we are advancing a new doctrine, for the same conduct is recommended by Augustine. "Christ," says he, "will reign in his servants for ever. God has promised this, God has said it; if that be insufficient, God has sworn it. Since the promise, therefore, is established, not according to our merits, but according to his mercy, no man ought to speak with anxiety of that which he cannot doubt." Bernard also says, "The disciples of Christ asked, Who can be saved? He replied, With men this is impossible, but not with God. This is all our confidence, this our only consolation, this the whole foundation of our hope. But certain of the possibility, what think we of his will? Who knows whether he deserve love or hatred? (*m*) Who has known the mind of the Lord, or who has been his counsellor? (*n*) Here, now, we evidently need faith to help us, and his truth to assist us; that what is concealed from us in the heart of the Father, may be revealed by the Spirit, and that the testimony of the Spirit may persuade our hearts that we are sons of God; that he may persuade us by calling and justifying us freely by faith : in which there is, as it were, an intermediate passage from eternal predestination to future glory." Let us draw the following brief conclusion : The Scripture declares that the promises of God have no efficacy, unless they be embraced by the conscience with a steady confidence ; and whenever there is any doubt or uncertainty, it pronounces them to be made void. Again, it asserts that they have no stability if they depend on our works. Either, therefore, we must be for ever destitute of righteousness, or our works must not come into consideration, but the ground must be occupied by faith alone, whose nature it is to open the ears and shut the eyes; that is, to be intent only on the promise, and to avert the thoughts from all human dignity or merit. Thus is accomplished that remarkable prophecy of Zechariah: "I will remove the iniquity of that land in one day. In that day, saith the Lord of hosts, shall ye call every man his neighbour under the vine and under the fig-tree;" (*o*) in which the prophet suggests that believers enjoy no true peace till after they have obtained the remission of their sins. For this analogy must be observed in the prophets, that when they treat of the kingdom of Christ, they exhibit the external bounties of God as figures of spiritual blessings. Wherefore also Christ is denominated "the Prince of peace," and "our Peace;" (*p*)

(*m*) Eccles. ix. 1.
(*n*) 1 Cor. ii. 16.
(*o*) Zech. iii. 9, 10.
(*p*) Isaiah ix. 6. Ephes. ii. 14.

because he calms all the agitations of the conscience. If we inquire, by what means; we must come to the sacrifice by which God is appeased. For no man will ever lose his fears who shall not be assured that God is propitiated solely by that atonement which Christ has made by sustaining his wrath. In short, we must seek for peace only in the terrors of Christ our Redeemer.

V. But why do I use such an obscure testimony? Paul invariably denies that peace or tranquillity can be enjoyed in the conscience, without a certainty that we are justified by faith. (*q*) And he also declares whence that certainty proceeds; it is " because the love of God is shed abroad in our hearts by the Holy Ghost;" (*r*) as though he had said that our consciences can never be satisfied without a certain persuasion of our acceptance with God. Hence he exclaims in the name of all believers, " Who shall separate us from the love of God which is in Christ?" (*s*) For till we have reached that port of safety, we shall tremble with alarm at every slightest breeze; but while God shall manifest himself as our Shepherd, we shall fear no evil even in the valley of the shadow of death. (*t*) Whoever they are, therefore, who pretend that we are justified by faith, because, being regenerated, we are righteous by living a spiritual life, they have never tasted the sweetness of grace, so as to have confidence that God would be propitious to them. Whence also it follows, that they know no more of the method of praying aright, than the Turks or any other profane nations. For according to the testimony of Paul, faith is not genuine unless it dictate and suggest that most delightful name of Father, and unless it open our mouth freely to cry, " Abba, Father;" (*u*) which he in another place expresses still more clearly: " In Christ we have boldness and access with confidence by the faith of him." (*v*) This certainly arises not from the gift of regeneration; which, being always imperfect in the present state, contains in itself abundant occasion of doubting. Wherefore it is necessary to come to this remedy; that believers should conclude that they cannot hope for an inheritance in the kingdom of heaven on any other foundation, but because, being ingrafted into the body of Christ, they are gratuitously accounted righteous. For with respect to justification, faith is a thing merely passive, bringing nothing of our own to conciliate the favour of God, but receiving what we need from Christ.

(*q*) Rom. v. 1.   (*s*) Rom. viii. 35, &c.   (*u*) Gal. iv. 6
(*r*) Rom. v. 5.   (*t*) Psalm xxiii. 4.   (*v*) Ephes. iii. 12.

END OF VOL. I.